THE SENATE
1789-1989

Volume Two

United States Senator and Mrs. Robert C. Byrd,
on the occasion of their fiftieth wedding anniversary,
May 29, 1987
Photo by Alan E. Porter

THE SENATE
1789-1989
Addresses on the History
of the United States Senate

Volume Two
Bicentennial Edition

ROBERT C. BYRD
United States Senator

Edited by
WENDY WOLFF
U.S. Senate Historical Office

U.S. Government Printing Office
Washington

100th Congress, 1st Session
S. Con. Res. 18
U.S. Senate Bicentennial Publication

Senate Document 100–20
U.S. Government Printing Office
Washington: 1991

The eagle device on the cover is based on details of the magnificent balustrades in the Senate wing of the Capitol. The two balustrades in the Senate and two in the House wing were designed by Constantino Brumidi, modeled by Edmond Baudin, and cast in Philadelphia by Archer, Warner, Miskey and Company between 1857 and 1859.

Library of Congress Cataloging in Publication Data
(Revised for vol.2)

Byrd, Robert C.
   The Senate, 1789–1989.

      (A U.S. Senate bicentennial publication) (Senate document; 100–20)
      "100th Congress, 1st Session, S. Con. Res. 18"—Verso of t.p.
      Vol. 2– : edited by Wendy Wolff.
      Includes bibliographical references and index.
         1. United States. Congress. Senate—History. I. Hall, Mary Sharon, 1944-   . II. Wolff, Wendy.
   III. Title. IV. Series. V. Series: Senate document (United States. Congress. Senate); No. 100–20.
   JK1158.B97   1988   328.73′071′09   88–24545

Cloth Cover Edition for sale by the Superintendent of Documents,
U.S. Government Printing Office,
Washington, DC 20402
Volume One–Supt. of Docs. No. 052-071-00823-3
Volume Two–Supt. of Docs. No. 052-071-00856-0

66,968

To My Wife Erma

And My Daughters Mona and Marjorie

Contents

Preface

The first volume of this work was published in January 1989, on the fourth day of the 101st Congress. During that Congress, the Senate Bicentennial Commission, which I chair, coordinated a rich assortment of projects in honor of the Senate's two-hundredth anniversary. Volume Two goes to press in late 1990, at the close of the 101st Congress. Taken together, these two books seek to explore the major institutional themes and the key personalities associated with the Senate's development during its first two centuries. The topical structure of the second volume is designed to complement the chronological organization of the first. Many of the addresses in this volume I originally delivered to the Senate in the early 1980's. By the end of that decade, I had revised and expanded each of these chapters to bring the story up to date through 1989. As with Volume One, I have retained the form of my remarks as they appeared in the *Congressional Record*, including an indication of the date on which I originally delivered the address and references to the presiding officer of the Senate as "Mr. President." In reproducing quoted material, I have retained the spelling and punctuation of the original source.

In the preface to Volume One, I expressed my appreciation to many of the talented and dedicated individuals who assisted me with this decade-long project. Most of those persons have also participated in the preparation of Volume Two. This work in its present form would not have been possible without the assistance of the professionals within the Senate Historical Office. I again acknowledge my gratitude to the director of that office, Dr. Richard A. Baker, to the associate director, Dr. Donald A. Ritchie, and to Secretary of the Senate Walter J. Stewart, under whose jurisdiction that office operates.

My deepest appreciation goes to Wendy Wolff, the editor of Volume Two. Her strong editorial hand has skillfully shaped this work from a disparate collection of speeches to what I believe is a carefully balanced and finely coordinated reference book. Tirelessly dedicated to this project from its inception, Wendy Wolff has maintained herein the editorial standards of Volume One and has convincingly guided the author away from tempting side roads. Her indexes to both volumes display a rich and impressively detailed knowledge of the Senate's historical structure.

Kathryne Bomberger indefatigably searched thousands of photographs in dozens of repositories to produce the illustrations on the pages that follow. These photographs attest to her resourcefulness and imagination. Others in the Senate Historical Office who contributed to this project include Diane Boyle, Anne M. Butler, John O. Hamilton, Jonathan Marcus, Mary Anne Moore, Jo Anne McCormick Quatannens, Elizabeth Strannigan, and Jonathan Warmflash.

I owe special thanks to the Senate Library, under the direction of Roger K. Haley, whose staff assisted in many ways. Reference librarians Ann Womeldorf, Greg Harness, Thea Koehler, Anne Sporn, Abbie Bradfield, Tom McCray, and Patti Schmid provided research on many points of fact and verified hundreds of footnotes and original sources. Library aides Mike Alion and George Costin delivered hundreds of volumes to support my research, as did Barbu Alim and Marcel Monfort from the Capitol Station of the Library of Congress.

The Office of Senate Curator was particularly helpful with the illustrations for this volume. The Architect of the Capitol's office generously lent photographs from its collection.

In transforming the original addresses into the chapters of Volume Two, I have relied heavily on key members of my own staff. Two who deserve special commendation are Charlotte Holt and Kathleen McNally. Charlotte Holt efficiently carried out literally hundreds of administrative assignments for me. As I drafted and redrafted numerous portions of each chapter, Kathleen McNally expertly prepared clean copy from my handwritten inserts and attachments. I particularly appreciated her cheerful attitude, uniformly evident despite the lateness of the hour or the intensity of other demands. Thanks are also due to Barbara Videnieks, my chief of staff, and Richard D'Amato, counsel to the Senate Appropriations Committee. I deeply respect their judgment and I am grateful for their help and suggestions. My former foreign policy counsel to the Democratic Policy Committee, Dr. Hoyt Purvis, is due a great amount of credit for the records of the foreign policy issues of my first term as majority leader. His excellent analyses and thorough notes were invaluable in my research.

Although many departments and individuals at the U.S. Government Printing Office combined to produce this volume, I would particularly like to thank three individuals there who made special contributions. Larry Boarman expertly guided the editorial staff in the use of a new, automated typesetting system; Bill Milans laid out the pages and illustrations; and Roy Morton devoted hours of his own time to this project.

ROBERT C. BYRD

EDITORIAL NOTE

This book, and the speeches from which it was drawn, represent syntheses of the works of the many scholars who have studied the United States Senate and the lives of individual senators. I have cited their books both in the text and in the notes, in order to encourage others to read the rich literature on the Senate and perhaps even to contribute to it themselves. After the publication of Volume One, I was distressed to discover that portions of five chapters drafted by a former staff researcher incorporated material from other authors without quotation marks. Although for the most part the sources of these passages were cited in the notes, the practice was clearly improper and ran contrary to my standards and those of the Senate Historical Office. Steps have been taken in the preparation of this volume to assure that all contributions are properly cited and that credit is given where credit is due.

R.C.B.

POWERS

In order to judge of the form to be given to [the Senate], it will be proper to take a view of the ends to be served by it. These were first to protect the people against their rulers: secondly to protect the people against the transient impressions into which they themselves might be led.

JAMES MADISON, JUNE 26, 1787 [1]

This power over the purse, may in fact be regarded as the most compleat and effectual weapon with which any constitution can arm the immediate representatives of the people, for obtaining a redress of every grievance, and for carrying into effect every just and salutary measure.

JAMES MADISON, FEBRUARY 20, 1788 [2]

This House is a sanctuary; a citadel of law, of order, and of liberty; and it is here—it is here, in this exalted refuge; here, if anywhere, will resistance be made to the storms of political phrensy and the silent arts of corruption; and if the Constitution be destined ever to perish by the sacrilegious hands of the demagogue or the usurper, which God avert, its expiring agonies will be witnessed on this floor.

AARON BURR, MARCH 2, 1805 [3]

Mr. President, I wish to speak to-day, not as a Massachusetts man, nor as a northern man, but as an American, and a member of the Senate of the United States. It is fortunate that there is a Senate of the United States; a body not yet moved from its propriety, not lost to a just sense of its own dignity, and its own high responsibilities, and a body to which the country looks with confidence, for wise, moderate, patriotic, and healing counsels.

DANIEL WEBSTER, MARCH 7, 1850 [4]

CHAPTER 1

Treaties

April 10, 1987, and April 29, 1987*

Mr. President, as we celebrate this year the bicentennial of the United States Constitution, I wish to draw attention to certain constitutional provisions unique to the United States Senate, which have played significant roles in shaping the history of this institution. I refer to the Senate's "advice and consent" authority on treaties and nominations. Today, I shall speak about the Senate and treaties and, at another time, I shall continue with remarks concerning the confirmation of nominations.

Article II, section 2, of the Constitution states that the president "shall have Power, by and with the Advice and Consent of the Senate, to make Treaties, provided two-thirds of the Senators present concur." These few words are the cornerstone to a major part of our system of divided powers, checks and balances. Yet, how were they decided upon? And what do they mean?

Under the Articles of Confederation, which preceded our Constitution, there was no executive branch, and treaties were negotiated by agents of the Congress. Even under that arrangement, no treaty could be entered into without the consent of nine of the existing thirteen states, or approximately two-thirds of the states. George H. Haynes, in *The Senate of the United States*, wrote: "Meantime the

new states were asserting and exercising powers of sovereignty. Thus, South Carolina specifically endowed its government with power to . . . enter into treaties." When the Constitutional Convention created an executive branch, it raised the issue of whether treatymaking should be a legislative or executive power. South Carolina's Charles Pinckney proposed that the upper house of the legislative branch have "the sole and exclusive power . . . to make treaties." Pinckney presumably chose the Senate because, under the new form of government, it would most closely conform to the old Confederation Congress' system of equal voices for all states, regardless of size. New York's Alexander Hamilton argued that the new executive should take the lead in foreign policy, suggesting that the president have the power to make treaties "with the advice and approbation of the Senate." [1]

James Wilson of Pennsylvania pressed the case for advice and consent by the House of Representatives as well as by the Senate. Roger Sherman of Connecticut, however, argued that secrecy would be required for the deliberation of sensitive foreign policy issues, and that the smaller, legislatively elected Senate would be more able than the larger, popularly elected House to conduct

* Updated, June 1989

The formal copies of treaties exchanged by nations are often elaborate documents adorned with heavy seals, as was the exchange copy of the Louisiana Purchase treaty. *National Archives*

its business in secret session. Virginia's James Madison offered an amendment to allow treaties of peace to be adopted by less than a two-thirds vote, or to permit two-thirds of the Senate to adopt a peace treaty without the concurrence of the president. Neither of Madison's proposals was adopted. Roger Sherman then proposed that treaties be approved by a majority of the Senate, rather than by a two-thirds vote. Hugh Williamson of North Carolina objected that this would be "less security than two-thirds." Sherman responded, "It will be less embarrassing." How many future presidents would second that opinion! But the convention retained the two-thirds margin. Finally, after much deliberation, the delegates adopted what was essentially Hamilton's proposal for presidential power to make treaties, with the advice and consent of the Senate.[2]

Hamilton defended his proposal in *The Federalist*, No. 75, which first appeared in the New York *Independent Journal* on March 26, 1788. Although the provision had raised some controversy, Hamilton declared it "one of the best digested and most unexceptionable parts of the plan." The essence of the legislative authority was to enact laws, wrote Hamilton, while the execution of the laws was the function of the president. But the power to make treaties was neither the enactment nor the execution of a law. "Its objects are contracts with foreign nations, which have the force of law, but derive it from the obligations of good faith." The power, therefore, properly belonged to both the executive and the legislature. The president was the most fit agent for negotiating treaties, "while the vast importance of the trust, and the operation of treaties as laws, plead strongly for the participation of the whole or a part of the legislative body in the office of making them."[3]

Mr. President, Roy Swanstrom, in *The United States Senate, 1787–1801*, said:

An 1801 Senate resolution established a standing rule relating to the reading of a treaty.   *National Archives*

The Senate power which aroused the gravest and most widespread apprehension was that associated with the *making of treaties.* Opponents of the Constitution expressed almost pathological fears that the Senate would use the treaty power corruptly and treasonably. A bare two-thirds of a Senate quorum—10 Senators—could in secret conclave sacrifice the dearest interests of the people, alienate the territory and commercial rights of the United States, even dismember the Union. Foreign gold would line the pockets of Senators, hungry for money and power. The Senate could usurp all the powers given other branches of the Government because under the Constitution treaties would supersede all laws.

Such fears were especially prevalent in the Southern States. Southerners feared that the Northern and Middle States would combine to pass treaties yielding the interests of the south to some foreign power. At Richmond, William Grayson, afterward a Senator from Virginia, anticipated that if southern Members were absent from the Senate floor for "just 1 hour," a treaty might be made yielding the navigation of the Mississippi to Spain, thus preventing the development of the Southwest and assuring the continued dominance of the North.

Virginia and North Carolina so opposed the Senate's treaty power that their conventions proposed identical amendments providing that no commercial treaties be ratified without the concurrence of two-thirds of the *whole number* of Senators (to prevent such tricks as Grayson envisioned) and that no treaties yielding any territorial, fishing, or navigation claims of the United States be ratified without concurrence of *three-fourths* of the *whole number* of the Members of *both* Houses—this in spite of the fact that James Wilson's motion to include the House in the treaty power had been defeated at Philadelphia by a vote of 10 States to 1.[4]

Mr. President, Roy Swanstrom's informative history of the first fourteen years of the "upper legislative body" was reprinted as a Senate document in 1988. In it, he pointed out that it is difficult to be sure of all of the framers' intentions, because so many decisions about the Constitution resulted from compromise rather than plan. He suggested, however, that they had three main purposes in giving the Senate a share of the treaty power:

(1) To restrain the President, who might otherwise use the treaty power in a despotic and arbitrary manner—in other words, this was part of the system of "checks and balances";

(2) To give the President "advice" in the sense of information and counsel;

(3) To defend the sovereignty of the States, of which the Senate was to be the special representative; giving this great power to the Chamber in which the States were equally represented was thus part of the "Great Compromise" of the Convention.[5]

Another interpreter of the advice and consent clause was Massachusetts Senator Henry Cabot Lodge, Sr., who, himself, played the leading role in defeating the Treaty of Versailles in 1919 and 1920. Senator Lodge took special note of the "carefully phrased section" of the Constitution which gave the president

absolute and unrestricted right to nominate, and the Senate can only advise and consent to the appointment of, a given person. . . . Very different is the wording in the treaty clause. There the words "by and with the advice and consent of" come in after the words "shall have power" and before the power referred to is defined. The "advice and consent of the Senate" are therefore coextensive with the "power" conferred on the President, which is "to make treaties," and apply to the entire process of treaty making. The States in the convention of 1787 agreed to share the treaty power with the President created by the Constitution, but they never thought of resigning it, or of retaining anything less than they gave.[6]

Well, Mr. President, it is one thing to interpret the Constitution and another to put that interpretation into practice. Neither the first Senate nor the first president was certain how to proceed. On August 6, 1789, the Senate appointed a committee, consisting of Senators Ralph Izard of South Carolina, Rufus King of New York, and Charles Carroll of Maryland, to confer with President Washington on the means of communication between them concerning treaties and nominations. Specifically, should that communication be written or oral? Two days later, the committee members met with the president and assured him that they sought a system most agreeable to him. But as Washington confided to James Madison (then a leading member of the House of Representatives), "I could plainly perceive notwithstanding, that oral communications was the point they aimed at."

Washington held his ground in favor of written communication on nominations. "It could be no pleasing thing I conceive, for the president, on the one hand to be present and

Chief Justice John Jay negotiated the controversial Jay Treaty with Great Britain. *Library of Congress*

The most important treaty that the Senate considered during the Washington administration was that negotiated by Chief Justice John Jay to settle disputes with Great Britain. Again, I refer to Roy Swanstrom's work.

By March 1794, relations between the United States and Great Britain had reached a critical point. Britain's intransigent attitude and the activities of the anti-British party in the United States combined to head the two nations toward the precipice of war. At this point, Senators Ellsworth of Connecticut, Cabot and Strong of Massachusetts, King of New York, and later Robert Morris of Pennsylvania, took the initiative in urging on the President appointment of a special envoy to go to London to try to secure recognition of American claims and adjust the differences which were tending toward an armed conflict. These five constituted the very core of the Federalist leadership in the Senate. They succeeded in convincing President Washington of the advisability of the mission, and after the latter had rejected their recommendation of Hamilton as politically unfeasible, successfully urged upon him, with Hamilton's own support, the selection of Chief Justice John Jay. . . .

Appointment of Jay was bitterly assailed by the Senate's minority—first, on the ground that an envoy extraordinary was unnecessary since negotiations could be conducted by our minister resident in London; second, on the ground that a Chief Justice should not be utilized for such a mission, and third, on the ground that Jay had expressed opinions contrary to the just claims of the United States. Perhaps an even greater practical reason for the Republicans' opposition was the fact that their party was sponsoring retaliatory commercial legislation as the means of protecting American rights. At any rate, this opposition gave the Senate opportunity to debate and pass upon not only the choice of envoy but also the question of the mission itself. However, the Senate as a whole did not have opportunity to pass on the instructions which were to govern the envoy's conduct of the negotiations since the Federalist leaders believed—no doubt correctly—that proposals regarding such instructions would provoke irreconcilable controversy and thus defeat the entire project. Consequently, a small group of Senators, including King, Ellsworth, and Cabot, together with Hamilton, met with Jay to discuss the instructions. Here again expediency dictated the procedure, and what amounted to a "Senate policy committee" rather than the Senate as a whole served as a "council of advice" to the President. . . .

Failure of the President to obtain the advice and consent of the Senate as a body before sending Jay to London did not pass unchallenged. The heads of the Treasury and War Departments approved the procedure, but Attorney General Edmund Randolph believed that it would abridge the rights of the Senate, following the current rule that a treaty approved by a nation's representative acting in compliance with his instructions must be ratified. The procedure was seized upon by the treaty's opponents as further evidence of bad faith on the part of the President and the treaty's proponents.

In 1795, after Jay had returned from England with the completed treaty and the President had submitted it to the Senate, Senator Aaron Burr moved that further consideration of the treaty be postponed and that the Senate recommend to the President further negotiations with Great Britain on the basis of seven propositions which he then submitted to the Senate. The Federalists defeated the motion—not because they considered it improper to recommend that the President attempt to secure a new treaty negotiated in accordance with the Senate's ideas, but only because the seven propositions contained demands so unacceptable to Great Britain as to defeat any prospect of a treaty. [There was great significance to] this motion's defeat:

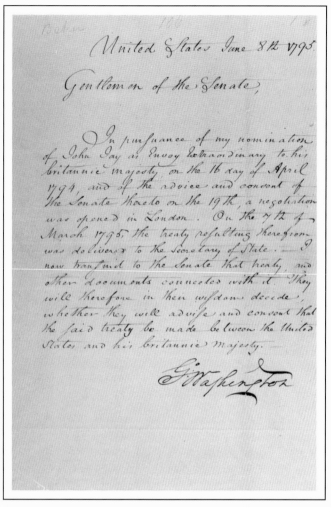

On June 8, 1795, President Washington submitted the Jay Treaty to the Senate. *National Archives*

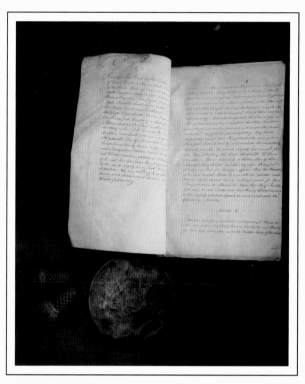

Senate approval of the unpopular Jay Treaty aroused a storm of public criticism. *National Archives*

Washington might well have considered passage of such a motion notice that the Senate would in the future expect to participate in framing the conditions under which a proposed treaty would be signed—at least it would have pointed out to him the expediency of always consulting the whole Senate before opening negotiations. The precedent might also have led the Senate to expect and demand such consultation in the future.[13]

Another significant precedent set by the Jay treaty was its injunction of secrecy.

When the Senate first received the completed treaty from the President, it adopted an order laying the Senators under an injunction of secrecy concerning the communications received from the President. After the treaty was approved, the Senate after much disputation adopted a resolution removing the injunction of secrecy but forbidding the Senators to give out any copy of the treaty or any of its articles. This action was apparently based on the belief that the question of publication was a decision which should be left to the President. However, since the resolution did not forbid Senators from making known the substance of the treaty, its contents gradually became widely known. After the appearance of an incomplete sketch in the *Aurora,* Senator Stevens T. Mason, of Virginia, sent a copy of the treaty to its editor, an act applauded by his fellow Republicans who had so bitterly fought the treaty, but denounced as a breach of faith by the Federalists.

Despite their scolding, the Senate's Federalists, took no steps to call Mason to account for disobeying the injunction. However, since it was a definite breach of a Senate order involving the secrecy of its proceedings, the President could hardly ignore such an act in considering the question of whether or not the Senate could be trusted with highly secret information. Washington as early as 1792 had expressed a low opinion of the Senate's ability to keep state secrets due to allegedly unguarded remarks of Senator Ralph Izard at a

Journalist William Cobbett, who used the pseudonym "Peter Porcupine," was caricatured for his attacks on the Jay Treaty.   *Historical Society of Pennsylvania*

dinner party. Such fears became even more natural when the Senate's membership became sharply divided between Federalists and Republicans, between friends of Great Britain and friends of France.

These doubts were shared by the State Department in the Adams administration. In reply to a list of questions posed by President Adams in 1797 regarding a possible mission to France, Secretary Pickering replied that it would be "highly expedient" to lay before the Senate for its approval a list of instructions for negotiating a treaty with France, as was done in the case of Spain in 1792, "if we could trust to the fidelity of *all* the members of the Senate." He explained his fears on that score by adding—"There was no inducement of passions or interest to betray the instructions to Spain;

but any instructions, alike communicated, for negotiating a new treaty with France, would reach the Directory sooner than we could send them our minister." [14]

The question of secrecy with regard to Senate treaties remained a problem for another century.

Throughout the nineteenth and early twentieth centuries the Senate attempted to deliberate on treaties in secret session. With regular efficiency, the newspapers managed to breach that secrecy and publish astonishingly complete accounts of the secret negotiations, sometimes printing the text of a treaty before the senators got their official copies. The Senate investigated, fretted, and howled but proved powerless to stop the leaks, which clearly came from the members themselves. Not until 1929 were executive sessions routinely opened to the press and the public. Today, we hold closed sessions only under the rarest of circumstances.

Approval of the unpopular Jay Treaty on June 24, 1795, brought the Senate under considerable public attack from newspapers and pamphleteers—indeed, media criticism of Congress in our times pales in comparison to the vitriol that was common in the eighteenth-century press. The treaty with England established reciprocal trading relations with certain restrictions, and England agreed to withdraw her garrisons from the northwestern frontier. But the treaty said nothing whatever about the stopping and searching of American ships by the British. Nor did it mention the matter of payment by the British for stolen slaves. The United States agreed that the debts owed to British merchants at the outbreak of the Revolution would be assumed by the federal government. Many people thought that Jay had made a bad bargain, and the treaty aroused intense anger in the United States. Both Jay and President Washington were severely criticized. Copies of the treaty were publicly burned, and the Senate was denounced as an aristocratic bastion. The House of Representatives used this fervor in an attempt to seize a large role in foreign affairs. While the Federalist supporters of the Jay Treaty held the majority in the Senate, the House was controlled by the Jeffersonian Republicans, who opposed the treaty.

Swanstrom wrote that the Senate faced a running threat to its treaty power from the House of Representatives, which jealously guarded what it considered its share of any authority involving the legislative power.

After the treaty had been signed in England by the American envoy and the representative of the British Crown, approved after full debate by a special session of the Senate, signed by President Washington, and officially ratified by representatives of the two Governments, the treaty was not yet ready to be put into full effect. A final obstacle was the Republican-controlled House of Representatives, to which (in addition to the Senate) the administration had to apply for the funds necessary to put certain provisions of the treaty into effect. . . .

. . . The House was naturally very jealous of its power over the purse, a power which the antitreaty forces claimed would be a nullity if the lower Chamber were duty-bound automatically to vote an appropriation for an object in which it did not have an agency. . . . As the popularly elected body, the House of Representatives had the same authority over the purse as the House of Commons enjoyed.

. . . the Federalists claimed that the House was under moral obligation to pass an appropriation necessary to put a legally adopted treaty into effect. . . . The Federalists also claimed that failure to put a legally adopted treaty into effect would be an act of faithlessness for which Americans would roundly condemn a foreign power. . . .

Finally, the Federalists claimed that if the House would not perform its plain duty and appropriate the necessary funds to put a constitutionally adopted treaty into effect, the Union would be at an end. The theory was that the Union would only hold together as each branch of the Government performed the duties required of it by the Constitution. . . .

In spite of the heat engendered by all these arguments, it should not be forgotten that the one paramount issue was the Jay Treaty itself. Should it, or should it not, be put into effect? The answer to this question depended, in turn, upon many economic, sectional, and social factors which cannot be discussed here. The Senate by a two-thirds vote had put itself squarely behind the treaty. What should the House do?

The constitutional House versus Senate issue was more clear cut in the vote on the resolution calling on the President to furnish the papers than on the appropriation issue itself, since many Members who were inclined to support the treaty on its own merits felt that the House had a constitutional right to pass upon the question of putting it into effect. Thus the former resolution was adopted by the respectable majority of 62 to 37. However, from a practical standpoint, the position of the House was relatively weak; Washington refused to furnish the papers and there was little the

House could do about it except adopt further resolutions defining what it claimed were its rights.

The President's reasons for rejecting the call for papers were four:

(1) Foreign negotiations require caution, often secrecy. Necessity for such caution and secrecy was a cogent reason for giving the treaty power to the President and Senate, the latter being a comparatively small body.

(2) The papers did not involve any purpose under the cognizance of the House, except impeachment, which the resolution did not cite as a purpose of the call. That treaties were fully completed when approved by the President and Senate had been the practice thus far, and had been so understood by foreign powers and acquiesced in by the House itself.

(3) The treaty power had been confined to the Senate as part of the "Great Compromise" of the Constitutional Convention in the interest of the smaller States.

(4) The Convention had explicitly rejected a proposal to make treaties binding only after being ratified by law. . . .

. . . the House having no practicable way of forcing the President to furnish the papers—the lower Chamber was far less helpless when it came to making or withholding financial provision for putting the treaty into effect. This was the all-important practical issue at hand.

Theodore Sedgwick opened this, the critical stage of the controversy, on April 13, 1796, when he moved that provision ought to be made by law for carrying into effect four recently ratified treaties—with Algiers, the Indian tribes northwest of the Ohio, Spain, and Great Britain. The obvious purpose, of course, was to link the Jay Treaty with the highly popular Pinckney Treaty with Spain. James Hillhouse, Federalist stalwart from Connecticut, announced that if provision for one of them were rejected, Federalists would feel justified in voting against provision for the others. Gallatin immediately punctured that bubble, however, by pointing out the obvious inconsistency between this strategy and the very basis of the Federalist position—the claim that the House was morally obligated to put all constitutionally adopted treaties into effect. The Republican majority thereupon quickly approved funds for the Indian, Spanish, and Algerine treaties, and the debate on the question of putting the Jay Treaty into effect was on again. The climax came on April 28, 1796, when Fisher Ames pulled his pain-racked body erect and delivered the address in favor of the treaty which was for decades remembered as the epitome of congressional eloquence—an address which moved to tears even two such old campaigners as Vice President Adams and Supreme Court Justice James Iredell, who sat in the crowded gallery. Ames based his arguments both on the merits of the treaty itself and on the constitutional duty of the House. Two days later the House by the narrow vote of 51 to 48 voted to approve the appropriation.

In spite of the sound and fury accompanying this "great debate," the final vote in a sense solved no question except that of approving appropriations for this one treaty. In the votes on the call for papers, on the resolutions answering the President's message refusing to furnish them, and on the Jay Treaty appropriation, the stand of the House majority was perfectly consistent. Its Members had claimed that when a treaty approved by the President and Senate required legislative action to put it into operation, the House had a constitutional right to weigh the treaty on its merits and pass, or refuse to pass, the necessary legislation as it saw fit. They had then weighed the Jay Treaty on its merits and had decided to vote the necessary funds. Among the 51 affirmative votes were those of many who claimed that the House had a perfect right to withhold the funds if it saw fit. Thus from the standpoint of constitutional theory, the vote was not a clear-cut victory for the exclusion of the House from the treaty power. The Constitution itself, by grant of powers mutually contradictory, had created the possibility of an impasse, and the theoretical powers of the House in this area were not then determined, nor have they been to this day.

From the standpoint of practical accomplishment, the outcome was a critical victory for the Senate's unique and vital role in the making of treaties. Had the outcome been different, the Senate's impact on the future conduct of foreign policy would have been greatly impaired, its place in the system of checks and balances largely diminished, and the constitutional separation-of-powers underpinning dangerously weakened. As Roy Swanstrom pointed out:

One of [the Senate's] most highly prized prerogatives—a prerogative which goes far to make the Senate the most powerful upper Chamber in the world today—had been challenged on an issue of the most critical importance by the best brains and most persuasive eloquence of the lower House, and yet had come through unscathed. And the precedent was a lasting one. While the great moral question remains undecided as to how far the House is bound in good faith to carry out by legislation and appropriations the provisions of treaties, the House has never yet failed to support a treaty pledging the good faith of the United States. On the other hand, if the House had successfully utilized this occasion to put into practical application its claim to pass upon treaties involving areas in which the lower Chamber had legislative power, the precedent would have been in the direction of nullifying the Senate's special treaty power, since most treaties would involve in some way at least one such area of legislation.[15]

Thus, Swanstrom concluded, "The Senate survived the ordeal with unimpaired powers."

As the new government evolved, new precedents shaped the treatymaking process. In 1794, the Senate "suspended" one article of the Jay Treaty as a means of preventing rejection of the whole. In 1803, Great Britain refused to accept an amendment that the Senate added to the King-Hawksbury Convention. Although the British foreign minister grumbled that the Senate's action was unprecedented, it was one which Great Britain and other nations would have to learn to tolerate.

The power to amend treaties rapidly replaced Washington's earlier expectation of Senate advice during the negotiations. This power to amend became so significant that, in 1868, the Senate changed its rules to permit amendments to treaties by a simple majority vote. As Professor Arthur Schlesinger has written: "This enabled senators to alter the text of treaties with greater ease. It also invited parliamentary maneuvers which, by uniting opponents of a treaty with a faction of its supporters on specific amendments, might produce a document unacceptable to original supporters on the final two-thirds vote." (The ability to amend by a simple majority vote can also, however, be the means of putting together the necessary two-thirds vote for final approval, as in the case of the Panama Canal treaties in 1978.) Professor Schlesinger noted that "the Senate exercised its power in this realm with relish, freely rewriting, amending and rejecting treaties negotiated by the executive. Indeed, it ratified *no* important treaty between 1871 and 1898."[16]

In rejecting a treaty with the Wabash and Illinois Indians, the Senate in 1794, for the first time, exercised its right to refuse its consent to a treaty negotiated by the executive branch.

In 1825, the Senate first rejected an international treaty, turning down, by a vote of 0 to 40, a convention with Colombia for the suppression of the slave trade. Leading to this defeat was a similar treaty with Great Britain in 1824, which proslavery advocates in the Senate had laden with amendments that the British refused to accept. Meanwhile, the United States had invited other nations to help it suppress the slave trade, and Colombia had responded. The Colombia treaty, however, was caught in the backlash of the British treaty. Having gutted the British treaty, the Senate entirely rejected the Colombian treaty on the same subject. Of the hundreds of treaties the Senate has considered in its two-hundred-year history, it has rejected relatively few. Of course, many have died in committee or been withdrawn by the president rather than face defeat.

Mr. President, one of the thorny issues that surfaced early in the Senate's history was whether the "advice and consent" of the Senate was required prior to the negotiations leading into the making of treaties. Reference has already been made to the controversy surrounding the Jay Treaty, in which Attorney General Edmund Randolph maintained that to proceed otherwise would abridge the rights of the Senate. On June 10, 1846, President James Polk sought the previous "advice and consent" of the Senate to a convention submitted by the British minister

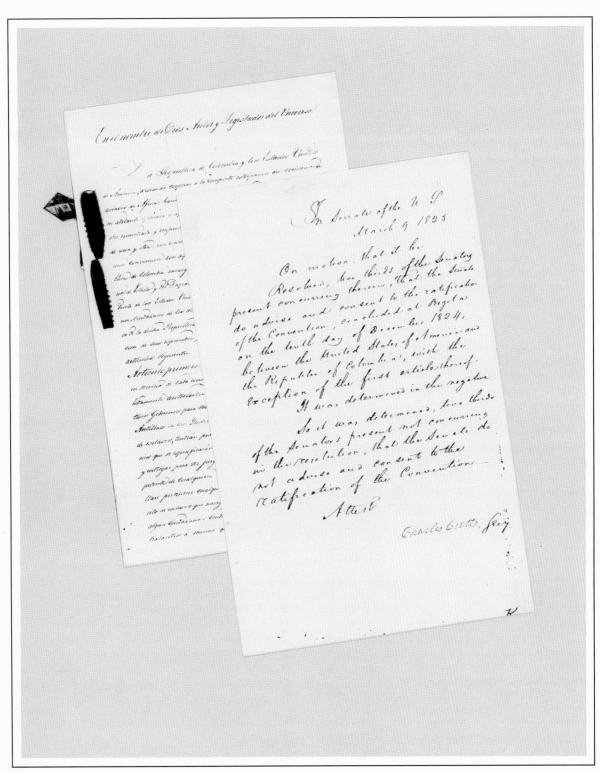

In 1825, the Senate refused to approve a convention with Colombia to suppress the slave trade. *National Archives*

in the dispute over the boundary of the Oregon Territory. Polk, in doing so, may have been trying to extricate himself from a political dilemma over the frustration of accepting or rejecting Great Britain's proposition to settle upon the forty-ninth parallel. If the Senate approved the treaty, it could not blame the administration for surrendering the extreme claims which demagogues in Congress had been making. Polk's message transmitting the British proposal said:

In the early periods of the government the opinion and advice of the Senate were often taken in advance upon important questions of our foreign policy. General Washington repeatedly consulted the Senate and asked their previous advice upon pending negotiations with foreign powers; and the Senate in every instance responded to his call by giving their advice, to which he always conformed his action. This practice, though rarely resorted to in later times, was in my judgment eminently wise, and may on occasions of great importance be properly revived. The Senate are a branch of the treaty-making power, and by consulting them in advance of his own action, upon important measures of foreign policy which may ultimately come before them for their consideration, the President secures harmony of action between that body and himself. The Senate are, moreover, a branch of the war-making power, and it may be eminently proper for the executive to take the opinion and advice of that body in advance, upon any great question which may involve in its decision the issue of peace or war. On the present occasion the magnitude of the subject would induce me under any circumstances to desire the previous advice of the Senate, and that desire is increased by the recent debates and proceedings in Congress, which render it, in my judgment, not only respectful to the Senate, but necessary and proper, if not indispensable to insure harmonious action between that body and the Executive. . . . For these reasons I invite the consideration of the Senate to the proposal of the British Government for the settlement of the Oregon question, and ask their advice on the subject. . . .

Should the Senate, by the constitutional majority required for the ratification of treaties, advise the acceptance of this proposition or advise it with such modifications as they may upon full deliberation deem proper, I shall conform my action to their advice. Should the Senate, however, decline by such constitutional majority to give such advice, or to express an opinion on the subject I shall consider it my duty to reject the offer.[17]

The Senate shrank from advising rejection and, by a vote of 37 to 12, advised the acceptance of the proposal. Later, Senate consent was given to ratification by a vote of 41 to 14.

On December 7, 1861, President Abraham Lincoln asked the Senate for advice concerning a treaty with Mexico proposed to Lincoln by the U.S. minister to that government. On February 25, 1862, the Senate, in a resolution, stated that "it is not advisable to negotiate a treaty that will require the United States to assume any portion of the principal or interest of the debt of Mexico, or that will require the concurrence of European powers."

Meanwhile, two treaties providing for a loan to Mexico had been signed by the U.S. minister, who had not received the delayed instructions, whereupon President Lincoln, on June 23, 1862, again sent to the Senate a message as follows, in part:

In view of the very important events occurring there, he has thought that the interests of the United States would be promoted by the conclusion of two treaties which should provide for a loan to that Republic. He has therefore signed such treaties, and they having been duly ratified by the Government of Mexico he has transmitted them to me for my consideration. The action of the Senate is of course conclusive against an acceptance of the treaties on my part. I have, nevertheless, thought it just to our excellent minister in Mexico and respectful to the Government of that Republic to lay the treaties before the Senate, together with the correspondence which has occurred in relation to them. In performing this duty I have only to add that the importance of the subject thus submitted to the Senate can not be overestimated, and I shall cheerfully receive and consider with the highest respect any further advice the Senate may think proper to give upon the subject.[18]

The treaties were promptly tabled.

President Ulysses Grant, on May 13, 1872, sent to the Senate a message requesting an expression concerning that body's disposition toward a proposal by Great Britain, in which he stated:

To the Senate of the United States:

I transmit herewith the correspondence which has recently taken place respecting the differences of opinion which have arisen between this Government and that of Great Britain with regard to the powers of the tribunal of arbitration created under the treaty signed at Washington May 8, 1871.

I respectfully invite the attention of the Senate to the proposed article submitted by the British Government with the object of removing the differences which seem to threaten the prosecution of the arbitration, and request an expression by the Senate of their disposition in regard to advising and consenting to the formal adoption of an article such as is proposed by the British Government.

The Senate is aware that the consultation with that body in advance of entering into agreements with foreign states has many precedents. In the early days of the Republic General Washington repeatedly asked their advice upon pending questions with such powers. The most important recent precedent is that of the Oregon boundary treaty, in 1846.

The importance of the results hanging upon the present state of the treaty with Great Britain leads me to follow these former precedents and to desire the counsel of the Senate in advance of agreeing to the proposal of Great Britain.[19]

The Senate gave its approval to the proposed article, but with an "understanding" which proved unacceptable to the British government.

Thus, Presidents Washington, Polk, Lincoln, Grant, and several others on occasion sought the advice of the Senate before entering into conventions and treaties.

Mr. President, another vexing issue that has surfaced many times in the history of the Senate's role in treaty ratification is whether senators should be involved in the actual negotiation of these treaties. The United States has sent some unusual treaty negotiators in

THE WAR DOESN'T SEEM TO BE OVER.
THE NEW ARRIVAL: " But, gentlemen, you know I am a Peace Treaty.

The peace treaty ending the war with Spain received a hostile reception in the Senate.   *Library of Congress*

the past. I noted, for example, that the chief justice of the United States negotiated the Jay Treaty.

During the War of 1812, Speaker of the House Henry Clay resigned from Congress to join the delegation (which also included Delaware Senator James Bayard) to negotiate the Treaty of Ghent. Bayard's presence raised the question of whether having senators on the negotiating team would make the Senate more favorably inclined to approve the treaty, or whether it would violate the separation of powers. That debate has gone on for many generations without being resolved.

Noting the frequency with which the Senate had rejected treaties during the last quarter of the nineteenth century, President William McKinley shrewdly named three U.S. senators to negotiate the treaty of peace with Spain in 1898. His action was roundly criticized by senators from both parties. Maine Senator Eugene Hale, one of the Republican floor leaders, said he did not want to see any more senators appearing as advocates of treaties that they themselves had negotiated. Democratic Senator Benjamin Tillman of South Carolina concurred, reminding the senators that they had once voted to prohibit the practice—at a time when two senators had been sent to negotiate a treaty with Hawaii. That vote was later rescinded in order to avoid embarrassing the two senator-negotiators.

Democratic Senator Augustus Bacon of Georgia and Republican George Frisbie Hoar of Massachusetts argued that the practice was blatantly unconstitutional—since the Constitution provides that no senator or representative should be appointed, during his term, to any civil office which was created during his term, and that no one holding such office could be a member of either House. Senator Hoar asked how a senator should discharge his duties "if he had already not only formed an opinion, but acted upon the matter under the control and direction of another department of the government?" And, he added, "If that practice continue, it will go far, in my judgment, to destroy the independence and dignity of the Senate." [20]

Now, these sentiments are all well and fine. But presidents, quite understandably, want to do everything possible to see treaties negotiated during their administrations approved by the Senate, and they will use every method at their disposal to do so. The peace treaty with Spain, negotiated by the three senators, was approved by the Senate.

A generation later, President Woodrow Wilson was roundly criticized for not including senators in the delegation that negotiated the Treaty of Versailles. For years thereafter, it became part of the American history catechism learned by schoolchildren that this

Foreign Relations Committee Chairman Henry Cabot Lodge bitterly opposed the Treaty of Versailles.
Library of Congress

senatorial omission contributed to the defeat of the Treaty of Versailles, which was twice rejected by the Senate. One cannot entirely blame President Wilson. In 1918, his party had lost control of the Senate, and the new chairman of the Foreign Relations Committee was his bitter political opponent, Henry Cabot Lodge, Sr. Had Wilson taken any senators, he could not have avoided taking Lodge.

With the Treaty of Versailles in mind, Wilson's successor, Warren G. Harding—who had served as a senator during the fight for the treaty's ratification—in 1921 appointed Senator Lodge and Senate Democratic Leader Oscar Underwood of Alabama as delegates to the Washington Arms Limitation Conference. For very much the same reason, Presidents Franklin Roosevelt and Harry Truman involved Tom Connally of Texas and Arthur Vandenberg of Michigan—the chairman and the ranking Republican of the Senate Foreign Relations Committee—in the creation of the United Nations.

Republican Senator Arthur Vandenberg played a leading role in foreign policy after World War II.
George Tames/New York Times

Senator Tom Connally chaired the Foreign Relations Committee during the creation of the United Nations. *George Tames/New York Times*

This action spared the UN the fate of the League of Nations; there were only two Senate votes against the UN Charter.

Francis O. Wilcox, who served as the first chief of staff of the Senate Foreign Relations Committee, accompanied Senators Connally and Vandenberg to the UN conference in the spring of 1945. Wilcox observed in an oral history that "we came back to Washington and the two senators were recognized as the authorities in the Senate on the Charter; they had been through all the negotiations, they knew the attitude of the Russians and the other delegates there. So there was no real problem getting it through the Senate." But Wilcox acknowledged that such direct senatorial participation had its drawbacks as well. He recalled that "Senator Vandenberg and Senator Connally spent two hundred and thirteen days . . . with Secretary of State [James] Byrnes, negotiating the peace treaties with the satellite countries. I think they found . . . that this took them away from their Senate duties too long at a time,

and after that there was a tendency not to get involved in these lengthy negotiations."[21]

That would certainly be a problem in today's Senate.

One solution to the problem of senators as negotiators has been for presidents to invite whole senatorial delegations to visit ongoing negotiations. In March 1957, Secretary of State John Foster Dulles invited a bipartisan delegation of senators to visit the London Disarmament Conference. Majority Leader Lyndon B. Johnson supported the idea but asked that the request come from President Eisenhower, with an indication of the urgency that required senators to consider the matter in London rather than in Washington. By then, however, Dulles had abandoned the idea as premature. In his closed-door testimony before the Senate Foreign Relations Committee, Secretary Dulles explained that "the main objective of going would be to sense the atmosphere a bit, which is always helpful; but that as far as the substance of the matter, that can be better learned here in Washington than it can be at London." Senator Hubert Humphrey added that sending senatorial advisers "would be like loading extra cargo on a ship." The give-and-take of that candid session, not published for another twenty years, provides an interesting insight into the pros and cons of senatorial delegations, which have been repeatedly proposed for subsequent arms limitations talks.[22]

On February 28, 1985, the Senate adopted a resolution, sponsored by Majority Leader Bob Dole of Kansas and cosponsored by me as minority leader, creating a Senate Observer Group to act as official observers at the Arms Reduction and Control Negotiations in Geneva between the United States and the Soviet Union, and designating Senators Ted Stevens of Alaska, Richard Lugar of Indiana, Claiborne Pell of Rhode Island, and Sam Nunn of Georgia as members.

In December 1985, the Senate, by resolution, added Senators Edward Kennedy of Massachusetts, Malcolm Wallop of Wyoming, Daniel Patrick Moynihan of New York, John Warner of Virginia, Don Nickles of Oklahoma, and Albert Gore, Jr., of Tennessee to the group, while Senator Dole and I continued to serve as ex officio members.

On January 6, 1987, the Senate adopted a resolution, which I introduced as majority leader with the cosponsorship of Minority Leader Bob Dole, reauthorizing and redesignating the bipartisan Senate Arms Control Observer Group. The negotiations resulted in the signing of the Intermediate-Range Nuclear Forces (INF) treaty in Washington on December 8, 1987. Senator Dole and I were invited by President Reagan to attend

Secretary of State John Foster Dulles consulted regularly with the Senate.   *George Tames/New York Times*

the ratification ceremonies at the Moscow summit meeting on June 1, 1988.

The senators in the observer group did not participate in the actual negotiations. They provided a continuing important link between the Senate and the Reagan administration's negotiators, keeping the Senate informed regarding developments and progress in the negotiations, and periodically advising and consulting with the U.S. negotiators. The work of the observer group was, indeed, praiseworthy, and its members received the plaudits of both the administration and their Senate colleagues.

On April 13, 1989, the Senate adopted a resolution, sponsored by Majority Leader George Mitchell of Maine and cosponsored by Minority Leader Bob Dole, reconstituting and reauthorizing the Senate Arms Control Observer Group to act during the 101st Congress as official observers at any formal arms reduction or control negotiations.

Mr. President, another aspect of the Senate's advice and consent powers is the constitutional requirement that the Senate consent to ratification of treaties by a two-thirds vote. The effect of that requirement is that successful treatymaking can never be a partisan affair, since only under the rarest circumstances has a party ever enjoyed a two-thirds majority in the Senate. It makes no difference which party is in the majority. The administration and the treaty's supporters will have to build a bipartisan coalition to win the day. This is as it should be: treaties must reflect a broad national consensus. Yet, it certainly adds to the burdens of the Senate leadership and requires a good deal of cooperation from the minority party. Looking back over two of the landmark treaties that were enacted during my years in the Senate, the Nuclear Test Ban Treaty of 1963—which I voted against—and the Panama Canal Treaty of 1977, neither could have been enacted without the support and assistance of the Republican minority leaders, respectively, Everett Dirksen of Illinois and Howard Baker of Tennessee.[23]

A half century ago, George Haynes wrote in his monumental history and analysis of the Senate that the two-thirds rule's

most calamitous effects are psychological. In the Senate it heartens any tiny group . . . to attempt by delays and bargaining to persuade enough colleagues to join them to make up "a recalcitrant one-third plus one." Such an *ad hoc* bloc in our Senate can and does exercise a "pathological obstruction" in the handling of our foreign relations such as is exercised by so small a minority in no other legislative body in the world.[24]

The Senate, itself, does not ratify treaties—actual ratification only takes place when the instruments of ratification are formally exchanged between the parties. When a treaty is submitted to the Senate for approval, it has several options for action. Depending on whether or not a two-thirds ma-

Faced with the 1963 Limited Test Ban Treaty, the Senate observes hopefully, "I guess the fine print's been read carefully." *Library of Congress*

jority votes in favor, the Senate may approve or reject the treaty as it has been submitted. It may make its approval conditional by including in the resolution amendments to the text of the treaty, reservations, understandings, interpretations, declarations, or other statements. The president and the other countries involved must then decide whether to accept the conditions and changes in the legislation, renegotiate the provisions, or abandon the treaty. Finally, the Senate may choose to take no definitive action, leaving the treaty pending in the Senate until withdrawn at the request of the president or, occasionally, at the initiative of the Senate.

On a number of past occasions, the Senate has exercised its role in the treatymaking process in such a way that treaties never entered into force. It is useful to distinguish among instances in which treaties were (a) rejected in a Senate vote; (b) approved with conditions subsequently refused by the ex-

Senate consideration of the Panama Canal treaties in 1978 involved an extended debate. *Library of Congress*

ecutive branch or other countries; or (c) never voted upon by the Senate.

In the case of most treaties submitted to the Senate, it has given its advice and consent to ratification, and the ratification has subsequently been signed and deposited by the president. From March 1789 through 1988, the Senate approved 1,546 treaties, approximately 90 percent of those submitted to it.[25] Only 20 treaties have been rejected by a Senate vote because they failed to receive the required two-thirds majority. Most often, the Senate has simply not voted on treaties that were deemed by the leadership not to

have sufficient support within the Senate for approval, and in general these treaties have eventually been withdrawn.

Of the many treaties approved by the Senate with amendments, reservations, understandings, or interpretations, forty-three never entered into force because the reservations or amendments were not acceptable either to the president or to the other country or countries party to the treaty.

Even after the Senate approves the ratification of a treaty, the president may decide that he does not want to go forward with ratifying the treaty. That would end the matter.

There have been at least eighty-five treaties that were eventually withdrawn because the Senate never took final action on them. Treaties may also remain in the Senate Foreign Relations Committee for extended periods. Since treaties are not required to be resubmitted at the beginning of each new Congress, there have been instances in which treaties have lain dormant within the committee for years, even decades, without action being taken.

Senate action is not the only reason that various treaties signed by the United States have remained "unperfected treaties" and never entered into force. In some cases, treaties have never been submitted to the Senate although they have been signed. In others, the ratification process has not been completed by the president, as I indicated a moment ago, even though the Senate has given its approval. In still other cases, treaties have not entered into force because of actions of other nations.

Several of the treaties rejected by the Senate received more "ayes" than "nays" but fell short of two-thirds. A number of treaties, including the Treaty of Versailles, were rejected twice.

In addition to treaties, which may not enter into force and become binding on the United States without the advice and consent of the Senate, there are other types of international agreements concluded by the executive branch and not submitted to the Senate. These are classified in the United States as executive agreements, not as treaties, a distinction that has only domestic significance. International law regards each mode of international agreement as binding, whatever its designation under domestic law. [26]

The difficulty in obtaining a two-thirds vote was one of the motivating forces behind the vast increase in executive agreements after World War II. In 1952, for instance, the United States signed 14 treaties and 291 executive agreements. This was a larger number of executive agreements than had been reached in all the years between 1789 and 1889 combined. Senate frustration with this situation boiled over into the so-called Bricker amendment. Introduced for the first time in 1951 by Ohio Republican Senator John Bricker, this proposed constitutional amendment would have required Senate consent to all executive agreements. Opposed by the Truman and Eisenhower administrations, the Bricker amendment failed to be adopted in the Senate by only a single vote. [27] Executive agreements continue to grow at a rapid rate. As of June 1989, the official treaty records of the Department of State indicated that the United States was a party to 890 treaties and 5,117 executive agreements.

Any of a number of factors may account for the growth in executive agreements. Among these are the sheer volume of business and contacts between the United States and other countries, coupled with the already heavy workload of the Senate. Many international agreements are of minor importance, relatively speaking, and would needlessly overburden the Senate if they were submitted to it for advice and consent. Another factor has been the passage of legislation authorizing the executive branch to conclude international agreements in certain fields, such as foreign aid, agriculture, and trade. Treaties have also been approved implicitly authorizing further agreements between the parties. According to one study, "88.3 percent of international agreements reached between 1946 and 1972 were based at least partly on statutory authority; 6.2 percent were treaties, and 5.5 percent were based solely on executive authority." [28]

Still another factor, on occasion, has been the knowledge that some international agreements that the president wished to conclude were unlikely to receive the approval of two-thirds of the Senate.[29]

When discussing the difficulties of winning a two-thirds vote approval in the Senate, and the power of the minority, I do not mean to imply that all treaties deserve to be approved. The Constitution clearly gives power to the Senate to withhold its consent, as well as to grant it, depending upon its interpretation of the best interests of the nation. The most recent treaty rejected by the Senate provides a good example.

On March 8, 1983, the Senate rejected the Montreal Protocols by a vote of 50 ayes to 42 nays, twelve votes short of the two-thirds of those members present and voting needed for approval. This treaty, negotiated during the Ford administration and supported by Presidents Ford, Carter, and Reagan, would have set limits on passenger damage awards in international air crashes. Supporters of this treaty believed that it would lead to swifter settlement of claims than under the current law. Opponents, led by Senator Ernest Hollings of South Carolina, called it an "outrageous assault on public safety and a sweetheart deal" for the foreign governments that own airlines. Although a majority supported the treaty, it fell far short of the two-thirds goal. The Senate would not consent.[30]

Upon several occasions, Senate amendments have proved fatal to treaties or conventions, either because they were not accepted by the president of the United States or because the other signatory party or parties were unwilling to ratify the modified contract. An amendment makes an actual change in the language of the treaty. Also available to the Senate are other options, short of outright rejection of a treaty. The terminology of these limiting actions varies. Although the labeling of the Senate's expression may be relatively unimportant in determining its legal effect, the most significant

actions, in order of their effect, are: amendments; reservations; understandings; interpretations; declarations; and statements, or similar wording such as clarification, recommendation, explanation, or sense of the Senate.

Regardless of what an action is called, the substance determines the legal effect. For example, language would constitute a *reservation* (or an *amendment*) when it would exclude or vary the legal effect of one or more of the provisions of the treaty. On the other hand, language which merely explains or clarifies the meaning of treaty provisions but which does not exclude or vary the legal effect of such provisions would properly constitute an *understanding* or *interpretation*. Often, there can be confusion in the use of a particular label or descriptive term for what is being done, but the substance is what counts, and there can, in fact, be little difference in effect between a reservation and an amendment, as I have shown, depending on its content. A reservation that limits the U.S. obligation may have the same effect as an amendment to the actual text of the treaty itself. Conversely, an understanding or declaration may often simply deal with some matter incidental to the operation of the treaty in a manner other than as a substantive reservation. Even though such language may have no effect on the international obligations of the treaty, however, the executive would communicate such interpretations or understandings to the other parties. If, regardless of its label, the U.S. government believes that the verbiage has the actual character of an amendment, condition, or reservation, it would be so treated and transmitted to the other signatory state or states, and it could be subject to further negotiations if not rejected outright by the other state.

Incidentally, on two notable occasions, the likelihood of failure to obtain the necessary two-thirds majority in the Senate led to the use of a joint resolution requiring a simple majority vote of both houses in order to accomplish the purpose sought by the proposed treaty. This occurred during the presidency of John Tyler, after the Senate had rejected a treaty for the annexation of Texas on June 8, 1844, by a vote of 16 to 35. Also, in the instance of Hawaii, an annexation treaty had been concluded with the provisional government in Hawaii, but its approval by the U.S. Senate was delayed by strong opposition. The outbreak of the war with Spain so strengthened the need for a mid-Pacific naval station that a joint resolution on the cession of Hawaii was approved in 1898.

Mr. President, while the Constitution explains how treaties must be ratified, it is silent about how treaties might be terminated. The breaking off of two treaties during the Carter administration stirred controversy. In 1978, the president terminated the U.S. defense treaty with Taiwan, to facilitate the establishment of diplomatic relations with the People's Republic of China. Also in 1978, the new Panama Canal treaties replaced three previous treaties with Panama. In one case, the president acted unilaterally; in the second, he terminated treaties in accordance with actions taken by Congress. But clearly it seems that the right to terminate belongs to the executive, the sole branch of government that communicates with foreign governments. Only once has Congress terminated a treaty by a joint resolution: that was a mutual defense treaty with France, from which, in 1798, Congress declared the United States "freed and exonerated." In that case, breaking the treaty almost amounted to an act of war; indeed, two days later Congress authorized hostilities against France, which were only narrowly averted.

Finally, by virtue of the supremacy clause of the Constitution (Article VI, clause 2), a treaty that is concluded compatibly with applicable constitutional requirements may have status as the "supreme law of the land," along with federal statutes and the Constitution itself. A treaty does not become effective as U.S. domestic law, however, automatically upon its entry into force on the international level. Instead, this occurs only where the instrument is "self-executing" and operates without any necessity for implementing legislation. The classic statement of this principle was given by Chief Justice Marshall in *Foster* v. *Neilson*:

. . . Our constitution declares a treaty to be the law of the land. It is, consequently, to be regarded in courts of justice as equivalent to an act of the legislature, whenever it operates of itself, without the aid of any legislative provision. But when the terms of the stipulation import a contract—when either of the parties engages to perform a particular act, the treaty addresses itself to the political, not the judicial department; and the legislature must execute the contract, before it can become a rule for the Court.

Let me conclude my capsule summary of the Senate's role in the treatymaking and treaty-ratifying process by emphasizing its importance in the American system of shared powers. When the thirteen colonies rebelled against the English king, they rejected the concept of monarchy on our shores. When the Constitution created an executive branch and a president of the United States, it gave him no unchecked or unconditional powers. The English king could make treaties exclusively on his own, but this would not be true for the American president. The Constitution, instead, made treatymaking a concurrent power. The United States Senate has carefully guarded its share of this power for two hundred years, as I trust it will continue to do, perpetually into the future of this Republic.

CHAPTER 2

Nominations

July 29, 1987*

Mr. President, whenever a nomination to the Supreme Court is made, it invariably happens that both the nation and this body are treated to the "sounding brass" and "tinkling cymbals" of claims that the appointment process is a presidential prerogative.

Notwithstanding that the Constitution requires appointment with the advice and consent of the Senate, White House spokesmen and their sympathizers begin the familiar refrain that the Senate's role is confined to confirming the president's choice unless the nominee is "manifestly unfit" for the post. Throughout the history of the Republic, this contention has been heard in regard to both cabinet and judicial nominations.

Those holding this view maintain that the president should be free to select any person he desires for even the most elevated and sensitive position, especially if the president was elected to office by a substantial majority. Furthermore, they assert that a Senate inquiry into a nominee's fitness for office is limited to qualifications, while such other areas of obvious concern as his or her personal philosophy or ideology are off limits to Senate scrutiny. Proponents of this view also claim that the Senate is obligated to place its stamp of approval on a nominee so long as he or she can demonstrate the requisite

minimum qualifications for the office in question.

All of these assertions have been made time out of memory but, unlike love, they do not become better or truer the second or third time around. Indeed, if anything, their repetition offends propriety, because they are transparent appeals to political expediency and opportunism and intended to deter the responsible exercise of the advice and consent function.

In recognition that the duty imposed on the president faithfully to execute the laws requires persons sympathetic to his programs, the Senate traditionally has given the president great leeway in choosing his policymaking subordinates, especially those in cabinet and subcabinet positions. The Senate has more or less uniformly followed this practice, as a matter of grace and in the spirit of cooperation, to ensure that the executive branch functions as a team in implementing and enforcing the laws.

What has been the fairly general practice with respect to the appointment of executive branch policymakers, however, has not applied to judicial nominations, and arguments to the contrary are at odds with the separation of powers doctrine, common sense, and history. The Constitution establishes a Su-

---

* Updated March 1989

preme Court and gives Congress power in its discretion to constitute inferior federal tribunals; nowhere in the blueprint of our government is it hinted that the high court or any other federal court is the president's court. Similarly, nothing in the Constitution suggests that either the justices or judges should be the president's men. In fact, the Constitution refutes this notion by granting federal judges lifetime tenure and making their compensation inviolable.

The Supreme Court not too long ago observed that "the principle of separation of powers was not simply an abstract generalization in the minds of the Framers: it was woven into the document that they drafted in Philadelphia in the summer of 1787." This principle appears especially in the clause dealing with appointments. "The Senate," the Court declared, "is a participant in the appointive process by virtue of its authority to refuse to confirm persons nominated to office by the President." Nothing in the Court's remarks regarding appointment intimates that the Senate is intended to be a rubber stamp; indeed, as just stated, the Court specifically recognizes the Senate's "authority to refuse to confirm persons nominated to office by the President." The involvement of the Senate in the process was not motivated by "etiquette or protocol," but, according to the Court, reflects the fact that "[t]he men who met in Philadelphia in the summer of 1787 were practical statesmen, experienced in politics, who viewed the principle of separation of powers as a vital check against tyranny." [1]

Can a rubber stamp be "a vital check against tyranny"? The question answers itself. A "Patsy Senate"—about which Mary McGrory, a columnist, writes from time to time—is neither an effective bulwark for liberty nor true to itself or to the American people. If, in truth, the framers had intended the Senate simply to endorse the president's selection, the Senate could have been left out of the process altogether. Clearly, the men who met at Philadelphia two hundred years ago had in mind a more substantive role for the Senate.

Under the Articles of Confederation, the Congress made all nominations, but when the Constitution established a separate executive branch, it divided responsibility for nominations between the president and the Senate. Some delegates to the Constitutional Convention had wanted the Senate to make all nominations of principal officers, while others thought the president should have exclusive power to make appointments. Although the language of the Constitution was a compromise between these positions, those supporting a strong executive felt the provision clearly favored the president.

Writing in *The Federalist*, No. 66, Alexander Hamilton argued that "it will be the office of the president to *nominate*, and with the advice and consent of the senate to *appoint*. There will of course be no exertion of *choice* on the part of the senate. They may defeat one choice of the executive, and oblige him to make another; but they cannot themselves *choose*—they can only ratify or reject the choice, of the president." [2]

In common with many provisions of the Constitution, the clause which provides that the president "shall nominate, and by and with the Advice and Consent of the Senate, shall appoint" is the result of a compromise between opposing views. One faction was afraid that giving the president the exclusive power of appointment would eventually lead to monarchy. These delegates believed not only that Senate involvement would reduce that danger but also that senators as a group might have information about a nominee not possessed by single individuals. John Rutledge of South Carolina, for example, was "by no means disposed to grant so great a power to any single person. The people will think we are leaning too much towards Monarchy." Charles Pinckney thought that the "executive will possess neither the requisite knowledge of characters, nor confidence of the people for so high a trust." [3]

Convention proponents of a strong executive felt that the president would be better qualified and more responsible in making appointments than the members of the national legislature. Supporters of an exclusive presidential appointments power saw no danger that it would lead to monarchy or despotism. Instead, they contended that appointments by legislative bodies have generally resulted from cabals, personal regard, and other considerations unrelated to qualifications. Persuaded that the power to nominate was for all practical purposes the power to appoint, the members of this group agreed to the compromise by which the president was given the power to nominate, with Senate approval required before an appointment could be made. Later, in *The Federalist*, No. 76, Hamilton explained that "every advantage to be expected from [the power of appointment] would in substance be derived from the power of *nomination*. . . . There can, in this view, be no difference between nominating and appointing." [4]

Although many of his views have stood the test of time, Hamilton's observation that a nomination is tantamount to appointment has not been vindicated. The role the Senate has actually played in giving its advice and consent has not been a mere passive review of the qualifications of the persons nominated by the president, as Hamilton had expected.

Hamilton, however, was convinced that Senate confirmation would be a welcome check on the president. He believed it "would have a powerful, though, in general, a silent operation. It would be an excellent check upon a spirit of favoritism in the President, and would tend greatly to preventing the appointment of unfit characters from State prejudice, from family connection, from personal attachment, or from a view to popularity." [5]

Although the debates at Philadelphia and in the state ratifying conventions leave unresolved such questions as what the framers may have meant by "advice," there is little doubt regarding the significance of the term "consent." Clearly, the framers intended to give the president the exclusive power to nominate. Just as clear is the fact that Senate "approval" was necessary in order for an appointment to become effective. In other words, the Senate was given an absolute negative. Thus, while senators could not choose an officeholder, they could defeat the president's choice and oblige him to make one or more others until senators were satisfied with the nominee's qualifications. Although the oft-stated phrase "qualified for office" is used in the sense of fitness for office, it is not limited to technical competence but extends to general suitability. A candidate's personal philosophy and ideology are, therefore, relevant considerations.

Over the past two hundred years, many a battle has been fought between the White House and the Senate over nominations. Although most nominations are approved, the Senate has more than once flexed its political muscles to reject a presidential nominee—including the rejection or withdrawal of fifteen cabinet nominations and twenty-six Supreme Court nominations. Confirmation power is one of the major constitutional provisions that separates the Senate from the House. It has been the subject of numerous articles, books, novels, and even motion pictures.

Indeed, as early as Henry IV (1399–1413), English parliaments effectively controlled the king's royal council and household. Several officials of Henry IV's household were dismissed at the insistence of the Commons.

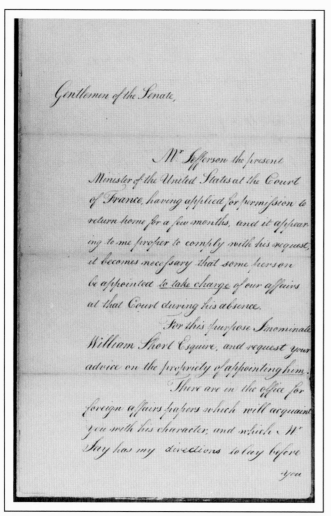

Gentlemen of the Senate,

Mr. Jefferson the present Minister of the United States at the Court of France, having applied for permission to return home for a few months, and it appearing to me proper to comply with his request, it becomes necessary that some person be appointed to take charge of our affairs at that Court during his absence.

For this purpose I nominate William Short Esquire, and request your advice on the propriety of appointing him. There are in the office for foreign affairs papers which will acquaint you with his character, and which Mr. Jay has my directions to lay before you

William Short was the first presidential nominee.
National Archives

Both the household officials and the members of "the great and continual council" were named in Parliament. For a time, Parliament almost completely controlled the king's council—the equivalent of today's American cabinet. Parliament lost some of its control over the council during the reign of Henry V (1413–1422), and especially under the powerful Edward IV (1461–1483), when Parliament had no control over the council's composition. With few exceptions, it would be over two hundred years before the modern cabinet system made the royal ministers responsible to Parliament.[6]

President George Washington sent his first nomination to the Senate on June 16, 1789. It was not a cabinet nomination but, instead, the appointment of William Short to become minister to the court of France. He was to take the place of Thomas Jefferson, then returning to the United States to become secretary of state. John Jay, who headed the Office of Foreign Affairs under the old Congress of the Confederation, and who was continuing to direct foreign policy until his successor arrived, carried this first appointment to the Senate chamber. The Senate deliberated for two days, taking into consideration both Short's qualifications and Washington's method of communication concerning nominations. On June 18, the Senate, voting by secret ballot, approved Short's appointment.[7]

The Senate appointed a special committee to consult with Washington about the form of presidential communications concerning executive business. There was considerable sentiment within the Senate that the president should appear personally in the chamber to seek advice and consent on treaties and nominations. Washington was rightly skeptical of this approach. He ruled out appearing in person for nominations, on the grounds that they were too numerous and would become too time consuming. Washington, however, did agree to meet with the Senate concerning treaties, although his first experience proved so disastrous that he and all future presidents abandoned the practice in favor of written communications. Only one chief executive strayed from this tradition. In 1921, Warren G. Harding, who was serving as a senator at the time of his election to the presidency, went directly from the inaugural platform to the Senate chamber to submit his cabinet nominations—a list which included several senators. Harding's ill-fated presidency, however, has never served as a model for his successors.

President Washington considered the appointment process "one of the most difficult parts of the duty of his office" and "the most irksome part of the executive trust." He fretted over pressures from unqualified office-seekers and turned away relatives who wanted federal jobs.

To one friend who wrote in support of a particular candidate, the president responded: "I am not George Washington, but President of the United States. As George Washington, I would do this man any kindness in my power; as President of the United States, I can do nothing." Later, Washington explained that he had aimed "to combine geographical situation and sometimes other considerations with abilities and fitness of *known* characters." The geographic balance of Washington's appointments can be seen in his selection of cabinet members from five states and Supreme Court members from seven states.[8]

Washington also worried about the precedents he was setting in relation to the Senate. In 1790, he conferred with James Madison, Thomas Jefferson, and John Jay about the propriety of consulting the Senate regarding geographic assignments for diplomatic representatives and the ranks they should hold. These able advisers agreed that the Senate had no constitutional right to interfere with either matter. Senators, they believed, were limited to the simple approval or disapproval of specific nominees. The senators themselves, however, were not so easily convinced. In 1791, when Washington nominated ministers to Paris, London, and The Hague, senators argued that they lacked enough evidence to determine whether it was in the best interest of the United States to place permanent emissaries at these capitals. Only after weeks of delay did Washington's nominees win a narrow approval.[9]

Another issue needing resolution was how senators would cast their votes for nominees.

Those favorable to the administration tended to prefer voice votes; those suspicious of the administration—notably Senator William Maclay of Pennsylvania—preferred secret ballots to prevent undue presidential influence. When the Senate considered its first nomination, that of William Short, it voted by secret ballot. This practice raised considerable criticism from those who feared cabals and too much Senate control over nominations. On August 3, 1789, when Washington sent a long list of nominations for collectors, naval officers, and surveyors for the ports, the senators once more debated the proper procedure. Again, they decided to vote by secret ballot but warned that "it should not be considered as a precedent." Washington himself preferred a voice vote, and, on August 21, the Senate adopted the recommendation of its special committee "that all questions [on nominations] shall be put by the President of the Senate, either in the presence or absence of the President of the United States; and the Senators shall signify their assent or dissent, by answering viva voce ay, or no." And so we continue to vote, two centuries later.[10]

It is important to remember that, even though the senators cast voice votes rather than secret ballots, they continued to meet entirely in secret session. Only the briefest minutes of executive sessions were published, in a separate journal, well after the fact. Even after 1795, when the Senate permanently opened its doors and allowed visitors to observe legislative business, it closed its galleries for all executive business. Until 1929, the Senate routinely debated nominations in closed session. Senators believed that this arrangement enabled them to discuss an individual's merits more freely, while also protecting nominees from unnecessary public embarrassment. Although these were noble purposes, they simply did not work all that well. News from secret sessions leaked

George Washington, *far right*, chose as members of his first cabinet, *left to right*, Henry Knox, Thomas Jefferson, Edmund Randolph, and Alexander Hamilton.

Library of Congress

out regularly during the first 140 years, causing the Senate no end of anguish. Secrecy also seemed to violate a key principle of a democratic republic: the right of the governed to know what their leaders were doing. Speaking for the public, the press waged a steady campaign against this secrecy until the doors to executive sessions at last swung open.[11]

Mr. President, there were not a great many federal appointments to be made in the early years of our republic, because the federal government was so small. In addition to cabinet secretaries and federal judges, there were diplomats, military officers, customs officers, and postmasters. But their numbers were minuscule by current standards. At the same time, there was no civil service system. All federal posts, no matter how small, were patronage positions, known to politicians as the "spoils of office." It was William L. Marcy, who served in the Senate from 1831 to 1833, who coined the slogan, "To the victor belongs the spoils." Much of a president's power rested in his ability to reward his supporters with federal appointments, but, as all presidents quickly discovered, patronage was both a blessing and a curse. From a twentieth-century perspective, it is amazing to read how much time eighteenth and nineteenth-century presidents spent listening to the pleas of officeseekers. Nor were United States senators immune to their entreaties.

Many early senators willingly submitted to President Washington the names of candidates for federal appointment. Quite often, senatorial intervention helped the candidate's chances, but Washington was not always swayed by congressional appeals. In 1794, House leader James Madison and Senator James Monroe three times appealed to Washington to appoint Aaron Burr as minister to France. But Washington refused to nominate the quixotic Burr. "I will appoint you, Mr. Madison, or you, Mr. Monroe," Washington responded apologetically. And, in fact, he did eventually send Monroe as minister to France.[12]

From the very beginning, the Senate insisted upon the practice that we commonly refer to as "senatorial courtesy." That is, the Senate generally will not confirm a candidate for a federal office within a state who does not have the support of his home state senators. This practice appears to date back to 1789, when President Washington nominated Benjamin Fishbourn to be naval officer in charge of the port of Savannah, Georgia. When Georgia Senator James Gunn opposed Fishbourn, the Senate rejected him. Washington conceded defeat and nominated a candidate acceptable to Senator Gunn.[13]

Senatorial courtesy grew even more deep-rooted during John Adams' presidential administration. Adams lacked Washington's national prestige and was even less able to withstand congressional pressures on nominations. He also faced the development of party organizations and, therefore, of organized opposition within the Senate. Although Adams made far fewer appointments than Washington, he had more of them rejected in the Senate. As Adams' weakness became more apparent, senators grasped for patronage power themselves. When one of Adams' own relatives recommended a nephew for appointment as a federal judge, the president responded, "If I were to nominate him without previous recommendations from the senators and representatives from your State, the Senate would probably negative him."[14]

Thomas Jefferson was a shrewder and more successful political leader than John Adams, but, within his first month as president, Jefferson complained that "nothing presents such difficulties of administration as offices." By the end of his presidency, Jefferson had concluded that the appointment power was a "dreadful burden" which oppresses a president. Jefferson was faced not only with the problem of appointing deserving Republicans (as his party was then known), but also that of removing Federalist officeholders. During the months after President Adams' defeat, Federalists had tried to pack as many offices as possible with their supporters. One of these last-minute appointees was William Marbury, scheduled to become a justice of the peace in Washington. When incoming Secretary of State James Madison found Marbury's commission still on his desk, he refused to deliver it. Marbury's suit set up the landmark case of *Marbury* v. *Madison*, in which the Supreme Court claimed the right to declare acts passed by Congress unconstitutional.[15]

Jefferson enjoyed majorities in the Senate throughout his term and had little trouble winning confirmation of his nominees. Ironically, however, Jefferson suffered the embarrassing rejection of his last nomination, that of William Short to be minister to Russia. This was the same William Short who was the first person George Washington had nominated in 1789. It does not appear that the Senate rejected Short personally or meant to rebuke Jefferson politically. Instead, senators were registering their displeasure over the establishment of permanent diplomatic posts in so many countries.

Jefferson, like Washington, was followed by a weaker president. James Madison began his term by losing a battle with the Senate over his desire to appoint Treasury Secretary Albert Gallatin as secretary of state. Strong opposition to Gallatin, spearheaded in part by Senator Samuel Smith of Maryland, led Madison reluctantly to nominate Smith's brother, Robert, as secretary of state. This proved to be a poor choice—one which weakened the administration in the difficult years immediately prior to the War of 1812. Later, when Madison gave Gallatin a leave of

Opposition from some senators prevented President Madison from nominating Albert Gallatin as secretary of state.   *Library of Congress*

absence from the Treasury Department and sent him to Europe to help negotiate peace with Great Britain, the Senate adopted a resolution protesting that the duties of secretary of the treasury and diplomatic envoy were incompatible. The Senate appointed a special committee to confer with the president on the matter, but Madison viewed this as an infringement upon presidential authority. In a special message to the Senate, he protested that "the appointment of a committee of the Senate to confer immediately with the Executive himself, appears to lose sight of the coordinate relation between the Executive and the Senate, which the constitution has established, and which ought therefore to be maintained." When the committee members persisted, Madison gave them a chilly reception and refused to discuss the Gallatin appointment.[16]

There is also evidence that the Senate voted to reject one of President Madison's cabinet nominations but then rescinded its vote to allow the president to save face. On March 1, 1815, President Madison nominated, as secretary of war, Henry Dearborn, who had previously held that post during the administration of Thomas Jefferson. Dearborn's abysmal record as a general during the recent war with Great Britain, however, had earned him so many opponents in the Senate that, on March 2, the president withdrew his name. In a letter to Dearborn, dated March 4, 1815, President Madison explained that he had first thought that the Senate would welcome the nomination, stating:

Contrary to these confident expectations, an opposition was disclosed in an extent, which determined me to withdraw the nomination. But before the Message arrived, the Senate very unexpectedly had taken up the subject and proceeded to a decision. They promptly however relaxed so far as to erase the proceeding from their Journal, and in that mode to give effect to the withdrawal.[17]

Mr. President, since the handwritten copy of the *Senate Executive Journal* at the National Archives gives no indication of any vote against the Dearborn nomination, we can assume the executive clerk that day did a thorough job of erasing the proceedings. I am unaware of any other similar tampering with the *Journal*, although, in 1837, the Senate did "expunge" its censure resolution of President Andrew Jackson. Nevertheless, I believe that we can trust James Madison's word that the Senate did indeed vote to reject the nomination of Henry Dearborn, making that the first overt rejection of a cabinet nominee in the history of this body.

During the one-party Era of Good Feelings, from 1817 to 1824, general harmony existed between the president and the Senate over nominations, but then open warfare broke out during the presidency of Andrew Jackson, which began in 1829. General Jackson came to Washington with a determination to "kick the rascals out" and to place his own supporters in federal posts. Foremost among these supporters were newspaper editors, who comprised a third of Jackson's appointments during his first session of Congress. Of course, as Jackson enthusiasts, these editors had offended Jackson's opponents in the Senate, who fought to deny them office.

Perhaps the most memorable Senate rejection of a Jackson appointee occurred in 1831. Jackson had nominated Senator Martin Van Buren, a New York Democrat, to serve as minister to Great Britain. But the highly partisan Van Buren had incurred the enmity not only of the opposition party, but also of Vice President John C. Calhoun. When the vote was taken, it resulted in a tie, and when the vice president cast the tie-breaking vote, he rejected his own president's nominee. Afterwards, Calhoun gloated to Senator Thomas Hart Benton: "It will kill him, sir, kill him dead. He will never kick, sir, never kick." Benton doubted that and prophesied, "You have broken a Minister and elected a vice president." Indeed, that is exactly what happened. When Jackson heard of the vote, he swore, "By the Eternal! I'll smash them!" In his campaign for a second term, Jackson dropped Calhoun and ran with Van Buren. And when Jackson retired as president, Van Buren succeeded him to the White House.[18]

Jackson's war with the Senate over the Bank of the United States led to the first officially recorded Senate rejection of a cabinet secretary. On June 24, 1834, the Senate voted 18 to 28 to reject Jackson's recess appointment of Attorney General Roger B. Taney as secretary of the treasury. Whigs in the Senate were offended by Taney's action—

In one evening, President John Tyler, *left*, nominated Caleb Cushing, *right*, three times to be secretary of the treasury, but the Senate rejected him each time.   *National Portrait Gallery and Library of Congress*

taken at the president's request—of removing federal funds from the Bank of the United States. By refusing to confirm Taney they were in fact rejecting Jackson. But the action neither changed Jackson's antibank policies nor damaged Taney's career. He went on to become chief justice of the United States in 1836, as Jackson's appointee, and served in that position until his death in 1864. Although battered by the Senate, Jackson felt he had emerged victorious. As he prepared to leave office, Jackson commented to a friend how much he looked forward to "the glorious scene of Mr. Van Buren, once rejected by the Senate, sworn into office [as President] by Chief Justice Taney, who also [had been] rejected by the factious Senate." [19]

Despite Jackson's satisfaction, after he left office, the Senate asserted its power over appointments and held the upper hand over the executive branch for the remainder of the nineteenth century. An example is the experience of John Tyler, the first vice president to become president on the death of the incumbent. Early in his administration, Tyler broke with the Whig majority in the Senate, which thereafter frustrated his efforts to appoint his own supporters to office. Nothing in the Senate's history has matched the spectacle that occurred on March 3, 1843, the last day of the Senate's session, when Tyler came to the Capitol to sign legislation and to submit last-minute nominations.

Tyler nominated Caleb Cushing to be secretary of the treasury not once but three times that night, and each time the Senate rejected Cushing by an even larger margin than before, the votes being, as recorded in the *Senate Executive Journal*, 19 to 27, 10 to 27, and 2 to 29. Three times, Tyler nominated Henry A. Wise to be minister to France, and

Wise, too, was thrice rejected. Senator Thomas Hart Benton reported that "nominations and rejections flew backwards and forwards as in a game of shuttlecock." In all, the Senate turned down four of Tyler's cabinet nominees—in addition to Cushing, David Henshaw as secretary of the navy, James M. Porter as secretary of war, and James S. Green as secretary of the treasury—and four of his nominees to the Supreme Court—John C. Spencer, Reuben H. Walworth, Edward King, and John M. Read—a record of rejection unmatched by any other president.[20]

When Democrat James K. Polk succeeded Tyler in the White House in 1845, he experienced tremendous pressure from members of Congress to follow their recommendations for appointments. "The passion for office among members of Congress is very great, if not absolutely disreputable, and greatly embarrasses the operation of the government. They create offices by their own votes and then seek to fill them themselves," Polk complained. He found his anterooms filled with officeseekers bearing signed letters of recommendation from congressmen. In one instance, Polk appointed a man recommended by a senator from Missouri to become surveyor of the port of St. Louis, only to have the individual rejected because of the opposition of the very senator who recommended him. When Polk pointed out this inconsistency, the senator replied, "Well, we are obliged to recommend our constituents when they apply to us."[21]

Mr. President, this incident calls to mind Representative James Buffin(g)ton, a Massachusetts Republican, who served in the House from 1855 to 1863 and 1869 to 1875. If we examine the 1971 edition of the *Biographical Directory of the American Congress*, we will find parentheses around the "g" in his name. The story goes that Buffin(g)ton could never say "no" to a constituent asking for federal appointment, no matter how incompetent or

Representative James Buffin(g)ton invented an ingenious way to indicate whether he genuinely supported the constituents he recommended for federal office.   *Library of Congress*

inappropriate the individual might be. So the congressman worked out a system that became well known among Washington clerks. When he signed letters of recommendation with a "g" in his name, that signaled that he considered the person worthy of appointment; when he signed without a "g," the recommendation should not be taken seriously. Either way, the constituent felt that his congressman had loyally supported his claim. Needless to say, Representative Buffin(g)ton was regularly reelected.[22]

President Abraham Lincoln had his own system of code for indicating the degree of his support for a given officeseeker. According to historian Allan G. Bogue, the types of comments he noted on an applicant's letter could be arranged in ascending order of priority, as follows:

I wish this paper called to my attention, when, if ever, the vacancy mentioned occurs.

I know James A. Briggs, and believe him to be an excellent man.

Let it be fairly considered.

As the appointment of a consul is desired by Mr. Hickman, who is much of a man, and does not trouble us much, I wish it to be made if it is within reasonable possibility.

I would like for these gentlemen to be obliged as soon as it can consistently be done.

I desire that [Congressman —] be obliged.

I shall be personally obliged if you will make the appointment.

I would like for [Mr. Nixon] to be obliged.

Oblige [Mr. Rollins] if you consistently can [consistent, that is, with propriety and the requests of others].

If consistent, let the appointment be made.

If at all consistent, let it be done.

Mr. Rice must be obliged in this.

Let the appointment be made [or] Let it be done.

"Only in the last three cases," Bogue observed, "did the president commit himself to action in the applicant's behalf." [23]

The patronage system worked well so long as presidents were in basic harmony with the majority in the Senate, but it caused rough times when presidents were at odds with the Senate. Recall the case of Andrew Johnson, who followed Abraham Lincoln to the presidency only to break with the Radical Republicans in Congress. A struggle over their sharply divergent goals for the reconstruction of the former Confederate states took on monumental proportions. It affected not only the president's appointments but also his efforts to remove certain individuals from office. Although the Constitution spelled out the procedures for nomination and confirmation of federal appointees, it left vague the question of how they should be removed. Did the president have unrestricted right to remove a person who had been confirmed by the Senate, or did he need the Senate's approval? Fearing that President Johnson would remove all officeholders sympathetic to Radical Reconstruction, Congress in 1867 enacted the Tenure of Office Act over Johnson's veto.

The firing of Secretary of War Edwin Stanton precipitated President Andrew Johnson's impeachment.
Library of Congress

This act provided that every civil officer confirmed by the Senate should hold office until a successor had been nominated *and confirmed.* It was Johnson's firing of Secretary of War Edwin Stanton, in violation of the Tenure of Office Act, that led to his impeachment. Significantly, the Tenure of Office Act remained the law for over fifty years, much to the discomfort of presidents from both parties. Finally, in 1926, the Supreme Court ruled the act unconstitutional, in the case of *Myers* v. *U.S.* This decision left unquestioned the power of presidents to dismiss all federal executive appointees except those with specific fixed terms, such as members of the regulatory commissions, whose independence would be compromised if they could be removed by the president for political or policy reasons.[24]

Henry Stanbery's devotion to his chief led him to sacrifice his position as attorney general in order to act as Andrew Johnson's counsel in the trial of the impeachment. Johnson's renomination of Stanbery for his old job following the trial was negatived by the Senate on June 2, 1868, in an atmosphere of bitterness and recrimination.

Andrew Johnson's successor, General U.S. Grant, should have had an easy time with nominations. He was a Republican, in sympathy with the Republican majority in the Senate; he was a hero with great popular support; and he came as a relief after the tense years of struggling with Johnson. But Grant was a political novice who had much to learn about the ways of Washington. The new president never bothered to consult with fellow party members in Congress about his cabinet appointments. The day after Grant's inauguration in 1869, the Senate received the president's cabinet nominees with some shock. It was a relatively unknown and undistinguished group of names. The most prominent individual on the list was Alexander T. Stewart, wealthy proprietor of the nation's largest department store, to be secretary of the treasury. But senators pointed out that the law prohibited anyone engaged in trade or commerce from serving as treasury secretary. Stewart refused to sell the business that bore his name, and the Senate would not accept his placing it in a blind trust. When faced with the prospect that the Senate would hold up the nomination in committee indefinitely, Grant reluctantly accepted Stewart's resignation.[25]

Further muddying the waters for Grant, his attorney general, Ebenezer Hoar, insisted that the president make judicial nominations without prior senatorial clearance, thus violating a venerable tradition. Hoar's choices of nominees were in fact quite excellent, but he made few friends in Congress for the administration. One can imagine the pleasure with which members of the Senate cast their votes to defeat Grant's nomination of Ebenezer Hoar to serve on the Supreme Court.[26]

In the late nineteenth century, patronage permitted several senators to become the undisputed political "bosses" of their home states. Memorable names on this list included Pennsylvania's Simon Cameron and Matthew Quay, New York's Tom Platt, Rhode Island's Nelson Aldrich, and West Virginia's Stephen Elkins. Those who wanted a federal appointment knew they must obtain the blessings of these powerful senators, and presidents dared not cross them unless they were prepared for a brutal political fight. The greatest of these battles occurred in 1881, when new President James A. Garfield decided to take on one of the most powerful members of his own party, New York Senator Roscoe Conkling. To the patronage-rich post of collector of the port of New York, Garfield nominated William Robertson, a former Conkling lieutenant who had broken ranks to support Garfield's nomination for the presidency. This audacious nomination set off a power struggle that ended tragically in Conkling's defeat and Garfield's death. Offended by the president's breach of senatorial courtesy, Senator Conkling resigned from the Senate and returned to Albany, hoping to persuade the state legislature to demonstrate its support by reelecting him. The legislature, however, rebelled and elected someone else. Meanwhile, in Washington, a demented officeseeker shot and fatally wounded President Garfield in the name of Conkling's "stalwart" faction of the Republican party.[27]

Garfield's death shocked the nation and sobered political leaders in both parties. For too long, they had allowed the patronage system to grow to scandalous proportions. Presidents had been hounded and now assassinated by officeseekers. At last, Congress accepted the need for a professional civil

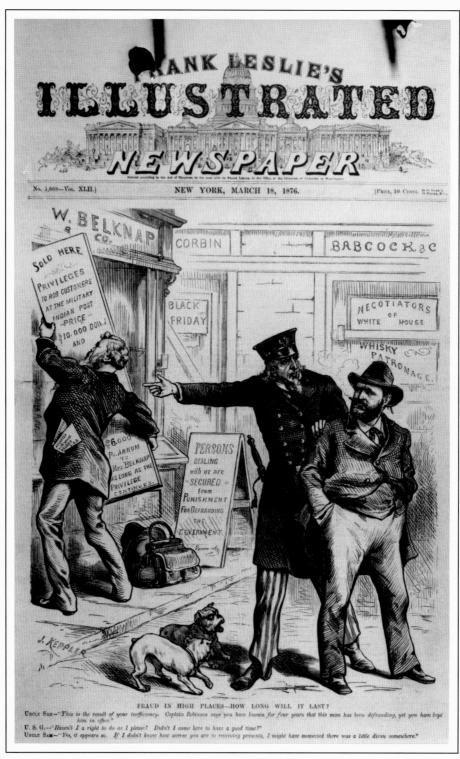

Cartoonist Joseph Keppler pictured official corruption in this caricature of, *left to right*, Senator Conkling, Uncle Sam, and President Grant.
Frank Leslie's Illustrated Newspaper, March 18, 1876

A HARMLESS EXPLOSION.

Senator Conkling's resignation from the Senate failed to produce the dramatic impact he expected.
Keppler/Puck, May 25, 1881

service. The Civil Service Act of 1883, known as the Pendleton Act because it was sponsored by Ohio Democratic Senator George Pendleton, removed a large segment of lower-level bureaucratic positions from the ranks of patronage appointments. A period of relative peace between the executive and the legislature followed, marred only by the actions of the Republican Senate to prevent Democratic President Grover Cleveland from making Supreme Court nominations toward the end of his second term.[28]

The next major battle, also involving a Democratic president's Supreme Court nom-ination, occurred in 1916 when Woodrow Wilson appointed Louis D. Brandeis as the first Jewish member of the Court. A brilliant Boston lawyer, Brandeis at that time had acquired a national reputation as the "People's Lawyer." A committed opponent of monopoly and a defender of consumers, he was the Ralph Nader of his day and equally controversial. Brandeis had advised Wilson during his campaign for the presidency and had helped to shape his "New Freedom" economic program. It should not have come as a surprise, therefore, that Wilson would nominate Brandeis to the Court when a vacancy occurred in 1916. Brandeis' many enemies, however, including conservative politicians and business leaders, denounced him as "ridiculously unfit" to serve as a judge. One who spoke out strongly was former President William Howard Taft—defeated by Wilson in 1912—who described Brandeis as "a muckraker, an emotionalist for his own purposes, a socialist."[29]

When the Judiciary Committee held public hearings, a string of witnesses denounced Brandeis. Fifty-five prominent Bostonians, led by Harvard President A. Lawrence Lowell, sent a petition to the committee, saying, "We do not believe that Mr. Brandeis has the judicial temperament and capacity which should be required in a judge of the Supreme Court." Quite clearly, anti-progressive and anti-Semitic undertones could be heard in these protests. To his credit, President Wilson stood firmly behind his nominee—a particularly notable action, since Wilson was running for reelection that year. In a letter to the Judiciary Committee, the president argued that the charges against Brandeis "threw a great deal more light upon the character and motives" of those who made them than on their intended target. "He is a friend of all just men and a lover of the right," the president wrote. "I knew from direct personal knowledge of the man what I

Woodrow Wilson called Louis Brandeis "a friend of all just men and a lover of the right."
Library of Congress

was doing when I named him for the highest and most responsible tribunal of the Nation." On June 1, 1916, the Senate voted 47 to 22 to confirm Louis D. Brandeis. He went on to become one of the greatest and most influential justices of that Court, serving until 1939 and thoroughly justifying Woodrow Wilson's decision.[30]

In the twentieth century, the Senate has rejected very few presidential nominations to either the Supreme Court or the cabinet. Only seven Supreme Court nominees have been withdrawn or have not been confirmed: President Herbert Hoover's choice of John J. Parker, President Lyndon Johnson's choices of Abe Fortas and Homer Thornberry, President Richard Nixon's choices of Clement Haynsworth and G. Harrold Carswell, and President Ronald Reagan's choices of Robert Bork and Douglas Ginsburg.

Parker, a North Carolina Republican, was accused of making antilabor and racist rulings, although his later record disproved those allegations. Fortas was sitting on the Court when President Johnson elevated him to chief justice and nominated Homer Thornberry to fill the vacancy. Since Johnson was not running for reelection, some members of Congress objected to a lame-duck president filling such important posts. Questions arose over Fortas' personal ethics, which caused him to resign; Thornberry's nomination was never acted upon.

Johnson's successor had equal difficulty in filling Supreme Court vacancies. Having been elected on the strength of his so-called "southern strategy," Nixon turned to lower-court judges from the South, picking Clement Haynsworth of South Carolina. Liberal senators mounted a strong challenge to Haynsworth for his questionable financial dealings, but, after defeating Haynsworth, they were confronted with Nixon's next choice of Harrold Carswell of Florida. With hindsight, some members, including myself, considered that they would have been better off with Haynsworth, who was a distinguished jurist, while even Carswell's supporters admitted his mediocrity. President Nixon was furious over these rejections. "If the Senate attempts to substitute its judgment as to who should be appointed," Nixon wrote, "the traditional constitutional balance is in jeopardy and the duty of the President under the Constitution impaired." After suffering two embarrassing defeats, however, the president wisely chose to nominate an able candidate, Harry A. Blackmun, who was easily confirmed in 1970. Nineteen years later, Justice Blackmun continues to serve on the Court, demonstrating that those bitter nomination fights were worth the effort.[31]

On July 1, 1987, President Reagan nominated Court of Appeals Judge Robert Bork for a seat on the Supreme Court. Considering

Charles Warren, Lewis Strauss, and John Tower, *left to right*, have been the only three cabinet nominees rejected by the Senate in the twentieth century.
Library of Congress and U.S. Senate Historical Office

that the Senate had previously confirmed three other conservative Reagan nominees for the Court, ideology was not so much the issue in Judge Bork's case. Rather, it was his perceived ideological inflexibility and intellectual aloofness that seemed to separate him from the very human elements of the issues that daily face the Court. Judge Bork's published opinions on civil rights and privacy particularly troubled many senators and contributed to his defeat. A motion in the Judiciary Committee to report his nomination favorably to the Senate was rejected by a vote of 5 to 9 on October 6, 1987. Later that day, a motion to report the nomination unfavorably carried by a vote of 9 to 5. On October 23, the full Senate voted 42 to 58 to reject Bork. Six days later, on October 29, President Reagan nominated—far too hastily as it turned out—another Court of Appeals judge, Douglas Ginsburg. Soon, however, reports surfaced in the news media about Judge Ginsburg's personal behavior, specifically his past use of marijuana, and, on November 7, 1987, the president withdrew his nomination.

Finally, the president nominated Judge Anthony Kennedy, who was easily confirmed and sits today upon the U.S. Supreme Court. Justice Kennedy is the 104th individual to serve on the Court.[32] Judge Ginsburg was the 26th person named to the court whose nomination was rejected, withdrawn, or not acted upon. Thus, some 20 percent of all Supreme Court nominees have not been confirmed. This strikingly large percentage speaks volumes about the Senate's attitude toward the independent status of the Supreme Court. By comparison, 541 individuals have served as cabinet secretaries, and only 15 have been rejected or withdrawn, less than 3 percent of the total. That is a remarkable difference.

Incidentally, the first Supreme Court had six members. The number was increased to nine in 1837 and to ten in 1863. In 1866, Congress was so bitter against President Andrew Johnson that it did not want him to have the privilege of making any appointments to the Court. When two vacancies occurred, Congress simply passed a law reducing the number of associate justices to seven. In 1869, the Court was again enlarged, and it has consisted of nine members ever since.

Only three cabinet nominations have been rejected since 1900. On March 10, 1925, the Senate turned down President Calvin Coolidge's candidate for attorney general,

Charles Warren. This was just after the well-publicized Teapot Dome investigation into government corruption, and progressive members of the Senate challenged Warren's connections with the "sugar trust." The vote was very close, and Warren lost only because Vice President Charles Dawes overslept that afternoon and did not get to the Capitol in time to cast the tie-breaking vote. Coolidge, fresh from an election victory at the polls, viewed the Senate's action as a challenge to his leadership and sent back the nomination, followed by a White House statement that the president would make a recess appointment of Warren if the Senate again rejected the nomination. This threat provoked a storm on Capitol Hill; the Judiciary Committee reported the nomination adversely and the Senate rejected it on March 16 by a vote of 39 to 46. Coolidge then abandoned his plan to give Warren a recess appointment and, on March 18, named John Sargent to the post.[33]

President Dwight D. Eisenhower suffered the humiliation of a cabinet-level defeat in 1959, when he nominated Admiral Lewis Strauss to serve as secretary of commerce. Admiral Strauss had previously served as chairman of the Atomic Energy Commission. Never a tactful man, he had alienated many senators, especially Senator Clinton Anderson of New Mexico. Anderson made it a personal quest to defeat Strauss' nomination and succeeded by a vote of 46 to 49.[34]

Most recently, on March 9, 1989, by a vote of 47 to 53, the Senate rejected the nomination of former Texas senator John G. Tower to be secretary of defense, following a party-line vote in the Armed Services Committee to report the nomination with an unfavorable recommendation. Opposition to the nominee was based on several concerns: a possible conflict of interest growing out of Tower's employment as a consultant to defense contractors after his service as an arms control negotiator; evidence bearing on a perceived pattern of excessive drinking in the not-far-distant past; and allegations and rumors of womanizing. All sides were in agreement that Tower, a former chairman of the Senate Armed Services Committee, was eminently qualified, regarding military and arms control matters, to be secretary of defense.

While the Tower nomination fight was a difficult experience both for members of the Senate and for the administration of President George Bush, it may have finally exploded some of the myths often perpetuated in the press. Although this occasion marked only the ninth time that a cabinet nominee has been formally rejected by a Senate vote and the first time that the Senate has rejected a former colleague for a cabinet office, three former senators—John J. Crittenden, George E. Badger, and George Henry Williams—had in the past been nominated but not confirmed as justices of the Supreme Court. Similarly, President Harry Truman's nomination of former Senator Monrad Wallgren as chairman of the National Security Resources Board had been tabled by the Senate Armed Services Committee. Clearly, former members are not excused from the Senate's scrutiny of nominations. Tower's rejection was also the first time that one of a new president's initial cabinet nominees was not confirmed—all other cases have occurred later in a presidential term. Again, the incident demonstrates that no president has the constitutional authority to "have his own team" without the consent of the Senate. While the Senate is willing to give the president far more leeway in choosing cabinet officers than in selecting Supreme Court nominees, it will not hesitate to reject a candidate it considers unfit.

Mr. President, I have concentrated here on cabinet and Supreme Court nominations and have not touched upon the thousands of lower level nominations that presidents send to Capitol Hill every session. Committees routinely consider nominations, and not all are reported out or reported out favorably. Some have been postponed indefinitely, while others have simply disappeared into the far reaches of committee file rooms.

Pat Holt, who served as chief of staff of the Senate Foreign Relations Committee in the 1970's, recalled the way that committee handled the nomination of Graham Martin, whom President Gerald Ford nominated to an ambassadorial post. Martin was our last ambassador to Saigon, and many committee members had been unimpressed with his performance in the job. When the committee met in executive session to consider the nomination, it was clear that the members did not intend to confirm him. Since they did not wish to reject Martin outright, they suggested holding the nomination while the staff conducted further investigation. "Is that clear, Pat?" someone asked. Holt replied, "Yes, it's very clear, and just to make it clearer, I'm not sure how long it will take the staff to do this." Several senators said, "Oh, don't hurry," and Senator George McGovern added, "Suppose we say the Fourth of July, 1990." [35]

In general, the better track record that presidents have enjoyed in recent years indicates that they—or at least their staffs—have developed a deeper appreciation of the Senate's role in the confirmation process, as well as a bit more finesse in presenting their candidates. Not long ago, the *New York Times* published a profile of Tom Korologos, who helped shepherd Reagan administration appointees through various nomination hearings. Korologos described his role in educating nominees.

"You have to scare 'em a little bit," he explained. Before sending nominees to a committee hearing, Korologos put them through a mock hearing. "I fire the rottenest, most in-

sulting questions in the world at them." He offered the following set of rules to all White House nominees:

(1) Model yourself after a bridegroom at a wedding: Be on time, stay out of the way, and keep your mouth shut.

(2) Between the day of nomination and the day of confirmation, give no speeches, write no letters, make no public appearances. Senators don't like to read about the grand plans of an unconfirmed nominee.

(3) You may have been a brilliant victor in the corporate world or some other field of endeavor, but the Senate expects you to be suitably humble and deferential, not cocky.

(4) There is no subject on earth that the Senate is not free to probe. Be ready with polite and persuasive answers. [36]

Mr. President, in my general overview of the past two hundred years of presidential-congressional relations regarding the appointment process, I have largely emphasized presidential problems and difficulties. I do not want to leave the impression that presidents are the only ones to suffer anguish over nominations. Certain nominations often place United States senators in very uncomfortable positions when they are forced to choose between their conscience and their president. A wrong decision, either way, can cause no end of trouble. In the Ninety-ninth Congress, we witnessed the fate of Senator Slade Gorton of Washington. Senator Gorton had been pressing the Reagan administration to nominate William Dwyer as a federal judge from his home state, but Dwyer was ideologically out of step with the White House. Then, the president nominated Daniel Manion to be a federal judge in Indiana. To win Senator Gorton's loyalty, White House lobbyists tied his vote on Manion to Dwyer's nomination. Senator Gorton swallowed hard and cast a vote that he might otherwise have cast differently. Manion was confirmed. Senator Gorton was defeated for reelection by voters who reacted negatively to the whole arrangement. Subsequently, Dwyer was nominated and confirmed as a federal judge, and, in 1988, Senator Gorton was again elected to the Senate.

The Senate often finds itself in positions where it will draw criticism no matter what it does. If the Senate probes too long or too deeply into a nominee's past, it is accused of denying the president the assistance he needs when he needs it. If the Senate rushes through a nomination without adequate investigation, it is accused of providing "consent without advice" or being "half rubber, half stamp." [37]

From years of experience, I would say that we do the country a disservice by rushing any nomination, unless there is a clear record as to the nominee's integrity, capability, and qualifications, as well as an overriding need for speedy action. If serious character flaws or damaging information about a nominee's past are to be uncovered, better that they become public knowledge before the individual is confirmed rather than afterwards. That is a hard message to deliver to any president of any party, but it is a lesson that has been learned too frequently to be forgotten. "History," wrote the poet Byron in *Childe Harold*, "with all her volumes vast, hath but one page." We should do well, then, to look backward into the past where we shall find that due diligence by the Senate in fulfilling its "advice and consent" responsibility in the appointment process has been, in Hamilton's words, "an efficacious source of stability" in the government of the Republic. For, as he wrote in *The Federalist*, No. 76:

The possibility of rejection [by the Senate] would be a strong motive to care in proposing. . . . [The president] would be both ashamed and afraid to bring forward . . . candidates who had no other merit, than that . . . of being in some way or other personally allied to him, or of possessing the necessary insignificance and pliancy to render them the obsequious instruments of his pleasure. [38]

In sum, the Senate must continue seriously and painstakingly to perform its constitutional responsibility of rendering advice and consent on presidential nominations if we are to maintain the unique system of checks and balances that has brought our democratic form of government to its bicentennial.

CHAPTER 3

Rules

*February 16, 1981**

Mr. President, someone has said that the difference between a lynching and a fair trial is procedure.

In his *Manual of Parliamentary Practice*, Thomas Jefferson quoted "Mr. Onslow, the ablest among the Speakers of the House of Commons" as follows:

> It was a maxim he had often heard when he was a young man, from old and experienced Members, that nothing tended more to throw power into the hands of administration, and those who acted with the majority of the House of Commons, than a neglect of, or departure from, the rules of proceeding; that these forms, as instituted by our ancestors, operated as a check and control on the actions of the majority, and that they were, in many instances, a shelter and protection to the minority, against the attempts of power.[1]

Jefferson himself wrote that whether the rules of a legislative body

> . . . be in all cases the most rational or not is really not of so great importance. It is much more material that there should be a rule to go by than what that rule is; that there may be a uniformity of proceeding in business not subject to the caprice of the Speaker or captiousness of the members. It is very material that order, decency, and regularity be preserved in a dignified public body.[2]

All legislative bodies need rules to follow if they are to transact business in an orderly fashion and if they are to operate fairly, efficiently, and expeditiously.

The first Senate understood this, and, on April 7, 1789, the day after a quorum of senators had appeared, a special committee was created to "prepare a system of rules for conducting business." The committee consisted of Senators Oliver Ellsworth of Connecticut, Richard Henry Lee of Virginia, Caleb Strong of Massachusetts, William Maclay of Pennsylvania, and Richard Bassett of Delaware. All five of these committee members were lawyers. Each had served in his state legislature, the procedures of which were indebted to colonial and English experience. Two had served in the Continental Congress, which was also indebted to colonial and English precedents, and three had participated in the Constitutional Convention, whose members had created the Senate.

Members of the committee charged with preparing a code of Senate rules recognized that the Constitution had already established fundamental rules of Senate procedure. The Constitution's framers determined, for example, that the vice president of the United States would be the Senate's presiding officer and that the Senate could choose all other officers, including a president pro tempore.

---

* Updated May 1989

Constantino Brumidi painted Thomas Jefferson in this mural located in the Senate wing of the Capitol.
Architect of the Capitol

margin of those present and voting to expel a sitting member. A similar "super majority" vote was necessary to approve treaties and to override presidential vetoes.

The proceedings of that first ad hoc Senate rules committee are lost to history, but the diary of committee member William Maclay suggests that there were disagreements in the course of its deliberations. The hot-tempered Maclay, a strident Antifederalist, prepared his own, more strict set of rules. They included a provision that the presiding officer should be in his chair a half hour before the Senate was due to convene each day and that senators "shall immediately take their seats in circular order, those from New Hampshire occupying the right of the Chair, and those of Georgia the left." Maclay was unsuccessful in these proposals and found little support for his rule to permit four senators to "move for the previous question" or to call for the question "in Case of a debate becoming tedious." Similarly, he was in the minority with his proposal to appoint as each committee chairman, the "Senator of the most northerly State of those, from Whom the Committee is taken."[3]

Perhaps his most strict proposal, also never adopted, was the final rule on his list of sixteen, which provided:

These Rules shall be engrossed on parchment, and hung up in some conspicuous part, of the Senate Chamber. And—every Senator, Who shall neglect attendance during a session; absent himself without leave, or withdraw for more than a quarter of an hour, without permission, after a quorum is formed, shall be deemed guilty of disorderly behaviour; and his name together with the nature of his transgression, shall be wrote on a slip of paper and annexed to the bottom of the Rules; there to remain untill the Senate, on his application or otherwise, shall take order on the same.[4]

The Constitution established that a majority of members would serve as a quorum to conduct business but that a minority could compel the attendance of absentees. The Constitution also set age, residency and citizenship requirements for senators. Otherwise, the Senate, like the House of Representatives, was to be the sole judge of the qualifications of those who presented themselves for membership. While the body could turn aside a senator-elect by a simple majority vote, it required a two-thirds

On April 13, 1789, the committee filed a report which "was read, and ordered to lie until tomorrow, for consideration." On April 16, the set of rules, nineteen in number, was voted to "be observed," and, on April 18, another rule, numbered XX, not reported by the committee, was adopted.[5]

In many instances, the Senate rules adopted in 1789 bore a close resemblance to those of its predecessors, the Continental Congress and the Congress of the Confederation. In fact, some of the rules were almost identical in wording. Hence, it is obvious that the Senate committee used the older rules as a pattern while preparing the rules of the Senate.[6]

A number of today's rules bear a striking similarity to those early Senate rules, as can be seen from the following table. The table compares certain rules of the Continental Congress with similar rules of the U.S. Senate, both in the First Congress and today.

1778 Rules, Continental Congress*	1789 Rules, United States Senate*	1989 Rules, United States Senate
3. No member shall read any printed paper in the house during the sitting thereof, without leave of Congress. 4. No member shall speak to another or otherwise interrupt the business of the house while the journals or public papers are reading for the information of Congress, or when any member is speaking in any debate. 5. Every member, when he speaks, shall rise from his seat and address himself to the Chair, and when he has finished, shall sit down again. 6. No member shall speak more than twice in any one debate the same day, without leave of the house. 7. When two members shall rise together, the President shall name the person to speak.	II. No member shall speak to another, or otherwise interrupt the business of the Senate, or read any printed paper while the journals or public papers are reading, or when any member is speaking in any debate. III. Every member, when he speaks, shall address the Chair standing in his place, and when he has finished shall sit down. IV. No member shall speak more than twice in any one debate on the same day, without leave of the Senate. V. When two members shall rise at the same time, the President shall name the person to speak; but in all cases the person first rising shall speak first.	XIX 1. (a) When a Senator desires to speak, he shall rise and address the Presiding Officer, and shall not proceed until he is recognized, and the Presiding Officer shall recognize the Senator who shall first address him. No Senator shall interrupt another Senator in debate without his consent, and to obtain such consent he shall first address the Presiding Officer, and no Senator shall speak more than twice upon any one question in debate on the same legislative day without leave of the Senate, which shall be determined without debate. * * *

8. No motion shall be debated until the same be seconded.
9. When a motion shall be made and seconded, it shall be reduced to writing, if desired by the President or any member, delivered at the table and read by the President, before the same shall be allowed to be debated.
10. While a question is before the house, no motion shall be received, unless for an amendment, for the previous question, to postpone the consideration of the main question, or to commit it.
	VI. No motion shall be debated until the same shall be seconded.
	VII. When a motion shall be made and seconded, it shall be reduced to writing, if desired by the President, or any member, delivered in at the table, and read by the President before the same shall be debated.
	VIII. While a question is before the Senate, no motion shall be received unless for an amendment, for the previous question, or for postponing the main question, or to commit, or to adjourn.
		XV. 1. All motions and amendments shall be reduced to writing, if desired by the Presiding Officer or by any Senator, and shall be read before the same shall be debated.
		* * *
		
		XXII. 1. When a question is pending, no motion shall be received but—
		  To adjourn.
		  To adjourn to a day certain, or that when the Senate adjourn it shall be to a day certain.
		  To take a recess.
		  To proceed to the consideration of executive business.
		  To lay on the table.
		  To postpone indefinitely.
		  To postpone to a day certain.
		  To commit.
		  To amend.
		* * *

11. If a question in debate contains several points, any member may have the same divided.	X. If a question in a debate include several points, any member may have the same divided.	XV. * * * 3. If the question in debate contains several propositions, any Senator may have the same divided, except a motion to strike out and insert, which shall not be divided; * * * * * *
18. No member shall leave Congress without permission of Congress or of his constituents.	XIX. No member shall absent himself from the service of the Senate without leave of the Senate first obtained.	VI. * * * 2. No Senator shall absent himself from the service of the Senate without leave. * * *

*Roy Swanstrom, *The United States Senate, 1787–1801*, p. 190

The nineteen Senate rules proposed by the Committee of Five in 1789, together with the twentieth rule adopted on April 18, were as follows:

I. The President having taken the chair, and a quorum being present, the Journal of the preceding day shall be read, to the end that any mistake may be corrected that shall have been made in the entries.

II. No member shall speak to another, or otherwise interrupt the business of the Senate, or read any printed paper while the journals or public papers are reading, or when any member is speaking in any debate.

III. Every member, when he speaks, shall address the Chair, standing in his place, and when he has finished, shall sit down.

IV. No member shall speak more than twice in any one debate on the same day, without leave of the Senate.

V. When two members rise at the same time, the President shall name the person to speak; but in all cases the member first rising shall speak first.

VI. No motion shall be debated until the same shall be seconded.

VII. When a motion shall be made and seconded, it shall be reduced to writing, if desired by the President, or any member, delivered in at the table, and read by the President, before the same shall be debated.

VIII. While a question is before the Senate, no motion shall be received unless for an amendment, for the previous question, or for postponing the main question, or to commit it, or to adjourn.

IX. The previous question being moved and seconded, the question from the Chair shall be: "Shall the main question be now put?" And if the nays prevail, the main question shall not then be put.

X. If a question in debate contain several points, any member may have the same divided.

XI. When the yeas and nays shall be called for by one-fifth of the members present, each member called upon shall, unless for special reasons he be excused by the Senate, declare, openly and without debate, his assent or dissent to the question. In taking the yeas and nays, and upon the call of the House, the names of the members shall be taken alphabetically.

XII. One day's notice at least shall be given of an intended motion for leave to bring in a bill.

XIII. Every bill shall receive three readings previous to its being passed; and the President shall give notice at each, whether it be the first, second, or third; which readings shall be on three different days, unless the Senate unanimously direct otherwise.

XIV. No bill shall be committed or amended until it shall have been twice read, after which it may be referred to a Committee.

XV. All Committees shall be appointed by ballot, and a plurality of votes shall make a choice.

XVI. When a member shall be called to order, he shall sit down until the President shall have determined whether he is in order or not; and every question of order shall be decided by the President, without debate; but, if there be a doubt in his mind, he may call for the sense of the Senate.

XVII. If a member be called to order for words spoken, the exceptionable words shall be immediately taken down in writing, that the President may be better enabled to judge of the matter.

XVIII. When a blank is to be filled, and different sums shall be proposed, the question shall be taken on the highest sum first.

XIX. No member shall absent himself from the service of the Senate without leave of the Senate first obtained.

XX. Before any petition or memorial, addressed to the Senate, shall be received and read at the table, whether the same shall be introduced by the President, or a member, a brief statement of the contents of the petition or memorial shall verbally be made by the introducer.[7]

The twenty Senate rules of 1789 consisted of approximately six hundred words. Today's forty-one rules run to at least fifteen thousand words. During the two centuries since 1789, the Senate has adopted only seven general revisions of its rules. These recodifications were agreed to as follows:

March 26, 1806 (40 rules)
January 3, 1820 (45 rules)
February 14, 1828 (48 rules)
March 25, 1868 (53 rules)
January 17, 1877 (78 rules)
January 11, 1884 (40 rules)
November 14, 1979 (50 rules, consolidated to 42 in 1980 and reduced to 41 in 1983)

Between the revisions, the Senate occasionally amended its existing rules and adopted various procedural orders, most of which were incorporated in the body of rules at the next general revision. Until the 1870's,

A subcommittee of the Senate Rules Committee met in 1913; shown are, *left to right*, Thomas Walsh, James Reed, Lee Overman, Knute Nelson, and Albert Cummins.   *Library of Congress*

the Senate followed the practice of creating a temporary committee each time it wished to consider a general revision of its rules. On December 9, 1874, the Senate made the select committee that had prepared the 1868 revision a permanent committee—the Committee on Rules. Within two years, that standing committee had produced another revision, adding twenty-five rules. Seven years later, in 1884, the Rules Committee submitted to the Senate a new set of rules, reducing the number from seventy-eight to forty. This reduction was accomplished by combining related rules and distinguishing them with numbered paragraphs. The use of numbered paragraphs within each rule made it necessary to revert to the practice, used previously only in the 1789 rules, of employing roman

numerals to identify individual rules. The Senate has continued to follow that practice since 1884.

The most recent general revision of the standing rules took nearly a century to accomplish. On May 10, 1976, the Senate adopted a resolution that I had submitted on May 15, 1975, to authorize the Committee on Rules and Administration to prepare such a revision. Assisted by Senate Parliamentarian emeritus Floyd M. Riddick, the committee conducted an exhaustive study of Senate rules, precedents, and practices. It ultimately produced a codification that consolidated the numerous piecemeal rule changes adopted by the Senate since the 1884 revision, as well as the provisions of the 1946 and 1970 Legislative Reorganization Acts. In the process, the committee dropped obsolete provisions, clarified arcane language, and grouped together related provisions from different rules to produce a clear, coherent, and consistent compendium.

After soliciting and reviewing comments of other senators, the Rules Committee unanimously agreed to the revision in November 1979. Committee Chairman Claiborne Pell fulfilled the committee's 1976 mandate by reporting a resolution, which I had submitted on behalf of myself, as majority leader, and Senator Howard Baker of Tennessee, the minority leader, to revise and modernize the Senate's standing rules. On November 14, 1979, the Senate voted 97 to 0 to adopt this resolution, which represented the first comprehensive revision in ninety-five years.

Mr. President, I shall now turn to a brief discussion of the Senate's defunct joint rules and its very much alive impeachment rules, as well as the precedents established over the years. I shall conclude with my personal observations about the operation of the Senate's rules.

JOINT RULES

Following common parliamentary practice, the House and Senate of the First Congress adopted a number of joint rules to expedite the handling of bills and messages between the two bodies. The Senate agreed to its first joint rules on April 15, 1789, the day before it adopted its initial nineteen standing rules. The joint rules governed the conduct of conference committees and the selection of chaplains.

From time to time, both houses added joint rules, as in 1822, when they provided that "each House shall transmit to the other all papers on which any bill or resolution shall be founded," and "no bill that shall have passed one House shall be sent for concurrence to the other on either of the last three days of a session." These and other joint rules were frequently suspended and, in 1876, several senators expressed concern over the legitimacy and continuity of the joint rules. They reasoned that, because the House expired each two years, so also did the joint rules. The Rules Committee proposed, and the Senate agreed to, a concurrent resolution adopting all former joint rules, except the twenty-second, which dealt with the method of counting electoral ballots. The House took no action but, several months later, sent over a concurrent resolution to suspend certain joint rules. The Senate immediately responded that, as the House of Representatives had done nothing to reinstitute the joint rules, none existed and, accordingly, there was no basis for action on the House resolution.[8]

In 1884, at the time the Senate revised its standing rules, it also adopted an updated code of joint rules. Among other provisions, this version prohibited including general legislation on appropriation bills and defined matter to be included in conference reports. The House failed to act on either this revision or several proposals that followed over the next five years. Since 1889, there have been no further efforts to revive the joint code, which has largely been replaced by statute law, as well as by custom and by individual orders pertaining to the operation of each body.

IMPEACHMENT RULES

The Senate's impeachment trial rules were modeled after those of state legislatures and the British Parliament. For the five impeachment trials that took place in the Senate prior to the 1868 proceedings against President Andrew Johnson, this body was guided by an informal set of rules. In 1868, in preparation for the Johnson trial, the Senate formalized its impeachment code, drawing upon the practices followed in the impeachment trials of Senator William Blount in 1797, Judge John Pickering in 1804, Justice Samuel Chase in 1804, Judge James Peck in 1831, and Judge West H. Humphreys in 1862. The Senate also adopted recommendations reported by the committee in charge of preparing rules for the trial of Johnson.[9]

The 1868 code has remained intact down to the present time with the exception of one amendment adopted in 1935 and the revisions of 1986. The 1935 amendment, now embodied in impeachment Rule XI, increased the number of rules to twenty-six and gave the Senate the option of creating a special twelve-member committee "to receive evidence and take testimony at such times and places as the committee may determine." This amendment was added at a time when many senators were concerned that trials of federal judges would severely cut into the Senate's normal legislative schedule. The Senate had just acquitted one judge, and the House was moving toward impeachment proceedings on another.

Nearly four decades later, in the summer of 1974, the Senate was faced with the prospect of another impeachment trial—the first for a president in more than a century. On July 29, 1974, I cosponsored a resolution, which the Senate immediately adopted, directing the Committee on Rules and Administration to review all existing rules and precedents that applied to impeachment trials in order to recommend any revisions to the rules that might be necessary. The resolution provided that the Rules Committee meet in closed session to prevent undue publicity and to avoid prejudging House action.

As chairman of the Subcommittee on Rules, I moved, on the day of our first meeting, to use the existing impeachment code "as working text to be amended, modified, revised, or approved as the Committee sees fit." I then asked Senator Howard Cannon of Nevada, chairman of the Committee on

Rules and Administration, to preside, in view of the fact that the full committee was present, and he assumed the chair. The committee proceeded, and the result of our work was an exhaustively researched publication entitled *Procedure and Guidelines for Impeachment Trials in the United States Senate*, as well as a report enumerating proposed revisions of the 1868 impeachment rules.

The committee's recommendations were laid aside after the president's resignation on August 9, 1974, spared the nation the ordeal of a second presidential impeachment trial, but they were later adopted by the Senate as it prepared for the trial of a United States district court judge in the summer of 1986. On June 26, 1986, I again introduced a resolution calling upon the Committee on Rules and Administration to review the impeachment rules. The committee reviewed the 1974 effort and, on August 12, 1986, reported a resolution to amend the Rules of Procedure and Practice in the Senate When Sitting in Impeachment Trials. This resolution, which consisted of the revisions proposed by the committee in 1974, was adopted by the Senate on August 15, 1986.

The 1986 amendments consisted primarily of technical, clarifying and conforming changes to the 1868 impeachment rules. However, several substantive changes were made to the rule governing the procedures for voting on impeachment articles. Under impeachment Rule XXIII, as amended, an article of impeachment "shall not be divisible for the purpose of voting thereon at any time during the trial." The Senate may not adjourn during the voting on articles of impeachment except "for a period not to exceed one day" or at the end of a session. However, once the Senate has voted to convict on any single article of impeachment, it may dispense with the voting and "proceed to the consideration of such other matters as may be determined prior to pronouncing judge-

In a lithograph entitled "A New Bill," artist William Gropper caricatured the Senate in action. *Library of Congress*

ment." Finally, the amended rule clarifies that the Senate's vote on an article of impeachment constitutes its final verdict: a motion to reconsider "the vote by which any article of impeachment is sustained or rejected shall not be in order." [10]

PRECEDENTS

Mr. President, when I first came to the Senate, I was advised by Senator Richard Russell of Georgia, himself an astute student of the Senate rules, that it was not enough just to know the rules but it was equally important to study the precedents of the Senate. At this point, therefore, I shall turn from the Senate's rules to a brief discussion

of its precedents. An intimate knowledge of Senate precedents is a vital component of the legislative effectiveness of the consummate floor leader. Precedents reflect the application of the Constitution, statutes, the Senate rules, and common sense reasoning to specific past parliamentary situations. In extreme cases, even the precedents from the British Parliament or the provisions in *Jefferson's Manual* may help to provide guidance.

There are several ways to establish a precedent. A senator may raise a point of order. The chair then has the responsibility either to rule on that point of order or to refer it to the full Senate for decision. If the chair makes a ruling, that ruling is subject to an appeal to the Senate, which is debatable except when the Senate is operating under cloture. If no appeal is taken, the chair's ruling becomes a precedent of the Senate. If the chair refers the question of order to the full Senate, under the provisions of Rule XX, the point of order is debatable. Points of order that raise constitutional issues must be referred to the membership. If the membership decides the point of order either initially or by supporting or overruling the chair on appeal, that decision also becomes a precedent. Additionally, the chair may establish a precedent through its own initiative if its action goes unchallenged. In a subsequent interpretation of precedents, greatest weight is given to those established by a vote of the Senate.

Throughout its history, the Senate has established thousands of precedents, most of which have stood the tests of time. In some cases, later rulings or subsequent decisions by the Senate have overturned a precedent, either because of changing circumstances or because of its incompatibility with other precedents. Over the past century, the Senate has compiled its key precedents for ready access by members. Senate Chief Clerk William J. McDonald prepared the first such compilation in 1881. Entitled *A Compilation of Questions of Order and Decisions Thereon*, this twenty-five page pamphlet includes sixty-nine entries, ranging from "Absent Senators" to "Yeas and Nays." [11] I am sure that the senators of 1881 particularly valued a publication on questions of order, since, at that time, they faced a deadlock in which both Senate political parties were equally divided.

In 1893, the Democratic party regained control of the Senate for the first time in twelve years. That transfer of power resulted in a turnover of committee chairmanships and created a receptive audience for a greatly expanded volume of Senate precedents. During that year, the Senate published a 350-page compendium entitled *Precedents Related to the Privileges of the Senate*, compiled by George P. Furber, clerk of the Senate Committee on Privileges and Elections. [12] That volume contained the following major topical sections, which nicely described the principal institutional concerns of the Senate in the 1890's: Secret Sessions; Privilege of the Floor; Witnesses; Contempts; Journal; Absentees; Order in Debate; Compensation of Senators; Franking; President of the Senate; Classification of Senators; Personal Privileges of Members; Limitation of Debate; Election of Vice-President; Right to Demand Papers on the Executive Files; Communication with the Executive; Communication with the House of Representatives; Appropriation Bills; Control of the Senate Wing of the Capitol; and Committees. Each section of the 1893 volume began with a historical overview of the topic, followed by the text of appropriate documentary authorities, including English parliamentary sources, the *Senate Journal*, and Senate committee reports.

Less than a year later, on May 17, 1894, the Senate created a special committee to investigate newspaper charges that senators had been bribed to oppose pending legislation designed to reduce tariffs and to institute an income tax. Because these allegations were construed as an attack on the integrity of the Senate and the House of Representatives, the Senate investigating committee prepared a publication with the richly descriptive title *Digest of Decisions and Precedents of the Senate and House of Representatives of the United States Relating to their Powers and Privileges Respecting their Members and Officers, and to Investigations, Contempts, Libels, Contumacious Witnesses, Expulsions, Writs of Habeas Corpus, Etc., With Decisions of the U.S. Supreme Court and Other Courts Related Thereto.* [13] This 975-page volume was prepared by Henry H. Smith, clerk of the special investigating committee. Along with George Furber's 1893 volume, this work offered senators of the late nineteenth century a wealth of information on Senate prerogatives and precedents.

In 1908, the Senate directed its chief clerk, Henry H. Gilfry, to prepare a volume, *Precedents: Decisions on Points of Order with Phraseology in the United States Senate*, which was published the following year.[14] The compilation covered the period from the First Congress through the end of the Sixtieth Congress (1789–1909). Decisions on points of order were grouped under eighty-five headings, such as: Amendments to General Appropriations Bills; Closed Doors; Morning Hour, Resolutions, and Unanimous Consent Agreements. Its section on Phraseology, a revision of a work first published in 1891, provided standard language for use on the Senate floor by presiding officers, committee chairmen, and other senators. For example, in the section on morning business, under the heading Opening of the Senate, the following guidance is offered:

Wendell H. Ford has chaired the Senate Rules Committee since 1987.   *Office of Senator Wendell Ford*

> The Presiding Officer enters the Senate Chamber accompanied by the Chaplain punctually at 12 o'clock meridian of the day to which the Senate has adjourned, and with the gavel raps once.
>
> (The Chaplain offers prayer.)
>
> The Presiding Officer takes the chair, and using the gavel says: The Senate will be in order. A quorum being present, the Journal of Proceedings of the preceding day's session will be read by the Secretary.
>
> (The Secretary reads the Journal, and such corrections as are necessary are made.)
>
> The Presiding Officer: The Journal will stand approved, if there be no objection.[15]

Gilfry updated his compilation of Senate precedents in 1914, 1915, and 1919. In the ninety years since publication of his first volume, several new and expanded editions of that work have appeared.

In 1958, Senate Parliamentarian Charles Watkins and the assistant parliamentarian, Dr. Floyd M. Riddick, prepared the first of the modern editions, entitled *Senate Procedure:*

Precedents and Practices. This volume, as described in the preface, "is a compilation of the rules of the Senate, portions of laws affecting Senate procedure, rulings by the Presiding Officer, and established practices of the Senate." [16] Like its predecessors, this vital reference source and the subsequent editions of 1964, 1974, and 1981 contain citations to decisions extending back almost to the First Congress. These volumes include comprehensive coverage of those decisions that have appeared in the Senate portions of the *Congressional Record* and the *Senate Journal* since December 3, 1883. Dr. Riddick was the sole compiler of the 1974 and 1981 volumes, and he is now at work with Senate Parliamentarian Alan S. Frumin on an edition that will update the precedents through the end of the One-hundredth Congress in 1988.

The rules of the Senate regularly come under assault by senators—usually new senators—who would like to change them. Many of these well-intentioned reformers come to the Senate from the U.S. House of Representatives or from state legislatures. They view the Senate as an antiquated institution, which ought to move on and be like other legislative bodies, where bills are passed quickly and the members can be off to the golf course or the fishing stream. Life as a senator is hectic and needs to be made better, they say.

These may be laudable objectives, but the United States Senate was never meant to operate like other legislative bodies. We were not told that life would be easy in the Senate. William Maclay of Pennsylvania, a senator in the First Congress, expressed it well in the final entry of his diary, written on March 3, 1791, at the close of his two-year term in the Senate:

As I left the Hall I gave it a look, with that kind of Satisfaction which A Man feels on leaving a place Where he has been ill at Ease. being fully satisfyed that many A Culprit, has served Two Years at the Wheel-Barrow, without feeling half the pain & mortification, that I experienced, in my honorable Station.[17]

Our problem is only two hundred years old! The people send us here to work. When we run for reelection to the Senate, we do not ask the people to vote for us so that we may improve the quality of life for senators. Back home, the voters ask how we can improve the quality of life for *them*—not for *us*. Not the quality of *life* in the Senate, but, rather, the quality of *work* should most concern us as senators.

Senators often criticize their leaders who schedule the work here. Some contend that the Senate should be more efficient and that the work should take less of our time. Perhaps so. But efficiency, from the standpoint

of the time utilized in doing its work, was not the Senate's *raison d'être*. The Senate was meant to be a deliberative body—a brake on the House of Representatives, a rock that would stand against the storms of passion that might, from time to time, sweep the country away from the center of logic, reason, and objective judgment.

As I have stated earlier, the Senate's rules have their roots in the rules adopted in the First Congress in 1789, the Continental congresses, and the Congress under the Articles of Confederation. They also reflect earlier influences from the English House of Commons and the American colonial legislatures. The Senate's rules were not dropped like manna from heaven overnight; as this chapter demonstrates, they are the product of time, trial, and experience, and we must proceed with caution when we seek to alter them. Much like the Constitution, the Senate rules should not be changed often or without compelling reason.

Dr. Riddick's book, *Senate Procedure*, containing the precedents of the Senate, may not be fascinating reading, but it is important. Every senator should study the Senate rules and precedents "to show thyself approved . . . a workman that needeth not to be ashamed." (2 Tim. 2:15)

Some Common Errors in Procedure

It is always amazing, sometimes embarrassing, to see senators who, having been here for years, reveal an utter ignorance of the rules. Some never learn, for instance, the difference between the "morning hour" and "morning business." Senators often loosely refer to the morning hour when they obviously have morning business in mind. Some apparently think that morning business is a period set aside for short speeches, whereas, in fact, senators are not permitted to make speeches in morning business, except by unanimous consent. Morning business, under Rule VII, is only for introducing bills, resolutions, petitions, memorials, and committee reports, as well as for laying before the Senate messages and communications from the president, the House, and heads of departments. It is not for speeches. Morning business can be utilized for short speeches only through the unanimous consent orders that the majority leader usually obtains, *permitting* senators to speak during that period.

There is a definite distinction between the terms morning business and morning hour. Neither occurs on a calendar day except when otherwise ordered by unanimous consent. Both automatically occur on a new legislative day (which follows an adjournment). Morning business follows the reading of the *Journal* and occurs in the beginning of the morning hour. The morning hour, as it appeared in the 1877 general revision of the rules, consisted of the "first hour of daily sessions." In the 1884 revision, there was no specific mention of a morning hour, as such, but, by implication, it was extended to include the first two hours ("each day . . . until 2 o'clock"). Today's Senate Rule VIII provides specifically for "the morning hour" as being "until 2 hours after the Senate convenes on [a new legislative] day."

The morning hour consists of the morning business, followed by resolutions coming "over under the rule" and then the "consideration of the Calendar of Bills and Resolutions."

The following are some procedural errors that too frequently occur in the Senate:

—When a senator asks for the immediate consideration of a bill or resolution, the chair should not say "without objection" before the clerk states the title of the measure. The title should first be stated, in order to inform the Senate what the resolution or bill is about, before the chair asks the Senate whether or not it will consent to proceed to consider the measure.

—Senators often send amendments to the desk and ask for "immediate consideration." This is not necessary. Senators need only to state that they send an amendment to the desk. The chair will take over from there.

—Senators, when called on to preside, should not speak from the chair. If the chair is complimented by a senator from the floor, the chair should not respond. When visitors from other countries are introduced in the chamber, the *chair* is not required or expected to address the visitors to make them feel welcome. That is not the chair's responsibility, nor is it desirable. All too often, members who should know better will unburden themselves of some pearly words of wisdom from the chair. This does not leave a very good impression. The chair is supposed to say as little as possible beyond making rulings on points of order, responding to parliamentary inquiries, making certain announcements, and securing order in the chamber and the galleries. A senator is not supposed to speak from the chair, even to answer criticism from the floor. The vice president—who is not a member of the Senate—may not address the Senate except by unanimous consent.

—Senators err in addressing other senators in the second person. It is not in order for them to do so. Senators in debate should address other senators in the third person, because it is impersonal, it is decorous, and it helps to avoid acerbities in debate. One does not appear to be, and one does not become, so personal by addressing another senator in the third person as by addressing a senator directly and in the second person. It is much like pointing the finger at someone else. Senators should address other senators through the chair: "Mr. President, will the Senator from West Virginia yield?"

—Senators should never read their mail or other matter while presiding. Doing so conveys an unfavorable impression concerning

Vice President Adlai E. Stevenson praised the Senate's rules and procedures. *Library of Congress*

the chair, who should at all times be attentive to the proceedings. After all, this *is* the United States Senate, and the chair should always be mindful that the American people are watching. They have the right to expect the *best* from the world's foremost upper legislative body.

—Senators sometimes "move" the adoption of an amendment, bill, or resolution. Such a motion has no parliamentary standing and is not recognized under the Senate rules. It is the duty of the chair to put the question of adoption when no other senator seeks recognition.

The foregoing common errors may seem insignificant, and perhaps, at times, they are, but they always serve to betray senators' lack of knowledge of Senate ways and Senate rules.

CONCLUSION

Mr. President, during my twenty-two years of service in various leadership posts in the Senate—secretary of the Democratic

conference, majority whip, majority leader, minority leader, again majority leader, and now president pro tempore—I have had the opportunity to become familiar with this body's rules and many of its precedents. As I have noted on other occasions, to know the rules and precedents is to know the Senate and its infinite capacity for flexibility in serving as a forum for reasoned deliberation and constructive action. To study the development of the Senate's rules over the past two hundred years is, indeed, to study the very history and institutional fiber of the Senate. The Senate's rules are milestones by which we can measure its struggle to meet the needs of a growing nation. With the passage of time, outmoded rules have fallen by the wayside, while those that have effectively promoted the Senate's business have survived in their original or modified form.

My experience with the Senate's rules compels me to appreciate the wisdom that Vice President Adlai Stevenson expressed in his farewell address to the Senate on March 3, 1897. I believe his observation is as fitting today as it was at the end of the nineteenth century.

It must not be forgotten that the rules governing this body are founded deep in human experience; that they are the result of centuries of tireless effort in legislative hall, to conserve, to render stable and secure, the rights and liberties which have been achieved by conflict. By its rules the Senate wisely fixes the limits to its own power. Of those who clamor against the Senate, and its methods of procedure, it may be truly said: "They know not what they do." In this Chamber alone are preserved, without restraint, two essentials of wise legislation and of good government—the right of amendment and of debate. Great evils often result from hasty legislation; rarely from the delay which follows full discussion and deliberation. In my humble judgment, the historic Senate—preserving the unrestricted right of amendment and of debate, maintaining intact the time-honored parliamentary methods and amenities which unfailingly secure action after deliberation—possesses in our scheme of government a value which can not be measured by words.[18]

CHAPTER 4

Impeachment

The Historical Development of Impeachment
1376–1789

June 19, 1987[*]

The president pro tempore [Mr. Byrd]. . . .

The Senate, having tried Walter L. Nixon, Jr., U.S. District Judge for the Southern District of Mississippi, upon three articles of impeachment exhibited against him by the House of Representatives, and two-thirds of the Senators present having found him guilty of the charges contained in articles I and II of the articles of impeachment, it is, therefore, ordered and adjudged that the said Walter L. Nixon, Jr., be, and he is hereby, removed from office.

Mr. President, on November 3, 1989, the foregoing judgment was entered in accordance with the order of the Senate.[1] Judge Nixon thus became the seventh person convicted by the Senate in its entire two-hundred-year history, but his was the second conviction within a space of only fifteen days. Another U.S. District Judge, Alcee L. Hastings of the southern district of Florida, was convicted and removed from office on October 20, 1989.

The Senate's powers of conviction and removal in impeachment trials flow from the U.S. Constitution, which deals with the subject of impeachment in several separate sections as follows:

Article I, section 2, clause 5:

The House of Representatives . . . shall have the sole Power of Impeachment.

Article I, section 3, clause 6:

The Senate shall have the sole Power to try all Impeachments. When sitting for that Purpose, they shall be on Oath or Affirmation. When the President of the United States is tried, the Chief Justice shall preside: And no Person shall be convicted without the Concurrence of two-thirds of the Members present.

Article I, section 3, clause 7:

Judgment in Cases of Impeachment shall not extend further than to removal from Office, and disqualification to hold and enjoy any Office of honor, Trust, or Profit under the United States: but the Party convicted shall nevertheless be liable and subject to Indictment, Trial, Judgment, and Punishment, according to Law.

Article II, section 2, clause 1:

The President . . . shall have Power to grant Reprieves and Pardons for Offenses against the United States, except in Cases of Impeachment.

Article II, section 4:

The President, Vice President and all civil Officers of the United States, shall be removed from Office on Impeachment for, and Conviction of, Treason, Bribery, or other high Crimes and Misdemeanors.

Article III, section 2, clause 3:

The Trial of all Crimes, except in Cases of Impeachment, shall be by Jury; . . .

---

[*] Updated December 1989

What were the influences that guided the Constitution's framers in their deliberations on impeachment? And what are impeachable offenses within the context of "high Crimes and Misdemeanors"?

According to Raoul Berger, one of the country's leading legal authorities on impeachment, the Founding Fathers, in considering the nature and purpose of impeachments, had the English experience very much in mind. In his authoritative book *Impeachment: The Constitutional Problems*, published in 1973, Berger wrote: "The Framers were steeped in English history; the shades of despotic kings and conniving ministers marched before them." [2] The impeachment of Warren Hastings, governor-general of India, was underway in the British Parliament in 1787, and George Mason referred to Hastings in a discussion of impeachable offenses at the Constitutional Convention.[3] According to Berger, the very terms "impeachment" and "treason, bribery, or other high crimes and misdemeanors" were "lifted bodily from English law." [4]

Let us examine the English experience. Berger explained that the English Parliament, by the use of impeachment, "after a long and bitter struggle, made ministers chosen by the King accountable to it rather than the Crown, replacing absolutist pretensions by parliamentary supremacy." [5] The first instance of the use of the weapon of impeachment occurred during the reign of Edward III. According to Goldwin Smith's *History of England*, the House of Commons, in the "Good Parliament" of 1376, registered its opposition to John of Gaunt's political machine by impeaching Richard Lyons, a customs officer and merchant, and other officials who had engaged in illegal activities "which would have been a horrible matter to rehearse in full." [6]

The impeachment process in England was a criminal process. The House of Commons, acting as a grand or accusing jury, would conduct an inquiry and bring charges against the king's minister or other person. The charges would be presented to the House of Lords for trial of the person impeached, and selected members of the Commons would serve as managers or prosecutors at the trial. If the Lords found the accused guilty, the penalties could be removal from office and punishment by fine, imprisonment, forfeiture of lands and properties, banishment, or death. Thus, removal from office and criminal punishment were united in one impeachment process which could cost a man both his office and his head.

Impeachment fell into disuse during the reign of the strong Tudor monarchs but was revived during the tyrannical rule of the Stuart kings in the seventeenth century. In 1621, the lord chancellor, Francis Bacon, was impeached for taking bribes and admitted his guilt. Bacon was convicted by the House of Lords, fined £40,000, imprisoned in the Tower, and, by judgment of the Lords, declared forever "incapable of any office, place or employment in the state." He could "never sit in parliament nor come within the verge of the court." According to Goldwin Smith, when Sir Edward Coke, a member of the House of Commons, brought the impeachment of Bacon, the Commons "were striking at [King James I's] claims of absolute power." [7]

Berger wrote that the impeachment of Sir Thomas Wentworth, the earl of Strafford, "constitutes a great watershed in English constitutional history of which the Founders were aware." [8] Wentworth had served as lord deputy of Ireland, where his ruthless policies had earned for him the sobriquet "Black Tom Tyrant." King Charles I recalled him from Ireland, made him earl of Strafford, and brought him into the counsels as a close adviser to the king. Strafford had long before shown his contempt for Parliament and his favor for despotic methods of government.[9]

When Charles, hard pressed for revenues, urged the King's Bench to uphold the extension of the Ship-Money Tax—previously levied on seaports—to inland towns, it was viewed as a move to end Parliament's power to tax and to legislate. According to Berger, Strafford advised Charles that "he was now absolved from law" and "urged the introduction of an Irish army to compel England to obedience."[10] Strafford was impeached by the Commons and charged with "subverting the fundamental law and introducing an arbitrary and tyrannical government." As Berger stated, Strafford's acts did not amount to treason against the king, because "they had his tacit consent, if not encouragement." After the charges had been made before the Lords and Strafford had been heard in his own defense, the Commons abandoned the impeachment and proceeded with a bill of attainder, on the same charges brought in the impeachment—a shift viewed by Berger as "an unsolved puzzle."[11]

Charles had vowed that Strafford would not die, but he broke his promise. Goldwin Smith's *History of England* reports that, "pleading the danger to his wife and children," the king signed the bill condemning his servant to death. On May 12, 1641, Strafford was beheaded on Tower Hill before the eyes of 200,000 people.[12]

Berger maintained that the Commons, in impeaching Strafford, "intended to pass judgment on a system of government as well as the man. For to them Strafford personified more than any other the injustice and misrule they meant to end."[13]

Berger wrote: "In truth, the gaze of the [Constitution's] Framers was concentrated on the struggles with royal oppression during the seventeenth century rather than on the system of parliamentary government fully achieved in the eighteenth. . . . Before

them marched a procession of ghostly despots; they were familiar with absolutist Stuart claims. . . ." Therefore, said Berger, "Fear of presidential abuses prevailed over frequent objections that impeachment threatened a President's independence."[14]

For an understanding of the experience with impeachment in the American colonies and under state constitutions prior to the Constitutional Convention, I highly recommend *Impeachment in America, 1635–1805*, written by Peter Charles Hoffer and N.E.H. Hull. Referring to "the Americanization of impeachment" as "fitting it to American needs,"[15] Hoffer and Hull wrote that "the connection between American law and English law was real enough but always tempered by American conditions and ideas."[16]

The settlement of colonies in America was taking place at the same time that impeachments were in their heyday in seventeenth-century England. Colonial assemblies had no legal right to initiate impeachments, but, as Englishmen, sitting in lower-house representative bodies far from the seat of royal power, they arrogated to themselves the same prerogatives as those of the English Commons at Westminster. John Adams clearly expressed this view in the eighteenth century: "But whence can We pretend to derive such a Power [to impeach]? From our Charter, which gives Us . . . all the Rights and Privileges of Englishmen: and if the House of Commons in England is the grand Inquest of the Nation, the [Massachusetts] House of Representatives is the Grand Inquest of this Province."[17]

Crown lawyers in England denied that the American colonies had been granted the right to impeach anyone for any reason. According to Hoffer and Hull, "The Privy Council noted that the correct alternative to impeachment in America was recourse to executive or judicial authority in England." Such action could take place through ap-

The British House of Commons, shown here as it appeared in 1741, established early precedents on impeachment that influenced the framers of the U.S. Constitution.   *Library of Congress*

peals; petitions; remonstrances; or addresses to either the crown, the Privy Council, or other administrative officers in the mother country. This rule was often followed by colonial governments. But colonial assemblies understood how useful impeachment could be in removing officials from office for corruption, misuse of power, violation of the public trust, or commission of felonies and misdemeanors. Hoffer and Hull explained that lawyers and legislators "had a sketchy familiarity with the major impeachment cases" underway in England, through pamphlets, newsletters, and word of mouth, since certain cases were much discussed throughout the colonies. When aggrieved private individuals brought their complaints to the assemblies, members would launch inquiries into the actions and conduct of public officials, thus carrying forward the high duty of representative government. But, as Hoffer and Hull related, "impeachment would not have been effective in practice or in theory if the upper houses and the governors of the colonies did not concede a certain degree of legitimacy to impeachment." [18]

According to Hoffer and Hull, colonial impeachment roots were deep. An action in 1635 involved Royal Governor John Harvey of Virginia, who was accused of misfeasance in office. Harvey was driven out of the colony and sent to England for judgment. Although the accusations were not termed an "impeachment" at the time, as seen in retrospect, "in all but name they were." It was in 1657, however, that the word "impeachment" was first applied to an assembly charge, when Roger Williams petitioned the general court of Rhode Island to "impeach" William Harris for "heresy and high treason." The assembly heard the case and referred the charge and Harris' defense to England for judgment. [19]

Both the Virginia and Rhode Island colonies had thus shied away from the final step

of trial, judgment, and punishment. The next series of impeachments, however, which occurred in Maryland between 1669 and 1683, went to judgment. The first resulted in acquittal and the second in loss of office. According to Hoffer and Hull, the third impeachment charged Charles James, sheriff of Cecil County, with "falsely swearing before a justice of the peace," inducing others to do the same, and assault and battery. For these offenses, he was removed from office by the council. The fourth impeachment in the Maryland series charged Jacob Young with "High Misdemeanors." Young was employed by the colony as an interpreter, and the assembly impeached him for "bringing the proprietary into disrepute among the Indians," "marrying an Indian," "leading raids against the Piscataway" tribe, and failing to mediate between the Indians in compliance with his "instructions as an officer of the government." In October 1683, the lower house sent managers to the upper house, where Young was tried, found guilty, and banished after suffering the loss of office. [20]

Seventeenth-century impeachments occurred in other colonies, as well. Hoffer and Hull reported that these proceedings were much alike in their most important aspects, with the lower houses "trying to protect the public against individual wrongdoing." The accusations ranged from common-law felony to "illegal conduct in office (with or without explicit statutory grounds), . . . or simply . . . some form of corruption." Although the colonists lacked information as to precise impeachment procedures, they endeavored to follow English precedent. [21]

Whereas impeachment in seventeenth-century America had concentrated on official misconduct, in the eighteenth century it became an instrument through which the colonial assemblies asserted their independence in the struggle with branches of government representing the imperial power. The colonists were aware of the ascendancy of the English Parliament over the monarchy, and of the supremacy of the Commons within the Parliament, and this knowledge spurred popularly elected lower houses to challenge appointed royal and proprietary officeholders. Impeachment became an important check against excesses by governors, councils, and judges appointed by authority of the crown, while continuing as an effective protection from malefactors among justices of the peace, sheriffs, and other locally elected officials. Although impeachment was not always successful, it spelled trouble for arrogant and arbitrary executives and judges, and it often resulted in resignation or censure of the individual accused of abusing the public trust. Hoffer and Hull, in their exhaustive study of early American impeachments, captured the last quarter-century of the colonial experience:

First, these cases were ultimately directed against English authority over the colonies. Second, they rested upon an assumption of the supremacy of the peoples' representatives, assembled in colonial lower houses, over other branches of government.[22]

Impeachment had thus become an effective weapon against the imperiousness of royal government, and, after independence, it became a fixture of American government in the newly formed states. Although the principle of separation of powers was contradicted by the mixing of legislative and judicial functions in the impeachment process, "only through impeachment and trial could a malfeasor be convicted of willful, knowing misconduct." This was the practical experience that had evolved during the colonial period, and it influenced the writers of state constitutions. Most of the states included impeachment in the first drafts of their constitutions. According to Hoffer and Hull, among those that did, "all except New York

had colonial cases or modeled their constitutions upon states with colonial precedents." Delaware and New Jersey, for example, were influenced by Pennsylvania's constitution, and Vermont, although not one of the colonies, "adopted the Pennsylvania provisions word for word."[23]

The states found impeachment and trial to be a practical means of dealing with mismanagement of public funds, fiscal misconduct, nonfeasance, malfeasance, misfeasance, abuse of the public trust, and other forms of unethical activity engaged in by officeholders. Conviction in the courts for crimes committed did not necessarily mean that the offender would be relieved of office, but the impeachment process could achieve this end and disqualify him from holding future public positions of honor and trust. For example, when Jonathan Fassett, a member of the Vermont assembly, led rioters attempting to close the county court in order to prevent debt collections, the assembly refused to reseat him and secured his impeachment. The council tried Fassett, found him guilty, and ordered him to pay the cost of "the prosecution of his impeachment." Although he had already been denied his assembly seat and thus could not be removed from office, the council barred him from holding future office. Fassett's was a case that had come before both the council and the courts but, according to Hoffer and Hull, "did not violate the double jeopardy clause of the constitution. The impeachment trial could only result in removal and disqualification and was thus a separate proceeding." A fine for the costs of an impeachment trial could also be imposed upon the defendant in both English and colonial cases; "it was not a punishment."[24]

The mere threat of impeachment alone had a positive effect, as Hoffer and Hull explained. The reminder that it was available "meant that the people did not have to take their complaints against officeholders into the streets. There was a well-tried, legal method for . . . trial of complaints against officials no matter how highly placed." Furthermore, impeachment "allowed state legislators to demonstrate publicly their commitment to honest government and their aversion" to incompetency, embezzlement, and corruption in high places. Several impeachments in New Jersey during the period from 1778 through 1782 resulted in removals of county magistrates for "malpractice" in office and other offenses in their "official capacity." Abuse of public trust and other offenses difficult for local courts to handle, because they might not be included in criminal codes, were nevertheless reachable through impeachment. "Misuse of power undermined the legitimacy of state government and impeachment effectively redressed such misconduct." [25]

Hoffer and Hull reported that other impeachable offenses included incompetence or lack of attention to duty, if they posed a danger to the state, but only if there was "evidence of intentional neglect or total incapacity to perform official duties." Although "well-meaning incompetence" was not enough cause for removal, the officeholder "often took the hint and resigned." In New Jersey, the official clothier, the army quartermaster, and two inspectors of confiscated lands all resigned when their inefficiency was brought to light by the assembly.[26]

The most famous inquiry for incompetence, according to Hoffer and Hull, was launched against Thomas Jefferson when he was governor of Virginia. The resolution of inquiry was introduced by assembly delegate George Nicholas, who was supported by Richard Henry Lee and Patrick Henry, both old rivals of Jefferson. In June 1781, Jefferson had fled the capital when the British invaded Virginia, and many in the revolutionary ranks had been angered by what they viewed as ineffective fiscal policy, inept administration of the conscription law, and controversy over Jefferson's handling of the Virginia militia. The investigation fizzled when nobody appeared to testify before the committee appointed to receive evidence. The committee acknowledged that the resolution of inquiry had been based on hearsay, and no formal motion for impeachment was ever made. Jefferson's friends maintained that the charges of incompetence "were animated by envy, spite, and partisanship." This was often true, conceded Hoffer and Hull, "but without proof of willful misuse of power (including failure to act when necessary), such charges fell to the ground." [27]

Between the 1776 Declaration of Independence from England by the thirteen colonies and the Constitutional Convention eleven years later in 1787, all but three of the original states included impeachment provisions in their state constitutions. The drafters of these constitutions were familiar with impeachment, both in theory and in practice, from their colonial experience. As Hoffer and Hull observed, they transformed impeachment "from a check against monarchical misdeeds to an instrument of republican government." [28]

Like the colonial models, the states' organic laws deviated from the British prototype in many ways, thus conforming impeachment to American concepts. Unlike the punishment by heavy fines, imprisonment, death, forfeiture of lands and other property that had often accompanied English impeachment and conviction, the only penalty that could flow from American impeachment was removal from office and barring from further office. In England, according to Raoul Berger, impeachment "was part and parcel of a criminal proceeding," [29] but in America, James Wilson, a leading framer of the United States Constitution, explained, "impeachments are confined to political characters, to political crimes and misdemeanors, and to political punishments." Wilson also stated that impeachments "come not . . . within the sphere of ordinary jurisprudence. They are founded on different principles, are governed by different maxims, and are directed to different objects."[30]

Hoffer and Hull noted that all of the state constitutions were markedly republican in their impeachment provisions. In Pennsylvania, for example, no ordinary citizen was subject to impeachment, while no state officer was immune from charges of maladministration, the only offense specified. Trial was by the president and executive council. As noted earlier, Vermont's provisions were identical to those of Pennsylvania. In New Jersey, judges and other officers could be impeached for misbehavior and tried by the executive council. In Delaware, specific categories of impeachable offenses were enumerated, but "danger to the public good" was the overriding element that distinguished such offenses from common crimes. In New York, all officers could be impeached for "mal and corrupt conduct" in office, with a two-thirds vote necessary to impeach. The 1776 North Carolina constitution made any official impeachable for "corruption and maladministration" and for "violating any part of the constitution." In the final version of the Virginia constitution, the supreme court was given the trial of impeachments for "offending against the state, either by Mal-administration, Corruption, or other means, by which the safety of the State may be endangered." Massachusetts limited impeachment to officeholders for maladministration and misconduct, with a two-thirds vote necessary for conviction. South Carolina, in its revised constitution of 1778, made state officers impeachable for "mal and corrupt conduct," with trial by the senate. According to Hoffer and Hull, "The New Hampshire lower house . . . styled itself 'the Grand Inquest' "; trial was by the senate for misconduct or maladministration, with all officers being impeachable. Georgia adopted impeachment in the 1780's, but Rhode Island, Connecticut, and Maryland did not add impeachment to their laws until the early 1800's.[31]

One hundred and fifty years of experience with impeachment in the colonies and newly formed states had, therefore, provided a background for the Constitution's drafters at the 1787 convention. As a result, the "prime movers behind incorporation of impeachment in the federal law," Hoffer and Hull wrote, "were intimately connected with state impeachment law and cases." They understood impeachment law and had first-hand knowledge of its effectiveness. Some, like Edmund Randolph, James Madison, and George Mason, "were closely associated with the evolution of impeachment law" in the states. Most important, they all agreed about certain basic precepts which had undergirded colonial and state practices. For instance, unlike the English precedent, "only officers could be impeached . . . with removal and disqualification the only punishments." As Hoffer and Hull observed, "these great differences between American and English impeachment law originated in the colonies and fully matured in the Revolutionary states." This shared background accounts for the apparent consensus among the delegates and for the relatively sparse recorded debate regarding most aspects of impeachment.[32]

Certain sticky points remained to be decided, however. What officials would be subject to removal? By what method would removal take place and in what forum? For what wrongdoings and under what limitations would removals occur?

According to the notes taken by James Madison at the Constitutional Convention,

Edmund Randolph of Virginia submitted a resolution on May 29 proposing a "supreme tribunal to hear and determine . . . impeachments of any National officers." The resolution was referred to a Committee of the Whole House for debate and action.[33] On June 2, John Dickinson of Delaware moved "that the Executive be made removeable by the National Legislature on the request of a majority of the Legislatures of individual States." The motion was rejected after James Madison of Virginia and James Wilson of Pennsylvania argued that it would enable a minority of the people to prevent removal of an officer viewed by the majority as a criminal and would encourage an officer to "pay court to particular States whose leading partizans he might fear, or wish to engage as his partizans." The convention then made the Executive "ineligible after seven years," and Hugh Williamson successfully moved to add the words "and to be removeable on impeachment and conviction of mal-practice or neglect of duty." [34]

On June 13, the Committee of the Whole reported on Randolph's propositions, one opinion of the committee being that "a National Executive . . . consist of a single person . . . to be removeable on impeachment and conviction of malpractices or neglect of duty." The national judiciary was to have jurisdiction over "impeachments of any National Officers." [35]

On June 15, William Paterson of New Jersey submitted an alternative to the Randolph, or Virginia, plan. Both plans were then discussed in the Committee of the Whole. The Paterson, or New Jersey, plan contained a provision for a plural "federal Executive . . . removeable by Congress on application by a majority of the Executives of the several States." There was also a judiciary with "authority to hear and determine . . . all impeachments of federal officers." [36]

At the Constitutional Convention, William Paterson submitted the New Jersey plan, which included a provision for impeachment. *Library of Congress*

Alexander Hamilton, who had thus far not entered into the convention debates, made a lengthy prepared speech on June 18, declaring his opposition to both the Randolph and Paterson plans, particularly the latter, and suggesting a plan of his own. Concerning impeachment, Hamilton proposed:

IX. The Governour Senators and all officers of the United States to be liable to impeachment for mal- and corrupt conduct; and upon conviction to be removed from office, & disqualified for holding any place of trust or profit—All impeachments to be tried by a Court to consist of the Chief or Judge of the superior Court of Law of each State, provided such Judge shall hold his place during good behavior, and have a permanent salary.[37]

Following Hamilton's address, the convention adjourned. The next day, June 19, the Paterson plan was discussed, and Madison delivered a long critique advising against it. The delegates then voted to again report the Randolph plan "as preferable" to the Paterson plan. The Randolph plan, as reported from the Committee of the Whole, still provided for impeachment and removal of the executive for "mal practice or neglect of duty" and "jurisdiction of the national Judiciary . . . [over] impeachments of any national officers." [38]

Madison's notes show nothing further concerning impeachment, other than an occasional peripheral reference, until a month later, on July 20, when the major recorded debate on the subject occurred. During consideration of the Randolph provision for impeachment and conviction of the executive for malpractice or neglect of duty, George Mason of Virginia, speaking for impeachment of the executive, asked, "Shall any man be above Justice?" Benjamin Franklin, who was a Pennsylvania delegate, supported impeachment on the strange grounds that, otherwise, as history had shown, "recourse was had to assassination." Madison believed it was crucial that the "Community" be defended "against the incapacity, negligence or perfidy of the chief Magistrate. . . . He might pervert his administration into a scheme of peculation or oppression. He might betray his trust to foreign powers." Elbridge Gerry of Massachusetts was for impeachments: "A good magistrate will not fear them. A bad one ought to be kept in fear of them." Gouverneur Morris of Pennsylvania, at first against impeachment, changed his opinion after listening to the arguments, saying that the executive "may be bribed . . . to betray his trust." Others, like Rufus King of Massachusetts and Charles Pinckney of South Carolina, were against including a provision for impeachment. On the question "Shall the Executive be removable on impeachments?" eight states voted aye, two states voted no.[39]

At the 1787 convention, Benjamin Franklin endorsed the concept of impeachment. *Library of Congress*

The records of the debate indicate that, by the latter part of July, the framers were almost exclusively concerned with removal of the topmost executive by means of impeachment, but there had been little discussion regarding removal of other federal officers. Not yet decided were the forum in which the trial should occur and the actions that would be impeachable.

The work of the framers was referred to the Committee of Detail on July 26, and the convention adjourned until August 6 to allow the committee time to prepare and report the Constitution.

John Rutledge's committee report at the Constitutional Convention outlined the process for impeachment. *Yale University Art Gallery*

On August 6, John Rutledge of South Carolina delivered the committee report, which contained the following concerning impeachment:

Article X, section 2. . . . [The president] shall be removed from his office on impeachment by the House of Representatives, and conviction in the supreme Court, of treason, bribery, or corruption.

The president would have power to grant pardons, but a presidential pardon would not "be pleadable in bar of an impeachment."

Article XI, section 3. The Jurisdiction of the Supreme Court shall extend . . . to the trial of impeachments of officers of the United States. . . .

Reference was also made to impeachment cases affecting "Ambassadors, other Public Ministers and Consuls."

Section 4. The trial of all criminal offences (except in cases of impeachments) . . . shall be by Jury.

Section 5 limited judgment in impeachment cases to removal from office and disqualification for any future "office of honour, trust or profit, under the United States," but the individual convicted would be subject to "indictment, trial, judgment and punishment according to law." [40]

Here, in the Committee of Detail's August 6 report, the impeachment process was being fleshed out: "officers" in addition to the top executive were impeachable; the House of Representatives would impeach, and the Supreme Court would conduct the trial; treason, bribery, and "corruption" were the impeachable crimes; impeachment was limited to persons holding office and did not bar trial and punishment in courts of law; and a presidential pardon for commission of a crime could not be a bar to further impeachment (as in the 1701 English Act of Settlement).

Nothing further appears in Madison's notes concerning the impeachment portion of the report until August 20, when Gouverneur Morris submitted various propositions. One of these provided that various officers (the chief justice of the United States and secretaries of departments) comprising a Council of State "to assist the President" be "liable to impeachment, & removal from office for neglect of duty malversation, or corruption." The propositions were referred to the Committee of Detail. Gerry moved that that committee also be instructed to report the "mode of trying the Supreme Judges" in cases of impeachment. Two days later, Rutledge reported the committee's recommendation that the trial of Supreme Court judges be "by the senate, on impeachment by the house of representatives." No further mention of impeachment appears until August 27, when the convention voted to postpone action on the impeachment clauses. Gouverneur Morris thought the Supreme Court an "improper" tribunal for trial of impeachment of the president.[41]

A new Committee of Eleven, one member from each state, was appointed, by ballot, on August 31 to consider all parts of the Constitution that had been postponed and any parts of reports that had not yet been acted on. Five days later, on September 4, David Brearly of New Jersey made a partial report for the new committee, including a major step forward. The committee recommended that the Senate "try all impeachments," with "two thirds of the members present" required for conviction. Furthermore, impeachment of the president "for Treason, or bribery" would be by the House of Representatives, and the chief justice would preside at the Senate trial.[42]

Earlier discussions regarding the forum for trial of impeachments had centered on the Supreme Court, while the debate concerning the method of selecting the president had raged between those delegates advocating his appointment by the Senate and those who urged other means, such as election by "the Executives of the States" or "election by the people."[43] But now the Committee of Detail was recommending his election by an electoral college, and, as a result, the Senate had moved to center stage as the trier of impeachments. According to Hoffer and Hull, the shift in direction

was part of a tangled debate over the manner of electing the president. When the committee of detail decided to create a college of electors, the Senate, which had been slated to name the president, could now try him upon an impeachment without being compromised by having named him in the first place.[44]

Thus, "the resulting availability of the Senate to hear trial upon impeachment of the president was a pleasant by-product" of the creation of an electoral college.[45] Gouverneur Morris, a member of the new Commit-

tee of Detail, stated that a strong reason for making the Senate instead of the Supreme Court the trier of impeachments "was that the latter [the Supreme Court] was to try the President after the trial of the impeachment," if he were subsequently indicted and tried for a crime.[46]

Action on the impeachment clauses was postponed until September 8. One important element, the definition of impeachable offenses, remained to be hammered out. In earlier debates and reports, references had been made to a number of possible grounds for impeachment, including: malpractice or neglect of duty; "mal- and corrupt conduct"; "incapacity, negligence or perfidy"; "treachery," "corrupting his electors, and incapacity"; "treason, bribery, or corruption"; "neglect of duty [,] malversation, or corruption"; and "treason, or bribery."[47] Most of the delegates were familiar with one or more of these as examples set forth in state constitutions or colonial cases.

In considering the clause specifying "treason and bribery" as the impeachable offenses, Mason complained that "treason as defined in the Constitution will not reach many great and dangerous offences." He therefore moved to add after "bribery," the words "or maladministration." Gerry seconded him, but Madison objected that "so vague a term will be equivalent to a tenure during pleasure of the Senate." Mason then withdrew "maladministration" and substituted the phrase "other high crimes and misdemesnors against the State," which was agreed to. A motion was then adopted making "the vice-President and other Civil officers" of the United States removable from office on impeachment and conviction for treason, bribery, or other high crimes and misdemeanors. The convention accepted a motion by Gouverneur Morris requiring members of the Senate to be "on oath" when sitting for trial of an impeachment. Finally,

George Washington presided over the Constitutional Convention.

the convention approved the clause, as amended, providing that the Senate would try all impeachments, conviction would require a two-thirds vote of members present, and members would be on oath.[48]

In the words of Hoffer and Hull, the vote in favor of the compromise phrase "other high crimes and misdemeanors" suggests that the framers

understood that the new terms included maladministration, corruption, and neglect of duty rather than excluding all but those offenses cognizable in regular courts of law. . . . The addition of misdemeanors to the list of offenses meant that the House of Representatives was permitted to charge officials with minor breaches of ethical conduct, misuse of power, and neglect of duty, as well as more prolonged, egregious or financially rapacious misconduct.[49]

During the September 8 debate on impeachment, Madison opposed Senate trial of the president, "especially as he was to be impeached by the other branch of the Legislature, and for any act which might be called a misdemesnor." The president, argued Madison, would thus be made improperly dependent on the two houses, and the Supreme Court would be preferable to the Senate as the trial forum. Gouverneur Morris, however, thought "no other tribunal than the Senate could be trusted," and the Supreme Court "were too few in number and might be warped or corrupted." Roger Sherman of Connecticut opposed trial of the president by the court "because the Judges would be appointed by him." When Madison moved to strike out the words "by the Senate," his

[71]

motion was soundly rejected by a vote of 2 to 9.[50]

A committee was appointed, by ballot, consisting of Dr. William Samuel Johnson of Connecticut, Hamilton, Gouverneur Morris, Madison, and King, "to revise the stile of and arrange the articles which had been agreed to." On September 12, Dr. Johnson, on behalf of the committee, reported "a digest of the plan," together with a proposed letter to the Congress to accompany the "plan." The convention then debated and made further revisions to various parts of the draft reported by the Committee of Stile and Arrangement. No further discussion concerning impeachments occurred until September 14, when Rutledge moved that persons impeached "be suspended from their office" until tried and acquitted. Madison opposed that motion. Stating that the president was being "made too dependent already on the Legislature," Madison declared that such an "intermediate suspension, will put him in the power of one branch only. They can at any moment, in order to make way for the functions of another who will be more favorable to their views, vote a temporary removal of the existing Magistrate." Rutledge's amendment was voted down.[51]

On September 15, after making further modifications, the convention unanimously agreed to the Constitution, as amended. On the seventeenth, the convention adopted one final amendment—increasing the number of representatives from one for every forty thousand to one for every thirty thousand—and then unanimously approved the engrossed Constitution.[52]

The convention then adjourned sine die. It had completed its work and had given the Senate a judicial role in a unique system of checks and balances under the proposed new Constitution.

Even though the debates and actions at the Philadelphia convention regarding impeach-

Dr. William Samuel Johnson headed the convention's "Committee of Stile and Arrangement."
Library of Congress

ment appear on the record to have been comparatively sparse, they seem to indicate clearly enough that the framers intended the phrase "high Crimes and Misdemeanors" to subsume corruption, maladministration, gross and wanton neglect of duty, misuse of official power, and other violations of the public trust by officeholders.

The interpretation of the Constitution's clause on impeachable offenses entered into the ratification debates. James Iredell, speaking at the North Carolina convention, declared that the "power of impeachment" given by the Constitution was "to bring great offenders to punishment. . . . for crime which it is not easy to describe, but which every one must be convinced is a high crime and misdemeanor against the government." Iredell, who would later serve as a Supreme Court justice, said that the "occa-

Artist Howard Chandler Christy depicted the delegates preparing to sign the U.S. Constitution.

sion" for exercise of the impeachment power "will arise from acts of great injury to the community, and the objects of it may be such as cannot be easily reached by an ordinary tribunal." The person convicted in an impeachment trial "is further liable to a trial at common law," noted Iredell, and could receive common-law punishment for the offense *"if it be punishable by that law"* (emphasis added).[53] As to impeachment of the president, he would be liable, said Iredell, "where he had received a bribe, or had acted from some corrupt motive or other" and "must certainly be punishable for giving false information to the Senate." Governor Samuel Johnston observed that impeachment "only extends to high crimes and misdemeanors in a *public office*. It is a mode of trial pointed

out for great misdemeanors against the public."[54]

General Charles Cotesworth Pinckney, who had been one of the Constitution's framers, assured the South Carolina ratification convention that "those who behave amiss, or betray their public trust" were impeachable. At the same convention, Edward Rutledge said that the president could be impeached if he "abused their [the people's] trust."[55]

Speaking at the Virginia convention, James Madison told the delegates that "if the President be connected, in any suspicious manner, with any person, and there be grounds to believe he will shelter him, the House of Representatives can impeach him." As to the vice president, "should he be sus-

[73]

pected," he, too, could "be impeached and removed." Madison, in discussing Senate approval of treaties, declared that, "were the President to commit any thing so atrocious as to summon only a few states [senators], he would be impeached and convicted," for most states would be affected by "his misdemeanor." Madison said that, in the British government, "the minister who advises [the king] is liable to impeachment" if there be "an abuse of this royal prerogative." In the United States, Madison asked, "Who is the minister? The President himself, who is liable to impeachment." Madison said that were the president, in the making of treaties, to fail to safeguard the interest of the states, "if he should seduce a part of the Senate to a participation in his crimes, those who were not seduced would pronounce sentence against him." [56]

George Nicholas, in referring to impeachment at the Virginia convention, stated, "This power must have much greater force in America, where the President himself is personally amenable for his maladministration." [57]

Alexander Hamilton, hoping to influence the critical New York decision on ratification, explained in *The Federalist* No. 65:

A well constituted court for the trial of impeachments, is an object not more to be desired than difficult to be obtained in a government wholly elective. The subjects of its jurisdiction are those offenses which proceed from the misconduct of public men, or in other words from the abuse or violation of some public trust. They are of a nature which may with peculiar propriety be denominated POLITICAL, as they relate chiefly to injuries done immediately to the society itself. . . .

What it may be asked is the true spirit of the institution itself? Is it not designed as a method of NATIONAL INQUEST into the conduct of public men? . . . In Great Britain, it is the province of the house of commons to prefer the impeachment; and of the house of lords to decide upon it. Several of the State constitutions have followed the example. As well the latter as the former seem to have regarded the practice of impeachments, as a bridle in the hands of the legislative

Alexander Hamilton described impeachment as "a bridle in the hands of the legislative body upon the executive servants of the government."
Library of Congress

body upon the executive servants of the government. Is not this the true light in which it ought to be regarded? [58]

Thus, the ratifiers at various state conventions appeared to emphasize the views of the founders in Philadelphia.

Once the federal Constitution was ratified, the legislatures of many states began revising their state constitutions. Like the delegates to the Philadelphia convention, the legislators, too, wrestled with the definition of impeachable offenses. The conclusions they reached varied. Georgia's 1789 constitution provided only that "the senate shall have solely the power to try all impeachments" and the house "shall have solely the power to impeach all persons who have been or may be in office." The 1792 revised Delaware constitution contained the words, "treason, bribery, or any other high crime or misdemeanor," similar to the federal language, as well as an additional phrase: "or any crime or misdemeanor in office." The constitutions of the new states of Kentucky and Tennessee were also influenced by the federal document. In the Kentucky constitutional convention debates, the delegates agreed that persons convicted in the regular courts of "bribery, perjury, forgery, or other high crimes or misdemeanors" were to be excluded from office and that legislators were to be removed from office if convicted of violating their oath of office or receiving or giving bribes. At the Pennsylvania convention in 1789–1790, the revised state constitution's language was influenced by the federal model, but the impeachable offenses were "any misdemeanor in office," a broader standard than the federal example.[59]

After 1789, the states were guided in bringing impeachment cases by their past experience. Thus, wrote Hoffer and Hull, the impeachments "resembled the state cases of the previous decade. . . . Gross, intentional, self-interested official misconduct, or some criminal act had to be alleged for the impeachment to go forward." State legislatures routinely handled impeachment inquiries, most of which were accusations of "infractions of law or ethics" against minor officials. In fact, the frequency of such inquiries was "overwhelming evidence that the ordinary citizens of the states came to the lower house when troubled by apparent official misconduct. The people trusted their assemblies."[60]

In retrospect, as shown by Hoffer and Hull's thorough analysis of impeachment in early America, most of the impeachment cases occurring between 1788 and 1795 were not brought on grounds that were indictable in the regular courts. Instead, they were based on such accusations as "mismanagement of funds, arbitrariness on the bench, and incompetence in office,"which fell into a "category of *general* offenses, that is, acts dangerous to the public weal or violating the public trust."[61]

Impeachment Trials in the Senate
1789–1989

Viewed from the vantage point of the Senate's two-hundredth anniversary, let us briefly examine the institution's experience relative to impeachment trials from 1789 through 1989.

The first impeachment case reached the Senate in December 1798. It concerned one of the Senate's own members, William Blount of Tennessee, the only senator ever to be impeached. In 1797, President John Adams accused Senator Blount of conspiring with the British to overthrow Spanish control of Florida and Louisiana. The Senate reacted by voting to expel Blount, by a vote of 25 to 1, on July 8, 1797.

Federalist leaders in the House, however, were not satisfied with Blount's expulsion. In January 1798, they initiated impeachment proceedings against him, eventually adopting five articles. On the surface, this action by Federalists at the height of their power in Congress to impeach Blount, a former North Carolina Federalist turned Tennessee Republican, seems an open and shut case of a partisan vendetta. While the case certainly contained this element, its significance runs deeper, since the Federalists apparently had little to gain from an impeachment trial if Blount was already out of office. Embedded in the passion of the Federalist managers of Blount's impeachment lay hidden political motives. If Blount, an elected officeholder, could be impeached and disqualified for *misconduct*, not for any actual crimes, all Republicans in Congress were vulnerable so long as Federalists controlled both houses. Blount's case might have been just the first step in a

major political assault under the cover of impeachment. What had at first seemed a clear-cut case of one man's reckless cupidity now grew into a highly technical case with broad repercussions.

Undeniably, Senator Blount had plotted against Spain. But did private plotting amount to an impeachable offense? Blount had acted in no official capacity, and neither his mania for land speculation nor his meddling in foreign affairs was uncommon or indictable in regular court. Nevertheless, by great leaps of imagination, the House Federalists managed to stretch Blount's harebrained scheme into a genuine peril: treason, a clearly impeachable offense spelled out in the Constitution.

Blount stayed away from his trial in the Senate. Speaking for him, his counsel argued that Blount was a private citizen, who had committed no crime. Federalists contended that it was irrelevant whether or not Blount still held office, but it was an issue they could not overcome.

In the end, the Senate voted 14 to 11 to refuse jurisdiction in Blount's case. Several of the Federalist senators voted against impeachment, perhaps fearing that other senators would become targets of impeachment by House members seeking their seats. If the Federalists were stung by the Blount case, Republicans were emboldened by it. Within a few years, Republicans, too, would try the game of political impeachment.[1]

In the elections of 1800, Republicans won the presidency and both houses of Congress. Now, it was time for the Federalists to

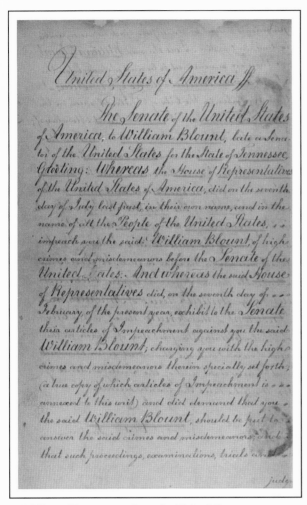

William Blount was the only United States senator to be impeached. *National Archives*

tremble, as Republicans looked to impeachment as a way to root out entrenched opponents. Their targets were Federalist judges, for the Federalists' greatest remaining strength lay in the judiciary. The Republicans were merely waiting for the right case before applying the doctrine of political impeachment themselves.

The first case to present itself concerned a drunken, mentally unbalanced federal judge, John Pickering of New Hampshire. Although elected to the Continental Congress, Pickering had refused to attend, as he suffered from a phobia about crossing water on a boat. When Pickering was made chief justice

of New Hampshire in 1790, his general mental imbalance became apparent. Pickering's strange behavior led the state legislature to vote to remove him from office in 1794, but the governor, a political friend of Pickering's, ignored the bill. Then Pickering was appointed to the federal judiciary, placing him within the grasp of congressional Republicans.

In 1803, Pickering was impeached in the House by a vote of 45 to 8—with all the dissenting votes cast by Federalists. Rather than charge him with madness, the House accused him of violating statutes and acting "wickedly, meaning and intending to injure the revenues of the United States." [2]

Senate Federalists sought to delay Pickering's trial, while Republicans seemed anxious to begin a general housecleaning of opposition judges. Finally, in March 1804, the Senate convened as a court of impeachment, and Pickering was summoned to attend. The judge responded by challenging President Jefferson to a duel. The judge's son pleaded that his father was "insane, his mind wholly deranged." He begged the Senate not to proceed, since Pickering was incapable of defending himself or of appointing counsel to defend him. The debate over whether the Senate could try an insane man raged for days. After a series of votes, a two-thirds majority of the Senate stood ready to regard Pickering's conduct as culpable, whether or not it met a strict standard of "high crimes and misdemeanors." Federalists knew that their case was lost. When the vote was to be taken, the entire House demanded entry to the Senate chamber and somehow managed to squeeze in. The Senate found Pickering guilty on all counts, making him the first individual to be removed from office by the Senate. [3]

The Federalists were badly shaken by Pickering's removal. Senator John Quincy Adams feared that any "trivial error" could

When Federal Judge John Pickering was impeached, this physician's statement was submitted as evidence that Pickering was insane.   *National Archives*

peached another Federalist judge. This time, the Republicans rested their arguments on what they termed "popular will," a doctrine that declared that impeachable offenses might be anything a lower house construed into a "high crime and misdemeanor." This doctrine, however, could not be used against any but the most unpopular Federalists; too many Republicans had proved loyal to a more moderate course in the Pickering case. The Republicans' target was the highly partisan and arrogant Federalist Supreme Court Justice Samuel Chase.

On the federal bench, Justice Chase displayed a mercurial temper. He showed Republican defendants, counsel, and witnesses no mercy, and, unlike a number of his Federalist brethren, he did not moderate his views and temperament after the Republican victories in 1800 and 1802. Chase's outspokenness finally got him into trouble in 1803, when one of his partisan charges to a grand jury was taken down and sent to President Thomas Jefferson. The president passed it on to the Republicans in the House, who initiated the process that led to Chase's impeachment. Federalists immediately shouted that the accusations were general, "not confined to any *specific charge*," as Senator William Plumer rightly argued. John Quincy Adams warned that a season of judge-hunting was upon them. In effect, Adams and Plumer were demanding that impeachment be above the very politics that their judges had practiced in the federal courts for so long.[5]

After bitter floor fights, Chase was impeached and his case sent to the Senate in December 1804. On January 4, 1805, Chase stood in the Senate to answer charges but was interrupted repeatedly by Vice President Aaron Burr. In despair, Chase pleaded for a three-month delay to obtain further evidence. The Senate granted him one month.

Early in February 1805, the proceedings began anew. In his opening remarks, Chase

become grounds for impeachment. But the Federalists had missed an important point. Republicans had removed Pickering because of his mental instability, not his politics. There simply was no other way to dismiss him from the bench. While some Republicans had plans for additional political prosecutions, Pickering's was not an entirely partisan case. It was actually the Federalists in the Senate who had voted as a bloc to protect a member of their party, no matter how incompetent. They themselves had politicized the Pickering case.[4]

It was easy to see why the Federalists were alarmed. Even while the Senate was removing Pickering from office, the House im-

[78]

Impeached by the House, Supreme Court Justice Samuel Chase was acquitted by the Senate.

Maryland Historical Society

did not dispute the essential facts in the charges but claimed that the concept of impeachment itself was at issue. His removal would be for strictly political reasons since, in his view of the law of impeachment, his acts showed no criminality. For almost a month, the House managers, led by Virginian John Randolph, who had made the impeachment of Chase a personal crusade, hammered away at the increasingly infirm justice.

The vote on Chase's impeachment was almost a party-line ballot. But enough Republicans deserted their party to prevent a two-thirds vote on any one of the eight articles. To the Federalists' surprise, Chase's victory was resounding. Now frail and destitute, Chase perhaps no longer seemed the harsh, mercurial, and high-handed bully he had appeared on the bench. He was humiliated by his impeachment in the House, while his chief prosecutors had acted with unbecoming bluster. Even President Jefferson stood back from the vindictiveness of the impeachers and did not call for party regularity on the vote to convict.[6]

After this flurry of partisan impeachments, almost thirty years passed before the House, in 1830, brought a single article of impeachment against a federal district judge from Missouri, James H. Peck. Peck was officially impeached for imprisoning an attorney for contempt, but, in fact, the case arose out of the highly charged issue of land grants in which the federal courts had become embroiled. Representatives opposed to Peck's land rulings had tried on two previous occasions to impeach him; only after three years of consideration, and after their numbers had increased, did they finally succeed in 1830. There was no suggestion that Peck had violated any criminal statute. Instead, the issues raised at his trial concerned wrongful intent and whether the judge had exceeded the authority granted by the Judiciary Act of 1789.

After a nearly two-month trial in the Senate, where sentiment over land-grant policy was not so fevered, Peck was acquitted.[7]

Thirty more years passed before another federal judge, West Humphreys of the District of Tennessee, was impeached. He was tried in the Senate in 1862 in the midst of the Civil War. Humphreys had accepted a judicial appointment in the Confederacy without bothering to resign his Union judicial assignment. The House adopted seven articles of impeachment charging Humphreys with, among other things, inciting revolt and rebellion against the government of the United States and aiding in the organization of an armed rebellion. Since Humphreys had already fled to the Confederacy, he did not attend his Senate trial. In a one-day trial, the shortest ever, the Senate convicted Humphreys on all charges except one and removed him from office.[8]

The bitter animosities growing out of the Civil War gave rise to the most famous of all impeachment trials, that of President Andrew Johnson in 1868. This case marks the only time in American history that a president has been impeached. The only other serious attempt at presidential impeachment came during the presidency of Richard Nixon. At the heart of the Johnson case, just as in the cases of Pickering and Chase, lay issues far larger than the individuals involved. The Johnson case revolved around the crisis of Reconstruction after the war.

When Johnson succeeded to the presidency in 1865, his ideas for a mild reconstruction of the southern states clashed with the wishes of a majority of the Congress, controlled by Radical Republicans who favored much stronger action. Throughout 1866, Johnson and Congress were locked in battle.[9]

The Tenure of Office Act, the violation of which was to be the legal basis for impeach-

Scenes during the impeachment trial of President Andrew Johnson show the vote being taken on the Senate floor, *below*, and, *above*, spectators in the Ladies' Gallery.

Frank Leslie's Illustrated Newspaper, June 6, 1868 and Harper's Weekly, April 18, 1868

ment, was passed over Johnson's veto on March 2, 1867. It required the approval of the Senate before the president could remove a civil officer appointed with the consent of the Senate. Despite the certain consequences, Johnson decided to rid himself of Secretary of War Edwin Stanton, an ally of the Radicals. On December 12, 1867, Johnson suspended Stanton, thus enraging the Radicals and setting in motion events that led the House to vote eleven articles of impeachment against the president.[10]

Johnson's Senate trial began in March 1868, with the defense immediately claiming that an indictable offense constituted the only grounds for impeachment. On May 16, after weeks of venomous argument, the Senate took a test vote on Article XI, a catch-all charge thought by the House managers most likely to produce a vote for conviction. The drama of the vote has become legendary. With 36 "guilty" votes needed for conviction, the final count was guilty, 35; not guilty, 19. Seven Republicans joined the twelve Democrats in supporting Johnson. Stunned by the setback, the Radicals postponed voting until May 26, when votes on Articles II and III produced identical 35 to 19 votes. To head off further defeats, the Radicals moved to adjourn sine die, and the motion was adopted, abruptly ending the impeachment trial of President Andrew Johnson.[11]

The next Senate impeachment trial was that of former Secretary of War William Belknap in 1876. Belknap, tipped off in advance that a House committee had unearthed information that he had accepted bribes in return for lucrative Indian trading posts, rushed to the White House at ten o'clock on the morning of March 2, 1876. Tearfully, he begged President Ulysses Grant to accept his resignation. Around three o'clock that afternoon, representatives, furious at both the president and Belknap for thwarting them,

decided by voice vote to impeach Belknap anyway. The Senate debated the question of its jurisdiction, given Belknap's resignation, and voted 37 to 29 that he could be impeached. At the end of Belknap's sensational trial in the summer of 1876, however, he was found not guilty of the charges. Although few senators believed Belknap innocent, most had decided they, in fact, had no jurisdiction over him, since he was by then a private citizen.[12]

The House impeached Florida District Judge Charles Swayne in 1904 for a variety of offenses that included filing false vouchers, wrongfully imprisoning attorneys on contempt charges, and not living within his district. When his trial ended on February 27, 1905, the Senate voted acquittal on each of the twelve articles. Doubtless, Swayne was guilty of some of the charges. Indeed, his own counsel admitted as much, though calling the lapses "inadvertent." The Senate, however, did not convict Swayne, because his eccentricities did not seem to be high crimes or misdemeanors.[13]

It was during the Swayne trial that the initial suggestion was made that a Senate committee, rather than the Senate as a whole, receive impeachment evidence. Senator George F. Hoar of Massachusetts, chairman of the Judiciary Committee, proposed that, except in an impeachment of the president or vice president, the presiding officer should appoint such a committee. While Hoar's proposal would eventually be embodied in Rule XI of the Senate's impeachment rules, in 1905 the resolution was referred to the Rules Committee, which took no action, and the trial proceeded without the use of a committee.[14]

The next impeachment trial was that of Judge Robert W. Archbald of the Commerce Court in 1913. Archbald was charged with numerous and serious acts of misconduct stretching over many years, including using his office to obtain advantageous business deals and free trips to Europe. As in the Swayne case, not one of the thirteen articles charged an indictable offense. Yet, apparently because of the seriousness and extent of his crimes, many of which he acknowledged, Archbald was convicted on five of thirteen articles. Archbald's counsel noted that the decision "determined that a judge ought not only to be impartial, but he ought so to demean himself, both in and out of the court, that litigants will have no reason to suspect his impartiality; and that repeatedly failing in that respect constituted a 'high misdemeanor.' " After the Archbald impeachment, Alexander Simpson, Archbald's counsel, again suggested that impeachment evidence be heard by a Senate committee, rather than by the Senate as a whole. Simpson argued that many senators were not in attendance when evidence was taken before the full Senate and thus had relied only on the printed record.[15]

In 1933, the House Judiciary Committee preferred censure to impeachment for federal Judge Harold Louderback of California, but a minority of committee members brought the issue to the full House, where they persuaded that body to adopt five articles of impeachment, charging Louderback with favoritism and conspiracy in the appointment of bankruptcy receivers. At Louderback's Senate trial in May 1933, a long parade of witnesses, including a faith healer who had to be brought into the chamber on a stretcher, filed through to testify. This occurred during the hectic Hundred Days legislative period of the early New Deal. Democrats charged Republicans with using the trial to delay a banking reform bill, a charge Republicans denied. Tempers in the Senate frayed, as witness after witness cast doubt on the charges. When the Senate finally voted on May 24, Louderback was acquitted on all five articles. Only on the fifth and last

charge, a summation of the preceding four, did the vote even reach a majority of 45 to 34, still eight votes short of the two-thirds needed for conviction.[16]

The trial of Judge Louderback again brought to the fore the problem of attendance at impeachment trials. After the trial, Representative Hatton Sumners of Texas, one of the House managers, noted the poor attendance of senators: "At one time only three senators were present, and for 10 days we presented evidence to what was practically an empty Chamber." As a result, Senator Henry Ashurst of Arizona, chairman of the Judiciary Committee, proposed what became Rule XI in 1935. The key words of Rule XI provide:

> That in the trial of any impeachment the Presiding Officer of the Senate, *if the Senate so orders*, shall appoint a committee of Senators to receive evidence and take testimony at such times and places as the committee may determine (emphasis added).[17]

Rule XI was not used in the next impeachment trial, that of Florida District Judge Halsted Ritter in 1936. Ritter was charged with a wide range of improprieties that included practicing law while a judge, filing false income tax returns, extortion, and general misconduct. Ritter's counsel argued that the judge had committed no offense that could be labeled a high crime or misdemeanor and was guilty only of exercising "poor judgment." In fact, Ritter was found "not guilty" by narrow margins on each of the first six charges. On the seventh, however, the omnibus article combining the previous six, exactly the required two-thirds of the senators found Ritter guilty of bringing, by his combined actions, "his court into scandal and disrepute." Said the *New York Times* of the decision, "The Senate is putting judges on notice that they will be removed if the sum total of their crimes shows unfitness for the bench regardless of whether a specific high crime or misdemeanor could be established under ordinary rules of evidence."[18]

In the summer of 1974, it looked very much as though there might soon be an impeachment trial of another president of the United States: Richard Nixon. The events of those weeks precipitated a more thorough scrutiny of the Senate's impeachment rules than they had ever undergone.

I was then a member of the Rules Committee and privy to the long hours of serious reflection about the solemn duty we believed we might be called upon to perform. In July 1974, the Senate adopted my resolution directing the Rules Committee to review the existing impeachment rules and precedents and to recommend revisions. We worked feverishly through the first days of that hot August. We were meeting on August 8, when President Nixon announced that he would resign the next day. Nevertheless, we continued with our work because we had a mandate from the Senate to file a report by September 1. The report contained our recommendations for primarily technical changes in the rules that had been adopted in 1868 for the presidential impeachment of Andrew Johnson. With the resignation of President Nixon, no further action was taken. The recommendations, however, were resurrected in the summer of 1986 to provide background for the debates on how to conduct the trial of a federal judge.[19]

Mr. President, this brings us to the recent impeachment trial of U.S. District Judge Harry E. Claiborne of Nevada. The Claiborne trial was the first in which Rule XI was put into practice. It was also the first impeachment trial in half a century. On July 22, 1986, Judge Claiborne became the first official to be unanimously impeached by the House, by a vote of 406 to 0. The first sitting federal judge ever to be jailed, Claiborne was then serving a two-year prison term for tax evasion. During September 1986, a twelve-

Each of the three federal judges impeached and convicted in the 1980's appeared on the Senate floor in his own defense. The above photographs taken from videotapes of the proceedings show, *from top*, Harry E. Claiborne, Alcee L. Hastings, and Walter L. Nixon.
National Archives and U.S. Senate Recording Studio

member committee took testimony, gathered evidence, and presented its findings to the Senate.

In the first two articles of impeachment, the House charged that Claiborne was "guilty of misbehavior and of high crimes and misdemeanors," based on his having "willfully and knowingly" made and subscribed false income tax returns for calendar years 1979 and 1980. The third article charged that Claiborne was "guilty of misbehavior and of high crimes in office," based on his having been "found guilty by a twelve-person jury" of filing false income tax returns for 1979 and 1980, for which he was sentenced to "two years imprisonment for each violation . . . to be served concurrently," and fined "$5,000 for each violation." Article IV charged Judge Claiborne with being "guilty of misbehavior and of misdemeanors in office," because, by "willfully and knowingly falsifying his income on his Federal tax returns," he had "betrayed the trust of the people of the United States and reduced confidence in the integrity and impartiality of the judiciary, thereby bringing disrepute on the Federal courts and the administration of justice by the courts." [20]

On October 9, the Senate voted to convict Judge Claiborne on the first, second, and fourth articles by votes of 87 to 10, 90 to 7, and 89 to 8, respectively, and acquitted him on the third article. [21] Judge Claiborne thus became the fifth person convicted by this body.

In August 1988, the House voted 413 to 3 to impeach U.S. District Judge Alcee L. Hastings of Florida. The seventeen articles of impeachment concerned an alleged bribery scheme, alleged lying under oath, and alleged leak of wiretap information. In March 1989, Hastings' lawyers argued before the Senate that the articles of impeachment should be dismissed, noting that Hastings had been acquitted of the charges by a jury. On March

16, the Senate, by a vote of 1 to 92, voted not to dismiss the articles and, as in the Claiborne case, appointed a special twelve-member committee to take evidence in the case. [22]

The House charged, in all seventeen articles, that Judge Hastings was "guilty of an impeachable offense warranting removal from office." In Article I, the offense was that Hastings had, in 1981, allegedly "engaged in a corrupt conspiracy to obtain $150,000 from defendants" appearing before his court, in return for "sentences which would not require incarceration of the defendants." In each of Articles II through IX, the alleged offense was "knowingly . . . [making] a false statement [under oath] . . . intended to mislead the trier of fact" during the 1983 trial in which Hastings was defending himself against the conspiracy and bribery charges. (The Senate, by unanimous consent of all parties, after votes had occurred on the first nine articles, agreed not to vote on the tenth through the fifteenth articles.) Article XVI charged that Hastings, in 1985, had revealed highly confidential information he learned as supervising judge of a wiretap. (Hastings had never been tried by the courts on the charge.) In Article XVII, the offense was that Hastings

did [through four separate allegations: corrupt relationship, lying under oath, fabricating false documents for evidence at his criminal trial, *and* improper disclosure of confidential wiretap] undermine confidence in the integrity and impartiality of the judiciary and betray the trust of the people of the United States, thereby bringing disrepute on the Federal courts and the administration of justice by the Federal courts. [23]

The Senate heard both the prosecution by the House managers and the case for the defense (Hastings and his counsel) on October 18 and debated the case for seven hours and fifteen minutes behind closed doors the next day. The following day, October 20, 1989, the Senate convicted Judge Hastings on eight of the eleven articles, acquitted him on Articles VI, XVI (wiretap), and XVII, and ordered his removal from office.[24]

The Senate voted 60 to 35 on Article XVII, four votes short of the two-thirds necessary for conviction. In my opinion, the article failed to receive the required number because it was confusing and poorly drawn. The four-fold allegations therein—which constituted the basis for the purported impeachable offense of undermining confidence in the judiciary, bringing it into disrepute, and betraying the people's trust—included the wiretap charge contained in the sixteenth article, which had just been rejected by a vote of 0 to 95. As indicated by the vote on the sixteenth article, senators unanimously felt that Judge Hastings was not guilty of the wiretap charge. Many senators interpreted Article XVII, as written, to require one to find Judge Hastings guilty of all four offenses listed in the article, including the wiretap. Illustrative of the point, the following inquiries of the chair and the president pro tempore's responses thereto occurred just prior to the vote on Article XVII:

Mr. [John H.] CHAFEE [of Rhode Island]. To find guilty on this article, does one have to agree with each of the four allegations?

The PRESIDENT pro tempore. This is for each Senator to determine in his own mind and in his own conscience and in accordance with his oath that he will do impartial justice under the constitution and law.

It is the Chair's opinion, if the Senator in his own conscience and based on the facts as he understands them determines that on any one of the paragraphs listed that Judge Alcee L. Hastings has undermined confidence in the integrity and impartiality of the judiciary and betrayed the trust of the people of the United States, he should vote accordingly. . . .

Mr. [Patrick J.] LEAHY [of Vermont]. Is the Senator from Vermont correct in understanding what the distinguished Presiding Officer said earlier that, if a Senator felt that to vote guilty on this he would have to find on each and every one, he would be within his rights to set for himself that as the standard?

The PRESIDENT pro tempore. The Chair has not rendered any such opinion. . . .

Mr. LEAHY. Mr. President, would a Senator be within his or her rights to interpret this as saying that a guilty or not guilty verdict would have to be based on a finding on each one of the four items as either guilty or not guilty?

The PRESIDENT pro tempore. The Senator would be within his or her right to so find.[25]

On this article, Senator Chafee voted to convict, and Senator Leahy voted to acquit Hastings. In my own personal judgment, any one of the four allegations was sufficient, if believed, to support a verdict of guilty on the article. The Senate had already voted to convict on three of the four allegations listed in the omnibus article. The use of the word "and" in joining the wiretap to the other allegations, however, was a tactical error by the House framers of the language and may have created confusion in the minds of senators, leading to the vote of acquittal on the article. I voted to convict on this and all the other articles.

Attendance at both the open and the closed sessions was good at all times, and the votes on the articles showed ninety-five senators voting. Senators Dan Coats of Indiana, James M. Jeffords of Vermont, Trent Lott of Mississippi, and Connie Mack of Florida recused themselves because they had previously voted on the impeachment question when they had served in the House. The only other senator not voting was Pete Wilson of California.

Judge Hastings was the first federal official to be convicted by the Senate after being acquitted by a jury at his criminal trial on related charges.

On May 10, 1989, by a vote of 417 to 0, the House voted to impeach U.S. District Judge Walter L. Nixon, Jr., of Biloxi, Mississippi, on three articles, each of which alleged that the judge was "guilty of an impeachable offense and should be removed from office."

Articles I and II related to charges that Nixon had made false statements before a grand jury, denying that he had attempted to influence local law enforcement officials in a drug-smuggling case that involved a business associate's son. Nixon had been convicted of two counts of perjury by a federal jury in February 1986. Two years later, the U.S. Judicial Conference recommended to the House of Representatives that Nixon be impeached, and, at the time of the House impeachment and the Senate trial, he was serving a five-year prison sentence.[26]

The Senate, on November 3, 1989, found Nixon guilty on each of the first two articles by votes of 89 to 8 and 78 to 19, respectively. It, however, acquitted him on Article III, the omnibus allegation that he had "undermined confidence in the integrity and impartiality of the judiciary, betrayed the trust of the people of the United States, disobeyed the laws of the United States and brought disrepute on the Federal courts and the administration of justice by the Federal courts [by lying under oath to agents of the FBI and Department of Justice and also before a grand jury]." The vote of 57 to 40 to convict on this article was short of the necessary two-thirds.[27] I voted "guilty," believing that the actions for which Judge Nixon had been convicted by a jury in a criminal trial did indeed betray the people's trust and bring disrepute on the federal courts.

Nixon, like Hastings two weeks earlier, was stripped of his judgeship and immediately lost his $89,500 annual salary. Nixon objected, as had Claiborne and Hastings, to the taking of evidence by an ad hoc committee rather than by the entire Senate, but the Senate, before acting on the impeachment articles, denied Nixon's motion for trial before the full Senate by a vote of 7 to 90.[28] Nixon and Hastings had both sued in the U.S. District Court for the District of Columbia, seeking to force a trial by the whole

Senate. On July 5, the case was dismissed as premature, and the dismissal was affirmed by the U.S. Circuit Court of Appeals for the District of Columbia on October 18. (Hastings had tried to restore his complaint on the day of his conviction, but his request was immediately denied by an appeals judge.) [29]

In its two parts, this chapter has traced the long history of impeachment over a period of 613 years, from the impeachment of Richard Lyons in 1376, during the reign of Edward III of England, to the impeachment and conviction of Walter L. Nixon, Jr., in 1989; it has examined impeachments in the American colonies and in the early American states; it has followed the debates at the Constitutional Convention in Philadelphia and during the ratification period; and, finally, it has reviewed the Senate record of two centuries. What conclusions may be drawn from the experiences of the past for the guidance of senators who will grapple with impeachment in the years and decades to come?

First, I believe it is clear from our study of history that, although the phrase "high crimes and misdemeanors" can include crimes indictable at common law, it does not require that they be so indictable. As Raoul Berger stated in his excellent work *Impeachment: The Constitutional Problems*, the phrase first appeared "in the proceedings against the Earl of Suffolk in 1386," at a time when "there was in fact no such crime as a 'misdemeanor.'" The impeachable misconduct with which the earl was charged—that he had "applied appropriated funds to purposes other than those specified"—was, wrote Berger, "patently not 'criminal' in the ordinary sense." [30] Other examples of impeachment (but not criminal) cases were, according to Berger:

Lord Treasurer Middlesex (1624), high crimes and misdemeanors: allowed the office of Ordnance to go unrepaired though money was appropriated for that purpose. . . .

As in the other recent impeachment trials, the Senate appointed a special twelve-member committee to hear evidence in the Claiborne case.

Duke of Buckingham (1626), misdemeanors, misprisions, offenses, and crimes: . . . procured offices for himself, thereby blocking the deserving; neglected as great admiral to safeguard the seas; procured titles of honor to his mother, brothers, kindred. . . .

Peter Pett, Commissioner of the Navy (1668), high crimes and misdemeanors: negligent preparation for the Dutch invasion; loss of a ship through neglect to bring it to mooring. . . .

Chief Justice North (1680), high crimes and misdemeanors: assisted the Attorney General in drawing a proclamation to suppress petitions to the King to call a Parliament. . . .

Lord Treasurer Middlesex was [also] charged with "corruption, shadowed under pretext of a New Year's-Gift" and with "using the power of his place, and countenance of the king's service, to wrest [from certain persons] a lease and estate of great value." [31]

The foregoing, Berger wrote, help to "delineate the outlines" of the rubric "high crimes and misdemeanors" in the English experience, for they cover "misapplication of funds (Earl of Suffolk)"; "abuse of official power (Buckingham)"; "neglect of duty (Buckingham, Pett)"; corruption and neglect of duty (Middlesex). [32]

My examination of the American experience from 1635 through 1989 likewise clearly reveals that impeachable conduct has been broadly understood, both in the colonies and in the state and federal constitutions, to include acts that are neither criminal, in the general sense, nor indictable. As to the impeachable offenses of treason and bribery, the former is defined by the Constitution. Bribery was made a federal crime for judges in 1790; not until 1853 was it extended to include members of Congress; and ten years later it was applied to other civil officers. According to the investigating committee of the Judicial Council of the Eleventh Circuit in the Alcee Hastings case, "This consideration strongly suggests that conduct not amounting to statutory bribery may nonetheless constitute the constitutional 'high Crime and Misdemeanor' of bribery."[33]

A misconception that has surfaced during impeachment trials is the notion that criminal or civil standards of proof are somehow required in voting to convict. Such standards run the gamut from the lowest threshold, proof by "preponderance of the evidence," which must be met by plaintiffs in most civil cases; to the next highest standard, proof by "clear and convincing evidence," employed in some classes of civil cases; to the most rigorous standard, "proof beyond a reasonable doubt," imposed for criminal cases. Of course, a senator may apply any standard of proof he or she desires, or may choose to apply no set standard whatever. But, given the history of impeachment in America and the fact that neither civil penalties nor criminal punishments are applicable in impeachment cases, any talk of standards of proof seems rather pointless and likely to be unproductive. Because the sole penalties are removal from office and, occasionally, disqualification from holding further office, the essential question remains: Is this person fit for a continuance in this office? The answer to the question calls for detached objectivity on the part of every senator, but, I believe, it also entails some subjective judgments. Senators should consider, for example, whether the respondent's continuance in office brings the political (or judicial) system into disrepute and undermines the people's trust and confidence in government. It is a question that requires sober reflection and eludes standards of proof. The chair's ruling in the Claiborne trial is instructive:

The PRESIDING OFFICER. Judge Claiborne has moved that the Senate establish a standard of evidence at the impeachment trial to be proof beyond a reasonable doubt. . . . It is the Chair's determination that the question of standard of evidence is for each Senator to decide individually when voting on Articles of Impeachment.[34]

Does a jury acquittal in a criminal trial preclude a subsequent impeachment, on the theory that it would violate the double jeopardy prohibition in the Fifth Amendment to the Constitution? In the light of history, it seems to me that the double jeopardy clause is irrelevant to an impeachment proceeding, which is noncriminal in nature. This is not to say that the previous findings by a jury should be ignored or not given any weight. But the Senate is not bound, nor should it be, by any previous jury or court verdict concerning an individual facing impeachment. As Joseph Story, an associate justice of the U.S. Supreme Court from 1811 to 1845, once observed:

There is also much force in the remark that an impeachment is a proceeding purely of a political nature. It is not so much designed to punish an offender as to secure the state against gross official misdemeanors. It touches neither his person nor his property, but simply divests him of his political capacity.[35]

Raoul Berger's truism, "Constitutional analysis need not depart from common sense," is applicable here, as is the analogy suggested by him:

Suppose that Jones runs a red light at eighty miles an hour and crashes into Smith, severely injuring Smith and destroying his car. Such reckless driving constitutes a criminal offense, but that does not convert a civil suit to recover damages on those facts into a criminal proceeding.[36]

"Impeachment," Berger wrote:

may be compared to deportation, which is attended by very painful consequences but which the Supreme Court held, 'is not a punishment for a crime. . . . It is but a method of enforcing the return to his own country of an alien who has not complied with the conditions' laid down for his residence, precisely as impeachment is designed to remove an unfit officer for the good of the government.[37]

The question of double jeopardy came up in the Hastings trial and was decisively laid to rest by the Senate. Judge Hastings filed a motion to dismiss Articles I through XV without trial, based on the 1983 jury verdict of acquittal and the lapse of time. Judge Hastings and his counsel, arguing for dismissal, contended that the Constitution's framers "authorized a second trial [impeachment] after a conviction [in the courts]"—as had occurred in the impeachment of Judge Claiborne—but that the constitutional mechanism did not work the same in reverse. "Where there is a conviction, two trials are authorized and may be required," they conceded, but "where there is an acquittal [in a court case], that should end the matter." They contended that "the function of a second trial in the Senate following a conviction in the courts is the function that protects the independence of the judiciary." [38]

Rejecting the contention that an acquittal in the courts served as a constitutional disposition of any subsequent impeachment proceeding, the House managers maintained that such a double jeopardy theory would "delegate to the judicial branch the Senate's authority to determine whether a civil officer should be removed from office." "Respondent's argument," said the House prosecutors, "rests entirely on a single false premise: that impeachment is somehow criminal in nature." But, the managers declared, the Constitution established "that impeachment is a remedial proceeding designed to protect the institutions of Government and the American people from abuse of the public trust." Texas Representative John Bryant, for the House managers, succinctly summarized the House's attack on the motion to dismiss:

In this country, impeachment has never functioned as a criminal process. Impeachment does not require an indictable offense as a basis for removal from office. Impeachment does not require proof beyond a reasonable doubt to establish the allegations. Impeachment does not call for trial by jury. Impeachment is not subject to

Presidential pardon. And above all, the purpose of impeachment is not to punish an individual, but rather to preserve and protect our constitutional form of Government. [39]

The House managers were persuasive in their arguments, and, by a 1 to 92 roll-call vote, the Senate denied the Hastings motion to dismiss. [40] The double jeopardy claim had been rejected.

The Hastings impeachment also resolved the question of whether lapse of time between alleged offenses and impeachment may be raised as a bar to impeachment—equivalent to the defense of laches in equity law. The Senate's 1 to 92 vote on Judge Hastings' dismissal motion impressively disposed of that issue, as well. In his rebuttal to the motion, Representative Mike Synar of Oklahoma stated unequivocally: "There is no statute of limitations applicable to the articles of impeachment. . . . the enforcement of public rights and the protection of the public interest cannot be terminated by the mere passage of time." [41]

Another question that has lingered over time—whether an impeachment proceeding begun in one Congress can be carried over to a succeeding Congress or must be conducted *de novo*—was determined in the Hastings case. Impeachment by the House occurred in the second session of the 100th Congress, but trial by the Senate was carried over to the first session of the 101st Congress.

Finally, I believe that the use of a twelve-member committee under the Senate's impeachment Rule XI has proved to be an efficient and meritorious procedure in impeachment trials. In my opinion, none of the respondents could realistically complain that the appointment of a committee to receive evidence and hear testimony on behalf of the full Senate prevented them from receiving a just and fair trial. Every effort was made to ensure that all senators and their staffs had access to the full evidentiary record during both trials. The Nixon and Hastings impeachment committees' hearings were transmitted by television to each Senate office by the Senate recording studio. Such an arrangement allowed senators not serving on the impeachment committees to watch the proceedings while remaining in their offices and attending to other pressing obligations. In addition, these videotapes were available for senators and their staffs to watch at their leisure whenever their schedules permitted. The committees met in open sessions, and senators and their staffs, as well as the public, were permitted to attend the hearings and listen to the testimony presented. The Senate also allowed sufficient time between the conclusion of the evidentiary hearings and the final arguments on the Senate floor to give senators an adequate chance to familiarize themselves with the record.

The Hastings impeachment committee held evidentiary hearings for eighteen days between July 10, 1989, and August 3, 1989; and the Nixon impeachment committee held evidentiary hearings for four days between September 7 and 13, 1989. Both hearings were well attended, and both the Nixon and Hastings committees declined to adopt the Senate standing rule that allows one committee member to take testimony. For each impeachment committee to meet and accept testimony, therefore, at least seven members had to be present. (There was one exception to this in the Hastings case. When the Senate was in recess, the one-member rule was invoked but was limited in scope to the receipt of testimony by William Borders, who refused the committee's summons to appear.)

As I close this chapter on impeachment, I return to its opening words: "The Senate, having tried . . . and two-thirds of the Senators present having found him guilty of the charges . . . it is, therefore, ordered and adjudged that [he] be, and he is hereby, removed from office."

The pronouncement is an awesome one. It severs neither life nor limb. It requires no forfeiture of lands or goods. It carries no prison sentence and levies no fine to be paid with silver or gold. Yet, for the person against whom this verdict is directed, the price to be paid is more than silver or gold can replenish, and the sentence more lasting than prison cell can claim. "A good name is rather to be chosen than great riches," and the impeached official's good name is gone. Honor, the respect of one's colleagues, public trust and confidence, are all intangibles that must be earned; they cannot be bought, and, once lost, they can never be restored to their former place. The sentence of shame and embarrassment that accompanies removal from an office of public trust leaves an indelible stain that will run through future generations. These are sobering thoughts, both for the impeached person facing the senators who will judge him and for those who must rise to cast their votes in judgment.

As a senator who has voted to convict three of the only seven individuals who have been convicted in the course of two hundred years, and as the only senator to have presided over two of the convictions, I was not impervious to these feelings. Nor can I agree with Raoul Berger (notwithstanding my great respect for his scholarship in this area) that

once initiated to topple giants—Strafford, Clarendon, Hastings—impeachment has sunk in this country to the ouster of dreary little judges for squalid misconduct. Our preoccupation with judicial impeachment tends to obscure the grand design of the Framers, to whom impeachment of judges was decidedly peripheral.[42]

English impeachments not only toppled giants, they also toppled some "dreary little judges." Federal judges are not little justices of the peace or county magistrates or presiders over local police courts. Their decisions often affect hundreds of thousands or millions of people and have an impact not only on their own judicial districts or circuits but on other jurisdictions as well. Nor can I believe that, to the framers, the impeachment of judges was simply "peripheral." While, admittedly, their chief concern was a runaway executive, they intended the impeachment weapon for other rogue officials as well. Otherwise, they would not have added the phrase "all civil Officers of the United States." In so doing, they shaped a net that could be cast in other troubled waters. Surely, William H. Rehnquist, chief justice of the United States, was not moved by a "preoccupation with judicial impeachment" when he transmitted to the Speaker of the U.S. House of Representatives a certificate, on behalf of the Judicial Conference and the Judicial Council of the Eleventh Circuit, stating that "consideration of impeachment" of Judge Alcee L. Hastings "may be warranted." [43] Nor could it have been such a "preoccupation" that impelled the Judicial Conference of the United States to address to the House Speaker a certification by the Judicial Council of the Fifth Circuit that Judge Walter L. Nixon, Jr., had "engaged in conduct which might constitute one or more grounds for impeachment." [44] Rather than springing from a "preoccupation with judicial impeachment," the actions of the two Judicial Councils arose from a concern for the integrity of the judiciary and are to be commended.

Voltaire is reported to have once said, "it is good to kill an admiral from time to time, to encourage the others" (a reference to Admiral John Byng, who was executed in 1757 for failing to relieve Minorca). [45] Similarly, it may reasonably be assumed that convicting impeached officials from time to time will remind other "civil officers" that a constitutional remedy exists for those who abuse the powers of office and violate the public trust.

There are some who advocate creating a system by which the judicial branch itself would remove judges, in order to spare the legislative branch the burden of work. I do not agree. The repository of impeachment should remain where the framers placed it. I do not believe that occasions for its use will arise so often as to greatly impede Congress in the fulfillment of its other duties. Furthermore, using the Rule XI committee has proved to be a fair and efficient way to deal with the hearing process when the need arises. Although, to date, only judges have been convicted, "civil officers" in the executive branch are also reminded that this constitutional sword remains in the temple. It is ready to be unsheathed by the elected representatives of the "people's branch" to hold accountable any who would subvert our system of government and who might otherwise be beyond the reach of common jurisprudence. Impeachment is the ultimate threat to the overreaching official whose unbridled self-interest or arrogant disregard for the public good renders him or her unfit to continue in elective or appointive office.

So grave is this power of impeachment, and so conscious is Congress of this solemn power, that impeachment proceedings have been initiated in the House only sixty-two times since Congress first met in 1789. Only sixteen federal officers have been impeached: one president, one cabinet officer, one senator, and thirteen federal judges. Two cases were dismissed before trial because the individuals had left office. Fourteen cases have reached the Senate. Of these, six ended in acquittal, one was dismissed, and seven resulted in conviction. Each of the convictions involved a federal judge.

The Senate has fulfilled its constitutional role in the impeachment process with a high sense of duty that is both commendable and in keeping with the framers' intent.

CHAPTER 5

Extended Debate

Filibusters, 1789–1917

October 13, 1989

Mr. President, Filibuster!—bane of Senate majority leaders, redoubtable weapon of legislative minorities, target of editors' and cartoonists' harpoons, the object of obloquy and scorn. The word is said to have come from the Dutch word *vrijbuiter*, or "freebooter," and passed into the Spanish as *filibusteros*, "who were West Indian pirates, using a small swift vessel called a filibote." [1] To the average American, it means obstructive tactics in a legislative body. While generally associated with the United States Senate, it is not unfamiliar to state legislatures around the country.

Obstructive tactics in a legislative forum, although not always known as filibusters, are of ancient origin. Plutarch reported that, when Caesar returned to Rome after a sojourn in Spain, his arrival happened at the time of the election of consuls. "He applied to the Senate for permission to stand candidate," but Cato strongly opposed his request and "attempted to prevent his success by gaining time; with which view he spun out the debate till it was too late to conclude upon any thing that day." [2]

Filibusters were also a problem in the British Parliament. In nineteenth-century Eng-

land, even the members of the cabinet accepted the tactics of obstruction as an appropriate weapon to defeat House of Commons initiatives that were not acceptable to the government. Opposition leaders had no qualms about using wordy speeches to delay and hinder the majority. In his article, "Parliamentary Obstruction," Georg Jellinek noted that Sir Robert Peel was reputed to have made "no fewer than forty-eight speeches in fourteen days" during 1831. [3] In 1881, during a period of 154 days, the House of Commons sat for 1,400 hours, 240 of which were after midnight. Debates on the Land bill "took up 58 sittings," and on the Coercion bill, 22 sittings, with 14,836 speeches delivered, 6,315 of them by Irish members. Nearly 2,000 points of order were raised during the session. Speaker Sir Henry Brand, on January 31, after a sitting of 41 hours, declared, "Mr. [Charles Stewart] Parnell [the Irish Leader], with his minority of 24, dominates the House. When will the House take courage and reform its procedure?" Speaker Brand then "simply put the question." [4]

That the members of the British Parliament were not alone in the use of lengthy speeches as a means of obstruction is clear from what Jellinek described as the "wonderful examples on record":

How modest seems the seven-hour obstruction speech of the Social Democrat, Antrick, in the German Reichstag, and even the twelve-hour oratorical effort of Dr. Lecher in the Austrian House of Deputies, compared with a twenty-six-hour speech which was delivered in 1893 in the parliament of British Columbia, or with the thirty-seven-hour address in which a delegate in the Roumanian Chamber of Deputies, in 1897, demanded the indictment of Joan Bratiano! . . . In April, 1896, a sitting of the Canadian House of Commons devoted to a bill dealing with the schools in Manitoba lasted a hundred and eighty hours, and in Chile a single speech is reported to have extended through ten days of a session.[5]

France, too, doubtless had her troubles, for the word *cloture* comes from the French.

In this country, experience with protracted debate began early. In the first session of the First Congress, for example, there was a lengthy discussion regarding the permanent site for the location of the capital. Fisher Ames, a member of the House from Massachusetts, complained that "the minority . . . make every exertion to . . . delay the business."[6] Senator William Maclay of Pennsylvania complained that "every endeavour was used to waste time," that Senators Richard Henry Lee, Pierce Butler, and William Grayson "refused to go on the Business as Gun was absent." When Senator James Gunn finally arrived, "then they wanted to go and see the Ballon let off," the reference being to a hot-air balloon that was one hundred feet in circumference, the ascension of which had been much advertised. (Incidentally, the balloon caught fire, and "the experiment ended in failure.")[7] Maclay observed that "there is really such a thing as Worrying weak or indifferent Men into a Vote," and that "no business ever could have a decision, if Minority Members, were permitted to move reconsiderations, Under every pretense of new Argument."[8]

Long speeches and other obstructionist tactics were more characteristic of the House than of the Senate in the early years. But the House, on February 27, 1811, "decided . . . that after the previous question was decided in the affirmative, the main question should not be debated."[9]

The Senate was a much smaller body, and its members were more staid and polite and dignified than were the members of the House, where, prior to the Jacksonian era, most of the action occurred and most of the spectacular battles were fought. With the election of John Randolph of Virginia to the Senate in 1825, however, the speechmaking landscape began to change. Randolph had served previously in the House, where he had been notorious for his extreme eccentricity and long-winded, vitriolic diatribes. Pity the person inside or outside the chamber who came under the lash of his biting sarcasm and merciless invective. Randolph had fought several duels and was a man of ungovernable temper, as well as great ability. According to Franklin L. Burdette, author of the classic study on Senate filibusters, Randolph engaged in "long and rambling discourses," but his friends "pardoned him as one half insane," while his enemies "ascribed his irrationality to drink."[10] One may marvel at the incongruity of Randolph's sentences, his perverted logic, his roving discourse, and the deluge of words that flowed with ease from his caustic tongue. His speeches brimmed with irrelevancies; yet, there were often flashes of brilliance in his long and desultory harangues.

Fragments from *Niles' Register* of August 26, 1826, demonstrate Randolph's elocutionary dexterity, as, during debate on a bill adding to the number of circuit judges, he managed not to utter a single word concerning the subject matter of the debate.

Randolph made a passing reference to difficulties "where the legislature or the judica-

John Randolph was one of the first senators to filibuster. *Library of Congress*

ture is separated by any long interval of space, an interval in practice, not an interval in distance—I count as the German store wagoners do, by hours, not by miles."

Then, after a brief reference to how the Whigs "always toasted the constitution, church and state," he made a quantum leap to the Dismal Swamp Canal bill and then to the gerrymanderings of states into districts by "canals and roads for the purpose . . . of pleasing men, and not for doing good to the public."

Randolph talked about the construction of roads in Ireland, after which his thoughts turned to the fortification of a town. "Leave it to a committee of carpenters," he declaimed, "and a bill will be brought in to fortify the city with wood; leave it to the tanner, and it will be leather; leave it to the stone-mason, and it will be stone." Randolph continued, "Then comes this bog trotter, with his spade on his shoulder, and his

wheelbarrow in his hand, and says there is nothing, my dear sir, like turf—all fortifications should be made of turf."

Randolph's vibrant loquacity knew no limits. "What is the Baconian philosophy?" queried the senator. "A philosophy of induction—of severe reasoning founded on severe experiment—founded not on one experiment" but on many. "Sir Joseph Banks," he announced, "made but one experiment to make the fleas into lobsters, according to Pindar, but they would not become lobsters, damn their souls." Wondered the irrepressible Randolph, "how do you know, if he had made another experiment, but he would have succeeded—perhaps the want of some acid or alkali prevented it."

Nor was the press to escape his excoriation. "The press is at this moment bribed—it is in the hands of some of the most profligate men of this country." As to abuse in the newspapers and anonymous letters, he never wasted his time on them. "Any man," declared Randolph, "who will write an anonymous letter . . . in the newspaper which he is afraid to own, would, if you would give him the opportunity, put poison in your drink."

The vast expanse of Randolph's prolixity knew no limits. His speech was clearly a stellar performance in verbal gymnastics, but there was never a word said about circuit judges! [11]

Randolph served in the Senate less than fifteen months, having been appointed to fill an unexpired term. Failing of reelection to the Senate, he was again elected to the House and later served a brief stint as minister to Russia, a post from which he shortly resigned. He was once more elected to the House, where he had served less than three months of his term when he died on May 24, 1833. Thus ended the life and career of this complex man whose volcanic temperament and virulent tongue could well have made

In the course of a Senate filibuster in 1841, William R. King, *right*, challenged Henry Clay, *left*, to a duel.

him, in a later age, the archfilibusterer of them all.

The dawn of complicated procedural filibustering in the Senate was yet a long way off when, at the opening of the Twenty-seventh Congress on March 4, 1841, the Whig majority determined to fire the Senate's official printers, Francis P. Blair and John Rives. A motion by Senator Willie P. Mangum of North Carolina to dismiss the printers of the *Congressional Globe* was debated from March 5 until March 11. The debate developed into what Burdette called a "prolonged and acrimonious contention, relevant to the subject but spun out by the Democrats through lengthy arguments based on grounds of constitutionality and expediency." [12] Among the most noted of the Democratic combatants were Senators John C. Calhoun of South Carolina, Thomas Hart

Benton of Missouri, William R. King of Alabama, and James Buchanan of Pennsylvania. The arguments were lengthy and heated, with King and Senator Henry Clay of Kentucky engaging in scathing personal attacks, as the following exchange, reported in the third person, will attest:

Mr. Clay. . . . If there was no other ground for his [Mr. Blair's] dismissal, he (Mr. Clay) would go on the ground of infamy of character of the print and the Printer. . . . It was but an attempt to prolong their [the Democrats'] power . . . and to force on them (the present [Whig] majority) unacceptable, unwelcome Printers. . . . The time had now come, and he trusted they [the Whigs] should avail themselves of it, and . . . adopt the resolution. . . .

Mr. King of Alabama said he was not disposed to enter into a long argument. . . . his indignant feelings would not permit him to reply to the imputation of motive by which it was alleged his side of the [Senate] were actuated. Such imputations were unworthy of the person who uttered them. . . . But who is this Mr. Blair, who has been so violently assailed on this floor? If his (Mr. King's) recollection served him aright, this man Blair resided years gone by in the State of Kentucky. . . . He was then the political friend of the Senator from Kentucky; his intimate associate. . . . Was he infamous then? He presumed not. He (Mr. King) knew nothing of Mr. Blair . . . until he made his appearance in this city some years past. Since that time, he had been on terms of social intercourse with him—had observed his conduct . . . and he felt bound to say, that for kindness of heart, humanity, and exemplary deportment as a private citizen, he could proudly compare with the Senator from Kentucky, or any Senator on this floor by whom he has been assailed. . . .

. . . Mr. Clay of Kentucky said . . . he believed the *Globe* to be an infamous paper, and its chief editor [Blair] an infamous man. . . . [B]ut a Senator [Mr. King], who he supposed considered himself responsible, had gone a step further, and had chosen to class him (Mr. Clay) with Blair, and to consider Blair as equal to him in every point of view—in reputation and every thing else. . . . and for the Senator from Alabama [Mr. King] to undertake to put him on an equality with Blair, constrained him to say that it was false, untrue, and cowardly.[13]

Clay's words were so offensive that King challenged him to a duel. Clay, who had once dueled with John Randolph, accepted the challenge. The duel was averted only when the warring senators were brought before a magistrate and placed under a peace bond. The March 11, 1841, *Newark Daily Advertiser* commented:

What a humiliating spectacle for the world to contemplate! Two American Senators arrested in the very temple of Liberty on an errand of murder!—How long will public sentiment tolerate men who thus publicly set at defiance the laws of God and man, and contemptuously violate the moral sense of the nation, in the very Halls consecrated to its protection!

Eventually, the filibuster ended, and the printers were dismissed.

Four months later, the Senate again experienced delaying tactics, this time on a bank bill, dear to the hearts of the Whigs but anathema to the Democrats. After the bill emerged from committee on June 21, 1841, the Democrats proceeded to debate it at length, greatly irritating Clay and other Whigs. On July 15, an annoyed Clay, believing that a limitation of debate would carry, announced that he would offer legislation permitting the majority to control the business of the Senate. When King of Alabama demanded to know whether Clay really intended to introduce such a measure to throttle debate, Clay responded, "I will, sir; I will." Defying him bluntly, King declared, "I tell the Senator, then, that he may make his arrangements at his boarding house for the winter," leaving little question that he was threatening an extended filibuster.

Joining the fray, an indignant Benton blasted the "design to stifle debate." "Sir," he declared, "this call for action! action! action! . . . comes from those whose cry is, plunder! plunder! plunder!" Calhoun, too, denouncing "a palpable attempt to infringe the right of speech," let it be known that he would resist any gag attempt.

Clay never pursued his announced proposal for limiting debate, as other Whig senators indicated that they would not support such a move. Debate on the bank bill continued for almost two weeks before the legislation finally passed on July 28.[14]

Five years later, in 1846, a lengthy debate was held over whether to terminate the Oregon Territory treaty with Great Britain. Long speeches delayed a decision for more than two months, until the Senate finally passed the resolution, and a peaceful settlement of the Oregon boundary was reached.[15]

Also in 1846, the United States declared war on Mexico, and President James Polk asked Congress to appropriate two million dollars as an initial payment to Mexico for territory that he hoped would be ceded to the United States. The House approved the request but attached the Wilmot Proviso—

named for its author, Representative David Wilmot of Pennsylvania—prohibiting slavery in any territory acquired as a result of the war. The appropriation bill came up in the Senate on the morning of August 10, with final adjournment scheduled for noon. When Senator Dixon Lewis of Alabama moved to strike out the antislavery provision, Whig Senator John Davis of Massachusetts took the floor. Since the House had adjourned in the meantime, the appropriation would not become law if the Senate failed to accept the amendment. Davis talked the bill to death, saying that if it passed, the president "will feel justified in prolonging the war until . . . additional territory is acquired." When Congress reconvened in December, Polk renewed his request for the money, and fierce debate again ensued. Senate delays tied up the appropriation for more than a month, but finally the bill was approved without the Wilmot condition.[16]

The Senate again engaged in extended debate in January 1850, when Senator Henry Foote of Mississippi introduced an omnibus bill designed to organize the western territories. The area covered included California, New Mexico, and Deseret (roughly encompassing Arizona, Nevada, and Utah). The bill proposed separating Texas into two states, as well as increasing southern representation in the Senate to balance the admission of California as a free state. The Judiciary Committee, on the same day, reported a bill to strengthen regulations regarding the capture and return of fugitive slaves. These measures, combined with proposals from the North to end slavery in the District of Columbia and from the South to enact a new fugitive slave law, set the stage for the historic debates which culminated finally in the Compromise of 1850. Henry Clay unveiled a set of eight compromise proposals, which he believed would settle the slavery issue for many years. As the Senate wrangled and de-

layed, Clay complained bitterly, "To postpone, to delay, to impede, to procrastinate, has been the policy of the minority in this body. . . ."[17]

Before the Senate finally passed the legislation, it deleted the admission of California and other proposals, leaving only the provision for the territorial government for Utah. Senator Stephen A. Douglas of Illinois then pressed for passage of a bill to admit California. That measure quickly encountered sudden and stiff resistance. In Franklin Burdette's words, "Dilatory motions to adjourn, postpone, lay on the table, amend, and so on were employed, although by no means exploited to their full possibilities."[18] The bill for California's admission passed on August 13, and the other compromise measures were adopted before the session ended. As soon as one proposal was settled, Douglas brought up another. Where Clay had failed to secure passage of his omnibus package of compromises, Douglas succeeded in having each enacted as a separate proposal, until the package was complete.[19]

In the midst of the Civil War, in January 1863, the Senate experienced a lengthy filibuster when Senator Lyman Trumbull of Illinois, chairman of the Judiciary Committee, called up a House bill to indemnify the president and other persons for suspending the writ of *habeas corpus*.[20] The administration had requested the legislation as a war measure. On January 27, during consideration of the bill as in Committee of the Whole, Senator Willard Saulsbury of Delaware, in lengthy remarks, referred to President Lincoln as "a weak and imbecile man; the weakest man that I ever knew in a high place." Saulsbury, stating that he had conversed with the president, repeated his assertion, "I never did see or converse with so weak and imbecile a man as Abraham Lincoln, President of the United States." Other senators charged Senator Saulsbury with transgress-

During the Civil War, when Senator Willard Saulsbury was ruled out of order on the Senate floor, he brandished a gun and threatened to shoot the sergeant at arms.   *Library of Congress*

ing the rules of the Senate, and the vice president, after Saulsbury accused other senators of "blackguardism," ruled the senator out of order "in attributing such language to members of the body," and ordered him to "take his seat."[21] Saulsbury appealed the ruling of the chair and proceeded to speak on the appeal. In the course of his remarks, he again attacked the president, saying, "if I wanted to paint a tyrant; if I wanted to paint a despot . . . I would paint the hideous form of Abraham Lincoln."

When the vice president ruled that Saulsbury's remarks were not pertinent to the question of order and again ordered him to take his seat, Saulsbury shouted, "The voice

of freedom is out of order in the councils of the nation!" The vice president then instructed the sergeant at arms to take Saulsbury in charge "unless he observed order." Saulsbury responded, "Let him take me," and the vice president ordered the sergeant at arms to "take the Senator in charge." The *Congressional Globe* reported that "the Assistant Sergeant-at-Arms, Isaac Bassett, Esq., approached Mr. Saulsbury, who was seated at his desk. After a brief conversation, they . . . left the Senate chamber." The vice president then put the question on the appeal, and the decision of the chair was sustained.[22]

As the debate continued on the *habeas corpus* bill, Senator Saulsbury persisted in his attempts to speak without leave of the Senate after having been ruled out of order. The presiding officer again ordered Saulsbury to take his seat and, upon the senator's refusal to do so, gave the order to the sergeant at arms to "take the Senator in charge." Saulsbury then said, "Let him do so at his expense." Here, the *Globe* recorded that the sergeant at arms approached Saulsbury, who was sitting at his desk, and that "it was understood that Mr. Saulsbury refused to retire, but at a subsequent period he left the chamber." This was a rather bland portrayal of what had, in reality, taken place, for Saulsbury had brandished a gun and threatened to shoot the sergeant at arms on the spot. Later in the day, Saulsbury again returned to the chamber, sought to gain the floor, and was again told by the presiding officer to take his seat. At this point, a roll-call vote occurred on an amendment, after which the *Globe* mentioned no further interruptions by Saulsbury.[23]

On the following day, January 28, Senator Daniel Clark of New Hampshire offered a resolution to expel Saulsbury from the Senate, charging him with having brought "a concealed weapon" into the Senate, having behaved "in a turbulent and disorderly manner," and having drawn "said weapon" and threatened "to shoot [the] Sergeant-at-Arms." Senator Clark asked that the resolution lie over until the next day.[24] On January 29, Saulsbury apologized to the Senate, not for what he had said about President Lincoln but for the "violation of the rules of the body," following which Senator Clark announced that he would not proceed with his expulsion resolution, and the matter was dropped.[25]

Meanwhile, the *habeas corpus* bill had passed the Senate on January 27 and had gone to a House-Senate conference. When the conference report was laid before the Senate on March 2, a heated debate again occurred, with Senator William A. Richardson of Illinois threatening to "express, at length, our opinions in reference to this whole measure, to which we are opposed." Senator Lazarus W. Powell of Kentucky expressed resentment at "an imputation that our object was to do what is commonly called filibustering."[26]

The debate continued throughout the day on March 2, with motion after motion to adjourn. At about five o'clock in the morning on March 3, Republican Senator Samuel C. Pomeroy of Kansas, who was presiding, executed a heavy-handed parliamentary action. Immediately following a roll-call vote rejecting a motion to adjourn, Pomeroy, in a voice scarcely audible, put the question: "The question is on concurring in the report of the committee of conference. Those in favor of concurring in the report will say 'ay'; those opposed 'no.' The ayes have it. It is a vote. The report is concurred in." Senator Trumbull moved quickly to take up another bill, and the motion was agreed to. Several senators had not heard the chair submit the question on the adoption of the conference report, and, amid the confusion, when Trumbull moved to consider another matter, Senator Powell, unaware that the report had

already been agreed to by a voice vote, insisted that the consideration of the conference report be continued and that the yeas and nays be taken on its passage. A heated discussion over what had transpired was ended only by an adjournment until noon that day.[27]

When the Senate reconvened at noon, the opponents of the *habeas corpus* bill heatedly insisted on reconsideration and a vote. When it was pointed out that the enrolled bill had already been signed by the Speaker and the Senate president pro tempore and was on its way to the White House, a staged vote was arranged. A motion requested the House to return the bill to the Senate for reconsideration, even though such an action was no longer possible. The purpose of the motion was to allow a test vote that would enable senators opposed to the bill to go on record against it by voting for the motion. Luckily, the request for return of the bill was rejected by a vote of 13 to 25.[28]

According to Franklin Burdette, the unsuccessful filibuster of 1863 was "the first in Senate annals which can be said without shadow of doubt to have been truly intense."[29] It failed because of slick maneuvering by the majority in the face of a small but determined minority.

The next filibuster of comparable magnitude occurred sixteen years later, in 1879, and marked an advance in methods of dealing with obstructive tactics. On June 16, the Senate took up a House appropriation bill containing a provision that no money in the act could be spent "for the subsistence" of the army "to be used as a police force to keep the peace at the polls at any election." Debate began on June 17 and continued the next day.

Republicans scathingly attacked the provision, with Senator Roscoe Conkling of New York leading the opposition. Repeated motions to adjourn, points of order, appeals,

A noted orator, Senator Roscoe Conkling once led an all-night filibuster.
Library of Congress

motions to table, motions to instruct the sergeant at arms, and breaking of quorums continued throughout the night of the eighteenth, until the Senate adjourned at 11:51 a.m. on June 19, only to reconvene nine minutes later at noon.[30]

When the dust from the all-night wrangling had settled, thirty roll-call votes and nine quorum calls had occurred after six o'clock on the evening of June 18, with little else to show for the all-night session. By June 20, tempers had subsided, and the bill was passed shortly before 2 a.m. on June 21.

The bitter filibuster had produced two new approaches to combating obstructive tactics in the Senate. When the Senate had

reconvened at noon on June 19, after the all-night session, the following discussion took place:

The President pro tempore called the Senate to order and said: "The Chair is informed by the journal clerk that owing to the length of the session yesterday and its prolongation during the night, the Journal . . . has not been finished; and the Chair suggests that the reading of it be dispensed with until it be finished."

Mr. CONKLING. "I object, Mr. President; and I insist upon the observance of the . . . rule . . . which requires the Chair to cause the Journal to be read, first of all, after calling the Senate to order." . . .

The PRESIDENT pro tempore. "The Journal can be read as far as it is made up; but what is not made up cannot be read. The Clerk will read the Journal as far as it is made up." . . .

Mr. CONKLING. "I object to anything being done until the Journal is read."

The PRESIDENT pro tempore. "The Journal will be read as far as it is made up."

Mr. CONKLING. "There will not be anything done until the rest of it is read."

The Journal of yesterday's proceedings was read in part.

The PRESIDENT pro tempore. "Petitions and memorials are now in order."

Mr. CONKLING. "Has the Journal been read?"

The PRESIDENT pro tempore. "All that has been written up has been read."

Mr. CONKLING. "I submit to the Chair that the rule requires that the Journal of the preceding day's proceedings shall be read. I demand the reading of the whole of those proceedings, and object to anything being done until the Journal is read.". . .

The PRESIDENT pro tempore. "It is the opinion of the Chair that the Senate cannot be prevented from transacting business by a failure to write up all the Journal, and that the rule does not require an impossibility. As far as the Journal has been written up it has been read. The rest of it, in the opinion of the Chair, must be read hereafter. Therefore, the Chair overrules the point of order made by the Senator from New York."[31]

Senator Conkling appealed the chair's ruling, and Senator Frank Hereford of West Virginia moved to table the appeal. On a roll-call vote, the appeal was tabled, 33 to 4. Because a quorum had not voted, the chair directed the clerk to call the roll to establish a quorum. A quorum of 48 senators being present, another vote was taken on the motion to table the appeal of the chair's ruling. The vote was 26 to 4 in favor of tabling, meaning that fewer than a quorum of senators had voted. The clerk again called the roll to establish a quorum, and 52 senators answered their names. Once more, the roll-call vote was taken on the motion to table Conkling's appeal of the chair's ruling, and the vote in favor of tabling was 32 to 3, again no quorum. At this point, Senator Thomas F. Bayard, Sr., of Delaware asked that Senator Zachariah Chandler of Michigan, being present but not having answered to his name, be required, under the rule, to assign his reasons for not voting. The Michigan senator responded that he viewed this "as an attempt in an unconstitutional manner to overturn . . . a standing rule of this body that cannot be overturned except in the regular way, and I will not vote to make a quorum to do an unconstitutional and wrong act." The presiding officer then stated it to be his duty to put the question to the Senate, "Shall the Senator from Michigan, for the reasons assigned by him, be excused from voting?" The yeas and nays were ordered, and by a vote of 0 to 33 the Senate refused to excuse Chandler. Again, a quorum of members had not voted, obviously because several senators who were present had remained silent, declining to vote when their names were called. The president pro tempore then announced:

"No quorum has voted. The Chair has counted the Senate. There is a quorum present, but no quorum voting. . . .

". . . The Chair does not think the fact that a quorum has not voted is conclusive evidence that a quorum is not present. On the contrary, in the opinion of the Chair, he has a right to count the Senate. He has counted the Senate and found that a quorum is in attendance; but a quorum has not voted." [32]

Thus, in the course of this 1879 filibuster, the chair had issued two important rulings: first, that the Senate could not be prevented from doing business when the *Journal* of the previous day had unavoidably not been completed; and, second, that, on a call to establish the presence of a quorum, the chair could count a quorum if one were physically present, though silent. The tactic that the Republicans had been using so effectively—sitting in their seats and refusing to answer to their names on a roll-call vote and then answering to their names on the quorum call that automatically followed—was known as "quorum-breaking."

Filibusterism in the Senate was now full-grown, but precedents were gradually being established to gnaw at its branches, if not yet at its roots. As Franklin Burdette pointed out, "To count a quorum present to allow the Senate to proceed to business, and to count a quorum on a vote in order to declare a motion carried, are different things." [33] The first step had been taken; the second step would not come for almost thirty years.

Two years later, in the closing days of the Forty-sixth Congress, the Democrats attempted repeatedly to take action upon nominations submitted by outgoing President Rutherford B. Hayes. But Republicans, in the minority, demonstrated their adeptness in the use of the filibuster weapon and resorted to obstructionist tactics to delay action until the new president, James A. Garfield, could fill the vacant offices. The Senate that met on March 4, 1881, was evenly divided, with 37 Republicans, 37 Democrats, and 2 Independents. In Volume I of *The Senate; 1789-1989*, I have already related the events which led to the victory of the Republicans when Senator William Mahone of Virginia, representing a breakaway faction—known as the "Readjustors"—within his state's Democratic party, joined with the Republicans to control the Senate. The Demo-

A senator of the 1870's is depicted conducting "an energetic filibuster."   *E. Alton, Among the Law-Makers*

crats, now in the minority, found the filibuster a useful tool to prevent the Republicans from replacing the Democratic Senate officers and staff. Two months later, when New York Republican Senators Roscoe Conkling and Thomas C. Platt resigned in May due to a patronage quarrel with President Garfield, the deadlock was broken. The Democrats had a two-vote majority and, in the interest of wrapping up the session, they agreed not to reopen the question of committee control. In return, the Republicans permitted the Democrats to maintain control of the Senate's officers and patronage.[34]

Nearly a decade later, another celebrated filibuster was launched when a so-called Force bill, or elections bill, was called up by Senator George F. Hoar of Massachusetts on December 2, 1890. The bill, designed to combat intimidation and disqualification of black voters in the South, provided for federal supervision of congressional elections. Republicans saw the legislation as a way to make political gains in the South, while to Democrats it represented an attack on states' rights. Democratic senators delivered lengthy speeches and vehemently resisted the bill. On December 23, Senator Nelson W. Aldrich of Rhode Island introduced a resolution permitting any senator, after a matter had been considered "for a reasonable time," to demand that debate be closed, after which, without further debate, a vote would occur on cloture. The resolution provided that a majority could invoke cloture, after which only motions to adjourn or recess would be in order. No quorum calls would be permitted unless, on a division or roll-call vote, a quorum was shown to be lacking. Every senator would be limited to one speech "not exceeding thirty minutes."[35]

The debate on the elections bill continued until December 31, with only a brief five-day recess over the Christmas holiday. After completing some other legislation, the Senate returned to the elections bill on January 14, 1891. The vote to proceed to the bill was a tie, 33 to 33, broken only when Vice President Levi P. Morton voted in favor. The Democrats, who thus far had resorted only to speechmaking, resolved to talk until the session ended on March 4. The Republicans were determined to overcome the minority by keeping the Senate in continuous session, leading to a contest of physical endurance.

The Senate remained in session throughout the day and night of Friday, January 16, and until 6 p.m. on Saturday. Senator Charles J. Faulkner of West Virginia nominally held the floor for eleven and one-half hours, during eight hours of which the Senate was unable to muster a quorum. Between midnight Friday and 9:30 a.m. Saturday, when the Senate was finally able to maintain a quorum,[36] the roll was called eight times, on procedural matters only. After the sergeant at arms was ordered to request the attendance of absent senators, he reported back to the Senate: seven members were too ill to comply; one said he was "much too fatigued to attend"; others would not answer the knock at their doors; Senator Matthew Butler of South Carolina simply "refused to obey the summons"; and Senator James H. Berry of Arkansas "requested me to report to the Senate that he would come when he got ready."[37]

After this exhausting session proved to be beyond the endurance of the majority, the Republicans abandoned the strategy of continuous session and concentrated, instead, on Aldrich's proposal for cloture, which he called up on January 20, 1891.[38] Concerned that a way would be found to throttle debate, the Democrats worked feverishly to displace the hated Force bill on the Senate agenda. By allying themselves with the silverites, they were able to accomplish this on January 26, when Senator Edward O. Wolcott of Colorado moved to take up a bill making an apportionment of representatives in Congress. The motion carried by the narrow vote of 35 to 34, thus killing the Force bill.[39] The filibusterers had succeeded in a battle they had waged from December 2 to January 26.

In August 1893, a less successful filibuster erupted on legislation to repeal the silver purchase provisions of the Sherman Silver Purchase Act. The country was in the midst of a financial panic, and the administration of Grover Cleveland supported repeal. Congress was called into session on August 7, and Senator Daniel W. Voorhees of Indiana led the fight for the administration. On August 29, Voorhees reported a House bill in the Senate, and the filibuster began. Republican Senator Fred T. Dubois of Idaho was one of the leaders of the obstructionist alliance in which silver Republicans joined with silverites and "farmer" Democrats. As Franklin Burdette assessed the situation: "Lines of battle were drawn; against the financial East, stood the Far West and most of the South. Silverites from the latter sections demanded more silver, not less. Free and unlimited coinage was their goal, their panacea for the financial ills of the country."[40]

On Wednesday, October 11, 1893, the Senate met at 11:00 a.m. and remained in session for thirty-eight hours and forty-five minutes before adjourning at 1:45 a.m. on Friday, the thirteenth. During this time, there were four roll-call votes and thirty-nine quorum calls, twelve of the quorum calls occurring between 6:20 p.m. Thursday and the adjournment early Friday morning. Senator William V. Allen of Nebraska held the floor throughout Wednesday night, until almost 8 a.m. on Thursday—some fourteen hours. The only interruptions during this time were eleven quorum calls, one roll-call vote, and speeches by colleagues. On Monday, October 16, the Senate met from eleven in the morning until ten at night. In

this period, there were twelve roll-call votes and thirteen quorum calls, as the filibusterers once more used the tactic of "breaking quorums." They would demand the yeas and nays, then remain silent when their names were called. When fewer than a quorum of members voted, the presiding officer would announce that no quorum was present, even though enough senators to make a quorum were in plain sight in the chamber. When he ordered the clerk to call the roll for a quorum, a quorum of members would answer, but when the roll-call on the vote was again taken, the filibusterers would decline to vote. Hour after hour, the ludicrous scene was repeated.

Finally, on October 24, the filibusterers yielded, and, six days later, on October 30, the bill repealing the Sherman Silver Purchase Act passed by a vote of 43 to 32. "For forty-six days, then, the filibusterers had performed upon the Senate stage," wrote Burdette, "and the endeavor failed only because some of its participants deserted the enterprise."[41] Democrats had felt the pressure from the administration and surrendered, leaving too few silverites to carry on the fight.

A one-man filibuster occurred on March 3, 1897, when Senator Matthew S. Quay of Pennsylvania attempted to include in a naval appropriation bill a maximum purchase price of $400 per ton for armor plate. On March 1, Quay had moved unsuccessfully to table an amendment by Senator William E. Chandler of New Hampshire lowering the price to be paid for armor from $400 to $300. Quay decided to filibuster the conference report on the naval appropriation bill when it came back to the Senate, hoping that, with the March 4 adjournment deadline approaching, he could force the Senate to agree to a figure higher than $300. On the night of March 3, even before the conference report was ready for Senate action, Senator Quay put the

In 1893, cartoonist Joseph Keppler suggested this method of dealing with senators who filibustered against repeal of the Sherman Silver Purchase Act.

Library of Congress

Senator Matthew Quay conducted a one-man filibuster in 1897.   *U.S. Senate Historical Office*

Congressional Record, filling 176 pages! [43] Not
only had Quay's exertions been in vain, but
another precedential arrow had pierced the
armor plate of the filibuster, thus strengthening the arsenal for combating such tactics.
From that time on, after a roll call that
showed a quorum present, a point of no
quorum could not immediately be made if no
business had intervened.

A more successful end-of-session filibuster occurred four years later, on the night of
March 3, 1901, when Senator Thomas H.
Carter of Montana blocked a rivers and harbors appropriation bill. With an automatic
adjournment deadline of noon the next day,
he had no trouble defeating the bill. [44]

Equally successful were the efforts of Senator Benjamin R. "Pitchfork Ben" Tillman of
South Carolina on March 3, 1903. Tillman
demanded the inclusion of $47,000 in a defi-
ciency appropriation bill as a claim for expenses his state had incurred in the war of
1812, and he threatened to filibuster all bills
before the Senate by talking until the noon
adjournment the next day. At his desk, he
had a pile of books, with a volume of Byron's
poems open and ready for use. In the face of
this threat, the Senate capitulated and included the $47,000 in the bill. [45]

When the conference report on the appropriation bill came up in the House, Representative Joseph G. Cannon of Illinois, on
behalf of the House managers, deplored the
Senate rules which permitted a single
member, by threat of a filibuster, to impose
his will on a majority of both houses.
Cannon reported that the auditing officers of
the treasury, in adjusting accounts, had
found that "the sum of 34 cents" was due to
South Carolina, but the Senate had proposed
granting the state $47,000. Stating that the
House conferees had objected, Cannon declared that, in the House, "we have rules . . .
by which a majority, right or wrong, mistak-
en or otherwise, can legislate." In the Senate,

Senate through one quorum call after another. When the Senate overrode the president's veto of a private relief bill by a vote of
39 to 7, with 44 senators not voting, Senator
Quay immediately suggested the absence of
a quorum. Irritated senators contended that
Quay was out of order in doing so, and, on a
point of order, the chair ruled that, once the
presence of a quorum had been established
by a roll call and no business had intervened,
a senator could not immediately thereafter
suggest the absence of a quorum. [42]

In the end, the House, which had supported paying $400 per ton for armor plate, re-
ceded from its position and concurred in the
Senate's lower figure, thus nullifying all of
Senator Quay's efforts. He had prepared a
lengthy speech designed to wear down his
colleagues, but, in light of the House's
action, he simply inserted his remarks in the

he complained, there were no such rules, so that "an individual member of that body can rise in his place and talk for one hour, two hours, ten hours, twelve hours." The House conferees, Cannon said, were unable to persuade the Senate to recede from "this gift . . . against the law, to the State of South Carolina." In a blistering attack on Senate procedures, Cannon asserted:

By unanimous consent another body [the Senate] legislates, and in the expiring hours of the session we are powerless without that unanimous consent. "Help me, Cassius, or I sink!"
Unanimous consent comes to the center of the Dome; unanimous consent comes through Statuary Hall and to the House doors and comes practically to the House. We can have no legislation without the approval of both bodies, and one body . . . can not legislate without unanimous consent. . . . Your conferees had the alternative of submitting to legislative blackmail at the demand, in my opinion, of one individual . . . or of letting these great money bills fail. . . .[46]

Cannon went on to argue that the Senate "must change its methods of procedure" or the House, "backed up by the people, will compel that change." Otherwise, the House would become "a mere bender of the pregnant hinges of the knee, to submit to what any one member of [the Senate] may demand of this body as a price for legislation." Although Representative Cannon concluded his remarks to prolonged applause and cheers, Senator Tillman's filibuster threat had prevailed.[47]

Another effective end-of-session filibuster began on March 2, 1907, as the Fifty-ninth Congress was coming to its close. Senator Jacob H. Gallinger of New Hampshire was pressing for an increase in the subsidy to American merchant shipping. Other senators opposed the subsidy as a burden on the taxpayers, and a Senate filibuster immediately threw a dark cloud over the adjournment landscape. Democratic Senator Edward W. Carmack of Tennessee, who was retiring

from the Senate, took the floor on Sunday, March 3, and his obstructive loquacity consumed that day and evening. When the Senate met early the next day, he showed up ready again to unload his oratorical guns on the subsidy target. Senator Gallinger, not wishing to see other legislation sacrificed in the remaining few hours of the dying session, abandoned the bill. In discussing Carmack's triumph, Franklin Burdette observed, "Senators had learned well the futility of opposing a determined filibuster in a short session immediately before the automatic 4th of March adjournment." (Incidentally, Carmack died in a gun fight in Nashville twenty months later.)[48]

A brief but bitter filibuster against the Aldrich-Vreeland bill to amend the national banking laws led to some significant interpretations of Senate rules that strengthened future efforts to oppose lengthy debates. On May 29, 1908, Senator Nelson W. Aldrich of Rhode Island presented to the Senate the conference report on the bill. Filibusters are inherently much more difficult to wage successfully on conference reports than on bills, because conference reports are not amendable. But opponents of the banking legislation decided to undertake a filibuster anyway, because they believed the bill would unfairly benefit the moneyed interests of the country. Republicans, on the other hand, considered it a way to deal with bankruptcies and other pressing financial problems facing the nation.

Senator Robert M. La Follette of Wisconsin, a Republican who distrusted Aldrich, led the opposition to the conference report, nominally holding the floor for more than eighteen hours.[49] During that time, however, his lengthy speech was interrupted often for colloquies, as well as for three roll-call votes and twenty-nine quorum calls, twenty-four of which La Follette himself demanded.[50] In those days, senators holding

Senator Robert M. La Follette used frequent quorum calls as a tactic in a 1908 filibuster. *Library of Congress*

the floor did not lose it when quorum calls occurred, and La Follette frequently suggested the absence of a quorum in order to force the majority to maintain a quorum while he rested during the quorum calls. That La Follette's tactics were not popular among his colleagues was evident from the numerous interruptions of his speeches for parliamentary inquiries and points of order, as well as for angry comments directed toward him by other senators during the time he held the floor.

Senator Aldrich proved to be an astute floor manager for the conference report and a resourceful opponent of filibustering. After the Senate had been paralyzed for hours by La Follette's torrent of words and time-consuming quorum calls, Aldrich, rising to a point of order, declared: "We have had 32 roll calls within a comparatively short time, all disclosing the presence of a quorum. Manifestly a quorum is in the building. If repeated suggestions of the want of a quorum can be made without intervening business, the whole business of the Senate is put in the hands of one man, who can insist upon continuous calls of the roll upon the question of a quorum." Continuing, Aldrich said, "My question of order is that, without the intervention of business, a quorum having been disclosed by a vote or by a call of the roll, no further calls are in order until some business has intervened.". . .

Mr. LA FOLLETTE. "Mr. President, I just wish to suggest, in order that it may appear upon the Record that debate has intervened since the last roll call."

Mr. ALDRICH. "That is not business . . . My suggestion was that debate was not business."

The vice president then submitted the question of order to the Senate, which sustained Aldrich's point of order by a vote of 35 to 8. Subsequently, Senator Lee Overman of North Carolina inquired of the chair "whether, after a speech has been made," the question of a quorum could be raised, to which the vice president replied, "The Chair is of the opinion that that is not in order."[51]

Thus, the Senate took an important step beyond the precedent established in 1897. At that time, Senator Quay had been ruled out of order for attempting a quorum call immediately after one had just been concluded, in a situation where no debate had intervened. Now, Aldrich was drawing the net of precedents tighter, so that such a tactic could not be used even when there had been some intervening debate.

The 1908 session also achieved a second crucial precedent: the chair would count silent members who were present in the chamber, in order to validate a division or roll-call vote on which a quorum did not vote. This decision occurred as Senator Charles Culberson of Texas had the floor. He was speaking when Senator La Follette rose to make a parliamentary inquiry.

The VICE-PRESIDENT. "Does the Senator from Texas yield to the Senator from Wisconsin?"

Mr. CULBERSON. "I prefer to go on, Mr. President." . . .

Mr. LA FOLLETTE. "It is not necessary for the Senator from Texas to yield to the Senator from Wisconsin when the Senator from Wisconsin rises to a parliamentary inquiry." . . .

Mr. ALDRICH. "I make the further point of order that in order to make a parliamentary inquiry a Senator must be in possession of the floor, and that he can not take the floor by asking to make a parliamentary inquiry and then make any motion."

When the chair ruled that Aldrich's point of order was well taken, La Follette appealed the ruling, stating that "a hundred times" he had seen senators rise and, "without any assent upon the part of the Senator who had the floor, raise the question that no quorum was present. Is it possible," he asked, "that important proceedings in the Senate, if one man can get the floor, may be conducted here for an unlimited period of time in the presence of the Presiding Officer and one single Senator, he declining to yield the floor?" Senator Aldrich moved to table the appeal, and, on a division, La Follette's appeal was tabled by a vote of 32 to 14, after which Senator Thomas P. Gore of Oklahoma contended that a quorum was not present.

The VICE-PRESIDENT. "The division disclosed the existence of a quorum."

Mr. GORE. "It takes forty-seven to constitute a quorum. . . ."

The VICE-PRESIDENT. "The Chair is of the opinion that a quorum is present."

Mr. GORE. "I should like to say that there are ninety-two members of this body . . . A division disclosed the presence of forty-six. As I understand, it takes one more than half to constitute a quorum."

The VICE-PRESIDENT. "There was present a Senator who did not vote. . . .

"In the present instance the Chair has counted the Senate, and there is a quorum present." [52]

This ruling expanded the earlier precedent of 1879—in which the chair had counted a quorum to determine whether enough senators were present to do business—also to include a count by the chair to declare a vote valid if a quorum was present, even though a quorum of members had not actually voted. With the filibuster broken, the conference report was adopted on May 30.

I should mention one other aspect of this historic, but brief, 1908 filibuster. Senator Aldrich demonstrated his parliamentary acumen by seeking and obtaining agreement for the yeas and nays before all debate was concluded. As a consequence, the Senate was ready to move immediately to a vote if an opportunity arose when no senator held the floor, thus bringing the filibuster to a sudden end. The usual course was to order the yeas and nays after all debate had ceased and just prior to taking the vote. The utility of Aldrich's forethought became evident later when Senator Gore, who was blind, completed speaking without realizing that Senator William Stone of Missouri, who was to relieve him in the filibuster, had momentarily left the chamber.[53] The vice president immediately put the question on adopting the conference report, and Aldrich, whose name was at the top of the alphabet, promptly responded. Senator Weldon Heyburn of Idaho, realizing what was happening, vainly sought recognition.

THE VICE-PRESIDENT. "The question is on agreeing to the report of the committee of conference."

Mr. ALDRICH. "I ask that the roll be called."

The VICE-PRESIDENT. "The secretary will call the roll."

Mr. HEYBURN. "Mr. President—"

The secretary proceeded to call the roll and Mr. Aldrich responded to his name.

Mr. HEYBURN. "I addressed the Chair before the commencement of the roll call."

Mr. ALDRICH. "The roll call can not be suspended."
Mr. HEYBURN. "I do not ask that it be suspended. It was started with undue haste. I was addressing the Chair." [54]

Heyburn had clearly sought recognition before Aldrich responded on the roll call, and, as Franklin Burdette observed, "it must be said that the filibuster was overcome by doubtful practice" and "for the first time since the practice had risen to great prominence in the Senate, a majority ruthlessly confronted filibusterism with restraints." [55]

In spite of the sharp practices that had been used, the 1908 rulings represented important milestones on the long road toward curtailing filibusters.

Filibusters continued to erupt intermittently before the cloture rule was adopted in 1917. The most prominent one in that period was the prolonged debate in 1915 over the ship purchase bill. The legislation authorized the United States to purchase, construct, equip, and operate merchant vessels in the foreign trade. World War I had begun in July 1914, after the June 28 assassination of the Austrian crown prince, Archduke Francis Ferdinand, and his wife, Sophie. The fighting had spread to the seas, with German torpedo boats and cruisers attacking shipping and German submarines roaming the oceans. Because shipping charges were high, due to a shortage of vessels, supporters of the legislation argued that expanding the merchant fleet would lead to a more rapid movement of goods and lower shipping costs. Opponents lined up with the shipping interests and attacked the bill as being socialistic.

The Republican minority in the Senate strongly opposed the measure and conducted a lengthy filibuster that dragged on for weeks. Discussions lasted into the evenings, and, on Friday, January 29, an all-night session occurred. Starting at eleven o'clock that morning, the session continued for thirty-six

During a 1915 filibuster, Senator Reed Smoot spoke without interruption for more than eleven hours.
U.S. Senate Historical Office

hours and fifteen minutes—until 11:15 p.m. on Saturday. Friday night was a night of wrangling and confusion, with the Senate tying itself in parliamentary knots on top of knots. There were points of order in layers, with appeals from the chair's rulings, motions to table, quorum calls, demands that senators be required to assign their reasons for not voting, warrants of arrest issued for absent senators, and votes on the motions. Senators disputed the chair's rulings and challenged the power of recognition by the chair without the right of appeal; there were questions of privilege, the calling to order of senators by the chair, and cries for the "regular order." The scene was one of wild uproar and chaos—a night to remember!

Finally, Senator Reed Smoot of Utah gained recognition, and the tumult subsided. Smoot opposed the bill, saying that he favored building an American merchant marine by the granting of subsidies. He called the pending bill "undemocratic, unrepublican, un-American, vicious in its provisions, and . . . dangerous and mischievous if it ever becomes law." Smoot's was one of the outstanding speeches in the history of filibusters. A *New York Times* story on January 30 stated that Smoot "settled down with evenly modulated voice to an address that lasted, without even the interruption of a rollcall, for 11 hours and 35 minutes." [56]

During Smoot's speech, Senator John Sharp Williams of Mississippi interrupted him to ask if he had "calculated the amount of money that he is costing the American shippers by his speech?" Williams opined that it was costing "$20,800 an hour" and that "if it continues much longer, he [Smoot] will very nigh bankrupt them." [57]

The Democratic majority had decided upon a strategy of continuous session, but, as always, the hours became as wearing upon the majority as on the minority. The *Times* reported that senators were sleeping "on couches in chamber" and catnapping "in cloakrooms." [58]

Finally, after thirty-six-and-a-quarter hours, thirteen roll calls, and five quorum calls, the Senate recessed until Monday, February 1. The filibuster then continued, with no sign of concluding. The session on February 8 began at noon and ran until 6:10 p.m. on February 10, a total of fifty-four hours and ten minutes, with thirteen roll-call votes and nine quorum calls. Six of the thirteen votes involved challenges to the chair's rulings, and four were on motions to adjourn or to recess—which gives some indication of the dilatory nature of the actions. [59]

At one point during the six-week-long filibuster, the Democrats found themselves having to delay action on the bill when several of their members joined the Republican opposition. Only after absent Democrats heeded urgent calls to return to Washington from distant parts of the country was the majority party again in a position to press for a vote on the legislation. Referring to the dilemma that had temporarily confronted the Democrats, Senator James A. Reed of Missouri said:

Mr. President, a few evenings ago we listened to a speech here that lasted all night, delivered by the Senator from Utah [Mr. Smoot]. The Republican side of this Chamber appeared to be well-nigh exhausted. It looked as though tired nature was to bring a surcease to our woes of waiting, when some Democrats entered into an arrangement with the Republican side of the Chamber whereby dilatory motions were to be offered to this bill and a combination effected between a small portion of the Democrats and nearly all of the Republicans; and then, having finally secured the attendance of Senators who have been brought here thousands of miles, who were absent for good and sufficient cause, we now witness the performance of last night, when, by a concerted action, nearly every Republican in this body went to his home, to his bed, with the understanding that the verbal stalwart who was then occupying the floor would hold it until a certain hour, when these gentlemen might rise from their couches, put forward another individual capable of talking several hours, a physical logician, an athletic orator, who could stand the exertion of remaining upon his feet and employing his vocal chords, the proposition being that again they would come here in relays, all of this . . . to deny the people whom this body represents any opportunity to have their will as so represented crystallized into law. [60]

In an effort to force the constant attendance of senators and thus avoid the loss of quorums, Senator Reed proposed that the Senate adopt the following standing order, to remain in effect until otherwise ordered:

All Senators are required to appear forthwith in the Senate Chamber and to remain in the Chamber until excused by the Senate. Any Senator disobeying this order shall be in contempt of the Senate and shall be brought to the bar of the Senate and dealt with as the Senate may order. [61]

Explaining the reason for his proposal, Senator Reed observed:

We have witnessed now for weeks not an attempt to do business, but an attempt to prevent the doing of business; not a purpose to come to a vote, but a deliberate conspiracy to prevent a vote. Senators have been arranged in relays, a part of them to retire to their downy couches of ease and to the embracing arms of sweet slumber, while one or two able-bodied and lung-experienced aerial athletes continue to pour forth a ceaseless flow of eloquence, which invariably would be characterized outside of this Chamber by language which is not here parliamentary, and therefore may not be employed. . . . it might be said that in the attempt to defeat this remedial legislation gentlemen were willing to obstruct the very machinery created by the law for the enactment of legislation for the expression of the will of the people.[62]

Senator Williams gave notice of his intention to move to amend Rule XXII of the standing rules as follows:

Any Senator arising in his place and asserting that in his opinion an attempt is being made on the floor of the Senate to obstruct, hinder, or delay the right of the Senate to proceed to a vote, the Chair shall, without permitting any debate thereon, put the question to the Senate, "Is it the sense of the Senate that an attempt is being made to obstruct, hinder, or delay a vote?" And if that question shall be decided in the affirmative, then it shall be in order, to the exclusion of the consideration of all other questions, for any Senator to move to fix a time for voting on the pending bill or resolution and all amendments thereto, and the said motion shall be decided without debate: Provided, however, That the time fixed in said motion for taking the vote . . . shall be at least two calendar days after the day on which said motion is made.[63]

Not surprisingly, neither Senator Reed's proposed order to force the constant attendance of senators nor Senator Williams' proposed cloture rule was ever approved, and the filibuster was eventually successful, after having raged for thirty-three calendar days. On February 18, the majority surrendered. A sizable and determined minority's opposition had proved insurmountable on the battlefield of the Senate floor. The ship purchase bill was dead.

The next major development in controlling filibusters was the adoption in 1917 of the Senate's cloture rule, which will be discussed in the next portion of this chapter. But the precedents established in the filibusters described here—particularly those of 1879, 1897, and 1908—together with other subsequent precedents, proved as important as the 1917 cloture rule itself in guiding the Senate through future stormy seas of filibusterism.

The Cloture Rule

March 10, 1981*

Mr. President, one of the greatest changes occurring in the Senate rules between the 1884 codification and the 1979 revision was the emergence and development of the controversial cloture rule. That rule is now contained in paragraph 2 of Rule XXII, and it commands a history unto itself. The origin, development, and evolution of the rule have constituted a long and stormy voyage on the Senate's parliamentary sea.

The practice of limiting debate dates to 1604 when Sir Henry Vane first introduced the idea in the British Parliament. Known in parliamentary procedure as the "previous question," it is described in Section XXXIV of Jefferson's *Manual of Parliamentary Practice* as follows:

When any question is before the House, any Member may move a previous question, "Whether that question (called the main question) shall now be put?" If it pass in the affirmative, then the main question is to be put immediately, and no man may speak any thing further to it, either to add or alter.[1]

The *Journals of the Continental Congress* record that the previous question was used in 1778. Section 10 of the rules of the Continental Congress read, "While a question is before the House, no motion shall be received, unless for an amendment, for the previous question, to postpone the consideration of the main question, or to commit it." [2]

Both the British Parliament and the Continental Congress used the previous question as a means of preventing discussion of a delicate subject. The Congress of the Confederation, on the practice of which the 1789 Senate drew heavily, specifically declared that the

previous question . . . shall only be admitted when, in the judgment of two States at least, the subject moved is in its nature, or from the circumstances of time or place improper to be debated or decided, and shall therefore preclude all amendments and farther debates on the subject, until it is decided.[3]

Jefferson, in his *Manual*, written while the 1789 rule was still in effect, stated:

The proper occasion for the Previous Question is when a subject is brought forward of a delicate nature as to high personages . . . or the discussion of which may call forth observations which might be of injurious consequences. Then the Previous Question is proposed; and in the modern usage, the discussion of the Main (pending) Question is suspended, and the debate confined to the Previous Question. The use of it has been extended abusively to other cases.[4]

The question of whether, in the last analysis, a minority should have the power to prevent legislative action by the majority had been discussed in America long before 1789. Even in the colonial assemblies, various forms of obstruction had been practiced, and the subject was mentioned in the Constitutional Convention.

Roy Swanstrom, in his in-depth study of the Senate's formative years, titled *The United States Senate, 1787–1801*, stated that a committee of the Congress of the Confederation, in 1784, "recommended stringent rules to prevent delays." The adjournment date having been set for June 3, and with much work to be done in the remaining two weeks, the committee recommended that

in this instance the President be authorized to take the following action to speed up business:

To take the sense of Congress with respect to putting any question without debate when he considered it desirable;

* Revised December 1989

To prevent any Member from speaking more than once or longer than the President deemed necessary;

To prevent more than two Members from speaking on one side of any question, and

To finish each day's business regardless of the hour of adjournment.[5]

The *Journals of the Continental Congress* "do not record that the recommendations were adopted," wrote Swanstrom, but they constituted proposals "far more stringent than the Senate was ever to consider."[6]

It is apparent that the Senate in the First Congress disapproved of unlimited debate, since Rule IV provided that "no member shall speak more than twice in any one debate on the same day, without leave of the Senate," and Rule VI provided that "no motion shall be debated until the same shall be seconded." Some senators, however, did resort to delaying tactics in 1789 against legislation providing that the national capital be located on the Susquehanna River.[7]

The next year, the bill to establish the permanent home of the capital again encountered dilatory tactics in both houses. According to Swanstrom, senators who opposed selecting Philadelphia as the capital "tried to spin out the time until the Rhode Island senators could arrive and vote against that site." In the House of Representatives, supporters of Philadelphia were contending with the weather. It was raining when the Philadelphia bill was under consideration in the House. "If the bill passed the House and was sent to the Senate before the rain stopped, its friends believed it would undoubtedly pass; if it reached the Senate after the rain stopped, it would be defeated." This unusual situation was due to the illness of Senator Samuel Johnston, an opponent of the Philadelphia location, who "could not safely be carried to the floor in the rain to vote against the bill, but could and would if the rain had ceased." Swanstrom explained that "the Senate was so evenly divided that

the ill Senator's vote could have meant the difference. . . . Supporters of the bill, therefore, tried to push the bill through the House while the rain continued."[8] According to Fisher Ames, a member of the House, Elbridge Gerry of Massachusetts and William Smith of South Carolina thwarted the effort by "making long speeches and motions" which prevented a decision until the next day.[9]

The rules adopted by the United States Senate in April 1789 included a motion "for the previous question." According to historian George H. Haynes, when Vice President Aaron Burr delivered his farewell address to the Senate in March 1805, he "recommended the discarding of the previous question," because, in the preceding four years during which he had presided over the Senate, it had "been taken but once, and then upon an amendment." When the rules were codified in 1806, reference to the previous question was omitted, since it had been used only ten times during the years from 1789 to 1806, and it has never been restored.[10]

In 1807, the Senate forbade debate on an amendment at the third reading of a bill—the last action it took to limit debate until 1846. Henry Clay, in 1841, proposed the introduction of the "previous question" but abandoned the idea in the face of opposition. When the Oregon bill was being considered in 1846, a unanimous consent agreement was used as a way to limit debate by setting a date for a vote. Such agreements are now often used to set the time for a Senate vote on a measure, without further debate, as well as to limit debate on amendments, appeals, debatable motions, and points of order if submitted to the Senate.

When Senator Stephen Douglas proposed permitting the use of the "previous question" in 1850, the idea encountered substantial opposition and was dropped.[11]

During the third session of the Forty-first Congress, in December 1870, Senator Henry

Anthony of Rhode Island introduced, and the Senate approved, the following resolution aimed at expediting business:

On Monday next, at one o'clock, the Senate will proceed to the consideration of the Calendar, and bills that are not objected to shall be taken up in their order; and each Senator shall be entitled to speak once, and for 5 minutes only, on each question; and this order shall be enforced daily at one o'clock 'till the end of the Calendar is reached.

Before adopting the so-called Anthony Rule, an important step in limiting debate, the Senate agreed to an amendment by Senator John Sherman of Ohio, adding at the end, "unless upon motion the Senate should at any time otherwise order." [12]

An effort to reinstitute the "previous question," on March 19, 1873, failed by a vote of 25 to 30.

On February 5, 1880, the Anthony Rule became Rule VIII of the standing rules of the Senate. In 1882, the Senate amended the rule, so that, if the majority decided to take up a bill on the calendar after objection was made, the measure would be subject to the ordinary rules of debate without limitation.

When Rules Committee Chairman William Frye of Maine reported a general revision of the Senate rules in 1883, the package included a provision for the "previous question," but it was eliminated by amendments in the Senate. [13]

On March 17, 1884, the Senate agreed to the following amendment to the rules: "The Presiding Officer may at any time lay, and it shall be in order at any time for a Senator to move to lay, before the Senate any bill or other matter sent to the Senate by the President or the House of Representatives, and any question pending at that time shall be suspended for this purpose. Any motion so made shall be determined without debate." [14]

Senator Henry Anthony introduced a rule in 1870 to limit debate.   *U.S. Senate Historical Office*

Between 1884 and 1890, fifteen different resolutions were offered to amend the rules regarding limitations of debate, all of which failed of adoption. In December 1890, when the Senate was filibustering Massachusetts Representative Henry Cabot Lodge's so-called Force bill, dealing with federal elections, Senator Nelson Aldrich of Rhode Island introduced a cloture resolution that stated:

When any bill, resolution, or other question shall have been under consideration for a considerable time it shall be in order for any Senator to demand that debate thereon be closed. On such demand no debate shall be in order, and pending such demand no other motion except one motion to adjourn shall be made. If such demand be seconded by a majority of the Senators present, the question shall forthwith be taken thereon without debate. [15]

According to a history of the cloture rule published by the Senate Rules Committee, five test votes were taken on Senator Aldrich's cloture proposal, and the votes "commanded various majorities, but in the end it could not be carried in the Senate because of a filibuster against it which merged into a filibuster on the 'force bill.' "[16]

In 1893, Henry Cabot Lodge, who had moved to the Senate that year, expressed his growing frustration over the delay, by excessive debate, on legislation he considered vital. In an article entitled "The Struggle in the Senate," Lodge wrote:

> Of the two rights (of debating and voting) that of voting is the higher and more important. We ought to have both, and debate certainly in ample measure; but, if we are forced to choose between them, the right of action must prevail over the right of discussion. To vote without debating is perilous, but to debate and never vote is imbecile. . . .
>
> . . . As it is, there must be a change, for the delays which now take place are discrediting the Senate, and this is something greatly to be deplored. The Senate was perhaps the greatest single achievement of the makers of the Constitution. It is one of the strongest bulwarks of our system of government, and anything which lowers it in the eyes of the people is a most serious matter. How the Senate may vote on any given question at any given time is of secondary importance, but when it is seen that it is unable to take any action at all the situation becomes of the gravest character. A body which cannot govern itself will not long hold the respect of the people who have chosen it to govern the country. . . .
>
> . . . No minority is ever to blame for obstruction. If the rules permit them to obstruct, they are lawfully entitled to use those rules in order to stop a measure which they deem injurious. The blame for obstruction rests with the *majority*, and if there is obstruction, it is because the majority permit it. The majority to which I here refer is the party majority in control of the chamber.[17]

Lodge would later change his mind. In 1903, he commented on the Senate's rules allowing full and free debate, declaring that he had "much rather take the chances of occasional obstruction than to put the Senate in the position where bills could be driven through under rules which may be absolute-

ly necessary in a large body like the House of Representatives . . . but which are not necessary here." It was Lodge's opinion that "here we should have, minority and majority alike, the fullest possible opportunity of debate."[18]

In 1897, the chair ruled that successive quorum calls could not be ordered unless some business had intervened, opening the way to a discussion of exactly what constituted "intervening business." This issue was finally joined in 1908 during a marathon filibuster led by Robert La Follette, Sr. On that occasion, Senator La Follette broke the previous endurance record by holding the floor for eighteen hours and twenty-three minutes. His accomplishment was made possible through the device of suggesting the absence of a quorum. Each quorum call lasted at least six minutes, giving him the opportunity to seek rest and relief.

On May 29, 1908, with the temperature above ninety degrees in the chamber, La Follette talked on into the night, fortifying himself with turkey sandwiches and eggnog from the Senate restaurant. At one point, he took a sip of eggnog and immediately cast it away, exclaiming that it had been drugged. (Chemical analysis later revealed that the amount of ptomaine in the glass would certainly have killed the Wisconsin senator, but the culprit was never identified.)[19]

After thirty-two roll calls, Senator Nelson Aldrich, whose bill was the target of Senator La Follette's filibuster, raised a point of order, based on the 1897 precedent, to the effect that no business had intervened since the last quorum call. Senator Aldrich argued that debate by itself was not "intervening business." The Senate upheld the point of order, 35 to 8, thereby reversing an 1872 precedent to the contrary. This ruling made it more difficult for La Follette to continue, and his filibuster finally came to an end a few hours later.

Again, in 1915, Utah Senator Reed Smoot set a new one-man record for the longest *continuous* filibuster, speaking for eleven hours and thirty-five minutes without rest and without deviating from the subject at hand. His action was part of a filibuster against the administration's ship purchase bill. The debate consumed thirty-three days and resulted in the failure of three important appropriations bills.[20]

In May 1916, the Committee on Rules reported a resolution providing for cloture by two-thirds of those voting, but the resolution, although debated, did not come to a vote.

In 1916, and again in 1920, the Democratic party's national platforms stated, "We favor such alteration of the rules of procedure of the Senate of the United States as will permit the prompt transaction of the Nation's legislative business."[21]

The final impetus for a cloture rule came as a result of a 1917 filibuster—one of the most famous in Senate annals—against an administration measure permitting the arming of American merchant vessels for the duration of the World War. Actually, this filibuster had been immediately preceded by the delaying tactics of Republicans, whose strategy was to stall the Senate's business and force a special session of Congress. As reported by the *New York Times* on February 23, 1917, "the Republicans in caucus this morning unanimously agreed on a course that means a general filibuster against practically all legislation, so that through the failure of this legislation to reach enactment by March 4 a special session would have to be called."

On the day of the Republican conference, President Woodrow Wilson issued a proclamation calling for a special session of the Senate, to begin at noon on March 5. The Republicans, however, "made it plain that what they wanted was a sitting of both houses," not just the Senate. For the Senate alone to sit in special session would permit only the consideration of treaties and nominations, matters under the Senate's sole jurisdiction. According to the *Times* story, Republican senators "dislike the idea of leaving President Wilson, clothed with large powers, to act for nine months in a great international crisis without legislative advice."[22]

Over the next several days, the Republicans held to the course planned. From February 23 through 28, they debated a revenue bill to defray the increased expenses of the army and navy. Meanwhile, on February 26, President Wilson appeared before a joint session to request legislation authorizing the arming of merchant ships. Referring to the sinking of two American merchant vessels, the *Housatonic* and the *Lyman M. Law*, the president stated:

No one doubts what it is our duty to do. We must defend our commerce and the lives of our people in the midst of the present trying circumstances, with discretion but with clear and steadfast purpose. . . . Since it had unhappily proved impossible to safeguard our neutral rights by diplomatic means against the unwarranted infringements they are suffering at the hands of Germany, there may be no recourse but to armed neutrality. . . .

. . . I request that you will authorize me to supply our merchant ships with defensive arms, should that become necessary, and with the means of using them, and to employ any other instrumentalities or methods that may be necessary and adequate to protect our ships and our people in their legitimate and peaceful pursuits on the seas. I request also that you will grant me . . . a sufficient credit to enable me to provide adequate means of protection where they are lacking, including adequate insurance against the present war risks.[23]

Debate on the revenue bill continued. Thirty-five roll-call votes occurred between the hours of 10:00 a.m. Wednesday, February 28, and 12:45 a.m. Thursday, March 1, when the bill passed. Thirty-three of these were back-to-back votes beginning at around eight o'clock on Wednesday evening and continuing over the next four hours and forty minutes.[24]

The Republicans ended their obstructionist tactics on March 1, following a prolonged reading of the *Journal*. According to Franklin L. Burdette, an expert on Senate filibusters, it was claimed publicly that "patriotic motives had prevailed to bring an end to dilatory tactics; but a skeptic in politics may wonder whether the regular Republicans had not simply realized that their filibuster would be conveniently assumed by other tongues."[25]

Later that day, Senator Henry Cabot Lodge of Massachusetts referred to an Associated Press news story reporting "a dispatch from the secretary of state for foreign relations in Germany inviting Mexico and Japan to unite with them in war upon the United States." Lodge introduced a resolution, requesting the president to inform the Senate whether the note signed "Zimmermann" referred to in the newspapers was "authentic" and calling on Wilson to supply the Senate with any other information "relative to the activities of the Imperial German Government in Mexico."[26]

News of the astounding and provocative German message electrified the country, and a wave of indignation swept the land, building strong popular support for action.

On March 2, the Senate began debating the Senate bill that had been reported from the Foreign Relations Committee, authorizing the president to supply American merchant ships with defensive arms. Because Senator William J. Stone, chairman of the committee, opposed the bill, he asked Senator Gilbert M. Hitchcock of Nebraska to act as its floor manager. The bill had less than forty-eight hours in which to pass or it would die with the session's end at noon on March 4.[27]

Senators George W. Norris of Nebraska, Asle J. Gronna of North Dakota, Robert M.

In 1917, Senator Gilbert M. Hitchcock led the fight for the Armed Ship bill, which was blocked by a Senate filibuster.   *U.S. Senate Historical Office*

La Follette of Wisconsin, and other opponents feared that if the legislation became law it would lead the country into war. The debate went on past midnight, and, at 12:40 a.m. on March 3, the Senate recessed until 10 a.m. the same day, when the debate was renewed. It raged furiously through the afternoon and night, right up to the stroke of noon on March 4, when the Senate adjourned sine die. Opponents of the armed merchant ship bill did not resort to dilatory tactics to defeat the legislation. Only one roll-call vote and six quorum calls interrupted the debate during the twenty-six-hour session.

Senator Stone, in opposing the bill, questioned its constitutionality:

The Constitution vests the war-making power alone in the Congress. It is a power the Congress is not at liberty to delegate. . . . I believe this law would contravene the Constitution. . . . The power to be granted [to the president] is granted in terms too broad, too sweeping. . . . No limit whatsoever is placed upon the "instrumentalities and methods" that the President may employ, and no direction whatsoever is given by Congress as to the manner in which this authority may be exercised. The President would be given an absolutely free hand to employ any instrumentality and to adopt any method he saw fit.[28]

Stone spoke for four hours against the bill. As the evening wore on, Senator Hitchcock sought in vain to obtain unanimous consent to vote at a given hour. He sought consent to limit speeches to fifteen minutes "beginning at 9 o'clock," "at 10 o'clock," "at midnight," "at 1 o'clock," "at 2 o'clock in the morning," "at 4 o'clock in the morning," but each time, his request was met with an objection. Finally, in exasperation, he stopped trying, saying: "Mr. President, I am not going to do anything here to kill time. I want to develop the fact that there is a deliberate intention to filibuster the bill to death. If Senators are willing to take that responsibility I want them to take it." Senator George Norris retorted that he "would not hesitate to kill the bill" if he could. "But the fact is," he said, "that most of the time has been taken up by those who favor the bill." Norris objected "to having the debate run on for a couple of days by those who are in favor of the bill and then an effort be made to gag those who are opposed to it. . . . I do object to a limitation of any kind."[29]

Invective flowed freely as the angry majority tried to silence the small but unsub-missive band of opposition senators, who accused the measure's supporters of monopolizing the time. Senator Wesley L. Jones of Washington referred to "the apparent filibuster that seems to have been carried on by those who profess to be friends of the bill. The Senator [Mr. Hitchcock] in charge of it wasted half an hour's time, that anybody might have known would be wasted, in trying to reach an agreement to limit debate and to vote. . . . the passage of this measure should not be hurried."[30]

At 3:20 a.m. on March 4, Senator Hitchcock asked Senator Joseph T. Robinson of Arkansas to present a statement for the *Record* "to show that nine-tenths of the Senate are ready to vote and anxious to vote and want to vote for this bill, but that they are being prevented by 12 Senators . . . who refuse us an opportunity to vote." When Robinson presented the statement, signed by seventy-five senators favoring the bill, Minnesota Senator Moses E. Clapp responded angrily,

I think it is unfair and unjust to men who have no purpose to delay this bill, who have sat here for over 24 hours seeking to get an opportunity to make a fair speech upon this question, to put them in the attitude of being responsible for delaying the bill, when the fact is we have not had an opportunity to speak upon the bill.

Clapp accused the majority party of displacing the bill "time and again" since it came "into the Senate Friday afternoon," thus denying senators the opportunity "of presenting their views to the Senate and to the country."[31] In his opinion, the bill represented "a step along that pathway which has wrecked every great republic." In fact, the nation was "so thoroughly today in the hands of commercialism that we propose to lend ourselves to a war for commercialism."[32]

Senator Harry Lane of Oregon deplored the "round robin," which had been signed

Senator George Norris helped to filibuster the 1917 Armed Ship bill.

by seventy-five senators. In his opinion, the statement had "caused a good deal of bitterness" and "left a bad taste in the mouths of some of those who signed it, as well as those who did not sign it," since its purpose was "to coerce" senators into supporting the legislation.[33]

Senator Norris gained the floor at 7:45 a.m. on March 4. Rejecting the charge that a filibuster was in progress, he stated: "[I]t seems to me it comes with poor grace to say, 'You are filibustering,' when the very means used in a filibuster have never been resorted to. You have had at least a dozen unanimous-consent agreements to expedite business during the night." Noting that there were "just five Senators on the Democratic side of the Chamber," Norris asserted, "if there were a filibuster . . . the Sergeant at Arms

would be scurrying around over the city, arresting Senators and bringing them in here. . . ." "Everybody concedes" an extra session to be "absolutely necessary," Norris declared, asking, "what is the great importance of hasty action on this legislation?"[34]

Expressing opposition to the bill, Norris said, "it abdicates our power; it gives to the President in effect the right to make war. . . . Do we want to surrender to the Executive the power that is ours under the Constitution?" Norris then quoted from *Constitutional Government: A Study in American Politics*, by none other than Woodrow Wilson himself:

Members of Congress ought not to be censured too severely, however, when they fail to check evil courses on the part of the Executive. They have been denied the means of doing so promptly and with effect. . . .

It is the proper duty of a representative body to look diligently into every affair of government and to talk much about what it sees.

Quoting further from Wilson's doctoral dissertation, Norris drove home the necessity for thorough discussion within the legislative body:

Unless Congress have and use every means of acquainting itself with the acts . . . of the administrative agents of the Government, the country must be helpless to learn how it is being served; and unless Congress both scrutinize these things and sift them by every form of discussion the country must remain in embarrassing, crippling ignorance of the very affairs which it is most important that it should understand and direct.[35]

As the hours of morning wore on, the filibuster shifted from the opposition to the proponents of the bill. With the noon hour approaching, Hitchcock sought to secure unanimous consent for a vote, but La Follette, who had been unable to get the floor, vowed to object to a vote until he was allowed to speak. According to Franklin Burdette, angry Democrats, realizing the futility of trying to reach a vote, "determined to talk themselves rather than give [La Follette] an opportunity to speak before crowded galleries in the final hours of the session."[36] At 11:43 a.m., Hitchcock made one final request to vote at 11:45. When La Follette objected, Hitchcock put in a quorum call to chew up additional time. The few remaining minutes of the session were spent in wrangling, with Hitchcock obstinately holding the floor against La Follette's vigorous protests. The clock struck twelve, the session ended, and the Armed Ship bill was dead.[37]

The bill's failure stimulated a great public outcry, which associated the Senate's right to free and unlimited debate with treason. President Wilson, on March 4, 1917, angrily responded to the Senate's action by making one of the most notable of presidential attacks on the Senate and its procedures. He said, in part:

The termination of the last session of the Sixty-fourth Congress by constitutional limitation discloses a situation unparalleled in the history of the country, perhaps unparalleled in the history of any modern government. In the immediate presence of a crisis fraught with more subtle and far-reaching possibilities of national danger than any other the government has known within the whole history of its international relations, the Congress has been unable to act either to safeguard the country or to vindicate the elementary rights of its citizens. More than five hundred of the five hundred and thirty-one members of the two houses were ready and anxious to act; the House of Representatives had acted by an overwhelming majority; but the Senate was unable to act because a little group of eleven Senators had determined that it should not.

The Senate has no rules by which debate can be limited or brought to an end, no rules by which dilatory tactics of any kind can be prevented. A single member can stand in the way of action if he have but the physical endurance. The result in this case is a complete paralysis alike of the legislative and of the executive branches of the government.

The inability of the Senate to act has rendered some of the most necessary legislation of the session impossible, at a time when the need for it was most pressing and most evident. . . . It would not cure the difficulty to call the Sixty-fifth Congress in extraordinary session. The paralysis of the Senate would remain. . . . The Senate cannot act unless its leaders can obtain unanimous consent. Its majority is powerless, helpless. . . .

Although as a matter of fact, the nation and the representatives of the nation stand back of the Executive with unprecedented unanimity and spirit, the impression made abroad will, of course, be that it is not so and that other governments may act as they please without fear that this government can do anything at all. We cannot explain. The explanation is incredible. The Senate of the United States is the only legislative body in the world which cannot act when its majority is ready for action. *A little group of willful men*, representing no opinion but their own, have rendered the great government of the United States helpless and contemptible.

The remedy? There is but one remedy. The only remedy is that the rules of the Senate shall be so altered that it can act. The country can be relied upon to draw the moral. I believe the Senate can be relied on to supply the means of action and save the country from disaster.[38]

Even before the filibuster which killed the Armed Ship bill, the president had planned to call the Senate into special session to deal with a pending treaty. Nonetheless, when the Senate met in extraordinary session the day following Wilson's inauguration, there was only one item of business on its members' minds: the cloture rule. Professor Thomas W. Ryley in his book, *A Little Group of Willful Men*, noted that, at the time, most senators did not want to undermine the filibuster, as many of them had taken advantage of it in the past, but "with an aroused public, there was almost as much resentment over the filibuster as there was over the fact that American rights had not been defended to the utmost." According to Ryley, when the president announced that the rules of the Senate would have to be revised before he would call a special session of the entire Congress to deal with the war emergency, "the fate of unlimited debate was sealed."[39]

The principal responsibility for the cloture resolution rested with the new Democratic majority leader, Thomas Martin of Virginia. Under his guidance, a bipartisan committee of the Senate's leaders drew up a proposal providing that a vote by two-thirds of those present and voting could invoke cloture on a pending measure. Under the new rule, cloture would begin with submission of a petition signed by sixteen members, followed two days later by a vote. If the requisite two-thirds approved the proposal, each senator could thereafter speak for a maximum of one hour, and no amendments could be made except by unanimous consent. Even if this rule had been in effect at the time of the Armed Ship bill filibuster, however, it could not have saved the measure, for the amount of time required under the procedure was greater than that remaining in the life of that Congress.

It was clear from the beginning of the March 1917 debate that the rule would pass by an overwhelming margin. But, as Burdette observed, senators were wary and cautious. "Public outcry against the Armed Ship filibuster might change the precedents of more than a century, but it should not be allowed to sweep them altogether away. Free speech in the Senate should still be the rule and cloture the exception." There were those who advocated cloture by a majority, but they were overridden by Democrats and Republicans who desired a more prudent change in the rules governing unlimited debate. Senate leaders would act to "curb filibustering, but drastic action they would not support."[40]

I think it is useful, in light of subsequent developments and considering the overstated nature of President Wilson's attacks on the Senate, to look at the arguments of the proposed rule's three lone opponents.

Illinois Senator Lawrence Sherman had been an avowed supporter of the Armed Ship bill. He took the position, nonetheless, that President Wilson's attack was unfair. On March 8, 1917, he declared: "There is in the memory of no person now having a seat in the Senate, delayed action or a filibuster which destroyed meritorious legislation, save during the last few weeks of the short (second) session, when Congress automatically adjourns on the succeeding fourth day of March of that year. . . . There is a limitation," he continued, "where mere exhaustion applies the cure. It is always in the power of the Senate to apply the remedy by continuous sessions, except the last few days named." Sherman argued that the rules were to be made "the scapegoat for the deficiencies of human nature," and that their amendment had been raised "solely for the purpose of breaking down the rule of the Senate and riveting Executive control on the Senate as firmly as on the House." Senator Sherman's basic point was that, if the administration had sent the bill in "due time, it would not have been possible," in his words, "for those senators to have defeated it by delaying a roll call until the adjournment." [41]

A second opponent, Senator La Follette, also took issue with the practice of holding important bills, such as appropriations measures, in committee until the eleventh hour in order to build up pressure for their speedy and uncritical consideration and passage. As the debate on the cloture rule was drawing to a close, La Follette presented a classic statement in defense of unlimited debate. He argued:

Mr. President, believing that I stand for democracy, for the liberties of the people of this country, for the perpetuation of our free institutions, I shall stand while I am a Member of this body against any cloture that denies free and unlimited debate. Sir, the moment that the majority imposes the restriction contained in the pending rule upon this body, that moment you will have dealt a blow to liberty, you will have broken down one of the greatest weapons against wrong and oppression that the Members of this body possess. This Senate is the only place in our system where, no matter what may be the organized power behind any measure to rush its consideration and to compel its adoption, there is a chance to be heard, where there is opportunity to speak at length, and where, if need be, under the Constitution of our country and the rules as they stand today, the constitutional right is reposed in a Member of this body to halt a Congress or a session on a piece of legislation which may undermine the liberties of the people and be in violation of the Constitution which Senators have sworn to support. When you take that power away from the Members of this body, you let loose in a democracy forces that in the end will be heard elsewhere, if not here. [42]

The third opponent, Senator Asle Gronna, complained that he had not been afforded the opportunity to speak on the Armed Ship bill. "The Senator [Hitchcock] having that bill in charge took up nearly all the time and

even refused to yield for questions. He occupied an hour and three-quarters . . . in denunciation of those who stood ready to carry out their honest beliefs." As to the proposed cloture rule, Gronna said that he did not wish "to do anything that will even have the slightest tendency to destroy in the smallest degree the liberty and freedom of this great Government of ours," concerning which he passionately declared, "too much precious blood has been shed to establish it; too many lives were sacrificed to perpetuate it; and I shall not by any act of mine do anything that will cause any disturbance or that will have the least tendency to destroy it as a democracy." Referring to those who spoke unkindly of the opponents of the Armed Ship legislation, Gronna exclaimed, "Forgive them, for they know not what they do!" [43]

By a vote of 76 to 3, on March 8, 1917, after only six hours of debate, the Senate adopted its first cloture rule.

In the months that followed, the United States entered World War I, and, during the second session of the Sixty-fifth Congress, the Senate broke all previous records by remaining in session for 354 days between December 1917 and the following November. By the time the war had ended in November 1918, it was becoming clear that the cloture rule was not going to be effective. Several months earlier, Senator Oscar Underwood of Alabama, soon to become the Democratic floor leader, introduced a resolution reestablishing the use of the "previous question" and limiting debate during the wartime period. The Rules Committee favorably reported the Underwood resolution, but it failed of passage by a vote of 34 to 41.

A year later, on November 15, 1919, the Senate adopted its first cloture motion and, four days later, brought to an end the fifty-five-day debate on the Treaty of Versailles.

In the years that followed, however, cloture was used only sparingly. From 1919

Senators Asle Gronna, *left*, and Lawrence Sherman, *right*, opposed adoption of the Senate's cloture rule.
State Historical Society of North Dakota and Library of Congress

through 1962, the Senate voted on cloture petitions on twenty-seven occasions and invoked cloture just four times.

On November 29, 1922, the Senate's Republican whip, Charles Curtis of Kansas, tried a new approach to limit debate. In the midst of a four-day filibuster against an antilynching bill, Democratic Leader Underwood, who supported that filibuster, moved to adjourn immediately upon the convening of the Senate. Curtis then raised a point of order that the motion was dilatory. He said, "I know we have no rule of the Senate with reference to dilatory motions. We are a legislative body, and we are here to do business and not retard business." He then observed that "it is a well-settled principle that in any legislative body where the rules do not cover questions that may arise, general parliamen-

tary rules must apply." He argued that in the House, Speaker Reed had ruled, in the absence of rules to the contrary, that dilatory motions were out of order. Vice President Calvin Coolidge, in the chair at the time, declined to rule on Curtis' specific point of order. Today, except in cases where the Senate is operating under the cloture rule, the rules and precedents do not specifically prohibit dilatory motions as such.[44]

One of the most notable of the earlier campaigns to devise an effective debate limitation rule began here in the Senate chamber on March 4, 1925. The occasion was the inaugural address of the new vice president, Charles Dawes. By that time, Dawes had already earned a reputation as an effective administrator due to his successful banking career and his service as the first director of

Vice President Charles Dawes in 1925 pressed for stricter Senate rules to control debate.

Library of Congress

the Budget Bureau. A man of commanding personality, the vice president was often called by his campaign nickname of "Hell an' Maria," one of his favorite expressions. During his term of office, Dawes participated more actively in the Senate's business than most of his predecessors.

Vice President Dawes began his activist role with a statement that shocked the assembled senators. He told them that it was his duty as their presiding officer "to call attention to defective methods in the conduct of (the Senate's) business." Accordingly, he observed that the existing cloture rule, "which at times enables Senators to consume in oratory those last precious minutes of a session needed for momentous decisions, places in the hands of one, or of a minority of senators, a greater power than the veto power exercised under the Constitution by the President of the United States, which is limited in its effectiveness by the necessity of an affirmative two-thirds vote." Filled with indignation, the vice president assaulted his audience with a barrage of rhetorical questions: *"Who would dare,"* he asked:

to contend that under the spirit of democratic government the power to kill legislation providing the revenues to pay the expenses of government should, during the last few days of a session, ever be in the hands of a minority, or perhaps one senator? . . . *Who would dare* oppose any changes in the rules necessary to insure that the business of the United States should always be conducted in the interests of the Nation and never be in danger of encountering a situation where one man or a minority of men might demand unreasonable concessions under threat of blocking the business of the Government? *Who would dare* maintain that in the last analysis the right of the Senate itself to act should ever be subordinated to the right of one senator to make a speech? [45]

On the following day, Senator Underwood introduced a resolution to replace the 1917 cloture rule. The proposed provisions, which harkened back to the original 1789 rule on the "previous question," were as follows:

1. There shall be a motion for the previous question which, being ordered by a majority of Senators voting, if a quorum be present, shall have the effect to cut off all debate and bring the Senate to a direct vote upon the immediate question or questions on which it has been asked and ordered. The previous question may be asked and ordered upon a single motion, a series of motions allowable under the rules, or an amendment or amendments, or may be made to embrace all authorized motions or amendments and include the bill to its passage or rejection. It shall be in order, pending the motion for, or after the previous question shall have been ordered on its passage, for the Presiding Officer to entertain and submit a motion to commit, with or without instructions, to a standing or select committee.

2. All motions for the previous question shall, before being submitted to the Senate, be seconded by a majority by tellers, if demanded.

3. When a motion for the previous question has been seconded, it shall be in order, before final vote is taken thereon, for each Senator to debate the propositions to be voted upon for one hour. [46]

To build support for his reform campaign, Vice President Dawes set out on a cross-country tour. In the spirit of his great-great-grandfather, William Dawes, who rode with Paul Revere on that fateful night in 1775 to warn of the impending arrival of British troops, Charles Dawes sought to sound the alarm against the dangers he perceived in the Senate's rules.

At one stop, in Boston, the vice president addressed a gathering on this subject. In the presence of Massachusetts Senator William Butler, he asked that those in the audience who favored a rules change stand up in order to make their views known to their senator. As the supportive cheers died down, the vice president literally pulled the embarrassed senator from his chair, exclaiming, "I want to hear what Senator Butler has to say about this." The freshman senator quickly observed that he was in favor of a reform of the Senate's rules, particularly the seniority rule.[47]

Several weeks later, Vice President Dawes announced that he intended to take his campaign to Kansas, home of Senate Republican floor leader Charles Curtis. There he promised to hold a "monster mass meeting," and he expressed the hope that the senator would be present to see his constituents "react." Senator Curtis, who was also chairman of the Rules Committee, told a reporter that he thought the Dawes-Underwood proposal stood little chance, even though he was willing to support it. Recalling his own earlier efforts to achieve majority or three-fifths cloture, Senator Curtis reminded the vice president that he had been able to find only two other Republican senators willing to join him in support of such a proposal. The Kansas senator correctly predicted that the Dawes campaign would fail.[48]

Later in 1925, Democratic Leader Joseph Robinson, joining members on both sides of the aisle, argued that no change in the rules was "necessary to prevent irrelevant debate." He noted that general parliamentary practice "contemplates that a speaker shall limit his remarks to the subject under consideration," and he called on the chair to require that debate be germane. (Prior to 1964, there was no rule requiring germaneness of debate, and the chair had ruled on numerous occasions that there was no requirement for debate to be germane.)[49]

Although executive branch reorganization acts in 1939 and 1945 contained provisions limiting debate to ten hours, equally divided between supporters and opponents, they applied only in the case of a concurrent resolution disapproving a presidential reorganization plan. The language of those statutes acknowledged the constitutional right of the Senate to change this requirement "at any time in the same manner and to the same extent as in the case of any other (Senate) rule." Later extensions of the Reorganization Act included similar limitations on debate.

By 1948, a series of rulings over the years had rendered the 1917 cloture rule almost worthless, particularly those rulings that held that it could not be applied to debate on procedural questions. On August 2 of that year, President pro tempore Arthur Vandenberg sustained a point of order against a petition to close debate on a motion to consider an anti-poll-tax bill. In doing so, he declared that, in the final analysis, the Senate had no cloture rule at all. He noted that "a small but determined minority can always prevent cloture under the existing rules." At that point, the Republican Conference appointed a committee of ten senators to recommend revision of the existing cloture rule.[50]

In 1949, control of the Senate returned to the Democratic party. Fresh from his surprise election victory, President Harry S. Truman sought to clear the way for a broad civil rights program, and his first step was to push for a liberalization of the cloture rule. His efforts produced a bitter battle at the beginning of the Eighty-first Congress.

After lengthy hearings in the Rules Committee, the majority leader, Scott Lucas of Illinois, moved on February 28 to take up the resolution. This action set off a filibuster

Senator Clinton Anderson contended that the Senate had the right to adopt a new set of rules at the beginning of each Congress. *Library of Congress*

which ran until March 15, when it was voluntarily halted. After three days of further debate, the Senate adopted a compromise measure that proved to be less usable than the one it replaced. It required that two-thirds of the *entire* Senate vote for cloture, rather than two-thirds of those present and voting. The new rule differed from the old in that it allowed cloture to operate on any pending business or motion with the exception of debate on motions to change the Senate rules themselves. Previously, the cloture rule had been applicable to those motions. This meant that future efforts to change the cloture rule would themselves be subject to extended debate without benefit of the cloture provision. Previously, under

the old rule, debate limitation on a rules change had at least been theoretically possible. This change led critics of the revised rule to develop a new strategy, which became apparent in 1953, at the beginning of the Eighty-third Congress.

At the opening of that Congress, opponents of unlimited debate argued that the Senate was not a continuing body. According to the Rules Committee's history of the cloture rule, they relied on a claim by Montana Senator Thomas Walsh in 1917 that "each new Congress brings with it a new Senate, entitled to consider and adopt its own rules." They planned "to move for consideration of new rules on the first day of the session and, upon the adoption of this motion, to propose that all the old rules be adopted with the exception of Rule XXII. Rule XXII was to be changed to allow a majority of all senators (49) to limit debate after 14 days of discussion." On January 3, 1953, Senator Clinton Anderson of New Mexico moved that the Senate begin considering the adoption of rules for the Senate of the Eighty-third Congress. Ohio Senator Robert Taft moved to table the Anderson motion. During the ensuing debate, Senator Paul Douglas of Illinois explained the advantages of the Anderson proposal over the existing system. He pointed out that the 1949 rule "ties our hands once the Senate is fully organized. . . . For under it any later proposal to alter the rules can be filibustered and never be permitted to come to a vote. . . . Therefore, if it be permanently decided that the rules of the preceding Senate apply automatically as the new Senate organizes, we may as well say farewell to any chance either for Civil Rights legislation or needed changes in Senate procedure." [51]

Opponents of the Anderson motion contended that the Senate is a "continuing body," bound by the rules of earlier Senates. To support their argument, they pointed out:

(1) Only one-third of the Senate is elected every two years.

(2) The Constitution did not provide for the adoption of new rules every two years.

(3) If the Senate had had the power to adopt new rules, it had lost that power through disuse.

(4) The Supreme Court . . . had decided that the Senate was a "continuing body."

The Anderson motion was finally tabled by a vote of 70 to 21, on January 7, 1953.[52]

On January 3, 1957, Senator Anderson moved, at the beginning of the Eighty-fifth Congress, to consider the adoption of new rules. On a motion by Senate Majority Leader Lyndon Johnson, the Anderson motion was tabled by a roll-call vote of 55 to 38. During the debate, however, Vice President Richard Nixon said that, in "the opinion of the Chair," although the Senate rules had been continued from one Congress to another, "the right of a current majority of the Senate at the beginning of a new Congress to adopt its own rules . . . cannot be restricted or limited by rules adopted by a majority of the Senate in a previous Congress." He said that, in his opinion, the current Senate could not be bound by any previous rule "which denies the membership of the Senate the power to exercise its constitutional right to make its own rules." Nixon stated his belief that the section of Rule XXII forbidding limitation of debate on proposals to change the rules was unconstitutional. He noted, however, that only the Senate could officially determine the constitutionality of the rule.[53]

During the Eighty-fifth Congress, in 1957 and 1958, eight resolutions were introduced to amend the cloture rule. At the beginning of the Eighty-sixth Congress, Senate Majority Leader Johnson offered, and the Senate adopted by a 72 to 22 roll-call vote, a resolution to amend Senate Rule XXII. Approved on January 12, 1959, after four days of debate, the resolution permitted two-thirds

of the senators present and voting to close debate, even on proposals for rules changes. It also added to Rule XXII, "The rules of the Senate shall continue from one Congress to the next Congress unless they are changed as provided in these rules."[54]

As a way to expedite business, the Senate, in 1964, adopted a requirement that debate be germane to the business before the Senate during certain hours of each day's session. Known today as the "Pastore Rule," this important innovation was proposed in a resolution introduced on February 19, 1963, by Senator John O. Pastore of Rhode Island. The Rules Committee held hearings and reported the resolution with amendments reducing the period of germane debate from four hours to three, limiting the germaneness requirement to only one period "on any calendar day," and preserving the practice of permitting nongermane amendments (except on appropriation bills, which continued to require amendments to be germane).[55] On January 10, 1964, the committee amendments were adopted en bloc without debate. That same day, Senator Pastore offered an amendment, which was agreed to, clarifying his intent that the resolution apply only to debate and not to the germaneness of amendments. He explained the need for some limitation on free-wheeling debate, saying:

It is incompatible with orderly, constructive procedure for a Senator who happens to have prepared a press release which he wishes to make public, in order to meet the newspaper deadlines, to proceed, in the Senate Chamber, to recite and discuss his press release while many other Senators wait to participate in the debate on the business pending before the Senate. Sometimes such interruptions occur hour after hour, while individual Senators talk about many other subjects, ranging perhaps from the price of eggs to conditions on the Great Lakes.[56]

Senator Everett Dirksen of Illinois was among those senators who opposed the rules change. His concern was shared by several of his colleagues, when he said that he had "great pride in the freedom of expression in the Senate" and that, if the adoption of the resolution did not "bring about what its sponsors hope it will achieve," they would "seek further modification of the rules in order to bring it about." The resolution was adopted, as amended, on January 23, 1964, by a vote of 57 to 25.[57]

Today, the provision constitutes paragraph 1(b) of Rule XIX of the standing rules. Although it has not had the effect on Senate debate that either its proponents had hoped or its detractors had feared, it, nevertheless, represented a useful change in the rules.

Efforts to amend the cloture rule failed again in the Eighty-eighth and Eighty-ninth congresses. On January 11, 1967, Senator George McGovern of South Dakota introduced a resolution providing for three-fifths of the senators present and voting to end debate. According to the Senate's published history of the cloture rule:

On January 18, Senator McGovern proposed that the Senate immediately vote to end debate on the motion to consider his resolution and if a majority vote occurred, the Senate would then debate the resolution itself. Mr. McGovern justified this procedure by arguing that the Senate under the Constitution could at the beginning of a new session, adopt new rules by a majority vote. Senator Dirksen raised a point of order against the McGovern motion. . . .

Supporters of McGovern had hoped for a favorable ruling from Vice President Humphrey, but Humphrey stated: ". . . the precedent, . . . namely, that the Chair has submitted constitutional questions to the Senate for its decision—the Presiding Officer believes to be a sound procedure. It has not been considered the proper role of the Chair to interpret the Constitution for the Senate. Each Senator takes his own obligation when he takes his oath of office to support and defend the Constitution. The Presiding Officer is aware of no sufficient justification for reversing this procedure."

Humphrey then asked the Senate if the point of order should be sustained. He also said this question was debatable but subject to a tabling motion, which is not debatable; whereupon McGovern moved to table the Dirksen point of order.[58]

According to the vice president, if the Senate had adopted the tabling motion, it would have acknowledged that the McGovern motion was constitutional, meaning that the Senate had the right to adopt new rules by majority vote at the beginning of a new Congress. The Senate, however, rejected McGovern's tabling motion by a 37 to 61 roll-call vote and then sustained Dirksen's point of order by a 59 to 37 roll-call vote. The Senate thus determined that McGovern's motion was unconstitutional. A subsequent attempt to invoke cloture failed.[59]

At the opening of the Ninety-first Congress, in 1969, those who sought to alter Rule XXII tried a different approach. Senators Frank Church of Idaho and James Pearson of Kansas introduced a resolution providing that cloture could be invoked by three-fifths, rather than two-thirds, of those present and voting. In order to succeed, their plan would need a ruling by Vice President Humphrey that cloture required only a simple majority when a rules change was being considered at the opening of a new Congress. On January 14, 1969, following the procedure outlined in Rule XXII, Senator Church and twenty-four other senators filed a cloture motion on the motion to consider the resolution. Senator Church then asked the chair whether a cloture vote by a majority of the senators present and voting—but less than the two-thirds required by Rule XXII—would be sufficient.

Church contended that requiring a two-thirds vote for cloture on a rules change was unconstitutional, because it restricted the right of a majority of the Senate, under the Constitution, to determine its rules at the beginning of a new Congress.

The vice president agreed, declaring, "On a par with the right of the Senate to determine its rules, though perhaps not set forth so specifically in the Constitution, is the right of the Senate, a simple majority of the Senate, to decide constitutional questions." Humphrey continued:

If a majority . . . but less than two-thirds, of those present and voting, vote in favor of this cloture motion, the question whether the motion has been agreed to is a constitutional question. The constitutional question is the validity of the Rule XXII requirement for an affirmative vote by two-thirds of the Senate before a majority of the Senate may exercise its right to consider a proposed change in the rules. If the Chair were to announce that the motion for cloture had not been agreed to because the affirmative vote had fallen short of the two-thirds required, the Chair would not only be violating one established principle by deciding the constitutional question himself, he would be violating the other established principle by inhibiting, if not effectively preventing, the Senate from exercising its right to decide the constitutional question. . . .

. . . the Chair informs the Senate that in order to give substance to the right of the Senate to determine or change its rules and to determine whether the two-thirds requirement of Rule XXII is an unconstitutional inhibition on that right at the opening of a new Congress, if a majority of the Senators present and voting but fewer than two-thirds, vote in favor of the pending motion for cloture, the Chair will announce that a majority having agreed to limit debate on Senate Resolution 11, to amend Rule XXII, at the opening of a new Congress, debate will proceed under the cloture provisions of that rule.[60]

Two days later, the Senate voted 51 to 47 to invoke cloture. Although the vice president ruled that cloture had been invoked by the majority vote, his decision was appealed and reversed by the Senate on a roll-call vote of 45 to 53. The Senate subsequently failed to achieve the necessary two-thirds vote to invoke cloture.

At the opening of the Ninety-second Congress, Senators Church and Pearson introduced a resolution to reduce the number of senators required to curtail debate from two-thirds to three-fifths of those present and voting. They again hoped the chair would rule that a simple majority was sufficient to invoke cloture on a rules change at the beginning of a new Congress. Vice President Spiro Agnew, however, preferred to refer such questions to the full Senate for its decision. The proponents of the Church-Pearson resolution, therefore, had to comply with the two-thirds requirement they hoped to change.

Attempts to invoke cloture failed, and debate on the motion to consider the resolution dragged on for six weeks in spite of efforts by a number of senators to achieve a compromise. Louisiana Senator Allen Ellender, for example, suggested that a three-fifths vote be allowed to end debate on conference reports and appropriation bills. I was majority whip at the time and suggested that cloture be invoked by three-fifths of all senators. Subsequent efforts to close debate, on March 2 and March 9, failed to achieve the necessary two-thirds, by votes of 48 to 36 and 55 to 39, respectively. Appealing the decision of the presiding officer, Allen Ellender, that the cloture attempt had failed to receive the necessary two-thirds majority, Senator Jacob Javits of New York again contended that the Senate could alter its rules by a simple majority at the beginning of a new Congress. Majority Leader Mike Mansfield successfully moved to table Senator Javits' appeal.

At the beginning of the first session of the Ninety-fourth Congress, Senator Pearson joined with Minnesota Senator Walter Mondale in sponsoring an attempt to change the cloture rule to enable three-fifths of the senators present and voting to invoke cloture. Once more, the strategy would need a ruling by the chair that debate could be closed by a simple majority on a rules change at the opening of a Congress. Senator Pearson made a lengthy multiple-part motion that the Senate proceed to consider the resolution, and that

under article I, section 5, of the U.S. Constitution, I move that debate upon the pending motion to proceed to the consideration of Senate Resolution 4 be brought to a close by the Chair immediately putting this motion to end debate to the Senate for a yea-and-nay vote; and, upon the adoption thereof by a majority of those Senators present and voting, a quorum being present, the Chair shall immediately thereafter put to the Senate, without further debate, the question on the adoption of the pending motion to proceed to the consideration of Senate Resolution 4.[61]

Senator Mansfield raised a point of order against the motion, because it prescribed an end to debate by a majority vote. Vice President Nelson Rockefeller submitted the Mansfield point of order to the Senate for its decision. When the Senate voted 51 to 42 to table the point of order, it was, in effect, endorsing the doctrine that cloture may be invoked by a majority to change Senate rules at the start of a Congress.

Senator James Allen of Alabama then moved that the motion be divided, since it contained distinct and separate clauses. The effect of Allen's motion was to permit debate on the individual parts of the motion, which could not be debated when considered as a whole. Amendments and intervening motions followed, so that, as the Rules Committee's history pointed out, "Although the principle of majority cloture had been [temporarily] endorsed, the parliamentary tangle which followed division of the motion prevented a majority cloture vote from being taken on the original Pearson resolution."[62]

During the debate, Senator Russell Long of Louisiana offered to compromise on a constitutional three-fifths cloture rule. I, therefore, introduced a resolution on February 28, providing that debate in the Senate be closed by a vote of "three-fifths of the senators duly chosen and sworn," except in the case of a measure or motion to change

the rules of the Senate, when a two-thirds vote of "senators present and voting" would be required to close debate. I requested immediate consideration of this resolution, but, in response to an objection, the resolution was held over.[63]

On March 3, 1975, the Senate voted to reconsider its February 20 action tabling Mansfield's point of order; rejected the motion to table the point of order; and, the next day, sustained the Mansfield point of order by a vote of 53 to 43. By this action, as the Rules Committee's published history stated, the Senate "erased the precedent of majority cloture established two weeks before, and reaffirmed the 'continuous' nature of the Senate rules."[64]

Also on March 3, I entered a cloture motion on the motion to consider the Mondale-Pearson resolution. Two days later, the Senate invoked cloture by a vote of 73 to 21—an affirmative vote by more than two-thirds of the senators present and voting—and voted 69 to 26 to consider the Mondale-Pearson resolution. The Senate then adopted the resolution that I had introduced on February 28 as an amendment in the nature of a substitute. I subsequently introduced a motion to close debate on the resolution as amended, and, on March 7, the Senate voted 73 to 21 for cloture. The same day, the Senate adopted my substitute providing that three-fifths of all senators chosen and sworn could invoke cloture. This provision applied to all measures except those amending the rules of the Senate, which still required a two-thirds vote of the senators present and voting.[65]

Four years later, on February 22, 1979, the Senate agreed to a resolution I introduced establishing a cap of one hundred hours of consideration once cloture had been invoked on a measure. When that time expired, the Senate would proceed to the final disposition of the measure or matter. Only amendments then pending and only a motion to table, a motion to reconsider, and motions necessary to establish a quorum were then in order.[66]

Under the resolution, each senator would be entitled to one hour of time. Senators could yield their time to the majority or minority floor managers of the bill, or to the majority or minority leaders. Except by unanimous consent, none of the designated four senators could have more than two additional hours yielded to him or her. These senators, in turn, could yield their time to other senators. If all available time expired, a senator who had not yielded time, and who had not yet spoken on the matter on which cloture had been invoked, could be recognized for ten minutes for the sole purpose of debate.

The resolution, as adopted, provided that no senator could call up more than two amendments until every other senator had had the opportunity to call up two amendments. The resolution was amended by Senator Ted Stevens of Alaska to provide that, after cloture was invoked, the reading of amendments would be waived routinely if they were available in printed form to members "for not less than twenty-four hours."

The former cloture rule made in order amendments introduced prior to the completion of the cloture vote. The 1979 resolution made in order only those first degree amendments submitted by 1 p.m. of the day following submission of a cloture motion, with second degree amendments (amendments to amendments) in order only if submitted in writing one hour prior to the beginning of the cloture vote.

In January 1985, I introduced a resolution relative to television broadcasts of Senate debates. In my resolution, I suggested a number of rules changes, one of which was to substitute a twenty-hour post-cloture time limitation for the one-hundred-hour cap. In October, the Rules Committee ordered the resolution reported to the Senate with all provisions stricken that did not relate directly to the issue of television in the Senate. In February 1986, the resolution was laid before the Senate and debated for several days. On February 20, the Senate adopted a motion to recommit the resolution to the Rules Committee with instructions to report back forthwith the twenty-hour post-cloture cap and other provisions contained in my original resolution. One week later, on February 27, 1986, Majority Leader Bob Dole, Rules Committee Chairman Charles Mathias, other senators, and I offered a leadership amendment in the nature of a substitute. That same day, the Senate adopted this amendment; it then agreed to the resolution as amended, by a roll-call vote of 67 to 21.[67] The substitute amendment contained the current overall limitation of "thirty hours of consideration" after cloture has been invoked. The thirty hours may be increased by a nondebatable motion adopted by an affirmative vote of three-fifths of the senators duly chosen and sworn. The amendment also provided that, after cloture, the reading of the *Journal* could be waived by majority vote on a nondebatable motion.[68]

Mr. President, the current cloture rule is the product of decades of trial and experience aimed at curbing the extremes in the use of filibusters to block Senate action. It has discouraged—though not eliminated—post-cloture filibusters and has also provided a more effective tool in overcoming all but the most determined filibusters carried on by a sizable minority. Its effectiveness is aided greatly by the strengthening precedents that have been established over the past century, some of which antedate the first cloture rule in 1917.

Filibusters, 1917–1964

Mr. President, the adoption of the cloture rule in March 1917 did not spell the end for filibusters. From 1917 through 1963, the Senate invoked cloture on only five occasions. And in the thirty-four years between 1927 and 1962, despite fourteen efforts, no cloture motion succeeded.

In 1919, a fierce controversy over the Treaty of Versailles resulted in the adoption of cloture for the first time. After many weeks of debate, Senator Gilbert M. Hitchcock of Nebraska, the ranking Democrat on the Foreign Relations Committee and acting Democratic leader, offered a cloture motion on November 13. Signed by twenty-three senators, that motion provided that the "debate upon the pending conditions and reservations proposed by Senator Lodge . . . and all substitutes, amendments, and additions thereto proposed, be brought to a close." [1] Two days later, in the debate preceding the cloture vote, Hitchcock stated that he had "made a computation of the space occupied by each Senator in the [_Congressional_] _Record_ during September and October in discussing the treaty," and "the supporters of the treaty during those two months" had consumed "27 per cent of the time" while the opponents had "consumed 73 per cent of the time." [2] The cloture motion was adopted by a vote of 78 to 16, [3] but the debate continued until November 19. On that day, the Senate rejected the resolution to ratify the peace treaty with Germany by a vote of 39 to 55. A motion to reconsider the vote carried, [4] but again the Senate rejected the resolution of ratification, by a vote of 41 to 51. Senator Oscar W. Underwood of Alabama, who sought President Wilson's support in his campaign to be elected Senate Democratic leader, then moved to adopt a resolution approving the ratification of the original treaty without conditions or reservations. Massachusetts Republican Senator Henry Cabot Lodge, the Foreign Relations Committee chairman—and archfoe of the treaty—made no point of order against the Underwood resolution on condition that a vote occur immediately. The Senate rejected the resolution, 38 to 53. [5] Thus, although a cloture motion requiring a two-thirds vote had been adopted by a majority of almost 5 to 1, the ultimate question at issue—the treaty—also requiring a two-thirds vote, had failed to garner even a simple majority, with or without reservations.

Three years later, on November 27, 1922, Senator Samuel M. Shortridge of California provoked southern senators into launching a vigorous filibuster when he moved to take up federal antilynching legislation which had passed the House. [6] The following morning, Senator Pat Harrison of Mississippi, a leader of the filibuster, objected to a request that the reading of the _Journal_ be dispensed with, a request normally granted. The clerk then proceeded with the time-consuming task of reading the _Journal_. Harrison interrupted the reading to suggest the absence of a quorum, but the chair sustained a point of order that the reading could not be interrupted by a quorum call, and the chair was upheld by a 60-to-1 vote of the Senate. After the reading was concluded, Senator Harrison continued with further delaying tactics regarding the _Journal_. At one point, for example, he moved to insert in the _Journal_ the names of localities in which certain North Dakota citizens lived who had, on the previous day, petitioned their senator, praying for

Senator Pat Harrison routinely filibustered against antilynching legislation. *Library of Congress*

the enactment of legislation to stabilize wheat prices. When this motion was rejected, Underwood then candidly announced to the Senate that "we are not disguising what is being done," and "you are not going to get an agreement to vote on this bill." He was "opposed to the passage of this so-called 'force' bill," which, should it ever become law, "would be the beginning of tearing down the last fabric left in the Constitution to support the integrity of the State governments."

Democratic Minority Leader Oscar Underwood, in sympathy with his fellow southerners, then laid down an ultimatum to the majority: "There are a large number of men whose names have been sent to the Senate, who have been appointed to important offices . . . and who ought to be confirmed;

but they are not going to be confirmed; we are going to transact no more business until we have an understanding about this bill. . . . You know you can not pass it." [7] After considerable debate had occurred, the *Journal* was at last approved and the Senate adjourned.

The next day, the dilatory tactics were resumed. Senator Harrison moved to amend the *Journal* of the previous day's proceedings by inserting the prayer of the preceding day as it appeared, in full, in the *Congressional Record*. He asked, "What if a hundred years from now your great-great-great-grandchildren should look over the *Journal* of yesterday and discover that no mention is made of the fact that there was prayer yesterday in opening this body, and then they should take the proceedings of the following day . . . and should read that their great-great-great-grandfathers voted against my motion to amend the *Journal* so that the prayer might be incorporated in the *Journal*?" Harrison, with feigned piety, then answered his own question. "Why, those children of tomorrow would hang their heads in shame over the action of their ancestors." [8]

Needless to say, Senator Harrison's motion to amend the *Journal* was agreed to. Harrison then moved that the *Journal* be amended to state the exact hour on the previous day "when the President pro tempore of the Senate relinquished the chair" and "exactly at what time the Vice President resumed the chair." [9] A lengthy debate followed, the transaction of business remaining at a standstill, until the Senate adjourned over Thanksgiving Day without having approved the reading of the *Journal*. "When any considerable number of Senators are satisfied," declared North Carolina Senator Lee Overman, "and conscientiously believe that any proposed legislation is unconstitutional, that it involves the integrity of the States and the liberties of the people, and if passed would undermine the very foundation stones of this Republic . . . they are fully justified in filibustering to prevent, if possible, a militant majority from roughshodding over a strong minority." [10]

It was obvious that the Democrats would not relent in their battle against the antilynching bill. For the discouraged Republican majority, there was no way to escape surrender. A determined and sizable minority blocked the transaction of any business, and the only reasonable expedient was to set the bill aside and go on to other things. Accordingly, on Monday, December 4, Senator Lodge moved to proceed to executive business, stating that the Republican conference had instructed him to say that "they would not press the bill further at the coming session or at the session which is just expiring." [11]

A week later, on December 11, another and longer filibuster began, this time over a ship subsidy bill pushed by President Warren Harding and Republican congressional leaders. The Senate Democratic minority strongly opposed the legislation, which had passed the House by a slim majority of only twenty-four votes. Leading the fight for the bill, Commerce Committee Chairman Wesley L. Jones of Washington pushed for early passage. Democratic Leader Oscar Underwood signaled the possibility of a filibuster. He pointed out that House Republican leaders had opposed the president's desire to pass the bill before the recent November elections, fearing the defeat of many Republicans because the measure was "unpopular with the American people." Even with the delay in House action, Underwood observed, "the result was an overwhelming defeat for the champions of the measure," nearly producing "a reversal of the political control of both Houses of Congress." Now, the Republican leadership sought to rush the bill through in the remaining weeks of the

Sixty-seventh Congress, which would end on March 4, before the newly elected members could be sworn into office and register their opposition to ship subsidies. Such an action, contended Underwood, was "in virtual defiance of public sentiment" throughout the country. [12] Underwood's ally, Senator Duncan Fletcher, a Florida Democrat and ranking minority member of the Commerce Committee, then forced a reading of the bill and the accompanying committee report, which consumed more than twelve pages of the *Record*, following which the Senate adjourned until noon the next day, December 12. [13]

The Christmas holidays came and went, and other urgent legislation consumed most of the Senate's time until mid-February, when Senator Jones announced that the ship subsidy bill would be pressed and not be set aside to take up other matters. Stating that the Republican leadership had "been twitted on this floor because we have laid the bill aside from time to time," Jones explained that it had been necessary to pass appropriation bills in order "to avoid an extra session." He knew there was "a strong desire in Congress for a vacation" and that working "day after day from early morning till late at night," as members had been doing, it was "no wonder that they are worn out." Jones lamented that "no man will know how many years have been taken from his life, but," said he, "we are sure that many men have had their lives shortened by their work here." [14]

Still, the talkathon droned on, with lengthy speeches on myriad subjects. Texas Senator Morris Sheppard began a speech on the League of Nations on Monday, February 19, and resumed it the next day, speaking for nearly four hours the first day and more than six hours the next.

Reporting on the filibuster, the *New York Times* stated:

At 9:20 o'clock tonight Senator Harrison made a point of no quorum and then followed a snarl that required an hour to straighten out. As soon as the clerk began calling the roll, the Democrats went into their cloakroom. . . . Their names were repeatedly called but not one emerged from the cloakroom.[15]

Determined to break the filibuster, Senator Jones then moved that the sergeant at arms be instructed to request the attendance of absent senators. According to the *Times*, Sergeant at Arms David S. Barry entered the Democratic cloakroom and "politely requested" Senators Thaddeus Caraway of Arkansas, Ellison Smith of South Carolina, Walter George of Georgia, Smith Brookhart of Washington and others in the room to appear in the chamber. "The reply," said the *Times*, "was a unanimous but smiling refusal." Administration supporters, who had promised to hold the Senate in session all night, gave up and recessed until the next day.

By late February, there was no longer any doubt that the obstructionists could and would keep the filibuster going until sine die adjournment at noon on March 4, throttling other legislation in the process. In the face of this threat, Senator Jones and the administration forces capitulated on February 28 by moving to take up a so-called filled milk bill, thus displacing the ship subsidy bill.[16] In the words of Alabama Senator J. Thomas Heflin, the "miserable measure" had "gone to its long, last sleep." It was "already dead."[17]

The next major filibuster broke out when the World Court Protocol was before the Senate in 1926. Opponents of the Court in the Senate included many of the so-called irreconcilables, who several years earlier had helped defeat U.S. membership in the League of Nations. Now they saw the Court as a back-door means of tying the United States to the League. They contended that the Court's power to render "advisory opinions" could undermine the nation's sovereign right to make its own laws. On January 15, Senator Coleman L. Blease of South Carolina launched into a speech, warming up with a folksy apology:

Mr. President, I think if we ever have a contest in the United States to determine who is its poorest reader, that I can easily win the prize. So if any Senator has any other business to attend to I shall not consider it the slightest discourtesy if he declines to listen to my reading.[18]

Blease proceeded to read George Washington's farewell address, interspersed with Blease's own extemporaneous words of earthly wisdom. Invoking the Bible and the names of Calhoun, Webster, Hayne, Theodore Roosevelt, Wilson, Jefferson, and others, Blease entertained his colleagues by heaping scorn upon international bankers, foreign embassies, members of foreign legations, evolution, and Prohibition. Of Prohibition, Blease said that "any man who thinks this country has prohibition is an ignorant fool. . . . The only man in this country that has prohibition is the poor devil who has not the money to buy liquor, and everybody knows it."

Blease's contempt for foreign embassies was blistering as he spoke of "liquor sent over from Baltimore under protection for foreign embassies that they and their people might have a big Christmas, drink liquor, drink wine and champagne, frolic, and have dances." Senator Blease, like George Washington, was against "foreign intrigue," and that also included the "league court," whose "foreign judges are going to decide against us."[19]

Senator William E. Borah of Idaho, chairman of the Foreign Relations Committee and a determined isolationist, stated that, although he had "spoken upon the subject three times," he had not spoken at great length. He had "been here 18 years" but had "never taken part in a filibuster" and was "not going to engage in any filibuster." He and others who were opposed to adherence to a world court only wanted "to present what we believe to be substantial arguments upon the proposition," after which "we will proceed to vote." When it came to fixing a date for a vote, however, he did not want to "cramp anybody."[20]

Other senators engaged freely in the loquacious sparring. On January 22, Senator Irvine Lenroot of Wisconsin, the most senior member of the Foreign Relations Committee to support the protocol, introduced a cloture motion signed by forty-eight senators. Meanwhile, Wisconsin Senator Robert M. La Follette, Jr., asked: "Why is so much pressure being exerted to force a vote on this resolution? What is the hurry? What interests of this country will be injured by considering this step fully?" La Follette reminded his colleagues that when the question of the League of Nations was before the Senate "the same kind of false alarm as to the impatience of the public over the debate was raised by the proponents of the league as is now being raised by the proponents of this court." On that occasion, said La Follette, "President Wilson demanded immediate action. He rebuked the Senate." La Follette further recalled, "It was stated then that the people were behind the President urging prompt, unquestioning approval of his demand that we join the League of Nations." The president went to the country, said La Follette, "confident that he would win an overwhelming victory," but the Wisconsin senator doubted if there had "ever been a more striking example of mistaken judgment or a more complete reversal of political fortune in the history of this Government." La Follette alluded to certain Republicans in the chamber who "personally have great distaste" for supporting the resolution approving America's entrance into the International Court of

the League of Nations. Yet, those same Republicans, he said, were supporting the protocol "because the Harding and Coolidge administrations have sponsored it."[21]

On January 25, 1926, for only the second time since the cloture rule was adopted in 1917, the Senate, by a vote of 68 to 26, invoked cloture and, two days later, agreed to the resolution by a vote of 76 to 17.[22] It took this action, however, only after Senate supporters had accepted five reservations, including restrictions on the Court's power to render advisory opinions. (These reservations ultimately blocked U.S. adherence to the Court.) Had not the administration and the Senate Republican majority been so willing to accommodate the opposition, this cloture effort would most certainly have failed. Cloture would not be easily applied in the future to curb filibusters.

Several months later, in the spring of 1926, a filibuster was conducted against legislation for migratory bird refuges, but the bill died after an effort to invoke cloture failed. Legislation for development of the Lower Colorado River Basin suffered a similar fate when, on February 26, 1927, cloture was rejected by a vote of 32 to 59. Two days later, however, the Senate did invoke cloture on a Prohibition reorganization bill, although a final vote on the bill was delayed for almost two days by the opponents of a resolution extending the life of a committee that was investigating charges of corrupt senatorial elections in Illinois and Pennsylvania. As Franklin Burdette, author of the study of filibusters, observed, "filibusterers against one measure had been able to make cloture against another serve their purposes for nearly two days!"[23] At one point, Senator J. Thomas Heflin of Alabama—who, incidentally, was an uncle of our own colleague and friend from Alabama, Senator Howell Heflin—ridiculed "obstreperous Republican filibusters" for obstructing action on the resolution for campaign investigations. "You are saying in your hearts," he declared with fine sarcasm:

Committee, spare that campaign boodle tree,
   Touch not a single bow;
In election times it shelters me,
   You must not harm it now.[24]

The filibusterers succeeded in killing the campaign resolution, along with a host of other measures which accompanied it to the parliamentary guillotine, when adjournment came on March 4.

As in the years before 1917, filibusters were most successful just prior to the mandated March 4 adjournment of a Congress. During a filibuster in March 1929 against a bill extending the life of the Federal Radio Commission, for example, Senators Coleman L. Blease of South Carolina and Royal S. Copeland of New York spoke at length in opposition to the measure. Blease said that he did not "know much about the radio business" and that he had "been opposed to the bill and the commission ever since it started." Then he informed his colleagues that he had "noticed recently that there is a report that it is intended to put a radio in the Capitol; in fact, in this very room." That Blease's feeling toward radios was indeed less than lukewarm, could be inferred from the following inquiry he made of Copeland, "I want to ask the Senator, who is an expert on radio, if that radio is put back in the corner of the Chamber here close to my seat whether it would be possible for one of these anarchists to send something through it and blow us all out of here?" Copeland's response was that it "would be a calamity too dire to contemplate."[25]

Were not the very lives of senators being put at risk by this contraption, the radio? asked Blease. "They might fill that thing up with gas, some deadly gas," he warned, "and just about the time the crowd assembled in this Chamber [for the inauguration of Presi-

dent Herbert Hoover], everybody in control of the Government of the United States, some fellow might turn on a machine down here and just gas out the whole business."

Blease's expressed fears may have been less than totally innocent, but his dislike for the Federal Radio Commission, for radios, and for the bill was not to be doubted.[26] Blease and Copeland succeeded in having the bill modified to shorten the time extension, and the filibuster ended.

In 1932, Huey Long burst upon the Senate stage. The junior senator from Louisiana was atomic energy in the flesh! Unflappable, irrepressible, indefatigable—here was the granddaddy of all filibusterers, those who had gone before and those who were yet to come. For wit, brass, and pure showmanship, Huey Long was in a class by himself. According to Franklin Burdette, not since the days of the eccentric John Randolph, over a century past, "had the Senate been treated to such a jargon of words."[27] The "Kingfish" had arrived! And, in January 1933, when the branch banking bill was before the Senate, he gave his colleagues a foretaste of things to come.

The bill, introduced by Senator Carter Glass of Virginia, dealt with Federal Reserve banks and national banking associations and the regulation of interbank control. Long vigorously opposed provisions permitting branch banks. On January 10, he spoke at length against the bill, and, typically, subjected its provisions to the fire and brimstone of passages from the Bible, quoting from the book of Isaiah,

Woe unto them that join house to house, that lay field to field, till there be no place, that they may be placed alone in the midst of the earth!

Having thus proved that the Lord was clearly on his side, Long made his point, declaiming, "All that it is necessary to put in

A natural showman, Senator Huey Long was noted for his lively, inventive filibusters.   *U.S. Senate Historical Office*

there are the words 'banking house to banking house and woe be unto them.' " Laughter in the galleries drew an admonition from the vice president in the chair.[28]

Flaying the "5 per cent" of the rich people of the country who owned "85 per cent of the wealth" and controlled "the other 15 per cent," [29] Long invoked the book of James:

Go to now, ye rich men, weep and howl for your miseries that shall come upon you.

Your riches are corrupted, and your garments are motheaten.

Your gold and silver is cankered; and the rust of them shall be a witness against you, and shall eat your flesh as it were fire.[30]

Long left no doubt that he was for decentralization of the banking authority "to take it out of the hands of the imperialistic financial manipulators, and to put the control back among the people of this country." And, again, what better authority than the Book of James!

Behold, the hire of the labourers who have reaped down your fields, which is of you kept back by fraud, crieth: and the cries of them which have reaped are entered into the ears of the Lord of Sabaoth. [31]

Having warned the Senate of the dangers of concentrating wealth in the hands of a few, Long announced that the wealth must be distributed: "The only way we are going to be able to get the people to spend more money is to give them something to spend." But instead of remedying the situation, he said, the government was "imposing a condition that means twofold more trouble on top of what we have already." The branch banking bill would "close the door so that there will be eternal trouble with a situation that admits of no correction." [32]

The next day, Senator Long renewed his oratorical forays against the bill. At one point, he sought to have the clerk read a res-olution adopted by the Country Bankers' Association, but Senator Glass objected to the request, saying, "We so much prefer to hear the mellifluous voice of the Senator from Louisiana that I am not willing to have the harsh voice of the clerk disturb us." The president pro tempore then put the question before the Senate, which rejected the request that the clerk read the resolution. Unperturbed, Long gleefully responded to the gentle reproof:

Mr. President, I thank Senators for this great expression of fealty which they have toward having my vocal strains resound through this Chamber. . . .

I do not know of anyone who has been told in the Senate, even against his own will, that the Senate desired to hear him, as I have been here this evening. It is a compliment which I truly appreciate. I shall carry with me, in what few days or few years I have in this body, appreciation for the Senator from Virginia; but I will read the resolution myself.[33]

Later in the day, when Long had yielded the floor, Glass declared that the Senate was "confronted with the question as to whether or not it shall be permitted to legislate." He served notice that, beginning the next day, he would "ask the Senate to sit until a reasonable hour in the evening in order that we may commence a deliberate consideration of the pending bill." [34]

Finally, after a unanimous consent agreement paved the way for passage of the Glass banking bill on January 25, 1933, the filibuster ended.

Huey Long participated in several filibusters over the next two years. On May 21, 1935, he undertook to prevent passage of a resolution providing for a joint session of Congress to hear President Roosevelt deliver a veto message. In the midst of a long, rambling discourse, Long referred to the effect that the wage scale set by the president for "works-relief" projects would have in Tennessee and other southern states. Senator

Exhausted senators doze, while one of their colleagues drones on and on.   *Library of Congress*

The galleries convulsed with laughter, which drew a stern admonition from the chair. Senator Alben W. Barkley of Kentucky appealed to the chair not to be too harsh with the occupants of the galleries, observing that "when people go to the circus they ought to be allowed to laugh at the monkey."

Long, ever ready to turn the tables on an adversary, quipped, "Now, Mr. President, I resent that statement about my friend from Tennessee." [35]

After he had talked for about five hours, Senator Long suggested the absence of a quorum and left the floor, whereupon Senator Thomas Connally of Texas gained recognition and claimed the floor. Long had made a technical error by walking off and thus had lost the floor. [36] The Senate then adopted the resolution authorizing the joint session.

Senator Huey Long had already proved himself to be one of the most resourceful filibusterers that the Senate had ever known. He was a superb debater—tough, gutsy, and brilliant—and his quick wit, folksy humor, and flamboyant style made him a crowd pleaser, whether on the campaign stump or on the Senate floor. In the clinches, he asked and gave no quarter. When Huey Long debated an issue, he was always center stage. He is perhaps most celebrated for his 1935 filibuster concerning the proposed extension of the National Industrial Recovery Act.

The Supreme Court had ruled the act unconstitutional, and the resolution before the Senate proposed to extend certain provisions of the original act until April 1, 1936. Having previously passed the Senate, it had been amended by the House and was back before the Senate on Tuesday, June 11, for further amendment. Senator Thomas Gore of Oklahoma had succeeded in having an amendment adopted to require Senate confirmation for any government officials appointed by the president whose salaries exceeded $4,000

Kenneth McKellar of Tennessee took umbrage at the mention of his state's name and admonished Long to "confine himself to Louisiana" and "let Tennessee alone." Continuing, McKellar angrily charged Long with never having "had a bill passed for Louisiana or for the country since he has been here." Moreover, the fiery Tennessean doubted that Long "could even get the Lord's Prayer endorsed in this body if he undertook to do so." Long liked to call himself the Kingfish, charged McKellar, and, while "he can be the 'Kingfish' in Louisiana . . . he is not the 'kingfish' in Tennessee, and he is not the 'kingfish' in this body; and his record proves that fact." McKellar's withering blast continued: "The Senator from Louisiana has an idea that he is a candidate for President. For Heaven's sake!"

per annum. Long, who supported the Gore amendment, had moved to reconsider the vote, a normal procedure, and Gore had moved to table Long's motion so as to conclude all action on the amendment and prevent any subsequent effort to overturn the vote. Alben Barkley, however, prevented a vote on Gore's tabling motion by recessing the Senate until the next day, Wednesday, June 12.

When the Senate resumed consideration of the matter on the twelfth, the tabling motion was rejected. Debate then began on the motion to reconsider the vote on the Gore amendment. Since it was apparent that the opponents had garnered enough votes to reverse the earlier decision and defeat the amendment, Long took the floor in an effort to block reconsideration of the earlier vote approving the Gore amendment.

Referring to the Roosevelt administration, Long charged that "they are promising every man in Louisiana who will say he is against Huey P. Long a job at $300 or $400 or $500 a head." Stating that one of the "Jim Farley-Roosevelt leaders down there" was operating "a tombstone and coffin club business," and that "this thumb-rigging, screw-driving character" would promise that "if a man paid 10 cents or 25 cents or whatever it was ever so often, that when he died they would give him a decent burial. They promised him a brass band at his funeral and a coffin and a tombstone and a shroud." But, said Long, "the little bird who was running this skin game" would go out on the night after a funeral "and dig up the coffin, take out the body, take the shroud off the body, put the body in a pine box, replace it in the ground, and then pack the ground down tight over it, and put the shroud and coffin on sale again and bury another man in them the next day." Long declared, "They do not dare bring that kind of character before the United States Senate for confirmation." [37]

Long continued his harangue against the administration's appointees in his state. Singling out another target, he spoke of a "little pot-bellied character down there" who reminded him very much "of a chicken snake." No one within the sound of his voice could have avoided amusement as the hilarious Huey Long recalled that

back in the old days in the woods, how we would hear the hens squalling and the chickens raising Cain out in the backyard at night, and we would run out and take a lamp and a shotgun to see what was the matter; and, lo and behold! We would raise up the hen and there would be a chicken snake that had swallowed every egg there was in the nest, and . . . he would be so puffed out in the stomach that you could hardly see how he could crawl away from there. This chicken snake would be about 1 inch around at one end and about 1 inch around at the other end, and about 8 inches around in the middle.

Long said that the chicken snake would then "crawl through a rail fence and break the eggs, so as to get the benefit of the nutrition that is in the eggs." This "little pot-bellied politician," Long averred, had been given the right to employ several thousand people, had jurisdiction over handling several million dollars of public funds, was "getting $500 or $600 a month" and had "grown so fat and so bloated, and his stomach has become so puffed, that they will have to get a rolling Chair, if things keep on as they are, to assist him in getting about."

Of course, Long's audience could not keep from laughing. His point had been made: "They do not dare bring these characters here and allow them to be fumigated" by the United States Senate. [38]

As to "that detestable, contemptible, despicable blue-buzzard N.R.A.," Long praised the nine men on the Supreme Court who had ruled the law to be unconstitutional and, in doing so, had "saved this country from Fascism and Bolshevism." He shouted, "God save and God bless those men to render service again! For every mistake they have ever made they are entitled to a million mercies." [39]

Long went on for hours, reading the Constitution, and commenting at length on section after section and clause after clause. Suffering interruptions from other senators from time to time, he would engage them in banter, sometimes derisive, sometimes cutting, often sarcastic, and always impervious to criticism or badgering from his would-be detractors.

Long continued to cover the oratorical waterfront, eventually getting around to a discussion of some of his down-home recipes. Oysters being a favorite, he regaled the galleries with a long-winded explanation of "the way to cook oysters." Then he thoughtfully advised his colleagues that "if every Member of the Senate will clip out of the Record tomorrow what I have said today and not give it to his wife"—and here he was especially considerate of senators' spouses—"learn how to do it himself and then teach his wife—he will know how to fry oysters better than most families in Washington." It was Long's opinion that there was "no telling how many lives have been lost by not knowing how to fry oysters," there having been "many times" he had heard of "some man who was supposed to have had an acute attack of indigestion or cerebral hemorrhage or heart failure, and the chances are the only thing that was the matter with him was that he had swallowed some improperly cooked oysters." [40]

Long then revealed his "recipe for potlikker." It was made from turnip or mustard greens, but turnip greens were preferable because they contained "more manganese." Of course, there was one problem: "Sand is always in them." His instructions were, therefore, that, "to get every vestige of dirt and sand and grit out of the greens you have to wash them many, many times." Then,

after he had described the quantity of water and the amount of "salted side meat" needed, he said the greens should be cooked "until they are tender." As to the potlikker? It was the "residue that remains from the commingling, heating, and evaporation." Interrupted by laughter, Long expostulated, "anyway, it is in the bottom of the pot!" [41]

After such a rhetorical smorgasbord of subjects had been disposed of to the obvious delight of his listeners—especially those in the galleries—the senator from Louisiana shifted his attention to the Schechter poultry case, in which the NRA had been declared invalid by the court. His comments on the "chicken coop case" were a classic in the use of trenchant wit as he systematically and methodically portrayed the NRA as a colossal act of folly.

According to Long, "When this coop of chickens got to New York," a man looked into the coop and decided that he liked "that pullet right over there, that frying-size pullet," but the man in charge said, "Hold on there . . . before you pull out that pullet hold on a minute; let us get down the N.R.A. rule book and look through it and see what the rule is before you take a chicken out of the coop." So, declared Long, "they got down the rule book . . . and it said there that no man could reach into a coop of chickens and pick out any particular chicken; that he had to blindfold himself and reach in and take whichever chicken came to hand. That is in the code." When the laughter subsided, Long reminded his colleagues, "that is a part of this wonderful thing that we are sitting here to reenact . . . as soon as I get through talking." But, disregarding the NRA and its rule book, Long proclaimed, the man proceeded to get the chicken he wanted, so "they indicted the poor devil and ordered him sent to the penitentiary because he got out of the coop the kind of chicken he wanted." The fellow "gets a lawyer, pays

Equipped with plenty of reading material, a senator
embarks on a filibuster.   *Carl Rose*

that the rules did not allow demonstrations
of approval or disapproval, but he added
that, if those in the galleries approved of
what he said, "it would be all right for them
to write me a nice letter," and, just in case he
should run for office, "you can enclose a
little contribution for the next election."
"Things like that," said Long, "are always in
the rules of the Senate," even though
demonstrations in the galleries were not
allowed.[42]

Of such stuff was Senator Long's filibuster
made. According to the *New York Times* of
June 14, 1935, when the tired but scrappy
Louisianian finally yielded the floor "at
about 4 a.m." on Thursday, June 13, he had
spoken for fifteen and a half hours at a cost
of "about $5,000." The speech consumed
eighty-four pages of the *Congressional Record*,[43]
including numerous interruptions—some
from senators hostile to Long, while others
came from senators eager to join in the prevailing carnival atmosphere.

That the feisty filibustering buccaneer was
an extraordinary showman was evident; his
story-telling, recipe-giving speech had elicit-
ed laughter ninety-eight times, and numerous admonitions had been directed to the
gallery occupants by the chair. But Long lost
the battle. The amendment requiring Senate
confirmation of administration appointees
was tabled by Senator Barkley soon after
Long's speech ended.[44]

The June 1935 speech is perhaps the most-
quoted filibuster example in U.S. Senate history, but it is also one of the most ridiculed
by critics of parliamentary obstructionism.
Within the Senate itself, administration
forces, together with a coalition of new senators, were strong in their denunciations,
while press comments regarding Long's tactics were generally unfavorable. A *New York
Times* column by Arthur Krock, headlined
"Long's Defeat in Filibuster Checks His
Senate 'Mastery,'" stated that, according to

him his cash, and gets convicted," all because
he had violated a provision in "rule book,
volume 6, page 641, paragraph z, subdivision
2" which provided, said Long, that a buyer
had to take chickens as they come, "he
cannot discriminate between chickens."
Laughter rang throughout the chamber, and
the chair once again reminded the galleries to
observe the rules of the Senate. Long agreed

"some observers," the senator from Louisiana "had let himself in for something foolish, something destructive to the reputation he has given himself . . . as the real master of the Senate." In Krock's view, "such spectacles as Mr. Long has often been permitted to make of the Senate and himself" were coming to an end. "He may try the same thing soon again. But he will be punch drunk when he enters the ring." [45]

Long did try again two months later, on the night of August 26, 1935, when the leadership was racing to pass a deficiency appropriation bill containing funds for the newly enacted social security program before a midnight end-of-session deadline. The Senate had previously added to the House bill provisions benefiting wheat and cotton farmers, which the House had refused to accept. When the bill came back to the Senate, Majority Leader Joe Robinson of Arkansas attempted to remove the amendments. Long objected and took the floor, hoping to force the leadership of both houses to find ways to accept the amendments rather than have the bill die with the impending sine die adjournment. The amendments, giving farmers minimum prices of 90 cents a bushel for wheat and 12 cents a pound for cotton, were supported by a coalition of western and southern senators. Complaining that "the chairman of a [House] committee has taken the deficiency bill and has served notice" that the committee would "not report the bill with the [cotton and wheat] amendment," [46] Long shouted: "I challenge all sides and beg all sides, the high, the mighty, the powerful, to let the House have a chance to vote. . . . Take this bill and send it back to the House. . . . and let the House vote on this matter tonight. . . . Let them vote. Who is afraid?" Otherwise, Long made it clear, the deficiency bill would die at midnight. "If you are in such a big hurry that you have to have it by 12 o'clock or not have

it at all," he declared, "then you let the House of Representatives vote on the bill." [47]

At one point, Long was forced to take his seat on a question of order raised by Washington Senator Lewis Schwellenbach, whose dislike for Long's tactics was well known. Schwellenbach complained that Long had transgressed Senate rules by referring to a member (Representative James P. Buchanan of Texas, chairman of the House Appropriations Committee) by name. On a motion by Senator Sherman Minton of Indiana, the Senate voted to permit the Louisiana senator to "proceed in order." [48] Unperturbed, Long resumed his efforts and, as time went on, his increasingly irritated colleagues repeatedly interrupted his speech with questions and parliamentary inquiries so phrased as to deliver stinging rebukes to the senator. Schwellenbach and Alabama Senator Hugo Black were especially caustic, taunting Long with derisive and scornful reproaches. Schwellenbach, in the guise of a parliamentary inquiry, asked the chair

whether the older men and women of this country . . . are to be deprived of an opportunity for a pension, whether the little children . . . are to be deprived of opportunity, whether the blind are to be deprived of the opportunity which this bill provides for them, simply because the Senator from Louisiana wishes to provide publicity for himself, and get himself in the newspapers, and talk to the occupants of the galleries.

The president pro tempore responded that "the Chair cannot answer that question at the present time." But Long answered by reminding his tormentors that it was he who had saved the bill and "kept it alive" on the preceding Saturday:

Ah! There was not a tear then. . . . Oh, the tears! How the salty tide runs around me. I can feel it in every pore, how there is weeping, how there is everything expressing deep sympathy, to induce me to pause long enough to allow the motion of the Senator from Arkansas to prevail, to take the wheat farmer and the cotton farmer out of the bill.[49]

Again and again, Long yielded to Black for a question, only to be upbraided. In one such instance, Senator Black said:

The Senator is fine on receiving laughter from the galleries, but I ask the Senator if he thinks he will receive laughter from the old people who are deprived of their pensions by his filibuster; from the crippled children who are deprived of their medicine by his filibuster; from the mothers who are sick . . . and who are deprived of their medical treatment on account of his filibuster; from the blind who are deprived of the money needed to take care of them by his filibuster; from the railroad men who desire to see their pension fund start in operation and who are deprived of having it done by his filibuster. Does he think they will smile and laugh at his witticisms and his smart sayings?[50]

Long repeatedly responded to such censure by insisting that he was for the bill but that the House should be forced to vote on the amendment to aid the cotton and wheat farmers of America. If the Senate leadership would send the bill back to the House for a vote, he would give up the floor. In Long's view, there was a simple solution for saving the bill: "There is one man in this body who can get it over there. If the Senator from Arkansas [Majority Leader Joseph Robinson] asks me to yield for the purpose of withdrawing his motion, so that the bill may go back to the House, I will yield."[51]

As the hours went by, even other senators who supported the amendment on wheat and cotton pleaded with Long to relent and let the bill pass. But he remained defiant to the last, impervious to entreaties and threats alike. At midnight, the gavel came down, the session ended, and the bill died.

Fifteen days later, Senator Huey Pierce Long was dead, shot by an assassin at the state capitol in Baton Rouge, Louisiana.[52] The Kingfish, who, even today, remains unrivaled in the annals of Senate filibusters, was gone forever.

A short, but successful, one-man filibuster was conducted on the night of Saturday, June 20, 1936, when Senator Rush D. Holt of West Virginia took the Senate floor to oppose legislation to regulate commerce in bituminous coal. Holt, with whom I served in the West Virginia legislature in later years, threatened to read from a volume of *Aesop's Fables* until final adjournment of the Congress, due to occur at the end of that day. The bill Holt was attacking was sponsored by his senior colleague from West Virginia, Senator Matthew Mansfield Neely, but the two senators had been feuding. Holt had been elected to the Senate on November 6, 1934, for the term beginning January 3, 1935, but not having yet reached the age of thirty, did not take his seat until June 21, 1935. Neely, a veteran of political wars in West Virginia, was a close ally of John L. Lewis, president of the United Mine Workers of America, with over 125,000 members in the state. Both senators were very articulate, outspoken, and tough infighters when it came to politics and debate.

When Senator Sherman Minton of Indiana asked Holt during the filibuster whether he expected to support Neely in the upcoming November election, Holt replied, "Mr. President, if I should say what I thought of him I would be violating the rules of the Senate, because I am not allowed to talk about my colleagues in that way."[53] It was clear that there was no love lost between the two West Virginia Democratic senators.

Holt spoke at some length against the pending coal legislation and then turned his attention to *Aesop's Fables*. Senators were to draw their own inferences from the fables, some of which, of course, were meant to apply to UMWA chief Lewis and Senator Neely. Holt droned on, from fable to fable: "The Elephant and the Assembly of Animals"; "The Dog, the Cock, and the Fox"; "The Wolf and the Lamb"; "The Ass That

In 1953, Wayne Morse held the floor for more than twenty-two hours.

Carried the Image"; and others, until Majority Leader Joe Robinson asked, "Is it the Senator's intention to continue his address?"

"I have a great many of Aesop's Fables to read," replied Holt.

"The Senator would not be willing to yield for a vote on the bill?"

"Oh, I would have to read all these fables," Holt maintained stoutly. "I desire to read them." [54]

Holt clearly intended to run the clock until the session's end. Soon afterward, the Senate adjourned sine die.

Filibusters continued to occur through the late 1930's, and in the 1940's and 1950's, with efforts to invoke cloture largely unsuccessful. In 1953, Wayne Morse of Oregon set a new record for long-windedness in the Senate when he took the floor at 11:40 a.m. on Friday, April 24, and spoke until 10:06 a.m. Saturday, a total of twenty-two hours and twenty-six minutes.

Morse opposed the pending offshore oil bill, and, according to the *New York Times* of April 26, 1953, "only once did he get a respite of as long as two minutes. . . . when he stopped for a colleague to make a brief statement in introducing a bill."

When he took the floor, Morse had already spoken twice on the bill but was given consent to speak again, in spite of the two-speech rule, after a warning by Majority Leader Robert A. Taft of Ohio that this would be Morse's "last speech." When asked by Taft how long he would speak, Morse replied, "I had a rather bad meal last night, which is going to handicap me somewhat, but I think I am good for from 8 to 12 hours." [55]

Morse talked about the educational needs of the country, the national debt, population growth, the REA, and, briefly, about his fondness for ring bologna and breeding horses. He spoke extensively about "the filibuster technique," or "prolonged debate," and the purposes to be served. "There is nothing improper about it, so long as it is done with good taste, with dignity, and with sincerity." [56]

When Morse yielded to Senator George Malone of Nevada for two minutes, by unanimous consent, for the purpose of introducing a bill, Majority Leader Taft asserted that Morse "will have to stand if he is to retain the floor." Morse replied that he "was merely sitting down in order to obtain a little rest" but that he would be glad to comply.[57]

Early on Saturday morning, Morse was called to order by Senator William A. Purtell of Connecticut, because of "the requirement that both feet be on the floor." [58] Morse had "placed a foot on a chair beside his desk and started to lean an arm on his leg." [59] Morse promised to proceed in order.

Senator Morse's record was exceeded four years later by Senator Strom Thurmond of South Carolina, who spoke in opposition to the Civil Rights Act of 1957. Thurmond began speaking at 8:54 p.m. on August 28 and completed his speech at 9:12 p.m. the next day—according to *Congressional Quarterly*, a total of "24 hours and 18 minutes." [60] Thurmond stated, at the close of his speech, that he had spoken "24 hours and 22 minutes," [61] but, in either event, he established

Strom Thurmond set the all-time filibuster record in 1957 when he spoke for more than twenty-four hours. *U.S. Senate Historical Office*

a record that remains unbroken today, thirty-two years later.

Thurmond spoke throughout the night of Wednesday, August 28, and all day Thursday against "the so-called voting-right bill." He discussed each of the forty-eight states' laws for the protection of voters. He then discussed the jury trial provisions in connection with criminal contempts of court arising out of civil rights cases, and expressed his opposition to the creation of a Commission on Civil Rights. Thurmond read at length from a treatise tracing the historical development of the jury system. His speech was interrupted many times for colloquies with friendly senators, like William Langer of North Dakota, and Thurmond yielded for the transaction of business for brief periods, as when the newly elected senator from Wisconsin, William Proxmire, took the oath of office on August 29. Thurmond confined his entire remarks to the bill and related subject matter. Shortly after his speech was completed, the Senate approved the bill by voting 60 to 15 to concur in the House amendments.[62]

Another of the longest speeches in Senate history occurred in 1981 when Senator Proxmire spoke sixteen hours and twelve minutes in opposition to legislation increasing the debt limit to over a trillion dollars. Beginning his speech at 6:15 p.m. on September 28, Proxmire spoke virtually nonstop until 10:27 a.m. on September 29.[63] He was not attempting to filibuster the bill, he said, assuring other senators that he would stop speaking "by 10:30 tomorrow morning [September 29]." He was making a "record" on what he felt was "a great watershed in our economic life when we go over $1 trillion national debt." [64] Proxmire only yielded twice to other senators while he held the floor—once to me for a brief statement lasting about four minutes, and once for a brief colloquy with Senator James J. Exon of Nebraska.

Proxmire was concerned about increasing the debt limit above a trillion dollars. What would be next, he wondered: "Are we going to go to a quadrillion? Mr. President, you know a quadrillion is a thousand trillion." After that came a quintillion, then "we go to a sextillion, then a septillion." At some point, supposedly, the "googol" would be reached. Proxmire explained, "a googol is 1 with 100 zeros after it"—a term "that is used with respect to measuring distances in outer space." [65]

Proxmire, who always kept himself physically fit through careful dieting and exercise, finished his speech in great shape.

Of the many talkathons that have occurred during the seventy-two years following the 1917 cloture rule, antilynching legis-

In a 1981 speech against raising the ceiling on the national debt, Senator William Proxmire talked throughout the night for more than sixteen hours.
U.S. Senate Historical Office

lation, creation of a Fair Employment Practices Commission, ending the poll tax, and other civil rights bills were the subjects of many filibusters. Following the passage of the Civil Rights Act in 1964 and the Voting Rights Act in 1965, however, the use of filibusters has shifted. Except for school-busing and equal job opportunity legislation, most cloture votes in recent years have occurred on legislation covering a broad range of issues, such as amending Rule XXII, permitting common-site picketing, establishing a consumer agency, and Export-Import banking. As we shall see, Senate filibusters have occurred far more often since 1964, as have the successful efforts to break them.

Filibusters, 1964–1989*

Mr. President, of the many filibusters during the past twenty-five years, I shall discuss only three: the 1964 civil rights filibuster, the 1977 natural gas deregulation filibuster, and the 1987–1988 filibuster on campaign financing reform.

The 1964 filibuster occurred on a House bill, the Civil Rights Act of 1963, which was designed to enforce the right to vote; to protect against discrimination in federally assisted programs and in public accommodations, public facilities, and public education; to extend the Civil Rights Commission; and to establish a Commission on Equal Employment Opportunity. It was, indeed, a major and far-reaching civil rights bill, which had President Lyndon Johnson's strong backing.

When the bill arrived from the House on February 26, 1964, it went directly to the Senate calendar, thus avoiding referral to the Senate Judiciary Committee, chaired by Senator James O. Eastland of Mississippi, an avowed opponent of civil rights legislation. Majority Leader Mike Mansfield moved on March 9 to take up the bill, and the motion was debated until March 26, when the Senate voted, 67 to 17, for the motion (my own vote being with those in the majority). From March 26 until cloture was invoked on June 10, the bill was before the Senate for a total of 77 days—including Saturdays, Sundays, and holidays—and was actually debated for 57 days, 6 of which were Saturdays. Still, the bill was not passed until 9 days after cloture was voted. Hence, 103 days had passed between March 9, when the motion was made to take up the bill, and final passage on June 19.

The southern senators opposing the bill, led by Senator Richard B. Russell of Georgia, were well organized, and their speeches were germane to the bill. The 1964 filibuster thus differed from other lengthy filibusters of the past, in that there was serious and informed "extended debate" over the entire period during which it was before the Senate. The discussion avoided the time-consuming dilatory tactics that had been the trademark of many earlier filibusters, and neither side resorted to parliamentary gamesmanship. Senator Hubert H. Humphrey of Minnesota led the forces supporting the bill, and he proved equal to the task. Majority Leader Mansfield played a low-key role, quietly courting Minority Leader Everett Dirksen's support, and avoiding all-night sessions, except for my all-night speech against the bill on June 9, 1964—the longest speech (fourteen hours and thirteen minutes) of the debate.[1]

Well-orchestrated, heavy and unrelenting pressure from the administration, civil rights groups, churches, labor organizations, and the media proved, in the final analysis, to be too much for the embattled southerners. In addition, Dirksen, who was the crucial factor in the outcome, threw his prestigious influence into the balance in support of cloture. When the vote came on June 10—the one-hundredth anniversary of Abraham Lincoln's nomination for a second presidential term—it was decisive: 71 to 29 for cloture. Except for Senators Carl Hayden of Arizona and Alan Bible of Nevada, I was the only nonsouthern Democrat who voted against cloture.[2]

Senator Russell reflected the views of the bill's opponents:

* Prepared December 1989

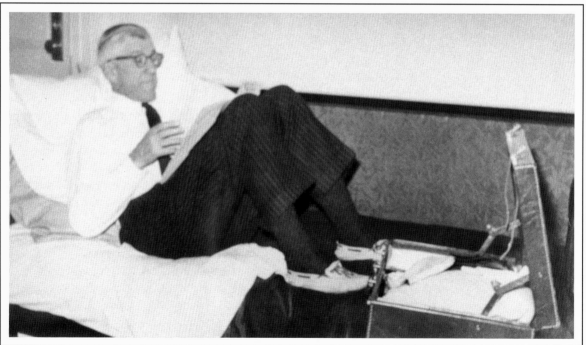

Senators made themselves comfortable during a filibuster in 1960; *above*, Pennsylvania Senator Hugh Scott and, *below*, Massachusetts Senator Leverett Saltonstall.   *U.S. Senate Historical Office*

Mr. President, what does equality mean?

. . . Equality does not mean that one person shall be admitted to a club merely because he desires to be. . . .

No, Mr. President, equal rights in this land of ours means that each citizen has an equal opportunity to acquire property through honest means, that once that property has been acquired he has a right to exercise dominion over it. . . .

Life, liberty, and property—in that order—are spelled out in the Constitution of the United States as our greatest civil rights. I care not how much politics may be involved, and it matters not how great may be the emotional appeal. We cannot strike down one of those rights without gnawing into the very vitals of constitutional government in this land. . . .

Mr. President, those of us who have opposed this bill have done so from a profound conviction that the bill not only is contrary to the spirit of the Constitution of the United States, but also violates the letter of the Constitution. . . .

. . . It confers upon the Attorney General the power to control many facets in the daily lives and in the private lives of the people of the United States. It greatly broadens Federal supervision and regulation—going into new areas—over the activities of business, commerce, and industry. . . .

One of the saddest aspects of the bill is the general enlargement of the Federal Government over affairs that have heretofore been considered the concern of the States and local governments.[3]

Senator Dirksen's comments mirrored the feelings of the bill's supporters:

The time has come for equality of opportunity in sharing in government, in education, and in employment. It will not be stayed or denied. It is here. . . .

. . . For many years, each political party has given major consideration to a civil rights plank in its platform. . . . Were these pledges so much campaign stuff or did we mean it? Were these promises on civil rights but idle words for vote-getting purposes or were they a covenant meant to be kept? If all this was mere pretense, let us confess the sin of hypocrisy now and vow not to delude the people again. . . .

. . . There is another reason why we dare not temporize with the issue which is before us. It is essentially moral in character. It must be resolved. It will not go away. Its time has come.[4]

The outcome, once cloture was invoked, was never in doubt. Again, the southern sen-

Minority Leader Everett Dirksen's support for cloture led to passage of the 1964 Civil Rights Act. Dirksen appears here with fellow Republican Senator John Tower. *George Tames/New York Times*

ators resorted to no parliamentary games or post-cloture delaying tactics. They offered serious amendments and accepted the verdict gracefully. Thirty-four roll-call votes occurred on June 16. On June 19, the bill passed, 73 to 27, mine being the only non-southern Democratic vote against the bill.[5]

The 1977 filibuster on the natural gas deregulation bill was shorter, more intense, and far more bitter than the 1964 civil rights filibuster. The bill came up on September 19, and Senators Lloyd Bentsen of Texas and James Pearson of Kansas offered a substitute providing for the eventual end of price controls on newly discovered natural gas. Cloture was invoked on the Bentsen-Pearson substitute by a vote of 77 to 17 on September 26, but a post-cloture filibuster immediately began, led by Senators Howard Metzenbaum of Ohio and James Abourezk of South

Senator James B. Allen developed the "post-cloture filibuster." *U.S. Senate Historical Office*

enabled a single senator, by husbanding the one hour to which he was entitled under the cloture rule, to tie up the Senate for days while he called up amendment after amendment, requested the reading thereof, asked for a roll-call vote thereon, and demanded a quorum call in advance of the vote. Following the vote on an amendment (or point of order or appeal), a roll call would be demanded on tabling the motion to reconsider the vote. Because the time consumed by roll calls, quorum calls, and reading of amendments was free time and not chargeable to the senator, this process, though mostly dilatory, could last indefinitely.

Senators Abourezk and Metzenbaum had not only mastered the technique, but they had also prepared themselves well in advance by drawing up myriad amendments and having them at the desk ready for use when cloture was invoked on the natural gas bill. Following cloture, vote after vote occurred on amendments, motions to adjourn, appeals, and tabling motions. Quorum calls were numerous.

After the bill had been before the Senate for twelve days (excluding Sundays) and one all-night session, I met with Vice President Walter Mondale to plan a strategy for breaking the filibuster. I asked the vice president to take the chair and rule on points of order—which I and other senators would raise—making various motions and quorum calls dilatory under cloture and peremptorily ruling amendments out of order "on their face" (for example, as being incorrectly drawn or not germane), thus avoiding the endless roll calls that could otherwise consume weeks.

Vice President Mondale took the chair, issued rulings on the points of order, and repeatedly and consistently recognized me, as majority leader, for the calling up of amendments which the chair then ruled out of order. Within a matter of minutes, thirty-

Dakota. As majority leader, I announced that there were "more than 500 amendments at the desk" and that there would be "late sessions" and "a great number of rollcall votes." [6]

In earlier years, once cloture had been invoked on a matter, the Senate had proceeded in an orderly fashion to dispose of the relatively few remaining amendments and go to a final vote. But when James B. Allen of Alabama came to the Senate in 1969, things changed in this respect. Senator Allen, courtly, soft-spoken, and highly intelligent, was also exceptionally knowledgeable about the Senate's rules and a man of courage and conviction. He developed what became known as the post-cloture filibuster. The technique

three amendments were ruled out of order that otherwise would have required days for disposition at the pace to which Senators Abourezk and Metzenbaum had slowed the Senate.[7]

Pandemonium broke loose as senators were denied recognition to appeal the chair's rulings declaring the amendments disqualified, and both the vice president and I were severely criticized for the extraordinary actions we had taken to break the post-cloture filibuster. Senators Edmund S. Muskie of Maine, Frank Church of Idaho, and Paul Sarbanes of Maryland vigorously protested the denial of senators' rights to appeal. Senator Gary Hart of Colorado charged that to be "foreclosed from an appeal" was an "abuse of leadership authority" and said that "the U.S. Senate has just seen an outrageous act." Senator Jacob Javits of New York raised a point of order making it out of order for the chair to successively recognize the majority leader so as to deny other senators the right to appeal the chair's ruling on a matter "raised in the course of the first recognition by the majority leader." [8] I asked consent for five minutes to discuss the point of order, but Senator John Culver of Iowa objected. Senator Sarbanes then asked that Senator Javits and I be given five minutes each to discuss the point of order before the chair ruled. That request was granted, and my remarks, in part, were as follows:

. . . Mr. President, we have come to a situation here in which it is not just the accommodation of a Senator that is involved; it is, rather, the accommodation of the Senate itself.

We have heard talk about the abuse by the leadership of its prerogatives. We have heard talk about the abuse of the custom of preferential recognition of the majority leader. What about the abuse of the rules to which every member of the Senate on both sides of the aisle has been subjected for the last 13 days and 1 night? What about that abuse of the rules? What about the abuse of the Senate itself, when we have stood here hour after hour. . . .

Now it came to the point that we saw we could not reason with a handful of filibusterers—and I have been on their side . . . on the basic issue of complete deregulation at this time. Time and time and time and time again, over the years, I have been the spear carrier, in fighting this able and honorable man, the Senator [James B. Allen] from Alabama. . . .

. . . I have gone on the battleground with this man because nobody else in the Senate was chosen to do so or was equipped to do so. I did it on the civil rights attorneys' fee bill; I did it on the anti-trust bill; I did it on [the resolution] that set up the Intelligence Committee; I did it on the extension of the Voting Rights Act; I did it on the fight to reduce the cloture votes from two-thirds to three fifths. Those of you who today charge the majority leader of having abused his prerogatives did not then raise your voice.

I would say that the Senator from Alabama . . . at that time had just as much right to say that I was abusing the rights of the leadership when I took him on. I was the majority whip then. But who stood up for him in that day? Nobody! Where were those then who now stand against me because I am now seeking to get this bill out of here, and because I am seeking to take a stand against the continued abuse of the U.S. Senate and every member of it? Where were they then? . . .

. . . I am trying to keep Senators from abusing the Senate, and I think it is self-evident that the ending of such abuse is long overdue. They have done too much of it already. . . .

In defense of the vice president, who, except by unanimous consent, is not allowed to address the Senate, I said:

. . . He is not here, as someone has said, to . . . pull the rug out from under us. The Vice President is here to get the ox out of the ditch. The ox is in the ditch! That is why the Vice President is here!

Reminding senators that President Jimmy Carter had publicly stated his intention to veto outright deregulation, I asked:

. . . What more do you want? You know you are going to win in conference. You know if outright deregulation gets through conference, the President will veto it. What kind of a charade do you think the American people are going to be fooled into thinking this is?

I say it is long past time, Mr. President, to stop this filibuster, and to stop the abuse of the Senate and its

During a lengthy filibuster, a weary senator rests on a cot set up in the old Senate chamber.

rules. It was for that reason that I, in this instance, took extraordinary advantage of my prerogative as leader to be recognized. One has to fight fire with fire when all else fails.

[Applause, Senators rising.] [9]

Senator Javits, at the suggestion of Senator Allen, withdrew his point of order. The struggle had left some deep wounds, but the strategy had been successful. The back of the filibuster had been broken, and agreement was soon reached for a final vote. The next day, on October 4, the Senate voted, 50 to 46, to accept a modified Bentsen-Pearson substitute, and the bill was passed. The bill had been debated for fourteen days, and, in the process, 130 roll-call votes had occurred, 111 of them after cloture was invoked.

This was the roughest filibuster I have experienced during my thirty-one years in the Senate, and it produced the most bitter feelings. Yet, some important new precedents

were established in dealing with post-cloture obstruction. One such precedent requires the chair to take the initiative, under cloture, "to rule out of order all amendments which are dilatory or which on their face are out of order." [10] Another precedent was established requiring the chair, under cloture, to take the initiative "to rule out of order all dilatory motions, including calls for a quorum, when it has been established by a quorum call or rollcall that a quorum is present and the Chair's count reaffirms that a quorum is still present." [11] A point of order was also made, and upheld by Senate vote, that a senator has "the right to recall his own amendments qualified and pending under cloture and have them removed from the desk prior to being called up," thus preventing them from being offered by another senator.[12] On another point of order, the Senate, by roll-call vote, held that, when op-

[156]

erating under cloture, "a request by a Senator to conduct business which the Senate declines to conduct, for instance, the making of a motion which is ruled dilatory, the offering of an amendment which is ruled out of order or dilatory, a request for the yeas and nays which is refused, is not the transaction of business for the purpose of calling another quorum." [13]

Never have so many attempts been made to break a filibuster as were made during the One-hundredth Congress in the effort to enact campaign financing reform. The legislation, proposed by Senator David Boren of Oklahoma and myself, was made the pending business before the Senate on June 3, 1987, and it immediately encountered stiff opposition from Senate Republicans. The bill had earlier been referred to the Senate Committee on Rules, chaired by Senator Wendell Ford of Kentucky, and, following hearings, had been reported back to the Senate in the form of a substitute. The bill provided for a voluntary system of spending limits and partial public financing of Senate general election campaigns; it limited contributions from political action committees (PACs); and it improved reporting and disclosure of campaign finance activities. The public financing would derive from a voluntary tax checkoff, a feature of presidential campaign financing, by which individual income-tax payers indicate on their tax forms that they wish to check off one dollar to go into the presidential tax fund.

Republican Senator Mitch McConnell of Kentucky, one of the leaders in the filibuster against the bill, was reported by a Kentucky newspaper to have stated that the Senate Republicans had met and agreed to bind themselves as a caucus to vote against any bill containing spending limits and public financing.[14] From the beginning, therefore, the division was along party lines, and, since the makeup of the Senate was 54 Democrats

and 46 Republicans, the outlook for cloture was bleak.

The first cloture vote occurred on June 9, and, with one senator absent, the vote was 52 to 47.[15] Two Republicans voted for, and three Democrats voted against, cloture. The missing Democrat, if present, would have voted for cloture, giving the proponents a total strength of 53. Four more cloture votes occurred in June—daily, the sixteenth through the nineteenth—and the overall strengths remained the same, 53 to 47—a majority but not the three-fifths needed for cloture. The lines had not budged! [16]

I decided to put campaign financing reform aside for the time being, so as to take up the budget conference report, the omnibus trade bill, and other measures that were beginning to clog the legislative pipeline. Meanwhile, negotiations with Republicans would continue in an effort to break the gridlock on campaign reform.

On August 3, the Senate resumed consideration of the election reform measure, after Senator Boren and I decided to modify the bill, hoping to mollify the Republican opposition. "We have completely removed public financing as a basis for supporting campaigns," said Boren, in explaining the change. "We have provided a bill with no net cost to the taxpayers." [17]

Debate continued on the bill and other measures through August 7, when the Senate adjourned until September 9 for the summer recess, with a cloture vote scheduled for Thursday, September 10.

On the September 10 cloture vote, supporters of campaign financing reform showed a gain of two votes, picking up one Republican and one Democrat. The vote was 53 to 42, and two of the five absentees were supporters of the bill; hence, the overall strength of the proponents had grown to 55.[18] Yet, a seventh cloture vote, on September 15, showed no further movement, with

51 yeas, 44 nays, and 5 not voting. Four of the missing senators were for cloture. With a legislative logjam in the making, I shelved the bill for the remainder of the session but promised to "revisit" the bill "next year." [19]

The Senate did, indeed, revisit campaign financing when, on February 1, 1988, I brought the bill back for further consideration. On the fourth, the Senate adjourned until February 15, for the Presidents' Day recess. Upon returning, the Senate renewed debate on February 17 on the financing reform bill. Meanwhile, a small group of senators, appointed by the majority and minority leaders, had been attempting to negotiate a compromise. Their efforts had not borne fruit.

On Tuesday, February 23, in Senate floor comments, I referred to the seven cloture votes in 1987, when "little interest was stirred because we had a very casual filibuster that lasted from 9 o'clock in the morning until 5 or 5:30 in the afternoon, and in the meantime we would take up other measures," and I said there was "no point in having a nice, easygoing filibuster here, carrying on a slow filibuster in the back rooms. Let us have it out here on the floor. . . . where the American people can see . . . that this is a filibuster." Stating that the other side had drawn a line against any limit on campaign spending, I said that "we on this side . . . are drawing a line also, and that line is there can be no genuine campaign financing reform in this country without a limit on campaign spending." I then stated:

Having drawn the lines in the sand, we have decided that we will just go around the clock. . . .

. . . there is no point in continuing the casual, gentlemanly, good-guy filibuster because it will just turn out as it did last year: Have a few cloture votes, everybody just takes it easy . . . everybody goes home and gets a good night's sleep, and everybody protects everybody else.

The American people will understand this is a filibuster. They will understand who is not willing to let the Senate vote on the bill. [20]

Senator Alan Simpson, the minority whip, and acting leader at the time, said that he saw no point "in going through the night" as we would "not accomplish anything," and he stated the position of the bill's opponents:

We cannot change the bill by amendment. Our amendments would be voted down by the same party line vote that has characterized seven cloture votes that we have had on this measure last year.

So we know what happens when we relinquish our position. . . .

. . . We are ready to go all night, we are ready to go all day. . . .

. . . we are prepared and we will have our sturdy SWAT teams and people on vitamin pills and colostomy bags and Lord knows what else we will have to have to improve our ability to stay here. [21]

So, indeed, the lines were drawn, and the debate continued into the evening and through the night, with Senators Robert Packwood of Oregon, Rudy Boschwitz of Minnesota, and other Republican senators doing most of the speechmaking. Floor attendance was poor, but, on a roll-call vote to have the sergeant at arms request attendance of absent senators, eighty-nine senators voted. On similar motions as the hours passed, first seventy-four senators and later seventy-eight senators voted. On a fourth motion to instruct the sergeant at arms to request attendance, the vote was 47 to 1 in favor of the motion, with 52 senators absent. Since not a single Republican senator voted, it was clear that the Republicans had decided to boycott the floor on roll calls designed to secure a quorum. I then moved that the sergeant at arms "arrest the absent Senators and bring them to the Chamber." The vote was 45 to 3, and, again, not one Republican was in the chamber for the vote.

After a long delay, two of the absent Democrats showed up. Finally, Sergeant at

Arms Henry Giugni located Republican Senator Packwood at his office and placed him under arrest. Packwood agreed to accompany Giugni to the Capitol but insisted on being carried into the chamber in order to make the point that he was not entering voluntarily. At 1:17 a.m. on Wednesday, the Oregon senator, gracefully accepting the action of the Senate and its sergeant at arms, allowed himself to be carried onto the Senate floor, thus making a quorum of 51 senators.[22]

At that point, I offered a cloture motion for the eighth time on the bill. In so doing, I commented, "We have seen that the opposition is not willing to vote on meaningful campaign financing reform, not willing to talk on the pending legislation, and ultimately not willing to stay on the job."[23] I then moved to go into executive session for a vote on a nomination, which attracted the attendance of sixty-four senators, after which the debate resumed on campaign financing reform.

Later, acting Republican leader Alan Simpson and I called a truce and agreed to restrict the activities on both sides to speeches by selected senators on the substance of the bill. The tensions subsided, and senators made lengthy speeches throughout the rest of Thursday morning, February 25. At noon on Thursday, Senator John McCain of Arizona yielded the floor briefly, and the chair announced that "the Senate having been in continuous session since yesterday, pursuant to the order of the Senate of February 29, 1960, the Senate will now suspend while the Chaplain offers a prayer."[24]

From the 10 a.m. convening on Tuesday until the Senate finally recessed on Thursday, February 25, at 7:24 p.m.,[25] only one brief respite had occurred: on Tuesday from 12:47 p.m. until 2 p.m. to accommodate party conferences. The Senate had been in continuous session for fifty-three hours and twenty-four minutes—more than two days

and two nights. When the cloture vote came on Friday, February 26, 1988, the bill's proponents showed no gains in overall strength. The vote was 53 to 41, with two of the five absentees being known supporters.[26] Three of 46 Republican senators had voted with the Democrats, while two of the 54 Democrats had broken from the fold and voted with the Republicans. Hence, party lines had remained almost intact throughout the controversy. Later in the day, I returned the bill to the calendar by unanimous consent and shelved it for the remainder of the One-hundredth Congress.[27]

The campaign finance filibuster had produced no new precedents, except for the number of cloture votes (eight). It had bridged more than eight months of the first and second sessions, although it was technically before the Senate for only twenty-seven days. In the apt words of Senator Warren Rudman of New Hampshire, "the events of the last 48 hours were a curious blend of 'Dallas,' 'Dynasty,' 'The Last Buccaneer' and the Friday night fights."[28] In accepting the bill's defeat, I paraphrased the Apostle Paul's words: "We have fought a good fight. We have finished our course. We have kept the faith."[29]

Some of the Republican members groused for a few days about my motion to "arrest" senators, but the Senate moved on to other business, and when the One-hundredth Congress ended at 3:16 a.m. on October 22, 1988, it was generally lauded as the most productive in over twenty years.

My discussion of Senate filibusters in this chapter has, by necessity, concentrated on only a few of the many talkathons that have occurred during the past 150 years. I have emphasized the longest speeches and the most dramatic of the filibusters, as well as those that were particularly illustrative. I have chosen to mention some incidents, for example, because of the precedents that were established, as in the filibusters of 1879, 1897, 1908; others I have selected because of the issues involved, like the 1917 Armed Ship bill that led to the first cloture rule; and some I have described because of the colorful senators who participated, such as Huey P. Long.

I have dwelt at length on the 1964 civil rights filibuster because of the orderly, dignified, and methodical way in which it was conducted, the total absence of dilatory tactics, its great length, and the historic legislation that was produced. It was also a filibuster that I experienced first-hand as a participant.

I have commented on the 1977 natural gas deregulation filibuster because of its fierceness, the several important precedents that were set, the dilatory tactics that were effectively employed, and because it was the classic and prime example of a post-cloture filibuster. Additionally, I was the majority leader at the time and was successful in breaking the filibuster.

During the filibuster on campaign financing reform, I was again the majority leader, but in that instance I lost the battle. That filibuster ran the gamut from low-key to very high visibility, from docile beginnings to a fire-storm ending, and it was conducted by a determined, unified, very large minority.

The 1964 civil rights and the 1977 gas deregulation struggles were not politically partisan, and the filibusterers failed to prevent the legislation from passing the Senate. In the 1987–1988 effort to enact campaign financing reform, however, the battle was highly partisan and the filibusterers succeeded in defeating the legislation.

Since filibusters generally commence without official declaration, no definitive list exists of all those that have occurred throughout the Senate's history. Cloture, on the other hand, is a formal action, and more reliable statistics are available concerning the number of cloture votes taken, although cloture has not been attempted against every filibuster since the rule's adoption in 1917.

Between 1917 and the 1960's, cloture was seldom attempted and, prior to 1971, it had succeeded only 10 times out of 49 attempts. From 1971 through 1989, however, cloture was invoked 87 times, a phenomenal increase. Hence, during the seventy-two years from the cloture rule's inception in 1917 through 1989, cloture was invoked a total of 97 times in 280 attempts.[30]

From these statistics, it is clear that the number of filibusters has increased greatly during the last nineteen years. Why such an increase? Having served in one leadership capacity or another during this entire period, and having offered more cloture motions than has anyone else, I must state that the statistics, standing alone, are a bit misleading. Cloture motions in recent years have frequently been offered, and adopted, in order to meet the mere challenge of a filibuster threat by a single senator or small group of senators. Resistance to a bill or nomination by a handful of senators who refuse unanimous consent to its consideration has often dissipated once cloture was invoked on the motion to take up the matter. After entering a cloture motion on a measure, I have, on several occasions, taken up some other matter rather than spend the Senate's time waiting until the second day after the filing of such a motion before a vote could be taken. If the cloture vote was successful, the legislation was then automatically back before the Senate until it was disposed of.

In a few instances, cloture has been applied solely to discourage nongermane amendments. Thus, as "the wicked flee when no man pursueth," so has cloture been applied many times when no actual filibuster was in progress.

Nonetheless, the number of filibusters has, indeed, increased considerably in recent

Two filibuster-related cartoons from the 1960's show, *left*, "The Senate battling the majority" and, *right*, Senator Dirksen reassuring the Senate that he is not planning a filibuster: "Don't panic—these are Lincoln Day speeches!"
Library of Congress

years, for a number of reasons, including the personalities and skills of certain senators and the intensity of particular political issues. Beginning in the early 1970's, filibusters were often led by Senators James Allen, Jesse Helms of North Carolina, or Howard Metzenbaum, all of whom proved to be aggressive, courageous, and very astute in the use of the Senate rules to block actions they opposed. The past two decades also saw a number of controversial issues, such as school busing to achieve integration, voter registration, a deadlocked election for a New Hampshire Senate seat, funding for the Export-Import Bank, establishment of the federal Legal Services Corporation, creation of a consumer protection agency, loaning federal funds to the Lockheed Corporation, energy legislation, and amending Senate Rule XXII. Such issues contributed to the proliferation of filibusters during the period.

Looking back across the past two hundred years, one must conclude that filibusters have played a significant part in the Senate's

history, but it was not until after the Civil War that filibustering became a weapon that was frequently and effectively employed by Senate minorities. Throughout the decades prior to the Civil War and Reconstruction, obstructionist tactics would have been considered out of place in an institution where dignity and courtesy prevailed and senators depended upon the logic and eloquence of forceful speeches to persuade their colleagues and the country to accept their views. As we have seen, filibustering came into vogue during the closing decades of the nineteenth century and was most successful when resorted to near a session's end, particularly the "lame-duck" sessions that automatically adjourned on March 4, when a single senator or small group of senators could exact concessions by threatening to obstruct passage of all legislation backed up in the adjournment rush. The Twentieth Amendment eliminated the notorious lame-duck session, but it did not eliminate filibusters.

Filibusters, or prolonged debate, have sometimes led to modifications that improved a bill or treaty. The mere threat of a filibuster has often resulted in a decision not to take up a bill or in the withdrawal of a nominee.

Arguments against filibusters have largely centered around the principle that the majority should rule in a democratic society. The very existence of the Senate, however, embodies an equally valid tenet in American democracy: the principle that minorities have rights. Furthermore, a majority of senators, at a given time and on a particular issue, may not truly represent majority sentiment in the country. Senators from a few of the more populous states may, in fact, represent a majority in the nation while numbering a minority of votes in the Senate, where all the states are equal. Additionally, a minority opinion in the country may become the majority view, once the people are more fully informed about an issue through lengthy debate and scrutiny. A minority today may become the majority tomorrow.

Moreover, the framers of the Constitution thought of the Senate as the safeguard against hasty and unwise action by the House in response to temporary whims and storms of passion that may sweep over the land. Delay, deliberation, and debate—though time consuming—may avoid mistakes that would be regretted in the long run. The Senate is the only forum in the government where the perfection of laws may be unhurried and where controversial decisions may be hammered out on the anvil of lengthy debate. The liberties of a free people will always be safe where a forum exists in which open and unlimited debate is allowed.

The most important argument supporting extended debate in the Senate, and even the right to filibuster, is the system of checks and balances. The Senate operates as the balance wheel in that system, because it provides the greatest check against an all-powerful executive through the privilege senators have to discuss without hindrance what they please for as long as they please. A minority can often use publicity to focus popular opinion upon matters that can embarrass the majority and the executive. Without the potential for filibusters, that power to check a Senate majority or an imperial presidency would be destroyed. It is a power too sacred to be trifled with. As Lyndon Baines Johnson said on March 9, 1949:

. . . if I should have the opportunity to send into the countries behind the iron curtain one freedom and only one, I know what my choice would be. . . . I would send to those nations the right of unlimited debate in their legislative chambers.

. . . If we now, in haste and irritation, shut off this freedom, we shall be cutting off the most vital safeguard which minorities possess against the tyranny of momentary majorities.[31]

As one who has served both as majority leader and as minority leader, as a senator who has engaged both in filibustering and in breaking filibusters during my thirty-one years in this body, I believe that Rule XXII today strikes a fair and proper balance between the need to protect the minority against hasty and arbitrary action by a majority and the need for the Senate to be able to act on matters vital to the public interest. More drastic cloture than the rules now provide is neither necessary nor desirable.

We must not forget that the right of extended, and even unlimited, debate is the main cornerstone of the Senate's uniqueness. It is also a primary reason that the United States Senate is the most powerful upper chamber in the world today. The occasional abuse of this right has been, at times, a painful side effect, but it never has been and never will be fatal to the overall public good in the long run. Without the right of unlimited debate, of course, there would be no filibusters, but there would also be no Senate, as we know it. The good outweighs the bad, and not all filibusters have been bad, even though they may have been exasperating, contentious, and perceived as iniquitous. Filibusters are a necessary evil, which must be tolerated lest the Senate lose its special strength and become a mere appendage of the House of Representatives. If this should happen, which God avert, the American Senate would cease to be "that remarkable body" about which William Ewart Gladstone spoke—"the most remarkable of all the inventions of modern politics."

LEADERSHIP

This is . . . a Senate of equals, of men of individual honor and personal character, and of absolute independence. We know no masters, we acknowledge no dictators. This is a hall for mutual consultation and discussion; not an arena for the exhibition of champions.

DANIEL WEBSTER, JANUARY 26, 1830 [1]

There are 100 diverse personalities in the U.S. Senate. O Great God, what an amazing and dissonant 100 personalities they are! What an amazing thing it is to harmonize them. What a job it is.

EVERETT McKINLEY DIRKSEN, 1964 [2]

. . . the only real power available to the leader is the power of persuasion. There is no patronage; no power to discipline; no authority to fire Senators like a President can fire his members of Cabinet.

LYNDON BAINES JOHNSON, 1960 [3]

The leaders are often the prisoners of their own troops and should ever expect the unexpected to happen and foil their best-laid plans.

ROBERT C. BYRD, 1989 [4]

CHAPTER 6

The President Pro Tempore[*]

Mr. President, in 1980, as the majority leader of the Senate, I delivered an address on the history of the Senate's president pro tempore. Now, nearly a decade later, as I occupy the office of president pro tempore myself, I wish to take this occasion to elaborate and expand upon my earlier remarks and to define more fully this constitutionally created office and its unique role in the history of the United States Senate.

The Constitution provides for two officers to preside over the Senate. The vice president of the United States is designated as the president of the Senate. In this capacity, the vice president was expected to preside at regular sessions of the Senate, casting votes only to break ties. From John Adams to Alben Barkley, presiding over the Senate was the chief function of vice presidents, who had an office in the Capitol, received their staff support and office expenses through the legislative appropriations, and who often were not invited to participate in cabinet meetings or other executive activities. It was Richard Nixon who changed the vice presidency in 1953 by moving his chief office from the Capitol to the White House, by directing his attention to executive functions, and by attending Senate sessions only at critical times when his vote, or ruling from the chair,

might be necessary. Vice presidents since Nixon's time have followed his example.

When we consider that the vice president used to be the Senate's regular presiding officer, we can better understand why the Constitution further provided that in the absence of the vice president the Senate could choose a president pro tempore to perform the duties of the chair. *Pro tempore* is Latin for "for the time being"; thus, the post was conceived as a temporary presiding officer. In the eighteenth and nineteenth centuries, the Senate frequently elected several presidents pro tempore during a single session. Since vice presidents presided routinely, the Senate thought it necessary to choose a president pro tempore only for the limited periods when the vice president might be ill or otherwise absent. While James Madison was president, the vice presidency was twice vacated, due to the deaths of Vice Presidents George Clinton in 1812 and Elbridge Gerry in 1814.

In 1841, the Senate for the first time faced the circumstance in which a vice president became president in mid-term, when John Tyler took office following the death of President William Henry Harrison. With no vice president, other presiding officers were needed during the remaining three years of

[*] Prepared December 14, 1989

[167]

Tyler's term. In other circumstances, however, the first presidents pro tempore served only for a few days, weeks, or months. During the Fourth Congress, for instance, there were three presidents pro tempore; there were five during the Fifth Congress; and there were four during the Sixth Congress, making a dozen different presidents pro tempore over a six-year period. Contrast that to one of my recent predecessors, Senator Strom Thurmond of South Carolina, who served as the sole president pro tempore during the six years from 1981 to 1987.

In discussing the relationship between our two constitutionally designated presiding officers, I should point out that the Senate had a president pro tempore before there was a vice president. In April 1789, when the Senate was struggling to achieve its first quorum, Vice President-elect John Adams waited back in Quincy, Massachusetts, for official notification of his election, just as President-elect George Washington waited at Mount Vernon. On April 6, 1789, when enough senators had arrived to constitute a quorum, their second order of business—after filing their own credentials—was to elect John Langdon of New Hampshire as president of the Senate, "for the sole purpose of opening and counting the votes for President of the United States." Once the ballots were read, Washington and Adams had to be notified, and, in their absence, the Senate once again elected Langdon president pro tempore. He served until John Adams appeared in the Senate chamber on April 21. On that day, Senator Langdon escorted Adams to the presiding officer's chair.[1]

The National Portrait Gallery's 1989 exhibit on "The First Federal Congress," which commemorated the congressional bicentennial, included a handsome oil painting of John Langdon, whose appearance suggested a well-dressed man with a strong chin and gentle countenance. Langdon was born the

John Langdon served as the Senate's first president pro tempore. *Library of Congress*

son of a farmer in Portsmouth, New Hampshire, in 1741. As a young man, he had served an apprenticeship as clerk and had learned his trade as a merchant and as captain of a cargo ship. Later, he served in the Continental Congress and helped to finance the American military effort during the Revolution, personally leading a company at the battle of Saratoga. Langdon was thrice elected "president of New Hampshire," and, in 1787, became one of New Hampshire's two delegates to the Constitutional Convention. He paid not only his own way to Philadelphia, but also the expenses of his fellow delegate, Nicholas Gilman. Although there were no official political parties in 1789, John Langdon might accurately be described as a Federalist. An admirer of George Washington's administration, he defended the financial programs of Treasury Secretary Alexan-

[168]

der Hamilton. He even supported Hamilton's plan for the federal government to assume state war debts, which was tremendously unpopular in New Hampshire, since the voters had already paid off their own state's debt and had little desire to shoulder the burden for other states as well.[2]

Professor Roy Swanstrom, in his dissertation on the first fourteen years of the United States Senate, speculated on how this institution might have developed had Vice President Adams or President pro tempore Langdon interpreted their duties differently. The Constitution is quite unspecific in its definition of the vice president's role as presiding officer. Suppose that, instead of being so concerned with titles and ceremony, Adams had devoted his energies to promoting specific legislation. Perhaps the position might have evolved into a "chief legislator." But Adams saw the presiding officer as a distinctly neutral figure, and what he began has remained constant over the past two centuries. I should add, however, that our first vice president actively exercised his single constitutional function. John Adams cast more tie-breaking votes—twenty-nine of them—than has any vice president who succeeded him. By contrast, during his eight years of service in that post in the 1980's, George Bush cast only eight tie-breaking votes.[3]

Perhaps the role as Adams viewed it is all we might reasonably have expected from vice presidents, but the situation of the president pro tempore is more ambiguous. Unlike the vice president, the president pro tempore is a duly elected member of the Senate, able to speak and vote on any issue. Perhaps this official was in a better position to assume leadership in the body, particularly in that era long before the creation of the posts of majority and minority leaders and party whips. (The vice president is not at liberty to address the Senate, except by unanimous consent. Nor should any senator speak while presiding, other than to make necessary rulings and announcements or to maintain order.)

The obvious limitation to the president pro tempore's role was that he presided only in the absence of the vice president, and those early vice presidents were rarely absent. Professor Swanstrom pointed out that, during the eighteenth century, the position of president pro tempore was "short and uncertain," with fourteen men filling the post in the years between 1789 and 1801. He suggested that John Langdon was elected not because of his leadership abilities but because of his admirable record during the Revolutionary War and his "gracious and sociable manner." As presiding officer, Langdon won praise for being "attentive, prompt, and impartial." He was reelected during Adams' absences in 1792 and 1793. But John Langdon eventually fell out of favor with the Federalists. His belief in republicanism, abhorrence of any traces of monarchy, and admiration for the French Revolution all caused Langdon to shift into the rival Antifederalist camp. As Swanstrom noted, "By 1794 he had become so much a Jeffersonian that Adams, believing that Langdon would again be named Presiding Officer in his absence, felt he could not leave the Capital." [4]

Since the end of World War II, with one exception in 1947, it has been traditional for the Senate to elect the senior member of the majority party as president pro tempore. In the earliest years, however, the Senate lacked both established parties and extended seniority. Presidents pro tempore, elected on a temporary basis, were chosen because of their personal characteristics, popularity, and reliability. During the Second Congress, for example, the Senate elected Richard Henry Lee of Virginia as president pro tempore. As a member of the Continental Congress, Lee had introduced the resolution that led to our Declaration of Independence. He served as a colonel in the Virginia militia and was a delegate to the Constitutional Convention—although he strongly opposed ratification of the Constitution it produced. It was Lee whose arrival in New York in 1789 finally created a quorum so that the Senate could begin its work.

Another Virginia senator, Henry Tazewell, was elected president pro tempore in February 1795. The remarkable fact here is that the forty-one-year-old Tazewell had only entered the Senate two months earlier, in December 1794! Moreover, he was a Jeffersonian Republican at a time when the Senate was controlled by the Federalist party. Could anyone imagine the election today of a young freshman member of the minority party as president pro tempore? It would be inconceivable! Senator Tazewell must have been a remarkable man. He was a Revolutionary War veteran, a state legislator who helped frame the Virginia state constitution and bill of rights, and a former chief justice of the Virginia Supreme Court. One biographer called him "perhaps the most popular Virginian of his day"—surely an impressive accomplishment in the era of Washington, Jefferson, and Madison. Tazewell might have become a more famous name in our history had he not fallen ill while traveling from Virginia to Philadelphia in January 1799 to begin his second term in the Senate. He died shortly thereafter at the age of forty-five.[5]

That the Senate took the post of president pro tempore seriously can be seen in the Presidential Succession Act of 1792. Should the offices of president and vice president both become vacant, then the president pro tempore would succeed to the presidency, followed by the Speaker of the House. Members of the House preferred a line of succession within the executive branch, with the secretary of state next in line, but increasing Federalist dismay over the policies of Secretary of State Thomas Jefferson and increas-

ing Republican dismay over the policies of Secretary of the Treasury Alexander Hamilton persuaded the Senate to insist on the primacy of the two congressional officials. This succession law remained in effect until 1886. The arrangement created a serious consequence on at least one occasion. When President Abraham Lincoln was assassinated in 1865, Vice President Andrew Johnson succeeded him, and the president pro tempore, Senator Ben Wade of Ohio, became next in line to the White House. During the impeachment trial in 1868, had the Senate voted to remove Johnson, Senator Wade would have become president of the United States. Senator Wade, it should be noted, cast his vote in favor of conviction, and President Johnson, after his acquittal, objected to placing the president pro tempore in the line of succession because he would therefore be "interested in producing a vacancy."[6]

Professor Hans Trefousse, the biographer of "Bluff Ben" Wade, discussed the reason a substantial number of Republican senators did not want to elevate their president pro tempore to the presidency. Ever since Wade came to the Senate in 1851, he had been one of the most consistently outspoken antislavery men. He had pressed Presidents Lincoln and Johnson to adopt more stringent federal Reconstruction of the defeated South. He had defended the southern freedmen from the various Black Codes that southern states had enacted immediately after the war, and he had similarly fought for racial equality in the North. These were righteous but not necessarily popular issues, especially in the postwar years when more conservative politicians wanted to quiet passions rather than stir them. Even more troubling to Republican conservatives, Senator Wade began to speak out on behalf of the laboring man and against society's inequitable distribution of wealth. The *Chicago Trib-*

Senators elected Henry Tazewell president pro tempore in 1795, soon after he became a senator.

Virginia Historical Society

Had the Senate convicted Andrew Johnson at his impeachment trial, President Pro Tempore Benjamin Wade would have succeeded him as president of the United States. *Library of Congress*

une, which endorsed impeachment, added that "the only doubt that has ever hung over the impeachment of Johnson has been raised by the consideration that Mr. Wade, with his infirmities of temper and speech, would be his successor." Fear of Wade as president, therefore, may have been the most significant factor in salvaging Andrew Johnson's cause in the Senate.[7]

Johnson's demands for changes in the order of presidential succession were ignored for two more decades. While the personality and politics of the president pro tempore lay at the heart of Johnson's complaint, vacancies in the office presented a far more pressing problem. In the eighteenth and nineteenth centuries, the Senate assumed that it was empowered to elect a president pro tempore only during the absence of a vice president. But what should senators do at the end of a session? Since Congress was out of ses-

sion for half of each year, what would happen if there were no designated president pro tempore? If the vice president became president, who would preside at the opening of the next Senate session? Rather than settle these problems by statute or rules changes, the Senate for decades relied upon an elaborate charade in which the vice president would voluntarily absent himself from the chamber at the end of the session to enable the Senate to elect a president pro tempore. Some vice presidents refused to perform this little courtesy. In 1813, when President James Madison was seriously ill, Vice President Elbridge Gerry refused to vacate the chair for the election of a president pro tempore, in order that House Speaker Henry Clay, rather than one of Madison's critics in the Senate, would assume the presidency should both Madison and Gerry die during the recess.[8]

A critical vacancy in the office of president pro tempore occurred in 1881. The previous occupant, Ohio Democratic Senator Allen Thurman, had lost his race for reelection the previous year. When the Senate met in special session in March 1881, the two parties were exactly divided—the only time that has happened in our history. There were 37 Republican senators, 37 Democrats, and 2 Independents. That same election made the Republican ticket of James Garfield and Chester A. Arthur president and vice president. One of the Independents announced that he would vote with the Democrats to organize the Senate, placing considerable pressure on the remaining Independent, Senator William Mahone of Virginia. Senate Democrats had high hopes that Mahone would side with them, giving them a 39 to 37 majority, but, at the dramatic moment in the roll call, Mahone switched to the Republican side of the aisle (in return for the chairmanship of the Agriculture Committee and considerable patronage power), splitting the

Senate 38 to 38. This gave Republican Vice President Chester Arthur the tie-breaking vote. With a number of Republicans absent because of illness, however, Republicans frequently could not muster a quorum or guarantee enough votes to carry their cause. Since it was not at all clear that they could elect a president pro tempore in Arthur's absence, the vice president remained consistently in the chair throughout the special session. There was, therefore, no president pro tempore when the Senate adjourned in May, or when President Garfield died of an assassin's bullet in September, making Chester Arthur president.[9]

When President Arthur called the Senate into session in October 1881, there was no presiding officer. On the day that the Senate convened, Senator Isham G. Harris, a Tennessee Democrat, took the chair and announced that he had "been requested by a number of Senators on both sides of the Chamber to call the Senate to order." Harris then presided while the Senate elected a president pro tempore. Since several resignations had occurred, the Democrats now had a majority of members, and when the votes were counted, they had elected Democrat Thomas Bayard of Delaware president pro tempore. When the senators returned in December for the regular session, they chose David B. Davis of Illinois as their presiding officer.

David Davis must be counted among the least regular politicians ever to serve in this body. He shifted his support from party to party and candidate to candidate as it suited his conscience. A man of impressive girth, Davis had managed his old friend Abraham Lincoln's nomination for president in 1860, and later Lincoln placed him on the U.S. Supreme Court. In 1872, while on the Court, Davis was nominated for the presidency by the Labor Reform Convention, but he withdrew when he failed to win the endorsement

In 1881, with the Senate almost equally divided between Republicans and Democrats, President Pro Tempore David Davis arranged a compromise that permitted the Senate to proceed with its business.
Library of Congress

of the small, reform-minded Liberal Republican party. In 1876, as a Supreme Court justice, Davis had been appointed to the special commission to determine the disputed presidential election of 1876. During those proceedings, Illinois Democrats elected him a United States senator, causing Davis to resign from the commission. His replacement, a more regular Republican Supreme Court justice, cast the deciding vote in favor of electing the Republican candidate, Rutherford B. Hayes, as president of the United States. In the Senate, Davis continued along his independent path. As president pro tempore faced with the deadlock between the parties in 1881, he concluded that, since the Republicans controlled the presidency and the House of Representatives, they should continue as chairmen of the Senate's committees, even though the Democrats held a two-vote majority. He did, however, permit the Democrats to continue in office their previously elected secretary of the Senate and sergeant at arms, a compromise that placated both sides.[10]

The election of 1884 put Grover Cleveland in the White House and made former Indiana Senator Thomas Hendricks vice president. Although Democrats held a majority in the House, Republicans had a nine-vote majority in the Senate. Presiding throughout the special session of the Senate that ran from March 4 to April 2, 1885, Democratic Vice President Hendricks prevented the Republicans from electing a president pro tempore. When Hendricks died in November 1885, before the opening of the regular first session of the Forty-ninth Congress, the House of Representatives for that Congress had not yet convened. Thus, the country was left with no vice president, no Senate president pro tempore, and no Speaker of the House.

Once again, the Senate convened without a presiding officer. On opening day, December 7, 1885, the secretary of the Senate, Anson G. McCook, sat in the presiding officer's chair, one of the very rare occasions when someone other than a vice president or senator has presided over the United States Senate. The Senate proceeded immediately to elect a president pro tempore, Ohio Republican John Sherman. Later in that session, Senator George F. Hoar of Massachusetts expressed concern about the frequency of such vacancies in the vice presidency and office of president pro tempore and called for a revision of the succession act. "The present arrangement is bad," he told the Senate, because "during a large portion of the term there is no officer in being who can succeed." Senator Hoar went on to argue that the Senate did not elect its presidents pro tempore on any consideration of their fitness to

become chief executive. The president pro tempore was by then a senior senator, chosen "for his capacity as a debater and a framer of legislation." Most likely, the president pro tempore would have "little or no executive experience." Hoar then pointed out that no president pro tempore had ever served as president, and only one, Lewis Cass, had even been a candidate for president. By contrast, six secretaries of state had been elected president. Following Hoar's reasoning, Congress in 1886 passed a new law that removed the president pro tempore and Speaker of the House entirely from the line of presidential succession, leaving at its head the secretary of state and the other cabinet members, all nonelected officials.[11]

This was the order of succession until 1947, when, at the urging of President Harry S. Truman, the law was again revised. Having served ten years in the Senate, Truman held the post of vice president only eighty-two days before Franklin Roosevelt's death propelled him into the White House. As a student of history and a fervent democrat, Truman was troubled that the next person in the line of succession was his secretary of state, Edward Stettinius. The secretary had never run for elective office, and as Truman stated, "it was my feeling that any man who stepped into the presidency should have held at least some office to which he had been elected by a vote of the people." Two months after becoming president, Truman proposed restoring the president pro tempore and Speaker of the House to the line of succession.[12]

An interesting feature of Truman's proposal was its reversal of the earlier order of succession, putting the Speaker of the House ahead of the president pro tempore. There were several reasons for this change. In his memoirs, Truman argued that the House Speaker, as an elected representative of his district, as well as the chosen leader of the

[174]

"elected representatives of the people," should stand next in line to the vice president. Of course, one could make the same argument for the president pro tempore, as the elected official of the people of his state and of the United States Senate. It is likely that specific personalities also played a role in Truman's thinking. The Speaker of the House in 1945 was Texas Representative Sam Rayburn, while the president pro tempore of the Senate was Kenneth McKellar of Tennessee. Rayburn was then a relatively young and vigorous Speaker, while presidents pro tempore were usually the oldest, or among the most senior, members of the Senate. McKellar's predecessor, Carter Glass of Virginia, had become so enfeebled that he had been unable to attend any sessions of the Senate during his last several years in office. McKellar himself was a cantankerous fellow, who simply did not stand as high in Truman's esteem as did "Mr. Sam." Truman had publicly declared that Speaker Rayburn was "probably the most influential man in the United States, next to the President." [13]

There may also have been an institutional factor in Truman's reversal of the roles. Between the 1886 removal of the president pro tempore from the order of succession and 1947, some entirely new leadership posts had evolved in the Senate: the majority and minority leaders and the party whips. Beginning in the 1920's, when the Democratic and Republican parties first officially designated floor leaders, such influential men as Charles Curtis of Kansas, Joseph Robinson of Arkansas, and Alben Barkley of Kentucky had been elected majority leader. By 1945, most Washington observers regarded the majority leader as the Senate's functional equivalent of the Speaker of the House of Representatives, while the president pro tempore had become more of a ceremonial office. Had Truman drawn a list of men, rather than offices, he would certainly have included

Alben Barkley in the line of succession—indeed, in 1948, Truman chose Senator Barkley as his vice presidential running mate. But, for the purposes of legislation, the president recommended inclusion of a constitutionally created officer, the president pro tempore, rather than a party-designated officer, the majority leader.

Truman's reversal of the two posts may well account for the alacrity with which the House embraced his proposal, as well as for the hesitancy of the Senate. The House immediately passed the presidential succession plan, but the Senate failed to act. Then, in the next Congress—the Republican Eightieth Congress—Truman resubmitted his proposal, much to everyone's surprise. The change in majorities in the House and Senate from Democratic to Republican meant that Truman was recommending succession by congressional leaders of the opposition party, rather than by his own cabinet officers. This "lack of partisanship" won great applause from Republicans, and the measure then passed both the House and Senate (the latter by a generally party-line vote of 50 to 35). Today, the president pro tempore continues to follow the Speaker of the House in the presidential succession, followed in turn by the secretary of state and the other cabinet secretaries. [14]

In terms of the president pro tempore's role in the Senate, an even more significant change took place in 1890, when the Senate adopted a resolution proposed by New York Senator William Evarts. Thereafter, presidents pro tempore were not elected just for the period of the vice president's absence, but they held the office continuously until the election of another president pro tempore. As a result, since 1890, with a single exception, each president pro tempore has served until he retired, died, or had the misfortune to see his party lose its majority. Thus, Senator John J. Ingalls of Kansas, who

[175]

The sharp-tongued John J. Ingalls served as president pro tempore from 1887 to 1891. *Library of Congress*

had previously been elected president pro tempore on four consecutive occasions, held the post without further election until he left the Senate in 1891.[15] The very first sentence of Rule I of today's standing rules of the Senate provides that the president pro tempore shall hold the office "during the pleasure of the Senate and until another is elected or his term of office as a Senator expires."

John J. Ingalls was a noteworthy senator. Today, few visitors to the Capitol are likely to recognize the statue of the tall, skinny man with mustache and goatee in Statuary Hall, but, during his years in Congress, he was an individual who demanded attention and recognition. Born in Massachusetts, Ingalls attended Williams College in Williamstown, Massachusetts. Restive at the school's requirement for compulsory chapel attend-

ance and its regular reporting to parents about students' deportment, Ingalls exacted his revenge in a commencement address he entitled "Mummy Life." In this oration, a forerunner of the many vituperative speeches he would deliver on the Senate floor, he vigorously castigated his college's oppressive church-dominated atmosphere.[16]

After studying law, John J. Ingalls migrated to the Kansas frontier, where he became active in antislavery politics. He lost two races for lieutenant governor and, in 1872, entered what was expected to be a losing race against incumbent Republican Senator Samuel Pomeroy. But, after a Kansas state legislator accused Pomeroy of offering a bribe to support his reelection, Ingalls won the contest. In the Senate, Ingalls was notable not as a productive legislator, but as a scathing speaker. One reporter noted that Ingalls' strength lay in "making vitriolic speeches that stung like the attack of a hornet. He was unique as a rhetorician. His vocabulary was inexhaustible, and as a word-painter he was unsurpassed in public life."[17]

Once, Senator John Sherman (who also served as president pro tempore) appeared before the Senate District of Columbia Committee to advocate the opening of a street that would enhance property that he owned. Sherman argued that Washington, like Rome, should be a beautiful capital. Senator Ingalls, who chaired the committee, replied contemptuously that he had never heard of a Roman senator who advocated improving the Appian Way at public expense for private benefit. During a heated debate with Senator Daniel Voorhees of Indiana, Ingalls snapped, "If this were a police court, the Senator from Indiana would be sent to the rock pile for being drunk and disorderly." Ingalls was clearly a senator with whom few would wish to cross verbal swords, and, yet, his colleagues thought highly enough of him

President Pro Tempore David R. Atchison liked to claim that he had been, technically, president of the United States for one day, before the swearing-in of Zachary Taylor. *Missouri Historical Society*

to elect him repeatedly as president pro tempore between 1887 and 1891.[18]

Few nineteenth-century presidents pro tempore served for any lengthy term, with a handful of exceptions. Among these was Alabama's William R. King, who served as president pro tempore between 1836 and 1841, and again from 1850 to 1852, following the death of President Zachary Taylor, when Vice President Millard Fillmore went to the White House. In 1852, Senator King was elected vice president, but he died in April 1853 and never presided over the Senate.

David R. Atchison of Missouri served as president pro tempore from 1846 through 1849, and again from 1852 to 1854. In Missouri, there is a statue of Senator Atchison that identifies him as president of the United States for one day, March 4, 1849. Since the traditional day for presidential inaugura-

tions, then March 4, fell on a Sunday that year, President-elect Zachary Taylor waited until Monday to be sworn in. Senator Atchison based his claim to the presidency that Sunday on the grounds that, as president pro tempore, he was next in the line of succession—although he never took the presidential oath. When asked later about his "presidency," Senator Atchison liked to say, "That was the honestest administration this country ever had." Although scholars dismiss Atchison's claim, he did in fact come close to becoming president four years later. In 1853, on his way to Washington, President-elect Franklin Pierce was in a train wreck that took the life of his only child. If Pierce had not survived the accident, David R. Atchison, as president pro tempore, would have succeeded to the presidency, since Vice President King died a month after the inauguration.[19]

Another memorable president pro tempore was Indiana's Jesse D. Bright, who served from 1854 to 1856, and again in 1860. Only two years later, in 1862, the Senate expelled Bright for his Confederate sympathies, because he had written a letter promoting arms sales by one of his constituents. Unfortunately for Senator Bright, he had written the letter to President Jefferson Davis of the Confederate States of America. When angry Senate colleagues learned of this treachery, they voted to expel their former president pro tempore. Like Bright's contemporaries, historians have a low regard for the senator. Professor William Gienapp recently characterized Bright as "hateful and extraordinarily ambitious"and noted that, "despite his belligerent personality, the senator often dodged controversial issues until it was clear which way the political winds were blowing, and his pro-southern sympathies (he owned a plantation and slaves in Kentucky) would ultimately subvert his leadership."[20]

A very different personality was projected by Rhode Island's Henry Anthony, publisher of the *Providence Journal* and president pro tempore from 1869 to 1873, and again in 1875. A charming, genial, dignified man, he was clearly popular among his Republican colleagues, who elected him president pro tempore. In 1875, the Republicans made Senator Anthony their caucus chairman, after which he declined to serve as president pro tempore, "no doubt pleased to be rid of its formal duties," as one historian has speculated. Clearly, the job of chairman of the party caucus—which, among other responsibilities, selected members of the powerful Committee on Committees—must have outranked that of president pro tempore in stature and desirability at the time.[21]

The longest-serving president pro tempore was William P. Frye of Maine, who held the post for fifteen years between 1896 and 1911. Senator Frye belonged to the small group of senators who dominated the national government at the turn of this century. Elected to replace James G. Blaine in the Senate, Frye took his seat on March 18, 1881, just two weeks after his Maine colleague, Eugene Hale, had been sworn in for his own first Senate term. Frye, the older of the two men, thereafter served for thirty years as the "junior" senator from Maine— "junior" in seniority to Hale, the "senior" senator. Both Maine senators were close allies of The Senate Four—Nelson Aldrich of Rhode Island, William Allison of Iowa, John Spooner of Wisconsin, and Orville Platt of Connecticut—who made up the conservative leadership of the Senate in the Progressive Era.

Twice during his tenure as president pro tempore, Frye presided over the Senate during vacancies in the vice presidency: first, after the death of Vice President Garret Hobart, and again when Vice President Theodore Roosevelt became president. In recognition of his genial service as presiding officer, the Senate presented him with a

Twice during William P. Frye's fifteen years as president pro tempore (1896–1911) vacancies in the vice presidency left him next in line for the White House.
U.S. Senate Historical Office

silver loving-cup in 1901. Senator Frye, however, was held in less esteem by the muckraking investigative journalists of his era. In his classic attack, *The Treason of the Senate*, David Graham Phillips dismissed Maine's senators Hale and Frye as tools of special interests. "Neither Hale nor Frye is in the Senate for the people," wrote Phillips. "In the vital matter, the people *versus* the confiscators of their property, Hale sits for his millions well invested with 'the interests,' and Frye for his dear friends in politics and social life."[22]

Senator Frye resigned as president pro tempore in April 1911, due to ill health, and died a few months later. When the Senate sought to elect his successor as president pro tempore, the Republican majority split, with progressive Republicans refusing to vote for the conservative Senator Jacob Gallinger of New Hampshire. The Democrats put forward the equally conservative Thomas Martin of Virginia. Progressive Republicans, therefore, nominated one of their own, Senator Moses Clapp of Minnesota. As a result of this three-way race, no candidate received a majority. The question was raised whether a plurality vote would be sufficient to elect a president pro tempore, but the presiding officer ruled that a majority vote was necessary, in the absence of any provisions to the contrary. The presiding officer also decided that the business of electing a president pro tempore was privileged and could not be interrupted by any other business. The Senate deadlocked on ballot after ballot between May 11 and May 17, 1911, and tried and failed again on June 5. Finally, senators sought a compromise to enable them to return to their regular business. On August 12, Republican Senator Reed Smoot of Utah proposed that Senator Augustus Bacon, a Georgia Democrat, serve as president pro tempore for a single day, Monday, August 15, during the expected absence of the vice president. Bacon was unanimously elected. Thereafter, Bacon and four Republicans, Charles Curtis, Jacob Gallinger, Henry Cabot Lodge of Massachusetts, and Frank Brandegee of Connecticut, alternated as presidents pro tempore for a few days or weeks at a time throughout the Sixty-second Congress.[23]

Still another contretemps occurred in 1923, after Vice President Calvin Coolidge succeeded to the presidency following the death of Warren G. Harding. The president pro tempore, Albert B. Cummins, was an Iowa Republican who had stood among the progressives during his earlier years in the Senate but had moved considerably to the right by the 1920's. "I saw him changing gradually, almost daily," observed the cru-

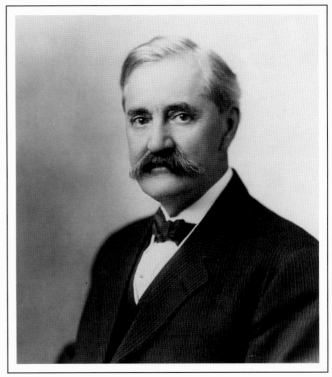

Originally a progressive Republican, President Pro Tempore Albert B. Cummins grew increasingly conservative.   *U.S. Senate Historical Office*

sading progressive Senator George Norris, "and it is one of the sad recollections of my public life to have seen this man, with his ability, gradually go over to the other side." Cummins had served as president pro tempore since 1919 and wished to continue in the post, but, when the first session of the Sixty-eighth Congress convened, he confronted three other candidates. With the conservative forces divided, the progressive Republicans held the balance of power. Pointing out that Cummins also chaired the Committee on Interstate Commerce, they objected to Cummins' holding two leadership posts. Progressives wanted him to relinquish his committee chairmanship, so that Senator Robert La Follette, Sr., could succeed him. Since this was a fate that conservative forces had no desire to endure, they encouraged Cummins to step down as president pro tempore instead. The contest lasted throughout December and was not resolved until January 1924. Cummins retained his post as president pro tempore, but the progressives threw their support behind a Democrat, Ellison D. "Cotton Ed" Smith of South Carolina, to chair the Interstate Commerce Committee.[24]

After Albert Cummins lost his race for reelection in 1926, he was succeeded as president pro tempore by New Hampshire's George H. Moses. An outspoken leader of the Republican "Old Guard," Moses had antagonized Republican progressives, whom he publicly dubbed the "Sons of the Wild Jackass." In December 1931, progressives were determined to defeat Moses as president pro tempore. Knowing that Moses lacked the votes, Republican Majority Leader James Watson did not call for election of a president pro tempore at the beginning of the Seventy-second Congress; but, with a smile, the Democratic minority leader, Joseph Robinson, called for a vote. Although the Republicans held the majority, the Democratic candidate received a plurality of the votes. The Senate stalled in deadlock for a month, unable to elect a new presiding officer. At last, the vice president ruled that the Senate could take up other pending business by majority vote and that the president pro tempore would continue in office until a successor was chosen. The Senate went on to other business, and Moses continued in his post.[25]

The Democratic victory in 1932 ushered in a new era in American political history and a new president pro tempore of the Senate. Nevada's Key Pittman was certainly one of the most colorful men to hold the office. Although he was born in Mississippi and educated at Southwestern Presbyterian University in Tennessee, Pittman's experiences as a prospector in the Klondike gold rush in 1897, district attorney in Nome, Alaska, and as a lawyer in the silver-mining town of Tonopah, Nevada, made him a product of the Old West. He served in the U.S. Senate from 1913 until his death in 1940, rising to become chairman of the Foreign Relations Committee and a major player in American foreign relations during the decade before World War II. He was a fierce supporter of silver purchases and inflation as a cure to national economic ills, and he was known to brandish his shooting irons against those who disagreed. A hard-drinking man who enjoyed relaxing at the racetrack, Pittman was elected president pro tempore in 1933.

When Pittman died in 1940, he was replaced as president pro tempore by William H. King of Utah. King had recently lost his race for renomination, and his election to a brief term as president pro tempore was meant as a final tribute from his colleagues.

When the new Congress convened in January 1941, the Democrats chose Senator Pat Harrison of Mississippi to be president pro tempore. Harrison had been defeated by only a single vote for majority leader in 1937, and his election as president pro tempore reflected his continued popularity among his colleagues.

Senator Carter Glass of Virginia was elected president pro tempore following Harrison's death later in 1941. Like most of his predecessors, Glass was a senior senator, but not *the* senior senator in his party. This marked the last occasion on which Senate Democrats chose someone other than the most senior member of their party for this position. Glass' successor, Kenneth McKellar, outranked all other members of his party in seniority in 1945 when he became president pro tempore. The Republicans similarly followed suit, with the exception of Senator Arthur Vandenberg of Michigan, who was second in terms of seniority in his party when he became president pro tempore in 1947, during the Eightieth Congress.

In recent years, some venerable senior senators have held the post of president pro

Kenneth McKellar was the senior Senate Democrat in 1945 when he became president pro tempore.

U.S. Senate Historical Office

tempore, including Walter George of Georgia, Carl Hayden of Arizona, Richard B. Russell of Georgia, Allen Ellender of Louisiana, James Eastland of Mississippi, Warren Magnuson of Washington, Strom Thurmond of South Carolina, and John C. Stennis of Mississippi. We should also add to that list Milton Young of North Dakota, who, at the end of his thirty-six years in the Senate, was elected president pro tempore for one day, on December 5, 1980, although his party was still in the minority. Of these men, Senator Hayden served the longest in the post, from 1957 until his retirement in 1969. He was also the last president pro tempore to hold the "patronage book," as they called it then. In those days, many of the positions around the Senate, from messengers to Capitol policemen, were political appointees rather than professional staff, and the president pro tempore, at least on the Democratic side, held considerable influence in the distribution of that patronage.[26]

The so-called powers of the president pro tempore, which have generally been more responsibilities than powers, have changed a good deal over the past two centuries. Since 1816, presidents pro tempore have received a larger salary than other senators, and, for a period after 1856, they were compensated at the same rate as the vice president. Since March 1969, the salary of the president pro tempore has been the same as that of the majority and minority leaders. During the early nineteenth century, between 1823 and 1863, presidents pro tempore appointed members of the Senate's standing committees, either indirectly or directly. Since 1820, the president pro tempore has had the power to name other senators to perform the duties of the chair in his absence. In modern times, presidents pro tempore have tended to ask new members of the majority party to preside over the Senate, a practice which enables freshmen senators to grow more accustomed

to the Senate's rules and procedures, and for which we present a "Golden Gavel" award for one hundred hours of presiding. (On October 20, 1989, I became the first president pro tempore to receive this award.)

In 1963, a resolution of the Senate made Senator Lee Metcalf of Montana the acting president pro tempore to assist Senator Carl Hayden. Senator Metcalf performed those duties under several presidents pro tempore. In 1977, the Senate created the position of deputy president pro tempore and elected former Vice President Hubert Humphrey to the post. By a sad coincidence, both the deputy and the assistant presidents pro tempore died within hours of each other on January 12 and 13, 1978. In January 1987, the Senate, upon my recommendation, elected Senator George Mitchell of Maine as deputy president pro tempore for the duration of the One-hundredth Congress.

Because the president pro tempore stands in the line of presidential succession, he is given a direct-access telephone to the White House and would receive special evacuation assistance from Washington in the case of a national emergency. On the Democratic side, the president pro tempore is an ex-officio member of his party's leadership, including the conference, the policy committee, and the steering committee, in which capacities he works closely with the Democratic floor leader. Various laws assign the president pro tempore authority to make appointments to an assortment of national commissions, usually with the advice of the majority leader. If there are minority appointments, the president pro tempore generally acts upon the recommendations of the minority leader in appointing individuals acceptable to the minority. In the absence of the vice president, the president pro tempore may administer all oaths required by the Constitution, may sign legislation, and may fulfill all other obligations of the presiding officer. Also, in the absence of the vice president, the president pro tempore jointly presides with the Speaker of the House when the two houses sit together in joint sessions or joint meetings.

The president pro tempore works closely with the secretary and the sergeant at arms of the Senate, directing the enforcement of the rules governing the use of the Capitol and the Senate office buildings. Jointly with the Speaker of the House, and at the recommendation of the Budget committees, the president pro tempore appoints the director of the Congressional Budget Office. As a staff assistant to Senator Warren G. Magnuson observed in 1981, the position of president pro tempore has "the honor and with it the responsibility." The occupant of the office, he said, "makes more or less out of it." [27]

As I said in 1980, long before I attained the post myself, "the election of a senator to the office of the president pro tempore has always been considered one of the highest honors offered to a senator by the Senate as a body." As I trust my remarks have indicated, that honor has been bestowed upon a colorful and significant group of senators during the past two centuries—men who stamped their imprint upon the office and upon their times. I am proud to join their ranks and to perform the duties of president pro tempore of the United States Senate.

CHAPTER 7

Party Floor Leaders

*April 18, 1980**

Mr. President, the majority leader is the dominant figure in the modern American Senate. According to political scientist George Goodwin, "the Senate has never formally entrusted any person . . . with as much power as the House did its Speaker . . . in some ways, however, the Senate majority leader comes close to the Speaker of the House. . . . No one questions the fact that the Senate is run from the floor and not the chair." [1] But this has not always been the case.

Although the offices of majority leader and minority leader in the Senate, as we know them today, are recent developments, former Senate Parliamentarian Floyd Riddick has written that, since 1789, various senators have "assumed leading roles" in determining "what the Senate would or would not do." Such senators exercised their power by virtue of their stature or influence or personality.[2]

From time to time, since the beginning of the Senate, caucuses have been called of senators who belong to a particular party, have a common interest, or come from a particular region. Such caucuses have served a variety of purposes, including determining a position or devising strategy on a particular issue.[3] For many years, the late Richard B.

Russell of Georgia, for example, was recognized as the head of the southern bloc of senators. He was the undisputed leader of that group, particularly in dealing with civil rights issues. Senator Russell had a great knowledge of the rules. He was highly respected by all senators on both sides of the aisle for his fairness, his evenhandedness, his level-headedness, his common sense and good judgment, and he was considered a superior tactician in the use of Senate rules and precedents. In the judgment of many who served with him in the Senate, including myself, Senator Russell could have been elected majority leader had he chosen to seek the office. That some observers outside the Senate shared this view was apparent from the following report in George Goodwin's book, *The Little Legislatures: Committees of Congress*:

It is said that Senator Richard Russell could have had the majority leader position in the 81st Congress but that he turned it down because it involved too much coaxing of prima donnas. (It would also have forced him to moderate his role as spokesman for the South.) [4]

During the nineteenth century, there was no particular officer, designated as the majority leader, who attempted to schedule the

---

* Updated July 1989

legislation or to enforce unity in voting. Although the conferences, or caucuses, frequently served as instruments of party leadership, Floyd Riddick noted that, well into the latter part of the nineteenth century, senators "usually performed their tasks without party superintendence." [5]

In the late nineteenth century, the senators of each political party began to organize and assemble separately to choose a representative of the party to serve as an agent in operating the legislative machinery. All records studied thus far by scholars of Senate history indicate that not until the twentieth century did the posts of Senate majority leader and minority leader become "official political positions." [6]

At various periods of our nation's early history, certain senators stood out as legislative leaders, although they were not selected by their official parties to act in that capacity. Senator William Maclay of Pennsylvania, to whom I have referred on earlier occasions, left an account of the proceedings of the First Congress. These notes indicate that, even in the earliest Congress, certain senators carried particular weight:

it was patching peicing altering & amending And even originating new Business. It was however only for Elsworth, King or some of Hamilton's People to Rise and the thing was generally done. [7]

Another senator without any official title as leader who left a characteristic impression upon the product of the Senate was Henry Clay of Kentucky. A colleague once remarked about Clay,

When that Senator (Clay) shakes his head and says, "I hope not," we know how the yeas and nays will stand as well as if they had been taken and counted. [8]

On one occasion, Clay commented, "I do not like to be a dictator in any sense." To this, a senator replied, "You do it so well, you

ought to like it." [9] Clay's leadership was not in the Senate alone. He was the leader of the Whig party throughout the Union.

Senator William B. Allison of Iowa became a power in the Senate during the more than thirty-five years he served in this body, from March 1873 until August 1908. He was chairman of the Appropriations Committee for twenty-four and one-half years and chairman of the Republican caucus for eight years. Of Allison's standing among his Senate colleagues, Senator Augustus Octavius Bacon of Georgia said, "In the final stages of almost every important controverted and difficult question, his were most frequently the words which in the end determined the fate of the measure, and, if successful, the shape it should finally bear." [10] Actually, during the first years of the twentieth century, the Senate was dominated not by one senator but by a collegial group of four senators that included Allison. The other members of "the Senate Four" were Nelson Aldrich of Rhode Island, Orville H. Platt of Connecticut, and John C. Spooner of Wisconsin. These were the "four bosses" of the Senate, whom I have described elsewhere as "the august and powerful senators with whom the brash young President Theodore Roosevelt would have to deal if he wished to enact his legislative program." [11]

Woodrow Wilson once wrote in the late nineteenth century: "No one is *the* Senator. No one may speak for his party as well as for himself; no one exercises the special trust of acknowledged leadership." [12]

By the early twentieth century, the party caucuses had chairmen, but neither party elected a leader as such, so that no one served as majority leader of the Senate. In 1903, the Democrats, and, in 1911, the Republicans, began electing a caucus chairman. [13] In 1905, for example, the Democrats elected Maryland Senator Arthur P. Gorman as caucus chairman, and, in 1906, the party elected

Senator Joseph C. S. Blackburn of Kentucky to be its caucus chairman but not its floor leader. On the latter occasion, the caucus adopted the following resolution:

> The Democratic Senators in selecting as the chairman of this conference Senator Blackburn of Kentucky, congratulate themselves and their several constituencies upon the fact that they have among their number one so well fitted by his marked capacity, his great acquirements, and his large experience in Congressional work, and especially by his power as an orator and as a debator, to render to his party associates the most signal and valuable services as their chosen official leader in the great forum of the Senate of the United States.[14]

In his history of majority and minority leaders, Floyd Riddick outlined the gradual evolution of the position of party floor leader, as follows:

> In March 1913, after Democrats had regained the majority in the Senate following two decades in the minority, they elected John W. Kern of Indiana as caucus chairman. Although serving in his freshman term, Kern was a nationally prominent Democrat closely allied with President Wilson's progressive wing of the party. His party sought effective leadership to hold together their narrow majority and to enact Wilson's ambitious programs. Kern's floor leadership antedated many of the later functions of that post, causing newspapers to refer to him as "Majority Leader Kern," and "the Democratic floor leader in the Senate," even though he lacked any official party designation other than caucus chairman.[15]

Thus, in the early years of this century, both parties elected chairmen for their respective party conferences or caucuses, but no senator was elected to be the majority leader or the minority leader as we know the offices today. As late as the 1920's, the chairmen of the standing committees were generally the ones to move that the Senate consider the legislation reported by their respective committees. The caucus chairmen at that time did not always occupy the center aisle seats. Nor were they always the spokesmen

Senate Democrats designated Oscar Underwood of Alabama as floor leader in 1920. *Library of Congress*

for their parties on the floor. They were chairmen of their party meetings and, in that capacity, they played an important role in determining legislation.[16]

According to Floyd Riddick, on January 15, 1920, for the first time, the Democratic Conference was called for the purpose of selecting "a 'leader' . . . and not just a chairman of the party caucus." In May 1920, "it was stated for the first time that the meeting was 'called to order'" by Alabama Senator Oscar Underwood, the "minority leader." [17]

Riddick related that, on March 5, 1921, at the beginning of the Sixty-seventh Congress, a meeting of the Democratic Conference "was called to elect officers of the party, 'including the Democratic leader.'" This action officially "established that the Democratic Party had created the office of party leader," who would serve as minority or majority leader, depending upon which party controlled the Senate.[18]

Charles Curtis of Kansas became the first official Republican floor leader in 1925. *Library of Congress*

"The story of the Republican conference was much the same," Riddick wrote. The conference minutes indicate that, "from 1911 until 1925," the Republican party, like the Democrats, "had elected one of [its] members to be chairman of [its] conference." Then, "on March 5, 1925, James E. Watson of Indiana nominated Senator Charles Curtis of Kansas to be chairman of the conference and floor leader." [19]

Although both Democrats and Republicans now elect their floor leaders, the Republican party's hierarchy of leadership is more diffused than that of the Democrats, being shared by various party members. In the Democratic party organization, the majority leader chairs the Democratic Conference, the Democratic Policy Committee, and the Democratic Steering Committee. I view this combined role as a matter of importance to Democratic leaders and to the party itself in the Senate. The Senate Republicans, unlike the Democrats, have long practiced a policy of shared leadership and have divided the chairmanships of party hierarchy committees among senators other than the leader. One reason may be that, except for a few brief intervals, the Republicans have been the minority party in the Senate for more than half a century. The combined chairmanships of the Democratic Conference and the policy and steering committees have constituted a major political tool in the hands of the leader of the party long in control of the Senate. Nonetheless, in January 1989, the new Democratic leader, Senator George Mitchell of Maine, chose to hand off the steering committee chairmanship to Senator Daniel Inouye of Hawaii and to share the leadership of the policy committee by appointing a vice chairman, Senator Tom Daschle of South Dakota.

The Democratic Steering Committee recommends assignments of Democratic senators to committees. The Democratic Policy Committee can aid in determining policy for the party, the shape and form of legislation, and whether or not certain legislation will be called up. The decisions of the Democratic Steering Committee are taken up before the Democratic Conference and are subject to its approval. Some decisions of the policy committee are likewise discussed in the Democratic Conference. When I first held the office of majority leader, from January 1977 through 1980, however, I made but little use of the policy committee and seldom called meetings. Instead, I established and chaired an informal committee of committee chairmen, which I convened from time to time in order to elicit the views of the chairmen with respect to the scheduling of legislation.

The length of time a senator serves before becoming Democratic leader has varied, as has the number of years a leader has held the post. My predecessor, Mike Mansfield of Montana, served sixteen years as majority leader, longer than anyone else in that posi-

George J. Mitchell of Maine and Bob Dole of Kansas served as Democratic and Republican leaders in the 101st Congress.

tion. Before becoming leader, Senator Mansfield had been in the Senate for eight years. Lyndon Johnson of Texas, who was Senator Mansfield's predecessor, and under whom I first served when I came to the Senate in January 1959, had been a senator for only four years before becoming leader. He held the post of leader for eight years. For my own part, I served four years as secretary of the Democratic Conference and six years as Democratic whip. Thus, I had been in the leadership for ten years, and in the Senate for eighteen, before I became majority leader.

The party floor leaders are selected to serve two-year terms by a majority of the senators of their respective parties assembled in conference. The majority leader must be on his good deportment all the time, because, at the beginning of each new Congress, he must face the judgment of his peers if he chooses to stand for reelection.

The majority and minority leaders are, as Floyd Riddick has pointed out, "spokesmen on the Senate floor for their respective political parties." Although "the office is a political one" and not created by the rules of the Senate, the rules and precedents confer certain "unique authority" on the majority and minority leaders.[20] For example, standing committees, except the Committee on Ap-

Democratic Majority Leader Mike Mansfield of Montana and Republican Leader Everett Dirksen of Illinois led their parties in the Senate during the 1960's.   *U.S. Senate Historical Office*

propriations and the Committee on the Budget, may not meet, without special leave, after the first two hours of Senate session. But the two leaders are authorized jointly to grant such consent without action by the Senate.[21]

By custom and practice, the two leaders also receive preferential recognition on the floor. The majority leader has first consideration from the chair, followed by the minority leader. Vice President John N. Garner, while presiding over the Senate in 1937, explained:

The Chair recognized the Senator from Kentucky because he is the leader on the Democratic side of the Chamber. He would recognize the Senator from Vermont, [Mr. Austin], acting Republican leader, in the same way.[22]

This power of first recognition is, by far, the most potent weapon in the majority leader's arsenal, enabling him to outflank any other senator in offering first- and second-degree amendments, substitutes, and motions to reconsider. Without it, he would be like the emperor without clothes.

The manager of a bill also is entitled to preferential recognition—not ahead of the two leaders, but following in line, and is accorded that recognition generally by the chair.

Since the 1920's, the majority and minority leaders have been assigned the first front-row seats on either side of the center aisle. Incidentally, Senate leaders have long been inscribing their names into the drawers of these desks. The first senator whose name is seen carved in the Democratic leader's desk drawer was Senator Joseph T. Robinson of Arkansas, followed by the names of Senators Alben W. Barkley of Kentucky, Scott W. Lucas of Illinois, Ernest W. McFarland of Arizona, Lyndon B. Johnson, Mike Mansfield, and, lastly, my own. The name of Senator George Mitchell, the current Democratic leader, has not, as of July 1989, been carved in the drawer, but it will undoubtedly appear there in due time.

One of the important functions of the Senate majority leader is to secure unanimous consent agreements limiting time, amendments, and motions on legislation called up for floor debate. I have probably secured more time agreements during my years in the leadership role—which includes my tenure in both the office of secretary of the Democratic Conference and the office of majority whip—than has any other senator in the history of the Senate. Even when I held these lesser offices, I arranged most of the time agreements.

As the majority leader in the Ninety-fifth and Ninety-sixth congresses, I made frequent use of the "two-track system," under

Arkansas Senator Joseph T. Robinson served as majority leader during the hectic years of the New Deal.

which the Senate would work on different pieces of legislation during the same day. The early part of the day would be spent on one measure, and later in the day the Senate would switch to another measure. We would continue in that fashion over a period of several days while those same pieces of legislation were being debated and acted upon.

The Senate majority leader, working with the minority leader, determines what matters or measures will be scheduled for floor action and when. He makes that determination based on his discussions with the committee chairmen, the subcommittee chairmen, or others who are going to manage the particular bills, resolutions, nominations, or other business. He also often touches base, through his staff, with senators who will be calling up amendments, and he seeks to keep the process moving in order to conclude the action and move on to the next item on the schedule.

The majority leader and the minority leader also need to keep themselves reasonably well briefed on fast-moving national and international events, and they often are called upon to receive and meet with heads of state and other foreign leaders who visit our country. They should be conversant with the rules and precedents and not wholly dependent upon the parliamentarians or floor staff for direction and advice. They must keep their respective memberships advised as to the legislative program and protect senators, to the extent possible, in scheduling votes. For their party members, the leaders and their policy committees act as clearinghouses for information about the status of pending legislation, while the majority leader generally alerts the full Senate on such matters.

The majority and minority leaders must stay on or near the floor most of the time, to protect the rights of their respective sides, keep the legislation moving, and participate in debate from time to time. Under the Senate's rules—unlike the House of Representatives—most legislation is called up by unanimous consent, after the majority leader has cleared it with the minority leader and members on both sides of the aisle. If it is not possible to call up a controversial bill by unanimous consent, the majority leader may call up the bill by motion, which, under ordinary circumstances, is debatable.

The personal relations between the majority and minority floor leaders are, therefore, very important. A great deal of cooperation between the two is required in moving legislation. In this body, courtesy, cooperation, and comity do much to keep the legislative process running smoothly. An element of compromise and forbearance is crucial if the Senate is to function properly—or if, indeed, it is to function at all.

Senator Howard Baker of Tennessee was the minority leader during my first two

Republican Leader Howard Baker of Tennessee and Democratic Leader Robert C. Byrd worked closely together in scheduling legislation.
George Tames/New York Times

terms as majority leader, from January 1977 through 1980. He was courtly, folksy, articulate, and smart, and possessed a keen political sense—a skillful and highly respected legislator and leader. Because most Senate business is taken up and transacted by unanimous consent, the minority leader's cooperation in the scheduling of legislation is critical to the expeditious handling of the heavy workload. To the extent that his own party leadership constraints and limitations allowed, Senator Baker cooperated by seeking and obtaining his party members' approval to schedule the legislation I wished to call up for Senate action. The legislative accomplishments of the Senate in the Ninety-fifth and Ninety-sixth congresses are a testament to his cooperation and to his leadership and statesmanship. As a leader, Senator Baker was necessarily partisan but not overly so, and I considered our leadership relations to be excellent.

When I again became the Senate majority leader at the beginning of the One-hundredth Congress, I found myself standing with a more partisan minority leader across the aisle: Senator Bob Dole of Kansas, who had been the majority leader in the preceding Congress. Senator Dole was congenial, witty, shrewd, clever, tough, and handsome, and, like Baker, he was a favorite with the news media. For the first six months, I felt that the relationship between the two of us was not the best and that the minority leader was keeping me on "a short leash" by delaying consent to call up bills. From time to time, on controversial matters, I was forced to position myself, using the rules, to make a non-debatable motion during the morning hour to take up legislation. Gradually, however, I sensed a decided improvement, and there developed a spirit of understanding and friendship between us that I shall continue to treasure. I could never have asked for a warmer and more cooperative relationship than that which existed between Bob Dole and myself as time went by. The outstanding legislative record of the Senate in the One-hundredth Congress is, in no small degree, due to the work and the assistance given by the minority party in the Senate under the leadership of Senator Dole and his assistant, Senator Alan K. Simpson of Wyoming.

Such a close working relationship between leaders of opposing parties has also existed at other times in the Senate's history. Former President Lyndon Johnson, for example, when he was majority leader of the Senate, described the way he worked with Minority Leader Everett M. Dirksen of Illinois:

Well, after I evaluate the bills on the calendar I ask him to make his recommendations. When I walk into the chamber every morning, he puts on my desk a memorandum stating what he thinks about each bill and what his policy group thinks and what his colleagues think—"This will be trouble," "This will be long debate," "This will have relatively little opposition," and so forth. And he marks the bills on the calendar in blue pencil. I evaluate mine and mark my calendar in red pencil. Then we exchange calendars. . . . I would say we spend a third or a fourth of every hour during the legislative day talking to each other and either trying to reach an agreement or to ascertain the points upon which agreement is not possible.[23]

The leader is the cement that holds his party group together. Lyndon Johnson, in a 1960 interview, stated that

. . . the only real power available to the leader is the power of persuasion. There is no patronage; no power to discipline; no authority to fire Senators like a President can fire his members of Cabinet.

Continuing, Johnson observed,

A good leader should not only know more about the workings of the committee and how the members arrived at the content of the bill as finally recommended, but he must also know the problems of each individual State and the temperament of each individual Senator.[24]

Senators' needs and egos being what they are and always will be, the burdens and trials of a Senate leader will never become less onerous than they are today. It is a fascinating and challenging job, and to be chosen by his peers as their leader in the Senate is an honor that has come to but few men. Yet, anyone who has ever held this unique position can lay true claim to a place on the honor roll of the university of "hard knocks." The Senate's rules and customs place a premium on the freedoms of individual members, and there are many ways in which they can make a leader's life difficult. Senators, for example, often block or delay what the leader hopes to accomplish, sometimes for no other reason than to accommodate their own personal convenience. The human and personal factors are always present, and both the majority leader and the minority leader are forced to deal with them. The leaders are often the prisoners of their own troops and should ever expect the unexpected to happen and foil their best-laid plans. Allen Drury, in *Advise and Consent*, said of the majority leader's tribulations:

He swiftly learned that his world began and ended in ninety-nine minds whose endless surprises he could never entirely anticipate. No sooner had he got somebody pegged in one place than he turned up somewhere else; his plans for steering legislation had to be constantly revised to accommodate the human material with which he had to work.[25]

Twenty-one persons have been elected party floor leader, fifteen of them as majority leader, of whom eight were Democrats and seven were Republicans. Of the six minority leaders who never became majority leader, one was a Democrat, five were Republicans.[26]

The styles of leaders vary, depending upon their political viewpoints and personalities.

One senator, in comparing the new majority leader, mild-mannered Mike Mansfield, with the hard-driving Lyndon Johnson, who had become vice president, said, "These fellows are about as similar as Winston Churchill and St. Francis of Assisi."[27] No two leaders are alike, but every leader must keep in mind every other senator's rights. It is crucial to recognize that senators are elected by differing constituencies and have to exercise their own independent judgments.

I found that patience is one of the greatest assets that one can possess in this often exasperating and tension-filled role, which I suspect is, in some ways, more difficult than that of president of the United States. Although I have never been president of the United States, I can attest that it is not easy to schedule legislation and run the Senate in a way that will satisfy the wishes and needs of ninety-nine other senators. Whenever a measure is scheduled, it will usually inconvenience one senator or another, and, as Lyndon Johnson lamented, the majority leader cannot fire any of them.

CHAPTER 8

Party Whips

May 9, 1980*

Mr. President, in May 1769, there was a great debate in the British House of Commons on a matter of considerable importance, and the king's ministers made vigorous efforts to round up their supporters from all quarters for the debate. Edmund Burke, who participated in the debate, referred to these efforts, describing the way the ministers had "whipped in" their absent colleagues.[1]

Burke's phrase, "whipping them in," was a reference to the "whipper-in," the person assigned to the task of keeping the hounds from straying off the field during the fox chase.[2] The public picked up the phrase, and, in due time, "whipper-in" was abbreviated into "whip," the political title given to the officials in the British parliamentary system whose responsibility it is to marshal the votes on a given issue when the showdown occurs.[3]

The term "whip" has long had another distinct parliamentary meaning in England, referring also to the written message dispatched to the party members throughout the realm. These messages were originally secret notices and were called "circular letters," "treasury notes," or "treasury letters."

Under the British system, both the government and the opposition have whips who

send to their respective party members this document—or notice—called a "whip," informing members of the legislative program for the ensuing days. Each legislative item in the whip notice is underlined in accordance with its importance. A one-line "whip" may indicate that there is not likely to be a vote on the issue. A two-line notice may indicate that the matter is important and that a vote may occur. A three-line "whip" would indicate that every member is expected to be on the floor and that a vote is scheduled.[4]

Shortly after my election to the office of majority whip, I wrote on March 11, 1971, to the Right Honorable Francis Pym, chief whip of the Conservative party in the British House of Commons, requesting information concerning the origins of "whipping" in the English Parliament. The chief whip responded promptly, in a letter dated March 23, enclosing "some notes which I hope will be of help to you." Pym stated that the "earliest whips I have seen recorded were sent to the King's friends in the House in 1621; they were underscored by as many as six lines." A royal "whip" issued on September 21, 1675, read as follows:

Sir J. Williamson to a Member of Parliament. The King being firmly resolved that Parliament shall meet

---

* Updated June 1989

13 Oct., that you may not be surprised with any contrary reports, nor be detained by the business of the sessions, which unhappily is near that time, has commanded me to give you this notice, and to desire you will not fail to be here at or before the time appointed, and I desire you will let me know as soon as you come to town, that I may acquaint the King how his commands to me have been executed.[5]

Although the whip system in the U.S. House of Representatives resembles that of the British House of Commons, party whips did not exist in the Senate until 1913. Certain legislators may have performed tasks roughly similar to those of our contemporary whips, but the office apparently did not become institutionalized until the twentieth century. One reason was that a strong political party structure evolved only slowly in the Senate.

In the early years of the nineteenth century, political parties on Capitol Hill were largely unorganized groups. Even as late as 1874, Senator Justin Morrill, Republican of Vermont, noted this lack of party organization when he declared: "I do not propose to act as 'the whip' of the Senate. I think the Senate are quite competent to express their own judgment without any whip. We have never had what is called a whip in the American Senate."[6]

In 1913, Senate Democrats officially designated their first party whip. Rather than turning to a senior member, they chose a senator who had taken his oath of office only two months earlier. He was J. Hamilton Lewis of Illinois, who said that, as far as he could learn, he "was the first Democratic whip appointed in the history of the United States Senate. It was during the first Wilson administration."[7] The *New York Times* of May 29, 1913, explained the reasons for creating the new post of whip:

As a further precaution against a snap division in the Senate by which the Democrats might find themselves in the minority, the caucus elected Senator J. Hamilton

In 1913, Senate Democrats chose J. Hamilton Lewis as their party's first whip. *U.S. Senate Historical Office*

Charles Curtis became the Senate Republican whip in 1915.

Lewis of Illinois today to serve as "whip," although designated as assistant to Majority Leader Kern in the capacity of floor leader. Mr. Lewis' chief duty will be to see that Democrats are present or paired at every rollcall.

The appointment of an assistant to Senator Kern, though brought about in a way to avoid wounding the majority leader's pride, is in fact partly explained by general dissatisfaction with Mr. Kern's leadership.

Others have said that poor attendance at some of the party caucuses angered Majority Leader John Worth Kern and resulted in the appointment of the party whip. In this regard, I quote from the 1918 biography of Kern by his secretary, the journalist Claude G. Bowers:

At times when the regular Democratic attendance had dwindled to a corporal's guard his impatience manifested itself in caucus, where on one occasion he supplemented his appeal with sarcastic protests, and a "party whip" was selected to assist him.[8]

Thus, two factors may have produced conditions which led to the creation of a party whip post: the dissatisfaction of the Democrats in the Senate with their party leader; and the need of their party floor leader for an assistant to ensure attendance at the party caucuses and on the Senate floor.[9]

Securing the attendance of senators was not an easy task for Kern, and one can imagine the frustrations that attended his efforts. Bowers illustrated the point:

Another senator who had been enjoying the shades of the verandas and wooded spaces of a summer resort was wired by Kern to return to Washington as he was needed. His secretary called upon [Kern] the next day to explain that his chief's return had been delayed by his inability to get a seat in the chair car. Taking from his vest pocket a number of clippings from *The Washington Post*, Kern dryly observed that the senator had been playing a good game of golf, had attended a number of dances, and given a dinner.[10]

[197]

Having observed the Democratic innovation in creating the office of whip, the Republicans, in 1915, appointed freshman Senator James Wadsworth of New York as their first party whip and as conference secretary. A week later, the party decided to divide the two positions, with Wadsworth remaining as secretary. Charles Curtis of Kansas was elected party whip.

Mr. President, during the years 1935 to 1944, no Republican served as party whip, because only seventeen Republicans were in the Senate following the landslide reelection of President Franklin D. Roosevelt in 1936 and only twenty-eight following Roosevelt's 1940 reelection.

Of the Democratic whips, J. Hamilton Lewis held the office for a total of twelve years, exceeded only by Alan Cranston of California, who is now in his thirteenth year. The Republican who served longest as whip was Thomas Kuchel of California, who held the post from 1959 to 1969. Charles Curtis served nine years, from 1915 to 1924.[11]

The whip appears to be next in line to succeed to the leadership of his party, but, according to political scientist Walter Oleszek, who has studied the whip system, "it should be stressed that this is a matter of probability" rather than certainty. "No fixed or formalized system of party advancement can be discerned" from a study of the political history of the whip institution in the Senate.[12] Only eight of the twenty-eight whips—four Republicans and four Democrats—have, as of 1989, gone on to become the leader of their party in the Senate.

Republican Whip Leverett Saltonstall of Massachusetts, for example, was bypassed for the leadership position in 1953, when Republicans elected Senator Robert A. Taft of Ohio as majority leader. Taft then appointed Senator William Knowland of California to be acting majority leader in his absence. When Taft died in mid-1953, Knowland became majority leader and Saltonstall remained as whip. Some political observers at the time believed that Saltonstall was not elevated to the office of acting majority leader because many conservative Republican leaders objected to the idea of a liberal in that position.

The whip's job, like the majority leader's, is often a thankless task, although the whips do receive some compensating benefits. Beginning in 1955, the legislative branch appropriation bill contained funds for two clerical assistants, one for the majority whip and one for the minority whip; today, there are four clerical assistants in each of the two offices. The whips are also given additional office space; they receive many invitations to social, diplomatic, and political functions; and they achieve increased public visibility through mass media coverage of the position.

Whips serve as acting floor leaders in the absence of their respective leaders. They also arrange voting pairs for senators on opposing sides of an issue to ensure that the absence of one will not influence the outcome of a vote. In recent years, however, that task has often been delegated to the secretary for the majority and the secretary for the minority. The whips' duties, which are determined largely by their relationships with the party floor leaders, usually include discussions of the legislation and the program from day to day and week to week. Individual whips have developed varied interpretations of the role.

J. Hamilton Lewis, nearly a quarter-century after becoming the first Democratic whip, indicated his views concerning the work of that official:

The duties of the Senate whip demand his presence on the floor as constantly as possible. Sometimes the long hours test his physical capacity, but generally he is devoted to "watchful waiting." He is ex-officio assistant floor leader, and in the absence of the floor leader, and other assistants, may be called upon to represent his party. At rollcalls he reports absentees and pairs which have been brought to his attention. He is not supposed to introduce bills lest they may divert his attention from his floor duties. While the parliamentary whip is not supposed to engage in debate, there is no such restriction on the congressional whips. In fact, as assistant floor leaders it often becomes necessary for them to do so.[13]

The chief whips and deputy whips of the Democratic and Republican parties today, of course, no longer are expected not to introduce bills. They introduce bills and resolutions just as do their colleagues on both sides of the aisle.

Senator Kenneth S. Wherry of Nebraska, who was Republican party whip from 1944 to 1949, viewed his responsibilities as follows, according to his biographer:

. . . Wherry saw himself as an official chosen by his party to assist in maintaining party discipline and united action in the day-to-day deliberations of the U.S. Senate. He viewed his position as being responsible for the attendance of party members and for the arranging and controlling of the "pairing" process. He reported the absentees, pairs, and voting attitudes of the members on rollcalls. He consulted with and worked under the party floor leader in arranging the order of business of the Senate; and he handled the details of the weekly and day-to-day legislative programs, consulting with the floor secretary of his own party and with the whip of the Democratic party.[14]

Leverett Saltonstall, the Republican whip from 1949 to 1957, said that the whip's chief responsibility was to do the "dirty work" as assistant floor leader; in other words, being on the Senate floor to protect the party's interests.

In summing up the majority whip's role shortly after I was elected to that post in 1971, I said on CBS's "Face the Nation," "The job of the whip, as I view it, is to do the floor work, assist the majority leader, and promote Democratic policy as formulated by the majority leader and the Democratic Policy Committee."[15]

Kenneth Wherry served as Senate Republican whip in the 1940's. *U.S. Senate Historical Office*

As in the case of other party leadership positions, that of party whip is not provided for in the standing rules of the Senate. The whips are elected by their colleagues in party conferences held at the beginning of each new Congress. In January 1989, the Democratic Conference began the practice of electing a chief deputy whip and regional assistant whips. Previously, these officials had been appointed by the whip after consultation with the Democratic leader. The regional whips are responsible for canvassing the party membership and are assigned a number of senators to contact.

The Republicans established a system of regional whips at the beginning of the 1970's. This action resulted from a meeting between Minority Leader Hugh Scott and

Former Senate Republican Whip Hugh Scott, *left*, passed the symbol of office to incoming Whip Robert Griffin in 1969.

U.S. Senate Historical Office

Minority Whip Robert Griffin, for the purpose of implementing what Walter Oleszek described as "Senator Scott's conception of 'shared leadership.' " [16]

The secretaries for the majority and minority also assist their respective party leaders by performing functions similar to those of the whips. For example, the secretary for the majority supervises the majority cloakroom and supplies the leader with daily attendance tallies, which indicate those senators who are expected to be absent and the time of their return, as well as the time of

departure of senators who may be leaving the city. The secretary also supplies attendance sheets for one or more days in advance, to assist the majority leader in determining the best day on which to schedule a particular vote.

The staff members who work in the Democratic and Republican cloakrooms telephone the various offices every morning to collect information about the plans of individual senators. From this data, they compile the attendance totals for that day and the next. The information gained is helpful to the respective leaders, since the expected attendance often varies from hour to hour during a particular day.

At the direction of the majority leader, the whip discusses with party members their positions on issues that will be coming before the Senate and provides a confidential tally sheet to the leader. The minority whip performs the same function for the minority leader. This arrangement enables the floor leaders to reach all members of the party quickly and to obtain a reasonable idea about how the majority of them will vote on a given matter. The leader, whip, and assistant whips can then concentrate their efforts on obtaining the support of any undecided senators.

The majority and minority leaders obviously must work closely with their respective whips. The whips are primarily responsible for keeping the members of their parties in attendance during the consideration of controversial issues. They operate on the cardinal principle of the need to have the right senator at the right place at the right time. To this end, it is often necessary for the party leadership to arrange to take a vote exactly at a certain time, after some members have returned to town and before others have left.

The party whips are often referred to as the "assistant leaders." On October 7, 1969, the Republican Conference agreed unanimously to change the title of "whip" to "assistant leader." Mike Mansfield, the Democratic leader at the time, changed the title of his party's whip as well, and the 1970 edition of the *Congressional Directory* identified Senator Edward Kennedy as the "assistant majority leader." [17]

When I was elected to the post in 1971, I reinstituted the title of "whip." I preferred that title because of its parliamentary and congressional history. As the history of the whip institution under the British parlia-

Democratic Whip Robert C. Byrd, *left*, confers with Majority Leader Mike Mansfield.
George Tames/New York Times

mentary system goes back to the 1600's, I felt that, with those deep historical roots, the title of whip should continue to be carried by the person in the party structure who fulfilled that traditional role in the legislative process.

In February 1971, I proposed ten ways to ensure more orderly floor procedure. With the concurrence of the joint leadership, I energetically enforced the following:

Ten Suggestions to Senators

1. Please do not seek unanimous consent for additional time beyond the 3 minutes allotted during morning business.

2. Speeches up to 15 minutes in length may be arranged for the first part of the day if Leadership is notified during the previous day's session. The Senate will come in early to accommodate a Senator who wants to

make such a speech. The Senate will come in early for colloquies of longer duration than 15 minutes if the Leadership is notified during previous day's session. Please contact the Leadership on the Floor or have your staff call Extension 53735 for an allocation of time. Please keep length of speeches and colloquies within the time requested by you.

3. Speeches of more than 15 minutes duration should be made toward the late afternoon.

4. Please observe the Pastore Rule concerning germaneness. It runs for 3 hours following "the conclusion of the morning hour or after the unfinished business or pending business has first been laid before the Senate on any calendar day." (Rule VIII.)

5. Please use your microphone. This will help the visitors in the galleries to better understand what is being said.

6. In debate, the rules prohibit addressing another Senator in the second person. He must be addressed in the third person.

7. No Senator shall introduce to or bring to the attention of the Senate during its sessions any occupant in the Senate galleries.

8. When presiding, remember that it shall be the "duty of the chair to enforce order on his own initiative and without any point of order being made by a Senator." (Rule XIX.)

9. Clerks to Senators are allowed the privilege of the Floor only "when in the actual discharge of their official duties." (Rule XXXIII.) A special gallery is set aside to accommodate Senators' staff members.

10. Twenty minutes is the maximum allotted for a yea and nay vote. A warning bell will ring at the end of 15 minutes to indicate that the vote will be announced 5 minutes hence.[18]

During my tenure as whip, I expanded the functions of the office in at least two important ways. First, I distributed to all Democratic senators a weekly whip notice (more frequently, even daily, when necessary) patterned after the British system, with frequent underscoring for emphasis. An example is the following notice, dated June 30, 1972.

SENATE DEMOCRATIC WHIP NOTICE

JUNE 30, 1972

The Program for today is as follows:
Senate convenes at 8:15 a.m.

Fifteen minute orders as follows:
Mr. Tunney.
Mr. Harry F. Byrd, Jr.
Mr. Proxmire.
Mr. Moss.
Mr. Robert C. Byrd.

DEBT LIMIT BILL

9:30 a.m.—rollcall vote on Bennett amendment (10 percent social security increase).

9:45 a.m.—rollcall vote on Church amendment (20 percent social security increase).

Resumption of debate and amendment to Debt Limit Bill (no time limitation).

Rollcall vote on final passage of Debt Limit Bill is sure.

PUBLIC WORKS APPROPRIATION BILL

Senate will take up Public Works Appropriation Bill under a time limitation (2 hours, 30 minutes on any amendment, etc.).

Rollcall vote sure on final passage of Public Works Appropriation Bill.

CONTINUING RESOLUTION

Senate will next resume consideration of Continuing Resolution under a time limitation (1 hour for debate, 1 hour on Proxmire amendment, ½ hour on any other amendment, etc.).

Rollcall vote on Proxmire amendment.

There will also be a rollcall vote on passage of Continuing Resolution.

GENERAL INFORMATION

(1) Conference reports will also be called up during the day.

(2) Foreign Assistance Act remains the unfinished business and action thereon will be resumed when Senate returns July 17.

(3) Minimum Wage Bill will be second track item when Senate returns on July 17.

REMINDER

At least 6 rollcall votes today, the first to occur at 9:30 a.m.

POST-DEMOCRATIC CONVENTION INFORMATION

The leadership urges all Senators to plan on lengthy sessions daily, six days each week, following the Senate's return July 17. A very heavy, tough and contro-

versial work load confronts the Senate at that time. For example, the following measures speak for themselves:
  (1) Foreign Assistance Act.
  (2) Minimum Wage Bill.
  (3) Welfare Bill.
  (4) No-Fault Insurance.
  (5) Maritime Bill.
  (6) Marine Mammals.
  (7) Military Construction Appropriation Bill.
  (8) Agriculture Appropriation Bill.
  (9) Supplemental Appropriation Bill.
  (10) Foreign Aid Appropriation Bill.
  (11) Defense Appropriation Bill.
  (12) Plus others.

Another way in which I expanded the role during my six years as majority whip was by attending the floor constantly. I was always there, doing floor duties for the majority leader, making the motions, and keeping the legislative process moving.

Additionally, during the early 1970's, Senator Mansfield and I instituted, with the approval and cooperation of Republican leaders, the "two-track system," an innovative device permitting the Senate to have two or more pieces of legislation pending on the floor almost simultaneously by designating specific periods during the day when each measure or matter would be considered. I also made increasingly frequent use of unanimous consent agreements to limit debate.

Although four "assistant whip" positions had been created by the Democratic Conference on January 11, 1966, I never made use of them during my tenure in the post, from January 21, 1971 through 1976. The action had been taken on a resolution offered by Senator Mansfield specifying that the four assistant whips were to discharge "such functions of leadership as may be requested of them from time to time by the majority leader or, in his absence, by the assistant majority leader," who at that time, was Senator Russell Long of Louisiana. As the *New York Times* reported, the work in the Senate had previously "been handled . . . by a single elected

The whip and majority leader consult: Democratic Whip Alan Cranston, *left*, with Majority Leader Robert C. Byrd.   *U.S. Senate Historical Office*

whip and one or more staff aides," while "the Democratic whip system in the House" included "a deputy and eighteen assistants." [19]

The whip system in the Senate has continued to develop. For example, Majority Whip Alan Cranston, the fifteenth Democrat to hold the position, instituted weekly whip meetings, attended by the chief counsel and staff director of the Senate Democratic Policy Committee, the secretary for the majority, and sometimes the majority leader. Senator Cranston outlines to the deputy and regional assistant whips the business that is expected to be taken up during the week and the ways in which they can assist him and the majority leader in carrying out the legislative program. Those whip meetings usually are scheduled for Tuesdays, following the weekly Democratic Conference luncheon. I commend Senator Cranston for adding this innovation to the whip system.

Senator Spark M. Matsunaga of Hawaii, who previously served in the House of Representatives, was chief deputy whip in the Senate for several years prior to January 1989, when he chose not to seek the post again. During his years in that position, Senator Matsunaga ably assisted in improving the whip system in the Senate. At the beginning of the 101st Congress, Senator Alan J. Dixon of Illinois was elected by the Democratic Conference to be the majority party's chief deputy whip.

During his time as Republican whip, from 1977 to 1985, Senator Ted Stevens of Alaska replaced the regional GOP whip system with a new assistant whip structure to ensure that the rights of Republican members were protected during Senate floor actions. All first-year Republican senators, along with several of their more experienced colleagues, were afforded the opportunity to become assistant whips. As minority whip, Senator Stevens introduced the practice of "double-teaming" the floor. In other words, a Republican whip was always present to assist the party's floor manager during Senate debate on legislation.

When Senator Alan K. Simpson of Wyoming became the Republican whip in January 1985, he continued the practice followed by Senator Stevens of maintaining liaison with the House Republican leadership. Senator Simpson also met periodically with Senate GOP committee staffs to craft legislation for quick action "before special interests mobilized . . . against spending cuts in their favorite programs," cuts that would be po-

In 1985, members of the Republican leadership posed in the old Senate chamber: *left to right*, Whip Alan Simpson, President Pro Tempore Strom Thurmond, and Majority Leader Bob Dole.   *Alan E. Porter*

litically risky as the 1986 elections drew closer. Simpson emphasized, "It's got to be done now [early 1985], or it won't get done." [20]

Mr. President, I believe that the institutionalization of the whip organizations is conducive to a more efficient functioning of the party apparatuses in the Senate and, thus, contributes to stronger party impact upon national policy.

In addition to his Senate leadership functions, a party whip may, from time to time, serve as the Senate spokesman for major White House policies when his party controls the presidency, especially in the absence of the party floor leader. Of course, the majority leader, even when his party controls the White House, does not at all times necessarily reflect the views of the president and his administration. The two may differ occasionally.

The relationship between the floor leader and the whip parallels, in some ways, the relationship that exists between the president and the leader of the president's party in the Senate. They are usually together, but not always. When I was majority whip, serving with Majority Leader Mansfield, there was never any friction, but, from time to time, we would differ in our votes—each of us owing a responsibility to his own constituents, to reflect their views. When I was majority leader, I had that same understanding and agreeable relationship with Senator Cranston, the majority whip.

Mr. President, just as vice presidential candidates have often been selected more for geographical balance than for ideological compatibility with the party's presidential nominee, so the same has sometimes been true with the selection of party whips in the Senate. Election to the office of party whip or, for that matter, floor leader, does not rest on the custom of seniority. It differs from time to time, based on many factors. In 1957, for example, the party leader, Lyndon Johnson, selected Mike Mansfield to be his assistant as party whip. A need for ideological balance may have been the major factor in the selection of Senator Saltonstall as minority whip in 1949, because he was a spokesman for the liberal elements in the Republican party. In the selection of Senator Hubert Humphrey for majority whip in 1961, President John F. Kennedy gave his support from the White House.

Incidentally, I do not think it is a good idea for the White House to attempt to influence the selection of any Senate party official. It could very well be counterproductive from the White House viewpoint.

Other factors that have influenced the selection of party whips over the years include legislative skill, persuasiveness, ability to get along well with colleagues, and knowledge of colleagues' interests and political viewpoints.

In conclusion, Mr. President, a proficient and effective party whip needs to possess a special combination of attributes: recognized competency in parliamentary procedure, organizational ability, an unlimited capacity for work, accurate political instincts, and the ability to count votes.

I expect that the position of Democratic or Republican whip will retain the considerable importance in the Senate that the office has gained in recent years. Likewise, senators will still aspire to become the chief party whip because they perceive the office as a stepping stone to the party leadership. Senator Russell Long, for example, observed:

When I ran for the position of majority whip, I had very much in mind the fact that men I had known like Lyndon Johnson and Mike Mansfield had served as whip before becoming majority leader. It's the logical stepping stone in that direction.[21]

CHAPTER 9

The Committee System

Committees, 1789–1845

*July 31, 1981**

Mr. President, when Woodrow Wilson published his study, *Congressional Government*, in 1885, he wrote that "it is not far from the truth to say that Congress in session is Congress on public exhibition, whilst Congress in its committee-rooms is Congress at work." At the time that Wilson wrote this study, the legislative branch was universally recognized as having taken a superior role over the executive branch, which had been presided over by a series of weak presidents since the Civil War. Within the legislative branch, Wilson identified the committees as the chief centers of power. "I know not how better to describe our form of government in a single phrase," Wilson wrote, "than by calling it a government by the chairmen of the Standing Committees of Congress." [1]

These sentiments reflected the conditions of the 1880's. As we know, there have been many changes in our political system in subsequent years, such as the growth of the modern presidency, the development of party floor leaders, the various committee reforms, and the spread of subcommittees. I have quoted Wilson's remarks to show the committees at their apogee, when they were the central force in the federal government of the United States. Today, I shall discuss the origins of these committees.

The Senate did not create its standing, or permanent, committee system until 1816, more than twenty-seven years after the Senate had begun to function. The United States Constitution did not mention or provide for committees in Congress. This does not mean, however, that there were no committees in the earliest years of the Senate, for, indeed, committees have operated since the very beginnings of Congress. Let me explain this paradox.

The use of committees in legislative bodies antedated the First Congress. We can find records of joint committees of the House of Lords and the House of Commons in the English Parliament as early as 1340. The first standing committee of Parliament was the Committee on Privileges and Elections, dating back to the reign of the first Queen Elizabeth. The Committee of the Whole originated in the House of Commons during the reign of James I, the first of the Stuart kings. The committee system expanded during the time of Oliver Cromwell, and eventually evolved into what has been called "that all-absorbing committee," the British

* Revised September 1989

The first Senate committee, appointed in 1789, was assigned to draft rules of procedure. *Above*, an artist depicted the Senate meeting in New York City's Federal Hall.
U.S. Capitol Historical Society

Cabinet. Members of the first Senate had not only the example of parliamentary committees, but also those of the Virginia House of Burgesses and other colonial and state legislatures and of the Continental Congress. It was, we may recall, a select committee of Thomas Jefferson, John Adams, and Benjamin Franklin that drafted the Declaration of Independence. Committees were, therefore, a fairly common way of doing legislative business.[2]

The House of Representatives, then as now the larger body of Congress, appointed

its first permanent committee in 1789. Like the first standing committee of Parliament, it was the Committee on Elections. By 1800, the House had five standing committees, and, during the next twenty years, it added twenty more. This proliferation of standing committees reflected the swelling size of the House as population grew and new states were added to the Union. In 1800, there were only 106 members of the House, but, by 1823, the number of Representatives had climbed to 213.[3] Of course, there was an even larger number of ad hoc committees appointed to handle single pieces of legislation. During the Third Congress, from 1793 to 1795, for example, there were some 350 such temporary committees in the House.[4]

The Senate, prior to 1816, appointed only four standing committees, all for "house-keeping" rather than legislative purposes. For the most part, the Senate relied on select committees, the first of which was the five-man committee appointed on April 7, 1789, to draw up the rules of procedure for the Senate. That committee filed its report on April 13, and, by April 18, the Senate had resolved that twenty rules "be observed." In those days, the Senate spent much of its time acting as a "Committee of the Whole," a device for controlling the legislation introduced and under discussion.

Today, we are accustomed to a rather straightforward way of introducing bills and resolutions whenever the Senate is in session. Rule VII provides for introduction of bills during the "Morning Business," and further states, in paragraph 6:

> Senators having petitions, memorials, bills, or resolutions to present after the morning hour may deliver them in the absence of objection to the Presiding Officer's desk, endorsing upon them their names, and with the approval of the Presiding Officer, they shall be entered on the Journal with the names of the Senators presenting them and in the absence of objection shall be considered as having been read twice and referred to the appropriate committees, and a transcript of such entries shall be furnished to the official reporter of debates for publication in the Congressional Record, under the direction of the Secretary of the Senate.[5]

By contrast, a senator in 1789 could introduce a bill only after he had given the Senate one day's notice of his intention to request permission to introduce the bill, and after a majority of senators had voted to give him such permission. According to Roy Swanstrom's dissertation, *The United States Senate, 1787–1801*, such permission was usually

granted, and, in fact, unanimous consent was sometimes given to dispense with the one-day waiting period. But, from such a rule, we can see how the majority could thwart the introduction of any bill it found distasteful or objectionable. For instance, when Senator James Monroe requested permission to introduce a bill repealing an article of the peace treaty with Great Britain, a majority of the Senate denied his request.[6] A more common form of initiating legislation was for a senator to move that a committee be appointed to report a bill to achieve a specific goal.

This method of introducing bills by permission allowed the majority party more control over legislation being deliberated, and it generally meant that most bills would be enacted once the committee reported them, since a majority had approved their introduction in the first place. During the first session of the Senate, only four public bills were introduced, and all were passed. (In the same period, thirty-three bills were introduced in the House.) In subsequent congresses, the number of bills increased, as did the number of rejections. With this growing volume of legislation came a corresponding need for committees. In addition, committees were appointed in each session of Congress to deal with the individual proposals of the president's annual State of the Union message.

There were several advantages to this system of introducing bills and forming committees. During the debate over granting permission for the introduction of a bill, the Senate's sentiments on the particular issue at hand would become clearer, providing better guidelines for the committee assigned to draft the final bill. When receiving legislation from the House, the entire Senate could participate in the amending process before the bill went to committee to be put in its final revised form. If this process sounds terribly unwieldy, I should point out that during the first session of the First Congress, the Senate had no more than twenty members present and voting at one time—and today several of our committees approach or exceed that size.

This improvisational system made the select committees completely responsive to the Senate as a whole. The Senate decided their jurisdiction and their membership, and they invariably complied with the will of the majority that had created them in the first place. Furthermore, the Senate could at any time create another committee to handle the same matter if it was not satisfied with the progress of a particular select committee. The system also was useful for its flexibility, as the Senate could, if it preferred, dispose of legislation and nominations without any committee referral. According to Professor Swanstrom, the Senate generally created committees to handle specific legislation, but, at times, it gave the committees broad areas to examine. In 1794, the Senate appointed a special five-member committee to report whatever legislation was necessary to promote the national defense. Some committees might be assigned several bills to draft, but they were usually bills revolving around a similar subject, such as military policy, finance, or national commerce.[7]

For the most part, Senate committees consisted of three members for routine business and five members for more important issues. During the first session of the First Congress, the largest committee, containing eleven members, was created to decide the salaries of the president and vice president (salary issues being as controversial then as they are now). In the first session, the entire membership of the Senate was divided into two large committees, with half on the committee to prepare legislation establishing the federal judiciary and the other half on the committee to define the punishment of crimes against the United States. These committees obviously contained more members than was usual, but Pennsylvania Senator William Maclay's diary tells us that, in the case of organizing the federal judiciary, a smaller subcommittee actually drafted the bill.[8]

Mr. President, today members of the Senate are accustomed to spending their careers as members of just two or three major committees, specializing in certain areas of legislation and gaining sufficient seniority to enable them someday to become committee chairmen. Things were different in the early years of the Senate. With scores of committees created during each Congress, it was more difficult to specialize and establish seniority. Even then, however, some members did specialize. Reading through the *Annals of Congress*, a forerunner of the *Congressional Record*, one notices the same names appearing and reappearing on certain types of committees. For instance, William Maclay served on a great many committees dealing with private claims bills. In his dissertation, Professor Swanstrom pointed out that certain other senators gained the reputation, from their committee service, of being "watchdogs of the Treasury." Merchant Robert Morris of Pennsylvania was most often a member of those committees handling commerce and shipping. Connecticut's Oliver Ellsworth, a framer of the Constitution who later became chief justice of the United States, served on practically every committee dealing with judicial matters during his Senate years. Other senators were likely to serve on committees relating to treaties and foreign affairs. From 1789 to 1797, nineteen separate committees with a total of sixty-eight members considered treaties. Yet, only twenty-four senators filled those sixty-eight positions. Members sympathetic to the views of the Federalist party predominated on these early foreign relations committees—particularly men such as Morris, Ellsworth, Rufus King of New York, and George Cabot of Massachusetts.[9]

Oliver Ellsworth frequently served on committees dealing with the judiciary. *Library of Congress*

The reappearance of certain senators on certain types of committees seems logical when we consider that the Senate as a whole elected members of each committee. We may assume that individual senators developed personal reputations for interest and expertise in particular areas that would lead their colleagues to include them on any committee considering a related subject. Other senators developed sufficient political prominence and reliability to encourage the members of the majority party to place them on committees where they would be the most effective. There was also a need to balance committee memberships according to regional and economic interests. Western senators, for instance, were generally included on the public lands committees. Northern senators were elected to committees on commerce and manufacturing. And senators from the thir-

teen original states often served on the Revolutionary War pensions and claims committees. Rarely did two senators from the same state serve on the same committee, except in the case of relatively minor private relief bills or legislation dealing specifically with their home state.[10]

With the great number of ad hoc committees appointed each session, the position of committee chairman was not as influential as it would become later with the establishment of standing committees. Chairmen were often the senators who introduced the legislation, since they had the most interest in the bill's passage. But, generally, the chairman was the senator who received the most votes in the balloting for committee members. In 1807, Senator John Quincy Adams of Massachusetts noted in his diary that this had become the "ordinary practice."[11] Under this system, it was possible for a member of the minority party (the Antifederalists or Republicans) to serve as committee chairman, despite the Federalist majority in the Senate. Senators who opposed the particular piece of legislation under consideration, however, were usually not appointed to the committee assigned to drafting and reporting it. Vice President Thomas Jefferson, in the manual of parliamentary practice he compiled while serving as president of the Senate, noted that the Senate's committee selections followed the principle that "the child is not to be put to a nurse that cares not for it."[12]

The chief disadvantage of the ad hoc committee system was that it permitted an unequal workload for senators. During the first session of the First Congress, for instance, Senator Oliver Ellsworth served on twenty-two committees. In the 1790 session of that Congress, Ellsworth was elected to thirty-six committees, while the average assignment was only about eleven committees. Several senators served on only one or two or no committees at all. One reads the diary of Senator John Quincy Adams with a sense that the man was eternally caught up in the work of one committee or another. One of his entries reads: "The whole of this month I have been so much engaged upon committees and their business that I have been obliged entirely to forego the continuation of my lectures." Adams noted that, since all the committees were chosen by ballot, the number of committees a senator served on was a fair measure of his influence and weight in the Senate. On the other hand, "as much of the labor of business is transacted in committees, an exemption from those which are important is also an exemption from toil, and leaves proportionable leisure." [13]

The unequal distribution of committee memberships continued from the Federalist to the Republican congresses, during the years prior to 1816. Dr. Mary Giunta, in her doctoral dissertation on the legislative career of Virginia Senator William Branch Giles, surveyed the committee memberships of senators from the Eighth to the Thirteenth congresses, from 1803 to 1815. During the Eighth Congress, Georgia Senator Abraham Baldwin, the Republican president pro tempore, served on forty-six committees, or 11 percent of the total number of committees appointed during that Congress. By contrast, the majority of senators served on fewer than fifteen committees. In the Ninth Congress, Senator Baldwin was elected to ninety-one committees, or 14 percent of the total number, while the majority of his colleagues served on fewer than eighteen. By the Thirteenth Congress, the last before the creation of standing committees, the range had been reduced considerably. Senator Rufus King served on the most committees, nineteen, while the majority of senators served on fewer than eight committees. [14]

When the Jeffersonian Republicans won control of the Senate for the first time in

During one Congress, Senator Abraham Baldwin served on ninety-one committees. *Library of Congress*

1801, they continued the system of ad hoc committees, although they instituted some changes. Early in the Seventh Congress, Senator John Breckinridge of Kentucky, one of the Jeffersonian floor leaders, gave notice that he would introduce a resolution to repeal the Judiciary Act of 1801, the first priority of the new majority and a major request of President Jefferson's State of the Union message. Breckinridge announced that he was prepared to offer his sentiments on the subject immediately, if his colleagues had no objection. Federalist Senator Uriah Tracy of Connecticut immediately rose to his feet to observe that the custom until then had been for the Senate to refer each portion of the president's annual message to a separate special committee, which would then prepare a report so that "the minds of the House would be drawn more precisely to the points involved in it, than could be expected from a resolution so loose as the present, which could only give rise to verbal discussions." Senator Stevens Mason of Virginia disagreed with Tracy. According to the *Annals of Congress*: "He believed the mode, now pursued, was perfectly correct, and conformable to a principle adopted this session, that the Senate was to be considered as in a committee of the whole on the President's Message, whenever taken up. Nor did he discern the necessity, in a body so select as this, of referring each subject to a select committee." [15]

Thus, while the House continued to refer separate portions of the president's message to separate committees, the Senate took up the message as in the Committee of the Whole. The Senate debated Breckinridge's resolution for six days, with some sixteen members speaking, indicating that the new procedure did not hamper debate on the issue. As Alex B. Lacy, Jr., wrote in his doctoral dissertation, "Jefferson and Congress: Congressional Method and Politics," "It can be said to the credit of the Republicans that during the Jefferson Administrations they never used their majority in either house to shut off debate unless the Federalists were pursuing dilatory tactics." [16]

Federalist Senator Jonathan Dayton of New Jersey moved to have the Judiciary Act repeal sent to a select committee to see if some compromise could be reached. The Republicans anticipated a victory, but the vote on Dayton's measure was 15 to 15, and Vice President Aaron Burr, a close friend of Dayton's, broke the tie in favor of referring the resolution to committee. In the jockeying to create a favorable committee, Professor Lacy noted: "The Senate broke one of its most rigid customs. . . . It was customary to place the original mover of a measure on any committee considering that measure. Usually, this member would serve as chairman of the

committee. Breckinridge missed election to the committee by one vote." [17] The Republicans were saved from embarrassment when an absent senator returned to the capital, giving them a sufficient majority to discharge the resolution from the select committee. Breckinridge argued against the committee on the grounds that the question was a matter of principle: whether the Judiciary Act should be repealed or not. Questions of principle, said Breckinridge, should be decided by the Senate as a whole. "A committee cannot, and ought not to settle principles. On the floor of this House alone ought principles, furnishing the ground-work of legislation, to be originated and settled. Details only are proper from your select committees." [18]

While the Senate was considering Jefferson's annual message as in a Committee of the Whole, it was changing its traditional practice by considering presidential nominations through select committees. At first, only controversial nominations went to committee, and, in the first session of the Seventh Congress, only eight were so referred. But by the Tenth Congress, the Senate routinely began to refer nominations to committees. In 1801–1802, three committees considered a total of eight nominations, while, in 1807–1808, four committees considered several hundred nominations. [19]

Committee meetings in the early years of the Senate bore some similarities to committee meetings today, but in other ways they differed. Committees met before and after, but not during, sessions of the Senate. Senators could attend meetings of committees of which they were not members, although, of course, they could not vote in them. Occasionally, a committee would hear testimony from witnesses, but this was quite rare. For instance, Secretary of State Thomas Jefferson appeared before one Senate committee to discuss President Washington's diplomatic nominations. No transcript of this or any other committee hearing was made at that time, nor, indeed, would any be made until well into the nineteenth century. Instead, the Senate would use the official report of the committee in its deliberation over legislation, nominations, and treaties.[20]

Mr. President, although no transcripts of these early committee meetings were kept, we are fortunate to have some fascinating inside glimpses of committee workings from the diaries of senators. These diaries are all the more important because of the sparseness of the *Annals of Congress*, which were prepared after the fact, from newspaper accounts and other contemporary sources. Let me give a graphic example from the diary of Massachusetts Senator John Quincy Adams. The *Annals of Congress* report that, on October 27, 1807, President Jefferson sent to Congress his annual message, which was devoted in large part to British naval aggressions against the United States. The next day, Senator Adams moved,

That so much of the President's Message as relates to the recent outrages committed by British armed vessels within the jurisdiction, and in the waters of the United States, and to the Legislative provisions which may be expedient as resulting from them, be referred to a select committee, with leave to report by bill or otherwise.[21]

On October 30, the Senate appointed a five-member committee composed of Adams, Samuel Smith of Maryland, John Milledge of Georgia, Samuel Mitchill of New York, and Joseph Anderson of Tennessee. Then, a few days later, on November 4, Senator Stephen Bradley of Vermont introduced a similar resolution calling for the appointment of another select committee.

Resolved, that a committee be appointed to inquire whether any, and, if any, what further and more effectual provisions are necessary in addition to the act, entitled "An act for the more effectual preservation of peace in the ports and harbors of the United States, and in the waters under their jurisdiction;" with leave to report by bill or otherwise.[22]

On November 9, Bradley's resolution was referred to the already appointed committee of five, but Senator Bradley and Senator Thomas Sumter of South Carolina were added to the committee. The *Annals* contain no more on the subject until November 24, when Senator Adams reported for the committee its bill relating to British aggressions and harbor defense. On November 26, the Senate debated the bill and "after progress, adjourned." The Senate never voted on the committee's report.[23]

Now, by contrast to this rather thin and uninformative official version, let me read from the diary of John Quincy Adams concerning the same events. Adams wrote:

November 20, 1807. The sub-committee on aggressions met, and [Stephen] Bradley presented a bill which he has drawn under the vote of the general committee, which I took home with me to examine and modify. I employed the evening in that work; but Mr. [Joseph] Anderson, who voted against me on the question, requested me this day to renew it—and told me that on further reflection he was convinced my project was the best. Mitch[i]ll told me that he voted with Bradley only to keep him in good humor, and to pledge him in support of a plan upon the idea that it was his own; and Mr. [John] Milledge urged me with some anxiety to renew the question upon my section; which, however, I shall decline. . . .

November 23. Met the sub-committee this morning at ten. Mr. Bradley had two or three additional sections to offer, which, with modifications, were agreed to, as was my bill, and all to be reported to the committee of seven. The Senate then sat. . . . Adjourned before *one*. Committee of seven met, discussed the bill of the sub-committee, and, with some alterations, ordered me to report it. I gave it accordingly to the clerks, to be copied by tomorrow morning.

Through the whole of this transaction I have had some difficulty to steer my way. I moved the first resolution, which has issued in this bill, the day after the President's message at the commencement of the session, merely to put the Senate upon some work. For I knew they would otherwise do nothing but what

In 1807, Senator John Quincy Adams recorded in his diary the political maneuverings within a committee he chaired. Adams appears here, thirty-six years later, in a daguerreotype taken during his service in the House of Representatives.   *Metropolitan Museum of Art*

should come from the House. I was obliged to leave it three or four days for consideration, and when the committee was appointed I was made its chairman. But Bradley not happening to be on the committee (though of five) immediately felt his pride piqued, and he determined to take the business out of my hands; so that, some days after, he moved for a new committee, substantially upon the same subject, though varied in form (a practice often used when the chairman of a committee of importance happens to be a federalist), and he took an opportunity to move this resolution when I was not in the House. From the moment it was made I saw its motive and object, but I saw that to attempt resistance against it was vain. So perfectly similar was it to my resolution in substance that it was noticed by a number of members, and he finally professed that he meant its reference to the *same* committee. I then moved the addition of two members to the committee, that he might be one of the number. When the committee met, he opposed the first principle upon which I wished the bill to be formed, and prevailed. He then proposed successively his own measures, most of which were adopted; and eventually I did scarcely any thing more than draw the bill. Even this, however, he has violently contested; and having drawn a mere proviso, upon the same principle in substance as one which I had drawn, and the committee having given the preference to mine, he broke into a passion, and told them he would vote against the whole bill, and would not vote upon any of the subsequent sections. I believe his purpose is to defeat the whole; and he has introduced some sections which he knows will be violently opposed, with the intention that they shall first fail, and then he will fly from the whole with great disgust at the *want of energy* in the Government. . . .

November 26. . . . The bill I had reported was taken up in committee of the whole. Bradley renewed his attack upon the proviso; Mr. [James] Hillhouse and Mr. [Timothy] Pickering immediately sided with him, and a debate of two hours ensued upon a few words which he moved to strike out. On the question taken, it was decided the words should stand—fifteen to fourteen. Mr. [John] Pope then moved to strike out the whole section, upon which a second debate arose as warm and as long as the first. It was finally closed by a motion to adjourn, which was agreed to. Bradley supported Pope's motion, with a view to have the bill recommitted, with instructions simply to *continue* the act of 3d of March, 1805, and then add *his* new propositions to it. His ultimate object is to defeat the whole bill. . . . The majority of the Senate, at the end of this day's debate, obviously wished for delay—procrastination; and I shall not hurry them on—they shall take

their own time. The bill itself, as it stands, is no favorite of mine, and I shall not be much concerned at the fate which awaits it.[24]

Mr. President, the diary of John Quincy Adams has obviously left us a far richer account of this incident than did the *Annals of Congress*. The two-hour debate on November 26, to which Senator Adams referred, is contained in exactly six lines in the *Annals*, merely noting that the Committee of the Whole took up the second reading of the bill, and that "after progress" the Senate adjourned without voting. Not only does Adams' diary tell us the story behind this debate, but it also reveals the apparently common practice of creating a second committee as a means of removing an unpopular or minority party chairman.

The increasing business of the committees, particularly in the handling of nominations, the pressing needs of national defense during the War of 1812, and the growing institutional needs of a body that was now over a quarter-century old, all pushed the Senate toward the creation of standing committees in 1816. Until that year, as I have mentioned, the Senate had appointed only four standing committees, all of which dealt with housekeeping functions. They were: the Joint Committee on Enrolled Bills in 1789, the Joint Committee on the Library in 1806, the Joint Committee on Engrossed Bills in 1806, and the Committee to Audit and Control the Contingent Expenses of the Senate in 1807.[25] The current Senate Committee on Rules and Administration may be seen as a successor to these first standing committees.

By contrast, the House of Representatives had appointed several standing committees, with both housekeeping and legislative functions, during the years prior to 1816. These included Enrolled Bills in 1789; Commerce and Manufactures, and Ways and Means in 1795; Public Lands in 1805; Post

Office, and District of Columbia in 1808; Judiciary, and Pensions in 1813; and Expenditures in Executive Departments in 1816. The House acted first because it was so large that it could not function effectively as a Committee of the Whole the way the Senate did. In addition, Republican representatives wanted to establish the House's legislative independence from the Federalist executive departments. The Jeffersonians opposed Treasury Secretary Alexander Hamilton's plan to have legislative proposals referred first to executive agencies rather than to congressional committees. Then, during the Republican-controlled Third Congress, from 1793 to 1795, Hamilton resigned as secretary of the treasury, and the House created its Ways and Means Committee. As Professor George Goodwin has written, "These steps put an end to a tendency that could have moved the country in the direction of British cabinet government."[26]

By the end of the War of 1812, the stage was set for the Senate to consider establishing its own system of standing committees. Meeting in temporary quarters—because the Capitol Building itself was under repair for damages which the British troops had inflicted upon it during the war—members of the Senate were most likely concerned about the permanency, continuity, and stability of governmental processes. Perhaps struggling with the issues of the war made members realize the need for greater expertise and a more specialized review of legislation. In addition, from the constant movement of representatives to the Senate, we may assume that former House members brought with them a preference for standing committee assignments. During the first session of the Fourteenth Congress, meeting in December 1815, the Senate appointed a series of select committees to report on various portions of the president's State of the Union message. Instead of allowing these select committees

In 1816, the Senate adopted a motion by James Barbour to create its first permanent legislative committees. *Library of Congress*

to disband after they had completed their immediate work, the Senate utilized the same committees for other business during the session. The select committee on finance, for example, which dealt with matters of finances and currency in the president's message, also handled the two most important issues of that session of Congress, the Tariff of 1816 and the rechartering of the national bank.[27]

During the second session of the Fourteenth Congress, meeting in December 1816, Senator Nathan Sanford of New York moved to have the president's annual message broken into its component parts and distributed to select committees for consideration, as was the usual practice. On December 5, Senator James Barbour of Virginia moved that the Senate, instead, create eleven standing committees: Foreign Relations, Ways and Means, Commerce and Manufactures, Military Affairs, Militia, Naval Affairs, Public Lands, Claims, Judiciary, Post Office and

Post Roads, and Pensions. On Tuesday, December 10, 1816, the Senate adopted Barbour's motion, although it changed the name of Ways and Means to Finance, a title it had used for such select committees in the past. By Friday of that week, the first appointments to standing committees were announced. Five members were appointed to each committee, with the exception of Commerce and Judiciary, each of which began with four members. On that same day, the president's message was referred to the appropriate standing committees, their first official business. Also on that day, five select committees were appointed to consider issues raised by the president's message that did not fall within any of the standing committees' jurisdiction: weights and measures, a national university, roads and canals, the slave trade, and the creation of a new executive department. On December 18, a committee on the District of Columbia was created.[28]

The appointment of standing committees permitted the Senate to assign long-term studies and investigations to committees, in addition to regular legislative duties. For instance, the Commerce Committee's first assignments consisted largely of compiling statistical reports and conducting investigations required by the Senate on harbor improvements, foreign trade, canal construction, and shipping regulations. Standing committees also spent much of their time handling presidential nominations and petitions from citizens.[29]

The significance of the change from ad hoc to permanent committees was perhaps little realized at the time. Walter Kravitz, a Library of Congress specialist in American government, observed, however, that the Senate's creation of standing committees was "a decisive moment in the institution's history," producing "an environment which eventually fostered profound changes in the chamber's working habits, floor practices and structure of internal authority." It is likely, of course, that such changes would have come about in any event, due to the rapid increase in the number of senators and the mounting demands of a nation that was swiftly spanning the continent. The sheer mass and complexity of the Senate's growing responsibilities required a division of labor and specialization impossible of attainment within the four walls of the chamber itself. With regard to the changed "structure of internal authority" suggested by Kravitz, there can be no doubt, for "instead of the Senate telling its committees what to put into legislation," as it did in the years prior to establishment of the standing committee system, "the committees assumed the prerogative of determining which substantive provisions the Senate should consider," and they became "policy-making bodies instead of merely technical aids to the chamber." Whereas the Senate formerly set the agenda, the committees came to be, "in effect . . . the Senate's agenda-maker."[30]

It is interesting to note that, in creating standing committees, members of the majority party did not appropriate all of the chairmanships to themselves. In 1816, the moribund Federalist party held the chairmanship of the Commerce and Manufactures Committee and had a majority of members on Finance.[31] Since the Senate as a whole elected members of each committee, and the member with the most votes became chairman, this nonpartisanship lingered on through the mid-1830's, when growing party spirit and factionalism finally made majority party leadership of committees the standard rule in the 1840's.

Members of the Senate found the balloting for committee membership at the beginning of each Congress an increasingly unappealing system. There was both an element of humiliation in the possibility of being turned down for a committee position by one's colleagues in the Senate, and also an annoyance with the tedious and time-consuming system of balloting. In 1823, Senators John Eaton and Andrew Jackson of Tennessee pressed the Senate to elect chairmen of five leading committees and then have the chairmen appoint all remaining committee members. This plan, however, lost to a proposal by Senator Barbour, the original author of the standing committee system, to have the presiding officer—either the vice president or president pro tempore—appoint all committee members. Until 1845, this system, interspersed with attempts to revive the balloting system, set the course for Senate committee memberships.

During the Mexican War, the system was finally changed. By a margin of one vote, in December 1846, the Senate removed from the presiding officer the power to appoint committee members. During the debate, Senator Willie Mangum, the Whig leader, accused the Democratic caucus of having prepared a "list made out and decided on by a meeting of members of this body belonging to a particular party." This was obviously what had been done, for when the Senate voted for committee chairmen they were selected by a strict party vote. By the following year, it had become the accepted practice for the members of each party, through their respective caucuses, to name their party members to the standing committees.[32]

Committees, 1845–1900

*August 1, 1983**

Mr. President, those who love this magnificent Capitol Building and who are fascinated by its history—architectural and artistic as well as political—would find great pleasure and edification in reading Glenn Brown's two-volume *History of the United States Capitol.*[1] Published in 1900 and 1902 as Senate documents, these handsome portfolio volumes present the creation and evolution of the Capitol, with lavish use of architectural drawings and photographs. Volume two contains four remarkable photographs of the interiors of Senate committee rooms at the turn of the century. Although taken over eighty years ago, these pictures will be instantly familiar to those of us who frequent the same rooms today. Yet, while the Brumidi frescoes and Minton tiles remain the same, a second look at these committee room photographs reveals many differences.

Take, for example, the photograph of the room used by the Naval Affairs and Philippines committees.[2] The very titles of these committees, which shared the same room, date the picture. Philippine affairs became a subject worthy of a standing committee's attention after the war of 1898, the Spanish-American War, when the United States acquired the Philippine Islands. In 1945, the Philippines received their independence, and shortly after that, the Naval Affairs Committee also ceased to exist as a separate entity, being merged into what is now the Armed Services Committee. In 1900, at the time this photograph was made, the Naval Affairs and Philippines committees occupied what is now numbered room S-127 on the ground floor of the Capitol. Countless visitors to the Capitol in recent years have stopped to marvel at this beautiful room, which is visible to the public via a glass paneled door.

In S-127, we find Constantino Brumidi's earliest ceiling and wall designs on the Senate side of the Capitol. Brumidi was hired in 1855 by Montgomery C. Meigs, superintendent of construction for the Capitol extensions, who encouraged him to produce classical themes appropriate for a naval affairs committee room. When the room was opened in 1858, a sign informed visitors, "The decorative paintings of this room are a specimen of the manner in which ancient Greeks and Romans ornamented their splendid buildings, some of which are still extant in the precious monuments of Pompeii and the baths of Titus." Indeed, looking around this room, which has been beautifully restored by the Senate Appropriations Committee, its occupant since 1911, we can find the Indian goddess America, adorned by a crown of stars; Neptune, Lord and Ruler of the Sea; Nereus, known as the Old Man of the Sea whose fifty beautiful daughters became sea nymphs; and assorted other gods and goddesses identified with the sea.[3] These frescoes are even more visible today than they were eighty years ago, since, in those days, the committee room was crowded with bookcases, screens, and other room dividers. The old gas chandeliers pictured in the turn-of-the-century photograph were replaced during the early twentieth century by large crystal chandeliers, modeled after those which hung in the White House. The Minton tiles have been carpeted over, to reduce the noise level. The committee table, which seated about nine, has been replaced

* Revised March 1989

In 1900, the Philippines and Naval Affairs committees met in room S-127 in the Capitol, now part of the Appropriations Committee suite.

Glenn Brown, History of the United States Capitol

with one large enough to seat the twenty-nine members of the Appropriations Committee today.

Room S-128, also assigned to the Senate Appropriations Committee in 1911, was originally occupied by the Committee on Military Affairs and the Militia, and the responsibility for the decorations had again been placed in the talented hands of Brumidi. A voucher dated October 19, 1871, records the payment to Brumidi "for painting in fresco three panels in Committee Room on Military Affairs . . . Washington at Valley Forge, Storming of Stony Point, Boston Massacre, @ $1000 each." Other scenes from the American Revolution are also depicted.[4]

Room S-129 was combined with S-128 and S-127 in 1911 to form a three-room suite for the Committee on Appropriations, which today occupies six rooms that span the entire west side of the north wing. Senate records of the 1850's indicate that S-129 was originally assigned to the Committee on Indian Affairs, with several other committees taking over the room during the ensuing dec-

Constantino Brumidi's frescoes adorn the walls and ceiling of room S-128, shown here as it appeared in 1900.
Glenn Brown, History of the United States Capitol

ades prior to 1911.[5] Rooms S-126, S-130, and S-131 were assigned to the Appropriations Committee in 1950.

A visitor wandering about a nineteenth-century committee room would find a roll-top, pigeonhole desk, overstuffed leather chairs, a chaise longue, and carved sideboards. Bookcases would cover the walls, and the tables would be cluttered with papers. These rooms had the appearance of a men's club, and, looking at these photographs, one can almost smell the cigar smoke that must have hung in the air.

Writing in 1898, in his study of congressional committees, Lauros McConachie imagined how one of the Founding Fathers might have reacted to a committee room of that era.

He would wonder at the silk gloves, the cork-screws, the quinine pills; he would shake his head over the Turkish rockers, the Smyrna and Axminster rugs, the antique oak French bevel mirrors. But the American of twentieth century aspirations, though today his pockets be empty as he treads Washington's beautiful halls, though he sees reflected in their golden domes the stintings of his coffee and sugar, rather condones and forgives it all in the proud sense that anything less were not worthy of a nation so rich and so grand—his own country.[6]

The committee rooms were the domain of their chairmen. Indeed, they were little fiefdoms. Committees functioned differently in the late nineteenth century from the way they do today. There were few formal meetings or hearings. Most committee staffs consisted of only one clerk, and the committee room served as the office, the only office, of the chairman. It was well known among the senators at the turn of the century that Senator Nelson Aldrich, chairman of the Finance Committee, would use the Finance Committee room for his afternoon nap, and woe be to the person who disturbed this powerful senator during his repose. Indeed, some committees apparently existed solely to give their chairmen a room in the Capitol and the use of space. For many years, the Senate kept alive the Committee on Revolutionary Claims—long after there were any Revolutionary War claims to process—only to provide meeting space for the Senate minority (and for the most part this meant the Democratic senators). This was a relatively large and conveniently located room next to the first floor entrance in the Senate wing, a room currently known as the Family Dining Room.[7]

A great proliferation of Senate committees occurred during the last half of the nineteenth century. In 1845, there were twenty-three committees; by 1890, there were fifty-five standing committees, eight select committees, and three joint committees. Among those committees established between 1845 and 1890 are such familiar names as Appropriations, Education and Labor (now Labor and Human Resources), and Rules and Administration. There were also many others that have since faded into history, such as Cuban Relations, Epidemic Diseases, Expenditures of Public Money, Geological Survey, Pacific Railroad, Philippines, Transportation Routes to the Seaboard, and University of the United States.[8]

During this period, the work of Senate committees became integral to the legislative process and crucial to the functioning of the

Sidney Breese in 1845 made a motion that the president of the Senate be given charge of making committee assignments. *Library of Congress*

federal government. As I noted in the previous chapter, the Senate in 1845 adopted a system by which the party caucuses would name their party members to the standing committees.

The preeminence of the party organizations in deciding committee assignments—a practice which continues today—ended years of debate over the subject. At first, the Senate as a whole had voted for the members of each committee; then came the practice whereby the vice president or president pro tempore appointed senators to committees. Senator Ambrose Sevier, a Democrat from Arkansas, was floor leader for the difficult birth of the new system of party organization assignments in December 1845. Senator Sidney Breese of Illinois had first moved that the president of the Senate make committee assignments, but this motion lost by one vote on December 4. Beginning on December 9, the Senate began voting on the membership of each committee. This was a tedious, troublesome process that continued through December 17. In some cases, positions on committees went to minority members by a plurality rather than a majority vote. Motions were made to change these positions, and the names of committee members were listed in "a special arrangement"—that is, distinguishing majority from minority members—which was adopted without dissent. It was at this point that leaders of the two parties agreed to present a common list, arranged in a manner acceptable to both the majority and minority.[9]

This system worked well so long as there were just two parties, the Whigs and the Democrats. But, after the Mexican War, the two-party system had been placed in jeopardy due to growing dissatisfaction over the slavery issue. In 1847, Senator John P. Hale, a Free Soiler from New Hampshire, refused to associate himself with either party caucus and would not accept the insignificant committee assignments offered him. A disgruntled lone member is hard to ignore in the Senate, and Hale made his protest known by objecting to the unanimous consent requests to suspend the rules and elect committee members in a group. Hale argued that he and Ohio Senator Salmon P. Chase had met in caucus and now constituted a third party, which should be consulted in making committee assignments. As a result of Hale's protest, Democratic and Whig leaders had to return to the tedious process of electing committee members individually by ballot. By December 1853, however, the parties had made a temporary peace with the independents, finding places for them on several committees.

By the mid-1850's, the Whig party was crumbling, and the ranks of the new Republican and American (Know Nothing) parties were swelling. As the *New York Times* reported,

the committee appointed by the Democratic caucus of the Senate to report a list of Senate committees to be voted for by the body have concluded that the Republicans and Know Nothings are "healthy organizations," sufficient at least to justify their sharing in the labors of the committee room.[10]

When the Republican party superseded the Whig party, its sectional nature posed some new problems for committee selection. Unlike the Democrats and Whigs, which spanned both North and South, the Republicans at first represented only northern states. Thus, with committee assignments favoring the majority party, a disproportionate number of appointments and chairmanships went to southern senators.

At the opening of the Thirty-fifth Congress, in December 1857, Senator Hannibal Hamlin objected to this arrangement. Hamlin, a Maine Democrat-turned-Republican, had studied the resolution assigning committee seats for that Congress and found it "unequal, unjust, and sectional." At that time, there were sixty-two members of the Senate, thirty from slaveholding states, and thirty-two from nonslaveholding states. There were 126 committee seats available for distribution on twenty-two committees. Senator Hamlin argued that "as the representatives of equal states, we are entitled to an equal representation in the organization of this body." In fact, the slaveholding states had been assigned 67 seats to 59 for the free states. Sixteen of the twenty-two committee chairmen came from slaveholding states. The South held a majority on thirteen of the committees. The nine committees on which free-state senators constituted the majority included such relatively unimportant committees as Enrolled Bills, and Audit and Control of the Contingent Expenses of the Senate.

"Here we have the Committee on Foreign Relations, that shapes and directs the foreign policy of the Government," said Hamlin.

We have the Committee on Military Affairs, that looks to its Army; we have the Committee on Naval Affairs, that has charge of its Navy; we have a Committee on the Judiciary, which gives constructions to laws and shapes the policy (so far as the legislature may) of the Government; we find them all constituted of a majority of men who represent the slaveholding states.

The Committee on Commerce, Hamlin pointed out, had a majority of southern members and no representation at all from the Northwest or from the Great Lakes region. The industrial Northeast was in the minority on the Patents Committee, even though that section produced by far the greater number of patent applications. "The majority of the Senate," Hamlin contended, "are entitled to a control in the organization of the committees. But it is this sectional manner of which we have right to complain."

Other Republicans protested that the *Congressional Globe* had inaccurately claimed that "the caucus of all parties in the Senate" had agreed to the list of committee memberships. In fact, there had been no Republican caucus. The Democratic caucus had met, chosen its own members, and left blanks on the list for the Republicans to fill in.

Democratic Senator James Bayard of Delaware rose to respond to Hamlin's accusations. "What is the first principle that enters into the organization of committees, and always must, in every political body?" Bayard asked. He then provided the answer to his own question: "The political party having the majority will necessarily control all the committees of the body, because they are responsible, as a party, for the business of the body."

James Bayard defended the committee assignments made by the Democrats in 1857.   *Library of Congress*

There was no deliberate discrimination against any section, Bayard insisted. The disproportions emerged only because the Republicans were a sectional party and because two-thirds of the Democratic senators came from the South. The Democratic majority had continued the practice of not displacing incumbent members of committees, in order to ensure experience and continuity. The Democrats had sought the best qualified members of the majority to fill new vacancies. Other than that, Bayard saw no way for the majority party to proceed.

Other Democrats pointed out that the Republicans had followed the same practices when they had controlled the House of Representatives during the Thirty-fourth Congress. Thus, Hamlin's objections were overruled when the Senate voted 30 to 19 to accept the committee memberships as presented by the Democratic caucus.[11]

Within four years, the political situation had reversed itself completely. Following Lincoln's election, the southern states seceded, taking with them the greater part of the Democratic majority in the Senate. For the first time, the Republicans controlled this body, and, in the Civil War Senate, they selected committee members who were just as disproportionately sectional, because now the Northeast and Northwest dominated the committees. We can be sure that Hannibal Hamlin watched these developments with pleasure from his new vantage point as vice president under Lincoln and president of the Senate.

Now it was time for the Democrats to complain. In March 1863, Democratic Senator Willard Saulsbury of Delaware insisted that it was "nothing but justice that the minority should be consulted and have the privilege of selecting their members upon the committee." [12] Senator Lazarus Powell, a Democrat from Kentucky, recalled that the custom had been for the majority caucus to make a list assigning its members to committees and to leave blanks for the minority to fill in their own members. In the face of these protests, Senator John P. Hale, now a member of the Republican majority and chairman of the Committee on Naval Affairs, rose to respond. "I think if there be a member here who has a right to speak of the experiences of being in a minority on this floor, I am that man."

Hale recalled that he had been omitted altogether from the committee lists at first and that he was eventually placed "at the tail end" of the Committee on Private Land Claims. "I could not render much service" on that committee, Hale reported. "A good many of those claims were found to rest in old Spanish grants; and, not being entirely conversant with the language, I had to trust to other agencies to find out what was intended. But I want to say, sir, that a claim to

anything of this sort comes with an ill grace from a party who thus ruled the Senate when they had power." [13] In a sense, Hale was reminding senators to be careful about setting precedents while in the majority, for they surely would reap them when they became the minority. Thus, as the southern senators returned at the war's end and the Democratic ranks grew, the Republicans saw the wisdom of reestablishing the old practice of allowing each party to choose its own committee members.

The late nineteenth century was also a period when party discipline became an issue that involved the Senate committees. Once a member was assigned to a committee, he remained on that committee unless he voluntarily withdrew, rising through its ranks according to seniority.

But, as the parties developed and attempted to enforce their collective will on individual members, there were some dramatic exceptions to the seniority rule. Senator Stephen A. Douglas of Illinois was removed as chairman of the Senate Committee on Territories in 1858. Douglas had broken with President James Buchanan over the organization of the Kansas territory. As the gulf between the senator and the president widened, Douglas found himself losing control of his committee. Although he was reelected chairman in December of 1857, the majority of the committee was stacked with Buchanan supporters. After Douglas' reelection in 1858, following his much publicized debates with Abraham Lincoln, he was seen as an even greater threat to the administration, and a concerted effort was begun to remove him from the chairmanship, his power base in the Senate.

When the Democratic caucus met on December 9, 1858, it was an open secret in Washington that Douglas would be dumped. As a result, many Democratic members boycotted the caucus rather than engage in the

An artist depicted a House-Senate conference committee at the turn of the century.

The Century Illustrated Monthly Magazine, May 1902

controversy. Thirty-one of the forty-four Democratic senators attended the caucus. Only seven of those who attended supported Douglas. After the caucus voted to remove the Territories chairman, Senator Robert Toombs of Georgia stormed out of the meeting calling the action vindictive and unworthy of the caucus. But the demotion of Douglas did not have its desired effect. Instead, it made him a political martyr. When Douglas returned to the Senate chamber on January 10, 1859, he was greeted by applause from the gallery and studied coolness from his colleagues on the floor. And in 1860, Douglas received the Democratic nomination for president (although the decision of Southern Democrats to nominate their own candidate, John C. Breckinridge, split the party and ensured Lincoln's election).[14]

Douglas was one of only two senators ever to be removed against their will as committee chairmen. The other was Charles Sumner, who, in 1871, lost his chairmanship of the Foreign Relations Committee. Like Douglas, Sumner has been a prominent subject of my speeches on Senate history. Entering the Senate as a Free Soil Democrat, he switched allegiance to the new Republican party and became perhaps the best known Senate advocate of emancipation and civil rights for the freedman. When the Republicans became the majority party in the Senate in 1861, Sumner assumed the chairmanship of the Foreign Relations Committee, a post he held for the next decade, exerting tremendous influence over the nation's foreign affairs. Sumner's relations with the Grant administration were poor from the start, per-

In March 1871, Senate Republicans removed Charles Sumner as chairman of the Foreign Relations Committee. The committee is shown here with Sumner presiding at the far end of the table. *Harper's Weekly, February 11, 1871*

haps because the imperious senator felt that he, rather than Ulysses Grant, should have been his party's candidate for president. Certainly, Sumner believed—as do some senators today—that he understood foreign affairs better than did the president.

The president and the Foreign Relations Committee chairman struggled over many issues, but none so passionately as Grant's proposal to annex Santo Domingo. Sumner succeeded in defeating the president's plans, but Grant retaliated by marshalling his forces in the Senate against Sumner. At the start of the Forty-second Congress in March 1871, the Republican Committee on Committees met to make committee appointments. According to Sumner's biographer, Professor David Donald:

The five-man Republican group consisted of two friends of Sumner's, Sherman [of Ohio] and Morrill of Vermont, and of two enemies, Pool, of North Carolina, a scalawag who was under Grant's thumb, and Nye, of

Nevada, for whose vulgarity and coarse anecdotes Sumner had showed marked distaste. Howe, of Wisconsin, once an admirer of Sumner but more recently an intimate of [Secretary of State Hamilton] Fish, had the casting vote, and he was subject to intense pressure from all sides.

The committee voted 3 to 2 to remove Sumner altogether from the Foreign Relations Committee and place him instead as chairman of the new Committee on Privileges and Elections. Twice the Republican caucus voted on the recommendation; each time, Sumner was defeated. On the Senate floor, the anti-Sumner forces held firm. "For the first time in ten years," wrote Professor Donald, "Sumner had no control over American foreign policy." [15]

The removals of Douglas and Sumner did not shake the seniority system, which grew even stronger over the following decades. But, while there were no other cases of chairmen being deposed, the party caucus occasionally exercised its prerogatives in making committee assignments. For example, there is the rather bizarre story of the Appropriations Committee chairmanship in the post–Civil War era. On March 6, 1867, the appropriations functions of the Senate Finance Committee were split off to form a separate standing committee on Appropriations consisting of seven members. Senator Lot Morrill of Maine became the first chairman of the Appropriations Committee. When Morrill left the Senate in 1869, Senator William Fessenden, also of Maine, succeeded to the chairmanship, but Fessenden died suddenly a few months later. Next in line among the majority members of the committee was Senator Henry Wilson of Massachusetts. The Republican caucus, however, skipped over Wilson and other ranking Republicans and awarded the chairmanship back to Morrill, who had returned to the Senate by appointment to fill Fessenden's seat. Apparently, the caucus felt that the state of Maine had been unfairly deprived of the chairmanship, and that Morrill, although then technically a freshman, deserved to head the committee again.

When illness forced Senator Morrill to relinquish the chairmanship of the Appropriations Committee, the next in seniority, Cornelius Cole of California, moved up. Two years later, Cole was defeated for reelection. At that point, in 1873, Senator William Sprague of Rhode Island stood next in line according to seniority.

Senator Sprague was a man with a seemingly unlimited political future. A handsome and wealthy textile manufacturer, he was married to one of the most beautiful women in Washington, Kate Chase Sprague, the daughter of Chief Justice Salmon P. Chase. Unfortunately, Sprague's private life was crashing down upon him. His mills teetered on the brink of bankruptcy. And his wife was making little effort to hide her affair

Because of his erratic behavior, William Sprague was denied the chairmanship of the Appropriations Committee. *W.H. Barnes, The American Government (1876)*

with Senator Roscoe Conkling. During March and April 1869, these pressures apparently became too much for Sprague and he lost control of himself, baring his soul to the world in a strange series of speeches on the Senate floor. They began mildly enough but grew increasingly frenzied. Sprague attacked other senators, bankers, lawyers, judges, women in the gallery, and the social elite in his home state. His shocked party considered him a traitor in the ranks, perhaps deranged, and certainly unfit to head the important Appropriations Committee. Thus, once again, Senator Lot Morrill was selected to head the committee, which he did from 1873 to 1876, when he resigned from the Senate to become secretary of the treasury.[16]

The first Democratic chairman, and the fourth person, to head the committee was a West Virginian, Henry Gassaway Davis,

UNITED STATES SENATE THEATRE.
Carl Schurz as Iago.

In 1872, Carl Schurz and other liberal Republican senators supported the presidential candidacy of Horace Greeley instead of their party's nominee, President Grant.   *Harper's Weekly, March 30, 1872*

who held that post from 1879 until 1881. His service on the committee extended from 1873 until his retirement in 1883. He was the father-in-law of Stephen B. Elkins, a senator from West Virginia, and the grandfather of Davis Elkins, also a senator from West Virginia. (Incidentally, I am the second West Virginian, the twelfth Democrat, and the twenty-third person to hold the chairmanship of the Appropriations Committee.)

In the 1870's, Senate Republicans had to contend with a splinter group of "liberal Republicans" who broke with the administration of President Ulysses S. Grant. In December 1870, the "regular" Republicans denied the liberal Republican Senator Carl Schurz of Missouri the chairmanship of the Committee on Retrenchment, which he was due by seniority. Then came the presidential

election of 1872, when liberal Republicans deserted Grant's candidacy in favor of the fusion ticket headed by Horace Greeley.

Following the election, the Republican caucus refused to give any committee assignments to seven liberal Republican senators: Carl Schurz, Charles Sumner, Lyman Trumbull, Thomas Tipton, Reuben Fenton, Joseph West, and Morgan Hamilton. "The Democrats," wrote Professor Clarence Berdahl, "did the unusually generous thing of offering most of these men committee places from their own meager allotment as the minority party, even at the cost of sacrificing some regular Democrats." Thus, Schurz received the only Democratic place on the Foreign Relations Committee, Trumbull on the Privileges and Elections Committee, and so on. "This was done," Professor Berdahl noted, "in spite of emphatic declarations by these Liberal Republican senators that they would not consider themselves Democrats and would not be bound by the caucus of either party, but would act independently and in accordance with their own best judgment on every question." [17]

Mr. President, I have been speaking about the organizational problems of the committees during this era, but I do not wish to minimize the work of these committees. Indeed, it was during the late nineteenth century that the truism developed that the real work of the Senate was done in committee. In my speeches on the Civil War, I cited the burst of significant domestic legislation enacted by those wartime congresses. With the Lincoln administration preoccupied by military matters, this legislation was the product of the hard-working committees of the Senate and House. Similarly, Reconstruction-era legislation was initiated in committee.

Although any senator could introduce legislation, and the Senate could debate such legislation without referring it to committee, committee referrals had in fact become a

Members of a joint House and Senate committee charged with finding a way to resolve the disputed Hayes-Tilden presidential election in 1877 are shown here signing their report.   *The Daily Graphic, January 26, 1877*

matter of course. Professor Michael Les Benedict has noted that twenty-three of the twenty-four major Reconstruction bills and resolutions that the Senate enacted between 1863 and 1869 were first reported from Senate or joint committees. In fact, Professor Benedict was able to trace the decline in influence of Radical Republican senators by examining the shift in committee jurisdiction over Reconstruction matters. During the Thirty-eighth Congress, Senator Ben Wade's Committee on Territories held jurisdiction over Reconstruction, and it was from this committee that the Wade-Davis bill, a Reconstruction proposal, was reported. At the same time, Senator Charles Sumner chaired the Select Committee on Slavery and Freedmen, which reported out the Freedmen's Bureau legislation. After 1865, however, the conservative Judiciary Committee took over Reconstruction matters, sharing jurisdiction

not with the Committee on Territories but with a new Joint Committee on Reconstruction. Members of the Committee on Territories and the Select Committee on Slavery and Freedmen were passed over by the Republican caucus when appointments to the new joint committee were made. Conservative Republicans were now firmly in control of Reconstruction matters by dint of their majority on the committees to which such legislation was referred.[18]

Jurisdiction remained critical to determining power in the Senate, particularly when it related to money matters. Without question, the two most powerful committees of the late nineteenth century were the committees on Finance and Appropriations. The former handled all tariff legislation at a time when most government revenues were raised from tariff duties and when tariff rates influenced the entire American economy. The latter de-

[231]

cided the level of funding of all legislation. The chairmen of these two committees were generally their party's leaders in caucus and on the Senate floor.

Power is rarely acquired or held without struggle. From time to time, members of the other committees sought to curtail the powers of the Appropriations Committee. In 1884, there was a major effort to remove from Appropriations' jurisdiction all appropriations for rivers and harbors, post roads, and the District of Columbia, and to refer them instead to the Committees on Internal Improvements, Post-Offices and Post-Roads, and the District of Columbia, respectively. Other motions were made to refer agricultural appropriations to the Agriculture Committee and military and naval appropriations to the Committees on Military Affairs and Naval Affairs.

"This is the beginning of a raid on the Appropriations Committee that if allowed to proceed cannot be resisted," warned Senator James Beck of Kentucky, an Appropriations Committee member. He explained that

each committee will claim that it has special knowledge and special information that the Committee on Appropriations does not have and can not have, because of the intimate relations of the various committees with the different Departments; and it will end in abolishing the Committee on Appropriations substantially. Perhaps that may be a good thing to do. It is a good way to get money out of the Treasury; there is no doubt about that.[19]

Such arguments appealed to the frugality of the late-nineteenth-century senators, and the raid on the Appropriations Committee was defeated. The House, in 1885, followed a different course, stripping its Appropriations Committee of jurisdiction over all but six of the fourteen general bills, referring the others to the appropriate legislative committees. Proponents argued that the new arrangement would further efforts to econo-mize the government and would reduce the practice of grafting legislation onto appropriations bills. They were also responding to complaints from the executive departments, which objected to the detailed itemization of appropriations, restrictions on their power to transfer funds, requirements for returning unexpended funds to the Treasury, forbidding of contract obligations in excess of appropriations, and other requirements set by the congressional appropriations committees. Although this movement was derailed in 1896, the Senate eventually followed the House's action. In 1899, the Senate removed rivers and harbors, military, Indian affairs, and Post Office appropriations from the Senate Appropriations Committee. The committee's six subcommittees continued to handle Deficiency, Diplomatic and Consular, District of Columbia, Fortifications, Legislative, and Sundry Civil appropriations. This time, the Senate adopted the changes by unanimous consent, without debate.[20] Not until 1922 was the Appropriations Committee's full jurisdiction restored.

Mr. President, I have concentrated on the Appropriations Committee, in part, because it is impossible to cover the activities of every Senate committee during this long period and also because the debate in 1884 provides us with some revealing insight into how the Senate committee system operated in the late nineteenth century. Take, for example, the remarks of Senator George Vest of Missouri. Senator Vest talked of the special relationships that developed between members of committees and the departments whose areas they oversaw and for which they considered legislation. "I assert," said Senator Vest:

what the experience of every Senator will confirm to be the truth, that just so soon as a committee is appointed, for instance in regard to the Navy, in regard to military affairs, or upon fiscal questions, that very instant the most intimate and, I admit, proper relations

George Vest, who complained that the Senate continually created new committees instead of referring new matters to existing committees, was portrayed in an unflattering cartoon.
New York World, March 5, 1888

begin between that particular department and the senators on that committee. . . . If one of my brother Senators today wanted a favor from the Navy Department, to what Senator on this floor should he go? It would be to the head of the Committee on Naval Affairs.

The result, Vest argued, was a rivalry between the committees to secure the biggest appropriations for their own areas of specialization.

Senator Vest also spoke of the trend toward creating new committees to meet new situations, rather than relying upon the regular standing committees. Rivers and harbors legislation, for example, was removed from the Senate Commerce Committee and assigned to a new committee on Internal Improvements. Vest recalled that

years ago, under the pressure of public opinion and the exigencies of the time, this Senate created a Committee on the Mississippi River and its Tributaries, and the argument made then was that the Commerce Committee could not consider this great question on account of

the river and harbor bill absorbing all its functions, and that a special committee should be created. It was created, and what has been the result?

. . . The record shows that nothing has been done. . . . Not one dollar has come from this special committee, not one single measure which has given relief to the people of the West upon this great question.

Public business would not be facilitated by the creation of new committees, said Senator Vest, but rather by the diligent attention of the committees already created.

Here, Senator Vest offered an argument that has been at the root of many Senate reforms over the years, the most recent being in 1977. He contended that the number of Senate committees had grown too large and needed to be reduced. In 1884, there were six standing committees of the Senate that had never considered a bill, resolution, or any other type of business. "They are all sinecure committees," Vest pointed out. "They were created simply to give secretaries to members of the Senate and a committee room." [21]

Senator Vest was echoed by Senator Richard Coke of Texas, who also objected to removing river and harbor legislation from the Commerce Committee. The problem was not that the Commerce Committee was inefficient, Coke asserted, but that the river and harbor bills never reached the Committee on Commerce from the House, where they originated, until the last eight or ten days of the session. To create a new Senate committee would not expedite matters at all. "It is well known, Mr. President," said Senator Coke:

that bills are passed much more rapidly and with much more facility through the Senate than through the House on account of the difference in the constitution of the two bodies, the one small and compact and the other large and unwieldy. It is also well known that with the expiration of every Congress large numbers of bills which have passed the Senate die on the Calendar of the House from non-action. I can not see the good to

John R. McPherson reported that he had served for three years on a committee that only met once.
The Daily Graphic, January 29, 1877

be accomplished by increasing the number of Senate committees, with the additional attendant expense, in order to increase the number of Senate bills to be ignored and permitted to expire without action in the House.[22]

As is usual in Senate debates, there was another side to be heard, and Senator William Frye of Maine responded to Senators Vest and Coke. The Committee on Commerce should not spend its time waiting for the House to act, said Frye, but should begin studying river and harbor matters from the very moment the session began. "The Senator from Texas says the committee has had ample time—" Frye noted, "the Committee on Commerce meets once a week, I believe on Thursday at 10 o'clock—ample time; only a week per session for the river and harbor bill! Show me, Mr. President, where the

Committee on Commerce has undertaken in that ample time to relieve American commerce, to restore our commerce to the ocean, to do those things that ought to be done in the interest of the whole country." [23]

As the debate continued, Senator John R. McPherson of New Jersey rose to report this interesting memoir of his committee service:

There are many committees in this body that have little or nothing to do. Committee-rooms are provided for them, clerks of committee. The same machinery, the same necessary expense is attendant upon a committee doing no service as is required for a committee doing a large amount of service. During three years of my service in this body I had the honor to be assigned to duty upon the Committee on Manufactures.

During that period of three years we never met but once. We were hastily called together one morning by the chairman of the committee to consider a bill which by some accident had been referred to us. No sooner had the consideration commenced than a messenger from the Committee on Finance appeared at the door and demanded that the bill be sent to the Committee on Finance, it being a revenue bill and properly belonging to that committee, and his authority showed the fact that the previous day the bill had been taken from the Committee on Manufactures and assigned to the Committee on Finance by the order of the Senate. During these entire three years, with the exception of this one bill to which I have alluded, the Committee on Manufactures had no bill, no resolution, no legislative matter of any character referred to it.[24]

Mr. President, in these days when United States senators must contend with conflicting committee and subcommittee schedules and demands upon their time, we may look back nostalgically upon the days when a senator could be assigned to a committee that conducted no business at all; although I seriously doubt that any currently serving senator would ever tolerate such a situation as Senator McPherson described. It is not at all surprising, however, to find that the Committee on Manufactures' only bill was whisked away by the clerk of the Committee on Finance. By comparison to the Committee on Manufactures, which did not meet and which did not consider legislation, the Finance Committee was an exceedingly powerful and busy committee, with jurisdiction over the national debt, currency, banking, and revenue. It was an amalgamation of today's committees on the Budget, Banking, Housing and Urban Affairs, and Finance. It handled the two most controversial areas of legislation in the late nineteenth century: currency and tariffs. It was not for nothing that the most powerful men gravitated toward the Finance Committee, and that Finance Committee members became the most influential senators. Henry Clay, Daniel Webster, and John C. Calhoun all chaired the committee before the Civil War. After the war, the chairmen of the Finance Committee generally served as their party's leaders on the Senate floor in the days before officially designated majority and minority leaders came into being. From 1865 to 1900, the list of Finance chairmen included Republicans William Fessenden, John Sherman, Justin Morrill, and Nelson Aldrich, and Democrats Thomas Bayard and Daniel Voorhees.

Senator McPherson mentioned the clerks of committees, which brings up another indication of the Finance Committee's stature. Beginning in the 1840's, the Senate authorized the Finance Committee to employ a clerk. When, in 1857, the Senate decided to extend this privilege to all standing committees, clerks were employed at a salary of $6.00 a day for every day the Senate remained in session. The clerk of the Finance Committee, however, was retained on an annual salary of $1,850. This reflected the scope of the committee's work, which increased dramatically during the Civil War when the first national paper currency was issued and revenue was needed to support the war effort. In the years after the war, the committee handled the tariff legislation which played such an important role in the industrialization of America. Although the

Constitution provides that bills to raise revenue must originate in the House, it does not limit the Senate's ability to add amendments, which the Finance Committee did on a regularly expanding basis. In 1872, for example, the House sent over a bill repealing the tariff on tea and coffee. The bill was four lines long. The Senate then added twenty pages of amendments.[25]

Mr. President, in discussing the committees of the Senate, I think I should say a few words about the party committees as well as the standing committees. In the years following the Civil War, we find party steering committees developing as a means of building party regularity and ensuring efficient handling of business in the Senate. The Republicans in 1874 and the Democrats in 1878 appointed ad hoc committees to recommend schedules of business for their respective party caucuses. During the 1880's, these committees were formalized as the Republican and Democratic Committees on the Order of Business, generally known as steering committees. Because the committees were strictly party creations, they filed no formal Senate reports and maintained no records. As a result, their exact dates of creation and early membership remain obscure.

The steering committees' control of the schedule required party members to consult with them before attempting to raise any matter on the Senate floor. The steering committees also requested committee chairmen to submit lists of bills which warranted immediate attention. They then notified the caucuses of the nature and the order of bills to be considered, frequently making recommendations on party policy concerning those measures. During the 1890's, such strong party leaders as Republican William Allison and Democrat Arthur Pue Gorman used the steering committees as instruments of party power, to keep their members unified behind the party's legislative program.[26]

The artist called this sketch "A Subcommittee meeting where the serious work is done."

The Century Illustrated Monthly Magazine, May 1902

In many ways, however, the strength of the Senate standing committees during these years militated against party unity and frustrated legislative-executive relations. Here, let me refer to Woodrow Wilson's classic study *Congressional Government*, published in 1885. Wilson, as we know, was an astute historian and political scientist who left academia for politics and was eventually elected president of the United States. This study was his doctoral thesis at Johns Hopkins University. Although there is no record that he ever traveled from Baltimore to Washington to observe Congress in action while writing this study, this fact does not diminish the value of his words.

Quoting Lord Rosebery, Wilson called the Senate "the most powerful and efficient second chamber that exists." But, at the same time, Wilson found that its committee organization denied leadership and fragmented the Senate. Each committee was an independent barony, with powers of "overlordship" of the executive departments. "The Committees are not the recognized constitutional superiors of Secretary A. or Comptroller B.," wrote Wilson,

but these officials cannot move a finger or plan more than a paltry detail without looking to it that they render strict obedience to the wishes of these outside, uncommissioned, and irresponsible, but none the less authoritative and imperative masters.[27]

To summarize, Mr. President, during the period from 1845 to 1900 the work of the Senate expanded greatly, and the number of its committees also expanded to handle that work load. New standing and special committees were appointed, more clerks were hired, more rooms were acquired. More bills and resolutions were considered, more amendments written and debated. The business of the Senate grew to match a geographically, economically, and industrially expanding nation. But, as many of these committees grew in power and influence, they created new problems of their own. They became magnets for lobbyists and special interests seeking to influence legislation, whether by legitimate or illegitimate means. They also became stumbling blocks for reform legislation. By the end of the nineteenth century, the Senate was recognized as the most powerful arm of the federal government. Yet, it was also seen as a "millionaire's club" that blocked legislation and frustrated the will of the people. By 1900, a dynamic new reform movement was getting underway which would bring great changes to the government as a whole and the Senate in particular. Committee reform became a major issue of twentieth-century political debate. But this is another story, deserving attention in detail, and I shall save it for another chapter in the history of the United States Senate.

Committees, 1900–1946

June 3, 1985*

Mr. President, the United States Senate does much of its work in committee, and all senators realize that their careers here will, in large part, be determined by the committee assignments they receive.

These days, every senator, no matter how new to this body, serves on at least one major standing committee. But it was not always this way. Only after Lyndon Johnson became Democratic leader in 1953 did Senate Democrats agree to place freshman senators on major committees before giving senior members second major assignments. Republicans did not adopt a similar practice until 1965. Because of this policy, when I came to the Senate in January 1959, I received a seat on the Appropriations Committee, an honor that other members of the Senate had waited years to achieve. I will always be grateful to Lyndon Johnson, and to Senator Carl Hayden of Arizona and Senator Richard Russell of Georgia, especially, for that assignment. My reception in the Senate, so far as committee posts were concerned, was, therefore, considerably different from the fate that befell some very prominent senators at the turn of this century.

Let me begin with a portrait of an ambitious young man, newly elected to the United States Senate at the age of thirty-six. The year was 1899; the senator was Albert J. Beveridge, Republican of Indiana. Senator-elect Beveridge personified the young man on the rise, with visions of national glory and the presidency fixed in his head. His eloquent speeches defending American expansion in the Philippines and the Caribbean had drawn national press coverage of his campaign in Indiana. Immediately after winning a Senate seat, Beveridge had sailed for the Philippine Islands to examine first-hand that newly acquired American colony. As a result of that trip and his already flourishing reputation, Beveridge believed he had earned an appointment to the Senate Foreign Relations Committee. He also wanted an assignment to the Committee on the Philippines—indeed, he expected to become its chairman. As if that were not enough, he also requested appointment to the Judiciary Committee. Senator Beveridge campaigned intensively for those posts, writing important senators and encouraging his friends to write letters and lobby on his behalf.[1]

Beveridge's efforts were almost for naught. While he was assigned to the Philippines Committee, the chairmanship went to a senior senator, Henry Cabot Lodge of Massachusetts. Beveridge, instead, became chairman of the Forest Reservation and Protection-of-Game Committee, which existed solely to provide him with an office and a clerk. The other committees he served on were Indian Depredations; Organization, Conduct, and Expenditures of the Executive Departments; Private Land Claims; Territories; and the Select Committee to Investigate the Condition of the Potomac River Front. None of these could be considered high-ranking committees. Theodore Roosevelt, then governor of New York, had been among the many who lobbied to put Beveridge on Foreign Relations. Roosevelt's friend Henry Cabot Lodge wrote back that he agreed Beveridge was "a very bright fellow, well informed and sound in his views." But Lodge

* Revised September 1989

As a new senator, Albert Beveridge, *left*, campaigned energetically but unsuccessfully for a seat on the Foreign Relations Committee. Freshman Senator Robert La Follette, Sr., *right*, was made chairman of a committee that had no business to conduct.
Success Magazine, January 10, 1910

added that Beveridge had "a very imperfect idea of the rights of seniority and . . . a large idea of what he ought to have." There would be no seat on Foreign Relations until a few years later when Beveridge had seasoned. For the time being, Senator Lodge observed that Beveridge was "fortunate" just to get on the Philippines Committee.[2]

A few years later, another man with powerful ambitions entered the Senate. Robert La Follette, a crusading reformer, had served as governor of Wisconsin before his election to the Senate, and he was used to executive prerogatives. In the Senate, however, La Follette started out on the bottom rung, no matter what his previous experience. He had received a form letter from the chairman of the Republican Committee on Committees

asking for his preference in committee assignments. La Follette replied that he had only one preference, and that was the Committee on Interstate Commerce. Considering his experience in regulating railroads in Wisconsin, this was an obvious choice, but it was the last place that the conservative Old Guard of his party intended to place him. Instead, La Follette was assigned to the committees on Census, Civil Service and Retrenchment, Claims, Immigration, Indian Affairs, Pensions, and the Select Committee to Investigate the Condition of the Potomac River Front, the latter of which he would chair.

"I had immediate visions of cleaning up the whole Potomac River front," La Follette later wrote,

The members of the Joint Committee on Interstate Commerce were photographed in 1916.

U.S. Senate Historical Office

until I found that in all its history the committee had never had a bill referred to it for consideration, and had never held a meeting. My committee room was reached by going down into the sub-cellar of the Capitol, along a dark winding passage lighted by dim skylights which leaked badly, to a room carved out of the terrace on the west side of the Capitol.

From his subterranean committee room, La Follette reflected on the nature of Senate committees. Some of the committees to which he was assigned, including the one he chaired, had no business to conduct at all. Others, especially Claims, Indian Affairs, and Pensions, were tremendously busy with a multiplicity of minor bills of a private nature. He could see the motives of the party hierarchy that controlled the Republican Committee on Committees. "We will give the gentleman so much routine work to do that he will not trouble us at all," he imagined them as saying. The real power and influence lay in other committees. "Of first importance is the great Finance Committee," La Follette observed, "which has charge of all bills affecting the tariff, currency and banking." At that time, the Finance Committee was chaired by Senator Nelson Aldrich of Rhode Island. "Other very powerful committees," La Follette went on, "are Interstate Commerce, with its control of bills relating to railroads, trusts and combinations, and the Committees on Rules, on Appropriations, on Foreign Relations, and on the Judiciary." [3]

In 1918, Secretary of War Newton D. Baker, *second from right*, met with the members of the Senate Military Affairs Committee.

Mr. President, at the turn of the century there were fifty-five standing committees of the Senate, eight select committees, one joint committee, and two joint commissions. That made a total of sixty-six committees and commissions for a Senate with ninety members. As Senators Beveridge and La Follette discovered, most of these committees were nonperforming. One way to sort out the working committees from those that existed only to provide their chairmen with some space, was to look at the committee staffs. Each committee was assigned at least one clerk. Those committees with more work were entitled to additional clerks and messengers. Using the staff as a standard, the Finance Committee ranked first on the list

with four clerks and a messenger. Appropriations and Pensions each had three clerks and a messenger. Committees with two clerks and a messenger included Claims, the District of Columbia, Foreign Relations, Judiciary, and Military Affairs. Those with two clerks were Immigration, Naval Affairs, Pacific Islands and Puerto Rico, the Philippines, Post Office, Printing, Public Buildings, and Territories. That suggests at least sixteen working committees.[4]

Location also indicated a committee's status and prestige. The Finance Committee, chaired by Senator Aldrich—by all accounts the most powerful senator of that generation—operated out of rooms on the second floor of the Capitol, S-208 and S-209, just off the Senate chamber. (From January 1977 through 1986, I occupied those same rooms as Democratic leader.) Only two other committees were located on the second floor off the chamber: Appropriations and the District of Columbia. The District Committee, which, at that time, essentially ran the nation's capital city, was located in what is now known as the Lyndon Johnson Room, S-211—a room currently assigned to the Democratic leader. Elsewhere on the second floor, important committees had rooms on the Capitol's west front, which had, until the 1890's, been occupied by the Library of Congress. The committees shared space there with the justices of the Supreme Court. Other committees of stature (or at least committee chairmen of stature) had rooms on the ground floor and the third floor of the Capitol.

Further down the pecking order, a senator like Robert La Follette would be assigned to dark and damp "committee rooms" under the terraces on the west front. Even more isolated were those freshmen and minority party senators who received committee rooms in the Maltby Building, which the Senate leased. That building stood approximately where the Taft Carillon is located today, but no subway or tunnel linked it to the Capitol. Senators assigned rooms there could be observed trudging across the Capitol grounds and streets. With the attainment of seniority, they would hope for more convenient quarters.[5]

Minority party members at times chaired committees. That practice has not carried over to our own day. But, when the Senate created committees as a device for providing office space and staff, it made some provisions for senior members of the minority. The easiest way to determine from the *Congressional Directory* whether a committee lacked any real business was to see if its chairman belonged to the minority party. Thus, in

1901, senior Democrats, then the minority party, chaired committees on Audit and Control of the Contingent Expenses of the Senate, Corporations Organized in the District of Columbia, Engrossed Bills, Private Land Claims, Public Health and National Quarantine, Revolutionary Claims, Additional Accommodations for the Library of Congress, Five Civilized Tribes of Indians, Transportation and Sale of Meat Products, and Woman Suffrage. We can assume that the Senate in 1901 had just as much likelihood of passing a bill to permit women to vote as it did of finding a Revolutionary War claimant at that late date.[6]

The growth in the number of standing committees was astonishing. Between 1863 and 1898, the Senate more than doubled the number of its committees—from twenty-two to forty-nine. Then, in 1899 and 1909, as the Library of Congress' government specialist Walter Kravitz pointed out, the Senate "indulged itself in two bursts of creation," creating twenty-three new standing committees. That is, they elevated a host of select committees to standing committee status. By 1914, the number of standing committees of the Senate had reached seventy-four (or seventy-five, if one counted the Joint Committee on the Library).[7]

This was all the more remarkable since the opening, in 1909, of the Senate Office Building, now known as the Richard B. Russell Building, alleviated a major reason for the multiplicity of minor committees. Every senator received an office in the new building, whether he was a committee chairman or not. Generally, these were two-room suites: one room for the senator and one room for his staff of two or three aides. We might have expected to see a housekeeping resolution in the Senate to abolish the non-meeting committees, but, instead, the Senate promoted them to standing committees. Senator Elmer Burkett, a Nebraska Republican,

Too many Senate committees did no work, declared Elmer Burkett, and were simply "graveyards to the great body of the senators." *Library of Congress*

counted "only about twenty" committees of the Senate that actually held hearings. The rest, he observed, were "graveyards to the great body of the senators." Graveyards or not, the Senate clung to its non-functioning committees as a source of extra patronage and hideaway offices in the Capitol.

In 1909, Senator Burkett introduced a resolution to reform the committee structure. By his estimate, there were seven powerful committees: Appropriations, Commerce, Finance, Foreign Relations, Interstate Commerce, Judiciary, and Rules. Then he counted thirteen second-level committees which also conducted business: Agriculture, Indian Affairs, Military Affairs, Naval Affairs, Pensions, Post-Offices and Post-Roads, Immigration, District of Columbia, Interoceanic Canals, Philippines, Privileges and Elections, Public Buildings and Grounds, and Public Lands. On the seven powerful committees there were eighty-nine seats. But twenty-eight senators held sixty-three of those eighty-nine places. This concentration of committee seats favored Republicans, especially those from states east of the Mississippi River. As the Nebraska senator pointed out, sixty-six of the eighty-nine seats went to eastern senators.

Combining both the primary and secondary level committees, Burkett found that 28 percent of the senators held 51 percent of the seats on functioning committees. Twenty-six senators served on more than two of these functioning committees; thirty served on two; twenty-two served on one; and fourteen served on none at all. Fourteen senators were, therefore, shut out of the real work of the Senate as done in committee. Yet, as Burkett pointed out, there were eighty-nine committee seats and ninety-two senators, almost enough for one to a senator. For that purpose, he introduced a resolution that no senator should serve on more than two of the seven most powerful committees or any other committee that handled appropriations bills. The Senate of 1909, however, had no desire to hear such heresy. Burkett's resolution was referred to the Rules Committee, and there it died.[8]

The staggering number of standing committees continued on through the First World War. In the aftermath of the war came a movement to streamline the operations of the federal government. It was at that time that the Bureau of the Budget was created (now the Office of Management and Budget) and the General Accounting Office was established, symbolizing the improved managerial attitudes. In that context, the Senate conducted some serious housecleaning.

On May 26, 1920, Pennsylvania Senator Philander C. Knox, chairman of the Rules Committee, gave notice of a proposed change in the Senate rules. The next day, Knox reported that the Rules Committee had unanimously voted to abolish "about forty" standing committees, effective at "the beginning of the Sixty-seventh Congress," in order to "cut out all the committees that rarely if ever meet." The total number of standing committees would be reduced to thirty-three. In addition, the Rules Committee voted to limit membership on each of the ten major committees to fifteen senators and reduced membership on the less important committees proportionately. This reform was adopted by voice vote after very little discussion, indicating that it was a noncontroversial and universally accepted proposal. Democratic leaders Oscar Underwood of Alabama and Joe Robinson of Arkansas, representing the minority, urged its adoption. For historical purposes, we might wish that the Senate had spent just a little time debating and explaining the proposed reform, but the Senate that day was debating agricultural appropriations, and Senator Wesley Jones of Washington, a supporter of that measure, objected to any discussion of the rules change. Since there seemed to be no opposition, proponents of the change gladly accommodated him. Hence, we have almost no record of one of the most sweeping committee reforms in Senate history—very different, I might add, from the reforms that followed in 1946.[9]

As one might expect from precipitous change, some of the results were unanticipated. The new committee structure had a profound impact on seniority in the Senate. Previously, what had been most significant was a senator's seniority within the Senate as a whole, not within a particular committee. Prior to the 1921 revisions, senators might be appointed chairmen of committees on which they had never served. After the revisions, with fewer committees in existence, seniority progressed strictly within each committee, just as it does today.

A second unexpected result of limiting the number of standing committees was the explosion of subcommittees. As Walter Kravitz observed, "The Senate discovered that reducing the number of standing committees under these circumstances was like squeez-

In 1920, Rules Committee Chairman Philander Knox oversaw a drastic reduction in the number of Senate committees. *Library of Congress*

ing a fistful of water: out squirted a stream of subcommittees." By 1946, sixty-eight subcommittees were in existence.[10]

Since the resolution cutting the number of committees had also cut the number of seats on those committees, the parties found it difficult to satisfy the demands of their members. This was especially true of the Republicans, who had recently regained the majority in 1918, after six years in the minority. At the time the Senate adopted the committee reforms, the Republicans held a slim 49 to 47 margin. But by the time the reforms went into effect, in April 1921, the Republicans had won a landslide election, putting Senator Warren G. Harding in the White House and increasing their margin in the Senate to 59 to 37. The Republican majority, wanting to

A subcommittee of the Foreign Relations Committee was photographed in 1924.   *Library of Congress*

satisfy its swelled ranks and to strengthen support for the new president's legislative programs, amended the new committee reforms to allow sixteen rather than fifteen members on each committee. The new positions would be filled, naturally, by Republicans.

Democrats, who until then had supported the committee reforms, now objected. Mississippi Democrat Pat Harrison asked, "Is it the object of the steering committee on the other side of the Chamber to grab all those 10 places [that is, one new seat on each of the ten major committees], or is it proposed to give to the minority half of them or any of them?" Republican Senator Frank Brandegee of Connecticut responded, "I would not use the word 'grab.' It is only our object to take them." Democrats charged that conservative Republicans wanted to increase their margin to diminish any effective Democratic oppo-

sition. No matter what their objections, Democrats lacked the necessary votes, and the majority party "grabbed" or "took" the additional seats.[11]

But Senate Republicans had their own internal problems as well. The party was divided between the majority conservative faction and a small but vocal progressive faction. The feuding between these two groups spilled over into committee assignments. In 1923, western progressive Republicans used Iowa Senator Albert Cummins' position as president pro tempore as a reason to deny him the chairmanship of the Senate Interstate Commerce Committee. President Harding having died, and Vice President Coolidge having gone to the White House, the president pro tempore now presided regularly. But this was simply an excuse. Cummins, a former progressive, had strayed into the conservative camp and had become a potent critic of the western agricultural bloc. Progressives viewed him as too close to the railroad interests to serve effectively as chairman of the Interstate Commerce Committee. Hence, the progressives called for a vote of the Senate on the chairmanship, and withheld their votes from Cummins, casting them for the next ranking Republican, Robert La Follette. With Republicans split and Democrats voting for their ranking committee member, South Carolina's Ellison Smith, it took the Senate a month to choose the chairman of the Interstate Commerce Committee. It was clear that progressives would not relent on their opposition to Cummins, but Republican regulars had no intention of making the insurgent La Follette chairman of the committee. Finally, on January 9, 1924, enough of the progressives threw their support to Smith (a thoroughly conservative gentleman) to make him chairman. Here, at least, was one case where neither side within the Republican ranks showed much allegiance to seniority.[12]

Later in 1924, Senator La Follette broke openly with the Republicans and ran for president on the Progressive party ticket against the Republican incumbent, Calvin Coolidge. La Follette lost badly. But victory at the polls did not satisfy party regulars; they wished to further punish those senators who had "bolted" from the party and supported La Follette. Some progressive Republicans, such as George Norris of Nebraska and Hiram Johnson of California, had clearly leaned toward La Follette but not openly endorsed him. No disciplinary action was taken against them. But Senators Edwin Ladd and Lynn Frazier of North Dakota and Smith Wildman Brookhart of Iowa had endorsed La Follette over Coolidge. The Republican Conference retaliated by voting not to admit them, or La Follette, to the conference. It stripped them of their committee seniority and voted not to assign them to Republican

vacancies on committees. Loss of committee seniority denied La Follette the chance to become chairman of Interstate Commerce, a post that went instead to a party regular, James Watson of Indiana, who chaired the Republican Committee on Committees. Ladd lost his chairmanship of the committee on Public Lands and Surveys. Brookhart, relatively low in seniority, lost little standing. Professor Ralph Huitt ably described the fate of Lynn Frazier:

In a move that today would scarcely seem like chastisement, but obviously ran counter to his preference, Frazier was transferred from Indian Affairs, whose business he understood, to Banking and Currency, whose business he did not. The reason given was forthright. With La Follette also on the [Indian Affairs] committee, the progressives and the Democrats together would control it; and since La Follette ranked him, Frazier had to go.[13]

These cases represent some of the very few occasions when any political party has attempted to discipline its senators, and such a draconian policy proved very difficult to maintain. In 1925, when Senator Robert La Follette died, he was succeeded as senator from Wisconsin by his son, Robert, Jr. The son had been active in his father's campaign and was clearly a party bolter. Should the Republicans welcome or bar him? Should they assign him to committees? While the young La Follette watched in silent bemusement, the Republicans squabbled over his fate. "It has been rather fun," he wrote to his brother, "to sit tight and watch them squirm." Finally, the conference found him room on three committees. Retribution against the revolt was clearly over.[14]

Mr. President, during the 1920's, Senate committees were quite fairly likened to feudal baronies. A committee could not meet except at the call of its chairman, and the chairman ran the proceedings as he wished. The behavior of chairmen ranged from dicta-

Henry Cabot Lodge ran the Foreign Relations Committee with a firm hand. *Library of Congress*

torial to benign. When the elder Henry Cabot Lodge ran the Foreign Relations Committee, for instance, President Harding, President Coolidge, other members of the committee, and the Senate all failed to pry from his committee a resolution calling for American membership on the World Court, which Lodge strongly opposed. Democratic Leader Joe Robinson complained that "the senator from Massachusetts has very effectively and, in my judgment, finally pigeonholed or entombed the proposal of the president respecting the World Court." On the other hand, fortunate were the senators assigned to the Rules Committee when Philander Knox served at its chairman. Arizona Senator Henry Ashurst glowingly recalled how Chairman Knox "served a sumptuous luncheon to his fellow committeemen" at committee meetings. That was, I suppose, at least one way of establishing a quorum! [15]

The basic structure of the Senate committee system remained unchanged in the decades following the 1921 reorganization. By contrast, the leadership of the committees changed dramatically. From 1919 through 1932, the Republican party held the majority in the Senate, with margins ranging from 59 to 37 in 1921, to 48 to 47 and one Independent in 1931. But with the election of 1932, which brought Franklin D. Roosevelt into the White House, the Democrats won control of the Senate, a majority they would hold for the next fourteen years.

Although causing a change in party, the 1932 election did not create as great an ideological shift as we might expect. A number of Republican committee chairmen had been members of the progressive wing of their party. Peter Norbeck of South Dakota chaired the Banking Committee; Hiram Johnson, Commerce; William Borah of Idaho, Foreign Relations; James Couzens of Michigan, Interstate Commerce; George Norris, Judiciary; Robert La Follette, Jr.,

Manufactures; and Gerald Nye of North Dakota, Public Lands and Surveys. The Democratic victory saw many conservative Democrats, especially those representing southern states, with sufficient seniority to move into the chairmanships. Ellison D. "Cotton Ed" Smith of South Carolina became Agriculture chairman; Carter Glass of Virginia chaired Appropriations; Josiah Bailey of North Carolina, Claims; Hubert Stephens of Mississippi, Commerce; Pat Harrison of Mississippi, Finance; Kenneth McKellar of Tennessee, Post Offices and Post Roads; and Walter George of Georgia, Privileges and Elections.[16]

Historians have noted that these Southern chairmen exerted a powerful influence during the New Deal years, forcing the Roosevelt administration to consider their wishes when planning legislation. In particular, the power of these chairmen helps to explain the New Deal's weak record on civil rights. But on economic matters, with the nation entrapped in its worst depression, these conservative chairmen generally supported the New Deal and managed its legislative initiatives on the Senate floor.[17]

A prime example was Pat Harrison, a talented and shrewd legislator who headed the powerful Finance Committee. By nature, Harrison was more conservative than was the New Deal; yet, he shepherded Roosevelt's tax proposals through the Senate, including the so-called "soak-the-rich" plan, no matter how unhappy he felt about it personally. Harrison also served as floor leader for the Social Security Act, one of the most significant pieces of New Deal legislation.[18]

Until 1937, President Roosevelt enjoyed a fairly united front among Senate committee chairmen, who were willing to put aside individual differences—at least publicly—to support the president's recovery and reform legislation. With Roosevelt's Supreme Court packing proposal, that consensus began to

dissolve, and, during his second term, Roosevelt had far greater difficulty in winning congressional support. The committee chairmen exerted more independence and became more baronial. In foreign policy, for example, as Roosevelt moved to an internationalist position, he could not always count on the support of Foreign Relations Committee Chairman Key Pittman of Nevada. As Professor Ernest May observed, "Consultation with Congress [in the 1930's] was largely a matter of catching Key Pittman, the chairman of the Senate Foreign Relations Committee, when he was sober."[19]

Another element of committee activity during the 1930's was the profusion of congressional investigations by both standing and select committees. The success of the Teapot Dome investigation in 1924 and the suspicions raised by the economic collapse in 1929 spurred Congress to investigate. Foremost among these investigations were: the Senate Banking and Currency Committee's probe of Wall Street, from 1932 to 1934, which was popularly known as the Pecora investigation after its chief counsel, Ferdinand Pecora; the Special Committee Investigating the Munitions Industry, chaired by Senator Gerald P. Nye in 1934; the Special Committee to Investigate Air Mail and Ocean Mail Contracts and the Special Committee to Investigate Lobbying Activities, both chaired by Alabama Senator Hugo Black in the mid-1930's; and the Senate Education and Labor Committee's investigation of unfair labor practices, chaired by "Young Bob" La Follette in 1938. As Telford Taylor, himself a staff member on several of these investigations, stated in his book *Grand Inquest: The Story of Congressional Investigations*, "Observing the immense success, both psychological and legislative, of the Pecora hearings, the leaders of the Roosevelt administration rightly concluded that investigations were unsurpassed as a means of formulating

In 1938, a joint congressional investigation of the Tennessee Valley Authority attracted a crowd of spectators.
U.S. Senate Historical Office

and awakening popular support for the governmental measures they had in mind." [20]

Indeed, the average citizen was more likely to be aware of these investigating committees than of the prestigious standing committees of the Senate. The special investigations drew the press, the radio broadcasters, and the newsreel makers (in those days, newsreels and such picture magazines as *Life* provided the visual side of the news that we now get from nightly television newscasts). The investigators sought the type of dramatic testimony and conflict that caught public attention and fixed itself in people's minds.

For most of the 1930's, these congressional investigations were a strong force in winning reform legislation and contributed to the public good. But, at the same time, an ominous cloud was forming. In 1938, the House of Representatives created the Special Committee to Investigate Un-American Activities. That committee, originally constituted to investigate pro-Nazi activities in the United States, quickly directed its attention to anticommunism and a renewed Red Scare. Its work, coupled with the excesses of investigations by Wisconsin Senator Joseph McCarthy in the 1950's, raised serious ques-

During the Army-McCarthy hearings in 1954, subcommittee counsel Roy Cohn, *left*, clashed with Senator Everett Dirksen, *right*.

George Tames/New York Times

tions about the tactics and ethics of congressional investigations that had not been foreseen in the 1930's.[21]

Although the number of standing committees had remained the same since 1921, the proliferation of subcommittees and special committees increasingly became a problem that called for reform and simplification. The demands of the Second World War further exacerbated matters. In 1942, for example, there were fourteen special committees, covering everything from wool production to gasoline shortages. The special committees performed essential services to meet the national emergency. Most notable among them was the Special Committee to Investigate the National Defense Program, better known as the Truman committee. This watchdog committee lifted its chairman, Missouri's Harry

S. Truman, out of obscurity and headed him on the road to the White House. The number of simultaneous committee meetings, however, wore down both the senators and the administration officials who were asked to testify. One official reported being called to discuss the rubber shortage with as many as seventeen different committees of the Senate and House. The war, wrote Walter Kravitz, "revealed how exasperating it could be to have more than thirty committees whose jurisdiction largely depended on their names and on outdated precedents."[22]

Staffing this profusion of committees also posed a problem. Because there was no provision for a permanent, professional staff, Senate committees began borrowing staff from executive agencies. By the end of World War II, Senator Kenneth Wherry of

Nebraska reported that thirteen committees had borrowed help from twenty-seven different departments of the executive branch, totaling ninety-six persons. The number ranged from one person borrowed for the Pensions Committee to twenty-three for the Small Business Committee. "I am convinced that the Small Business Committee needs all the personnel it has today in order to do its work," said Senator Wherry, adding,

> I am also of the opinion that if the employees were employed directly, they would be loyal beyond any question. I do not mean to say they are not loyal now; but being employed by a department, to a certain degree they have a loyalty to that department which otherwise they might give to the Senate committee in a study of the problems covered in the investigations.[23]

Dual loyalty of borrowed staff was clearly a problem, but understaffing created similar difficulties. The Foreign Relations Committee in 1945, during the debate over the founding of the United Nations, had only three regular staff members, two of whom worked just part time. Naturally, the committee depended upon the Department of State to draft reports and supply information for its hearings. Independent action under such limitations was no easy feat. When the chairman and ranking member of the com-

mittee left for San Francisco to attend the opening meeting of the UN, they borrowed a staff member to accompany them. Francis Wilcox was the foreign policy specialist of the Legislative Reference Service, the tiny predecessor of the current Congressional Research Service. Wilcox continued to devote much of his time to the committee during the next two years—a critical period in American foreign policy—eventually becoming the committee's first chief of staff in 1947.[24]

The mechanism which allowed the committee to hire Wilcox and other professional staff members, rather than to borrow them, was the Legislative Reorganization Act. Perhaps the single most important reform in the history of the United States Senate, this act set the course for the institution we know today. The Reorganization Act increased the size of each senator's personal staff and provided for a full-time, permanent, nonpartisan, professional staff for committees. It reduced the number of Senate committees to fifteen and defined specifically, for the first time, each committee's jurisdiction, in what is now Rule XXV of the Senate's standing rules. The Legislative Reorganization Act did not solve all the problems of the Senate, but it changed and strengthened the institution, especially its committee structure.

Committees, 1946–1989

February 23, 1987[*]

The subject of the modern Senate committee system is as rich and complex as that of the Senate itself. Although political scientists have written extensively about the development of House committees in the years since World War II, there are few genuinely historical accounts of Senate committees. This is surprising, for never has so much information about the operations of individual committees been as readily available.

Since 1946, committees have kept full transcripts of their deliberations, and the National Archives is virtually bursting with their records. In 1980, the Senate adopted a resolution, which I introduced, that opened to researchers the majority of the Senate's records at the Archives twenty years after their creation. This access policy is the most liberal of any branch of the government. Anticipating the bicentennial of the Senate, the National Archives prepared the first full inventory of these valuable unpublished materials. In recent years, the Congressional Information Service, a commercial publisher, has issued comprehensive indexes to committee records, providing efficient access to a vast body of documentation.[1]

As a senator who, for more than three decades, has been a close observer of the operation of the Senate committee system, I shall focus my remarks today on its recent history. In making these observations, I shall devote particular attention to two major reform efforts in 1946 and 1977.

The natural starting point for consideration of the modern Senate committee system is the 1946 Legislative Reorganization Act. As I explained in an earlier address on congressional reform, that act laid the foundation for the operations of Congress as we know it today.[2] Based on the assumption that Congress should have access to independent expertise of a quality equal to that of the executive branch, the 1946 law authorized nonpartisan, permanent professional staff for all committees. It consolidated overlapping and conflicting committee jurisdictions and reduced the number of Senate committees from thirty-three to fifteen. Each of these committees was to have thirteen members with the exception of Appropriations, which was given twenty-one. The number of assignments to major committees per senator dropped from six to two. The act also spelled out in the Senate rules, for the first time, each committee's jurisdictional responsibilities.[3]

Framers of the Legislative Reorganization Act sought, in particular, to curb the power of autocratic chairmen. They did this in a number of ways: by including provisions for regular committee meeting dates, public disclosure of committee action, and the requirement that a majority of members be physically present before a committee could vote to report measures to the full Senate. Once a measure had been approved, it was the duty of the committee chairman to report it promptly. In the interest of public disclosure, the act specified that committee hearings would be open unless the panel took specific action to close them. Markup sessions, however, were to remain closed. Witnesses were required to file advance written statements to enable committee staff to prepare digests, so that even the most junior minority member would have the opportunity to formulate appropriate questions.

---

[*] Updated March 1989

The Reorganization Act also underscored the need for more effective legislative oversight of executive agencies. The law directed that committees shall

exercise continuous watchfulness of the execution by the administrative agencies concerned of any laws, the subject matter of which is within the jurisdiction of such committee; and, for that purpose, shall study all pertinent reports and data submitted to the Congress by the agencies in the executive branch of the Government.[4]

The operation of the Senate committee system in the years following 1946 is distinguished by two structural developments: the explosive growth of staff and the proliferation of subcommittees. The size and role of committee staffs had changed very little between the appointment of the first committee clerks in the 1850's and the passage of the Reorganization Act nearly a century later. The responsibilities of these small staffs were limited to handling correspondence, overseeing the printing of committee documents, and setting up hearings. Generally, they relied on executive agencies to generate information, reports, and even drafts of speeches on proposed legislation.[5]

The 1946 statute provided that each standing committee of the House and Senate (other than the Appropriations committees) could appoint up to four professional staff members, at annual salaries ranging from five thousand to eight thousand dollars, and up to six clerical aides, who would earn from two thousand to eight thousand dollars. These individuals were to be recruited "without regard to political affiliations and solely on the basis of fitness to perform the duties of the office." They were to work under the supervision of the chairman and ranking minority member and could only be discharged by a majority vote of committee members. Professional staff members were forbidden to accept any executive branch ap-

pointment for the period of one year after leaving congressional employment. The Appropriations committees of the two houses were "authorized to appoint such staff . . . as each such committee, by a majority vote, shall determine to be necessary."[6]

Democrats controlled the Congress that passed the Legislative Reorganization Act, but Republicans controlled the Congress that, in 1947, had to implement its lofty objectives. As a result, the goal of hiring independent professional staffs was taken seriously, for Republican congressional leaders otherwise would have had to rely on technical data and policy information supplied by executive agencies within the Democratic administration of Harry Truman. The adversarial nature of relations between President Truman and the Republican Eightieth Congress made such an arrangement unlikely.

When Senate committees began building professional staffs in 1947, there were a total of 232 committee employees. Of this number, 46 worked for the Post Office and Civil Service Committee and 41 for the Rules Committee. In both committees, most staff members were found in the clerical and patronage ranks. Among the committees with fewer than 10 staff members were Banking with 9; Labor, 9; Commerce, 8; Foreign Relations, 8; Interior, 7; Finance, 6; District of Columbia, 4; and Agriculture, 3. To get ahead of my story a bit, I should add here that, within thirteen years, by 1960, the total number of committee staff members would double, rising to 470. During that same period, the ratio of professional to clerical staff increased at an even greater rate. Between 1960 and 1974, the number of staff had again doubled to 948. The peak was reached in 1979 with 1,269.[7]

Mr. President, the second major change in the operation of Senate committees after 1946 was the dramatic growth in the number of subcommittees. In 1945, there were just 34

Secretary of State Dean Acheson, *right*, testified before the Foreign Relations Committee. *U.S. Senate Historical Office*

subcommittees for thirty-three standing committees. Immediately following implementation of the Reorganization Act, the fifteen Senate committees gave birth to 44 subcommittees. Several years later, in 1950, the family of subcommittees had grown to 66, and, by 1976, nearly 140 subcommittees competed for the attention of the Senate's increasingly harried members.[8]

To personalize the growth reflected in these statistics and to capture the thoroughgoing transformation that took place in the years immediately following World War II, one could read with profit the memoirs of the late Dr. Francis O. Wilcox, first chief of staff of the Senate Foreign Relations Committee. Dr. Wilcox epitomized the kind of professional civil servant that the framers of the 1946 Reorganization Act had in mind.

When he came to the Senate in 1946 from the Library of Congress' Legislative Reference Service, the Foreign Relations Committee staff consisted of a full-time clerk, a half-time clerk, and a half-time secretary.

Dr. Wilcox entered his new position with the committee under political circumstances that many staff aides would have found ideal. In 1947, both the chairman of the committee, Republican Arthur Vandenberg of Michigan, and the ranking Democrat, Tom Connally of Texas, believed they had individually talked him into taking the job! As he recounted the story:

Senator Connally said to me one day: "Would you like to be the committee staff director? We're going to set up a new staff. Under the Legislative Reorganization Act of 1946, as you know, we're entitled to set up

[254]

a professional staff." I replied that I hadn't thought about it, but it would be interesting and I would be glad to consider that. He said, "I think I can talk Old Van"—that's the way he referred to Senator Vandenberg—"I think I can talk Old Van into it. I'll see what I can do." Well, the next day, before Senator Connally had a chance to talk to Senator Vandenberg about me, the Senator from Michigan called me in and asked me if I would like to become the director of his new staff. I immediately accepted the invitation. This meant, in effect, that Senator Connally was under the impression that he had gotten me the job, and I was therefore his man; and Senator Vandenberg had asked me, regardless of what Senator Connally had said or done after the event. So, in effect, I was more or less welcomed by both the Senate committee leaders, which put me in a very good position, because I was a good friend of Senator Connally and also of Senator Vandenberg. There's nothing more helpful to a Senate staff member than to be *persona grata* to both majority and minority leaders.[9]

Under the Legislative Reorganization Act, as I have noted, each committee was entitled to hire four professional staff aides. Wilcox explained that, for the Foreign Relations Committee, this authorization came not a moment too soon; otherwise, the committee would have been completely flooded with work. "We had," he later recalled, "the United Nations Charter, the peace treaties with the satellite countries, the peace treaty with Japan, the program of aid to Greece and Turkey, the interim aid program, the Marshall Plan, the NATO Treaty, and a whole host of important issues, including the specialized agencies of the UN." The committee was helping to create the framework of the country's postwar foreign policy.[10]

Chairman Vandenberg gave Wilcox a free hand in staff recruitment, with the clear impression that he would hold him totally responsible both for the staff's successes and for its shortcomings. The chairman insisted that Wilcox take the title of chief of staff. When Wilcox suggested that staff director or executive director would be sufficient, Vandenberg countered: "It's got to be more important than that. I want to make an impres-

sion on the State Department. . . . [Chief of staff] sounds bigger and better and stronger. . . . I want you to be an important figure."[11] Thus began a whole new generation of Senate committee staff aides. Many of these professionals rose to positions of great responsibility within their committees, and a good number of them remained through the mid-to-late 1970's.

As the figures I cited earlier demonstrate, the proliferation of subcommittees sharply distinguished this period of Senate committee history. Early in his tenure, Francis Wilcox recommended to his chairman that subcommittees might make the committee's operation more efficient. He believed they would relieve the full committee of considerable detail and would channel many requests from the executive branch directly to subcommittee chairmen, relieving the burden on the full committee chairman. Consequently, from 1950 to 1975, the Foreign Relations Committee maintained a series of ad hoc consultative subcommittees, one covering each area for which the State Department had designated an assistant secretary.

These subcommittees would meet periodically with the assistant secretaries for off-the-record discussions of key issues in the respective geographic or functional areas. The discussions were designed to reduce the need for extensive full committee meetings. On balance, the idea of consultative subcommittees—the term *investigative* was considered too adversarial—produced indifferent results. Their successful operation depended largely on the interests of the particular subcommittee chairmen, as well as on the prominence and urgency of the issues within their jurisdictions.[12]

Mr. President, although the Legislative Reorganization Act of 1946 was intended to reform Senate committee structures for all time, it merely began the process. Early in 1948, the Committee on Expenditures in the

Former Senator Robert La Follette, Jr., testified in 1948 that subcommittees performed a useful service in the work of the Senate. *Library of Congress*

Executive Departments, the forerunner of our Governmental Affairs Committee, held hearings to see how well the year-and-a-half-old act was working. Senate Republican Policy Committee Chairman Robert Taft of Ohio believed the act had functioned quite well and said, "I think it has improved the character of the work done by committees [and] certainly the character of the experts employed by committees." He added, however:

I don't feel that it has particularly succeeded in relieving Senators of multifarious duties, because there are just so many subjects, and if you don't consider them in different committees, you consider them in subcommittees. I am afraid there is no way in which Senators may be able to do less work, but certainly with the expert assistance which has been given, they have been able to do very much better work.[13]

Former Wisconsin Senator Robert La Follette, Jr., one of the Reorganization Act's architects, told the committee that he saw

nothing wrong with the trend toward a larger number of subcommittees. Many of them merely substituted for ad hoc subcommittees that had been called to consider particular bills and then disbanded. By creating standing subcommittees, most of which served as issue-oriented study groups, the Senate was assuring itself that a reservoir of expertise would be available for efficient use as related issues presented themselves. By the same token, La Follette strongly opposed creation of special investigating committees on the grounds that standing committees possessed sufficient expertise to oversee the executive agencies within their jurisdiction.

La Follette concluded,

The essential and important difference between a hodgepodge committee system and an integrated scheme is not in the relative number of subcommittees, but rather in the formalization of fixed channels and definite jurisdictions so that each new piece of legislation in any given field can have the benefit of the staff work and specialized experience of Members of Congress.

The former senator continued:

As I see it, there is much less likelihood of wasteful duplication in legislative studies, or of uncorrelated activities, under the present committee structure. I venture the prediction that it will work even better as the professional staff members, many of whom are relatively new, gain additional experience in their specialized fields of legislation.[14]

To this observation, Representative Mike Monroney added, "One difficulty Congress has found is that, never having worked with well-trained staff members, they do not know how to use them for maximum benefit."[15]

Three years later, in June 1951, the Committee on Expenditures in the Executive Departments held a second hearing to evaluate further the act's effectiveness. Again, members focused on intended reforms of commit-

tee operations. Senators agreed that these reforms were far from complete. They felt that
committee work loads continued to be distributed inequitably. Some proposed to
exempt members of the Appropriations and
Foreign Relations committees from service
on any other committees. Most realized,
however, that this arrangement would eliminate the coordination that occurred by
having members of those key committees sit
on related committees.[16]

Despite the reformers' desire in 1947 for
committees to hire nonpartisan staff experts,
Republican chairmen, with a few exceptions,
hired Republican staff. When the Democrats
regained control of Congress two years later,
they kept approximately two-thirds of these
individuals. At the time, Professor Gladys
Kammerer contended that "many committees were headed in 1949 by conservative
southern Democrats who maintain policy
stands identical to those of their Republican
predecessors." She concluded that the low
staff turnover might be "linked to the seniority system for selection of committee
chairmen which frees them from any feeling
of party responsibility."[17] This situation
dissatisfied Democratic Senator J. Howard
McGrath of Rhode Island, who commented
that it just might be necessary to find some
more Democratic experts. Ernest Griffith, director of the Legislative Reference Service,
reported: "Some committees have survived
changes in party control without impair-
ment, largely in instances in which party
considerations did not influence the original
appointments. In other instances, a reasonable stability has been secured by the division of appointments between the parties.
Others have been partisan."[18]

The framers of the 1946 Reorganization
Act placed great faith in the usefulness of
joint committee action. The plan was to establish joint panels or to have the corresponding committees of each chamber meet

jointly, whenever possible, to reduce duplication of effort by members, staff, and witnesses. Creation of roughly parallel committee systems, with similar jurisdictions in
both houses, stimulated occasional joint
hearings and staff collaboration. This was
particularly the case for committees concerned with foreign economic policy, military aid, public housing, and the District of
Columbia. Hopes for more creative uses of
the joint panels that had been established ultimately died, however, as members of both
houses sought to preserve the prerogatives of
their individual chambers and to set their independent agendas.[19] Most formal collaboration was limited, therefore, to the eight
joint standing committees.[20] Until 1953,
senators generally chaired joint committees.
Growing irritation among House members
led to the practice, after that time, of alter-
nating chairmanships between the bodies
from one Congress to the next.

There were a number of other deficiencies
in the operation of the 1946 act. Combining
committees with overlapping jurisdictions
did little to eliminate conflict on major issues
related to defense, the economy, and social
welfare. Two-thirds of the Senate's fifteen
committees claimed an interest in national
security affairs. The committees on Finance
and Labor fought over control of veterans'
legislation, while others quarreled over aid to
small business.[21] The Senate began routinely to waive the act's prohibition on holding
committee meetings during full legislative
sessions—a provision designed to ensure
maximum attendance on the Senate floor.
Hearings were frequently called without sufficient notice, so that the provision requiring
submission of written testimony in advance
often went unheeded. Committee chairmen,
in general, paid little attention to the requirement for regular meeting dates.

In *Citadel*, his classic study of the Senate,
New York Times correspondent William S.

Senator Joseph Clark coined the term "the Senate establishment."   *U.S. Senate Historical Office.*

White described Senate committees of the mid-1950's:

A Senate committee is an imperious force; its chairman, unless he be a weak and irresolute man, is emperor. It makes in its field in ninety-nine cases out of a hundred the real decisions of the Institution itself. What bills it approves are approved by the Senate; what bills it rejects are rejected, with rare exceptions. . . . To override, say, the Committee on Foreign Relations or the Committee on Finance involves a parliamentary convulsion scarcely less severe, as the Senate sees it, than that accompanying the overturn, say, of a British government.[22]

White was pessimistic about chances for genuine change in committee operations, observing, "Reform in this field, as in a good many others, in short looks much easier the farther one stands from the facts."

A growing number of senators in the late 1950's and early 1960's did not share White's view of the limited possibility for genuine committee reform. Pennsylvania's Democratic Senator Joseph Clark referred to White as "the poet laureate of the Senate establishment." By 1963, Clark believed the days of the Senate establishment were numbered.[23] In a series of floor statements in February of that year, he set forth a reform program designed to unhorse what he believed to be the conservative Old Guard and to widen the circle of senators involved in institutional decision making. With reference to committees, Clark proposed to curtail the power of chairmen by allowing a majority of a committee's members to convene a meeting, requiring chairmen to step down at the age of seventy, and providing for election of chairmen by secret ballot of committee members. The frustration that energized Clark's campaign led, in 1965, to the establishment of the Joint Committee on the Organization of the Congress, the first significant effort at institutional reform since the Reorganization Act of 1946.

That panel, under the cochairmanship of Oklahoma Senator A.S. Mike Monroney and Indiana Representative Ray Madden, confronted a committee system in great disarray. As political scientist Roger Davidson summarized the situation: "Some of the problems were external . . . : mismatches between committee jurisdictions and emerging public issues, and the dispersed committee system's failure to aggregate related pieces of a policy. Yet internal . . . difficulties occurred as well—in the form of jurisdictional rivalries and scheduling conflicts."[24] The joint committee issued its findings in 1966. The Senate, in 1967, quickly devised a series of proposed rules changes to incorporate the major portion of the joint committee's recommendations. The House, however, deferred until 1970 the necessary legislation to institute these reforms.

In that year, Congress passed a new Legislative Reorganization Act. Among the most notable changes for Senate committees, the act authorized a majority within a committee to call a meeting if the chairman had ignored such a request for at least ten days. All committee meetings were to be open to the public except for executive sessions held to mark up bills or to vote. All committee record votes were to be publicly reported. The act permitted elimination of general proxies for absent members in committee voting and allowed committees to ban proxies altogether on a vote to report a measure. It placed no limits on the use of proxies in subcommittees.

The 1970 Legislative Reorganization Act limited newly elected senators to membership on two major committees and one minor one, with no member serving on more than one of the committees on Appropriations, Armed Services, Finance, and Foreign Relations. No senator could chair more than one full committee. The 1970 act required Senate committees to adopt and publish rules of procedure and to issue annual reports of their accomplishments. It mandated that a committee report on a bill must be available at least three days—excluding Saturdays, Sundays, and holidays—before the full Senate could consider the measure. This provision did not apply to certain urgent categories of legislation, and it could be waived, in any case, by agreement between the two floor leaders. Committees were required to announce hearings at least one week in advance, except in unusual circumstances.

The 1970 act is best remembered for the changes in committee practices that I have just described. It accomplished little by way of structural reform, except to establish the Senate Committee on Veterans' Affairs and to permit each standing committee to increase from four to six the authorized number of permanent professional staff.[25]

On March 11, 1975, intensifying pressures for further significant committee reform compelled fifty-seven senators to cosponsor a resolution establishing a Temporary Select Committee to Study the Senate Committee System. Although the Rules Committee deferred action for a year, the Senate accepted other committee-related changes during that time. Senate Democrats agreed to permit use of a secret ballot in selecting committee chairmen if one-fifth of the party conference called for it. Two years earlier, Republicans had decided to select their senior committee members by vote of their party conference. For the first time, the Senate permitted public access to committee meetings in addition to hearings. This included markup sessions and joint House-Senate conference committees, although either chamber could vote to close specific conference sessions.

In a move that had major significance for the operation of its committees, the Senate, in 1975, provided junior senators with up to three personal staff members to assist with their committee work. This was in addition to the requirement of the 1970 statute that two of the six committee professional staff be assigned to the minority. The net effect of these two changes was to limit the power of committee chairmen, who previously had the final word on staff selection. That power flowed increasingly to members of both parties with less seniority.

In 1975, major reform activity centered around the special Commission on the Operation of the Senate. Chaired by former Senator Harold Hughes and composed of nine private citizens, one Senate officer, and one Senate employee, this panel carried a mandate to examine every area of Senate activity except the jurisdictional responsibilities of committees. At the end of 1976, the Hughes commission submitted its report, addressed principally to the modernization of Senate administrative practices. With regard to committee operations, the commission recommended that major committees be charged with the responsibility for conducting long-range analyses of pressing national issues. It also urged the Senate to centralize executive agency oversight responsibility within the then Government Operations Committee.[26]

As is often the case with advisory commissions that take on highly complex issues, the recommendations of the Hughes commission met with mixed success. The Senate subsequently adopted two of the commission's proposals related to committee operations. One was a plan to consolidate the budget requests of all Senate committees (with the exception of the Ethics Committee) into a single funding resolution. The other was a recommendation to set up a computerized clearinghouse for scheduling committee meetings.

Early in 1976, the Subcommittee on the Standing Rules of the Senate, which I chaired (and which I later moved to abolish), held a hearing on the 1975 proposal to establish a temporary select committee on the committee system. Part of my overall strategy, as majority whip, was to facilitate the business and improve the image of the Senate, and I was determined to see the work of the temporary committee succeed. Consequently, the Committee on Rules and Administration approved that measure, and the full Senate adopted it on March 31, 1976. As the principal sponsor of the authorizing resolution, Illinois Senator Adlai E. Stevenson III was appointed chairman, and Senator William Brock of Tennessee served as cochairman of the Temporary Select Committee to Study the Senate Committee System, more commonly known as the Stevenson committee.

Senator Stevenson eloquently described the difficulties arising from the committee system's antiquated jurisdictional assignments. He noted that they had remained relatively unchanged since the 1946 Legislative Reorganization Act despite major changes in executive branch structure. With the proliferation of subcommittees and the lack of jurisdictional realignment, Stevenson observed: "We sometimes end up reinventing the wheel simultaneously in different sub-

committees. And we often end up dealing with parts of an issue with no mechanism to put the parts together." [27]

The six Democratic and six Republican senators on the Stevenson committee were relatively junior and reform-oriented, and none chaired major Senate committees. The panel included no members from the Rules Committee or from the powerful committees on Foreign Relations and Judiciary. During the remainder of 1976, the panel examined proposals for restructuring and reducing the number of committees, rotating chairmanships and memberships, and creating major new committees on science and technology, energy, and national security. [28]

Following extensive hearings and an exhaustive series of interviews, the temporary committee, in September 1976, produced a set of recommendations. Picking up a familiar theme of congressional reformers, its members urged the abolition of all select, special, and joint committees, with the exception of the newly created Intelligence Committee. It advised eliminating four committees: District of Columbia; Post Office and Civil Service; Aeronautical and Space Sciences; and Veterans' Affairs. The temporary committee further recommended restructuring the panels that had responsibility for issues related to energy, environment, and transportation. This recommendation led to creation of the Committee on Energy and Natural Resources—from the old Interior Committee—and the Committee on Environment and Public Works. The panel also advocated placing strict limits on the number of chairmanships and committee assignments for each member, and it sought to improve scheduling of committee meetings. [29]

Prospects for passage of this reform measure brightened with the election, in November 1976, of eighteen new senators. Shortly after the election, I met with Senator Stevenson and Oregon Senator Bob Packwood,

Senator Adlai E. Stevenson III headed an effort in 1976 to reorganize Senate committees.
U.S. Senate Historical Office

who had replaced Senator Brock as cochairman. Along with Rules Committee Chairman Howard Cannon of Nevada, we agreed that a resolution incorporating the temporary committee's recommendations would be referred to the Rules Committee for hearings and reported out to the full Senate not later than January 19, 1977.

In a major step to protect the reform proposals, we decided that no new permanent assignments to committees would be made until after reorganization was completed. On the first day of the Ninety-fifth Congress, as I began my service as Senate majority leader, Senator Stevenson introduced a resolution embodying the reform proposals. Newly elected senators were decidedly unhappy

that they would have to wait for permanent assignments. To expedite committee business, the Democratic Conference decided to assign new senators of the majority party to committees by lot. These assignments would expire on the day the Senate completed action on reorganization.

The hearings before the Rules Committee proved to be stormy.[30] Many senators and others who testified agreed, in general, with the need for reform but feared the impact on their own committee assignments. I realized that this entire effort might collapse unless senior chairmen relaxed some of their opposition. Accordingly, I arranged two lengthy private meetings with committee chairmen so that Senator Stevenson and those of us with overall leadership responsibilities could work out a solution acceptable to the majority. This approach resulted in a series of agreements that preserved the major provisions of the reform package.

The agreements cleared the way for adoption of Senator Stevenson's resolution early in February 1977, by a vote of 89 to 1. In the process, the Senate modified the Stevenson committee's proposals in several respects. It retained the Joint Economic Committee and the Joint Committee on Internal Revenue Taxation but withdrew the Senate's members from the Joint Committees on Atomic Energy, Defense Production, and Congressional Operations. The Senate also established the Special Committee on Aging, while abolishing the Committees on the District of Columbia, Post Office and Civil Service, and Aeronautical and Space Sciences. The Committee on Standards and Conduct was renamed the Select Committee on Ethics.[31]

The structural accomplishments of the 1977 committee reform effort are impressive by any standard. The number of standing committees was reduced by 23 percent from thirty-one to twenty-four. Subcommittees

Members of the Joint Committee on Atomic Energy celebrated the committee's twentieth anniversary in 1966.
U.S. Senate Historical Office

were cut 33 percent, from 174 to 117. Each senator was limited to service on two major committees and one minor one. Senators were permitted to serve on not more than three subcommittees for each major committee (other than the Committee on Appropriations) and two for each minor committee to which they were assigned.[32]

Although it might seem that service on a total of eleven committees and subcommittees is excessive, that number compared favorably with the previous volume of committee and subcommittee assignments, which had often exceeded twenty and occasionally even exceeded thirty. In a move to spread leadership responsibility among a committee's majority party members, the Senate agreed to permit full committee chairmen to chair only one subcommittee within the parent committee. Committees were also required to obtain approval of the full Senate before setting up new subcommittees.

Restriction on subcommittee membership served to reduce the number of subcommittees. During 1976, for example, the Judiciary

Committee, composed of fifteen members, had fifteen subcommittees. Senator John McClellan of Arkansas served on eleven of these subcommittees and chaired two. Chairman James O. Eastland of Mississippi chaired three subcommittees. Under the reorganization, with each majority member limited to one subcommittee chairmanship, the Judiciary Committee, in 1977, abolished five subcommittees, merged two and created one, for a total of ten subcommittees. Among that committee's eleven-member majority, I, because of my duties as Senate majority leader, chose to chair no subcommittee.

In a major step in the direction of partisan staffing, the Senate agreed that staff ratios should reflect the relative size of the majority and minority party assignments to individual committees. Committee minorities were permitted to have at least one-third of a committee's funds, beyond those used for clerical staff and central resources, placed under their control.

For the first time in three decades, the Senate had succeeded in bringing about an internal reorganization of its committee

In 1976, Senator John McClellan, *left*, chaired two of the Judiciary Committee's fifteen subcommittees, while Committee Chairman James Eastland, *right*, chaired three subcommittees. *U.S. Senate Historical Office*

system. "Widespread skepticism about prospects for reorganization persisted almost until the eve of approval," wrote Judith H. Parris, a member of the staff of the Temporary Select Committee and, later, an adjunct professor of government at American University.[33] Although there had long been inner rumblings of frustration about the committee system, the chances for effective change appeared slim. Institutional inertia and the entrenched positions of senior members, chairmen, and ranking members of committees and subcommittees constituted a formidable roadblock to any major structural alterations in the system. That several major changes did indeed occur was due, in great measure, to the dedication, persistence, and hard work of Senator Stevenson, who stated, on behalf of supporters of reorganization, "We're not asking, we're demanding." [34]

"Undoubtedly," said Parris, "winds had been blowing in the direction of institutional change." For several years, the country had been moving toward governmental reform. Nonetheless, such internal reform as the Stevenson committee recommend-

ed faced more than the usual odds against changing the status quo. Except for Common Cause and editorial writers for the *Washington Post*, the *Washington Star*, and a few other publications which "solidly supported the Stevenson Committee's efforts, other public interest forces were either equivocal or silent." [35]

"The most important constituency for change," declared Parris, "was the Senators themselves." Restructuring the system was favored by a "heterogeneous coalition" of members for various reasons, among which, according to Parris, were "modernization, efficiency, rationalization, benefits to junior senators, benefits to the minority, responsiveness, more limited government, a better public image, and making their own work more convenient and productive." Moreover, and very importantly, "few senators (or groups . . .) perceived themselves as seriously affected adversely" by the legislation as ultimately enacted. "Provisions that damaged vital interests of preeminent actors in particular subsystems," as Parris correctly observed, "had been deleted." [36]

[263]

Members of the Veterans' Affairs Committee received testimony in 1977.   *U.S. Senate Historical Office*

In explaining why reorganization succeeded, Parris stated:

Leadership is necessary to galvanize support. Senator Stevenson assumed responsibility for developing the issue, immersed himself in the subject, engineered a series of widely acceptable proposals, and proved convincing when it counted—particularly in marathon sessions with senior Democrats and in the Rules Committee and floor deliberations. Also crucial was the support of Senator Robert Byrd in establishing the Select Committee, reaching agreement for consideration of its recommendations, arranging the sessions with the committee chairmen, and expediting the proposal in committee and on the floor. Similarly essential to success was the leadership of Chairman [Howard] Cannon in agreeing to take up reorganization, building a consensus on the resolution in the Rules Committee, and managing it jointly with Senator Stevenson on the floor. In the Republican ranks, articulation of the need for reform by Senator Brock and active backing from the minority leader [Senator Howard Baker of Tennessee] and GOP members of the Rules Committee were instrumental.[37]

Press comments concerning the 1977 reorganization were generally modest in their assessments of the changes brought about. The Stevenson committee's recommendations had not been fully accepted, and several worthwhile features had fallen by the wayside: for example, the Committee on Veterans' Affairs was restored in response to the pressures that were encountered. But, while the glass was half empty, it, was also half full. As Senator Stevenson summed it up, the strategy was "to ask for 150 percent in order to get as much as possible."[38]

Mr. President, conflict between tradition and innovation has characterized the Senate's entire two-hundred-year history. The committee reforms of 1977, as with those of 1946, were undertaken with an appreciation of the need for continuity, and a deep respect for institutional tradition and the rights of individual senators. They were also conceived in the need to constantly adapt to modern challenges. None of these efforts settled all of the problems they set out to address. In the intervening years, there have been additional study groups dedicated to improving the operation of the Senate and its committee system. As the United States Senate enters its third century, its leadership and members must continue to struggle for a creative balance between tradition and innovation. There is no better example of the Senate's fundamental ability to strike that balance than that provided by the steady evolution of its modern committee system.

ORGANIZATION

Resolved, unanimously, That the Senate, from a sincere desire of testifying their respect for the long and faithful services of their late Secretary, Samuel A. Otis, Esq., who performed the duties of that office with punctuality and exactness, from the commencement of this Government until the close of the last session of Congress, will go into mourning for one month, in the usual method of wearing crape round the left arm.

SENATE RESOLUTION, OCTOBER 7, 1814 [1]

. . . there were no secretaries to senators at that time [1855–1859]; so after adjournment each day members had their correspondence to detain them. It was required of the pages to stay until every senator had left the chamber. All letters for the mail were handed to us to be sealed. The table where the sealing was done was situated in the lobby, and a candlestick and sealing wax were always at hand.

CHRISTIAN ECKLOFF,
Memoirs of A Senate Page, 1909 [2]

The Senate was about to tell me to go out and arrest the senators and bring them in. But I knew where Senator Cliff Hansen of Wyoming was in his hideaway. I went to get him, and I said, "Senator, I don't like to have to come and get you. Why don't you come in so we can break this. After all, I'm a new man on the block. It makes the Senate look bad and it makes me look bad." He said, "You talked me into it." He came in and we were able to get the vote and we didn't have to arrest anybody.

NORDY HOFFMANN,
SENATE SERGEANT AT ARMS, 1975–1981 [3]

CHAPTER 10

Secretary of the Senate

June 13, 1980 *

Mr. President, the duties of a United States senator are very demanding, from multiple committee and subcommittee assignments to Senate floor work and constituent services. We cannot do everything by ourselves. Senators have their own office staffs to assist them, and committees also employ professional staffs to assure the efficient conduct of committee business. Yet, there is another body of Senate employees who are less known by those outside this chamber, but whose services are equally vital to the legislative process.

Some of these people are seated before us today on the dais below the presiding officer. These are the bill clerk, the journal clerk, the legislative clerk, and the parliamentarian. Also, here beside me is a reporter of debate, taking down my words as I speak, for publication tomorrow in the daily *Congressional Record.*

While each of these staff members performs a very different task, each is under the supervision of the secretary of the Senate, and it is about the secretary of the Senate and his myriad responsibilities that I wish to speak today. I shall also discuss many of the twenty-five individuals who have held the post since 1789.

The secretary of the Senate is one of the Senate's five elected officers, the others being the sergeant at arms, the chaplain, and

the majority and minority secretaries. The secretary holds a most demanding position. Not only is he in charge of hiring and supervising the various clerks and official reporters in this chamber, but he also oversees the Senate document room, where recent bills, resolutions, and other documents are stored for distribution. In addition, he oversees the Senate stationery room, the Senate library, the Senate curator's and historian's offices, and even the Senate disbursing office. The Senate places much trust in its secretary, who is charged with such diverse functions as supervising the education of our pages, registering all lobbyists, and arranging the transfer of our historically valuable documents to the National Archives. The secretary compiles a semiannual report on the salaries, expenses, and other financial transactions of the Senate, in order to make sure that this information is fully available to the public.

Under the Federal Election Campaign Act, the secretary is an ex-officio member of the Federal Election Commission. All candidates for the Senate must file financial reports through the secretary's office, detailing their political contributions, their political expenditures, and their sources of income.

The secretary also serves as executive secretary to the Senate Commission on Art, which oversees preservation of the Senate's

---

* Updated April 1989

collection of paintings, furniture, and other artifacts.[1]

The Senate would have a most difficult time operating without a secretary. The post goes back to the earliest days of congressional history—indeed, before the establishment of the Congress of the United States.

The Senate inherited the position of secretary from the Continental Congress, which served as our national legislature from 1774 until 1789—from before the Declaration of Independence until the Constitution was adopted. During those years, there was no executive branch of government, and the equivalent of today's cabinet secretaries reported to the Congress. First among the secretaries, ranking just behind the members of Congress, was the secretary of the Congress, which was, at that time, a unicameral body. Throughout the entire history of the Continental Congress, this post was filled by one man: Charles Thomson of Philadelphia, an Irish immigrant, businessman, politician, and classical scholar. He was a truly remarkable man.[2]

Thomson sat to the right of the president of the Congress, where he oversaw the keeping of the *Journal* and its printing and distribution, took the roll, made special reports to Congress, and even occasionally served on its committees. He also kept the Seal of the Congress and placed it upon all official documents (it was Thomson who designed the Great Seal of the United States). Thomson received all public and secret documents of the Congress. He filed, transmitted, and protected these documents as the Congress moved from city to city, first to evade the British armies and then to find the most hospitable environment for its work.

When the Constitution took effect in 1789, each house of the new Congress established a post similar to that which Thomson held: the clerk of the House of Representatives, and the secretary of the Senate. On

Samuel A. Otis was the first secretary of the Senate.
National Gallery of Art

April 8, 1789, two days after the United States Senate established its first quorum, the Senate elected its first secretary, Samuel Allyne Otis of Massachusetts.

Otis began immediately to function officially in the office without having taken any oath. The instance is unique and explained by the fact that, at the time, there was no oath to administer. The act regulating the administering of the oath supporting the Constitution was signed into law on June 1, 1789, and Otis was sworn on June 3.

The new secretary was responsible for keeping the Senate's legislative journal, as required by Article I, section 5, of the Constitution. At each session, he took the minutes in his own hand. Since this was in the days before shorthand was perfected, we have no verbatim accounts of those early proceedings. The secretary's rough journal was then read to the Senate for corrections before the clerks copied it into a "smooth journal," which Otis would deliver to the printers.

The secretary also became the Senate's business manager. Otis purchased the ink, quills, parchment, and other supplies that the new senators required. He handled the disbursement of salaries and travel allowances to the Senate and its staff at a time when senators received six dollars for each day they were present in the chamber. After the Senate completed work on a piece of legislation, the secretary personally would carry the bill to the House. He was further entrusted with receiving and transmitting all presidential messages and vetoes.

Mr. President, much of what we know about the operations of the Senate during the First Congress comes to us from the diary of Senator William Maclay. The Pennsylvania senator profoundly disliked Secretary Otis, but his observations are worth recounting.

Maclay would comment from time to time about Otis' inaccuracy in writing the minutes of the *Journal*. For example, Maclay's diary for April 25, 1789, reports the following:

attended the House Ceremonies endless ceremonies the whole business of the day. I did not embark warmly this day. Otis our Secretary makes a most miserable hand of it, the grossest Mistakes made on our minutes and it cost Us an hour or Two to rectify them. I was up as often I believe as was necessary and certainly threw so much light on Two Subjects, that the debate ended on each.[3]

On May 8, 1789, Maclay wrote as follows:

attended a joint Committee on the removing the papers of the old Congress, made progress in the Business, agreed to meet half after ten on Monday, and report, Senate formed the Secretary as Usual had made some Mistakes which were rectifyed.[4]

On May 9:

Senate formed it took a long time to correct the minutes. Otis keeps them miserably.[5]

On August 26:

attended the Senate the minutes were lengthy but I was surprized to find no notice taken, of my presenting the Draught of Lancaster the letter, and my nomination of the other places in Pennsylvania, altho I had put in Writing, the Whole Matter and given it to the Secretary. When he had read about half way of his Minutes, I rose and called on him to know Why he had not inserted them. he said he was not come to them but seemed much confused. he however got the letter and handed it to the President. to read it and it was read.[6]

On August 29:

I know What a Wretch Otis is, I therefore called on him to see how he had made up the Minutes of Yesterday, on the 3 sets of Yeas and Nays, all was right. This I thought necessary.[7]

And on August 31:

after What had passed with Otis notwithstanding I before knew him to be a Villain, I scarce could suspect him of practising anything now. when [in reading the minutes] he came to the Motion however he read it, That the pay of the Senators should be 5 dollars and that the pay of the Representatives should be six. I heard him with Astonishment. but there was no time to be lost. I moved the necessary Alteration and had it inserted. [Izard] attempted to Support the Secretary. I staid a While. but found myself too sick to attend. I came out of a Window and found Otis in the Corner room, I called on him to explain this business. he hum'd haw'd said his Memory was bad, I put him in mind of my having called on him on Saturday, and that then it stood right. I made him however copy it on a Peice of paper. . . . He said it was, so in the other book went to fetch it but did not return—[8]

Mr. President, we can conclude from the comments of Maclay that he was convinced that Otis was the instrument and creature of the vice president. In fact, Maclay wrote on June 4, 1789, that "the Minutes are totally under the direction of our President or rather Otis is his Creature—"[9] On January 20, 1790, Maclay stated:

I am not disappointed in Otis, every Word respecting the Bill was suppressed in Journals read this Morning, the Entry stood Ordered that Mr. King Mr. Strong &ca. be a Committee to report a bill to regulate Processes &ca. It would have been considered as manifesting a Spirit of Contention, if I had attacked the Minutes, and I let it pass. but if they endeavour to make any Use of it. I will then be at liberty to act, and make the most of Circumstances.[10]

Under date of March 5, 1790, Senator Maclay wrote:

This day gave a fresh instance of the Rascallity of Otis. the Committee on Baily's bill. reported Yesterday and said not One Word more nor was another word said in the Senate, but Otis had on the Minutes Ordered that the Report be accepted. I did not immediately observe it, but I called on him about it. his Excuse was. Mr. Adams had Ordered him to do So.[11]

Maclay referred to what he considered to be the untruthfulness of Otis. Under date of January 27, 1791, he commented:

I have hitherto, attended only to the part acted by some Persons whose Conduct, from Appearances, is not very consistent. I called on Otis for the Papers, he said Butler got them and had Given them to One of the Representatives, a minute after I saw them in the hands of Mr. Dalton. But Otis is really so Stupid, That I know not Whether he lyed or Blundered.[12]

Senator Maclay wrote in a profoundly frank manner, viewing individuals and their motives in his own somewhat jaundiced way; not all observers or participants would have agreed with his sour assessments.

When George Washington arrived in New York to be inaugurated as the nation's first president, Samuel Otis held the Bible on a crimson cushion for the ceremony. Samuel Otis served as secretary for the first twenty-five years of this body's history and never missed a single day that the Senate was in session. I wonder what Senator Maclay would have said of Otis' attendance record. Known for his courtly manners and scrupulous devotion to duty, Otis held his post even after control of the chamber passed

Secretary of the Senate Asbury Dickins in 1837 carried out the Senate's order to expunge its earlier censure of President Andrew Jackson.
U.S. Senate Historical Office

from the Federalists to the Jeffersonians. To show the respect that the members of the Senate had for their secretary, when Otis died on April 22, 1814, the Senate went into mourning for a month, with each member wearing a black crepe band around his left arm in memory of Otis' long and effective service.[13]

Before the Senate had the opportunity to elect a successor to Otis, the British, in August 1814, launched an assault on Washington. Realizing that the invading army might well burn the Capitol, Lewis Machen, a young clerk in the secretary's office, took matters into his own hands. Commandeering a farmer's wagon, he hastily loaded the valuable records of the Senate's first twenty-five years. With great difficulty, he removed them to the countryside just in time to escape the conflagration that consumed much of the Capitol and most of the House's old records.

Our current secretary, Walter J. Stewart, is required to be as shrewd in his oversight of the stationery operation as was his mid-nineteenth century predecessor, Asbury Dickins. In 1845, Dickins wrote to an American manufacturer of penknives that

[your penknives] afford evidence of great improvement in that branch of American industry. I think, however, you will admit that they do not quite equal . . . the best work of the English cutlers. . . . I will give a preference to the manufacturers of our own country when ever I can properly do so. In providing penknives for the Senators it will not do to incur any avoidable risk as to the tempers and quality of the blades.[14]

Mr. Dickins, as secretary, was also the man to whom the Senate turned to provide maps of Texas and Oregon when the Senate debated adding those new territories in 1845.[15]

In 1837, shortly after Dickins took the oath as secretary, he played a major part in one of the most dramatic moments in the Senate's entire history. Three years earlier, on March 28, 1834, the Senate had taken the extraordinary step of passing a resolution of censure against President Andrew Jackson, charging him with "assuming authority and power not conferred by the Constitution and laws, but in derogation of both." This occurred at the instigation of Henry Clay, as a result of Jackson's refusal to provide the Senate with documents related to his withdrawal of government funds from the Second Bank of the United States. In 1837, Jackson's allies in the Senate, principally Senator Thomas Hart Benton, succeeded in persuading the Senate to adopt a resolution expunging the earlier censure. In an emotion-charged Senate ceremony, Secre-

For two days in 1947, Secretary of the Senate Leslie Biffle presided over the Senate.
U.S. Senate Historical Office

tary Dickins produced the 1834 *Senate Journal* and, with the galleries packed to capacity, drew black lines around the original censure resolution. He then wrote across its face "Expunged by order of the Senate this sixteenth day of January 1837."[16] Following the ceremony, senators supporting Jackson withdrew to an adjacent room for refreshments to celebrate their victory. One observer noted that "several Senators showed by their actions that they were not members of the then newly organized Congressional Temperance Society."

The secretary of the Senate is also authorized to preside over the Senate in the absence of the vice president and pending the election of a president pro tempore. Such an event last occurred in 1947 at the opening of the Eightieth Congress, when the secretary, Leslie Biffle, performed the duties of the chair for two days. Biffle served in the days when the secretary was considered a "legislative mechanic," who was called in to help the passage of legislation through the chamber. One of his practices, from time to time, was to invite various senators to lunch in his office just before the start of the day's session. A senator who particularly enjoyed those repasts was Harry S. Truman of Missouri. On the day Truman became president in 1945, the first phone call he placed from the White House was to Leslie Biffle asking him to arrange a luncheon the next day with his former senatorial colleagues.

The relationship between the new president and Leslie Biffle had deep roots. Biffle, who had come to Capitol Hill in 1909 as a legislative aide and later worked as superintendent of the Senate folding room, was elected secretary for the Democratic majority in 1933. He rapidly won the respect of senators from both parties for his knowledge of Senate operations and his courteous manner. He was particularly helpful to freshmen senators, including Harry Truman in 1935. In 1945, upon the death of Secretary of the Senate Edwin Halsey, the Senate unanimously elected Biffle to that post. Known as the "sage of Capitol Hill," Biffle was an able administrator and a walking encyclopedia of Senate information.[17]

In 1948, when the Republicans controlled the Senate and Biffle served as secretary to the Senate Democratic Policy Committee, President Truman asked him to conduct an informal and highly unusual presidential preference poll. As of 1948, opinion sampling had not reached the level of sophistication that its supporters claim for it today. George Gallup earned international and everlasting fame shortly before the 1948 presidential election by predicting the victory of Governor Thomas E. Dewey. In any event, what became the "Biffle Poll" made no claim to sophistication. Dressed in a droopy straw hat and overalls, Leslie Biffle

set out in an old chicken truck to sample grassroots sentiment for the president's candidacy that year. Occasionally buying chickens and eggs, the usually dapper Biffle talked to farmers in West Virginia, northern Ohio, Indiana, and Illinois. As a result of his tour, Biffle was one of the very few in Washington to correctly predict Harry Truman's subsequent victory. In 1949, when the Democrats regained control of the Senate, Biffle returned to the secretary's office—the only person ever to be elected secretary of the Senate for two nonconsecutive terms—and remained in that post until his retirement in 1952.

In addition to Leslie Biffle, a procession of talented and dedicated men have held this office. Two were former senators—Charles Cutts and Walter Lowrie—four were former members of the House of Representatives. James M. Baker had been assistant Senate librarian before becoming secretary. Edwin A. Halsey (who served for the entire New Deal era), Carl A. Loeffler, J. Mark Trice, and Walter J. Stewart all started as Senate pages. Felton "Skeeter" Johnston arrived on Capitol Hill as a senator's stenographer.

I would be remiss if I did not pause to note the services of two former secretaries whose devotion and length of service to this institution were nothing short of remarkable. One was a Democrat and the other a Republican.

Colonel Edwin Halsey, secretary of the Senate for twelve years, from 1933 until his death in office in January 1945, watched Franklin D. Roosevelt's New Deal unfold in this chamber. His twelve years as the Senate's secretary, however, were only a small part of the forty-eight years that he served the Senate.

Colonel Halsey was born at Tye River, Virginia, in 1881, and first came to Washington with his uncle, Senator John Daniel of Virginia, to become a Senate page when he was sixteen. In May 1898, not long after he

Four men who served as secretary of the Senate posed at the Capitol; *left to right*, Mark Trice, Leslie Biffle, Felton Johnston, and Carl Loeffler.

U.S. Senate Historical Office

arrived, he and the other pages were on hand to see the Senate as a whole rise and cheer when word came that Admiral Dewey had bottled up and defeated the Spanish fleet at Manila.

In 1917, Colonel Halsey heard Woodrow Wilson deliver his epochal address asking Congress for a declaration of war against Germany, and, in December 1941, he heard Franklin Roosevelt make a similar grim request.

From his appointment as a page, Colonel Halsey advanced step by step until he became secretary of the Senate. A colonel by virtue of appointment to the staffs of two Virginia governors, Halsey was a devoted Democrat, but his talents and efficiency were recognized by members of both parties. Along the way to the secretary's post, he served as sergeant at arms of the Democratic National Committee and as aide to the Democratic Senatorial Campaign Committee.[18]

When Colonel Halsey died suddenly on January 29, 1945, the Senate adjourned in his honor. For many of the younger senators

Colonel Edwin Halsey, secretary of the Senate from 1933 to 1945, signed a tax bill with Senate Finance Committee Chairman Walter George looking on.

swept into office with the Roosevelt land-slide, he was the only secretary they had known, and many felt they had lost an extraordinary friend.

Carl Loeffler served as secretary for only two years, from 1947 to 1949, but he assisted the Senate in a variety of responsible positions for a total of fifty-nine years.

Carl Loeffler was born here in Washington on January 12, 1873. His first home was in the shadow of the White House. By the time of his death on January 30, 1968, at the age of ninety-five, Carl Loeffler had achieved the status of an institution within an institution.[19]

Although Loeffler received his formal education from public schools and Columbian University, now George Washington University, his political education began when he was still a small child. His father, Major Charles Loeffler, served as one of President Grant's personal aides in the White House. Major Loeffler was also later an aide to President McKinley. Young Carl ate his dinner at a table buzzing with discussion of national politics and the White House.

Loeffler's own personal look at the political process began when he was just sixteen. In 1889, he was appointed a Senate page by the powerful Republican senator from Pennsylvania, Matthew Quay. While the Carl Loeffler who greeted senators in the chamber in the 1940's was a courtly and dignified figure, his first days in the chamber were quite rowdy. Once, he and some other rambunctious pages brought their bows and arrows into the chamber. They affixed gum to one end of the arrows and long paper streamers to the other, and took as their target the glass panels that used to be in the ceiling above us. The arrows struck their mark and remained there, trailing streamers until ladders could be brought in by workmen to remove the offending decorations.

Loeffler grew up with his nation. During his first years in the Senate, he witnessed the bitter debates over the Force bill governing election laws in 1890, the stormy Spanish-American War, and the annexation of Hawaii. He was here when President William McKinley was assassinated and Theodore Roosevelt assumed the presidency.

In 1913, Loeffler was elected acting assistant doorkeeper of the Senate and, in 1919, he became assistant doorkeeper. This was a period, in the wake of the First World War, that produced vastly increased legislative activity in the Senate. These were years which

For nearly six decades, Carl Loeffler served the Senate, from page to secretary of the Senate.

U.S. Senate Historical Office

required great stamina, and Loeffler maintained his own by bicycling, a sport in which he won several medals.

In 1928, Loeffler became assistant sergeant at arms, and a year later he became majority secretary for the Republicans. With a Democratic majority in 1933, he became secretary for the minority. His other positions in the Senate included the secretaryship of the Republican Committee on Committees and the Republican Steering Committee.

Although Loeffler was an ardent Republican, he had devoted friends on each side of the aisle. He went out of his way to help the uninitiated of both parties at the beginning of each Congress. During his fifty-nine years

of service to this institution, he came to know over half of all the United States senators who had ever served up to that time.

In 1947, Carl Loeffler was elected secretary of the Senate, the position which capped his long career on Capitol Hill. When the Republicans lost control of the Senate in 1949, Loeffler retired, taking with him the tributes and affection of those whom he had served so long and so well.

Our most recent secretaries have been Francis R. Valeo, J. Stanley Kimmitt, William F. Hildenbrand, Jo-Anne Coe, and Walter Joseph Stewart.

Frank Valeo served in the U.S. Army during World War II. Having seen duty in the China theater, he was a specialist on the Far East and was chief of the Foreign Affairs Division of the old Legislative Reference Service before coming to the Senate as a consultant to the Foreign Relations Committee. He then became an assistant to Senator Mike Mansfield and, in 1963, was elected secretary for the Democratic majority. On September 30, 1966, Valeo was sworn in as secretary of the Senate, serving in that position until 1977.

J. Stanley Kimmitt spent the earlier years of his career in the United States Army, from which he retired as a colonel in 1966, having won the Silver Star, Legion of Merit, Bronze Star, and other important decorations. In 1966, Stan Kimmitt became administrative assistant to Senator Mike Mansfield, the majority leader. Like six of his predecessors as secretary, he then served as his party's secretary in the Senate before his election as secretary of the Senate in January 1977.

When the Republicans took control of the Senate in 1981, Bill Hildenbrand was elected secretary. Any senator from either party who had spent an appreciable amount of time on the Senate floor was well acquainted with Bill Hildenbrand. He had come to the Senate as a staff member for Delaware Senator J.

The most recent secretaries of the Senate have been: *top row, left to right*, Emery L. Frazier, Francis R. Valeo, J. Stanley Kimmitt; *bottom row, left to right*, William F. Hildenbrand, Jo-Anne L. Coe, and Walter J. Stewart, the current secretary.   *U.S. Senate Historical Office and Office of the Secretary of the Senate*

Caleb Boggs in 1961 and spent much of his time in the Senate chamber, keeping an eye on the floor proceedings. In 1969, he became an assistant to the new Republican whip, Hugh Scott of Pennsylvania. When Republican Leader Everett Dirksen died later that year, Senator Scott became minority leader. When J. Mark Trice retired at the end of 1973, after many years as secretary for the Republican minority, Bill Hildenbrand succeeded him in that post. After his many years of superior service on the floor, it was only natural that Bill Hildenbrand would be elected secretary of the Senate when the Republicans organized the Senate in the Ninety-seventh Congress.

When Senate Majority Leader Howard Baker of Tennessee retired in 1985, Bill Hildenbrand also ended his Senate career. Senate Republicans elected Bob Dole of Kansas as the new majority leader in the Ninety-ninth Congress, and Senator Dole proposed one of his most trusted assistants to fill the vacancy in the office of secretary of the Senate. The Senate's election of Jo-Anne Coe meant that, for the first time in its almost two hundred years of history, a woman would serve as secretary of the Senate. She had been office manager for Senator Dole during almost his entire time in the Senate, save for two years that she spent on the staff of the Commodity Futures Trading Commission.

The election of 1986 once again shifted the party majority in the Senate to the Democrats. Walter J. Stewart—who first came to the Senate as a page in 1951 and had most recently served as secretary for the Democratic majority from January 15, 1979, to January 5, 1981, and as secretary for the Democratic minority from January 5, 1981, to August 1981—returned to be elected secretary of the Senate on January 6, 1987. Joe Stewart is the twenty-fifth person to hold the office, and his service to the Senate as its secretary is superb. He is acclaimed by all for his efficiency, his dedication to the Senate, and the strict attention that he gives daily to his Senate duties.

In recent years, the operations of the Senate have been modernized in order to increase its efficiency. Staff positions that were traditionally filled by political patronage are now professional posts held by specialists in their various fields. Computers, microfilm, and other products of modern technology have been introduced to speed procedures in nearly every department, from the disbursing office to the stationery store, as well as in the publication of our annual legislative and executive journals. The Senate library, which, since 1871, has collected significant books and documents for the Senate's use, now operates a bank of computer terminals providing Senate offices with up-to-the-minute information on pending legislation and bibliographical materials for our research projects. The curator's and historian's offices use computers to prepare catalogs of the art and antiquities in the Senate's possession and to compile the locations of former senators' papers, as research tools for scholars and others interested in the history of the Senate.

Technically, the secretary of the Senate serves under the president pro tempore. Since the secretary is elected by a majority of the members, however, he or she responds in great measure to the Senate through the majority leader, often in consultation with the minority leader, on matters of concern to all senators.

Today, as throughout the Senate's history, the secretary provides services to all members regardless of their party affiliation. Back in 1852, when Whig Senator Willie Mangum of North Carolina, a member of the minority party, retired from the Senate, he wrote (with tongue in cheek) to Secretary Asbury Dickins:

I go off this evening not half prepared. . . . I have not taken my things out of my drawer in the Senate Chamber, . . . there may be many treasonable things in it, . . . and although you are a [D]emocrat I hardly think you would take pleasure in seeing the neck of an old friend stretched.[20]

This is just a sample of the confidence that we as senators have so often placed in those who have served this institution as its secretary.

CHAPTER 11

Sergeant at Arms

May 12, 1989

Mr. President, the sergeant at arms is the principal law enforcement and protocol officer of the United States Senate. His various powers and responsibilities are derived, and have developed over time, from several primary sources: from the statutes; from rules and regulations adopted by the Senate; from policies, regulations, and guidelines approved by the Committee on Rules and Administration; and from customs and precedents that have evolved over the Senate's two hundred years of operation.

On April 7, 1789, the day after senators established their first quorum, they elected James Mathers of New York as "Door-Keeper," a post similar to the one he had held for the Continental Congress. The "Door-Keeper's" position was particularly significant because the Senate barred the public and kept its proceedings secret from 1789 to December 1795. It was not until 1798 that the Senate adopted the designation "Sergeant-at-Arms," following the practice of the English Parliament and the U.S. House of Representatives.

The new title reflected the growing responsibilities of the post. On March 23, 1790, an appropriation bill from the House had included $192 for Gifford Dally, the House doorkeeper, "for Services during the

Vacancy." Pennsylvania Senator William Maclay, in his diary, reported that the Senate "divided this Sum," giving half to Dally and "96 to Mathers our Door keeper." The House would not agree to this arrangement, and, according to Maclay, the Senate then "continued the 192 Doll. to Dally and put in 96 for Mathers." [1] On March 3, 1791, when the First Congress was preparing to adjourn, it passed a resolution authorizing Mathers to take care of the Senate chamber and committee rooms in their absence, "and also to make the necessary provision of fire wood for the next Session." [2]

Even more significant for the evolution from "Door-Keeper" to sergeant at arms was the authorization of James Mathers to compel attendance of senators and to arrest others sought by the Senate. The framers of the Constitution in 1787 had been profoundly disturbed by the chronic absences that had crippled the Congress under the Articles of Confederation. Accordingly, in Article I, section 5, they provided that, in each house of the new Congress, a smaller number than a quorum "may be authorized to compel the attendance of absent members, in such manner and under such penalties as each House may provide." A member of one state ratifying convention observed, "When it is known of how much importance attendance is, no senator would dare to incur the universal resentment of his fellow citizens by grossly absenting himself from his duty." [3]

Senators of the First Congress did not need to be reminded of the consequences of the inability to compel members to attend sessions. Those eight who arrived on March 4, 1789, the appointed day for the beginning of the new government, constituted only two-thirds the number necessary to form a quorum. Nearly five weeks passed before the twelfth senator arrived and a quorum was achieved on April 6. One of the first orders of Senate business was the preparation of a set of rules of procedure. The drafting committee borrowed heavily from the 1778 rules of the Continental Congress, Rule 18 of which provided that "no member shall leave Congress without permission of Congress or of his constituents." In revised form, that provision became Senate Rule XIX, adopted on April 16, 1789: "No member shall absent himself from the service of the Senate without leave of the Senate first obtained." Today, that ancient cornerstone of Senate operations appears in slightly modified form in Rule VI. [4]

From March 1789 through the end of 1801, the Senate achieved an opening-day quorum during only half of its first fourteen regular sessions. In 1794, following a delay of fifteen days in obtaining a quorum, the Senate established a committee to revise its rules to compel attendance of members; but there is no record that the committee ever made a recommendation. So frustrated was the House of Representatives at the Senate's delay on this occasion, that it proceeded to conduct business without waiting for the Senate to organize. Near the end of the first session of the Third Congress, in May 1794, five senators left the Senate chamber and "retired to the lobby" during a vote on a peace treaty with Great Britain. Vice Presi-

dent John Adams angrily described their action in intentionally avoiding a vote as the "greatest curiosity of all." But, under the existing rules, Adams lacked specific authority to compel senators' attendance. [5]

In July 1797, Senator William Blount faced charges of conspiring with the British to incite Indians to seize frontier lands in Spanish Florida and Louisiana. As a result, the Senate conducted an inquiry into the truth of the allegations. When Blount was slow in returning to the Senate to respond to the charges, Vice President Thomas Jefferson, by order of the Senate, wrote to him, stating, "You are hereby required to attend the Senate in your place, without delay." [6] Blount returned the next day, but, after the Senate expelled him and the House impeached him, he fled to Tennessee. [7]

On February 5, 1798, as the Senate prepared for Blount's impeachment trial, it resolved that James Mathers, the doorkeeper of the Senate, "be, and he is hereby, invested with the authority of Sergeant-at-Arms, to hold said office during the pleasure of the Senate, whose duty it shall be to execute the commands of the Senate, from time to time, and all such process as shall be directed to him by the President of the Senate." [8] Then, on March 1, the Senate issued a warrant for Blount's arrest, and Mathers journeyed to Tennessee to find him. While there, Mathers "was received courteously" by Blount and by state authorities, but he "was also firmly assured that Blount could not be taken from Tennessee." [9] Mathers returned the warrant to the Senate, which proceeded with the impeachment trial.

Four months after establishing the position of sergeant at arms, the Senate added to its standing rules provisions that empowered him, in the absence of a quorum, to round up members not in attendance. "In case a less number than a quorum of the Senate shall convene," the rule read, "they are hereby au-

HARPER'S WEEKLY.

A

JOURNAL OF CIVILIZATION.

Vol. XII.—No. 587.]   NEW YORK, SATURDAY, MARCH 28, 1868.   [SINGLE COPIES, TEN CENTS. $4.00 PER YEAR IN ADVANCE.

Entered according to Act of Congress, in the Year 1868, by Harper & Brothers, in the Clerk's Office of the District Court of the United States, for the Southern District of New York.

GEORGE T. BROWN, SERGEANT-AT-ARMS OF THE SENATE, SERVING THE SUMMONS ON PRESIDENT JOHNSON.—Sketched by C. H. Davis.—[See Page 195.]

In 1868, Senate Sergeant at Arms George T. Brown notified President Andrew Johnson of his impeachment trial in the Senate chamber.

Harper's Weekly, March 28, 1868

[283]

thorized to send the Sergeant-at-Arms, or any other person or persons, by them authorized, for any or all absent members." During the next half century, Senate orders to its sergeant at arms were expressed in direct and assertive language. He was to "summon and command the absent members of the Senate to be and appear before the Senate immediately," taking "all practicable means to enforce their attendance." As time passed, the tone of these orders softened, so that the sergeant at arms was simply to "request the attendance of absent members." [10]

The first sergeant at arms, James Mathers, a man of tact and patience, was well suited to these duties. A native of Ireland, he came to the American colonies shortly before the start of the Revolutionary War. He enlisted to serve under George Washington and participated in combat throughout the war. He was wounded several times, once severely. In recognition of his valor, Mathers earned appointment as sergeant at arms and doorkeeper to the Continental Congress and later to the United States Senate. By all accounts, the Senate chose well. Mathers served faithfully for nearly twenty-three years until his death in 1811 at the age of sixty-seven. [11]

Although Mathers had authority to "take all practicable means to enforce" the attendance of senators, the Senate's records for those early years do not reveal any occasion when a senator was physically compelled to enter the chamber, or fined for his absence. By the middle of the nineteenth century, reflecting the failure of efforts at compulsion, the Senate modified its rules to the effect that the sergeant at arms be directed to "request" the attendance of absent members. Nevertheless, in the face of chronic absences during the crisis years of the Civil War, Senator John P. Hale of New Hampshire supported restoration of a rule, similar to the practice of the House of Representatives, to "compel" attendance of absentees. Senator

Hale disliked the "cautious, guarded, and modest shape" of the language then used to invite members back to do their duty. Senator John Conness of California was among those senators who successfully blocked Hale's motion. Conness observed that "all these rules will prove ineffective unless the minds of Senators and the feeling of duty that they owe to the country keep them in their seats." The California senator believed, perhaps naively, "that it should only be necessary on this subject to direct the attention of Senators to the degree to which the public business is retarded by their absence in order to have their presence in the Senate hereafter."

In 1864, Senator William Pitt Fessenden of Maine, who at the time was de facto leader of the Senate by virtue of his position as chairman of the Finance Committee, proposed publishing a list of absentees. "The fact of the frequent want of a quorum in this body has become notorious," he declared in frustration. "It is shameful and discreditable to the body. . . . The fact that it occurs so frequently, day after day, especially at this [late] period of the session when we have so much important work to do, is discreditable." Until that time, the *Congressional Globe* (forerunner of the *Congressional Record*) included only the yeas and nays for each roll-call vote. The Senate then adopted Fessenden's half-way measure, providing that, in the *Congressional Globe*, there should appear a separate listing of "the absentees in each call for ayes and noes" to embarrass members into attendance. This arrangement remained in effect until about 1892, when the Senate removed some of the sting of this listing by substituting the words "not voting" for "absent." [12]

Still, the various sergeants at arms of the period remained uncertain about the extent of their powers to secure senators' attendance if their initial "request" failed to have the desired effect. During a Saturday evening session on April 20, 1872—the quality of life in the Senate not being then what it is now—the presiding officer ruled out of order a motion, in the absence of a quorum, that the sergeant at arms "compel the attendance of absentees." He made this ruling on the grounds that the minority of members present did not have the power to change the existing rules. Judiciary Committee chairman Lyman Trumbull asserted: "We have no way of forcing the attendance of Senators; we can only request them to attend; and that has always been supposed in the history of the Senate to be a sufficient summons for a Senator to attend. It has always been supposed that a Senator acting upon his honor would report himself when his attendance was requested by the Senate."[13]

Finally, as part of a general revision of its rules in 1877, the Senate adopted a rule that was designed to remove this obstacle by providing that, in the absence of a quorum, "a majority of the Senators present may direct the Sergeant-at-Arms to request, and, when necessary, to compel the attendance of the absent Senators, which order shall be determined without debate; and, pending its execution, and until a quorum shall be present, no motion, except a motion to adjourn, nor debate, shall be in order." This rule received the unanimous recommendation of the Rules Committee. Maine's Senator Hannibal Hamlin, whose Senate service extended back to 1848, successfully argued that the authority to compel attendance, although included in the Constitution, must be spelled out in Senate rules. This action would end the frustration of having to adjourn when members failed to answer their colleagues' pleas to attend.[14]

Yet, the problem of compulsion persisted. On a winter evening in February 1883, the sergeant at arms informed the Senate that "a number of senators are reported to be at a

Sergeant at Arms E.K. Valentine had little success persuading absent senators to return to the chamber during an all-night filibuster in 1891.
Library of Congress

dinner party at Secretary [of the Navy William E.] Chandler's, where the host refuses admission to the officers sent to notify them." After repeated futile efforts to convince the dining senators to answer their call to duty, the Senate adjourned at 10:00 p.m.[15] Several years later, on Friday, January 16, 1891, a coalition of southern Democrats and a minority faction of western Republicans stayed away from the Senate in an ultimately successful effort to block passage of a so-called Force bill providing for federal supervision of elections. Shortly after midnight on a cold, rainy Saturday, the Republican leadership secured enough votes to direct the sergeant at arms, E.K. Valentine, "to use all necessary means to compel the attendance of absent Senators." At various times during the all-night session, the sergeant at arms reported that seven members were too ill to comply with the Senate's request, that one said he was "much too fatigued to attend," and that others simply refused to answer the knock at their doors. The sergeant at arms related how he had found Senators James Berry and Matthew Butler in the Democratic cloakroom, and that Berry had "requested me to report to the Senate that he would come when he got ready," while Butler "refused to obey the summons." At 5:44 a.m., the chair announced that a quorum was present, and debate resumed briefly before a quorum was again lost.[16]

In the ensuing debate, senators were unable to decide by what means the sergeant at arms was to "compel" absentees, or what might be the penalties for absenteeism. Following inconclusive discussion, the Senate finally secured a quorum at 9:30 a.m. and proceeded in an unsuccessful attempt to shut off the minority's filibuster.[17]

Matters had changed little by 1915. That year, in the midst of a filibuster on President Woodrow Wilson's ship purchase bill, a frustrated Senate debated a proposed rules change that would require senators to remain in the chamber unless excused by the Senate and would hold violators in contempt of the Senate. Although this rule was not adopted, the thirty-three-day filibuster, which prevented passage of three major appropriations bills, did lead to enactment of the Senate's first cloture rule in 1917.[18]

A dozen years later, at "twelve o'clock and 45 minutes a.m." on February 22, 1927, during a filibuster that had snarled legislation to harness the water resources of the lower Colorado River, Senator Matthew M. Neely of West Virginia moved successfully that warrants of "arrest" be issued for absent senators. The sergeant at arms was ordered to bring the absent senators before the bar of

the Senate. At 2:40 a.m., the president pro tempore announced that fifty senators had answered to their names and a quorum was present. No arrests were made. Prior to the arrest order, the Senate, on a motion by Senator Neely, had ordered the sergeant at arms "to compel the attendance of absent senators." After doing his best to comply with the order, Sergeant at Arms David S. Barry reported that he had received an interesting variety of excuses: one senator was preparing to attend a funeral; one said he would come later, if necessary, but he was already in bed; another responded that he would not come because he was too tired; and another said he would think it over.[19]

A more explosive event occurred on the afternoon of Saturday, November 14, 1942, during a Senate debate on anti-poll-tax legislation. Shortly after 1:00 p.m., with only forty-four members present, the Senate agreed to Majority Leader Alben Barkley's motion to direct the arrest of missing senators. In the course of this action, additional senators arrived, reducing the number needed for a quorum to five. Forty-three senators were out of town, so the search narrowed to the remaining eight members believed to be in Washington. The missing eight were all Democrats: Kenneth McKellar of Tennessee, Burnet Maybank of South Carolina, Berkley Bunker of Nevada, Lister Hill of Alabama, Wall Doxey of Mississippi, W. Lee O'Daniel of Texas, Richard Russell of Georgia, and John Overton of Louisiana. Sergeant at Arms Chesley Jurney sent his men to the Senate office building now named for Senator Richard Russell. Jurney deputized the custodian to unlock the office doors of the missing senators; but only Senator Bunker was found, and he walked to the Senate chamber. A deputy sergeant at arms drove to the home of Senator Maybank, who, without objection, agreed to return to the Capitol. Senators Aiken and Herring, both of whom had been reported as being out of town, returned to the chamber on their own, apparently unaware of the sergeant at arms' search.[20]

Kenneth McKellar, the Senate's third most senior member, was resting at his apartment at the Mayflower Hotel when another deputy sergeant at arms, Mark Trice, arrived with his warrant. After the seventy-three-year-old senator failed to answer the house telephone, Trice appealed to a hotel maid, who persuaded McKellar to open his door. The senator seemed taken aback to see Trice standing in the hall but willingly accepted his offer to ride back to the Senate. Trice never mentioned the warrant, but, as they approached Capitol Hill, the Tennessee senator realized that he was being used to help the leadership thwart the tactics of his fellow southern senators. As a Senate press gallery official later recalled, "His face grew redder and redder. By the time the car reached the Senate entrance, McKellar shot out and barrelled through the corridors to find the source of his summons. . . . He was so angry with [Majority Leader] Barkley that he would not speak to him for months." With the arrival of Senator McKellar, a quorum was present, but the Senate still failed to end the filibuster. It continued to fail when the legislation was brought up again in 1944, 1946, and 1948. Not until 1962 were the anti-poll-tax provisions enacted by Congress to become the Twenty-fourth Amendment to the Constitution. Senator McKellar did not quickly forget his "arrest." At the Democratic caucus at the beginning of the next Congress, McKellar advanced his own candidate for sergeant at arms, and Jurney resigned rather than face a contest. Ironically, the new sergeant at arms was former Senator Wall Doxey, who, himself, had been among the absent senators that night in 1942.[21]

It was after two o'clock on the morning of Saturday, June 10, 1950, when, having

A former senator, Wall Doxey became sergeant at arms in 1943. *Office of the Senate Sergeant at Arms*

adopted a motion by Majority Leader Scott Lucas, the Senate again issued warrants for the arrest of absent senators, as members answered quorum calls and then returned home. Simply issuing warrants was sufficient to produce the missing senators, only four of whom were needed to make a quorum, and no arrests were necessary.[22]

More than a quarter century passed until October 1, 1976, when, as majority whip, and in the absence of Senator Mike Mansfield, I moved for the issuance of "warrants of arrest for absent senators." It was during the hectic conclusion of the last day of the Ninety-fourth Congress, before adjournment for the 1976 elections. Several important actions remained, obstructed by the threat of a filibuster. At that time, I said:

"We are playing games. There are senators in the greeting room and cloakroom who have not come to the floor." Apparently my words reached enough ears, and the vote on my motion to arrest senators was 46 to 11. Absent senators hurried into the chamber, and a quorum was quickly established. The chair then ruled that the sergeant at arms would not have to issue warrants, and we were able to complete our work and adjourn the Ninety-fourth Congress.[23]

Nordy Hoffmann was then serving as sergeant at arms. In a recent oral history, he recalled:

The Senate was about to tell me to go out and arrest the senators and bring them in. But I knew where Senator Cliff Hansen of Wyoming was in his hideaway. I went to get him, and I said, "Senator, I don't like to have to come and get you. Why don't you come in so we can break this. After all, I'm a new man on the block. It makes the Senate look bad and it makes me look bad." He said, "You talked me into it." He came in and we were able to get the vote and we didn't have to arrest anybody.[24]

Our current sergeant at arms, Henry Giugni, was not quite as fortunate. On February 23, 1988, during a filibuster against a bill to curtail the cost of senatorial campaigns, I made a motion "that the sergeant at arms be instructed to arrest the absent senators and bring them to the chamber." The motion carried by a vote of 45 to 3, with 52 senators not voting. Around midnight, Sergeant at Arms Giugni and several Capitol policemen moved through the Senate office buildings and Capitol hideaway offices to round up hiding senators. Some members ran when they saw the sergeant at arms. Some refused to accompany him. Senator Bob Packwood agreed to walk to the chamber with the sergeant at arms, but would not enter it. Two policemen, therefore, carried him into the chamber, thus establishing a quorum of 51 senators.[25] Needless to say,

this incident drew considerable press attention. Since the Senate so rarely has ordered the arrest of its own members, the media treated the incident as if it were unprecedented. But, as I have pointed out, there were precedents for the issuance of such warrants, and only the physical carrying of a senator into the chamber was really unique on this occasion. Senator Packwood, I should note, had only praise for the conduct of the sergeant at arms, who, he conceded, was simply doing his job, as directed by the Senate.[26]

Senators are not the only people subject to arrest by the sergeant at arms. Whenever the Senate has called a reluctant witness to testify, whether before a committee or before the Senate as a whole, the sergeant at arms has been sent out on the manhunt. This was true in 1800 when the sergeant at arms brought William Duane, editor of the Philadelphia *Aurora and General Advertiser*, before the bar of the Senate; it was still true in 1951, when Sergeant at Arms Joe Duke won some national notoriety for rounding up such underworld figures as Jacob "Greasy Thumb" Guzik, one of Al Capone's mobsters, to testify before Estes Kefauver's crime investigating committee. Of course, Joe Duke had some help from the FBI, especially since he had sworn in J. Edgar Hoover as a deputy sergeant at arms of the Senate.[27]

As the chief law enforcement official of the Senate, the sergeant at arms can be empowered to arrest any member of the Senate, including the leadership, the president of the Senate, and, indeed, even the president of the United States. It was the Senate's sergeant at arms who presented President Andrew Johnson with the notification of his impeachment trial in the Senate chamber.

Furthermore, sergeants at arms have even served as jailers. Twice in the nineteenth century, the Senate held newspaper correspondents prisoners in committee rooms

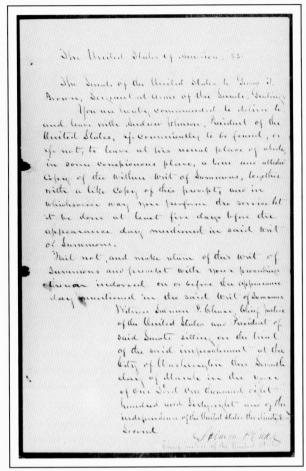

Chief Justice Salmon P. Chase directed Senate Sergeant at Arms George Brown to serve a summons on President Andrew Johnson for his impeachment trial.
National Archives

inside the U.S. Capitol, hoping to force them to divulge sources of Senate secrets they had published. John Nugent, Washington correspondent for the *New York Herald*, was held for leaking the still-secret Treaty of Guadalupe-Hidalgo to the *Herald* in 1848. At that time, Senate Sergeant at Arms Robert Beale placed the prisoner in the Committee on Territories room at the Capitol and took him home in the evenings to feed him dinner and make sure he had a good night's sleep. Similarly, in 1871, the sergeant at arms held two reporters for the *New-York Tribune* in the room of the Senate Committee on the Pacific Railroad while the Senate waited for them to tell

who gave them the still-secret Treaty of Washington. Again, the sergeant at arms provided a comfortable environment for the prisoners, who had daily visits from their wives and friends, received books and flowers, and dined in the Senate restaurant. In fact, the prisoners were entrusted with the key to their own committee-room cell! In neither case, by the way, did the correspondents divulge the source of their secret information, and the Senate since then has wisely abandoned the practice of arresting newspaper correspondents, at least for that reason.[28]

Today, the sergeant at arms is a member of the Capitol Police Board (along with the sergeant at arms of the House and the architect of the Capitol), which oversees the policing of the U.S. Capitol Building and grounds by the Capitol police. In addition, since 1867, the Senate sergeant at arms has had the authority to make any regulations necessary to preserve the peace and prevent the defacement of the Capitol and the Senate office buildings, and to protect the public property in these buildings. Since 1878, the sergeant at arms has been empowered to prevent any part of the Capitol grounds and terraces from being used as a playground, thereby protecting the turf. As part of his policing responsibilities, the sergeant at arms, a member of the Capitol Police Board, shares control over traffic around the Capitol, including parking and impoundment of vehicles. These are not matters to be taken lightly, for it has often been stated that the two most important issues on Capitol Hill are neither political nor legislative but, rather, office space and parking space.

Mr. President, when one tallies them up, the number of responsibilities that the Senate assigns to its sergeants at arms appears staggering. The sergeant at arms is in charge of the doorkeepers, who maintain order in the galleries and in the surrounding lobbies. He greets and escorts important visitors to the Capitol, including presidents, prime ministers, kings, and queens. The sergeant at arms directs the work of such Senate facilities as the service department (once known as the folding room), which prepares printed material for mailing to constituents; the computer center; telephone and telecommunications services; the Senate recording studio; and the Senate post office. He also supervises the leasing of official Senate automobiles and the rental of home state offices for senators. In addition, the sergeant at arms directs the work of the maintenance workers, janitors, housekeeping staff, restroom attendants, elevator operators, cabinetmakers, upholsterers, and locksmiths; he is in charge of selling or disposing of surplus or worn-out office equipment and other furnishings; and he is in charge of the Senate barbershops and beauty salon.

The sergeant at arms, along with the secretary of the Senate, leads the formal processions of the Senate, whether to a joint session, an inauguration, or other ceremonial events. He accompanies us even unto death, at least as far as the cemetery, since, by custom, the sergeant at arms heads the delegation representing the Senate at the funeral of a deceased member. Nordy Hoffmann recalled that he was in charge of a great many funeral arrangements as sergeant at arms. The largest funeral he oversaw was for Senator Hubert Humphrey, who died in Minnesota but who lay in state in the Capitol Rotunda. Hoffmann arranged with the White House for the use of the presidential jet to bring the coffin and the senator's family to Washington and then coordinated activities with the military and other federal agencies involved. What he most remembers from that event, however, was meeting Ambassador to Japan Mike Mansfield at the airport. "Isn't this a long way to come for a funeral?" he asked the former senator. "No place is too

far to come for a friend," replied Senator Mansfield, underscoring the seriousness with which this collegial institution treats such occasions.[29]

With all these responsibilities, which keep growing, the Senate has been fortunate to have had outstanding individuals serving as sergeant at arms. After the first sergeant at arms, James Mathers, we had such men as Mountjoy Bayly, who served twenty-two years, including that fateful August in 1814 when British troops burned the Capitol Building. George T. Brown was sergeant at arms during the Civil War and Reconstruction, when special security was needed at the Capitol—considering that some of the war was fought in the suburbs of Washington. There was Daniel Ransdell, a Civil War veteran whose arm was shattered at the battle of Roseca, and who served as sergeant at arms from 1900 to 1912. Known as the "Pooh-Bah of the Senate," Ransdell prided himself in being the Senate's chief housekeeper, making sure that senators were always comfortable. According to the newspapers, no matter what problem arose around the Senate, the answer would always be the same: "Ask Ransdell about it."

One of the most colorful men to hold the post was David S. Barry, author of a fascinating memoir, *Forty Years in Washington*, which he published in 1924 while serving as sergeant at arms. Barry first came to the Senate in 1875 as a page, recommended by Senator Isaac Christiancy of Michigan. Young Barry made the most of his service as a page, using his time off to learn stenography from the official reporters of debate. Later, he was employed as secretary to a number of senators and representatives, most notably to Senator Nelson Aldrich of Rhode Island, long the unofficial Republican leader of the Senate and, by the way, the maternal great-grandfather of my distinguished colleague from West Virginia, Jay Rockefel-

David S. Barry, *right*, shown here with Senator Henry Cabot Lodge in 1923, served as sergeant at arms for four-teen years.   *Library of Congress*

ler. In 1879, Barry also became the Washington correspondent for the *Detroit Post* and the *Detroit Tribune*, beginning a forty-year career as a newspaper reporter. Over the years, he wrote for major papers in Chicago, Detroit, St. Louis, Cleveland, Cincinnati, and New York, and became editor in chief of the *Providence Journal*, then a major Republican paper. During all those years, he built many friendships in the Senate and the House. In 1919, when the Republicans returned to the majority in the Senate, they elected David Barry as sergeant at arms.[30]

Fourteen years later, when the Republicans were swept out of the majority by the Great Depression, Barry made plans to retire. During the long interregnum that then existed between the November election and the March inauguration (before the Twentieth Amendment to the Constitution advanced the date to January), Barry drafted several articles containing his observations on Congress. He sent these to the *New Outlook* magazine, with the stipulation that they not be published until he left office. Unfortunately, one article entitled "Over the Hill to Demagoguery" appeared in print a month too soon and contained an especially injudicious sentence, "There are not many Senators or Representatives who sell their votes for money, and it is pretty well known who those few are."

Offended senators called sergeant at arms Barry to the floor of the Senate to explain himself. The Senate Judiciary Committee held two days of hearings on the matter, and, while Barry argued that he had really written in defense of the majority of members of Congress, the committee was not mollified. It voted to recommend his removal as sergeant at arms, which the Senate agreed to by a vote of 53 to 17 on February 7, 1933. The then-chairman of the Judiciary Committee, George Norris of Nebraska, commented that, had the statement been written by a newspaper correspondent, the Senate would have paid it no attention. David Barry, however, was an officer of the Senate, elected by a roll-call vote, and his impropriety cost him his position.[31]

Barry's departure left his young deputy, J. Mark Trice, as acting sergeant at arms for a month. That month included the inauguration of Franklin D. Roosevelt as president of the United States, which was, indeed, a trial by fire for a staunch Republican like Mark Trice. But Trice was equal to the challenge. Later, during the Eighty-third Congress, he served as secretary of the Senate, and for many years he was the secretary for the Republican minority in the Senate.

When I first came to the Senate in 1959, I was greeted warmly by the then-sergeant at arms, Joe Duke. Duke learned of the difficulties associated with arresting unwilling persons early in his life. In 1930, while a student at the University of Arizona, he held a part-time job with the Miami, Arizona, police department. One day while pursuing fugitives, he was ambushed and shot in the stomach. He managed to struggle into his automobile and drove to town for medical aid, arriving just in the nick of time. Several years later, he came to the Senate; he served first on the staff of Arizona Senator Henry F. Ashurst, and then with Senator Carl Hayden. In 1949, he became Senate sergeant at arms, a post he held until 1965, except for the two years of the Republican Eighty-third Congress. Hubert Humphrey once referred to Duke as "the Houdini of Washington, who can produce the almost impossible on short notice."

When I first became Senate majority leader, in January 1977, I could always count on the able assistance of Nordy Hoffmann. In fact, I had known Nordy for several years previously; he served for eight years as executive director of the Democratic Senatorial Campaign Committee, and, earlier, he was

Deputy Sergeant at Arms J. Mark Trice gave the Senate's gavel a last-minute polishing before the opening of a Senate session.
U.S. Senate Historical Office

an official of the United Steelworkers of America. Anyone who has ever seen Nordy Hoffmann can attest that he *looked* like a sergeant at arms. He has a football player's physique, and, indeed, he played football at Notre Dame from 1929 to 1931, under the legendary coach, Knute Rockne. Hoffmann was named guard on the top All-American selections in 1931 and starred for the East in the East-West Shrine Football Classic in San Francisco. In 1978, I was pleased to add my name to those of all one hundred senators and Presidents Gerald Ford and

Jimmy Carter in recommending that Nordy be recognized by the National Football Foundation; and, indeed, he was inducted into their Hall of Fame. As sergeant at arms, he stood six foot, three inches, and weighed 290 pounds, which was big enough to arrest and bring to the Senate chamber any member.[32]

When a star of the movie *The Knute Rockne Story* was elected president in 1980, Hoffmann's experience of having been coached by Rockne gained an added dimension. The change in party in the Senate during that

[293]

Joseph C. Duke, *left*, served as sergeant at arms for fourteen years; Nordy Hoffmann, *right*, who was a former All-American football player, held the post from 1975 to 1981.   *U.S. Senate Historical Office*

election also meant a change in sergeants at arms, and Howard Liebengood replaced Nordy Hoffmann. Hoffmann told a story about greeting President-elect Ronald Reagan when he arrived at the Capitol before the inauguration. As they waited for the limousine, Liebengood realized that he did not know what title to use in addressing a president-elect. "Do you call him 'President-elect,' 'Governor,' or what?" he asked the Republican leader. Senator Howard Baker responded, "Well, watch Nordy, he knows." When the limousine pulled up and Ronald Reagan emerged, Nordy Hoffmann said, "Hiya, Gipper." "I couldn't do that!" said Liebengood, who decided to address the president-elect more formally. But, as Nordy Hoffmann explained, "Well . . . he wasn't President, it wasn't an insult. He liked to be called the Gipper"—especially, one imag-

ines, by someone who actually knew the legendary Coach Rockne.[33]

During the six years that the Republicans held the majority in the Senate, from 1981 to 1987, there were three sergeants at arms: Howard Liebengood, who had first come to the Senate as a staff member of the Watergate committee; Larry Smith, at thirty-four the Senate's youngest sergeant at arms; and Ernest Garcia, the first Hispanic-American to serve in the post. As Senator Mark Hatfield said, in commending Smith's service: "The Senate Sergeant at Arms must be a politician along with the best of us. His constituency, however, is made up of 100 Senators with ample egos to be massaged." Certainly, most of these sergeants at arms performed their constituent services admirably, in the tradition set by predecessors dating back to James Mathers.[34]

Henry Kuualoha Giugni was elected sergeant at arms—the thirtieth to date—on January 6, 1987. A native of Hawaii and the first Polynesian-American to become sergeant at arms, Giugni had previously served for twenty-four years, from 1963 to 1987, as administrative assistant to Senator Daniel Inouye. He knows the Senate, its members, its staff, its physical plant, and its multitude of needs. The deputy sergeant at arms is Mrs. Jeanine Drysdale Lowe, who has ably served the Senate in that position for over two and one-half years, and who previously represented the Democratic minority in the sergeant at arms' office for almost five years.

From modest beginnings, the office of sergeant at arms and doorkeeper of the Senate has developed over two centuries into the largest single entity within the Senate. Today, that office comprises an administrative services organization involving a dozen major departments and activities and employing, as of this date, 1,465 persons. This number includes 689 officers and civilians in the Capitol police force attending the Senate. The Senate would have a difficult time functioning without its Capitol police, computer

Henry K. Giugni became Senate sergeant at arms in 1987. *Office of the Senate Sergeant at Arms*

specialists, janitors, postal workers, parking attendants, carpenters, or barbers, all of whom perform their duties under the careful eye of the Senate sergeant at arms.

CHAPTER 12

Senate Chaplain

June 25, 1980*

Mr. President, today I shall speak about another of the elected officers of the Senate, the Senate chaplain.

Let me preface my statement on the chaplain by referring to a portion of the scriptures: "Except the Lord build the house, they labour in vain that build it: except the Lord keep the city, the watchman waketh but in vain." [1]

Mr. President, the Founding Fathers believed that God was the Ruler of the universe and that the destinies of nations were guided by His hand. Faith in God was their guiding light. We can see from the Mayflower Compact and the other great documents in our early history—the Declaration of Independence and the Constitution of the United States—a spiritual awareness on the part of the men and women who founded this nation. This spiritual sense runs throughout the nation's history as an unbroken thread. In times of adversity, it has given strength to those who have built this great country.

I point, as an example, to Benjamin Franklin, who rose at the Constitutional Convention on June 28, 1787, at a time when the convention seemed likely to fall apart and end without success. Addressing the assembly, which General George Washington chaired, the aged but still eloquent and witty Franklin declared:

I have lived, Sir, a long time, and the longer I live, the more convincing proofs I see of this truth—*that God governs in the affairs of men.* And if a sparrow cannot fall to the ground without his notice, is it probable that an empire can rise without his aid?

Franklin continued, observing that, unless the founders drew upon spiritual strength for guidance, "we shall succeed in this political building no better, than the Builders of Babel." [2]

While the convention was surprised to hear such views expressed by Franklin, a Deist, the sentiments he voiced were shared by most of his colleagues in Philadelphia that June. We should continue to be mindful of that spiritual awareness on the part of our forefathers as the chaplain opens our daily sessions with prayer.

The custom of opening sessions of the Senate and House with prayer is a very old one. Indeed, it dates back to the Continental Congress, before the Senate and House even existed. The Continental Congress first met in Philadelphia on September 5, 1774. When the members convened on the second day, the fiery radical from Massachusetts, Samuel Adams, was among those who rose and proposed to open the session with prayer. The suggestion touched off a heated debate over the religious diversity of the colonies, which would prevent selection of a chaplain from

---

* Updated April 1989

The custom of opening congressional sessions with an invocation dates from September 1774, when the Reverend Jacob Duché led the Continental Congress in prayer.
Library of Congress

any one denomination. The furor was not stilled until Adams delivered a stirring speech in which he proclaimed, as John Adams reconstructed the events for Abigail, "he was no bigot, and could hear a prayer from a gentleman of piety and virtue, who was at the same time a friend to his country." After this emotional plea, Adams' motion carried, and the Reverend Jacob Duché of Philadelphia's Christ Church came to the chamber to lead the Congress in prayer.[3]

From Philadelphia, John Adams once wrote home to his wife that "the business of the Congress is tedious beyond expression." On this particular day, however, he reported

to her that he had never seen a more moving spectacle. After reading the formal Episcopal service, Duché broke into an extemporaneous prayer, which "filled the bosom of every man present. I must confess, I never heard a better prayer, or one so well pronounced." The prayer, Adams informed Abigail, "has had an excellent effect upon every body here." The appreciative members appointed Mr. Duché as their first chaplain.[4]

When the first Senate under the new Constitution, meeting in New York City, finally mustered a quorum of twelve members on April 6, 1789, one of its first orders of business was the matter of selecting a chaplain.

The Senate selected the Right Reverend Samuel Provoost, Episcopal Bishop of New York, as its first chaplain. *Library of Congress*

On April 7, a committee composed of Senators Oliver Ellsworth of Connecticut, Richard Henry Lee of Virginia, Richard Bassett of Delaware, Caleb Strong of Massachusetts, and William Maclay of Pennsylvania was formed to confer with a similar House committee. Their task was "to prepare a system of rules to govern the two Houses in cases of conference, and to take under consideration the manner of electing Chaplains." [5]

This committee reported back in just seven days with a recommendation to elect two chaplains of different denominations—one from the Senate and one from the House—who would alternate between the chambers on a weekly basis. The recommendation was accepted and, on April 25, the Senate chose the Right Reverend Samuel Provoost, Episcopal Bishop of New York, as its first chaplain. Five days later, in his new capacity, the Reverend Mr. Provoost presided over a most historic occasion. On April 30, 1789, George Washington stood before the members of

the new Congress at Federal Hall and solemnly took the oath of office as the first president of the United States. Immediately following the ceremony, President Washington, his vice president, John Adams, and the members of the Senate and House proceeded to St. Paul's Chapel, where Chaplain Provoost led them in a prayer asking for Divine Providence to watch over the new government. [6]

The Senate's first chaplain was as ardent a patriot as the men he served. Born in New York City in 1742, he was a member of the first graduating class of King's College, now Columbia University, in 1758. After graduation, young Provoost sailed for England to study for the Episcopal priesthood. He returned to New York as assistant minister at prestigious Trinity Church. Provoost, however, was a passionate Whig, and his sympathy for the colonies against English rule did not sit well with his wealthy, loyalist congregation. Before long, his patriotism cost him his parish. During the Revolution, Provoost and several of his neighbors in Dutchess County, New York, narrowly escaped capture and death at the hands of the British. It must have been very satisfying to the minister when, after the British evacuated New York and his former Tory parishioners had fled, the little band of patriotic vestrymen who remained invited him to return as head of Trinity Church. [7]

Samuel Provoost served as the Senate's chaplain until Congress moved on to Philadelphia in the winter of 1790. For the next ten years, while the Senate met in Congress Hall, Senate sessions were opened with prayers by the Senate's second chaplain, the Right Reverend William White, first Episcopal Bishop of Pennsylvania.

In 1800, Congress moved to its permanent home along the Potomac. On November 27, in a room one floor below me, now the beautifully restored old Supreme Court chamber,

Bishop William White of Pennsylvania served as the Senate's second chaplain.

Historical Society of Pennsylvania

the Senate elected its third chaplain, the Right Reverend John Thomas Claggett, first Episcopal Bishop of Maryland.[8]

When the seat of government moved to Washington, the nation's capital was little more than a tiny village. In 1800, it offered only two churches: a small frame Catholic chapel on F Street and an Episcopal church, formerly a tobacco warehouse, at the base of Capitol Hill. Although more churches sprang up as the population grew in the early nineteenth century, the House of Representatives chamber, which today serves as Statuary Hall, was the scene of some of the city's most interesting Sunday services.

These religious services were conducted alternately by the chaplains of the Senate and the House, or by distinguished visiting clergymen, and they were open to the public. From contemporary accounts, we know that the public took full advantage of the opportunity to come to the Capitol, though it is not always clear that worship was foremost in their minds. In 1837, recalling the city's first three decades, the brilliant Margaret Bayard Smith wrote:

I have called these Sunday assemblies in the capitol, a *congregation*, but the almost exclusive appropriation of that word to religious assemblies, prevents its being a descriptive term as applied in the present case, since the gay company who thronged the H[ouse] [of] R[epresentatives] looked very little like a religious assembly. The occasion presented for display was not only a novel, but a favourable one for the youth, beauty and fashion of the city, Georgetown and environs. The members of Congress, gladly gave up their seats for such fair auditors, and either lounged in the lobbies, or round the fire places, or stood beside the ladies of their acquaintance. . . . Smiles, nods, whispers, nay sometimes tittering marked their recognition of each other, and beguiled the tedium of the service. . . . The musick was as little in union with devotional feelings, as the place. The marine-band, were the performers. Their scarlet uniform, their various instruments, made quite a dazzling appearance in the gallery. The marches they played were good and inspiring, but in their attempts to accompany the psalm-singing of the congregation, they completely failed and after a while, the practice was discontinued—it was *too* ridiculous.[9]

Mrs. Smith also told a good story about the Senate's thirteenth chaplain, the Reverend John Brackenridge, a stern Presbyterian who served from 1811 to 1814, years that saw the new nation embroiled in another war with England. Chaplain Brackenridge used the forum of the Sunday services in the House chamber in the summer of 1814 to deliver a sermon that proved quite prophetic. His subject was the observance of the Sabbath, and he launched into a vehement denunciation of those who violated its holiness. According to Mrs. Smith:

Bishop John Thomas Claggett of Maryland became the Senate's chaplain when Congress moved to Washington in 1800. *Maryland Historical Society*

He unshrinkingly taxed those then listening to him, with a desecration of this holy day, by their devoting it to amusement—to visiting and parties, emphatically condemning the dinner-parties given at the whitehouse, then addressing himself to the members of Congress, accused them of violating the day, by laws they had made, particularly the carrying the mail on the sabbath.

Brackenridge ended dramatically:

"It is not the people who will suffer for these enormities. You, the law-givers, who are the cause of this crime, will in your public capacity suffer for it. Yes, it is the *government* that will be punished, and as, with Nineveh of old, it will not be the habitations of the people, but your temples and your palaces that will be burned to the ground."

At the time of John Brackenridge's sermon, no one had the remotest apprehension that the British might ever reach Washington. But shortly thereafter, on August 24, 1814, British troops did capture this city and set fire to this very building, as well as to the White House. Dolley Madison told Mrs. Smith that, upon her return to the city after the British had left, she chanced to meet Chaplain Brackenridge one day and said to him, "I little thought, Sir, when I heard that threatening sermon of yours, that its denunciation would so soon be realized." "Oh, Madam," Brackenridge replied, "I trust this chastening of the Lord, may not be in vain." [10]

Until 1853, the House and Senate went on regularly electing their chaplains. But in that year, the House received several memorials requesting that the offices of chaplain in the "army, navy, at West Point, at Indian stations, and in both houses of Congress, be abolished." The memorials argued that the position of chaplain, supported by tax dollars, violated the constitutional provision for separation of church and state. They were referred to the House Judiciary Committee, which, in March 1854, reported that its members were "not prepared to come to the conclusion desired by the memorialists," and proceeded to explain why. After a lengthy discourse on the constitutionality of the chaplaincy, the committee declared:

If there be a God who hears prayer—as we believe there is—we submit, that there never was a deliberative body that so eminently needed the fervent prayers of righteous men as the Congress of the United States. There never was another representative assembly that had so many and so widely different interests to protect and to harmonize, and so many local passions to subdue. One member feels charged to defend the rights of the Atlantic, another of the Pacific coast; one urges the claims of constituents on the borders of the torrid, another on the borders of the frigid zone; while hundreds have the defence of local and varied interests stretching across an entire continent. . . . If wisdom from above . . . be given in answer to the prayers of the pious, then Congress need those devotions, as they surely need to have their views of personal importance daily chastened by the reflection that they are under the government of a Supreme Power, that rules not for one locality or one time, but governs a world by general laws, subjecting all motives and acts to an omniscient scrutiny, and holds all agents to their just rewards by an irresistible power.[11]

And there the matter ended for the time.

Several years later, there arose a more serious, internal challenge to the offices of Senate and House chaplain. In 1855, the House decided to discontinue its practice of electing a regular chaplain. Instead, various members of the District of Columbia clergy were invited to take turns opening each session and preaching the sermon on Sundays. In 1857, the Senate followed suit. The reasons behind this change appear in the floor discussion recorded in the *Congressional Globe.* Senator James Mason of Virginia summed up the problem:

Every Senator, I have no doubt, has had some experience (I think it is very unfortunate, but perhaps it is incident to the subject-matter) that a sort of competition has grown up by the usage of the Senate in electing a Chaplain, which I have thought is not altogether consistent with the office of a clergyman or a pastor. I will not say, by any means, a competition so much among the clergymen themselves, perhaps, as amongst Senators, who desire to prefer particular persons; but the fact is that it has become a matter of that kind, and it is not entirely agreeable to me, certainly, and I dare say is not to other Senators, to have that state of things existing.[12]

The appointment of the chaplain, as Senator Mason pointed out, had fallen into the realm of political patronage. At the beginning of each session, sometimes a dozen or more senators placed in nomination the names of favored clergymen.

Senator Mason had touched a sensitive nerve. Many senators rose to support his proposal for rotating local clergymen who would receive no salary. Senator Clement Clay of Alabama was one of the few to object, saying, "We should not 'muzzle the ox that treadeth out the corn.' " He did not think, as he put it, "in these degenerate

days," anyone would come to pray over the Senate for free. He felt that chaos would ensue and that "oftentimes we shall have to go to work without prayers." Despite Clay's objections, the Senate decided to try the new plan for one Congress.[13]

While the House experimented with the new system from 1855 to 1861, the Senate, after only two years, returned to its old practice of selecting an official chaplain. Had Senator Clay been right? Partly. It seems there had been problems arranging for an orderly succession of daily prayers by disparate individuals willing to volunteer their services. But Senator Henry Wilson of Massachusetts expressed another concern. In an eloquent plea to return to the old system, he said:

I know, sir, there was complaint in the Senate and in the country before we adopted the plan of inviting the clergymen of the city to officiate here. That grew out of electioneering; out of the fact that clergymen came to this city seeking the place of Chaplain here. The plan was adopted of inviting clergymen of Washington city to officiate, I think, for the purpose of correcting that evil. It has been corrected; but it seems to me that to bring the clergymen of this city without pay to the Capitol to officiate, is imposing a burden on them. Besides, these clergymen cannot become acquainted with us. We cannot look to them as we should look to a Chaplain of the Senate. I think the plan of the last Congress is a very poor substitute for the former plan of having a Chaplain of the body, to whom we can look and consider as such; a Chaplain who would become acquainted with us, and who would know the interests and wants of the body. I hope, therefore . . . that the Senate will elect a Chaplain.[14]

After only brief discussion, Senator Wilson's colleagues granted his request and adopted a resolution to elect a chaplain. They then proceeded to elect the Reverend Phineas Gurley, a Presbyterian of Washington, as the Senate's fortieth chaplain.

In more recent times, charges of "electioneering" have been raised about the chaplaincy, and some have complained about the

The Reverend Richard C. Halverson has served as Senate chaplain since 1981. *Office of the Senate Chaplain*

money spent for the chaplain's salary. But I think Senator Wilson understood the importance of the office. The Senate needs a chaplain who is well acquainted with it, who knows its interests and knows its members. Our current chaplain, the Reverend Richard C. Halverson, is the sixtieth individual to hold the office of chaplain of the Senate, and he is a good example of what I am talking about. He has been our chaplain for many years now, and during that time he has gotten to know the Senate and to know us, his flock.

During my three decades in the Senate, I have known three Senate chaplains: Dr. Halverson and his two immediate predecessors, the Reverend Edward Lee Roy Elson and the Reverend Frederick Brown Harris. I should now like to tell senators a little more about the first two of these chaplains who served during my time.

The very first day that I stood before the Senate was Wednesday, January 7, 1959. I was a green freshman in the Senate that day. Before my credentials were presented and before I took the oath of office, the session was opened with a prayer by Chaplain Harris. His words moved me deeply.

Summoned by a new year and a new session to face matters that pertain to the nation's welfare, before we talk to one another and to a listening world, we would turn to Thee, without whose guidance and help our feeble hands will fail and our striving will be losing.[15]

Although I was new to the Senate, the Reverend Mr. Harris had already been its chaplain for almost fifteen years and would continue for another decade. This tenure of nearly twenty-five years, beginning in 1942, was broken only by the two-year chaplaincy of the Reverend Peter Marshall from 1947 to 1949. Harris was thus the longest-serving chaplain in the Senate's history.

Tall, with gray hair and a lean, craggy face, the Reverend Frederick Brown Harris looked like just the man to lead such a diverse flock. He was born in England in 1883, the son of a minister, and came to the United States as a small boy. He was raised in New Jersey, studied for the Methodist ministry at Dickinson College in Pennsylvania, and was ordained in 1923. In 1924, he was assigned to historic Foundry Methodist Church here in Washington and stayed on for thirty years, retiring in 1955.

Frederick Brown Harris once learned that his job as the Senate's chaplain was not without some peril. Around 1:30 p.m. on the afternoon of July 18, 1961, just after he had left the chamber, there was a terrible crash in the hallway. The whole chamber shook. Senator John Pastore of Rhode Island stopped speaking in mid-sentence. Majority Leader Mike Mansfield rushed into the hallway and took charge of the situation. An enormous temporary wall, covering the

The Reverend Frederick Brown Harris was the longest-serving Senate chaplain. *U.S. Senate Historical Office*

entire area where the public elevators are now located, had crashed, trapping and injuring several tourists and employees. Harris was one of the most seriously wounded, with two severe gashes over his eye and behind his ear. Six days later, however, after several stitches and a little rest, Chaplain Harris returned to the Senate.

My most vivid memory of the Reverend Mr. Harris is from that terrible day of November 22, 1963, when we learned that President Kennedy had been shot. The Chaplain rushed to the Hill when he heard the news. I was in the chamber when he arrived to pray with us, and I shall never forget his theme from the lines of one of my favorite poets, Edwin Markham:

    And when he fell in whirlwind, he went
      down
    As when a lordly cedar, green with boughs,

    Goes down with a great shout upon the hills,
    And leaves a lonesome place against the
      sky.[16]

When Frederick Brown Harris retired as our chaplain in 1969, he was succeeded by the Reverend Edward Lee Roy Elson, who had originally planned to go to West Point but answered, instead, the call to the ministry. After serving as an army chaplain during World War II, he was called to Washington in 1946 as pastor of the National Presbyterian Church. A few years later, he officiated at a very special baptism. In February of 1953, he baptized President Dwight D. Eisenhower, the first president ever baptized while in office.

Elson told this story of the events leading up to that day. The president had been raised in a religious family belonging to the Church of the River Brethren, a small denomination that only baptizes adults. By the time Eisenhower was old enough to be baptized, he was traveling all over the country and, later, the world. During his 1952 campaign, several of his aides urged him to join a church but he replied, "I'd no sooner join a church during a campaign than I'd join a labor union." He said he would wait until it was clear he was acting out of conscience, not expediency, and shortly after his first inauguration, he sought out Chaplain Elson.

As chaplain, Elson introduced several important "firsts" into the Senate. In 1971, he invited the first woman minister to pray in the Senate, and, later, he invited the first nun, and then the first American Indian holy man, an eighty-three-year-old Sioux who brought his peace pipe.

The duties that chaplains, from Samuel Provoost through Richard Halverson, perform for us are not all written down, but they are numerous and have evolved over two centuries. Just about all the chaplain is required to do in the Senate chamber is to

The Reverend Edward Lee Roy Elson, Senate chaplain during the 1970's, appears here with Senators Hugh Scott, *left*, and Mike Mansfield.

U.S. Senate Historical Office

open our daily deliberations with a prayer. Incidentally, before 1939, prayers were delivered only at the start of each new Legislative Day. Because Legislative Days—then as now—often ran for a number of calendar days, it was not unusual for many days to pass without an opening prayer. In February 1939, the Senate adopted a resolution which provided that "the Chaplain shall open each calendar day's session of the Senate with prayer." On February 29, 1960, the Senate adopted a resolution providing that, during round-the-clock continuous sessions, "the Presiding Officer shall temporarily suspend the business of the Senate at 12 o'clock noon each day for the . . . daily prayer by the Chaplain of the Senate." Senators have, from time to time, delivered the prayer.[17]

The Reverend Peter Marshall once said he sometimes felt that the chaplain was a little like a bit of parsley garnishing the political platter. But his prayers could often help members who were caught up in their own immediate battles to put the nation's needs into perspective. His prayer of June 17, 1947, is a case in point. Aware that the day's schedule promised to bring heated debate over a host of relatively inconsequential items, Marshall began with this prayer: "Since we strain at gnats and swallow camels, give us a new standard of values and the ability to know a trifle when we see it and to deal with it as such." [18] This is a good example of what Peter Marshall believed was the unspoken rule regarding Senate prayers, "Keep it short!" He once noted, "I find that the Senators appreciate my prayers in inverse ratio to their length."

In addition to the daily prayer, the chaplain schedules and instructs the many guest chaplains whom senators occasionally nominate to come before us. Although the number of guest chaplains is now limited to two per month, there was once no ceiling on the number. This prompted the Reverend Mr. Harris to note to Majority Leader Lyndon Johnson that he had been replaced seventeen times in just a few weeks. "Now look here, Reverend," Senator Johnson consoled, "if you want me to call a halt to this sort of thing, you let me know, and we'll just restrict the number of visiting preachers." Harris did not remind Johnson that he already had two requests from the senator's office on his desk requesting the privilege for two Texans.[19]

Another of the chaplain's duties is to perform our weddings and, sadly, our funerals. Chaplain Harris once performed a wedding at a specially constructed altar in the Caucus Room of the Russell Building for a sixty-nine-year-old Western Union messenger and a sixty-year-old widow. During his term as

On February 21, 1939, the day the Senate began opening each daily session with a prayer, Senate Chaplain ZeBarney Thorne Phillips offered the invocation. *U.S. Senate Historical Office*

Senate chaplain, in addition to conducting the funerals for several senators, he also led the funerals of General Douglas MacArthur, Vice President Alben Barkley, and President Herbert Hoover. Chaplain Elson conducted the funerals of Presidents Eisenhower and Johnson, and of FBI Director J. Edgar Hoover, as well as those for several of our former colleagues.

While a sad subject, the history of Senate funerals is an interesting one. The first senator to die in office was William Grayson of Virginia, who died on March 12, 1790, just a year after taking office. Although he had lived only fifty years, he had fought under Washington at the Battle of Monmouth and had been a member of the Continental Congress before coming to the Senate.

The first official action taken by the Senate on the death of one of its own was in 1799 when Senator Henry Tazewell of Virginia died. Since Tazewell died in Philadelphia, far from friends and family, his funeral

and burial at Christ Church in Philadelphia were supervised by a committee of his friends in the Senate.

From time to time, especially in the nineteenth and early- to mid-twentieth century, the families of deceased senators have chosen to have the funeral services performed in the Senate chamber. With the casket placed in the open space before the dais, in front of the reporters' tables, the services were conducted by the chaplain of the Senate. Often, the president and his cabinet, justices, ambassadors, and members of the House joined senators in paying their respects to their fallen colleague. A doorkeeper announced the groups of dignitaries as they entered. When the services were concluded, a committee of senators would accompany the remains back home for burial.

One of the most elaborate of the more recent funerals in the chamber was that of Senator Joseph Robinson of Arkansas in 1937. At the time of his death, Senator Rob-

On September 10, 1969, the body of Senator Everett Dirksen lay in state in the Capitol Rotunda.

Architect of the Capitol

inson was the Democratic majority leader and had been a member of this body for twenty-four years. His friends were legion, and the chamber was overflowing with floral tributes. The most recent such funeral service in the chamber, conducted by Chaplain Harris, was that of Senator William Langer, whose family requested the privilege in 1959.

Senators have also been among the twenty-four individuals whose remains the nation has honored in the Rotunda of the Capitol. The first was Henry Clay of Kentucky, who lay in state in the Rotunda on

July 1, 1852, after a funeral service in the old Senate chamber down the hall. He was followed in 1874 by Charles Sumner of Massachusetts and in 1875 by Vice President and former Senator Henry Wilson of Massachusetts, who died in the Vice President's Room right outside this chamber. Senator John Logan of Illinois, whose funeral took place in this chamber, lay in state in the Rotunda in 1886, followed by President and former Senator Warren Harding of Ohio in 1923, Robert Taft, Sr., of Ohio in 1953, President and former Senator John F. Kennedy in 1963, Everett Dirksen of Illinois in 1969, President

Architect Benjamin Latrobe designed the massive sandstone cenotaphs that stand as memorials in Congressional Cemetery. *Library of Congress*

and former Senator Lyndon Johnson in 1973, Senator and former Vice President Hubert Humphrey in 1978, and, most recently, former Senator Claude Pepper in 1989.

A particularly impressive site to visit in this city is the burial ground of several of the early senators. I do not mean Arlington National Cemetery, but the less-well-known Congressional Cemetery at the far end of East Capitol Street. In 1817, the vestry of Washington's Christ Church set aside one hundred burial sites within its parish cemetery for the interment of members of Congress. Until the 1860's and the beginnings of Arlington, Congressional Cemetery was the national burial ground.

When one visits this peaceful spot, the first things to strike one's eye are the long rows of the so-called Latrobe cenotaphs, om-

inous sandstone memorials to those congressmen who died in office from 1807 to 1877. The second architect of the Capitol, Benjamin Henry Latrobe, designed these massive square bases with conical caps. Although several hundred of these memorials were erected, one for each congressman who died in office, only eighty bodies were actually interred under them. In many cases, burial in Congressional Cemetery was only temporary, until seasons changed and the dirt roads leading home became passable once more.

Occasionally, the government would erect a cenotaph to a private citizen. One bears the name of Push-Ma-Ta-Ha, a Choctaw chief who died of diphtheria while in Washington to negotiate a treaty. Carved on his cenotaph are his last words, "When I am gone, let the big guns boom over me." In accordance with his wish, he was given a full military funeral.

The practice of erecting these curious four-and-one-half-foot-tall monuments to each deceased congressman's memory was halted in 1877, largely because of a speech by Senator George Frisbie Hoar of Massachusetts, who said that the thought of being buried beneath one of them added a new terror to death.[20]

Although largely overlooked today, Congressional Cemetery remains the final monument to a fascinating assortment of famous Americans. When I recently visited the cemetery, I found the tomb of Vice President Elbridge Gerry, a signer of the Declaration of Independence and delegate to the Constitutional Convention. Gerry, for whom the "Gerrymander" was named, was stricken while riding in his carriage to preside over the Senate. William Thornton, who designed the Capitol Building, and Samuel A. Otis, the first secretary of the Senate, are buried there. So, too, are Civil War photographer Mathew Brady, Marine Corps bandmaster John Philip Sousa, and FBI Director J. Edgar Hoover.

Also in Congressional Cemetery stands a recent cenotaph erected in memory of Hale Boggs, the Democratic majority leader of the House of Representatives who disappeared on a flight that went down somewhere between Anchorage and Juneau, Alaska, in October 1972. Since Boggs' body was never recovered, his widow, Representative Lindy Boggs, believed that a cenotaph in Congressional Cemetery would be a fitting memorial. And, indeed, Hale Boggs seems very much at home among monuments to Henry Clay, John C. Calhoun, and others whose lives were so thoroughly identified with the history of Congress.[21]

We are all familiar with, and grateful for, the opportunity we are afforded of offering tributes from the floor to our friends in the Senate when they are taken from us by death. Many of us have had occasion to rise in the chamber on the days set aside for such tributes and pay homage to some friend. Our parting words are gathered together in a bound volume for family and friends as lasting evidence of our esteem.

Until the mid-1950's, a special memorial service would be held near the beginning of a new session to honor all the members who had passed away since the last such service. These services sometimes took place here in the Senate chamber, and sometimes in the House chamber.

I can remember, when I served in the House, attending memorial services conducted in the House chamber, at which a quartet of representatives would gather in the well of the House and sing the old familiar hymns. I was very impressed with those memorial services and with the harmony of the hymns that were sung by the House quartet.

I believe that the last memorial ceremony (as opposed to a funeral service) held in the Senate was in 1948, and the last joint service, in which Senator Brien McMahon of Connecticut was honored along with several members of the House, was in 1953. These ceremonies were generally conducted by the chaplain and were indeed moving. The walls would reverberate with the notes of an organ and of voices raised in sacred song. The 1953 service, conducted in the House chamber, began with a quartet of representatives, accompanied by a colleague at the piano, singing the excellent verses of "Have Thine Own Way, Lord."

There were two especially poignant moments during these ceremonies. One was the solemn reading of the roll of deceased members. As each name was read, a lovely rose was placed in a vase in the front of the chamber. Finally, the program ended with a serviceman playing the mournful notes of Taps, which echoed through the halls.

From 1827 to 1882, senators took the oath of office on this Senate Bible. *United States Senate Collection*

sentative Brooks Hays of Arkansas and Senator Mike Monroney of Oklahoma conceived the idea of setting aside a room in the building where members could go to sort out their thoughts and pray, away from the turmoil of the floor and their offices. This peaceful room was designed by Architect of the Capitol George Stewart, who skillfully achieved a non-denominational decor. The room was officially opened in the spring of 1955.

I believe the Prayer Room's most impressive feature is the beautiful stained-glass window, a gift from a group of California craftsmen. In the center of the window, against a ruby background, is the kneeling figure of George Washington, representing the people of America at prayer. Above and below the kneeling Washington are the two sides of the Great Seal of the United States. There are no services in this room, nor is it generally open to the public. It is a room for us, for members of Congress, as Speaker Sam Rayburn said at its dedication, "who want to be alone with their God."

The chaplain visits senators when they go to the hospital, represents the Senate in appearances before church groups across the nation, and is host to visiting religious figures who come to the Capitol. On occasion, chaplains of the Senate have led groups of saffron-robed Tibetan monks on tours of the building.

In closing, I would like to repeat something from that 1854 report vindicating the office of the chaplain:

If there be a God who hears prayer—as we believe there is—we submit, that there never was a deliberative body that so eminently needed the fervent prayers of righteous men as the Congress of the United States.

To that I say, Amen!

The same chaplain who is there to conduct our happy and sad services is also always available to counsel and provide information to us, our families, and our staffs. The chaplain often gets calls such as, "Where is the passage in the Bible about the seven fat and seven lean years?" or "What is the name of the Roman Catholic archbishop of . . . ?"

With his counterpart in the House, our chaplain shares responsibility for the beautiful Capitol Prayer Room. I hope that senators have all had the chance to visit this quiet retreat just off the Rotunda. In 1952, Repre-

CHAPTER 13

Reporters of Debates and the *Congressional Record*

July 21, 1980*

Mr. President, at this moment as I speak, my words are being recorded by an official reporter of debates. By tomorrow morning, these remarks and all other items of business conducted on the Senate floor today will have been transcribed and printed in the *Congressional Record*. This daily volume, which may run to several hundred pages, will then be distributed to the offices of every member of the Senate and the House, to various federal and state agencies, and to individual subscribers—many of them public and university libraries—all across this nation and abroad. Currently, more than 21,000 copies of the *Record* are printed for each day that Congress is in session. Within approximately three years, today's proceedings, and the record of all other daily sessions of the Senate and House during this session of Congress, will be bound in the permanent volumes of the *Congressional Record*.

This is a remarkable achievement which, because of its speed and reliability, we may possibly take for granted. The *Record* is a vital instrument of the legislative process without which our work would be greatly hampered. We rely on the *Record* to follow the progress of legislation in both houses, from a bill's introduction to its passage or defeat. When we are busy with committee meetings or other Senate business, we depend on the *Record* for a complete account of the floor discussion we might have missed. When we have completed our work, the *Record*, together with the *Senate Journal* and committee reports, preserves the legislative histories to which the courts, long into the future, will refer in determining the congressional intent behind the laws we have written.

Mr. President, the *Congressional Record* is a symbol of our democracy through which the people may observe the making of their laws and may hold their lawmakers accountable for their words and deeds. I, therefore, wish to discuss today the men and women who have served as our official reporters and the evolution of the *Congressional Record*.

The Constitution provides that each house of the Congress shall keep a journal of its proceedings, a mandate that both the House and the Senate have faithfully upheld since the beginning of the First Congress in 1789. These journals are, in effect, minute books or summaries of the floor proceedings pub-

_____

* Updated April 1989

[311]

lished after each session of the Congress is completed. The *Record*—as distinguished from these journals—has grown and been perfected over the years as necessity and political sensibility have required, even though there is no requirement in the Constitution for its publication.

The Senate, for the first almost seven years of its existence, kept its doors closed to both the press and the public (except for a few days during the debate regarding the seating of Albert Gallatin). From the outset, however, the House of Representatives, following the practice of various state legislatures, admitted both press and public to its deliberations. The smaller Senate, which envisioned playing an advisory role to the president, chose to observe the custom of the earlier Continental and Confederation congresses and the Constitutional Convention by conducting its business in secret. Yet, outsiders, particularly those from the press who were interested in the Senate's activities, had little difficulty in learning the substance thereof from its talkative members.

The greatest pressure for open sessions came from the state legislatures, whose duty it was, at that time, to elect United States senators. Virginia and other southern states, especially, believed that they could keep track of their senators' legislative behavior only through open sessions. For the first five years, however, their efforts were turned back by a majority of senators who argued that secrecy ensured their freedom of discussion. Indeed, the Senate chamber in New York had no galleries for reporters or other visitors, nor did the Senate chamber in Philadelphia have galleries until late in 1795.

In 1794, a major debate took place in the Senate over whether Pennsylvania Republican Senator-elect Albert Gallatin, a financial wizard and thorn in the side of President George Washington's Federalist administration, had satisfied the Constitution's nine-year residency requirement for senators. Meeting in Philadelphia, the Senate came under increasing public pressure to open its doors for the debate over the seating of a Pennsylvania senator. After agreeing to admit the public only for the Gallatin debate, the Senate, almost immediately, decided to open legislative sessions permanently following the construction of suitable galleries. These galleries were built in the summer of 1795 and opened to the public that December. Shortly afterward, the first substantive debates of the Senate were published in the Philadelphia newspapers. Unfortunately for those interested in the Senate's early history, however, they were not the verbatim accounts to which we have become accustomed today. Since these first accounts were prepared by newspaper reporters, they often reflected the partisan biases of their editors. Nor were the reporters admitted to the Senate floor; they sat in the galleries and often missed remarks that were difficult to hear.[1]

To rectify this situation, the Senate, by a vote of 16 to 12, on January 5, 1802, resolved that stenographers and note takers should be admitted to the Senate floor and assigned to "such place . . . as the President shall allot." Three days later, the debates of the Senate began to appear regularly in the columns of the *National Intelligencer*, a tri-weekly Washington paper that provided the first reports of debate.

The founder of the *National Intelligencer* was Samuel Harrison Smith, a close ally of President Jefferson. Upon Smith's retirement in 1810, the paper was taken over by Joseph Gales, Jr., and William W. Seaton, two stenographic reporters. Seaton reported on the House of Representatives, while Gales was the sole reporter in the Senate from 1807 to 1820.[2]

The *National Intelligencer* published its notes on the debates, which other newspapers

William W. Seaton, *left*, and Joseph Gales, Jr., *right*, published congressional debates in the *National Intelligencer*.
National Portrait Gallery

around the country then clipped and reprinted. While the *Intelligencer* generally performed a creditable job, shorthand reporting was still in a primitive stage, and the results were often haphazard. The reporters had their political favorites and nonfavorites, and their coverage varied accordingly. Some senators neglected to submit copies of their speeches or to correct the early drafts of the reporters' notes. Others, such as Daniel Webster, would visit the offices of Gales and Seaton after the Senate had adjourned to correct and elaborate upon versions of their speeches. It is also alleged that, on one occasion, "a reporter of the *National Intelligencer* fell asleep while taking a member's speech. After a half hour's sweet restorer, the reporter, refreshed, resumed his reportorial work. Another honorable member had the floor but the reporter did not distinguish. Appeared as one speech parts of two speeches, different in character, emanating from the same speaker."[3]

The *National Intelligencer* held its position by patronage, both houses of Congress having elected Gales and Seaton as their official printers. In the 1820's, Gales and Seaton expanded their activities by publishing the *Register of Debates*, which provided fuller reports on congressional debates and proceedings than those which appeared in their newspaper. The *Register of Debates*, a private venture, was thus the forerunner of our current *Congressional Record*.

In 1829, the political tides turned, and Gales and Seaton lost their position as congressional printers. Deeply in debt, they looked for new projects to raise revenue, publishing first the *American State Papers*—a remarkable collection of early American historical documents—and then the *Annals of Congress*, which went back to the First Congress and filled in the gap for congressional proceedings through May 1824 when the *Register of Debates* began. The *Annals*, in forty-

Francis P. Blair, shown here with his wife, published the proceedings of the House and Senate in the *Congressional Globe* starting in 1833.   *Library of Congress*

two volumes, were printed between 1834 and 1856.

In 1833, rival publishers, Francis Blair and John C. Rives, won the title of official printers for Congress and launched the *Congressional Globe.* Blair and Rives hired their own stenographers, and, for the next four years, both the *Globe* and the *Register* published the Senate and House proceedings. Finally, in 1837, Gales and Seaton terminated the *Register of Debates.* The *Congressional Globe* continued its work from 1833 until 1873.[4]

During those years, the reporters of debates worked directly for their newspapers. Not until 1873, when the Government Printing Office began the *Congressional Record*, did Congress directly hire its own reporters, although reporters had been paid at public ex-

pense since 1855. They have remained as Senate and House employees since that time.

It was during the era of the *Congressional Globe*, in 1848, that verbatim reporting became standard. Senate reporters used handwritten shorthand—either the Pitman or Gregg system of pen shorthand—exclusively from 1848 until 1974 when the stenotype machine first made its appearance on the Senate floor. On March 31, 1989, an era in the reporting of Senate debates ended with the retirement of William D. Mohr, a Pitman writer who served the Senate for more than twenty years. Today, all of the reporters use machine shorthand, just as the gentleman who stands within reach of me is doing at this time.

Over the years, the format of the published proceedings has gradually developed into the style of the current *Congressional Record.* By 1862, the role of the shorthand reporters was so well defined that the Confederate Congress also adopted the same procedure. In 1865, Congress provided that the *Globe* should be published daily and delivered to the members of both houses at their next meeting.

Mr. President, the official reporters of debates came into existence on March 4, 1873, as a result of the recommendations of a commission headed by Senator Henry Anthony of Rhode Island. Since then, they have performed their work efficiently and unobtrusively in the crossfire of debate in this chamber. They should not, however, be seen as an anonymous group. It is possible to trace the various individuals who have performed this task and to mention some of the most outstanding among them.

The founder of the Senate's corps of verbatim reporters was Richard Sutton, who sat in the gallery of the British House of Commons with Charles Dickens when both were young shorthand writers for the press. Sutton came to this country in 1838 and

The verbatim record of Senate debates was made by shorthand reporters such as the one depicted here in the midst of "A Stormy Sitting."   *Harper's Weekly, September 15, 1888*

Stenographer Dennis Murphy reported Senate debates for nearly fifty years. *U.S. Senate Historical Office*

worked as the Washington correspondent for the *New York Herald.* In December 1848, Sutton and a group of shorthand writers began reporting the proceedings of the Senate for the *Congressional Globe.* Among those working for Sutton was fourteen-year-old Dennis F. Murphy, hired on the advice of Senator John C. Calhoun. Upon Sutton's retirement in 1869, Murphy became head of the corps of reporters.

It is worth pausing a moment to make special reference to Dennis Murphy and his family and their remarkable record of 112 years of continuous service to the Senate. Dennis Murphy continued as a reporter of debates from 1848 until his death in 1896. His brother James served as a Senate reporter for twenty years, and another brother, Edward, served nearly thirty years, from 1890 until his death in 1919. Edward's son, James W. Murphy, joined the corps of re-

porters in 1896, became chief reporter in 1934, and remained on the job until his retirement in 1960. James Murphy was chief reporter when I first came to the Senate, and I find it startling to think that his uncle had been appointed by John C. Calhoun.[5]

Other significant figures who have served as reporters have included Theodore Shuey, who labored for sixty-five years, from 1868 until 1933. Shuey had participated in the battle of Gettysburg during the Civil War and had kept a detailed diary of his experiences in Pitman shorthand. At the time of his Senate service, he was considered the most scholarly reporter in the world. For over sixty years, he did not miss a single session of the Senate.

Some of my colleagues will recall John D. Rhodes, who retired as chief reporter of debates in 1963, after forty-five years of service. Rhodes arrived during the tumultuous debate over the Versailles Treaty in 1919 and retired in the year of the Nuclear Test Ban Treaty in 1963. There was also Gregor MacPherson, known as "Mr. Mac," who served for thirty-two years, until his death in 1966. Following MacPherson as chief reporter was Charles Drescher. From 1974 to 1988, our chief reporter was G. Russell Walker, who was succeeded by C.J. Reynolds.

Seven reporters of debates actually appear on the floor of the Senate to record the proceedings. Supporting them are three staff assistants, the chief reporter, and six expert transcribers. The chief reporter and his assistants are under the jurisdiction of the secretary of the Senate.

Mr. President, all of us who serve in the United States Senate owe a great debt to the reporters of debates. This debt was most eloquently described by Senator Everett Dirksen, who said:

It baffles me when I think of the readability of the *Congressional Record,* because, when all is said and done, I

Trucks from the Government Printing Office lined the front of the Capitol in the 1920's, ready to unload copies of the *Congressional Record*.

think it will be agreed that Congress is really the home of the split infinitive, where it finds its finest fruition; this is the place where the dangling participle is certainly nourished; this is the home of the broken sentence; and if there were no dashes I do not know what our distinguished official reporters would do. This is the home where, with impunity, we can ignore the comma and the period, we can ignore the colon and the semicolon, we can ignore the exclamation mark and the question mark; and yet, somehow, out of this great funnel it all comes out all right, and it is always readable.

It was readable, Senator Dirksen concluded, because of the endeavors of the official reporters of Senate debate.[6]

These reporters watch out for us. They check our grammar and double-check our quotations. Since Scripture is often quoted on the Senate floor, the reporters keep a Bible at hand to authenticate our verses and citations—and, by the way, it is my favorite, the King James Version. I understand that this handsome Bible was given to the reporters in the 1930's by Senator Huey P. Long, the father of Senator Russell Long from Louisiana. When he gave the Bible to the reporters, Senator Huey Long related how his wife had been reading his speeches in the *Congressional Record* and told him:

[317]

I want to see those wonderfully educated reporters of the Senate who take those supposed quotations you are making from the Bible and fit them into your speeches exactly as they are in the Scripture! [7]

All the reporters sign this Bible on the day they are appointed, and the dates of their retirements and deaths are also noted therein.

The reporters of debates live by the rules and make the members of the Senate live up to the rules which we have set for the *Congressional Record.* Profanity and obscenities in debate are prohibited. Indeed, in 1921, one member of the House of Representatives, Thomas L. Blanton of Texas, was censured by his colleagues—after a motion to expel him had been rejected—for having printed in the *Record* a letter from a GPO employee which contained profane language. [8]

Maps, diagrams, or illustrations may not be inserted in the *Record* without the approval of the Joint Committee on Printing. On only one occasion has an editorial cartoon appeared in the *Congressional Record.* It was introduced on October 3, 1913, by Senator Benjamin Tillman of South Carolina. "Senator Tillman's Allegorical Cow," as the cartoon was entitled, portrayed two large cows spanning the continent. The first cow was shown being fed by farmers in the West and being milked by Wall Street in the East. The second cow, facing in the opposite direction, showed western and southern farmers as being "disappointed" because they could not feed the cow on "income tax[es]" paid by New England and Wall Street moneyed interests fed by the farmers' cow. A few weeks later, senators were criticizing the inclusion of "cows in the Record." [9]

No member of the Senate is permitted to speak disparagingly of any other member or of any other state in the Union. A member may make no more than one revision of his or her remarks for the permanent *Record*; it shall consist only of corrections of the origi-

nal copy; and it shall not include deletions of correct material, substitutions for correct material, or additions of new subject matter. No italics, boldface, capitals, or unusual indention—except where appearing in quoted material—may be used for emphasis. No full reports of committees will be printed in the *Record* if previously printed elsewhere. No material in a foreign language may be printed, except with the permission of the Joint Committee on Printing.

Mr. President, the reporter who is taking down my words as I speak is normally here on the floor for just ten minutes at a time. After ten minutes have elapsed, this reporter will be replaced by another reporter and, at that time, will return to the office of the official reporters, where the notes will be dictated onto dictating machine discs, or, in the case of the stenotype machine reporters, the notes will be either dictated or note-read. The dictation or the stenotyped notes will be transcribed by a team of six expert transcribers.

The typed transcript is returned to the reporter, who compares it with the original notes, inserts appropriate headlines, checks for conformity with the *Government Printing Office Style Manual* and Senate procedural requirements, and makes minor grammatical corrections.

The transcript is then submitted to the chief reporter for further editing, collating, indexing, and arrangement for printing in the *Congressional Record.*

Remarks made by senators in the Senate chamber are usually available in typewritten form within one-half to three-quarters of an hour after delivery. Under the rules of the Senate, senators are then permitted to make minor alterations but are not supposed to make substantive changes in their remarks.

Senators will often help out the reporters by making available to them the prepared statements—just as I am doing now—out-

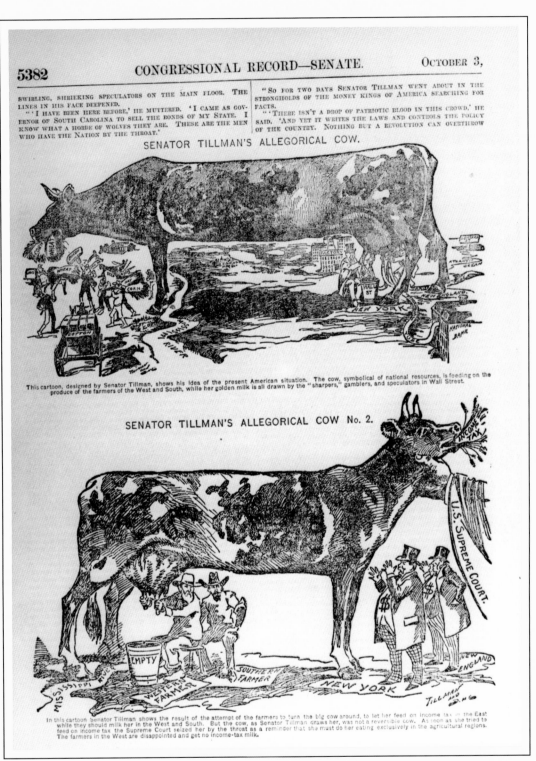

Senator Benjamin Tillman's cow is the only editorial cartoon ever to appear in the *Congressional Record*.

Congressional Record, October 3, 1913

Reporters of debates—whether using shorthand in the past or stenotype machines today—spend ten minute shifts on the Senate floor.

U.S. Capitol Historical Society

lines, or other material they used when they addressed the Senate. We can be assured that the reporters appreciate this assistance as they try to cope with senators who whisper and senators who shout, and with the wide and sonorous range of regional accents. In fact, Gregor MacPherson used to refer to any senator who handed a prepared copy of his remarks to the reporters as a "statesman." [10]

When a debate gets especially fast and furious, we sometimes make it difficult for the reporter to follow our colloquies. Once when the late senator from Michigan, Philip Hart, was presiding, he found it necessary to gavel the Senate to order and said:

Gentlemen, gentlemen. The reporter is having difficulty; you are both talking at once. Even I am having trouble understanding what you are saying.

Some senators are known for their particularly rapid rate of speech. The late senator from Minnesota, Hubert Humphrey, was an eloquent speaker, but his rapid-fire words could be quite intimidating to all but the most experienced reporters. One newcomer to the corps of official reporters related how the senior reporters warned him, "Oh, wait until you get Humphrey; wait until you get Humphrey!" But they also gave him a useful tip: while Senator Humphrey spoke very rapidly, he frequently repeated himself for emphasis. Senator Humphrey, I understand, never had any complaints about the quality of their reporting. [11]

In addition to prepared remarks, senators may submit to the legislative clerk prepared statements, which they do not intend to read, for inclusion in the body of the *Record* under the headline "Additional Statements," or as "Extensions of Remarks" at the back of the *Record*, although this section is used primarily by members of the House of Representatives. A statement that is inserted but not read is indicated in the *Record* by a small black circle, a printing symbol known as a "bullet," so that readers will know that it was not actually spoken on the floor of the Senate.

Mr. President, this last innovation, the "bullet," was added in 1977, as part of a

Photographs taken in 1908 show reporters of debates reviewing their transcripts, *above*, and dictating their notes, *below right*.
Library of Congress

series of so-called reforms to improve the readability of the *Record* of the Senate proceedings. In 1985, the House discarded the "bullet" in favor of different type sizes to indicate speeches inserted without being read. The Senate continues to employ the "bullet."

I must say that I am not so greatly pleased in one respect, at least, with the changes we have inaugurated. A senator is required to read at least the opening sentence of a statement in order to prevent the bullet from being used. For this reason, many senators now come to the floor and read sections of a speech, or at least the first sentence, in order to avoid the bullet, even though the full speech is not read into the *Record*. This takes up the time of the Senate needlessly and denies our television viewers the full flavor and content of the speech. For these reasons, I cannot fully subscribe to the use of the bullet as a very useful reform.

At any rate, that is the way it is.

Since early in 1970, senators who announce live pairs on votes are listed under a heading "Present and Giving a Live Pair as Previously Recorded," with their positions shown as for or against the particular measure. This was done at my request during the time Mike Mansfield was majority leader.

The program announced by the majority leader is placed in the *Record* immediately prior to the recess or adjournment for the day. Listed at the very end of the Senate proceedings are executive nominations received and executive nominations confirmed during the day's session.

Messages from the House and the president are collected during the day and printed in one place in the morning business, rather than sprinkled throughout the proceedings.

The Daily Digest at the end of the *Record* includes an entry showing the record votes taken, together with a running total. This is another innovation which I brought about during the leadership of Senator Mansfield, because I felt that it would be useful to senators if they could find in one place in the *Record* every day the total number of roll-call votes that had occurred during the session up to that time.

Mr. President, I would like to briefly summarize the makeup of the *Congressional Record*, which consists of Senate Proceedings, House Proceedings, Extensions of Remarks, and the Daily Digest.

The Senate Proceedings are alternated with the House Proceedings on a daily basis, as far as possible, with the Senate being first in the *Record* one day and the House first the next day. Pages for each of these components are numbered consecutively from the first day of each session. Senate page numbers are preceded by an S, House pages by an H, Extensions of Remarks pages by an E, and Daily Digest pages by a D.

The Extensions of Remarks and the Daily Digest are always the last portions of the

Record. Between them, one will often find what might be called "filler" material. This material includes: Laws and Rules for Publication of the *Record*; a listing of representatives and senators and their office numbers; officers of the House and Senate; committee assignments of members; and members of the Supreme Court and certain federal courts.

The Daily Digest was the product of the Legislative Reorganization Act of 1946—which, in so many ways, helped to streamline and "modernize" the Senate's work. By the mid-1940's, the *Record* had become so thick that without some sort of daily index it was becoming practically unusable. Dr. Floyd M. Riddick, who was already a specialist in congressional procedure, recommended to the Special Committee on Legislative Reorganization that they create a digest to be added to the *Record* with the highlights of each day's activities as a handy reference. His proposal became part of the Legislative Reorganization Act of 1946, and, at the beginning of the Eightieth Congress in 1947, Dr. Riddick was invited to become the Senate editor of the first Daily Digest, a post which he held until he became the assistant parliamentarian in 1951.[12]

Starting the Digest was no easy task. Committee clerks, already burdened with their own work, resisted taking the additional notes for Digest citations. Yet, the Digest had only one staff member covering all the Senate committees and another covering the Senate chamber. Eventually, through persistence, a system was developed, and the Digest became the integral part of the *Record* that it is today.

To ascertain what Senate business was transacted on the previous day, the reader of the *Congressional Record* should turn to the Daily Digest and look under the heading "Senate." There, one will find the chamber action, such as bills introduced and reported and measures passed, as well as a brief description of the legislation. Also included, if applicable, are messages from the House, presidential communications, committee meetings and lists of witnesses who presented testimony, committee hearing notices, appointments, confirmations, and record votes. With the indicated page numbers, the reader may use the Daily Digest to find the location of the desired material in the Senate proceedings.

The Senate proceedings appear chronologically in the *Record*, with several exceptions. All material and statements relating to routine morning business are assembled in one or more sections, usually near the beginning and again toward the end of the proceedings. This category includes messages received during the day from the House and the president, measures introduced, additional cosponsors, resolutions submitted, petitions and memorials, and other morning business transactions permitted by the Senate rules. Statements on introduced bills appear in a particular section of the *Record*, together with the bill titles, but if a senator introduces a measure under a special order to address the Senate, his remarks remain in the *Record* at the place where they were given.

The chief reporter may also place unspoken statements, when properly submitted, so that they appear in the *Record* during the consideration of the measure to which they refer.

In the debate portion of the proceedings, one page of the *Record*, as a general rule, covers approximately ten minutes of free-flowing uninterrupted debate.

Over the last decade, inflation has increased the cost of producing the *Record* rather sharply as it has everything else. For its value to the nation, however, the *Congressional Record* is surely worth its cost.

Mr. President, one cannot speak of the *Congressional Record* without taking into account the periodic criticism it has received from those who insist that it must be a verbatim record. Back in the 1950's, Oregon Senator Richard Neuberger, himself a former journalist, argued that the *Congressional Record* was not really a record, due to the additions, deletions, and revisions that members were permitted to make. In a somewhat more inflammatory tone, James Nathan Miller repeated the charge in his 1983 *Readers' Digest* article, "Congress' License to Lie," assaulting the *Congressional Record* as "what may be the most outrageous cover-up in Washington." In 1985, the Freedom of Information Center published a report on "Editing the *Congressional Record*," which argued that "control of the *Congressional Record* should be completely removed from the grasp of Congress," in order to prevent congressional "tampering."[13]

These arguments tend to fall into several common errors. First, critics assume that the Constitution mandates Congress to keep a verbatim *Congressional Record*. It does not. The Constitution mandates only that both houses keep journals, which are summarized minutes of their proceedings. As I have pointed out, the *Congressional Record* evolved over time from a private to a governmental publication, and—as stenographic arts improved—from abstracts to a substantially verbatim account. Some critics also believe that the members' revision of the *Record* is a recent phenomenon, whereas, in fact, it has two hundred years of history behind it. Indeed, Representative James Madison, father of our Constitution, warned against hiring official reporters of debates in the Congress because members would ever after bear the onerous responsibility of editing their remarks for publication.

From the very beginnings of Congress, members of both houses have felt the need to edit the written record, both to correct inaccuracies, and to ensure that it adequately captures the spirit of the remarks. A famous case was Senator Daniel Webster's reply to Robert Hayne. As one of his biographers, Irving Bartlett, noted, "The peroration in the reply to Hayne, which thousands of schoolboys over several generations would commit to memory, was not a verbatim report of what Webster said in the Senate, but a consciously literary effort which Webster revised afterward." Webster delivered his peroration in the Senate on January 27, 1830, but his remarks were not published in the *National Intelligencer* until a month later. Webster expressed disappointment that the notes taken by Joseph Gales, and transcribed by Mrs. Gales, did not capture the emotional appeal so evident in the chamber on that memorable day. Over the next few weeks, Webster diligently reworked the speech for publication. We can document his editing, because the Boston Public Library contains Joseph Gales' original shorthand notes, Mrs. Gales' transcription, and Senator Webster's numerous corrections and changes. Claude Fuess, another of Webster's biographers, reported that "a detailed comparison between Mrs. Gales' version and that finally perfected by Webster shows that the latter, in preparing the speech for the press, omitted many sentences, added others, and modified his phraseology so that it was very different from the original." Professor Fuess therefore concluded that "it is obvious that the speech, in its generally accepted phrasing, is not that which was delivered on the floor of the Senate." [14]

A third error is that critics falsely assume that stenography has become an exact art, perhaps even a science, into which members should not intrude. To the contrary, it has been my experience that the reporters of debates welcome all the help they can get, from an advance copy of a senator's remarks, to editing by the senator or his staff to prevent the type of common, irritating, and misleading errors that inevitably emerge in an enter-

prise as large and demanding as the daily *Congressional Record*. There are typographical errors in an average *Congressional Record*, as there are in an average issue of the *New York Times* or *Washington Post*. Still, no member wants to see his words garbled, or risk the consequences. In one speech, for example, I made a reference to politicians "kissing babies," which, to my dismay, appeared in the *Record* as "killing babies." The right to edit one's remarks, therefore, can be an asset to accuracy rather than a detriment.

Many critics also believe that, by making deletions from the *Record*, members are somehow hiding something from the public. In my thirty years in this chamber, I can attest that very little escapes public notice. Senators may delete an offensive remark, or erase an embarrassing exchange, in their efforts to restore some parliamentary civility after the heat of a debate, but, almost without fail, the next morning's newspapers will publish a full account of the deleted words. Members of Congress certainly cannot edit what the press gallery reports, nor retract words that are broadcast over C-SPAN.

Underneath much of the criticism, I suspect, is a fear that the *Congressional Record* tells less about what goes on than it should. On the contrary, the *Record* generally tells more than what happens, giving full texts of bills not read on the floor, and speeches and articles similarly inserted without being read. If members were required to read every statement they prepared for the *Record*, the Senate often would need to be in session twenty-four hours a day. After all, just as one must stand behind a check that one writes, so must the senator who inserts a speech into the *Record* stand behind, and be responsible for, every word, just as if the speech were delivered orally. Some items simply do not need to be read aloud, even though it is important to circulate them among the members of Congress and others who follow its proceedings, to establish a full record for both sides of every debate.

Regardless of this logic, some people remain dissatisfied with the system. In 1984, three members of the House of Representatives went so far as to ask the courts to declare the allegedly corrupt *Congressional Record* unconstitutional, on the grounds that it deprived them of their First Amendment right to receive a faithful account of what was actually said during congressional debates. Both the U.S. District Court and the U.S. Court of Appeals for the District of Columbia wisely dismissed these charges. I note that Judge Abner Mikva, a distinguished former member of the House of Representatives and scholar of its proceedings, cited my initial 1980 address on the reporters of debates as one of his sources for explaining the historical evolution of the *Congressional Record*.

In addition, noting the separation of powers, the court declined to review the way Congress reported its own legislative business and affirmed the dismissal of the private appellants' complaint, stating, "There simply is no first amendment right to receive a verbatim transcript of the proceedings of Congress." [15] Any future changes in the manner of reporting the debates of Congress must, therefore, take place just as they always have in the past, by the deliberation and decision of the members of the Senate and House.

As I close my dissertation on this subject, I would like to express my gratitude—and I am sure I speak on behalf of all my colleagues—to the excellent team of official reporters and to all of the staff who work with them to make the *Congressional Record* readable, informative, and useful, not only to senators but also to the great American public.

CHAPTER 14

Capitol Police

February 3, 1981*

Mr. President, during the spring and summer months, as many as ten thousand persons visit the Capitol Building each day. They come from every state in the Union and from all parts of the world to see for themselves this structure, which has become the symbol of the highest ideals of representative government. Those of us who have visited legislative bodies in other nations never cease to marvel at the wide access that visitors enjoy to this seat of government.

Many come with specific issues or grievances that they wish to discuss with those of us whom they have elected to be their representatives. Others simply want to explore, at first hand, this great citadel of democratic government. Just as our visiting citizens have a right to the widest possible freedom of movement and expression in these halls, so do we, their representatives, have the right to conduct our business without undue delay and without fear of restraint or reprisal.

To maintain this often delicate balance, we are fortunate to have the assistance of a dedicated and well-trained Capitol police force. Today, in my continuing series of statements on the United States Senate, I shall discuss the development of the Capitol police from a single watchman in 1801 to its current posi-

tion as a highly professional law enforcement organization.

During Congress' first twenty-five years in Washington, the Capitol was protected by a single guard, whose charge was simply "to take as much care as possible of the property of the United States." The first guard, John Golding, and his immediate successors lacked the customary police authority to make arrests. We must assume that the solitary guards had frequent occasion to wish that they could call on more than simply the force of their individual personalities. We do know that, from time to time, the guard had to seek assistance from the nearby Marine barracks.[1]

By late 1824, as the construction of the Capitol's Rotunda neared completion, the number of visitors to this building had increased significantly and, accordingly, so had the need for police protection. The arrival of one of this nation's greatest foreign friends, the Marquis de Lafayette, must have placed a great burden on the Capitol guard. On December 10, 1824, Lafayette became the first foreign dignitary to address Congress. Several months later, the commissioner of public buildings complained bitterly about the difficulties the Capitol's guard had in expelling

* Updated May 1989

Police posed at the Capitol in the 1860's.   *Architect of the Capitol*

from the building "disorderly persons, vagrants and beggars." A fire in the Capitol's library, on December 22, 1825, demonstrated the growing need for increased surveillance. Fortunately, no one was hurt, and only a few books were damaged in the blaze, which was ignited by a candle in one of the galleries. The ensuing investigation pointed clearly to the importance of systematic professional protection to avoid the recurrence of what might surely have been a disaster.[2]

Action finally came in 1827, when President John Quincy Adams directed that a regular watch force be established. That force consisted of four men—two for daytime duty, one for the nighttime, and one relief man. The next year, on May 2, 1828, the city

of Washington's police regulations were extended to include the Capitol and adjacent grounds. This action occurred several weeks after the president's son, serving as his father's private secretary, was accosted and beaten in the Capitol Rotunda. The outraged president sent both houses heated messages that deplored the lack of protection, and it is likely that the incident prompted the city's action. The year 1828 appears prominently on the shoulder patch of today's Capitol police force, signifying the date of its "founding."[3]

For the next quarter century, however, the force remained small, consisting of a captain and three men. They worked fifteen-hour shifts when Congress was in session and ten hours at other times. Although not required to wear uniforms, the police were directed to be "neat and tidy and present a gentlemanly appearance at all times; to be stern with violators of the laws, but courteous to officials, citizens, and strangers." Due to the force's small size, its area of responsibility was confined to the Capitol Building and its immediately adjacent walks and drives. In addition to providing general security inside the building, the police served as tour guides and were, by all accounts, knowledgeable and helpful, just as they are today.[4]

A major source of irritation for the police came from the hack drivers who, in their zeal to pick up passengers, refused to keep their carriages within designated areas. The greatest difficulty, however, lay beyond the walkways, over the course of the Capitol grounds. Although the grounds were surrounded by a large iron fence, the gates of which were closed each evening, the many secluded areas offered ample opportunity for holdups and other crimes. In those days, the grounds to the east of the building, covered with more than six hundred trees, sloped upwards from the building to the eastern boundary line. First Street was then graded seven feet below the boundary, so that it was difficult, if not impossible, to see the Capitol or most of its grounds from the street. During daylight hours, a single watchman, usually an elderly man unsuited for arduous duty, patrolled the grounds. At night, it was every man for himself.[5]

Throughout most of the nineteenth century, the Capitol police had to rely on the District of Columbia's fifteen-member Auxiliary Guard to control demonstrations and stop disorderly conduct on the grounds. Unlike the Capitol police, the Auxiliary Guard did have uniforms, which were gray with flowing capes and a profusion of brass buttons. The "AG," as they were known, were armed with fearsome wooden sticks topped with iron spearheads. The weapon was said to resemble an ancient javelin. Both the Capitol and the city forces were provided with "whirligig rattles" instead of whistles. When twirled, these rattles reportedly emitted "a most unearthly noise."[6]

The need for an expanded force became acute by 1851. During that year, construction began on the Capitol extension that was to consist of wings housing our current Senate and House chambers. When completed later in the decade, the extension would more than double the available working space in the building, making it virtually impossible for a handful of men to guarantee the security of members and visitors alike.

As 1851 drew to a close, another fire broke out in the congressional library. This time, the damage achieved disastrous proportions. When the blaze was finally contained, more than 35,000 of the library's 55,000 books were destroyed, including two-thirds of Thomas Jefferson's original collection. In a building containing 45,000 gas jets and hundreds of candles, the likelihood of additional fires was exceedingly great.[7]

A year later, in 1852, the Capitol police force, which was subsequently described as "an ununiformed squad of ancient watchmen," was enlarged to include a captain and eight men. It was then that the term "Capitol police" first appeared in the statutes, and one might consider 1852 as the real beginning of the evolutionary process through which the small guard force grew into a professional police organization. By 1854, the police, armed with heavy hickory canes, had begun to wear uniforms, possibly borrowed from the military. Not until the start of the Civil War in 1861, however, were they authorized to wear badges, symbolic of their police authority.[8]

The increased activity that came in the wake of the wartime emergency, as well as the continuing construction work on the

Capitol extension and the new dome, necessitated further expansion and the issuance of more detailed regulations for the police. Although supplemented by military troops stationed in and around the building, the force was increased to constitute three six-man watches. Each watch was on duty twelve of every thirty-six hours, with an hour's relief for meals. At that time, the Capitol Building was open to the public from sunrise to sunset. Children under the age of twelve were not permitted on the grounds or in the building, unless, in the language of the regulations, they were accompanied by "parents or some discreet person." [9]

In 1867, as the country slowly struggled to recover from the tragedy of the Civil War, responsibility for the Capitol force was transferred from the commissioner of public buildings to the sergeants at arms of the Senate and the House. As one of their first acts, those officials authorized the design of new uniforms to distinguish the police from the members of the general public, many of whom were attired in old military garb, and to instill a sense of esprit among the men. Salaries were raised to one thousand dollars per year, and three men were added to help with the increased flow of visitors to the top of the recently completed dome.

With the expansion of the force came the inevitable criticism that it was getting too large and that its membership, which included a large number of Civil War veterans, was not suited to the heavy responsibility of protecting the Capitol. Mark Twain was one of the force's most prominent critics. In February 1868, he speculated that "[t]he days of the picturesque, blue-uniformed, brass buttoned Capitol Police are numbered." He argued that they cost the government eighty thousand dollars per year and were not worth the money. Mark Twain reported that the force's members "have grown fat and comfortable dozing in chairs and scratching

their backs against marble pillars." He suggested that protection be provided, when necessary, by regular army troops. [10]

At the time Mark Twain made his observations, the services of the police were very much in demand. On February 24, 1868, the House voted to impeach President Andrew Johnson. From early March until late May, the Senate sat as a court of impeachment. This unprecedented event drew huge crowds from across the nation. The police provided added security, screening visitors to ensure that only those with proper credentials were admitted to the Senate galleries. Senators found it difficult to move in and out of the chamber, despite the best efforts of the police to keep the corridors clear.

In 1873, the Capitol Police Board was established, adding the architect of the Capitol to the force's governing body. The board assumed responsibility for a force consisting of one captain, three lieutenants, twenty-seven privates, and eight watchmen. In addition, it supervised a newly created and separate guide force. The guides were allowed to offer their services to the public for not more than fifty cents an hour. [11]

The following year, in 1874, Congress appropriated $200,000 for a major redesign of the troublesome and unsightly Capitol grounds. Up to that time, the shoddy appearance of the grounds confirmed Lord Bacon's observation that "men come to build stately sooner than to garden finely." The soil consisted of poor clay which "turned to powder in dry weather and to mortar in wet." The west front of the building had been particularly neglected. From the earliest years, it had been assumed that the city would develop to the east. Consequently, little attention was paid to the western portion of the Capitol until 1873, when Congress acquired seven acres on Capitol Hill's western slope. The Senate and House retained nationally prominent landscape architect Frederick Law

Olmsted to prepare a suitable plan for both the east and west grounds of the building. As work proceeded on Olmsted's plan, Congress adopted a resolution "to prevent any portion of the Capitol grounds and terraces from being used as playgrounds or otherwise, so far as may be necessary to protect the public property, turf and grass from destruction and injury." Congress also moved to keep the public from climbing onto the exterior statues and walls by making the offense punishable by a one-hundred-dollar fine and sixty days in jail.[12]

In making its arrangements to resolve the disputed presidential election of 1876, Congress decided additional police protection was necessary for the congressional members of a special electoral commission. In January 1877, the Senate and House agreed to an appropriation of ninety-nine hundred dollars to hire one hundred temporary policemen. When a House member questioned this large expenditure of public funds, a colleague reminded him that eight hundred special police had been required to ensure good order during the recent 1876 centennial exhibition. "We do not anticipate any difficulty," he said, "but we thought it wise that the officers of the two Houses should have power to keep a way clear between the Senate and the House, so that the Senate on retiring to consult may have the opportunity of passing to their Chamber without difficulty. It is also possible," the member continued, "that there may be a class of men known as pickpockets here, and we desire to protect those who come to witness the proceedings."[13]

Fire continued to plague the building during the last quarter of the nineteenth century. The most serious, and the last, gas explosion occurred at 5:13 p.m., on November 6, 1898, in the vicinity of the first-floor room now restored as the old Supreme Court chamber. Two bicycle policemen, stationed at Second and C Streets, Southeast, heard the explosion and saw a sheet of flame rise from the windows along the east front at the basement level. The police officers saved valuable minutes by quickly sounding the alarm. Just before the blast, a policeman inside the building detected the smell of gas. As the Capitol was honeycombed with gas pipes, that odor was not considered uncommon. Nevertheless, the officer set out to investigate. Just as he left the Senate side and headed toward Statuary Hall, the accumulated gas, which had leaked from the service pipes beneath the crypt, ignited. The force of the explosion heaved upward the very floor that the officer had just crossed. The resulting fire raced up an elevator shaft adjacent to the Supreme Court chamber, causing considerable damage on both the first and second floors.[14]

Although the building and its furnishings suffered approximately $25,000 in damage, the severest loss was a priceless collection of manuscript copies of Supreme Court decisions for the period 1792 to 1832. The court itself was not slowed by the calamity. It met the following day in the District of Columbia Committee's room on the second floor of the Capitol, now known as the Lyndon B. Johnson Room. By 1900, electricity had replaced gas for purposes of illumination and, thereafter, all gas lines to the Capitol were closed to avoid what was then becoming an altogether too frequent occurrence.

Less than seventeen years later, another explosion rocked the Capitol. On that occasion, however, it was hardly accidental. On July 2, 1915, at 11:40 p.m., Erich Muenter, a former German language instructor at Harvard University, stood in front of Union Station, his eyes fixed intently on the Capitol. At that moment, an ignition device set off three sticks of dynamite which Muenter earlier had placed behind the Senate's telephone switchboard, located adjacent to the west wall of the Senate Reception Room. The explosion caused major damage to the room, smashing windows, chandeliers, and mirrors. Officer Frank Jones, a thirty-year-veteran of the Capitol police force, was stationed at the Senate door on the first floor. The severity of the blast nearly knocked him off his chair. The only other policeman on duty in the Senate wing was Officer George Gumm. Only ten minutes earlier, Officer Gumm had closed a window in the Reception Room just inches from where the dynamite lay concealed. Meanwhile, Muenter, pleased with his dramatic protest against the United States' aid to Great Britain in World War I, quickly boarded the midnight train to New York City.

On the following day, the *Washington Star* carried two banner headlines. The first recounted the Capitol bombing and reprinted an anonymous letter in which the writer expressed the hope that the explosion would "make enough noise to be heard above the voices that clamor for war and blood money." The writer, expressing his opposition to America's faltering efforts at neutrality, concluded that "this explosion is the exclamation point to my appeal for peace." The other page one news story told of the shooting of financier J. P. Morgan, Jr., at his Long Island estate. Morgan was not seriously hurt, and his assailant was arrested. His attacker's motive was to strike a symbolic blow against J. P. Morgan and Company, Great Britain's chief purchasing agent in the United States for war munitions and supplies. Morgan's assailant was none other than Erich Muenter, who, several days later, committed suicide in jail.[15]

Explosions and bombings aside, the life of a Capitol policeman at the end of the nineteenth and into the twentieth centuries contained a large measure of boredom. This was a particular problem late at night, after the building had closed and the members and

visitors had departed. Perhaps this situation accounts for a variety of ghost stories about the Capitol that have been told down through the years.

One of the oldest stories is recounted by newsman John Alexander in his book of Washington ghost tales. It concerns the infamous denizen of the Capitol's lower reaches, "Demon Cat." As the story goes, Demon Cat always waits until its victim is alone. Members of the Capitol police force are, generally, the animal's prey. One victim told of encountering the infamous cat on a winter's eve. As it walked toward the policeman, the cat began to swell.

The guard felt paralyzed as he stared into the glowing, piercing eyes that came closer and closer and grew larger and larger. The animal swelled to the size of a giant tiger, yet never lost its unmistakable catlike form. Its purring changed to a ferocious snarl. There was a deafening roar as the monstrous animal leaped—with claws extended—toward its victim. The guard couldn't move. His feet seemed nailed to the floor. He covered his face with his arms as the giant animal seemed just inches away from landing on him. He screamed.

Nothing happened. The Demon Cat vanished into thin air as the man screamed.

The trembling guard stood alone, the corridor deserted, the silence pierced only by his breathing. His limp body was covered in a cold, clammy sweat. He felt drained. The narrow marble hallway now reminded him of a tomb. The guard shuddered, tried to pull himself together, and headed back to his desk. For some reason he just didn't feel like finishing his rounds.[16]

This grisly feline was blamed for an elderly guard's fatal heart attack. The cat is reputed to appear only on the eve of a national tragedy, or upon the changing of presidential administrations!

There are other stories of footsteps echoing through darkened halls, belonging, perhaps, to long-since departed members of the police force, still faithfully keeping watch over their posts. In the 1890's, a policeman entered Statuary Hall, the former House

According to a Washington ghost story, a Capitol policeman once entered Statuary Hall on New Year's Eve and found the statues dancing.
Architect of the Capitol

chamber, at midnight and allegedly interrupted the entire ghostly membership of a much earlier Congress in solemn deliberation. In the same chamber, one New Year's Eve, as the clock struck twelve, the marble and bronze statues were reported to have drifted off their pedestals in order to dance. A terrified guard fled from the chamber and into the still night air. On the following day, he recounted the eerie event to his supervisor. The captain immediately ordered the private to take "a long, long rest." I have heard, however, that, even in recent times, the police tend to avoid Statuary Hall on New Year's Eve!

The ghost of General John Alexander Logan, of Civil War fame, has also reportedly been seen wandering through the lower recesses of the Capitol. Logan served in both the House and Senate, and he chaired the old Committee on Military Affairs. It is said that Logan's spirit has haunted the precincts of the room where the Military Affairs Committee conducted its meetings, and, when

[333]

seen in the corridor, he was still wearing "his famous slouch hat" and appeared to be listening intently to what was going on in the committee room.[17]

Other Capitol Hill ghosts that have been the subjects of conversation down through the years include the "silent specter of a workman . . . gliding through a hallway," who had fallen from the scaffolding in the giant Rotunda. According to John Alexander, "On the anniversary of his fall, the worker, clad in his faded overalls and carrying his wooden tool kit, retraces his journey through the hallway en route to the Rotunda."[18]

Some of today's younger Capitol police members—especially if they are inclined to doubt the existence of ghosts—may refuse to believe the stories that have been handed down from earlier times. But even the bravest and the biggest of such doubting Thomases would feel their eyeballs pop and their hair stand on end should they be walking the dark basement corridors some night while alone and suddenly come face-to-face with a stonemason who "has been seen—trowel in hand—passing through a wall . . . on the Senate side of the building." It is said that, while the Capitol's north wing was under construction, the stonemason "had the misfortune to lose an argument to a hotheaded carpenter who smashed in his head with a brick and used the man's own trowel to seal his tomb."[19]

The supernatural has always excited the imagination of most of us—especially those among us who are law-abiding citizens, and senators. We can, of course, expect to encounter a few cynics who will slough off these reports of ghosts as pure fantasies embedded in Senate folklore. But I, for one, refuse to be intimidated by the cynics. I prefer, instead, to be intimidated by the ghosts, whose nonexistence has yet to be proven. Besides, what have I to fear as long as there is a Capitol policeman around!

Members of the Capitol police force posed for this group photograph in 1900.
U.S. Capitol Police Yearbook, 1973

In 1896, twelve privates were added to the force, and seven watchmen's positions were abolished. The outbreak of the Spanish-American War two years later served as reason for adding eighteen more privates. Although they were intended to be temporary, in 1901 they became part of the permanent force. Thus, by the beginning of this century, the Capitol police force had grown impressively. Including a newly established detective force, it consisted of sixty-seven men. Half the privates were selected by the Senate and half by the House. Of this number, four officers were assigned to the dome, due to its popularity among the tourists. During the height of the season, more than two thousand persons each day climbed the stairs for a breathtaking view of the surrounding city of Washington. That was quite a hike: from the basement, on the Senate side of the Capitol, there are 399 steps to the top of the dome. The grounds were, at that time, patrolled day and night by a bicycle squad to give chase to those who drove their two-wheelers at high speeds, and to catch, and send to the pound, all unlicensed dogs.[20]

In 1902, the *Washington Star* pronounced the force's evolution complete. In that paper's judgment, the Capitol police represented "the finest body of indoor policemen in the world." Each member of the force was then attired in a natty, dark blue, regulation army frock coat and was armed with a billy club, pliable handcuffs called "nippers," and a distress whistle. They carried revolvers only when on "important service" or when assigned to the grounds at night. Apparently, not all of the officers liked their natty uniforms, for a number of appropriations acts of that period included the admonition that "the officers, privates, and watchmen of the Capitol Police shall, when on duty, wear the regulation uniform."[21]

By 1911, the force was again the target of strong criticism because of its continuing expansion. Several years earlier, the Senate and House had opened their new office buildings, those which we know today as the Russell and Cannon Buildings. Together, they required an additional twenty-six officers. For some reason, the House took only ten, while the less populous Senate claimed sixteen. One senator contended the reason was that the 391 House members were more orderly than the 92 senators![22]

The House, following the lead of its Democratic caucus, reported a bill in 1911 to reduce the size of the force by 50 percent. The measure's proponents argued that most of the recent increase had been intended as temporary, due to the Spanish-American War. Senator Clarence Watson of West Virginia agreed with the reduction plan. He noted the presence of many "sleepy-headed officers sitting around that never would be allowed in a real business institution." He claimed that they were "of no use to anybody, even themselves, except to draw their

salaries." Democratic Senator John Sharp Williams of Mississippi concurred, accusing the policemen, whom he believed to be the appointees of the Republican majority, of being "political hangers-on." He said, "to them we intrust the safety of this great national property, and they attend to it with such little efficiency that although there are 67 of them hanging around between here and the House somewhere, somebody came in here the other day and ruthlessly cut one of the pictures in the Capitol all to pieces."[23] Senator Williams was referring to an incident on December 19, 1911, in which a vandal cut a thirty-inch-long strip out of the "Battle of Lake Erie" painting, located in the marble stairway to the east of our chamber. In 1955, that same painting suffered a similar outrage.

Unfortunately, the paintings and statuary in this building have frequently been the target of mindless mutilation, a fact which presents a strong argument for an adequate and vigilant police force. In 1912, Senate Appropriations Committee Chairman Francis Warren of Wyoming expressed the sentiment of a majority of his colleagues when he told them he would rather pay the price of a sufficient police force than to risk the consequences of less protection.[24]

After extensive debate, the Senate, in 1912, decided not to concur in the House's force reduction plan. Senators realized that the younger men, who had been recently hired, would have to be the first fired. That would have left a core of Civil War veterans, most of whom were in their late sixties, the very men who were the targets of the complaints about inactivity. Few senators were willing to take the action necessary to fire these old war veterans, from both the Union and Confederate armies. Their heroic deeds in days gone by were familiar to the senators, many of whom had served as their comrades in that tragic struggle. The veterans were allowed to remain, and the records of the Senate Democratic Conference indicate that, as late as 1918, there were still a few Civil War veterans guarding our doors.[25]

Back in those days, the police were given fifty days of annual leave. One senator thought he saw a way to save funds by reducing the number of leave days to thirty. His plan foundered, however, when another senator explained that those fifty days were from the entire year, barely giving the men each Sunday off! Even today, the official policy of the Capitol Police Board is that leave is a privilege rather than a right.

The police had great responsibilities on the eve of the First World War. They had to protect the Capitol, then valued at seventeen million dollars. The grounds had been expanded to cover fifty-nine acres, and an estimated one million visitors traversed these halls each year. Among the particularly sensitive posts were: Statuary Hall, to guard against chronic vandalism; the Senate gallery, where two officers worked to reduce congestion; and the upper dome, "for the preservation of order, to protect the Dome from defacement, and to guard sightseers from dangerous places." A final important post was the northeast portion of the grounds, where a patrol was assigned "to protect the lawns from trespassers and the roadways and plaza from invasion by unauthorized vehicles and from fast driving of all kinds."[26]

As I noted earlier, World War I created the need for additional security. The bombing of the Reception Room in 1915 was directly related to the war. In 1917, when the United States entered the conflict, the Senate attempted to add fifty men for the duration of the emergency. The House, however, refused to go along with the Senate's plan. One representative interviewed the chief and quoted him as saying that 50 percent of the force was absolutely inefficient, due to the patron-

By 1935, the Capitol police were attired in modern-era uniforms. *U.S. Capitol Police Yearbook, 1973*

age system of appointment. He argued that "a large number of the force are entirely unacquainted with the duties of policemen. . . . [T]hey do not know how to make an arrest, . . . and a large number are physically incapable of performing the duties of their office."[27]

In 1935, at a time when the area of the Capitol grounds had just been increased from 59 acres to 126 acres, the chief of police appealed to the Senate and House for 24 men to supplement his 132-man force. He reported to the House Appropriations Committee that his force was severely handicapped, due to the large number of underaged or elderly policemen and the lack of service standards. He estimated that one-third of the force did all the work. At that time, the men ranged in age from nineteen to seventy-five. One officer was six feet, two inches tall and weighed all of 120 pounds! During the previous year, the police had made 600 arrests, and there were 112 automobile accidents. One of the force's two automobiles, a four-year-old Ford with forty thousand miles to its credit, was constantly out of service, leaving the other vehicle to make all the rounds.

The chief recommended that the force adopt the standards of the metropolitan Washington Police Department and require all new men to be between the ages of twenty-one and fifty. He indicated that he would be happy to have World War I veterans, because "they know how to shoot and know how to take orders." The House sergeant at arms supported the chief's request and added that he saw no need for the additional men unless they complied with the standards. He noted that standards would make the work of the congressional patronage committees easier, allowing them to turn down the unqualified candidates of influential members. Subsequently, both houses agreed to allow the Capitol Police Board to establish specific qualifications. Today, candidates for appointment must be within the twenty-one to fifty-year age bracket recommended earlier. Officers must have a high school education, and they may not be less than five feet, four inches, nor more than six feet, five inches, in height and of proportional weight.[28]

In setting those standards, the police board was well aware that the Capitol would, unfortunately, continue to be the setting for periodic acts of violence.

On December 13, 1932, a twenty-five-year-old department store clerk entered the House gallery, waving a loaded pistol in the air. He dangled one foot over the railing and demanded the right to speak. There followed a mad scramble for the cloakrooms. Minnesota Representative Melvin Maas, who had been trained as a psychologist, gently talked the man into turning over his weapon. When asked later by a reporter whether he had had experience in handling deranged persons, Maas observed, "Why not? I've had six years in Congress."[29]

On July 12, 1947, just before noontime, Senator John Bricker of Ohio left his suite in the Senate office building and headed for the old monorail subway for a ride to the Capitol. As he boarded the car, a man with a twenty-two-caliber target pistol fired at him twice from a distance of fifteen feet. Neither shot hit Senator Bricker, who had the presence of mind to duck under the car's front seat and to tell the operator to "step on it." Arriving at the Capitol end of the subway, the senator nonchalantly headed for the chamber, stopping only to phone his secretary and neglecting to mention the incident. Meanwhile, the subway car operator returned to the office building terminal, only to find the assailant waiting and very much alone. The gunman quickly fled in a taxi, but, thanks to the combined efforts of the metropolitan and Capitol police forces, he was arrested within the hour. The man had recently lost his patronage position as a Capitol policeman. (The nature of his previous employment led several cynics to observe that the danger was minimal of his being able to hit the senator!) The assailant, when questioned as to his motive, said that he was just trying to "refresh" Senator Bricker's memory about a savings and loan association's failure fifteen years earlier in which the man had lost a considerable sum of money.[30]

For as long as there has been an organized Capitol police force, there have been public demonstrations to test that body's training and experience. Many of us recall the Vietnam-era protest marches and rallies that ebbed and flowed across this federal city. In the early 1980's, farmers traveled with their families, and often with their tractors and livestock, from the nation's heartland to deliver to their government a message of concern and frustration. Almost without exception, the Capitol police have handled these demonstrations with, in the words of the police manual, "coolness and firmness," mindful of the participants' rights under our Constitution and laws.

Earlier demonstrations were not always managed with such professionalism and restraint. A good example was the march on Washington in the spring of 1894 by General

Jacob Coxey and his "army" of five hundred men, women, and children. Coxey, a successful Ohio farmer and businessman, provided an outlet for the frustrations of thousands of unemployed Americans who were victims of the economic distress that gripped the nation following the panic of 1893.

On March 19, 1894, Senator William A. Peffer, a Kansas Populist, introduced two bills embodying Coxey's scheme for national economic recovery. They provided for an elaborate system of public works projects financed by a large new issue of paper money. At that point, Coxey announced his plans to assemble a contingent of one hundred thousand persons to march from Ohio to Washington as a "living petition" to Congress for his proposals.

On a biting-cold Easter morning, Coxey set out with one hundred followers and a forty-seven-man press escort for what was certain to be a well-publicized, if arduous, journey. One observer noted that the "army" consisted "for the most part of men who inspired more sympathy than respect." As Coxey moved toward his ultimate destination, officials in Washington prepared for the worst. Some feared a howling mob of tens of thousands who would attempt to seize the government's supply of gold, silver, and paper currency. Sharpshooters prepared to defend the Treasury Building. Fifteen hundred army troops were alerted for duty. At the Capitol, two hundred special police were sworn in, and the guard in and around the building was doubled.

Senator Peffer and other sympathizers sought in vain to secure adoption of a resolution to establish a special Senate committee to receive petitions from "bodies of citizens visiting Washington," in an effort to curb what he believed was the prevailing notion that the Senate was an "American House of Lords" out of touch with the needs of the people.

When Coxey arrived in Washington, he obtained a parade permit but was informed that it was illegal to parade on the Capitol grounds, to walk on the grass, and to "display flags, banners, or devices designed or adapted to bring into public notice any party, organization or movement."

Reference to this law did not deter Coxey. Asserting the constitutional rights of free speech and assembly, he gave his "troops" orders to prepare to march.

On May Day 1894, Coxey's army was joined by twenty thousand generally sympathetic spectators who lined Pennsylvania Avenue in anticipation of the protest's climactic moments. They were not disappointed. As Coxey approached the Capitol, he found the grounds encircled by a solid phalanx of mounted police. He and two companions left the main body of marchers and headed toward the Senate wing. Mounted police galloped in pursuit, followed by an agitated and curious crowd. Coxey, alone, succeeded in reaching the Senate's front steps where he was surrounded. His request to speak denied, he threw a written statement of protest to nearby reporters and was quickly led away by the police. The excited crowd of onlookers surged forward, causing the police to charge into their ranks. Fifty spectators were either trampled or beaten. Coxey and the other leaders were soon released, and he returned to his headquarters to issue "Special Order Number 1." In it, he proclaimed that:

Liberty lies weltering in her own blood in the Nation's Capitol City to-night, stabbed in the home of friends and supposed guardians. Free speech has been suppressed and police clubs have taken the place of the scales of justice. . . . Brothers, we have entered upon the beginning of the end.

After the May Day drama, Coxey and several key followers were tried for violation of the 1882 Capitol Grounds Act. They were

In 1894, Coxey's army marched across the nation to the Capitol.

found guilty of trampling the Capitol's grass, and Coxey spent twenty days in jail for his trouble.

Although most members of Congress disagreed with Coxey's specific remedies for the nation's economic difficulties, many deeply resented the treatment he and his followers were accorded. Ohio Representative Tom Johnson expressed this attitude in denouncing as disgraceful the fact that "the representatives of this Nation should have no better reception for a peaceful body of poor,

unemployed men, no matter how erroneous their economic views, than to meet them with the upraised clubs of police." [31]

Nearly four decades later, another "army" made a dramatic march on Washington. Conscripted by the Great Depression's agents of unemployment, starvation, and despair, twenty-five thousand World War I veterans and their families traveled here in the spring of 1932 from all parts of the nation. They came to urge Congress to amend a 1924 act that would have provided

World War I veterans who sought immediate payment of their veterans' bonuses marched near the Capitol in 1932.

veterans' bonuses in 1945. The members of this rag-tag "Bonus Expeditionary Force" wanted their bonuses, amounting to five hundred dollars apiece, immediately.

From May until late July, the bonus marchers lived in camps along the Anacostia River, in abandoned buildings, in garbage dumps, and, even in the shadow of this building, near the Library of Congress. Congress adjourned on July 16 without responding to the veterans' demands. As the summer's heat intensified, so, too, did concern within the Hoover White House that matters might soon get out of hand. Up to that point, the marchers had conducted themselves with restraint. This prompted Will Rogers to observe that they held "the record for being the best behaved of any hungry men assembled anywhere in the world."

The available evidence indicates that the Capitol and metropolitan police acted with sympathy towards the veterans. The latter arranged to serve hot meals to the marchers for a nominal cost. Police Superintendent Pelham Glassford counseled the White House to let the demonstration run its course; President Hoover, however, feared that that course might prove to be contrary to the nation's best interests. Accordingly, on July 28, 1932, he ordered the metropolitan police to clear out marcher-occupied buildings on the present site of the National Gallery of Art. In the ensuing encounter, the police killed four veterans. This led President Hoover to order the use of whatever force was necessary to remove the marchers from the area. Cavalry troops and tanks arrived from Fort Myer. As the mounted soldiers charged into the demonstrators, one of those trampled was Senator Hiram Bingham of Connecticut, himself a veteran of World War I.

Throughout the remainder of that sad day, the demonstrators were chased, clubbed, gassed, and shot in what Major Dwight Eisenhower, who was then serving as an aide to chief of staff Douglas MacArthur, observed was a reaction to a political manifestation rather than to a military threat. By day's end, the marchers' Anacostia camp lay a smoldering ruin. The battered veterans were given police escorts through the neighboring states of Maryland and Virginia to ensure that they would not regroup and return.

Although the Capitol police played no direct role in this sad drama, they witnessed the tragic consequences of an overreaction to an essentially peaceful protest. Senators William Borah of Idaho, Hiram Johnson of California, and Hugo Black of Alabama, in particular, were outraged by the army's heavy-handed use of force. They undoubtedly agreed with New York Representative Fiorello La Guardia's telegram to the president that "soup is cheaper than tear gas bombs and bread is better than bullets in maintaining law and order in these times of Depression, unemployment, and hunger." [32]

Over the past three and one-half decades, several demonstrations have taken the form of direct assaults on Congress. They have necessitated tightening of security and further expansion and professionalism of the Capitol police.

On March 1, 1954, four terrorists belonging to a Puerto Rican nationalist group invaded the gallery of the House of Representatives and fired approximately thirty shots in the direction of the nearly 150 members who, according to press reports, were then present. Five representatives were wounded but, fortunately, all recovered. I was sitting in the chamber at the time and witnessed it all. [33]

As a result of that outrage, five plainclothes policemen from the metropolitan force were stationed in the public galleries of each chamber, and visitors since that time have been required to check all packages before entering the House and Senate galleries. Shortly after the attack, the Committee on House Administration, of which I was then a member, met to consider legislation to institute stringent recruitment and training procedures in the mostly patronage-dominated force. At that time, new recruits were issued revolvers without having had any formal training, although the majority were war veterans. Captain William Broderick told the committee he believed that only 35 to 40 of his 157-member force would be qualified to continue serving, once the proposed reforms were instituted. He indicated that it took at least two years to train a man to be a professional policeman, and then the patronage appointee usually moved on to other employment. [34]

Although security was tightened after the 1954 attack, the broader package of reform proposals was not immediately adopted. The Capitol police came to rely more heavily on the metropolitan department's professionals for assistance as needed. In 1958, Congress added twenty men to the force to provide security for the newly opened office building

During the Vietnam War, protesters regularly gathered at the Capitol.   *U.S. Capitol Police Yearbook, 1973*

which was subsequently named for Illinois Senator Everett Dirksen.[35] By that time, the Capitol police force was headed by a chief and other high-ranking officers who had been permanently detailed from the metropolitan force. That arrangement continued until February 1, 1980, at which time these key positions were brought under the exclusive control of Congress. Meanwhile, the old patronage system had been terminated, the last entry for a Senate patronage position being October 1971, according to the Capitol police appointment books.[36]

One event that I remember particularly well occurred in this chamber on September 11, 1967. A few minutes after the Senate convened, five spectators threw from the galleries a number of anti–Vietnam War leaflets. The message in the leaflets promised "sustained disruptions of government apparatus" until the United States withdrew from Vietnam. The demonstrators were arrested and removed.

On the following day, I noted that such action constituted "a threat to substitute an-

archy for law and order." I suggested that it was "a contemptible effort at coercion, one that strikes at the foundations of the orderly processes that protect the rights of all Americans including the group that made the threat." I reminded my colleagues that there was, at that time, no statute on the books that specifically prohibited demonstrations inside the Capitol. Shortly thereafter, Congress passed, and the president signed, an act to make such disorderly activities, including forcible entry into the Senate and House chambers and surrounding rooms, a felony punishable by a fine of up to five thousand dollars and/or imprisonment of up to five years. Although I regretted then, as I do today, the necessity for such strict measures, events before and since have made them essential.[37]

On March 1, 1971, exactly seventeen years after the attack in the House chamber, a violent explosion ripped through a ground floor rest room in the oldest portion of the Senate wing, not far from the site of the 1898 gas explosion. The device had a force equivalent to twenty pounds of dynamite. Fortunately, no one was injured. The damage, amounting to $300,000, consisted of cracked walls, broken windows, weakened floors, and injuries to artwork. A group known as the Weather Underground immediately claimed credit as a symbolic protest against the United States' policies in Southeast Asia. To date, no one has been brought to justice for that craven act.[38]

Before the 1971 bombing, police did not routinely check staff and visitors to the Capitol for weapons or other potentially dangerous devices. In its wake, a number of steps were taken to improve the building's security. Everyone who entered the Capitol and the office buildings, with the exception of members, had to submit handbags, briefcases, and packages to police inspection. A closed-circuit television system was installed. With more than one hundred cameras, it permits around-the-clock monitoring of all areas of the building, including the most obscure back halls. The tunnels from the Capitol power plant have been wired with an alarm system. A hazardous device unit was established within the Capitol police force to respond to bomb threats and to search the grounds as necessary. Electronic metal detectors have been installed at all gallery entrances.

On November 7, 1983, shortly before 11 p.m., terrorists again struck the Capitol. A powerful bomb exploded in an alcove several feet from the entrance to S-208, the Capitol office which I then occupied as minority leader, and thirty feet from the Senate chamber. The explosion blew out a wall partition and sent a potentially deadly shower of wood, brick, plaster, and glass into an area that had been occupied only a little while earlier. The doors to my office were blown off their hinges, and windows in the Republican cloakroom were shattered. Although the building sustained no significant structural injury, major damage was done to floors, walls, and furnishings. Two chandeliers, the "Ohio Clock," and several paintings were severely damaged. The face of Daniel Webster was blown from John Neagle's handsome painting nearby, and only the quick action of the Senate curator kept the pieces of this treasure from being swept away with the surrounding debris. Fortunately, it was possible to restore these priceless treasures to nearly their pre-blast condition.

The Senate had been expected to meet late into that evening, but we had progressed faster than anticipated on the pending legislation and were able to adjourn at 7:02 p.m. The adjacent Mansfield Room had been crowded with a reception just hours before the blast. Refusing to be intimidated by such a heinous deed, we convened the Senate early the next morning as investigators sifted through the rubble and workmen began the cleanup process.

A group calling itself the "Armed Resistance Unit" claimed responsibility for the bombing, saying the action was in retaliation for U.S. military "aggression" in Grenada and Lebanon. In May 1988, seven militant activists associated with this group were indicted. The case is presently awaiting trial in the U.S. District Court in Washington.[39]

Several days prior to the bombing, I had scheduled a meeting with Senator Howard Baker, then the majority leader, to discuss increased security procedures. This action had been triggered by an October 18 incident in which a visitor to the House gallery had been arrested after threatening to blow up the building with a homemade bomb which he had concealed under his clothing. That incident, combined with the bombing, fostered greatly tightened security arrangements. Metal detectors, which previously had been used only outside the chamber galleries, were placed at designated public entrances to the Capitol and office buildings. (In 1988, police seized 148 weapons, including knives, clubs, blackjacks, and guns.) Hallways outside the Senate and House chambers were closed to general traffic. Identification badges were devised for staff and accredited members of the media, and visitors to the Capitol's non-public areas were required to register at a special desk and to be escorted to their respective destinations.

The restriction of citizens' access to their elected representatives is intolerable in a democracy. Equally intolerable are the substantial threats of violence directed against those representatives. As we review proposals for additional security measures, such as a fence around the Capitol and bullet-proof glass in the galleries of our chambers, we strive to keep in mind the necessary balance between access and security. We deplore the necessity for such measures, and we applaud the sensitivity of the Capitol police to their implementation.

As of May 25, 1989, the Capitol police force numbered 1,335 men and women—646 on the House side of the Capitol, 689 for the Senate. The first two female officers on the Capitol police force were hired on September 16, 1974. After first becoming plainclothes police, Nancy B. Yount and Patricia K. Rinaldi were promoted to detective in 1978 and 1979, respectively. Karen J. Magee, who joined the force in 1978, became the first woman appointed to the rank of lieutenant on March 1, 1987.

Frank Kerrigan, the current chief of the U.S. Capitol Police, was appointed to that post in August 1987. A native of Parkersburg, West Virginia, and the son of a police officer, Frank Kerrigan joined the Capitol police in 1966 as a patrol officer. Immediately prior to his appointment, Chief Kerrigan had earned special distinction for his direction of security operations for the Iran-Contra hearings.

On December 29, 1981, the jurisdiction of the Capitol police expanded from the Capitol Building and grounds to encompass the entire nation. On that occasion, the police received specific statutory authority to protect members and officers of Congress when those officeholders and their families travel away from Capitol Hill. This is comparable to the Secret Service's longstanding mandate to protect presidents and vice presidents and their families wherever they travel. Prior to 1981, members had to rely on piecemeal security arrangements outside of Congress' institutional control. There was, for example, no specific authority for protecting congressional committees when those panels held field hearings.

Congress provided this expanded protection at a time of increased threats against individual members, and as the Reagan admin-

Capitol police officers posed with their motorcycles on the Capitol grounds in 1973.
U.S. Capitol Police Yearbook, 1973

istration was warning of a suspected Libyan terrorist operation, possibly directed against members. This authority may be implemented only on a case-by-case basis, when the Capitol Police Board, in voluntary consultation with the Federal Bureau of Investigation and the Secret Service, determines that it is necessary.

This expanded jurisdiction has been invoked only rarely. It facilitated planning for a special July 1987 bicentennial meeting of Congress in Philadelphia. In the early stages of that planning, it was assumed that the entire Congress would convene in actual legislative sessions at Independence Hall. Ultimately, more than two hundred members did participate in ceremonial sessions. The event proceeded flawlessly, thanks, in great measure, to the smooth coordination between the Capitol police and state and city protective services.[40]

Today, all members of the force must undergo rigorous training, both in marksmanship and in the latest law enforcement methods. That training includes a special sixteen-week program, eight weeks of which are spent at the Federal Law Enforcement Training Center in Glynco, Georgia, with periodic refresher courses. Capitol police officers must qualify annually on the firing range, a part of the local training area often affectionately referred to as "Rayburn U," located in the basement of the Rayburn House Office Building.

Mr. President, if John Golding, the first Capitol guard, were able to return here today, he would undoubtedly be envious of his successors. No longer merely guards, today's Capitol police are equipped with the latest in uniforms, weapons, and technical proficiency. In the mid-1980's, the Police Board adopted a uniform consisting of a dark blue shirt with brass buttons, a gold badge, and a round military-style cap. In August 1988, this new uniform won a national award, conferring upon the Capitol police the distinction of being the best-dressed government agency security force.

The Capitol police can be counted upon to exhibit equal dexterity in controlling demonstrations and in guiding bewildered visitors with sensitivity and effectiveness. I think it is particularly appropriate that the Capitol police manual gives equal emphasis to both functions. When one considers that some ten million people visit the Capitol Building each year, one appreciates their tasks all the more.

I think that all members of the Senate and the Senate staff have found the Capitol police to be good friends. They are the first to greet us when we arrive each morning, and they bid us farewell as we leave at night. Senate work often spills over into the late evenings and early morning hours, and it is particularly reassuring to see the Capitol police on those dark nights. The Capitol police can be counted upon to find a parking space for a hurried staff member at mid-day; to produce a coat hanger to open a car door when the owner has locked his keys inside; to point out a tire going bald and in need of replacement; and to assist senators and tourists in boarding the subway cars. They are a dedicated and valiant group of men and women, and we are fortunate to have their service.

CHAPTER 15

Congressional Salaries

July 14, 1989*

Mr. President, much has been in the news in recent months about a congressional salary increase. Last winter, irate citizens besieged the offices of senators and representatives with letters and telephone calls protesting the substantial pay increases for federal employees that were recommended by the Commission on Executive, Legislative, and Judicial Salaries and endorsed by President Ronald Reagan. While the proposed pay increase would have affected thousands in the executive and judicial branches, it was the increase to members of Congress that aroused the wrath of so many Americans. The story has been the same since the beginning of our Republic.[1]

The subject of congressional pay generated considerable discussion in 1787 at the Constitutional Convention in Philadelphia. The records of the convention reveal that the question of compensation for members of Congress plagued that forum's delegates from the very beginning. In late May 1787, Delegate Edmund Randolph of Virginia presented what became known as the Virginia plan for the future government. Point three of the Virginia plan provided "that the National Legislature ought to consist of two branches." The next point specified that the members of these two as-yet-unnamed branches were "to receive liberal stipends by

which they may be compensated for the devotion of their time to public service."[2] As debate progressed, the word "liberal" was removed from the phrase "liberal stipends." Next, several delegates questioned whether members of the "second branch"—the Senate—should be compensated at all. This, after all, was to be the branch of Congress dominated by the elite of the nation. That proposal was quickly abandoned.

Virginia delegates James Madison and George Mason sought to depart from the system of congressional compensation that had existed under the Articles of Confederation, in which individual states determined the salaries of their representatives. They, and others at the Constitutional Convention who favored strengthening the central government, believed that it was essential to pay congressional salaries from the national treasury. The records of the convention note:

[Madison] observed that it would be improper to leave the members of the Natl. legislature to be provided for by the State Legisls because it would create an improper dependence; and to leave them to regulate their own wages, was an indecent thing, and might in time prove a dangerous one. He thought wheat or some other article of which the average price throughout a reasonable period preceding might be settled in some convenient mode, would form a proper standard.

* Updated December 1989

In the Constitutional Convention, James Madison supported the use of federal, rather than state, funds to pay congressional salaries. *Library of Congress*

Col. Mason seconded the motion; adding that it would be improper for other reasons to leave the wages to be regulated by the States. 1. the different States would make different provision for their representatives, and an inequality would be felt among them, whereas he thought they ought to be in all respects equal. 2. the parsimony of the States might reduce the provision so low that as had already happened in choosing delegates to Congress, the question would be not who were most fit to be chosen, but who were most willing to serve.[3]

After much debate during that long hot summer of 1787, the issue of compensation was finally decided. Or, perhaps it would be more accurate to say that the framers—in their infinite wisdom—chose not to decide the issue. Article I, section 6, of the Constitution provides that senators and representatives "shall receive a Compensation for their services, to be ascertained by Law, and paid out of the Treasury of the United States."

Of course, the matter was not really settled at all. Just as Madison and others had feared, having members of Congress vote on their own pay quickly caused trouble. In the First Congress, the legislative compensation bill provoked intense controversy. While the bill was in the House, several representatives brought upon themselves charges of demagoguery by urging a cut in the six-dollar-per-diem compensation recommended by the committee charged with determining the amount to be paid. Next, James Madison and John Page of Virginia earned the enmity of many of their House colleagues when they suggested that senators receive a higher rate of pay than representatives because greater service was likely to be demanded of members of the upper house.

In the Senate, a special committee considered the House-passed compensation bill and made its recommendations on August 27, 1789. The committee proposed to strike out the House provisions that each senator and representative receive six dollars for each day he attended a regular or special legislative session and six dollars per twenty miles of distance traveled "by the most usual road" from his residence to the capital. The committee then proposed a substitute for the House version to provide that, when the Senate was called into special session to consider executive nominations, its members be paid eight dollars daily and eight dollars per twenty miles of travel. This plan would remain in effect until the start of the Fourth Congress in 1795. William Maclay submitted an amendment to reduce the daily rate to five dollars. He argued that it was folly for the Senate to think it might increase its dignity in the public's eyes by taking a salary higher than that of the House. Voting 14 to 4, the full Senate defeated Maclay's amendment.[4] When Senator Oliver Ellsworth sought unsuccessfully to reduce the House rate to five dollars, Vice President John Adams became so agitated that he was unable to sit still. Three times he interrupted Ellsworth, suggesting that the former Congress under the Articles of Confederation had degenerated in part because of inadequate pay. The Senate then reduced to seven dollars the eight-dollar rate that senators would receive for special sessions.[5]

The House refused to agree to a salary differential, and a conference committee convened on September 10, 1789, to try to find common ground. Senate conferees held fast in support of a differential, but, by way of compromise, they proposed that the compensation act be limited to seven years and that the differential for senators apply only for the seventh year—from March 4, 1795, to March 4, 1796—but for regular as well as special sessions. Senate conferees added that, if House members did not like this arrangement, they should pass a separate law providing for their own compensation. These suggestions provoked an acrimonious debate and howls of protest from the House, which rejected the conference report on a 24 to 29 vote. On the following day, the House reconsidered and reversed its earlier action, passing the measure by a narrow 28 to 26 margin. President Washington signed the act on September 22.[6]

The act, as finally passed, provided that, prior to March 4, 1795, at every session of Congress—and at every meeting of the Senate when Congress was in recess—each senator was entitled to receive six dollars for every day in attendance. In addition, at the commencement and end of every such session and meeting, each senator was allowed six dollars for every twenty miles "of the estimated distance by the most usual road from his place of residence to the Seat of Congress." From March 4, 1795, until March 4, 1796, senators were to be paid seven dollars for every day of attendance at sessions of Congress and meetings of the Senate in recess, as well as seven dollars at the beginning and end of every such session and recess meeting for every twenty miles to and from the seat of Congress. Representatives, on the other hand, were not to share in the increased pay and travel allowance accorded to senators between March 4, 1795, and March 4, 1796. They were to receive six dollars per day of attendance at sessions and six dollars for every twenty miles to and from the seat of Congress throughout the duration of the act until March 4, 1796.[7]

The legislative compensation act also provided salaries for congressional staff. The chaplain of each house would receive an annual salary of five hundred dollars. The secretary of the Senate and the clerk of the House would be paid fifteen hundred dollars, plus two dollars for each day their respective houses were in session. The Senate's principal clerk and its doorkeeper would be paid only during sessions at three dollars per day, while the engrossing clerk and the assistant doorkeeper would receive two dollars per day.

Though they had addressed the question of compensation for the moment, few members of Congress believed the matter settled for good. In the fall of 1789, the issue found its way into a proposed amendment to the Constitution. On September 28, 1789, Congress sent twelve proposed amendments to the states for ratification. The second of those amendments read as follows:

No law, varying the compensation for the services of the Senators and Representatives, shall take effect, until an election of Representatives shall have intervened.[8]

On December 19, 1789, Maryland became the first state to ratify the congressional salary amendment. North Carolina followed on December 22, South Carolina and Delaware in January 1790, Vermont and Virginia in 1791. And that was it! Long after ten other amendments in the package had been incorporated into the Constitution as the Bill of Rights, the congressional salary amendment, and an amendment related to congressional apportionment, languished. Eighty-two years passed before Ohio, in 1873, became the seventh state to ratify it. Although the amendment languished, it did not die. Because the amendment was proposed without a ratification deadline, it is technically—as I shall discuss later—still pending before the states.

Why, we may wonder, did this amendment not win easy ratification if interest in congressional pay was keen? Constitutional scholars believe that the congressional pay and apportionment amendments were just too different from the other ten, which guaranteed what we now take for granted as our basic freedoms and over which there was such passionate debate in the ratifying conventions. Compared to freedom of speech, freedom of religion, and freedom against unlawful search and seizure, congressional pay and apportionment seemed mere housekeeping details.

Although the Constitutional amendment regarding congressional pay made little headway, the question of specific salary rates continued to trouble members. Inevitably, the issue would surface again. It did, in 1796, when the seven-year compensation bill expired, with its provision for a differential in the senators' favor during the seventh year only—March 4, 1795, to March 4, 1796. This time, there was little taste for acrimony or arguments over superiority. On March 1, 1796, the House sent to the Senate "an act for allowing compensation to the members of the Senate and House of Representatives of the United States, and to certain officers of both Houses." The Senate passed the bill

on March 4, the day the old measure was to expire.

The new compensation act, signed into law by President Washington on March 10, 1796, provided that "at every session of Congress, and at every meeting of the Senate in the recess of Congress . . . each Senator shall be entitled to receive six dollars for every day he shall attend the Senate; and shall also be allowed, at the commencement and end of every such session and meeting, six dollars for every twenty miles of the estimated distance, by the most usual road, from his place of residence to the seat of Congress." Except for the phrase about extra sessions of the Senate, the wording for the Representatives was identical. Gone was any pay differential. All members of Congress would receive six dollars per day. And their salaries remained at that level for the next twenty years! [9]

The six-dollar per diem worked out to an annual salary of between nine hundred and one thousand dollars. But even this seemingly modest sum drew fire from the press, which pointed out that members of the British House of Commons were paid the equivalent of less than a dollar a day.

In 1816, in view of the increased cost of living, a bill was introduced in the House that provided for an annual salary of fifteen hundred dollars. The argument was made that an annual salary, in place of the per diem of six dollars, would shorten sessions and thus save the government money. The measure's chief sponsor, Representative Richard Johnson of Kentucky, argued that members were deliberately extending their speeches. This delayed essential bills and made it necessary to call special sessions, which would allow members to collect more money.

After lively debate, both houses passed, and President Madison signed, the measure. This new law sparked a fire storm of criticism. Members who voted for the yearly salary were denounced from one end of the nation to the other. In Georgia, senators were hanged in effigy. In Tennessee, citizens demanded that the entire state delegation resign. The elections of 1816 proved a disaster for members who had backed the pay raise, as they were turned out of office in large numbers. To gauge the impact of this issue, one simply has to compare the number of members of the Senate and House who did not return to Congress following the elections of 1814 (93 members), 1816 (128 members), and 1818 (88 members). The 1816 number was 38 percent greater than in the previous election and 45 percent larger than in the following contest.[10]

At the next session of Congress, the Senate and House quickly repealed the fifteen-hundred-dollar yearly salary, and the amount reverted to six dollars per diem. In 1818, the per diem was raised to eight dollars, where it remained for thirty-eight years. In 1856, Congress finally established an annual salary rate—three thousand dollars; then, in 1857, the salary was set at $250 monthly while in session. For twelve months, this amount would equal three thousand dollars, but, in actuality, members received less, because Congress was not in session every month. Nine years later, in 1866, during the days of wartime inflation, members raised their salaries to five thousand dollars.

The provision for docking members' pay for the days that they did not attend originated in 1856 as part of the plan to abandon the per diem in favor of an annual salary. Some members opposed changing from the daily rate to an annual salary because they feared it would further stimulate the already high rate of absenteeism. They anticipated, not without justification, that a few of their colleagues would simply collect their salaries and spend much of their time at other pur-

suits. To combat that argument, the House added a provision to the salary bill authorizing the secretary of the Senate and the sergeant at arms of the House to dock absent members' pay "unless such Member or Delegate assigns as the reason for such absence the sickness of himself or of some member of his family."[11] The statute remains on the books even today, but it quickly became a "dead letter" because it was clear then, as it is now, that members' services are not confined to the floors of their respective houses.

In 1873, congressmen proposed raising their salaries from five thousand to seventy-five hundred dollars a year. The public furor unleashed by the proposal has not been equaled before or since. More explosive than the size of the increase was a provision making the raise retroactive for two years. That meant that every member of Congress, even those retiring or voted out of office, would receive a tidy windfall of five thousand dollars.

The press quickly dubbed the 1873 salary increase proposal the "salary grab" and the "back-pay steal." But despite heavy criticism, members pressed ahead. They could not argue, as they had argued half a century before, that the increase would actually save the government money. Quite simply, they argued that they desperately needed additional funds. Cries of poverty went up from the House and Senate, and from both parties. Richer members offered impassioned pleas on behalf of their poorer colleagues.

"Take the expense of any member of Congress that lives with a family in the most economical style here," argued millionaire Nevada Senator William Stewart, who allegedly spent more than five thousand dollars on a single Washington party, "and he cannot live on his $5,000." Oregon Senator Henry Corbett, a rich merchant, banker, and railroad promoter, spoke out for "justice," "toward those living a great way off who

A cartoonist contrasted Congress' "salary grab" in 1873 with the low pay of congressional clerks.

come here a great distance from their homes, who are obliged to bring their families here and establish them and make a home." [12]

Senator Simon Cameron of Pennsylvania, stating that he would vote for the amendment mainly because "the salary of the President ought to be increased," described how costs had escalated during his three decades of government service in Washington. "As to the pay of members of Congress, I do not care a button about it [the additional $2,500] myself," explained the millionaire Pennsylvania political boss, who was living at the Willard Hotel, but he sympathized with the plight of the poorer members. "I came here first at eight dollars a day [in 1845

when he became a senator], and that pay covered all my expenses then," Cameron reminisced. "I boarded at Gadsby's, and we had canvas-back ducks on the table every day in the season, and everything else in proportion, and I only paid ten dollars a week board. . . . After a while I got $3,000 a year, and it took all of that to pay [his expenses]; and now I get $5,000 a year, and although I have no family here except my wife and myself it costs me twenty-five dollars a week more than I receive from the Government for my board." Cameron cited specific examples of the increase in the cost of housing in Washington: "a member of the Cabinet [Secretary of State Hamilton Fish] now lives in

[352]

Millionaire Senator Simon Cameron, *left*, supported the 1873 congressional salary increase, but Senator Justin Morrill, *right*, opposed the increase because "We ought to set an example of frugality at the capital of our country." *The Daily Graphic, March 8, 1888, and U.S. Senate Historical Office*

the house I occupied when I filled a place in the Cabinet [secretary of war, 1861–1862]. . . . I had the furniture and the house for $100 a month. Now he pays $6,000 a year rent for the same house without furniture." [13]

Senator George G. Wright of Iowa based his opposition on the need for economy in government:

> . . . every day we have had evidence of the difficulty of the Government in . . . paying for the actual wants of the Government in its actual and necessary administration. We know that so far as the taxes are concerned, . . . it is almost impossible to pay the actual running expenses of the Government in connection with the interest upon our public debt. All over this land there is a complaint of taxation, and want, and suffering. Every day the cry comes to us from the people. . . . [salaries] are high enough already. There never has been a time yet but that good men throughout the land have sought these places at the salaries fixed by law." [14]

Some members, like Senator John Scott of Pennsylvania and Senator Justin Morrill of Vermont, both wealthy men, took the moral high ground, arguing that men should not aspire to a seat in Congress with an eye to a high salary, but out of selfless desire to serve the public. Seeing that his lofty argument was getting nowhere, however, Senator Morrill eventually adopted the more practical argument of unseemliness. "I believe," said the Vermont senator, who had just moved into a handsome mansion on Thomas Circle, "we ought to set an example of frugality at the capital of our country. . . . Certainly it seems to me not only wrong in itself but wholly inopportune, and I trust the Senate will reach the same conclusion." [15]

The majority of Morrill's colleagues did not reach the same conclusion, and many grew irritated by the sanctimonious speeches of the opponents of the increase. Senator

Senator Matthew Carpenter's support for raising congressional salaries cost him his Senate seat.

Library of Congress

Matthew Carpenter, a wealthy lawyer from Wisconsin and one of the unabashed champions of the increase, managed to take a few well-aimed swipes at his high-minded colleagues while presenting an unvarnished assessment of the importance of wealth to a political career:

The expense of living has advanced fearfully beyond what it was in the days of the Revolution. . . . The people of Wisconsin if they send a man here to represent them in the Senate wish him to live how? In the garret of a five-story building on crackers and cheese, to dress in goat skins and sleep in the wilderness? No. When they come here and ride by the mansions of my honorable friends from Vermont [Mr. Morrill and Mr. Edmunds] up on the Circle, see their elegant houses, brilliantly lighted, surrounded by acres of pavement, parks, fountains . . . and then come to the homes of

the "poor white trash" of this Senate and find their own Senators among them, they will not like that. [Laughter.] They have manly pride; and expect to find their Senators living like other Senators. . . . The people of Wisconsin know that the services of a competent cashier of a bank or president of an insurance company cannot be secured short of a salary of $10,000 a year. They believe a Senator ought to have as much brains as a cashier of a bank or president of an insurance company. And they are willing to pay accordingly. . . . There is great sublimity undoubtedly in the idea of rising above all the accidents of human nature, looking at things in the abstract, and regarding a man dressed in goat skins precisely as one dressed like a gentleman; but unfortunately the sentiment is not respected in practical life. Would my honorable friend from Vermont, [Mr. Morrill,] or my honorable friend from New Jersey, [Mr. Frelinghuysen,] if he was about giving a party, invite even a good man who was so eccentric as to defy all the canons of society in dress and demeanor? [16]

If the arguments for and against the salary bill of 1873 sound familiar to my colleagues today, perhaps those who lament the current plight of federal judges will take comfort in the fact that history is merely repeating itself. Senator Corbett's remarks 116 years ago are strikingly reminiscent of those we heard in January and February of this year:

I know of district judges who are receiving but $3,500 a year who ought to receive at least $5,000; and if we cannot provide for the judiciary of this country by giving them respectable salaries in order that they may maintain themselves in their integrity and place them beyond want and temptation, I think we had better not vote ourselves salaries. [17]

Despite the public outcry, the salary increase passed; and President Ulysses Grant signed the bill, thereby also doubling his own salary, from $25,000 to $50,000. Senator Carpenter and the other senators and representatives who claimed that their constituents supported increased salaries were sadly mistaken. Quite the contrary. The storm of abuse that broke over members of Congress

[354]

when the odious bill passed on March 3, 1873, reflected their constituents' lack of sympathy with their plight, especially in the midst of a deepening economic depression.

Startled by the ferocity of the outcry, members rushed to return their back pay to the Treasury or donate it to charity. In January 1874, congressmen who worried about reelection that fall, including Senator Carpenter, voted to repeal the salary increase. But the damage had already been done. That November, in bitter campaigns focusing on the "salary grab," constituents voted out member after member who had supported the "back-pay steal." Senator Matthew Carpenter's head was one of those that rolled.

Not until 1906, a third of a century after the infamous "salary grab," did Congress again seriously consider an increase in congressional pay, which had remained at five thousand dollars throughout the intervening decades. With little fanfare, representatives and senators quietly voted themselves an increase of twenty-five hundred dollars a year, and their new salary of seventy-five hundred dollars took effect in 1907.

In 1925, the Senate attached a rider to the legislative appropriation bill, providing that the pay of members would be increased to ten thousand dollars. There was not a word of debate on the amendment, and the vote was taken unexpectedly at an evening session when several senators who opposed the proposal were absent. Senator George Norris of Nebraska tried, without success, to secure its recall from the House. The House passed the provision after a half-hour of debate, without a recorded vote. President Calvin Coolidge was placed in an embarrassing dilemma, however, because the salary increase ran counter to the economic program he had been urging. Yet, he knew that if he vetoed the bill, Congress would delay or prevent other badly needed appropriations. Consequently, he signed the legislation.

When it comes to salaries, what goes up seldom comes down. But, in 1932 and 1933, at the height of the Great Depression, members of Congress voted to reduce their own salaries, along with those of other federal workers, as part of a package of measures to cut government spending. The Economy Act of 1932 reduced members' pay 10 percent, from $10,000 to $9,000; and, in 1933, their compensation was further lowered to $8,500. As economic conditions improved, salaries rose again in 1934, first to $9,000 and then to $9,500, and in 1935 they were restored to the 1925 level of $10,000. In 1945, a nontaxable annual expense allowance of $2,500 was enacted—which, essentially, amounted to a salary of $12,500. In 1946, Congress increased its pay to $12,500, effective on January 3, 1947, and continued the additional $2,500 nontaxable expense allowance, making a total of $15,000. That is what the salary was when I came to the House of Representatives in January of 1953. In 1953, the nontaxable expense allowance became taxable and part of the $15,000 salary.

Then, in 1955, Congress voted an 80 percent increase to $22,500. Coming at a time of economic prosperity, the action raised little outcry.

Periodic pay increases have continued: in 1965, to $30,000; in 1969, to $42,500; in 1975, to $44,600; in 1977, to $57,500; in 1979, to $60,662.50; in 1983, to $69,800; in 1984, to $72,600; and, in 1985, to $75,100. In 1987, there were two increases that brought the annual salary to its 1989 level of $89,500.

On October 1, 1965, for the first time, a slightly higher salary rate was established for Senate and House majority and minority leaders. Prior to 1969, the Senate president pro tempore received the same salary as other senators, except when there was no vice president. During such vacancies, his salary was the same as the vice president's. In 1969, the president pro tempore's rate was

A 1969 cartoon illustrates a popular view about the benefits of serving in Congress.

tied to that of the majority and minority leaders. In 1989, that rate is $99,500.

In 1983, for the first time since March 4, 1796, members of the Senate and House received differing rates of compensation. For the first six months of 1983, the Senate declined the higher legislative rate that had taken effect on January 1. Consequently, House members received an annual rate that was $9,137.50 higher than that paid to senators. On July 1, 1983, the congressional rate of $69,800 was extended to senators.

In the two hundred years from 1789 to November 1989, there had been a total of only twenty-two actually funded pay increases for senators, although, in recent years, several additional pay raises have been authorized but never funded. Of these twenty-two increases, two were quickly repealed (in 1816 and 1873), and three (in 1934 and 1935) constituted a restoration of reductions that occurred during the height of the Great Depression, leaving a net total of seventeen salary increases in two hundred years.

In November 1989, each house separately voted itself an increase. The House of Representatives, acting first, overwhelmingly voted to raise its members' pay to an annual rate of $96,600, effective February 1, 1990—a 7.7 percent increase. House members could continue to accept honoraria amounting to 30 percent of their 1989 salary level ($89,500) through 1990. The legislation provided that, effective January 1, 1991, House members' salaries would be increased 25 percent, to $120,750 annually, but with total elimination of honoraria.

Senate leaders had hoped to pass similar legislation for the Senate, but a last-minute whip check indicated the votes were lacking. Legislation was then adopted increasing senators' salaries 9.7 percent to an annual rate of $98,400, effective February 1, 1990, but, unlike the House, without an automatic further increase in January 1991. Also, unlike

the House, honoraria would be reduced from 40 percent of salary to 27 percent on February 1, 1990, and would only be phased out over time, dollar for dollar, as (and if) cost-of-living increases were permitted to take effect.

The failure of senators to match the courage of their House colleagues was regrettable, first, because it would result in a disparity in salaries favoring senators over House members in 1990, followed by a disparity favoring House members over senators in 1991 that would widen rapidly thereafter. Second, it was most unfortunate that the Senate did not eliminate honoraria completely. As a result, senators would continue to supplement their salaries with "back-door" income paid by special interest groups for speeches, a practice that has undermined the Senate in the public's esteem.

Pay raises have been achieved in three ways, and a fourth route may be in the making. During the eighteenth, nineteenth, and early twentieth centuries, members had to go on record as voting specifically to raise or not to raise their salaries. In recent decades, however, senators and representatives have adopted an intricate series of mechanisms designed to shift recommendations for pay increases to independent commissions appointed by the president.

The record 80-percent increase in 1955 was suggested by an independent commission, formally called the Commission on Judicial and Congressional Salaries, that had been set up by Congress two years earlier. In order to be approved, the panel's proposals required a vote by Congress. In 1967, Congress established the President's Commission on Executive, Legislative, and Judicial Salaries, referred to as the "quadrennial commission," which would make salary recommendations every four years. Unlike the system with the earlier panel, this commission's rec-

After two hundred years, congressional salaries remain the subject of controversy.   *Inter-IKEA Systems B.V., 1990*

ommendations would become law unless either chamber passed a resolution to block them.

The third method by which congressional pay has been increased was established in 1975, when Congress voted to make members eligible for the same annual cost-of-living increases given to other federal employees. Members would still, however, have to vote on appropriations to fund the increase. Then, in 1981, Congress devised procedures whereby members could receive the cost-of-living increases without having to vote on appropriating the funds.

In 1985, the quadrennial commission process underwent revision, because the old procedure by which either chamber could block the president's recommended pay raise was upset by the Supreme Court ruling (*Immigration and Naturalization Service* v. *Chadha*), which

banned such "legislative vetoes." Congress, therefore, rewrote the law to conform to the Court's decision. Now, to block a recommended pay increase, both chambers are required to pass a resolution of disapproval— which the president may sign or veto— within thirty days of the date the president submits his budget.

At present, another procedure is slowly making headway to render congressional pay raises more palatable. It involves resurrecting an idea that has been around for two hundred years: the proposed congressional salary amendment to the Constitution that I mentioned earlier. The notion is simple: keep members from pocketing a salary increase until after they face voters in the next election. I shall repeat the amendment: "No law, varying the compensation for the services of the Senators and Representatives, shall take effect, until an election of Representatives shall have intervened." Unlike most modern attempts to change the Constitution, the salary amendment had no time limit for state ratification. Technically, the amendment still needs only a thirty-eight-state majority for ratification. Since the original six states ratified the amendment between 1789 and 1791, twenty-six additional states have ratified it—nineteen of them in just the last five years—bringing the total, to date, to thirty-two, six shy of the required number.

It remains unclear whether Congress or the courts would allow an amendment, slowly ratified over two hundred years, to take effect. Is an amendment to the Constitution still viable after two centuries? While the answer to that question is as yet unknown—and there are other questions to which the answers are equally uncertain—one thing is clear: interest is strong on all sides, and we will undoubtedly continue to struggle with the salary issue as Congress moves into its third century. It is an issue that has, from the beginning, borne the curse of political grandstanding, posturing, hypocrisy, and demagoguery—by members, the news media, and others—thus feeding public opposition to congressional pay increases, and, in all probability, it will continue to do so.

CHAPTER 16

Archives and Records

December 4, 1980 *

Mr. President, inscribed in stone at the entrance to the National Archives building, which stands halfway between the Capitol and the White House on Pennsylvania Avenue, are the words, "What is Past is Prologue." This is an important sentiment for the lawmakers of this nation to consider as we grapple with the problems of our society today and look toward the future. We cannot, and should not, forget our history, for, in the words of the philosopher George Santayana, "Those who do not remember the past are condemned to repeat it."

These concerns have led me to address the Senate on a regular basis regarding its historical development, so that we may not forget the heritage of this great institution, and so that we may build upon the successes of the past and not repeat the failures.

Our predecessors have left for us, and we leave for posterity, a bountiful record of words and accomplishments. These are in the form of our speeches and actions in the *Congressional Record,* and the bills and resolutions, reports, and other documents we submit for the record and to the Senate during each session of Congress. Those who study our actions and words—historians, political scientists, sociologists, lawyers, and many others—will scrutinize this record

carefully. But they will want more. They will want to see the correspondence and memoranda, the minutes and transcripts, and other background material that shaped the legislative history of the laws we have enacted and other actions we have taken.

Such records are being compiled every day by every senator's office, by the Senate committees, and by the clerks and other staff members whom we see before us here in the Senate chamber. Today, I would like to direct our attention to the making and the preservation of these records, and all of the records of the United States Senate since 1789.

When the public records of the Senate were transferred to the National Archives in 1937, the examiner who surveyed the collection reported to the archivist of the United States: "From the standpoint of historical as well as intrinsic interest, this is perhaps the most valuable collection of records in the entire Government. It touches all phases of governmental activity, and contains a vast amount of research material that has never been used." [1]

The records of the Senate may be small by comparison with the voluminous paperwork turned out by the executive departments, but, in content, they are even more rich and

---

* Updated April 1989

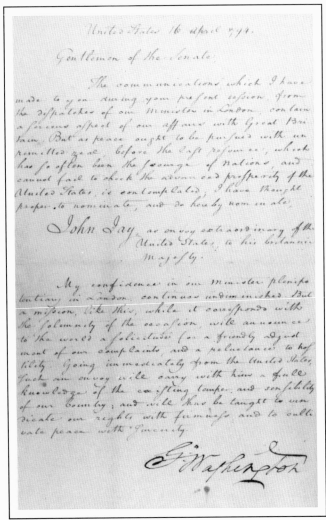

George Washington's nomination of John Jay as envoy to Great Britain is one of many documents from the First Congress in the care of the National Archives. *National Archives*

from the first presidential election; petitions from citizens, including Revolutionary War veterans seeking benefits; and handwritten drafts of the first legislation introduced in Congress. One outstanding example is the Judiciary Act of 1789, which established our federal court system. There is the rough copy of the first *Senate Journal,* badly water damaged, perhaps due to a leaky roof in Federal Hall where the Senate first convened (or to a spilled teakettle), and also the smooth copy of the *Journal* with its elegant eighteenth-century script, as overseen by the first secretary of the Senate, Samuel A. Otis.

This is the stuff of which history is made. It is awe inspiring to hold in one's hands the documents signed by Washington, Alexander Hamilton, Thomas Jefferson, and James Madison, or by those three great leaders of the Senate in its so-called "Golden Age," Henry Clay, Daniel Webster, and John C. Calhoun. Unlike the early records of the House of Representatives, many of which were lost, either through the carelessness of its clerks or in the raging fires which gutted the Capitol during the War of 1812, Senate records dating back to 1789 are essentially intact. Considering the treatment these records have received over time, this is truly a miracle.

During its early years, the government of the United States moved about in search of a permanent home and carried its records about with it. Because of the poor roads in those days, the records were packed in trunks and cases and strapped to the decks of flatboats, which hauled them first from New York to Philadelphia in 1790 and then from Philadelphia to Washington in 1800. The papers of Congress arrived on the docks of Alexandria, Virginia, some months before the House and Senate convened in November of 1800 and were carted up to the still unfinished Senate wing of the Capitol. There they remained until August of 1814, when

rewarding. For example, in the legislative records division of the National Archives, just seven blocks from here, one may open a small metal box and find the records of the Senate in the First Congress, which convened in March 1789. There are actual documents sent to the Senate by President George Washington—some written in his own hand—nominating his cabinet officers, making diplomatic appointments, and transmitting treaties and other executive communications. There also are the electoral ballots

In recent years, the *Senate Journal* from the First Congress has been carefully preserved by the National Archives, but in the previous century-and-a-half it suffered severely from water damage and fading. *National Archives*

word reached Washington that British troops had broken through the American lines at Bladensburg and were advancing on the city. Chaos reigned, and many of the clerks of Congress were pressed into service by the local militia. All available carts and wagons were also gathered up for military needs.

In the Senate, the long-time secretary, Samuel Otis, had recently died and his successor had not yet been elected. Fortunately, a young clerk, Lewis Machen, had the presence of mind to take charge. Commandeer-

ing a farmer's wagon, he piled the Senate's valuable records into it and made haste for his farm near Centreville, Virginia; thus, the records of the Senate were saved. In the House, the remaining clerks were frantically loading records onto an ox cart on the very eve of the invasion. In their haste, they lost most of the petitions and private papers for the years 1789 to 1799 and also the House's secret journal, which was consumed by the flames set by the British troops. The House, bitter about the destruction of these records, appointed a select committee to investigate

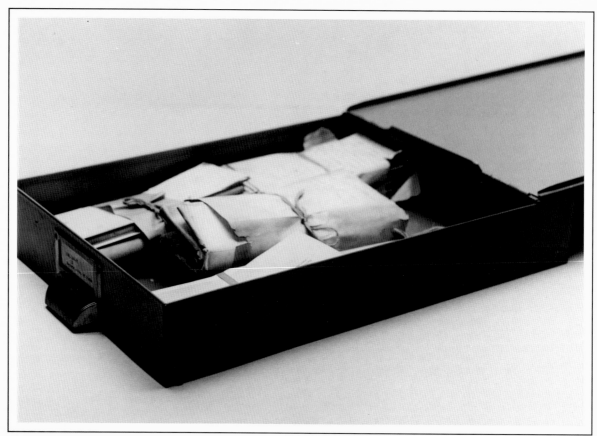

In the nineteenth century, government documents were folded and tied with red tape for filing or storage.

the matter. When the committee branded the clerk of the House, Patrick Magruder, as having been derelict in his duty, he resigned, expressing the hope that his successor might have "an easier and happier time in the discharge of his duties" than he had had.[2]

Even more hazardous to the records of the Congress than dangerous sea voyages and invading armies was the century of neglect which followed.

Busy senators and their very small clerical staffs had no use for documents once the legislation was enacted and the Congress had adjourned; they, therefore, consigned the records of the Senate to the darkest, dankest rooms of the Capitol basement, those that were unfit for human occupation or for stor-

ing supplies. Here, in vault-like chambers, the records piled up. The papers lay on wooden racks, while bound volumes were stacked on the floor. There were no windows in these rooms, and their brick and steel walls and ceilings afforded protection against fire but not against dampness. Since the nineteenth-century brickwork is porous, the records grew damp and moldy. A survey conducted by archivists in 1937 found that

Rooms scattered throughout the basement contain bound volumes of engrossed copies of Senate Bills, originals of Minutes and Journals of Legislative proceedings of the Senate, Bill Books, Account Books and other Legislative and Administrative records. Most of these have been subjected to severe hazards. Some of the volumes are stacked on the concrete floor. Water has seeped through the floor of the terrace above and cock-roaches and other insects have damaged many of the documents.[3]

I should point out that, in the nineteenth century, it was the custom to fold all government documents roughly into thirds and then tie them with thin red ribbon—hence, the expression "red tape"—for convenient stacking in the pigeonholes of the clerks' desks and other receptacles. Stored in such damp and unventilated conditions, the documents became so dirty and brittle that there was danger they would literally fall apart in one's hand should they be unfolded. Before the Fiftieth Congress, in 1887, documents were not stored in envelopes. As a result, they were out of sequence and scattered about in no particular order. The lack of indexes and inventories made them, for all practical purposes, irretrievable and of no possible research use, either to the Senate or to private scholars.

Indeed, while some records of the House had been deposited in the Library of Congress, for years it was said of Senate records that they were "somewhere around the Capitol." Now, I am not talking about a few file cabinets of documents. The records of the Senate at that time totaled some 6,638 linear feet—over a mile long. This is small by today's standards, but still quite a collection to be lost "somewhere around the Capitol."

A fortuitous appointment to the Senate staff, in 1927, set in motion a massive rescue operation for these valuable records. Secretary of the Senate Edwin Pope Thayer, an Indiana Republican, hired as a file clerk a young man named Harold Hufford. From Thayer's home town, Hufford took the job with the Senate to support himself while a student at the George Washington University law school. One day, in search of some needed documents, Hufford ventured down into the basement rooms under the west front terrace. Cautiously opening the door,

he found himself faced with a mountain of papers, in filing cases, stacked in boxes, or just scattered about the floor. He reported that his entrance disturbed a host of mice and swarms of fat roaches. Groping his way across the dark room, he reached for the light switch. When the single yellow bulb came on, Hufford looked down and saw that he was standing on an official-looking document. Picking it up, he found two markings on it: "the print of my rubber heel and the signature of Vice-President John C. Calhoun." Said Hufford: "I knew who Calhoun was; and I knew that the nation's documents shouldn't be treated like that."[4]

From that day on, the preservation of the Senate's records became both an obsession and a career for Harold Hufford. Each day, he would go about his regular duties as a filing clerk for the secretary of the Senate and attend law school classes, but, in every free moment, he would search out Senate documents and haul them up to the Senate attic.

At the beginning of the twentieth century, the Capitol roof was lifted as part of a renovation program. This created a large storage space. As early as 1904, the Office of the Secretary of the Senate began transferring noncurrent records to the attic, and Hufford added to them his new discoveries. There in the attic, he would pore over the material and attempt to place the records into some order. His search took him to unlikely places in some fifty to seventy-five different areas of the Capitol. Nor was he the first to find many items. Autograph hunters had often beaten him in his search and snipped off the signatures from presidential messages and other documents. Other items were missing and lost, probably forever; President Wilson's message on the outbreak of World War I and President Franklin Roosevelt's handwritten message on the soldiers' bonus were among the most prominent of these.

The National Archives building attracts many visitors to view the Declaration of Independence and the Constitution.

For a while, Hufford was unable to locate any Senate records from the Fortieth and Fiftieth congresses, but then one day some construction workers tore down a wall while remodeling a room and uncovered the missing records. These, as with the others he had been collecting, the young clerk carried up to the attic.

Harold Hufford's one-man search and salvage operation brought together in one place, and in reasonable order, the many thousands of historical records of the Senate. But the story does not stop there. While the Senate attic was an improvement over the many dingy basement hideaways, and was large enough to house the entire collection in one place, it, too, was unsuitable for proper preservation of the records. Dust and sooty grime sifted through the roof; rain seeped through the skylights; and temperatures were too extreme to guarantee the survival of these fragile documents.

Finally, in 1936, the newly completed massive National Archives building in the Federal Triangle stood ready to receive the records of the national government. It is startling to realize how long it took this nation to correct the careless and cavalier treatment of its precious historical resources. As cases of documents were being carried out of basements at the State Department and other executive agencies—many thousands of records having already been lost in tragic fires during the nineteenth century—the United States Senate arranged to ship its own files from the Senate attic to the Archives building.

Under a resolution agreed to on March 25, 1937, the Senate authorized its secretary, Edwin Halsey, to transfer to the Archives all records he did not deem necessary for current business. On April 2, 1937, a truck and five workmen arrived at the Capitol's Senate wing to haul away Harold Hufford's laboriously assembled collection.[5]

Mr. President, I am happy to say that Hufford's efforts to preserve Senate records continued. In 1935, he had become one of the first employees of the National Archives, and, when the records of Congress arrived there, he became director of the legislative section. With a staff of nine assistants, he began placing the records of the Senate, and later the House, into archival containers in fireproof surroundings, with proper temperature and ventilation for long-term preservation. Many of the older documents were unfolded, laminated, and placed in envelopes. In addition to organizing, storing, and inventorying the records, Hufford believed in fast and efficient service to the Congress. He argued that misplaced or inaccessible records were as bad as no records at all. Former Representative Ralph Harvey of Indiana recalled at the time of Hufford's retirement that the archivist could always be counted upon for prompt service. "Many times, upon receiving a request from the Hill, he located the desired records, ran into the street, hailed a taxicab and, at his own expense, delivered the records into the hands of those who requested them." Expressions of astonishment at such fast service were not infrequent. The result was that many on Capitol Hill said that they could receive faster service on their noncurrent records from the National Archives than they could by keeping and servicing the records themselves. That remains true today.

During World War II, the Senate Special Committee to Investigate the National Defense Program called upon Hufford to handle records searches in the mammoth files it had compiled on all aspects of wartime defense production. Hufford put in an eight-hour day at the Archives and then another eight hours at the committee, until he finally collapsed from exhaustion. Harold Hufford continued his valuable service on behalf of the records of Congress until his retirement on August 31, 1961. He died in 1970. At the Archives, he was succeeded by two of his assistants, first Buford Rowland and then George Perros. Perros spent nearly forty-five years in federal service, most of it devoted to the records of Congress.

While the Senate sent its records to the Archives in 1937, the House did not follow suit for another decade. In June 1937, the House Library Committee favorably reported a resolution to move House records from the Library of Congress and eight other locations in the Capitol and House office buildings down to the National Archives. Due to the objections of its clerk, however, the House did not act on the resolution. The clerk in those days considered the records of little historical interest, thought the transfer would be an unnecessary expense, and feared that the records would be less accessible to the House. In 1946, however, the special committee which drafted the Legislative Reorganization Act considered it incongruous for Senate records to be housed at the National Archives while House records were elsewhere, and the act required that the secretary of the Senate and clerk of the House oversee the transfer of all noncurrent records of Congress to the National Archives. That provision, as it relates to this body, has been incorporated into Senate Rule XI.

The transfer of records to the National Archives is a continuous process. At the end of each two-year session of Congress, Senate committees routinely ship their noncurrent records to the Archives. These committee records comprise the largest share of Senate records at the Archives and also pose the greatest problems in archival management. Even before the first transfer of records to

Bound copies of the *Senate Journal* are stored on shelves at the National Archives.   *U.S. Senate Historical Office*

the Archives, Senate rules required that all records on measures referred to committees and not reported upon be returned (for safekeeping) to the secretary of the Senate at the close of each session. This apparently was done; but the rule made no provision for the transfer of papers which the committees had received directly, such as letters from the president or communications between the chairman of the committee and the executive departments, nor was correspondence from the public included. Some committees returned all of their files to the secretary, while others retained or destroyed their records.

There are no remaining records at all for many committees in a number of congresses, and only the most perfunctory material sur-

vives for many others. I am told that the surviving records of the Foreign Relations Committee covering much of the 1930's, when important neutrality issues and other foreign policy matters were under discussion, can be fitted into a single envelope—and this material was saved only because it was discovered behind a file cabinet some years later. Conversely, for many other committees, there is an abundance of material. Students of Indian policies, for instance, have good reason to thank Albert A. Grorud, clerk of the Senate Indian Affairs Committee from 1927 to 1952. While the official papers of the committee for those years are infinitesimal, Grorud saved his own files on the committee's activities, which fill 141 boxes in the Archives.

Citizens' petitions sometimes bear thousands of signatures and take unwieldy forms, like this one received in 1924.

Library of Congress

Other committees have retained their past records in storage spaces here in the Senate office buildings, often to be forgotten for many years. At the direction of then-Chairman John Stennis, the Senate Armed Services Committee, a few years ago, shipped to the Archives some nine hundred boxes of its noncurrent papers—some dating back to the Military Affairs and Naval Affairs committees in the early part of this century. These records comprise a magnificent testimony to our nation's defense policies in the twentieth century and will be of immeasurable use to military historians in the future. Carefully inventoried and screened

for sensitive and classified materials, this collection is being made available to researchers on a case-by-case basis.

For those committees which transfer their noncurrent records at regular intervals, there are also many troublesome considerations. What should they save? What will be useful to researchers in the future? And what will merely waste space? Recently, the Senate Historical Office published an excellent guidebook for Senate committees, with recommendations on the types of records to save and those to discard.[6] But this is a very sensitive chore, for one cannot completely predict the research needs of the future.

For example, a great many of the congressional records at the Archives are from citizens exercising their right under the First Amendment "to petition Government for a redress of grievances." These petitions come in all shapes and sizes, from a single sheet of paper signed by one or more persons to great rolls of paper with thousands of signatures. Recently, a professor from the State University of New York at Oswego, Judith Wellman, made use of the petitions received from women abolitionists in upstate New York during the 1830's. By carefully examining the signatures on the petitions and the addresses they gave, Dr. Wellman was able to describe in considerable detail the distribution of women abolitionists in that critical period of pre–Civil War agitation. For the period after 1840, however, she found that many of the petitions were destroyed. She related that "the late Dr. C.H. Van Tyne used to tell his classes at the University of Michigan how, when he was making his *Guide to the Archives of the Government of the United States*, he found a caretaker in the Capitol keeping his stove hot with bundles of antislavery petitions. 'There were so many of them,' the caretaker said, 'that those he used would never be missed.' " [7]

Today, Senate records are in constant use by a wide variety of researchers. During 1988 alone, the National Archives provided photocopies of approximately five thousand pages of documents in response to research requests for information found in the Senate records. Besides the academic user, there are also law firms that consult judicial nomination files to study federal judges, and even prisoners who write to the Archives for background information on the law that they were convicted of violating. Among the largest continuing research projects are the various publications of the National Historical Publications and Records Commission within the National Archives. These massive

searches to find, edit, and publish the papers of great Americans have included the edited writings of such senators as John C. Calhoun, Henry Clay, Jefferson Davis, Andrew Jackson, Andrew Johnson, and Daniel Webster, as well as microform editions of the papers of Albert Gallatin, Timothy Pickering, and William Plumer. In addition, the editors of many other publications projects, covering the lives of Americans great and humble, have combed through Senate records. [8]

Prior to 1980, access to the Senate's records at the National Archives proved troublesome for researchers. Some Senate committees were willing to open their records as soon as they were transferred to the Archives. Others kept them closed for many decades. Even within each committee, policies proved inconsistent, depending on the momentary judgments of the chairman, staff director, or clerk who was called upon to decide individual requests. Recognizing this situation, the Temporary Select Committee to Study the Senate Committee System, in 1977, recommended that the "Senate adopt a resolution directing that all noncurrent committee records be opened within a certain reasonable time after their creation except where a committee declares that personal privacy, national security, or other national interest requires continued confidentiality." [9]

In response to this recommendation, I, as the then-majority leader, sponsored a Senate resolution that set a policy governing access to all Senate records at the National Archives. Adopted by the Senate in December 1980, that policy provides public access to the vast majority of Senate records at the Archives. Unless an individual committee takes specific action to the contrary, by majority vote, its routine records are made available after they become twenty years old. Records containing information that is potentially detrimental to personal privacy or to nation-

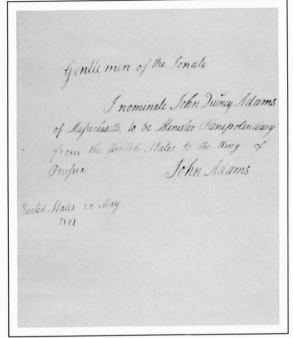

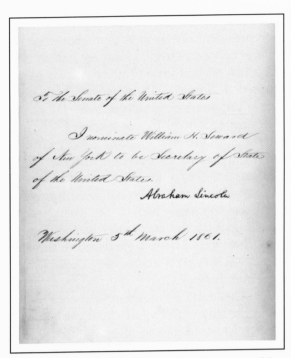

Among the handwritten presidential documents in the Senate's collection at the National Archives are, *left*, a nomination by John Adams of his son John Quincy Adams and, *right*, Abraham Lincoln's nomination of William Seward to be secretary of state.

National Archives

al security interests are opened after fifty years.[10] Adoption of this resolution has greatly increased the public use of Senate records since 1980.

In 1982, a special Senate study group, charged with planning activities to commemorate the Senate's 1989 bicentennial, recommended publication of a guide to permanent Senate records at the National Archives. The panel concluded: "Dating from 1789, these materials are fundamental sources for the study and understanding of the Senate's history and role in the legislative process and of the general history of the American people. They are a basic component in the Senate's institutional memory."[11] Beginning in 1983, the National Archives' legislative records division made this project its top priority, along with a companion guide for House records. At the Senate special bicentennial session, on

April 6, 1989, the result of this labor became evident to all. On each senator's desk there appeared a handsome 356-page hard-bound volume entitled *Guide to the Records of the United States Senate at the National Archives, 1789–1989: Bicentennial Edition.*[12] This work, published as a Senate Document to ensure the widest possible distribution, contains individual chapters describing the historical records of each Senate committee, together with an excellent essay on conducting research in the records of Congress.

Mr. President, I should also like to give some flavor of the records of the Senate that are housed in the National Archives. One of the most fascinating groups of papers is the so-called "McCook Collection." This collection of particularly rare presidential papers was initiated by Secretary of the Senate Anson McCook, who culled them from the larger body of Senate records during the

[371]

1880's. He chose at least one document from each president. There is Washington's list of cabinet officers. There is John Adams' nomination of his son John Quincy Adams to be minister to Prussia. There is Abraham Lincoln's nomination of Ulysses S. Grant as Lieutenant General in the Army. There are Supreme Court nominations ranging from John Marshall to Thurgood Marshall. There is John Kennedy's message concerning the Nuclear Test Ban Treaty. To turn the pages of these volumes—which, for years, were maintained by the secretaries of the Senate until they were finally transferred to the Archives—is to travel across two centuries of American history.

Mr. President, although my remarks today deal primarily with the official records of the Senate, I should like to mention briefly another important body of material without which it would be impossible to study and fully understand the nation's past. I am referring to the papers of the 1,792 men and women who have served as members of this body during its two-hundred-year history. Technically, these papers belong to the senators in whose offices they were assembled and created. More appropriately, however, they belong to the nation. In this spirit, senators over the years have deposited and eventually donated their office files and personal papers to approximately 350 universities, colleges, historical societies, and other educational institutions across the length and breadth of our country. Recently, for example, I made arrangements to deposit my papers with the West Virginia University in Morgantown, in the hope that future generations will benefit from them.

In 1978, the Senate sponsored a Conference on the Research Use and Disposition of Senators' Papers. In addressing that gathering of 250 historians, archivists, and congressional staff, I noted that "certain senators, it is sometimes acknowledged, and it is a fact,

have eclipsed even sitting presidents in the influence they exerted on our national destiny, and have long since been remembered when presidents have been forgotten." I reminded those present that "many important documents from the records and files of such senators have vanished, or have been destroyed over the years," and I called for action to establish preservation standards for senatorial records.[13] In 1985, the Senate Historical Office published an invaluable document entitled *Records Management Handbook for United States Senators and Their Repositories*.[14] Drawing upon the experience of historians, archivists, and those who work with these records here in the Senate, this publication has become an indispensable resource for all senators.

In 1983, the Senate Historical Office published an extensive catalog of locations of former senators' papers. The product of five years of labor, this publication was designed to facilitate the use of these valuable collections.[15]

Mr. President, I came to the United States Senate as a senator from West Virginia in January 1959. Thirty years later, at the beginning of the 101st Congress in January 1989, only one other sitting member of the Senate—Strom Thurmond—had been serving that long or longer. When I arrived, the Senate included such figures as Lyndon Johnson, Richard Russell, John F. Kennedy, Harry F. Byrd, Sr., Everett Dirksen, and Hubert Humphrey. They now belong to history. From January 1959 to January 1989, 213 Americans took the oath to become senators of the United States. The membership of the Senate that convened in January 1989 includes 62 senators whose service began within the past decade. Our collective memory of men and events in this institution is growing shorter. We should, therefore, take care that our records are preserved, here on the floor, in our personal offices, and in our committees. We owe this to those of generations yet unborn, who will someday stand in our places, and whose pathway will be lighted by the lamp of written history we leave behind. Without that record, there would be, for them, no prologue to span the void.

> Alone I walked the ocean strand;
> A pearly shell was in my hand;
> I stooped, and wrote upon the sand
>   My name, the year, the day.
> As onward from the spot I passed,
> One lingering look behind I cast;
> A wave came rolling high and fast,
>   And washed my lines away.
> And so, methought, 'twill shortly be
> With every mark on earth from me;
> A wave from dark oblivion's sea
>   Will sweep across the place
> Where I have trod the sandy shore
> Of Time, and been to be no more,
> Of me, my day, the name I bore,
>   To leave no track nor trace. . . .[16]

CHAPTER 17

Senate Pages

September 8, 1980[*]

Today, I shall explore the history behind a group of Senate employees we see every day. Each morning that the Senate is in session, we see before us, sitting on the risers, the fresh faces of our young pages. They have already been up, attending school and on the job, for several hours before we set foot in this chamber, and no matter how late into the night we remain in session, the pages are always with us. All we need to do is to beckon, and a page will respond to our every request. I am afraid that we sometimes take these young people for granted, so, in partial remedy, I shall tell my colleagues of the pages' long history of service to this institution—a history that tells us much about the institution itself.

The term "page" is of Middle English origin. According to the *Oxford English Dictionary*, the word dates from the fifteenth century when it meant a youth employed as a personal attendant to a person of rank. Hence, because of the similarity of their ages and the services they provide to members of Congress, the word "page" is the term used to describe these young congressional employees.

One of the earliest references to pages in Congress is found in a report on House pages issued by the Twenty-seventh Congress in 1842. The report noted:

From the origin of the present Government, in 1789, to the present time, they [messengers] have been employed under the orders and resolutions of the House, and experience has attested the necessity of their services. . . . from the first session of Congress held at the city of Washington, they have continued to be employed, with the approbation of the House.[1]

The report also stated that, in 1827, the House employed three young pages to wait on its members, and that the number had steadily increased.[2]

The original messengers were usually adults. The practice of appointing young boys to serve as pages apparently began with Senator Daniel Webster of Massachusetts in the late 1820's. The first Senate page, appointed by Webster, was nine-year-old Grafton Dulany Hanson, who was descended from John Hanson of Maryland, a president of the Continental Congress. Grafton Hanson, grandson of Senate Sergeant at Arms Mountjoy Bayly, grew up in the office of page, serving for more than ten years. He moved on to other jobs in the Senate and only left to fight in the Mexican War, where he was decorated for bravery.[3]

[*] Revised September 1989

Sixteen Senate pages posed in the chamber around 1904.

In 1831, Daniel Webster appointed a second page, twelve-year-old Isaac Bassett, who spent the next sixty-four years in the Senate, serving as messenger and later as assistant doorkeeper. I shall have more to say of Bassett in a later address.

These early pages wore blue uniforms with shiny brass buttons. They, like those who followed them, had a variety of duties to perform which might not occur to us today. Pages still keep our desks supplied with writing materials and retrieve documents for us, but, in the nineteenth century, this job required knowledge of what type of quill pen and ink each senator preferred. Daniel Webster, for example, used a broad-nibbed pen, but Henry Clay liked his sharpened to a fine point. Since ink did not come in convenient bottles in those days, pages had to mix it up and achieve the proper con-

sistency to satisfy the senators. There were also individual blotting-salt shakers to be filled. Some of us may have wondered what these little shakers here on our desks are for; the salt—actually a mixture of ground-up cuttlefish bone known as pounce—was used to blot the ink.[4]

There were other needs of the senators to which the pages catered. The flamboyant Sam Houston of Texas used to stride into the old Senate chamber wearing such eye-catching accessories as a leopard-skin waistcoat, a bright red vest, or a Mexican sombrero. Senator Houston required special attention. He would while away the time in the old chamber by whittling, creating a pile of shavings beneath his desk, and pages would bring him his pine blocks and then clean up the shavings.[5] There is a charming description of Houston in a book by a Senate page

Even in Washington, Senator Sam Houston of Texas did not forsake his sombrero.
Archives Division, Texas State Library

during the 1850's. In *Memoirs of a Senate Page*, Christian Eckloff related:

"Sam" Houston was one of the gentlest and most kindly natures I have ever known. A true friend and a gallant gentleman. Day after day, during spare moments, he sat there in his seat carving hearts out of soft pine wood. They were pieces about the size of the hand. When he had completed one of these works of art, he would summon a page, and pointing toward some fair spectator in the gallery, would say: "Give this to that lady up there, with General 'Sam' Houston's compliments.['"] [6]

In addition to keeping General Houston supplied with whittling blocks, which "were especially prepared for the general by the Senate cabinetmaker (Mr. Griffith)," [7] the pages also had to keep the Senate snuffboxes filled, a service they continue to perform—although to a much lesser degree—to this day.

Until the late 1840's, a single snuffbox was kept on the vice president's desk. After that, two small snuffboxes were placed on either side of the presiding officer's chair, a position which two similar small boxes retain today. Senators would use a "pinch" to "gratify the nostrils and clear the mind." [8] According to Eckloff: "A number of senators were very fond of snuff. Seward, Foot, Collamer, Cass, Evans, and Butler were so much addicted to its use, they could not speak well without it." [9]

The pages themselves sometimes had a good time with the snuff. One nineteenth-century page, Edmund Alton, who also wrote a charming book about his years in the Senate called *Among the Law-Makers*, noted that when things got dull in the chamber, a page would sneak a large pinch of snuff and pass "his hand beneath the noses" of his fellow pages as they sat in the front of the chamber like a row of solemn "penguins," throwing them into a fit of sneezing. [10]

As the Senate grew in the 1840's, it hired two additional pages to help out with the expanding workload. One of the new boys, an eight-year-old orphan named Baker A. Jamison, also wrote about his life as a page. In his book, *Memories of Great Men and Events, 1840–1861*, Jamison gave his impression of the senators of that era: "On the floor of the Senate . . . were congregated men of high character and eminent ability, distinguished as statesmen . . . and forming a galaxy of talent of which any nation might be proud." [11]

In those early days, pages were usually paid $1.50 for each day the Senate was in session. [12] Sometimes, however, the sessions lasted late into the night, and the sleepy pages had to remain at their posts. Night sessions meant a great deal of extra work for the boys. Oil had to be brought for the lamps on the walls, candles for the desks, and continuous supplies of hickory wood were needed for the fireplaces and stoves in the old chamber. In the wintertime, the pages were responsible for keeping the fires blazing away night and day. Christian Eckloff described the scene:

One winter I recall—the winter of 1855–1856, if I am not mistaken—was extremely severe, with frequent snows and the mercury trying hard to get out at the bottom of the tube. Woolen shawls were then the fashionable garment for both men and boys, and they were heavy and warm; of somber hues, principally grey and brown, with a little variety in Scotch plaids. It was a common sight to behold the revered dignity of the Senate wrapped head and all in these big shawls, and comfortably retaining them in the chamber on very cold days. Many of the older men in their efforts to keep warm made frequent pilgrimages to the open grates, and were far more interested in the state of the fires than in any State of the Union.[13]

At the end of each session, the Senate usually voted to award the pages a bonus of two hundred dollars each. Baker Jamison recalled receiving, at the conclusion of the 1846 session, a small pile of twenty-dollar gold pieces. "This," he noted, "was a large sum for a small boy to carry through the streets of Washington, so the careful and thoughtful Secretary, Mr. Ashbury Dickens, had the money sewed up in our vest pockets and sent us home in the Senate mail wagon."[14]

As one might imagine, enterprising pages soon hit upon another way of earning a little extra money. Their route to wealth lay through the autograph books that soon became a plague to senators. Tourists seeking senatorial autographs were willing to tip pages to help collect the signatures. Sometimes, a visiting lady in the gallery would send the page in with her personal autograph book, seeking an inscription. The going rate in the 1850's was six cents a name. Pages would trade names among themselves, trying to get a complete set, which might bring as much as ten dollars. Most senators willingly cooperated until the demands became too frequent, but some were annoyed by the clamor for their signatures from the first. Henry Clay and John C. Cal-

houn were particularly reluctant to give their autographs, and to get them required considerable strategic maneuvering by the pages.[15]

Many of the pages retained into their later careers the energy and enterprise shown in their entrepreneurial activities. Baker Jamison grew up to become a lawyer and serve in the Maryland legislature. John M. Wilson, who was also a page at the time, went on to West Point and became a brigadier general during the Civil War. A more colorful former page was Henry Burgevine, an adventurer who became a soldier of fortune in China, where he was eventually killed—tied up in a bag and thrown overboard—after leading rebel forces against the emperor.[16]

Another page from Maryland, Arthur Pue Gorman, showed early signs of the political skills that would later make him a powerful Senate leader. As a young House page in 1852, he caught the eye of Senator Stephen Douglas, who had him transferred to the Senate page force. The story goes that, during a recess, Gorman carved his name in one of the stone columns of the old chamber with his penknife. Years later, when Gorman was a senator, he went back and claimed he found the evidence of his youthful misdeed.[17]

Gorman, a Democrat, rose quickly in politics, holding a number of appointive posts before becoming a member of the Maryland legislature and leader of the state's Democratic party. In 1880, he was elected to the U.S. Senate, where he served for some twenty years. Although an extremely influential senator, Gorman never forgot his days as a page.[18]

The Civil War brought dramatic changes to the Senate, where pages, like senators, tended to sympathize with either the northern or southern cause. After secession, most pages from the South returned home, and their places were filled by pages from the North who were considerably younger.

In those days, pages were responsible for making their own living arrangements, and some of their boardinghouses apparently lacked bathing facilities. At one point, the pages' appearance became so objectionable that officers of the House and Senate tried to enforce a rule that every page take two baths a week in one of the huge, cold, marble bathtubs in the Capitol basement. The pages tried every trick in the book to avoid the baths. To prevent escape, a ticket system was devised. Each boy was issued two tickets; upon entering the baths, he was to turn one in, which would be credited to his name, with a tally taken each week. But the clever boys took to selling their tickets to city boys who were eager to say they had had a congressional ablution.[19]

After the Civil War, the pages found still other ways to make extra money. A thriving business in autographs continued, especially during the impeachment trial of President Andrew Johnson, when they were also able to sell as souvenirs such leftover trash from the trial as programs and ticket stubs. At night, pages could earn money working in the folding rooms, sorting and folding the Senate's outgoing mail.

The best sideline of all, however, was arranging for the printing and dissemination of senators' speeches. When a senator gave an important speech, he would select a page to handle its distribution. The page would collect orders for the speech, set a charge, hire a printer, and keep the profit. Christian Eckloff reported that, in the years before the Civil War, an address by Douglas, William Seward, Charles Sumner, or some other nationally famous personality, with a subscription list of over fifty thousand copies assured, could bring a page as much as thirty dollars! Eckloff also noted that his fellow page, Arthur Pue Gorman, headed the organization formed to handle the printing orders. Such money-raising ventures have long since departed the scene, as my colleagues of today can attest, and the $1.50 per diem of Jamison's early days as a page (raised to $2.00 in 1846) has been supplanted by a yearly rate, which currently is $9,090.[20]

We senators of today have electric folding and sealing machines, electric letter openers, and all kinds of computerized equipment available to us. How was it way back then? Eckloff wrote:

. . . there were no secretaries to senators at that time; so after adjournment each day members had their correspondence to detain them. It was required of the pages to stay until every senator had left the chamber. All letters for the mail were handed to us to be sealed. The table where the sealing was done was situated in the lobby, and a candlestick and sealing wax were always at hand.[21]

One of the most colorful accounts of life as a page in the post–Civil War Senate can be found in Edmund Alton's *Among the Law-Makers*, to which I referred earlier. Alton described Washington and the Senate as he saw it from his perch on the steps before us.

Alton became a page on December 2, 1872. On his first day, he dutifully showed up in the required attire: dark blue knee breeches and jacket; long, ribbed stockings; and white blouse shirt. Here is Alton's description of his first few minutes in the chamber:

The prayer was hardly finished when nearly all the Senators began to clap their hands in every part of the Chamber, making quite a racket. They had a habit of doing that immediately after the opening exercises, and, on one occasion, caused an old man in the gallery to exclaim, "Wall, I'll be hanged ef I saw anything pertikerlerly fine about that prayer!" But they were not applauding the prayer—they were merely calling for pages.

Alton continued:

When the clapping commenced, the other pages began running zigzag and in every direction, and at

A young page from the 1840's is shown at work.
E. Alton, Among the Law-Makers

first I became confused and did not know what to do. At last I saw one Senator look at me and clap, but as I started to walk another page ran ahead of me. I was about the only new page, and more timid and modest than the other boys. They wished to "show off," and they ran as fast as they could every time; and as I was a little fellow, with short legs, of course they distanced me. I tried about a dozen times to answer calls, but was beaten by the other boys.

I think several of the Senators must have observed my embarrassment, for after a while Senator Conkling beckoned me with the forefinger of his right hand— that was the way he always called a page—and I moved toward him at a quick but respectful gait. . . . He was then standing behind his desk holding a letter, and a number of boys rushed and put up their hands and grabbed at the letter, and almost fought for it. The Senator made a gesture for them to go away, and when I came up he reached over their heads and gave the letter to me, with instructions as to what I should do with it. After that episode, I felt all right.[22]

It did not take Alton very long to feel at home in the Senate. Only a few days later, he played a bold trick on a senator. Here is what he said he did:

. . . a Senator came into the Chamber just as his name was reached by the Clerk who was calling the roll on some question. He looked around, and did not know what was going on or what he should do, and I pitied him and called out from behind him, "Vote 'No!'" And he did! Of course he thought it was some responsible Senator speaking to him.[23]

Alton intersperses his history of the times with one amusing story after another (albeit with a slight touch of hyperbole, one may suspect), and I think the stories give some idea of just what sort of mischief boys can get into, in case some of us may have forgotten. I will only mention a few incidents, however, since I do not want to give our current pages too many ideas!

When things were slow in the chamber, Alton recalled that the boys would play marbles virtually under the vice president's chair:

Sometimes the Senators could not think of anything to send the pages for, and we would have an easy time; and, instead of sitting, as we ought, in an erect and dignified position, we would kneel down upon the soft carpet and play marbles. I have often gone up on the Republican side to where the Vice-President sat, as on a throne, and played marbles with a page on the Democratic side, almost under the Vice-President's chair. It would make some of the Senators angry to see us do this, especially Senator Anthony, who of late years was called the "Father of the Senate," a distinction given to the senior member in continuous service. But most of the Senators believed in letting us do whatever we pleased, so long as we kept still, while the young ladies in the gallery usually paid more attention to what we did than to what the lawmakers were doing. Perhaps it was this that used to annoy Senator Anthony.[24]

When things got very dull, we are told, the page boys would dare one another to see who was brave enough to sneak a cap under the presiding officer's gavel. The next rap of the gavel brought a small explosion which certainly enlivened the chamber and enraged many senators.[25]

Evening sessions seemed to bring out the worst in the pages. They warmed to their mischief by first clearing the chamber of bats:

> On warm summer nights the bats would fly through the open windows of the Marble Room, and, crossing the lobby, dash about the Chamber in a bewildering style. Their gyrations were as nothing, however, in comparison with the antics of the chasing pages endeavoring to drive them from the room.[26]

Once the bats were removed, the pages would run about, gleefully hiding the senators' hats, coats, and canes. The slick marble banisters outside the chamber presented an irresistible temptation. To the horror of visiting ladies, it is said, pages would slither down them head first, shrieking all the way. Some would crawl out onto window ledges and howl like banshees or snake their way through the ductwork.

> We would take up the registers in the cloak-rooms and crawl all about, through the ventilating flues, under the floor of the Senate-chamber, among pipes and other heating and lighting contrivances that, like net-work, ran in every direction, looking for—no one knew what! The fact that we were in utter darkness and that there was an air-well into which we might fall and break our necks, added to the pleasure of such an excursion.[27]

Usually, the pages would play tricks on one another, sparing the senators. A favorite pastime on long evenings was to find an unwary page asleep in some corner and cover him with mucilage or ink spots. Senators even entered into the game on occasion and would reveal to the "glue crew" the whereabouts of nodding pages.[28]

The most fun, however, whether day or night, was to be had in mock sessions (a few

Edmund Alton and other pages would sometimes play marbles "almost under the Vice-President's chair." *E. Alton, Among the Law-Makers*

of which I, in my own time here, have had the rare privilege to observe), mimicking the senators they served. Some boys were so good at their imitations that the senators they modeled themselves after would come to watch. One page would preside and others would play the roles of their favorites in the chamber. Often, one "senator" would begin with a motion to toss the previous day's journal into the waste basket, and it always carried.[29] During the 1920's, Vice President Charles Dawes gave some official status to these mock sessions when he presided at meetings of an organization the pages formed, known as the Little Senate.[30]

We learn of some early twentieth-century page pastimes in a book by another former page, Richard Riedel. After arriving in the Senate as a nine-year-old page in 1918, Riedel stayed on for forty-seven years, ending as Senate press liaison. Riedel reported that, in 1918, "we would see who could

Richard Riedel, shown here as a thirteen-year-old page, remained a Senate employee for forty-seven years. *United Press International*

launch a paper clip with a rubber band hard enough to hit the glass ceiling. A champion launcher could make the old roof ring or hit a paddle arm on one of the electric fans that were suspended from the ceiling before the era of air conditioning."[31]

Let me hasten to add that, lest we begin to think that the life of pages in the past was all play and no work, they had some very arduous tasks to perform in the days before the automobile and an abundance of telephones. Before the installation of the legislative buzzers and signal lights, pages raced through the halls and through committee rooms, announcing an impending vote as they ran.[32]

There were also "riding pages." Before telephones were invented, communication with the executive departments was by mail.

Consequently, the first riding pages, mounted on horseback, delivered letters of an urgent nature. For communications around Capitol Hill, there were pages known as "telegraph pages," who were equipped with fashionable high-seat bicycles to deliver telegrams.[33]

Before pages were assigned to cover certain areas of the chamber and certain senators, a hand clap from a senator could bring a stampede of pages eager for his attention. Half a dozen small boys would collide in front of a senator's desk, and the one who sustained the least shock and picked himself up first got to run the errand. Alton recounted that senators often amused themselves when they required a page's aid by folding their messages, sailing them "into the air," and watching the pages jump for them. Once, in his exuberance to aid Senator Oliver Morton of Indiana, "one of the pages went over into the Senator's lap." Former page Alton recalled that Senator Daniel Pratt's method of summoning pages once got him into trouble:

Senator Pratt occupied a seat on the back row, and every day he used to roll up his heavy *Record* into a tight package, ready for mailing, and toss it to the pages. . . . Once, when he wished to have some extra fun, he stood up and threw the package, apparently with all his might. But either he did not take good aim or his arm slipped, for the *Record* whizzed through the air and struck Senator Anthony on the back of the head. With a cry of pain, that venerable Senator jumped to his feet, his eyes glistening with astonishment and vengeance. Turning fiercely around (expecting, perchance, to fasten the guilt upon a page), he saw Mr. Pratt bowing profoundly and profusely, the other Senators smiling. So Mr. Anthony forced a smile to his own face, and with an elegant obeisance, . . . resumed his seat. But he rubbed his head for an hour or more.[34]

From Senator Charles Sumner of Massachusetts, pages often had to endure pinches on the ear. The gesture was an affectionate one, but sometimes, as in Alton's case, it had the opposite effect:

Often have I attempted to pass the Senator, while he would be walking to and fro on the floor of the Senate, only to have both my ears seized good-naturedly. . . . I shall always remember one of these adventures. He had sent me on an errand. Having returned, reported to him the answer, and received his deep-voiced thanks, I started to move away, but he had caught me, and continued his slow march—I in front, Indian file. As he was a tall man and I a very small boy in comparison, I had to walk on tiptoe to ease the pain, and even then it seemed as if my ear would come off my head. The worst of it was that he at once became so lost in thought that he forgot he had hold of me, and mechanically paced up and down, with his long strides, while I danced a mild war-dance for some minutes—it seemed to me hours—to the intense amusement of all who observed it.[35]

Having already quoted Alton somewhat at length, I should move on, but not before leaving my colleagues on both sides of the aisle with his incisive differentiation between a Democrat and a Republican: "A Democrat is a man who thinks the country ought to be governed in a particular way, and a Republican is one who thinks the Democrats are always wrong." A penetrating observation, I must say![36]

Since the turn of the century, much about the Senate pages' life has changed. Yet, much remains the same. Pages still find it advantageous to know the likes and dislikes of those they serve. In the 1940's, one page had to remember that Senator Kenneth McKellar of Tennessee preferred a special brand of mineral water and fruit-flavored chewing gum. Senator Harley Kilgore of West Virginia liked a certain cola drink. And Senator Carter Glass of Virginia liked a piece of apple pie with cheese at two o'clock in the afternoon. Senator Joseph O'Mahoney of Wyoming liked an unusual brand of cigarettes, while Senator Charles Tobey of New Hampshire liked cigarettes with filters.

Senators still like to tease the new pages. When Richard Riedel was a page in 1919, Senator Charles McNary of Oregon, a great

Lost in his thoughts, Senator Charles Sumner continued to grasp a young page by the ear as he paced the floor. *E. Alton, Among the Law-Makers*

friend of pages, had a special initiation for them. Riedel reported:

In a serious Senatorial voice he instructed the novice to find "Senator Sorghum" for him immediately, said statesman having last been seen in the Senate restaurant. The waiters, elevator operators, and clerks were all in on the joke and sent the unsuspecting page to every corner of the Capitol on hearing that "Senator McNary wants to find Senator Sorghum." Eventually the page had to report back to McNary empty-handed. Another day, he would send a gullible new page to the Document Room for a nonexistent bill stretcher, but McNary failed to trick me the second time.[37]

The fictitious "bill stretcher" was a favorite ploy. It was used on Riedel in 1918, and Bobby Baker, later secretary for the majority, reported that Senator Robert Wagner of New

Pennsylvania Senator George Wharton Pepper enjoyed a game of baseball with the Senate pages. *Library of Congress*

York sent him for a "bill stretcher" in 1943 when he was a new page. I, too, have sent new pages for "bill stretchers" and "left-handed scissors," but I have later shown due contrition by having lunch with them, followed by a photo session on the Capitol steps.[38]

In the midst of first day confusion, one senator always liked to give some dazed page a quarter and tell him to go down to the barbershop and get him a haircut. The young man would be halfway there before realizing he had been had!

But, while senators have had fun at the pages' expense, they have had fun *with* them, too. Senator McNary used to adopt each page, in turn, for a weekend of football, baseball, or theatergoing. Senator James Davis of Pennsylvania shared with pages the candy he kept in his desk, and Senator Rufus Holman of Oregon shared his comic books.

In 1913, Vice President Thomas Marshall began what was to become a custom of the vice president, giving a Christmas dinner in the Capitol for the pages. Vice President Calvin Coolidge continued the tradition, at-

Vice President Charles Dawes entertained the Senate pages at Christmas dinner in 1925. *U.S. Senate Historical Office*

tending the dinner in 1921 with his sons, John and Calvin. In return, the pages presented Coolidge with a gavel. In 1929, however, they gave Vice President Charles Curtis a tomahawk instead, in recognition of his Indian heritage, explaining, "history credits [it] with having imposed silence on many men." [39]

Since nine-year-old Grafton Hanson became the Senate's first page in the 1820's, there have been a number of changes in the age limit for pages. In 1854, the Senate adopted a resolution requiring pages to be between the ages of thirteen and seventeen. In 1870, the age span was changed to twelve-through-sixteen years. And, in 1949, a new age limit was established permitting appointment of pages from the ages of fourteen through seventeen.[40] At present, Senate pages are required to be juniors in high school. There have always been exceptions to the age limits, however. Richard Riedel

was only nine when he became a page in 1918, although pages were then supposed to be from twelve to sixteen years old. Riedel explained that he was accepted because of the influence of his sponsor, Senator Boies Penrose of Pennsylvania.

Senators in those days could waive rules and customs just as grandly as they could wave the flag. Boies Penrose, the czar of Pennsylvania politics who personally had to approve a generation of Republican presidential candidates, could have put a toddler on the rostrum if he had wanted to.[41]

While pages do have to leave today when they have completed their junior year in high school, they are no longer required to depart because of their height. There was an unwritten rule in the nineteenth century that no page could be taller than the shortest senator. In the Supreme Court, which until just a few years ago had pages, one of the stipulations for the job was that the young-

[385]

Appointed in 1965 by Senator Jacob Javits, *left*, the Senate's first black page, Lawrence W. Bradford, Jr., was greeted by Senator Everett Dirksen.

Wide World Photos

sters not be higher than the justices' chairs, so that they could scurry about unnoticed by the audience.[42]

No matter what their age, the road to becoming a Senate page remains the same. Whether it was Grafton Hanson appointed by Senator Webster in the 1820's, Richard Riedel by Boies Penrose in 1918, or the pages who serve us today in this chamber, they all became pages because a senator appointed them. The majority party is able to appoint the majority of the pages.

Pages may still be young, and they may still be our appointees, but they are no longer all boys. That tradition was brought to an end in 1971, when Senator Jacob Javits of New York appointed the first female Senate page. Senator Javits had also appointed the first black page in 1965.[43]

While there was some question about what the girls would wear, they did not have to worry about the scratchy knickers that the Senate pages had worn until 1947. For the first time in many years, the Republicans won a majority in the Senate in 1946, and they set about putting their own stamp on the era. One of their first acts was to change the pages' uniform to a dark blue suit and tie.

This was an enormous relief to the Senate pages, because they had endured merciless teasing from the House pages, who had switched to long pants several years earlier.[44]

Although the pages no longer wear knickers, and their duties no longer include chasing bats from our chamber and bringing us whittling sticks, they still have to sit up nights with us, and there are plenty of other duties to keep them busy. The pages are principally messengers—carrying documents, messages, and letters to and from the chambers of the House and Senate, members' offices, committees, and the Library of Congress, and running other errands to assist senators.

When their school day is over—around 10:30 a.m., unless the Senate has convened earlier—the pages report to the Senate cloakrooms to which they have been assigned. A page then begins a typical day by placing on each senator's desk the latest *Congressional Record*, calendar of business, executive calendar, and bills, resolutions, reports, and other matters that are scheduled before the Senate.

On the House side, there is an electronic light system to summon pages, but, here in this smaller chamber, senators still clap their hands, nod their heads, wave, or snap their fingers. Our pages make sure our microphones are working and that the lines are not stretched out so we will trip and fall over them. They also place phone calls, deliver messages, and bring us a glass of water when we become parched or cough in the midst of a speech.

One of the Senate pages' special duties occurs only every four years when they take part in the ceremony of counting the electoral ballots after a presidential election. Two pages, one from each party, carry the wooden boxes containing the ballots from the Senate to the House where the votes are tallied.[45]

During the ceremony of counting presidential electoral ballots, pages carry the ballot boxes to the House chamber for tallying. *U.S. Senate Historical Office*

Once the Senate convenes, the pages sit on the steps to the right and left of the presiding officer's desk, waiting to be summoned for assistance. The pages appointed by Democratic senators sit to the presiding officer's right, and those appointed by Republican senators to the presiding officer's left.

One of the biggest changes in the twentieth century pages' life has been the beginning of a school for pages. I think we might all be more forgiving of the occasional yawn escaping from a weary page during a long evening session when we stop to realize that they must be up, dressed, and *in school* by 6:15 a.m.

[387]

No one gave much thought to the pages' education until 1925, when Congress passed legislation requiring boys in the District of Columbia to remain in school until the age of fourteen. Because pages' congressional duties prevented them from attending regular public schools during the day, the House doorkeeper established a special school for them, run by a single teacher, in the basement of the Capitol. The boys paid tuition to attend the school, where they were drilled in the rudiments of reading, writing, and arithmetic. The curriculum also included occasional field trips. In March 1928, for example, in eight cars borrowed from members of Congress, twenty-two pages motored to Atlantic City.

In 1929, the Devitt Preparatory School of Washington took charge of educating the pages. Transporting them from the Capitol to the school each day, however, proved impractical, and, in 1931, the pages returned to school in the Capitol. By 1937, the school, approved by the District of Columbia school board, had grown to encompass five classrooms beneath the west terrace of the building.[46]

Conditions in this subterranean page school were far from ideal. Senator Harold Burton of Ohio happened upon the school rooms by chance in 1942 and was most distressed by what he saw. Testifying before the Joint Committee on the Organization of Congress in 1945, Senator Burton recounted his visit:

I visited the school a couple of years ago, and found it housed in the most disreputable and unsuitable conditions. Dickens' Do-the-boys school had nothing on it at all. It was under the terrace of the Capitol Building looking west. The room that the elementary boys used was one that the newspapermen used for a card and smoking room.

The main room was at the center of the Capitol. There were desks, but water was dripping from the ceiling onto the desks, and the plaster was falling down. A piece that had fallen had recently just missed a boy. There were no blackboards in the room, and there was no adequate lighting. The whole place looked as disreputable as it could be.[47]

Senator Burton's speech must have had an effect. When the Joint Committee issued its report, it recommended improvements in the school. As a result, Congress included in the Legislative Reorganization Act of 1946 provisions for the tuition-free education of its pages in a school that would be part of the District of Columbia school system. Plans were also made for the school to move to more suitable quarters on the third floor of the Library of Congress, starting in 1949.[48]

Beginning with the 1983–1984 school year, the House and Senate decided to have separate schools for their respective pages. Both schools continue to meet in the Thomas Jefferson Building of the Library of Congress, but, rather than try to cover material appropriate for the ninth through twelfth grades, they now offer a curriculum for only the junior year of high school.[49]

Today, the Senate Page School is part of the District of Columbia school system and is fully accredited by the Middle States Association of College and Secondary Schools. There are currently four teachers, a program director, and an administrative assistant. The school starts in September and runs through June, but the number of students there at any one time may fluctuate, since some pages come for as little as two months and others remain for as long as a year. The college preparatory curriculum includes courses in social studies, English, science, and mathematics, as well as tutoring in foreign languages.

Students are expected to maintain a B average. A powerful incentive to do so may be the fact that students' report cards are issued not only to the pages and their parents, but also to their sponsoring senators and the Senate sergeant at arms.

In 1953, the staff of the page school's newspaper posed for a yearbook photo. The editor that year, Walter J. Stewart, *seated center in white shirt*, later became secretary of the Senate.   *The Congressional, 1953*

I think most of us realize the many things the pages do for us. But what do the pages get in return for the miles of legwork they put in? Former Senator Harold Hughes of Iowa once told a group of pages:

Actually you probably know more about what is going on in the House and Senate chambers than we members do. You have heard virtually all of the speeches and parliamentary dueling that goes on, while we members, owing to committee hearings and other demands on our time, hear only part of the action.[50]

Lyndon Johnson once described the chance to be a page as "a chance to see government without glamour—to learn that ideals alone don't make programs; that dreams do not automatically become reali-

ty." The pages seem to agree with these assessments of their job. As one page described it: "It's having a chance to watch day by day that counts. It's fascinating to see how one thing balances against another, the compromises, the need to give way on this to get that." From her vantage point right on the floor of the Senate, she said, she had come to realize the complexities of government. "It's like a puzzle. When you look at just one piece—one day—it means nothing, but after a while you discover how it all fits and locks together."[51]

When the 1965 graduating class of the old Capitol Page School went to the White House to meet President Lyndon Johnson, he reminisced about the Senate and complimented the pages on the nature and quality of their work. I think we all would agree that his assessment is still fitting. The president said:

Woodrow Wilson said that the office of President requires the constitution of an athlete, the patience of a mother, and the endurance of an early Christian. Personally, I think he may have overstated the requirements of the Presidency. But from very long and close observation of thirty-four years, it seems to me that President Wilson may have been describing the requirements for a congressional page.[52]

Mr. President, from this brief account of the history of Senate pages, we see that many changes have occurred over the years since Daniel Webster initiated the Senate page system; yet, much remains the same. For instance, the advice given to Senate page Carl A. Loeffler in 1889 by his appointing senator, Matthew S. Quay of Pennsylvania, is as wise today as on the day those words were spoken. Quay told him, "My boy, if you wish to succeed, keep your eyes and ears open, and your mouth shut." (That is good advice for senators, too, who hope to continue in the service of their constituents!)[53]

Incidentally, Loeffler, who began as a page in 1889, remained with the Senate for fifty-nine years, eventually becoming secretary of the Senate before his retirement in 1949. Unfortunately, his memoir of those years remains unpublished in 1989.

And so, Mr. President, from the page undergoing training for knighthood in medieval times to Webster's page, Grafton Dulany Hanson, to today's pages who run our errands and bring us a glass of water—all are inseparable strands woven into the majestic fabric of history.

Of one thing we may be certain, as we watch our young friends go about their daily tasks here: the Senate could not function very well without them. Moreover, the nation itself benefits from their labors, for, as Milton so wisely observed: "They also serve who only stand and wait."

SETTING

As I left the Hall I gave it a look, with that kind of Satisfaction which A Man feels on leaving a place Where he has been ill at Ease. being fully satisfyed that many A Culprit, has served Two Years at the Wheel-Barrow, without feeling half the pain & mortification, that I experienced, in my honorable Station.

WILLIAM MACLAY, MARCH 3, 1791 [1]

. . . Wherever we sit we shall be the Senate of the United States of America—a great, a powerful, a conservative body in the government of this country, and a body that will maintain, as I trust and believe, under all circumstances and in all times to come, the honor, the right, and the glory of this country.

JOHN J. CRITTENDEN, JANUARY 4, 1859 [2]

Winding in and out through the long, devious basement passage, crawling through the corridors, trailing its slimy length from gallery to committee room, at last it lies stretched at full length on the floor of Congress—this dazzling reptile, this huge, scaly serpent of the lobby.

NEWSPAPER ATTACK ON LOBBYISTS, 1869 [3]

CHAPTER 18

Meeting Places of the Senate

New York and Philadelphia, 1789–1800

August 18, 1980*

Mr. President, no matter how many times I enter the Capitol Building and walk its marbled halls, I never fail to be struck by the beauty and history around me. I am sure this is true of my colleagues as well. We never quite lose the awe we felt when we first entered this hallowed building and the Senate's own chamber, for this is a very special place.

We come to this building day after day and sit at these antique desks, many of them dating back to the early nineteenth century. Sometimes, it seems that this building and this chamber are timeless—that this is how it has always been—but that is not the case. The city of Washington was, in fact, the third stop of the congressional cavalcade that opened briefly in New York City and moved on to Philadelphia for a decade before settling here.

Once in Washington, as we can see from the various rooms in which it met, the Senate was still restless. We see the beautifully restored old Supreme Court chamber on the first floor where the Senate met during the first decade of the nineteenth century. We

also often pass by the lovely old chamber, just down the corridor on the second floor here, where the Senate sat from 1810 to 1859, with the exception of five years when it was forced out of the building entirely after the British set it ablaze in 1814.

I shall talk today about the first two meeting places of the Senate: New York and Philadelphia. It is a tale of grumbling architects and conniving city fathers—a story that mirrors the early chapters in the nation's history.

The story begins in New York City when, at sunset on March 3, 1789, the big guns along the Battery thundered out the message that the weak government under the Articles of Confederation was about to expire. The next day, huge crowds gathered to cheer the news that eleven states, all of the original thirteen except North Carolina and Rhode Island, had ratified the Constitution. A new national government had been born.

The waning days of the Confederation Congress had witnessed a long and inconclusive debate about the site for the new gov-

---
* Revised August 1989

The First Congress met in Federal Hall, formerly New York's city hall.　　　　*New-York Historical Society*

ernment's home. Given the disagreement, the question was postponed. For the time being, the new Congress would simply assemble in New York City, where the old Congress had been meeting. The city fathers were overjoyed. While serving as the temporary seat of the new government was a great honor, it also gave New York City a chance to prove itself fit to be the government's permanent home as well, a position which would, it was believed, mean vastly increased revenues for the city that was finally chosen.

New York in 1789 was the young Republic's second largest city—Philadelphia being the largest. During the Revolution, it was oc-

cupied by the British and suffered severely from fire and looting. Within the decade after the war's end, however, New York was back on its feet, a boom town well on its way to surpassing Philadelphia as the new nation's number one city. The mayor of New York lost no time in providing Congress with proper facilities. He placed at the government's disposal the city hall, which was located on Wall Street, opposite Broad Street, just a short walk north of the Battery.

Built between 1699 and 1704, the city hall had been remodeled in 1763 and had managed to survive the Revolutionary War unscathed. Now it was to have another facelift. The plans selected were submitted by a thirty-five-year-old Frenchman, Major Pierre Charles L'Enfant. A volunteer officer in the Continental army, L'Enfant was destined later to play an important role in the development of the city of Washington. The work of enlarging and remodeling city hall began on October 6, 1788. By the deadline of March 1789, the old building had been transformed into a handsome, elegantly decorated capitol and renamed Federal Hall. The project eventually cost sixty-five thousand dollars.

After the renovation, which almost tripled the size of the old city hall, Federal Hall measured 145 feet by 95 feet. The architectural details of its interior and exterior were unique to America and placed it in the vanguard of a new federal architectural style. In this style, L'Enfant tried to combine European classical forms with details symbolizing American independence.

No sooner had Federal Hall been completed than both praise and scorn were heaped upon it. Much of each was motivated by politics rather than aesthetics. Antifederalists viewed the grand structure as a symbol of Federalist aristocracy. House Speaker Frederick Muhlenberg, a Pennsylvanian who hoped the permanent capital would be in his state, sarcastically referred to Federal Hall as "really elegant & well designed—for a Trap" and expressed his hope that "however well contrived we shall find Room to get out of it." [1] The Federalists, on the other hand, were delighted with their new home. Once the noble eagle was affixed to the frieze overlooking the portico, the pro-Federalist *Gazette of the United States* pronounced that "the general appearance of this front is truly august." [2] A visiting Englishman, perhaps more impartial, noted that Federal Hall was an "elegant and grand building well adapted for a senetorial presence." [3]

Because Federal Hall was torn down in 1812, we must rely for descriptions of what it looked like on contemporary accounts, drawings, and an excellent 1970 study of the old records by Louis Torres. One depiction of Federal Hall appeared in the *Massachusetts Magazine* in June 1789:

This building is situated at the end of Broad Street, where its front appears to great advantage. The basement story is Tuscan, and is pierced with seven openings; four massy pillars in the center support four Doric columns and a pediment. The frieze is ingeniously divided to admit thirteen stars in the metopes; these, with the American Eagle and other insignia in the pediment, and the tablets over the windows, filled with the 13 arrows and the olive branch united, mark it as a building set apart for national purposes.

After entering from Broad Street, we find a plainly finished square room, flagged with stone, and to which the citizens have free access; from this we enter the vestibule in the center of the pile, which leads in front to the floor of the Representatives' room, or real *Federal Hall*, and through two arches on each side, by a public staircase on the left, and by a private one on the right, to the Senate Chamber and lobbies. . . .

After ascending the stairs on the left of the vestibule, we reach a lobby of nineteen by forty eight feet, finished with Tuscan pilasters; this communicates with the iron gallery before mentioned, and leads at one end to the galleries of the Representatives' room, and at the other to the Senate Chamber. . . .

The Senate Chamber is decorated with pilasters, etc. which are not of any regular order; the proportions are light and graceful; the capitals are of a fanciful kind, the invention of Major L'Enfant, the architect; he has appropriated them to this building, for amidst their foliage appears a star and rays, and a piece of drapery below suspends a small medallion with U.S. in a cypher. The idea is new and the effect pleasing; and although they cannot be said to be of any ancient order, we must allow that they have an appearance of magnificence. The ceiling is plain, with only a sun and thirteen stars in the center. The marble which is used in the chimnies is American, and for beauty of shades and polish is equal to any of its kind in Europe. The President's chair is at one end of the room, elevated about three feet from the floor, under a rich canopy of crimson damask. The arms of the United States are to be placed over it. The chairs of the members are ranged semi-circularly, as those in the Representatives' room. The floor is covered with a handsome carpet, and the windows are furnished with curtains of crimson damask. [4]

It seems a shame to have lost that building, which must have been beautiful as well as historic.

Let us examine more closely the Senate chamber in which our predecessors first convened. The *New-York Journal* of March 26, 1789, describes the Senate chamber as being "neatly wainscotted." [5] The same article mentions fireplaces, but not how many. Judging from early drawings of the building, which show two chimneys above the chamber, there were probably two fireplaces to help ward off the bitter winter chill. Hanging in the lobby just outside the chamber were numerous works of art including American artist John Trumbull's portraits of George Washington, Alexander Hamilton, and George Clinton. A poem of the period describes the scene in this lobby of the Senate. In verse we learn of senators who

> . . . desert their seats,
> And walking forth as if for air,
> Strait to the anti-room repair,
> View Trumbull's forms sublimely blasé,
> And feel the paint—with wondering gaze,
> Justly admire the glowing work,
> A lasting honor to New York;
> An honor to our corporation,
> A future honor to our nation. [6]

I have taken great pleasure in reading from the marvelous diary kept during the first two years of the Senate's life by William Maclay, the strongly opinionated, Antifederalist senator from Pennsylvania. Maclay seems to tell us something about everything in those busy days, and his discerning eye roved over Federal Hall. Maclay made numerous references to a committee room on the second floor and implied that it adjoined the Senate chamber. He referred to the office of the secretary of the Senate, and to an audience room as well.

Maclay mentioned still another room on that floor—the "machinery room." His entry for September 28, 1789, begins:

felt pretty well in the morning dressed and went to the Hall. sat a little While but had to get up and walk in the Machinery room. Viewed the pendulum Mill, a Model of which stands here. it really seems adapted to do Business, returned and sat a While with the Senate but retired and came home to my lodgings. [7]

Since Congress passed on new inventions and patents, Federal Hall was a logical place to exhibit such models, and this is apparently what Maclay saw.

After months of wrangling over a permanent location for the capital, the First Congress, in July 1790, adopted a compromise in which Philadelphia would serve as a temporary capital for ten years. At the end of that time, the government would move to a new city that would be built on the shores of the Potomac River.

On August 12, 1790, the Senate met for the last time under the ceiling with the sun and stars in its chamber in Federal Hall. The final item before adjournment was the following resolution:

Resolved unanimously, That the thanks of the Senate be given to the Corporation of the City of New-York, for the elegant and convenient accommodations provided for Congress. [8]

On December 6, 1790, Congress reassembled in William Penn's City of Brotherly Love. With fifteen senators present, there were enough members for a quorum, and the third session of the First Congress was under way. Many of the senators present were no strangers to Philadelphia. In the uncertain first days of nationhood in the early 1780's, several, like Benjamin Hawkins of North Carolina and Oliver Ellsworth of Connecticut, had been in Philadelphia as members of the Continental Congress. Others, like Pierce Butler of South Carolina and William Few of Georgia, had been members of the Constitutional Convention in 1787.

The thriving city of Philadelphia served as the nation's capital from December 1790 until 1800.

The Philadelphia which greeted the Congress in 1790 was a larger, but quieter, city than New York. It was the capital of Pennsylvania and would remain so until Harrisburg won the honor in 1812. The first American city with regularly laid out streets, thanks to William Penn, its sedate squares were lined with trees and the stately homes of prosperous Quaker merchants.

Although it lacked the excitement of New York, Philadelphia offered more of the urban amenities. Indeed, Philadelphia had been in the vanguard of many colonial city improvement efforts. By 1744, every house in the city had its own well. Streets had been cobbled and, in 1751, a night watch was ordered

and plans made for "enlightening the city." In 1768, the first arrangements were made for regular trash collections and street cleaning. Philadelphia led the nation in fire protection as well.[9]

For the next ten years, the House and Senate would meet in the recently constructed Philadelphia Court House. Begun in 1787, just to the west of the State House and opposite Carpenter's Hall, the Court House had been finished only in March 1789, in time for a meeting of freeholders to nominate candidates for the office of alderman.

Courtrooms on the first and second floors of the two-story red brick structure would serve, respectively, as the chambers for the

While in Philadelphia, the House and Senate convened in Congress Hall.

Independence National Historical Park

House and the Senate. Even though the building was brand new, the county commissioners graciously renovated it and ordered special furnishings for its new occupants. They built a dais for the Speaker in the bay window of the House chamber, which was furnished with mahogany writing desks and black leather armchairs. A spectators' gallery designed to hold as many as four hundred people overlooked the room.[10]

Once again, as in New York, the Senate was the "upper chamber." It was to meet in the smaller, but more elegantly furnished, chamber on the second floor. Two lesser rooms, on either side of the second floor hallway, served as a Senate committee room and as an office for the secretary of the Senate, Samuel Otis.

I am happy to report that, unlike New York's Federal Hall, which was razed over a century and a half ago, Congress Hall, as the Court House came to be known, still stands.

It has been beautifully restored and, along with Independence Hall and Carpenter's Hall, it is an important part of Independence National Historical Park. The National Park Service has done a magnificent job with these buildings. It is a moving sight to view the silent, cracked Liberty Bell; to visit the room where Jefferson, Adams, and Franklin worked through that sweltering June of 1776 to write the Declaration of Independence; and to stand in the second Senate chamber where our predecessors struggled with questions of procedure and public law, just as we do today. I hope all of my colleagues—indeed, all Americans—will have the opportunity to view it and feel the history it radiates.

A local cabinetmaker, Thomas Affleck, who created the representatives' desks and chairs, also made thirty-two desks for the senators. When the Senate first convened in Congress Hall, there were only thirteen states, with twenty-six senators. By 1800, the admission of Vermont, Kentucky, and Tennessee had brought the total to sixteen. The desks in this chamber were the first the senators had, for, in New York, they had been given only chairs, placed in a row facing the vice president's big chair.

Affleck was also responsible for the senators' thirty-two mahogany armchairs. Amazingly enough, although they had to be retrieved from all over the nation, twenty-two of these chairs have been returned to Congress Hall, where they can be seen today. One even has some of the original upholstery tacks! The senators' chairs were covered with crimson morocco and crimson moreen—a watered wool.

The available records are not clear on how the seating arrangement for senators was determined. William Maclay leads us to believe that, during the First Congress when he served, members selected their seats at random. Senator Roger Sherman suggested

The Senate chamber in Congress Hall has been restored by the National Park Service.

in a memorandum that seating was based on length of federal service, a view that does not seem to square with other contemporary accounts. Writing a hundred years later, Senator William Peffer asserted, from unspecified sources, that senators sat geographically, beginning on the right with New Hampshire and ending on the left with Georgia.[11]

The vice president, first John Adams and then Thomas Jefferson, presided over sessions in the chamber from a red leather chair beneath an impressive crimson damask canopy, lined with green silk, in the bay of the room. Adding more color was the vice

president's table, covered with tasseled green silk, and lavish crimson curtains. Covering the windows were wooden Venetian blinds, then very fashionable, made by David Evans of Philadelphia. Evans was also commissioned, in 1790, to make fifty "spitting boxes" for Congress, to be divided among the rooms.[12]

The ceiling of the chamber was decorated with a plaster centerpiece made by Thackara and Jones, Philadelphia plasterers. Flickering candlelight from the candlesticks on each desk, the chamber's only illumination, would play softly over the plasterwork during sessions that extended into the twilight hours.

While John Trumbull's portraits remained in Federal Hall in New York, his skill was nonetheless represented in the new Philadelphia chamber. In 1799, he donated to the Senate two prints made after his paintings—"The Battle of Bunker Hill" and "The Death of General Montgomery in the Attack on Quebec." They probably hung over the two fireplaces where, Maclay wrote, senators liked to congregate to thaw out and converse on blustery days. It is uncertain whether coal or wood was burned in the fireplace stoves; Secretary Otis purchased considerable quantities of each.

While the vice president's crimson canopy and Trumbull's prints attracted considerable attention, the most dazzling feature of the Senate chamber at Congress Hall was its beautiful carpet. This elaborate rug was made especially for the room, in 1790, by William Peter Sprague of Philadelphia. A visitor to Sprague's factory in 1791 reported:

The Carpet made for the President, and others for various persons, are masterpieces of their kind, particularly that for the Senate Chamber of the United States. . . . The whole being executed in a capital stile, with rich bright colours, has a very fine effect. . . .[13]

The carpet was quite large, about forty by twenty feet. The *American Daily Advertiser* for June 6, 1791, gave a detailed description of the complex, colorful design:

The device wove in . . . is the Crest and Armoreal Atchievements appertaining to the United States. Thirteen Stars, forming a constellation, diverging from a cloud, occupy the space under the chair of the Vice-President. The AMERICAN EAGLE is displayed in the centre, holding in his dexter talon an olive branch, in his sinister a bundle of thirteen arrows, and in his beak, a scroll inscribed with the motto E PLURIBUS UNUM. The whole surrounded by a chain formed of thirteen shields, emblematic of each state.

The sides are ornamented with marine and land trophies, and the corners exhibit very beautiful Cornu Copias, some filled with olive branches and flowers expressive of peace, whilst others bear fruit and grain, the emblems of plenty.

Under the arms, on the Pole which supports the Cap of Liberty, is hung the Balance of Justice.[14]

Seated in their red leather armchairs, and treading on this elaborate carpet, the senators entered upon their ten-year stay in Philadelphia.

During the period between George Washington's second inauguration in March 1793 and the December 1793 convening of the Third Congress, several changes were made in Congress Hall. The House of Representatives needed additional space, since reapportionment after the 1790 census had substantially expanded its membership, from 65 to 106. The building was therefore enlarged by twenty-six feet at one end, giving the Representatives much more room for their three semicircular tiers of seats. The Senate gained more space as well, both in its chamber and in the addition of two committee rooms.[15]

When the Fourth Congress convened on December 7, 1795, the doors of the Senate were permanently opened to the public. To accommodate the spectators, a narrow gallery was constructed, with a capacity of, at most, fifty people, and the chamber floor, which was too weak to bear the added strain of visitors, was repaired and raised.

The first session of the Sixth Congress, which opened on December 2, 1799, was the last held in Congress Hall. In the spring, ships full of government documents began to leave Philadelphia's harbor, bound for the new capital on the Potomac. Word filtered back to Philadelphia that the site was far from ready. The new capital was said to be filled with mud and mosquitoes. Federal buildings were rumored to be unfinished and sinking into the mire. Unfortunately, most of the rumors were true. No handsome building like Congress Hall, which had sheltered the senators for ten years, awaited them there.

No civilized city like Philadelphia with its broad streets, elegant homes, and sophisticated cultural life beckoned from the south.

No wonder senators were more than a little reluctant to set off for the unknown, some said nonexistent, federal city. It must have been with heavy hearts that on May 14, 1800, many senators attended their final session on the second floor of Congress Hall. Their very last act was to adopt this heartfelt resolution:

Resolved, That the thanks of the Senate of the United States be presented to the Commissioners of the City and County of Philadelphia, for the convenient and elegant accommodations furnished by them for the use of the Senate, during the residence of the National Government in the city.[16]

With that done, the senators dispersed to their homes. When next they gathered, on November 17, 1800, it would be in the new federal city. But that is another story, best left for another day.

Washington, 1800–1859

*August 25, 1980**

Mr. President, when I last spoke of the meeting places of the Senate, we left the nation's thirty-two senators in Philadelphia on May 14, 1800, the last day of the first session of the Sixth Congress and the last time they would meet in Congress Hall. When they reconvened six months later, it would be in the half-finished Capitol Building in the new federal city. Today, I should like to pick up the story in Washington. This is for us, perhaps, the most exciting part of the Senate's saga because it unfolded not only in this city, where we still meet, but also within this very building. Over the past 189 years, the great events in the history of this body were played out in various rooms within sixty yards from where I stand.

As the senators prepared to leave Philadelphia, where they had been meeting for the past decade, government officers were loading the records, archives, and furniture of the infant Republic onto sloops that would carry them to the new capital. When the first ships arrived at their destination on the Potomac River, however, they found few signs of a city. After Philadelphia's broad streets and stately mansions, the federal city was a rude shock. There were no decent streets, let alone tree-lined avenues, nor, at first glance, did there appear to be any suitable buildings.

Despite the ten years of planning and building that had preceded the government's move, there was little to show for the effort. The skyline was meager. Above the marshy, malarial, tidal flats rose the sandstone Executive Mansion, flanked by the brick Treasury and the partly completed building to house the departments of State and War, with a few brick houses for company. A mile to the southeast, perched on Jenkins Hill, arose just one wing of the Capitol, surrounded by miscellaneous small houses. Between these two landmarks stretched what was optimistically called Pennsylvania Avenue. The city's architect, Major Pierre Charles L'Enfant, who had designed Congress' earlier meeting place, Federal Hall in New York, intended Pennsylvania Avenue to be the city's main, grand thoroughfare. In the summer of 1800, however, it hardly fulfilled these dreams. John Cotton Smith, a representative from Connecticut, thoroughly disappointed with his new surroundings, reported:

Instead of recognizing the avenues and streets portrayed in the plan of the city, not one was visible, unless we except a road with two buildings on each side of it, called the New Jersey Avenue. The Pennsylvania Avenue, leading, as laid down on paper, from the Capitol to the President's Mansion, was then nearly the whole distance a deep morass, covered with alder bushes, which were cut through the width of the intended avenue during the then ensuing winter.[1]

In a building census of the new city taken that first summer, its commissioners could count only 109 brick and 263 wooden houses. Oliver Wolcott, who, in 1795, succeeded Alexander Hamilton as secretary of the Treasury, moved to the capital about four months before Congress was slated to convene.[2] On July 4, 1800, he complained in a letter to his wife, back home in Connecticut, that there was at that time

one good tavern about forty rods from the Capitol, and several other houses are built and erecting; but I do not perceive how the members of Congress can possibly secure lodgings, unless they will consent to live like scholars in a college, or monks in a monastery, crowded ten or twenty in one house, and utterly secluded from

---

* Revised September 1989

When Congress arrived in Washington in 1800, only the north wing of the Capitol had been completed.

society. The only resource for such as wish to live comfortably will, I think, be found in Georgetown, three miles distant, over as bad a road, in winter, as the clay grounds near Hartford.[3]

The arrival of executive officers and the public records that summer caused little excitement. Local citizens, fearful that the Federalists might still somehow manage to shift the capital to the north, were cautiously waiting for Congress to convene in November before celebrating. They did, however, turn out to welcome President Adams when he arrived at the district line, on June 3, and escorted him to Union Tavern. After inspecting the half-finished public buildings and the Executive Mansion, still full of plaster dust and workmen, but soon to be his home, Adams paid a call on the recently widowed Martha Washington at Mount Vernon. The nation's first president had died the previous December, and partisan bickering had been stilled as the nation paused to mourn. After only ten days in the District of Columbia, Adams departed for Massachusetts to help Abigail and the family prepare for the move south.

In the last few months before Congress arrived, conditions gradually changed for the better in Washington, with the institution of such entertainments as dancing assemblies, outdoor band concerts, and a brief, unsuccessful attempt at starting a theater. Samuel Harrison Smith, a friend of Thomas Jefferson, opened a newspaper, the *National Intelligencer*. Smith's wife, Margaret Bayard, became an early Washington hostess, bringing a touch of gentility to the young city.[4]

[403]

Many members of Congress resided in small boardinghouses on Capitol Hill.   *Architect of the Capitol*

Some of the best descriptions of early Washington are the excerpts from Mrs. Smith's letters and diary, containing her first impressions of the city. Her trip to Washington was her wedding journey; she and Samuel had been married in New Jersey on September 29, 1800. Although undoubtedly disposed to think the best of her new home, she could not hide her disappointment upon her arrival on October 3:

At last we drew near this, our future abode. We left the woods, among which a boundary stone, marked the beginning of the city. We entered a long and un-shaded road, which rises a hill and crosses a vast common, covered with shrub oak and blackberries in abundance. I look in vain for the city. I see no houses, although among the bushes I see the different stones which here and there mark the different avenues. . . . At last I perceive the Capitol, a large square ungraceful white building. Approaching nearer I see three large brick houses and a few hovels scattered over the plain. One of the brick houses is the one where we lodge. We drive to it. It is surrounded with mud, shavings, bricks, planks, and all the rubbish of building. Here then I am.[5]

Washington clearly still remained a far cry from urbane Philadelphia. As Oliver Wolcott foretold, the first members of Congress to arrive at the new capital did indeed have to live like monks and scholars. As he searched for lodgings in the frontierlike settlement, Senator Gouverneur Morris of New York remarked that the new capital only lacked "houses, cellars, kitchens, well informed men, amiable women, and other little trifles of this kind to make our city perfect." [6]

Members of Congress found themselves lodged two to a room in the boardinghouses established by enterprising citizens on Capitol Hill. Representative Manasseh Cutler of Massachusetts described the "congressional mess," which he shared with seven others, relating that each chamber had "two narrow field beds and field curtains, with every necessary convenience for the boarders." As Speaker of the House, Representative Theodore Sedgwick was not required to share a room. At Conrad and McMunn's hostelry near the Capitol, Vice President Jefferson enjoyed the even greater luxury of a sitting room in addition to his own bedroom. Jefferson believed that there was no real need for members to live in Georgetown, as many did, since there were adequate and comfortable lodgings for all on Capitol Hill. The Capitol Hill Tavern, in fact, even offered shuffleboard and a ninepin alley. [7]

Residents of the District of Columbia looked forward to November 17, 1800, the date set for the first convening of Congress in its new home. Leading citizens laid plans for a formal parade to welcome the 32 senators and 106 representatives of the Sixth Congress. Unfortunately, nothing went as intended. A heavy snow blanketed the woods, fields, and unfinished buildings of Washington the day before the scheduled activities. The snow, combined with a disagreement over the choice of a grand marshal, caused the planned parade to be abandoned. It was probably just as well. Only 15 of the 32 senators appeared on November 17. For lack of a quorum, the Congress had to postpone its opening for four days. Actually, in view of the difficulty of getting to the new capital, it was remarkable that a quorum could be mustered so soon. Even under the

best of conditions, which seldom prevailed, the stage journey from Philadelphia to Washington took a minimum of thirty-three hours. [8]

Finally ready to begin, Congress notified President Adams that a quorum was present on November 21, and he appeared the next day to address the senators and representatives assembled in the Senate chamber. While members complained about the conditions, which Representative Roger Griswold of Connecticut called "both melancholy and ludicrous," Adams congratulated Congress "on the prospect of a residence not to be changed":

Although there is cause to apprehend that accommodations are not now so complete as might be wished, yet there is great reason to believe that this inconvenience will cease with the present session. [9]

Some members of Congress were not as confident. The quarters that actually greeted the senators and representatives that November in 1800 were far from complete, even though construction had been going on for seven years. In 1792, the commissioners of the District of Columbia had announced a competition to select a design for the building to crown Jenkins Hill and house the Congress. A prize of five hundred dollars and a city lot would go to the winner. The first entries, however, were very disappointing. One envisioned a squat building topped by an enormous weathervane. Neither President Washington nor Secretary of State Jefferson was satisfied with any of the designs received by the July 15 deadline.

In November, a letter arrived from William Thornton, a young physician, who was also an artist and an architect. Could he please, he wrote, submit a late entry? Within two months, he sent to George Washington his design for a long, classical building with a low central dome. The president was delighted with it, and so was Jefferson. The only person not pleased was Stephen Hallett, whose design had been the best of the earlier entries. To soothe his pride, Hallett also received a five-hundred-dollar prize, as well as the assignment of overseeing construction, a position that inevitably led to endless quarrels with Thornton.

On September 18, 1793, George Washington laid the cornerstone for the new building. After an elaborate Masonic ceremony, construction of Congress' permanent home began. Almost immediately, Hallet began to slip slight alterations into the design to make it more like his own unsuccessful entry. He had to be dismissed in 1794 and was replaced by George Hadfield. But Thornton was also critical of Hadfield, who was replaced in 1798 by James Hoban, designer of the Executive Mansion.[10]

Hoban made frequent reports to the city's commissioners on the building's progress. In May of 1799, he noted that, since the previous November, the following improvements had been made to the Senate chamber:

The window frames are all put up, except one, which is circular at top, and which is not yet finished; four of the columns are raised on the arcade, the ground work to receive the entablature is put up and fixed, and bracketing getting ready to receive the cornice; the girders, binding, bridging, and ceiling joists are all put up, and the trimmings for doors and windows three-fourths finished.[11]

Six months later, he could report even more progress:

. . . its lobby and gallery are floored; the door-ways are trimmed with framed jamblinings, soffits and architraves; . . . the arcade piers, on a semi-eliptic plan, are trimmed with pannelled work, and the columns raised on the arcade, sixteen in number with two semi-pilasters to correspond, of the ancient ionic order, two feet three inches in diameter; the entablature is finished with stucco ornaments, and the walls and ceiling finished, two coats of mortar floated, and one coat of stucco.[12]

Despite Hoban's optimistic reports of progress, by the summer of 1800, with Congress scheduled to arrive in just a few short months, only the building's north wing, what we know as the old portion of the Senate side of the Capitol, was finished. Until the central section and southern wing could be completed, it would have to serve as a cramped home for the Senate, House of Representatives, Supreme Court, Library of Congress, and the circuit court of the District of Columbia. That summer, even this north wing was beset with problems. It had sprung leaks everywhere. In July, Thornton wrote to the responsible contractor, describing the situation and demanding satisfaction:

Sir, After every Rain, fresh leaks are observed in the lead-work of the Capitol, and we have so repeatedly sent Persons to endeavour to find out the Leaks that we see no end to this business. The walls are in many places exceedingly injured. The plaster in some places falling off, and we fear the Building will be in every respect so damaged by a further delay in compleatly correcting the lead-work, that we desire, you will examine, in the most minute manner, every part of it, and render it Water-tight. If you should not do it effectually, we shall be under the necessity of enforcing the fulfilment of yr. Engagement, by a law suit.[13]

After examining Congress' new home that summer, Oliver Wolcott reported to his wife that the temporary House chamber on the second floor was "inelegant," but the Senate chamber, on the ground floor, was "magnificent in height, and decorated in a grand style."[14] Although smaller than the room they had left in Philadelphia, the Senate chamber measured approximately eighty-six by forty-eight feet and, with its forty-one-foot ceiling, was indeed magnificent in height. Encircling the senators' desks and red leather chairs was an arcade with sixteen paneled piers upon which the visitors' gallery rested. Again, as in New York and Philadelphia, the motif was red.[15]

This chamber was located where the restored old Supreme Court chamber is today, one floor below us, on the east side of the building. The Supreme Court occupied that chamber after the Senate moved to the floor above in 1810.

As President Adams delivered his address to the Congress in the Senate chamber on November 22, the portraits of Louis XVI and Marie Antoinette, gifts to the Continental Congress from the unfortunate French monarch in 1784, looked down at him from the walls. That day, they gazed upon a chamber so crowded that, as Mrs. Thornton reported, the ladies overflowed the gallery and sat and stood on the main floor among the assembled senators and representatives. Although elegant, the chamber was not warm. After a month in Washington, on December 17, the senators ordered "that the Doorkeeper of the Senate be directed to procure and put up two stoves, with suitable apparatus, in the Senate Chamber, and that the expense be defrayed out of the contingent fund." [16]

Taking a break only for the Christmas holidays, the Senate met in its new and chilly chamber throughout the winter of 1800–1801. On February 11, the Speaker of the House, followed by all the representatives, proceeded to the Senate chamber to witness the opening and counting of the electoral votes for president and vice president. Republicans Thomas Jefferson and Aaron Burr emerged from the tally with seventy-three votes each, incumbent John Adams with sixty-five, and his fellow Federalists Charles Cotesworth Pinckney and John Jay with sixty-four and one, respectively. Jefferson, as vice president and president of the Senate, announced that, since there was no clear victor, the Constitution mandated that the House of Representatives choose between Jefferson and Burr for president. [17]

The House members arose and filed back upstairs to their own chamber to begin, behind closed doors, to ballot by state. Six acrimonious days and thirty-six ballots later, Jefferson emerged as the third president of the United States, with Aaron Burr as his vice president. In order to prevent a recurrence of such a deadlock, the states, in 1804, ratified the Twelfth Amendment, providing that the electors should vote separately for president and for vice president. [18]

Before dawn on March 4, 1801, a bitter President John Adams left the Executive Mansion and quietly headed home to Massachusetts to nurse his wounded pride. At noon, his successor, the enemy of all Federalists, Thomas Jefferson, walked to the Capitol from his nearby boardinghouse. In the Senate chamber, he read his inaugural address to the gathered members of the Seventh Congress. Seeking reconciliation between the warring political factions, he urged his fellow citizens to "unite with one heart and one mind," declaring: "We are all Republicans. We are all Federalists." [19]

The new Republican senators brought a change in the atmosphere of the institution. While the Senate still remained more formal than the House, its new members behaved more casually than their older Federalist colleagues. In his history of Congress, Alvin Josephy described the way "newcomers from the West and South munched on apples and cakes in the Senate chamber and strode around the floor, often walking unconcernedly between members engaged in debate with each other. The House was cruder, dominated by Republican members whose brashness, slovenly dress and manners, . . . addictive use of chewing tobacco, and loquacious belligerency dismayed foreign diplomats." [20]

One of these, an Englishman, complained in a letter home, "This undoubtedly is a miserable place, but the elect of all the states are assembled in it, and really such a gang to have the affairs of an empire wanting little of

The Senate and House wings of the Capitol were completed before the central portion containing the Rotunda.
Library of Congress

the size of Russia entrusted to them, makes one shudder." [21] Another sneered:

To judge from their Congress, one should suppose the nation to be the most blackguard society that was ever brought together. . . . [The] excess of the democratic ferment in this people is conspicuously evinced by the dregs having got up to the top. [22]

The "excesses" of the Senate transpired in the chamber I have just described. The House, however, in 1802, moved out of its cramped second floor quarters, which, shortly thereafter, became the site of the Library of Congress. Since the House's wing of the Capitol had not yet been constructed, it met in an oval-shaped temporary brick room, inside the area that would become the House wing. Representatives called the place the "Oven," claiming they were baked in it during all seasons except the winter. [23]

In 1803, a new architect took over responsibility for work on the Capitol when President Jefferson authorized Benjamin Latrobe to begin construction on the House wing. Since this task would require demolishing the temporary oval Oven, the representatives moved back to their earlier quarters in

the north wing for several years. Latrobe also undertook to remodel that wing, which was experiencing leaks and falling plaster after only a few years of use. In 1804, Latrobe submitted his report on the north wing to Jefferson, telling him the bad news:

On a careful survey of the north wing of the capitol it was found, that the want of air and light in the cellar story, had begun to produce decay in the timbers, that the roof was leakly, and the ceilings and walls of several of the apartments were thereby injured, that it would be impossible to render the Senate chamber, the extreme coldness of which was a matter of complaint, more warm and comfortable without the construction of stoves or furnaces below the floor, for which purpose it would be necessary to carry up additional flues, and to remove a very large quantity of rubbish from the cellars; and that the skylights were extremely out of repair. [24]

Since Latrobe had constructed the handsome new House chamber on the main floor of the south wing, it seemed inappropriate that the Senate, traditionally the "upper chamber," should meet on the lower level of the building. Latrobe, therefore, produced a design for moving the Senate chamber to the second floor and creating an elegant chamber for the Supreme Court below it in the space where the Senate formerly met. Funds were appropriated, and work began in 1808. The new floor of the chamber was erected and became the ceiling of the Supreme Court chamber below.

Tragedy then struck during the construction. Latrobe had appointed his friend and fellow Englishman John Lenthall to take charge of the work on the Capitol when he was away on his frequent trips. In September of 1808, while the Senate was in recess and Latrobe was not in Washington, Lenthall prematurely ordered the removal of the braces holding up the beautiful vaulted ceiling of the Supreme Court chamber. The ceiling and the floor over it crashed to the ground, crushing Lenthall to death. Out of respect and affection for both Lenthall and Latrobe, the Capitol workmen voted to donate a week's labor toward repairing the damage.[25]

Because of the construction work, the Senate was forced to find temporary quarters when it reconvened in November 1808. For a few weeks, it met in a room on the west front of the ground floor on the north side. While comfortable in winter, the space would clearly be unbearable in summer. On February 18, 1809, Latrobe submitted a detailed report to the Senate committee charged with finding more suitable quarters for the session that was due to begin in May. Latrobe provided an excellent description of the Senate's temporary quarters, which,

. . . being on the west side of the house, and exposed to the afternoon's sun, without the means of complete ventilation; and being besides low, and almost entirely filled by seats and tables of the Senators, will probably be a very hot, unpleasant, and unwholesome apartment during the summer months; and although an external awning, or shed, might in some degree prevent the effect of the sun's rays, the other inconveniences cannot be remedied.[26]

He recommended to the committee:

The library above stairs, although at present in a very dilapidated condition, and much too large in its present state, for the purpose of the session of the Senate in May next, is the only room in the capitol adapted to the object of your inquiry. It is lofty and airy, and having two ranges of windows, will not be darkened by the blinds that exclude the western sun.

I therefore propose to you . . . to enclose in the centre of the room an area of about 50 feet by 35, by a slight partition of scantling, . . . board, canvass and paper, to place within it the present seats and tables of the Senators, and thus, at a moderate expense, to provide a chamber which will unite every requisite of convenience and comfort, and will enable the Senate to await, without being in the smallest degree incommoded by the delay, the completion of their permanent chamber.[27]

The Senate was persuaded by Latrobe's report and authorized him to proceed. The refurbished Library Room, which is marked today by a plaque on the wall near the Republican leader's office just down the hall from our doors, awaited the senators when they returned to Washington in May, and served as their home until they adjourned a month later.

Latrobe and his workmen labored feverishly throughout the summer to prepare the new Senate chamber for occupancy by January 1, 1810. On June 12, 1809, he wrote to Vice President George Clinton, assuring him that the room would be ready but pointing out that there were few furnishings available worthy of the new chamber:

. . . no provision whatsoever has been made for furnishing the Senate chamber, its committee rooms, lobbies, and offices. Of the furniture now on hand, no part is applicable to the new apartments, excepting chairs of various descriptions, and a few tables. The desks of the Senators are inconvenient from their size, and being each of a different length and form cannot be adapted to the regular distribution so necessary to the economy of space. . . .

An artist caricatured the plight of President Madison as the British troops captured Washington in 1814.
Library of Congress

The carpets now in use, have in general undergone the wear of several years; and although a few of them may be made useful, there will be required at least 800 yards of new carpeting of a more durable kind than that now in the Senate chamber.

Excepting the draperies of three windows there are no hangings fit for use.

In order to prevent the echo, which is the great cause of difficulty in hearing and speaking in large apartments, it will be necessary to hang at least the circular wall of the chamber with drapery. These hangings will form a considerable item in the furniture required.[28]

Again, Latrobe was granted his appropriation and bought the desks, chairs, curtains, and carpets he wanted. On January 2, 1810, the senators happily settled into their new two-story, domed chamber. Upon viewing the elegantly finished room that year, a visi-tor observed that "the drapery, hangings and carpets, and indeed the whole chamber [are] finished in a superior style of splendour and brilliancy."[29] The color scheme was the buff and blue of Revolutionary War uniforms, instead of the crimson used in the earlier chamber. Unfortunately, the senators were not destined to enjoy their new home for long.

During the first two years of fighting that followed the United States' declaration of war on Great Britain in 1812, the chief effect on Washington was economic hardship due to the British blockade of the Chesapeake. But, in August 1814, the British fleet, commanded by Rear Admiral George Cockburn, sailed up the Patuxent River toward the nation's capital. Cockburn's men, joined by a force of forty-five hundred British regulars under General Robert Ross, began marching on Washington. On August 24, at Bladensburg, they encountered American forces under General William Winder and Major John Armstrong. The result was an ignominious rout of the Americans, derisively nicknamed the "Bladensburg Races." The British pressed on toward Washington.

News of the defeat at Bladensburg and the sight of soldiers fleeing through Washington, abandoning government buildings to the mercy of the enemy, was the signal for general panic. Every sort of vehicle was pressed into service to cart off valuables from private homes and public offices. After stuffing all available trunks full of cabinet papers, Dolley Madison fled the Executive Mansion, stopping only long enough to gather up the silver and Gilbert Stuart's portrait of General Washington. On Capitol Hill, the clerks scattered in all directions. An alert Senate clerk, Lewis Machen, collected the priceless Senate records and loaded them into a commandeered wagon, which he then hastily drove across the river to Virginia and safety.

At dusk, the redcoats entered the city and the Capitol. Admiral Cockburn led his men into the House chamber, sprang into the Speaker's chair in his muddy boots, and, calling his troops to order in mock solemnity, shouted derisively: "Shall this harbor of Yankee democracy be burned? All for it say 'aye.'"[30] Not surprisingly, agreement was unanimous, and the order to burn was cheerfully obeyed. Desks, carpets, heaps of books from the library, portraits, and furniture were piled in the various chambers, and both wings of the Capitol were set ablaze. Only a violent storm late in the evening, which drenched the city's smoking buildings, prevented complete destruction and made the British soldiers' stay a brief one.[31]

Within weeks of the British departure, President Madison called the Thirteenth Congress back into session. The returning senators found that not only had the Capitol's wooden floors and roofs burned, but even the stone columns were severely damaged. The heat in the House chamber had been so intense that the glass from the lamps had melted.[32]

On September 19, 1814, a shaken Congress met in the Patent Office Building in downtown Washington. Popularly known as Blodgett's Hotel, the three-story brick building had been used for a theater, a tavern, and a boardinghouse before the Patent Office and Post Office moved in. According to legend, this public building had been spared the British torch through the heroism of William Thornton, the designer of the Capitol. Seeing the building, containing hundreds of patent models, about to be burned, Thornton dashed up its stairs, barred the door with his own body, and eloquently persuaded the British officer in charge to spare its priceless contents.

Meeting in their cramped quarters, with the city in ruins around them, some senators and representatives began to discuss rebuilding the capital in another city, with Philadelphia and Lancaster, Pennsylvania, having the strongest advocates. Although the motion to relocate was quickly defeated, the residents of Washington were badly shaken. In the summer of 1815, fearing that the capital might yet be moved if members of Congress were forced to meet for long in such inadequate quarters, Thomas Law, a large property holder in the city and a relative, by marriage, of George Washington, raised a subscription from other nervous citizens to build a large brick building. It was offered to Congress as a meeting place until the Capitol could be rebuilt. Congress readily accepted the offer and, in December 1815, moved into what became known as the Brick Capitol, lo-

The fires set by British troops not only consumed the Capitol's wooden floors and roofs but even damaged some of the stone columns.

cated on the present site of the Supreme Court Building.

For the next four years, while they waited for the Capitol to be repaired, the senators and representatives met in this temporary location. Because the House and Senate could not agree which chamber in the Brick Capitol should be used for President Monroe's inauguration on March 4, 1817, the event was, for the first time, held outdoors.[33]

In the meantime, Latrobe was recalled from Pittsburgh, where he was building steamboats with Robert Fulton, to inspect the ruins of the Capitol and superintend its reconstruction. Latrobe filed an extensive report on what he found, containing this tragic description of the Senate side of the building:

The north wing of the Capitol was left after the fire in a much more ruinous state than the south wing. The whole of the interior of the west side having been constructed of timber, and the old shingle roof still remaining over the greatest part of the wing, an intensity of heat was produced which burnt the walls most exposed to it, and, being driven by the wind into the

Senate chamber, burnt the marble columns to lime, cracked every thing which was of freestone, and, finding vent through the windows and up the private stairs, damaged the exterior of the wing very materially.[34]

Instead of simply rebuilding the Capitol, Latrobe also undertook some alterations. For example, he designed the present Statuary Hall as the chamber for the House of Representatives. As directed by the Senate, he enlarged its chamber's design as well, for the nation's expansion was reflected in growing space requirements for the legislators. Tensions developed, however, between Latrobe and the commissioner of public buildings, Samuel Lane, who was concerned that Latrobe was spending too much money. Since many members of Congress agreed with Lane, Latrobe was soon forced to resign. In his place, President Madison appointed Charles Bulfinch, the noted Boston architect who was responsible for the Massachusetts statehouse.[35]

By December 1819, all was finally ready for Congress' return to its own building. Representatives were greeted by the resplendent columned Hall of Representatives, hung with tasseled, crimson curtains to muffle a terrible noise problem and adorned with a theatrical crimson canopy above the Speaker's desk. The chamber awaiting the senators was equally elegant. Fortunately, we can still see and appreciate its attractiveness. Located fifty-five paces down the hall from where we meet today, the chamber was restored to the height of its mid-nineteenth century beauty under the direction of the Senate Commission on Art and Antiquities in the early 1970's. When senators stop by, they will see its windows draped with crimson, just as they were in 1819.

The most dramatic sight to greet the senators was the vice president's chair, or "throne" as some offended Republicans labeled it. An early guidebook recorded that "a screen of columns stretches on each side of the President's chair, which is placed in a niche on an elevated platform." From this raised dais in the center of the chamber, vice presidents from Daniel Tompkins to John Breckinridge presided over the assembly.[36]

Each senator found a handsome new desk awaiting him. In 1819, "48 desks for Members, each $34," made of mahogany, were ordered from Thomas Constantine, a New York cabinetmaker. Each held a silver-topped inkwell and small bottle of blotting sand. Constantine also supplied the low-backed mahogany armchairs upholstered in red leather.[37]

In the early nineteenth century, a senator's only office was his desk in the chamber. Beginning in the 1830's, three-inch-high mahogany writing boxes were added to the desks to provide additional storage space. One senator, however, objected to the change. Daniel Webster is said to have insisted on keeping his desk as it was, and, to this day, that desk still lacks the writing box that was added to all the others. Since 1974, Webster's desk has been assigned by resolution to the senior senator from New Hampshire—his native state.[38]

Another historic desk still in use in this chamber is the Jefferson Davis desk, which Senator John Stennis of Mississippi held until his retirement at the end of the One-hundredth Congress. This desk almost did not survive the Civil War. While Union soldiers from the Sixth Massachusetts Regiment were camped in the chamber in April 1861, one of them used his bayonet to attack the desk that had been used by the president of the Confederacy when he had been a senator. Luckily, Assistant Doorkeeper Isaac Bassett caught the miscreant in the act. "Stop that; stop that; what are you doing?" Bassett shouted. "That is not Jefferson Davis' desk, it belongs to the Government of the United

In 1844, William MacLeod painted the Capitol rising
from a bucolic landscape.
Diplomatic Reception Rooms, U.S. Department of State

Daniel Webster refused to allow his Senate desk, *left*, to be changed in the 1830's when writing boxes were added to the other desks, *right*. His desk remains unaltered to this day. *United States Senate Collection*

States. You were sent here to protect Government property, and not to destroy it." Bassett later had the desk repaired so well that the only visible evidence of the damage is a small inlay over the mark of the bayonet.[39]

One of the first pieces of art the Senate purchased to grace its chamber still hangs above the marble gallery in the old chamber. This is the handsome portrait of George Washington, painted by Rembrandt Peale, which the Senate purchased in 1832 for the sum of two thousand dollars. Peale dressed his subject in black cloak and jabot and framed the first president with a painted stone porthole surrounded by an oak wreath and topped by a keystone bearing the head of Jupiter. Peale hoped that this, the first of his porthole portraits of Washington, would become the first president's standard likeness. Art historians regard it as one of Peale's finest works.[40]

The senators, glad to leave the Brick Capitol, settled into the new chamber in December of 1819 for what would turn out to be an uninterrupted stay of four decades. These would be years of excitement and anxiety for the nation.

Washington, in the mid-1800's, was still a small town, with little in the way of entertainment other than the business of legislation and government. Viewing Congress in action was one of the most important and liveliest diversions of the day. The prominent ladies of the city often spent their afternoons in the House and Senate visitors' galleries watching the debates below. On the day a burning issue was to be debated, the galleries in the Senate would begin to fill early. When the time came for the debate to begin, the more gallant senators would give up their desks to the belles who could not crowd their way into the galleries. On warm days, the poorly ventilated chamber would

Thomas Doney portrayed a session of the Senate in 1847.

heat up quickly, and fruits and beverages were sometimes passed on long poles up to the sweltering spectators.

Margaret Bayard Smith describes the scene in the Senate chamber in 1830 as the Webster-Hayne debates were about to begin:

. . . every inch of ground, even the steps, were *compactly* filled, and yet not space enough for the ladies—the Senators were obliged to relinquish their chairs of State to the fair auditors who literally sat in the Senate. One lady sat in Col. Hayne's seat, while he stood by her side speaking. I cannot but regret that this dignified body should become such a scene of personality and popular resort, it was supposed yesterday that there were 300 ladies besides their attendant beaux on the floor of the Senate. The two galleries were crowded to overflowing with *the People*, and the house of Reprs. quite deserted.[41]

The senators appear to have conducted themselves with more dignity than did their audience, although each had his own particular style. John C. Calhoun dressed very simply in black, while Daniel Webster preferred the colors of blue and buff, and Thomas Hart Benton wore a long blue coat with an enormous collar. [42]

Snuff taking was fashionable in this period, in the Senate as elsewhere. Henry Clay, in particular, was noted for the "grace and ease" with which he indulged in a pinch of the powdered tobacco. He also found the habit politically useful on occasion, as when

[417]

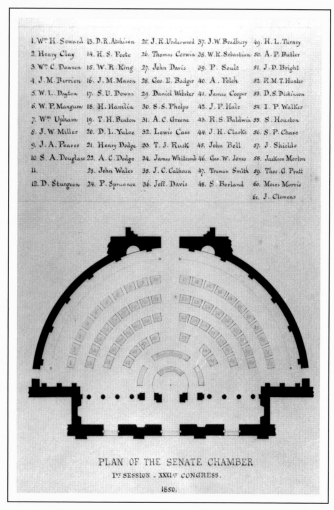

Senators were seated according to this plan during the debates over the Compromise of 1850.

United States Senate Collection

Vice President Martin Van Buren reported that "Mr. Clay left his seat, on one of his snuff-taking expeditions, his common resort, when anything was going on, of which he wished to wash his hands, and occupied his time in badinage."[43]

After visiting Washington, Charles Dickens noted another custom common in the city and the Senate. "Washington may be called the headquarters of tobacco tinctured saliva . . . ," he wrote. "In all public places of America, this filthy custom is recognized." The English writer Frances Trollope observed in her *Domestic Manners of the Americans* that "the senators, generally speaking, look like gentlemen . . . I would I could add they do not spit." Because of the prevalence of tobacco chewing, a cuspidor was placed by every desk in the chamber.[44]

In the gallery, hand-lettered signs cautioned visitors not to put their feet on the railing, "as the dirt from them falls upon the Senators' heads."[45]

The beautiful chamber that the senators entered in 1819 was the setting for what has been called the Senate's Golden Age, the era of brilliant oratory, as the Senate and the nation wrestled with divisive issues like nullification and extension of slavery into the western territories. In that chamber was forged the Missouri Compromise of 1820. A decade later, Senators Robert Hayne of South Carolina and Daniel Webster of Massachusetts debated the right of a state to nullify a federal law.

Then, twenty years later, the harsh debates of 1850 brought together for the last time the three mighty legislators of the era—Webster, Clay, and Calhoun. Returning to the Senate at the age of seventy-three, Henry Clay sought one last compromise to save the Union. His principal opponent, John C. Calhoun of South Carolina, was too ill to deliver his own speech but sat in the Senate chamber while Senator James Mason of Virginia read it for him. Newspaper reporter Ben: Perley Poore, who was present, described Calhoun as wrapped in a cloak, "his eyes glowing with meteor-like brilliancy as he glanced at Senators upon whom he desired to have certain passages make an impression."[46]

The Senate was packed on March 7, the day Daniel Webster responded to Calhoun's speech. Calhoun himself attended to hear Webster answer his arguments and support the Compromise of 1850. Although Webster was denounced by the North for his accommodating words that day, and though his

In the 1850's, construction began on two new wings of the Capitol to provide larger chambers for the House and Senate.
Architect of the Capitol

chances for the presidency were shattered, the Senate adopted the Compromise of 1850, which its creators hoped would bind the nation back together. But introduction of the Kansas-Nebraska bill by Senator Stephen A. Douglas of Illinois in 1854 renewed the passions over the extension of slavery into the territories, and, in May 1856, Massachusetts Senator Charles Sumner fiercely attacked the "Crime against Kansas" in a speech on the Senate floor.

Among the many whom Sumner viciously attacked in this speech was Senator Andrew Butler of South Carolina. Representative Preston Brooks, a relative of Butler's, was outraged at Sumner's words, and felt duty-bound to avenge the honor of his aged kins-

man and of his home state. While Sumner sat at his desk a few days later, shortly after the Senate had recessed, Brooks entered the chamber and beat him repeatedly with a heavy gold-headed cane. Sumner was seriously injured and did not return to the chamber for more than three years.[47]

In 1859, with the nation on the verge of Civil War, the Senate vacated the chamber that had served it for forty years and moved to the large new one that we use today. As the country had grown and acquired new territory during the first half of the nineteenth century, the size of Congress had doubled. When William Thornton designed the Capitol Building in the early 1790's, there were only 30 senators and 105 repre-

[419]

By 1863, the Capitol had expanded considerably, with the spacious House and Senate wings and a massive new dome.

Architect of the Capitol

sentatives from fifteen states. By the mid-1850's, the Union had grown to thirty-one states, and 62 senators and 233 representatives served in Congress. With both the Senate and the House chambers crowded, the building clearly needed to expand. Congress decided to add a new wing for each house, one on either end of the building. Eventually, the plans would also include a new dome, the one we see today, which was designed to be more in proportion to the newly enlarged building.

The project took form under the guidance of architect Thomas Walter of Philadelphia. When the cornerstone was laid for the new wing, President Millard Fillmore presided, and Daniel Webster, who had left the Senate to become secretary of state, delivered the principal address. It would be one of his last pleas for national unity, for he died the following year.[48]

Work on the new wings progressed rapidly, and the House moved into its new cham-

ber in late 1857. By January 1859, the new Senate chamber was ready for occupancy. Despite bad weather, the Capitol, on January 4, 1859, was filled to capacity with people eager to watch the ceremony as the Senate moved from the old chamber to the new. The crowds overflowed into the halls, prompting Senator Charles Stuart of Michigan to move that some of the ladies, "who . . . have great anxiety to witness these proceedings," be allowed onto the floor. He said,

We have plenty of seats here, and I move (I hope there will be no objection to it) that they be admitted to seats on the floor.[49]

There *was* an objection. Senator Hannibal Hamlin of Maine barred the ladies' admission and gave his reasons why:

It may be an ungracious, it is an unpleasant task, to object to the motion . . . ; but I have seen so many occasions when ladies were admitted to this Hall when the result was only to interrupt the legitimate business

[420]

of the session, that I feel compelled to enter my objection. We passed a resolution on the last day of our meeting excluding all persons, except the members of the House of Representatives, from being admitted to the Senate Chamber; and I think it is too early now to depart from that resolution.[50]

Before the assembled senators arose to file out of their old chamber for the last time, Senator John Crittenden of Kentucky, the longest-serving member of the Senate at the time, offered a moving eulogy to the room that had been the Senate's home for the past forty years, "This place, which has known us so long, is to know us no more forever as a Senate."[51] Crittenden brought tears to the eyes of his colleagues as he evoked the memories of their illustrious predecessors, then dead. Their lives and their words had consecrated, he told them, the chamber they were about to leave to the cause of liberty and freedom.

After Vice President John Breckinridge offered another farewell to the chamber, he led the secretary and the sergeant at arms of the Senate and the senators as they solemnly marched down the corridor and into this chamber where we, their successors, continue to meet today.

Washington, 1859–1989

September 3, 1980 *

Mr. President, we occupy the chamber in which senators have met since January 4, 1859. When the Senate moved to this chamber, there were sixty-four senators from thirty-two states. When I arrived here in 1959, the body had grown substantially, so that there were ninety-six senators from forty-eight states. After I became a member, Alaska and Hawaii were admitted into the Union, and their senators brought the total number to the one hundred we have today.

The *New York Herald* of January 5, 1859, gave a detailed description of the spacious new chamber that awaited the sixty-four senators, and of the marvel of a heating system installed to serve it:

> The general aspect of the new hall is light and graceful. In shape and dimensions it is similar to the new Hall of Representatives, but to the eye appears more finely proportioned. . . . The inner roof or ceiling, of iron, is flat, with deep panels, twenty-one of which are fitted with ground glass, having in the centre of each pane a colored medallion representing the printing press, steam engine, cornucopia, and other symbols of progress and plenty. The light is supplied wholly through this window in the roof. . . . The gas apparatus is placed above the ceiling. . . . The ceiling is thirty-five feet from the floor, but presents an appearance of greater altitude. It is encrusted with floral and other embellishments in high relief, and all of iron. The floor of the chamber is covered with 1,700 yards of tapestry carpeting, having a large pattern of flowers on a purple ground. . . .
>
> The heating and ventilating arrangements are said to be the largest in the world—those of the English House of Parliament not excepted. Every portion of the Capitol—that mountainous mass of marble—is at once ventilated and warmed by one apparatus. . . . The air is graduated according to the atmospheric temperature without, and the political excitement within—during a sectional debate never to exceed 90 [degrees], and on ordinary occasions to range between 70 [degrees] and 73 [degrees].[1]

Carpets and color schemes have changed over the last 130 years, but much about our chamber has remained the same. Our desks, for example, are the same style as those used by Clay, Webster, and Calhoun. Nearly all of the desks purchased from Thomas Constantine in 1819 followed the senators into this chamber in 1859, and new ones, copied after the old, were added with the admission of each new state.

The custom of grouping senators' desks by party is very old but not always rigidly followed. In the old Senate chamber, an equal number of desks were placed on either side of the aisle, without regard to party size. During the 1840's and 1850's, Democrats could be found sitting at random on the Whig side. And when the Senate moved into this chamber, the system of dividing the desks equally continued for almost two decades. In 1877, the practice developed of moving desks back and forth across the center aisle to permit all the members of each party to sit together, with Democrats on the chamber's west side and Republicans on the east side.

Occasionally, however, one party has elected such an overwhelming majority that some of its members had to sit with the minority. For instance, during the Sixtieth Congress (1907–1909), ten of the Senate's sixty-one Republicans sat on the Democratic side, while, during the Seventy-fifth Congress (1937–1939), thirteen of the seventy-six Democrats sat on the Republican side. Such seating became known as the "Cherokee Strip," suggesting that the overflow of majority party senators were off their reservation. The seating of the majority and minority leaders at the front-row desks on either side of the center aisle is another rela-

---
* Revised September 1989

[422]

In 1859, *above*, desks for senators from the thirty-two states occupied only part of the floor in the new Senate chamber. After 1959, *below*, desks for one hundred senators from fifty states nearly filled the chamber.

Harper's Weekly, December 31, 1859, and U.S. Senate Historical Office

[423]

tively recent Senate tradition, dating back to 1927 for the Democrats and 1937 for the Republicans.[2]

One of the few changes to our desks, in addition to the writing boxes added in the 1830's, has been the introduction, in 1969, of the inconspicuous apparatus for our public address system which better enables us to be heard elsewhere on the floor, in the galleries, and in our offices.

There is a quiet dignity and a rich tradition associated with this Senate chamber. Although it has been renovated and redecorated over the years, its historical details have been preserved. Today, we conduct the nation's affairs against a background of cream and dark red marble, gold silk damask walls, and the rich gleam of our carefully preserved mahogany desks.

On a raised dais at the front of the chamber stands the mahogany desk used by the vice president of the United States when he presides as president of the Senate. His chair is flanked by red marble pilasters, above which is carved the motto *E Pluribus Unum*— One Out of Many—in cream colored marble. During the One-hundredth Congress (1987–1989), the chamber's furnishings were modified to accommodate requirements of television, which was introduced in 1986. A curtain, U.S. and Senate flags behind the presiding officer's desk, damask wall panels, and a new carpet were added.

The secretary for the majority sits in the chair to the right of the presiding officer, and the secretary for the minority sits to the left. In front of them, on either side of the presiding officer's desk, sit the secretary of the Senate and the sergeant at arms.[3]

At the long marble desk on the dais sit the legislative clerk, the assistant legislative clerk, the parliamentarian, and the journal clerk. During official functions, the assistant secretary of the Senate replaces the assistant legislative clerk at the desk.

As presiding officer, the vice president sits behind the mahogany desk at rear; the parliamentarian and clerks sit at the long marble desk; and the mahogany tables in the foreground are assigned to the official reporters of debates. This view shows the dais as it looked in the 1960's.   *Architect of the Capitol*

Two long mahogany tables below the rostrum are assigned to the official reporters of debates, although these tireless employees of the Senate rarely get a chance to sit down while on the Senate floor. For example, the reporter of debates who is here now, taking down what I have to say, is standing.

Usually, the assistants to the majority and the minority sit at these mahogany tables to inform senators about the vote count, and about the issue on which senators are voting.

The current rostrum is relatively new to this chamber, being a product of the 1949–1950 restoration. At that time, a little part of the Senate chamber found its way to Kentucky. In 1950, the Senate resolved to honor Vice Presidents John Breckinridge and Alben Barkley, who were the first and last to use the vice president's desk before it was removed from the chamber during the refurbishing. Since both vice presidents were from Kentucky, the Senate presented the historic desk to Vice President Barkley for the remainder of his lifetime, after which it would be given to the Commonwealth of Kentucky. Today, it is on display in the Alben Barkley Collection at the University of Kentucky in Lexington.

In 1951, the Senate further resolved that the clerk's desk, measuring fifteen feet by three feet, which had matched the vice president's desk, should follow it to Kentucky. Until the 1970's, it was located in the old capitol building in Frankfort. After that building was remodeled, the clerk's desk was moved to Western Kentucky University in Bowling Green, where it is handsomely displayed.

Another historic artifact in the chamber is the Senate gavel. A small, handleless piece of solid ivory, it is only one and three-eighths inches in diameter and two and one-half inches long. Although the record is not entirely clear, the gavel is believed to have been used by Vice President John Adams during the meetings of the first Senate in 1789, and it is known to have been used at least as early as 1831.[4]

In 1947, after more than a century of hard use, the gavel started deteriorating. Silver disks were added to each face to try to strengthen and preserve it, but the ravages of time could not be halted. In 1954, during a late night debate, the gavel began to fall apart as it was being used to call the Senate to order. The silver disks came loose, and the aging yellowed ivory splintered.

In seeking a replacement, Senate officials hoped to match the style of the old gavel. When no piece of ivory large enough could be secured through commercial sources, the sergeant at arms appealed to the Indian embassy for assistance. India came to the rescue, both providing the ivory and having it carved into a new gavel in the same shape and size as the old one. On November 17, 1954, the vice president of India formally

When the Senate is in session, the mended historic gavel, left, rests in its box while its replacement is used to call the chamber to order.
U.S. Senate Historical Office

presented it to the Senate. In accepting the gavel, Richard Nixon, who had been wielding the old one when it fell apart, announced:

For the benefit of those who have been in the galleries in the past, and those who will be there in the future, we shall place the old gavel . . . in a box which will be kept on the Senate rostrum while the Senate is in session. We shall use in its place the gavel of solid ivory which has been presented to us, it seems to me quite significantly and appropriately, by the largest democracy in the world.[5]

Before the Senate convenes, a page brings the case with the two gavels from the office of the sergeant at arms to the chamber, placing it on the vice president's desk, with the new gavel ready for use in calling the Senate to order.

Two other relics of the Senate's past, so small that they are easily overlooked, remain

Senate pages make sure that the two tiny lacquered snuffboxes in the Senate chamber are always filled with snuff.

United States Senate Collection

here in the chamber. They are two tiny lacquered snuffboxes resting on the marble ledges flanking the rostrum. Though I have never seen any of my colleagues take a pinch, the snuffboxes are kept filled by our pages. I am not sure that all senators are aware of the presence of these lacquered snuffboxes, but for the benefit of senators, pages, and others who may be watching and listening, one of the snuffboxes is sitting here. It contains some snuff, of which I shall now take a pinch. The other lacquered box sits in a similar place to the right of the presiding officer, and today it happens to be empty of snuff! The pages will, before the day is over, see that the snuff supply is renewed in that box.

At one time, in the early 1800's, there was only one snuffbox in the old Senate chamber. Former page Isaac Bassett, who, by the late 1800's, had risen to the post of assistant doorkeeper, recalled in his memoirs how the tradition of the two snuffboxes arose. It was always his custom, he said, to keep a snuffbox on the vice president's desk. The senators used to step up to the desk to get a pinch of snuff, and they would stop to chat awhile with the vice president. Sometimes, two or three senators would be standing at the rostrum, each with a pinch of snuff in his fingers, deep in conversation. One day in 1849, Vice President Millard Fillmore complained to Bassett in desperation: "I want you to take this snuff box away from here. I can't under-

[426]

stand what is going on in the Chamber because of the interruptions and the conversations of Senators who come here for snuff." Fillmore suggested that boxes be placed on either side of the chamber, and Bassett complied with little boxes like the ones we see today.[6]

There are two kinds of snuff: the sniffing kind and the dipping kind. One is dry and the other is moist. The moist snuff in the can, which is delivered to the sergeant at arms and used in the Senate snuffboxes, was first manufactured in 1911.

For the benefit of those who may never have tasted snuff, may I say that snuff is a pulverized form of tobacco that is either inhaled through the nose or chewed. Snuff is made mainly from heavy-bodied grades of dark, fire-cured tobacco leaves and stems. The preparation may be moist or dry, the former being known as rappee and the latter as Irish, Scotch, or sweet snuff, among other names. I used to sell snuff—sweet snuff, Scotch snuff, Copenhagen—and it used to be a popular item. When I visit the stores in rural areas of West Virginia now, I always look on the shelves to see if they are still selling snuff—and they are.

Today, while we have no senators who use snuff, the assistant to the secretary for the majority, Patrick Hynes, is a user of snuff, so that those who read the history of this institution a hundred years from now may know that snuff was not something that was entirely unknown to this august body in the 1980's.

The habit of snuff-taking in the Senate chamber is as old as the Senate. For those today or in the future who would cast a jaundiced eye at the use of snuff, we might pause to be reminded that, during the first half of the nineteenth century, most members of this body carried their own boxes of finely ground tobacco, and some even kept two boxes on their persons, one containing a

mixture for personal use and another, usually a milder type, which was offered to friends. Washington's leading presidential hostess, Dolley Madison, is reported to have carried as many as three snuffboxes at White House receptions.

On each desk is a container of blotting salt. Originally, the Senate used a blotting substance known as pounce. From the Middle Ages to the present day, pounce has been made from the ground-up bone of the cuttlefish. The limestone in the bone is the absorbent element.

The cost of importing pounce probably led eventually to the use of an alternative sand, either silicate or biotite. The Senate curator's office, some years ago, tested the sand on one of the desks and found that the blotting sand was indeed silicate.

When I first came to the Senate in 1959, there was ink in the inkwells. There were still some pens that used the ink, and we would write on stationery and then use the silicate as a kind of blotter.

Seven sets of double doors lead into this chamber: one set to the presiding officer's immediate left, one to his immediate right, one to the east, one to the west, and three sets to the south—to the Democratic Cloakroom, to the Republican Cloakroom, and to the corridor leading to the Rotunda and the House chamber.

We are surrounded by Latin inscriptions, which our citizens carry daily on the reverse side of the one-dollar bill. The sculpture *Patriotism* and motto *Annuit Coeptis*—He (God) Has Favored Our Undertakings—appear over the east entrance; *Courage* and the motto *Novus Ordo Seclorum*—A New Order of the Ages—are over the west entrance; and *Wisdom* and our national motto—In God We Trust—appear over the south-central entrance.

On the upper level of the chamber, above these doorways, are the galleries of the

Many of the Latin inscriptions in the Senate chamber also appear on the one dollar bill.

U.S. Senate Historical Office

Senate, which can seat over six hundred people. The press gallery occupies the north side of the chamber, with the northeast corner designated for Senate staff. The various other galleries are reserved for diplomats and their guests, senators' families, and the general public, with a special section set aside to accommodate visitors in wheelchairs. This is where America comes to witness our deliberations. Here we are on view to those to whom we are accountable.

Some of our visitors may wonder why they are not permitted to lean on the railings. This is a security precaution dating back to the suffrage movement in the early part of this century. On December 5, 1916, as President Woodrow Wilson addressed a joint session in the House chamber, the galleries were full, particularly the one east of center, with ladies intent upon the suffrage debate. Suddenly, some of the women, representing the Congressional Union for Woman Suffrage, lowered a golden satin banner over the railing. Startled members looked up to read, "Mr. President, What Will You Do For Woman Suffrage?" Consternation swept the

chamber. House doorkeepers tried to reach the ladies only to find the aisle blocked by suffragettes. In a few minutes, James Griffin, one of the assistant doorkeepers of the House, moved toward the banner. According to the *New York Times*, he jumped twice "in an effort to haul it down" but failed. His third attempt was successful and, giving the banner "a vigorous jerk," he pulled it "out of the hands of the six women who held it." The ladies watched in disappointment as their banner disappeared from the chamber. It was reported that President Wilson "smiled just a little, but there was no break in the reading of his address." As a result of this experience, the Senate has prohibited individuals from leaning over the railings of our own galleries.[7]

Highlighting the gallery walls above us are marble busts of twenty vice presidents, resting in marble niches. The Senate first authorized placing these busts in 1886, and, by 1898, all available niches were filled. Since that time, busts of vice presidents have been placed in the halls surrounding the Senate chamber. The two most recently placed are those of Nelson Rockefeller and Walter Mondale.

Leaving the chamber through either of its doors on the northern side under the press gallery, one enters the Senate lobby. The lobby is furnished with couches and offers teletype machines, bringing us the latest news from around the nation and the world. The lobby is lined with seven beautiful crystal chandeliers. But the outstanding pieces of art there are the two large Sèvres porcelain vases, placed on either end of the lobby. These huge vases—nearly six feet high—of green, blue, and crystal on a light background were a gift of the French government in 1918 in "sisterly gratitude for America's timely help" in World War I.[8]

At the west end of the Senate lobby is a beautifully decorated room known as the

The Senate lobby is situated adjacent to the northern side of the chamber.   *U.S. Senate Historical Office*

President's Room. It is one of the most elaborately finished rooms in the Capitol, with a floor of beautiful Minton tiles that were manufactured in England. In the past, when presidential terms and congresses both expired on March 4, the president would use the room to sign last-minute legislation, because bills passed at the conclusion of a Congress would only take effect if they were signed before the end of the president's term. Since 1937, under the provisions of the Twentieth Amendment, the term of a Congress and the term of a president no longer expire on the same day, and the room is no longer needed for its original function. It is now used occasionally for meetings and ceremonies.[9]

The room is also used by members of the Senate and representatives of the press for interviews. Senators are often called out into the President's Room by the press to answer questions or to have pictures taken—especially after passage of controversial bills, when the principal participants will pose for press photographers.

Early in 1865, the President's Room was the scene of a dramatic event with broad implications. In the closing days of the Civil War, General Robert E. Lee sent a message to General Ulysses S. Grant asking for a meeting and an exchange of views about the possibility of submitting "the subjects of controversy between the belligerents to a convention." Not empowered to seek a peace, Grant immediately telegraphed the secretary of war, asking for instruction. His dispatch was sent to President Lincoln who, at the time, was in the President's Room signing eleventh-hour bills. At midnight, after consulting with his secretaries of war and state, Lincoln wrote the following response, which was signed by Secretary of War Edwin M. Stanton:

The President directs me to say to you that he wishes you to have no conference with General Lee, unless it be for the capitulation of General Lee's army, or on some minor and purely military matter. He instructs me to say that you are not to decide, discuss, or confer upon any political question. Such questions the President holds in his own hands, and will submit them to no military conferences or conventions. Meantime you are to press to the utmost your military advantages.[10]

A century later, on August 5, 1965, President Lyndon Johnson signed the historic Voting Rights Act in the President's Room.

A dramatic feature of the President's Room is the enormous chandelier suspended from the ceiling. When originally installed in 1864, it burned gas. In 1896, the President's Room was electrified, and, in 1915, the chandelier was enlarged with the addition of six arms holding twenty-four more globes, making it twenty-three feet in length by twenty-one feet in width. It nearly fills the small room.

Until 1937, presidents regularly visited the President's Room to sign last-minute legislation at the conclusion of a Congress. Here, President Grant is depicted in the room with members of his cabinet. *U.S. Senate Historical Office*

A mahogany grandfather clock, purchased in 1887 and known as the "gold clock" because of its decorations, graces one corner. The clock's gold hands, however, were stolen in the late nineteenth century, and the replacements are black. The room is furnished with comfortable couches and chairs and a large walnut table, dating back at least to the 1880's.[11]

The rich decorations on the walls are the work of Constantino Brumidi, the Italian painter who began work on the Capitol Building in 1855 and continued until his death in 1880. Among the rooms he beautified, in addition to the President's Room, are the Senate Reception Room—to the northeast from where I stand—the Brumidi corri-

dor on the first floor, and the Rotunda. Brumidi once said: "I have no longer any desire for fame and fortune. My one ambition and my daily prayer is that I may live long enough to make beautiful the Capitol of the one country on earth in which there is liberty."[12] Brumidi did not live to finish his work in the Capitol, but he certainly made the building beautiful.

In the President's Room, Brumidi decorated the ceiling with portraits of William Brewster, elder of Plymouth Colony, Christopher Columbus, Benjamin Franklin, and Amerigo Vespucci. Four groups depicting Religion, Executive Authority, Liberty, and Legislation also adorn the ceiling. In medallions between the large ornate mirrors on the

[430]

walls he placed portraits of George Washington's first cabinet members: Thomas Jefferson, Alexander Hamilton, Henry Knox, Samuel Osgood, and Edmund Randolph.[13]

Opening off the center of the lobby behind this chamber is the Marble Room, which is reserved for the use of senators only. The room earned its name by being constructed almost entirely of smooth, cool marble of various hues. The ceiling, pilasters, and fluted columns are of veined Italian marble, and the walls and wainscoting are of native, dark brown marble from Tennessee. The mirrors placed at the ends of the room reflect, and endlessly multiply, the marble columns and crystal chandelier. In 1869, *Harper's Magazine* reported that "when the soldiers were quartered at the Capitol the enormity was committed . . . of hanging this white place full of flitches of bacon, slices of which our hungry sentinels toasted on their jack-knives at roaring fires in the chimney-place."[14]

In the Marble Room, senators find newspapers from their respective states, enabling them to read each day the news from home. They also may use the dictionary and other volumes that are in the room, or they may open the doors and go out onto the portico and, in the summertime, possibly read the newspapers outside the Marble Room.

To the right of the Marble Room is the entrance to the Vice President's Room. Like the President's Room, the Vice President's Room is dominated by a large chandelier and huge gilt mirror. The chandelier was originally purchased for the White House by President Grant and was moved to the Capitol during the administration of President Theodore Roosevelt. This was reportedly the chandelier under which President Grover Cleveland married Frances Folsom in their 1886 White House wedding.[15]

In that room behind the lobby, just to the left of the presiding officer, one vice president took the oath of office as president and another one died. On September 22, 1881, following the assassination of President James Garfield, Vice President Chester Arthur was sworn in as president of the United States in that room in the presence of former President Grant, justices of the Supreme Court, and various senators and representatives. In November 1875, Vice President Henry Wilson suffered a stroke while at the Capitol and was carried to the Vice President's Room, where he remained ill for several days. Finally, in the early morning of November 22, 1875, the vice president died.[16] A bust of Wilson is mounted on the wall to one side of the massive wooden desk, which was placed in the room in the late nineteenth century and used by every vice president until 1969. Below his bust is a plaque bearing the following inscription:

> IN THIS ROOM
> HENRY WILSON
> VICE PRESIDENT OF THE UNITED STATES
> AND A SENATOR FOR EIGHTEEN YEARS,
> DIED NOVEMBER 22, 1875
>
> The son of a farm laborer, never at school more than twelve months, in youth a journeyman shoemaker, he raised himself to the high places of fame, honor and power, and by unwearied study made himself an authority in the history of his country and of liberty and an eloquent public speaker to whom Senate and people eagerly listened. He dealt with and controlled vast public expenditure during a great civil war, yet lived and died poor, and left to his grateful countrymen the memory of an honorable public service, and a good name far better than riches.[17]

In 1969, the vice president's desk was moved to the oval office of the White House, where it remained until 1977, when it was returned to the Vice President's Room. On the other side of the desk rests a bust of Senator Lafayette Foster, who was president pro tempore of the Senate and second in line for the presidency from 1865 to 1867.[18]

Once used to quarter Union soldiers during the Civil War, the Marble Room today offers senators a peaceful refuge.

U.S. Senate Historical Office

Artist Constantino Brumidi painted the walls and ceiling of the Senate Reception Room, shown as it appeared at the turn of this century.
Glenn Brown, History of the United States Capitol

At the east end of the Senate Lobby is the Senate Reception Room. Like the President's Room, this area owes much of its beauty to the brush of Brumidi. On the northern portion of the ceiling are four groups representing Peace, Freedom, War, and Agriculture. In the southern half of the room are depicted the cardinal virtues: Prudence, Justice, Temperance, and Fortitude. On the south wall, we find George Washington with two of his cabinet officers, Alexander Hamilton and Thomas Jefferson.[19]

Brumidi left eleven blank spaces on the walls and ceilings of the Reception Room. The most prominent were the five "portholes" on the walls at eye level. In 1955, the Senate authorized a special committee to determine which five of all those who had served in the Senate should be honored by having their portraits inserted in the empty medallions. The selection of the five was fraught with political peril. Each senator and almost every other prominent politician and historian had suggestions. The committee chairman was Senator John F. Kennedy, who had recently completed his book *Profiles in Courage*, which examined the lives of eight famous senators. Other members of the committee were Senators Richard Russell of Georgia, Mike Mansfield of Montana, Styles Bridges of New Hampshire, and John Bricker of Ohio.[20]

In 1957, after the committee reported its choices and selected artists to paint each portrait, work began on the paintings. I recall the dedication ceremony that was held on March 12, 1959, in the presence of many living relatives of these great men, to honor the five selected senators. The men chosen were Henry Clay of Kentucky, Daniel Webster of Massachusetts, John C. Calhoun of South Carolina, Robert A. Taft of Ohio, and Robert M. La Follette, Sr., of Wisconsin. There still remain six vacant spaces on the Reception Room walls. Perhaps, at some future date, the Senate will again convene a similar committee and select additional senators to be so honored by their successors.

Except for several brief occasions, the Senate has met continually in this chamber ever since January 4, 1859. At the times when it did have to find a temporary home, the Senate returned to its old quarters—the chamber down the hall, which had been used by the Supreme Court from 1860 to 1935.

In 1938, the Senate learned that the chamber's ninety-ton ceiling and the roof over it were in danger of collapsing. Since World War II intervened to prevent immediate reconstruction, extra steel supports were added to strengthen the ceiling. While these were being put into place, the Senate met in its old chamber. Then, for nine years, starting in January 1941, the senators conducted their business in this chamber beneath a network of temporary braces.[21]

Special braces supported the unsafe ceiling of the Senate chamber from 1940 to 1949.   *Architect of the Capitol*

As long as extensive work was needed on the chamber, collateral studies were conducted on other aspects of the chamber's environment. A subcommittee of the Committee on Public Buildings and Grounds was empowered to examine acoustics, redecoration, and better lighting systems. It became clear during the hearings that the old ceiling, though lovely with its stained glass panels of cornucopias, printing presses, and steam engines, was the source of many of the chamber's problems. It was through this glass ceiling and the skylight above it that sunlight filtered into the room. Unfortunately, after passing through the greens and blues of the stained glass, it imparted a murky glow to the room which made it look uncomfortably like an aquarium.

The situation at night was not much better. "In olden days," according to Isaac Bassett, whose Senate employment as page, messenger, and assistant doorkeeper spanned the years from 1831 to 1895, "candles were used in the Senate, and . . . a common brass candlestick stood on each Senator's desk. These and two large brass oil lamps on either side of the Vice President formed the whole light in the Chamber." Later, the candles were supplanted by gaslights located above the ceiling, and, in 1888, electric lighting was installed that cast an uneven, shadowy glare onto the desks below.[22]

The hearings also revealed that the glass and iron ceiling was the source of many of the Senate's acoustical problems as well. Was the ceiling, asked Senator Charles Andrews of Florida, the reason "[we] can hardly hear anyone speak a few yards away from us in the Senate today?" "Yes, sir; I think it is," agreed the consulting engineer.[23]

The new ceiling, shown during construction in 1950, was designed to improve both acoustics and lighting in the Senate chamber.
Architect of the Capitol

Not only would a proposed ceiling of plaster, with its indirect lighting, ease problems of hearing and seeing; it would also incorporate some changes to improve the chamber's air conditioning system. For seventy years, from 1859 to 1929 when an air conditioning system was installed, senators had been plagued by hot, stuffy air in the chamber. The only sure method of beating the summer heat had been to adjourn in the spring. The consultants who testified at the hearings hoped that replacing the skylight and the glass ceiling over the chamber with a solid roof and a plaster ceiling that could be insulated would reduce the heat "transmitted through the ceiling during the summer season" and thus improve the effectiveness of the air conditioning. The system involved using equipment in the basement to force air

into the attic and then into the chamber through slots in the ceiling. The air exited the chamber through grilles in the floor. In the course of the renovation, the air conditioning equipment was also updated to improve the functioning of the system and enable the Senate to carry on through the summer months in comfort.[24]

Construction work in the chamber finally began in July 1949, and, once again, the senators moved back to their old meeting place down the corridor. While the old chamber had been ample space for the Senate of 1819, it was overwhelmed by the Senate of 1949. There was room for desks for only the majority and minority leaders; the remaining ninety-four senators—there were only ninety-six senators at that time—were lucky to have chairs. The marble gallery, jammed with air-conditioning equipment, hung precariously over Vice President Alben Barkley's head. Again, in 1950, while work in its own chamber was being completed, the Senate met in the old quarters. The senators returned to their newly refurbished chamber, with the ceiling we see today, for the first session of the Eighty-second Congress on January 3, 1951.[25]

More recent occasions on which the Senate met in the old Senate chamber are ones which many of my colleagues will well remember, for I know they made a great impression on me. On June 16, 1976, the Senate convened in its old chamber to mark the completion of that room's restoration. Sitting beneath that beautiful crimson balcony, under the watchful gaze of Peale's portrait of Washington, one had a sense of the majesty of the Senate during the mid-nineteenth century. Again, on March 29, 1988, we convened in the old chamber to hold a closed session on the Intermediate Nuclear Forces (INF) treaty. Due to the vast amount of electronic equipment in the present chamber, it was felt that the old chamber would offer greater security for discussing classified information. On April 6, 1989, the Senate returned to the old chamber for a ceremony commemorating the two-hundredth anniversary of its first quorum and the beginnings of our legislative history.

The hopes and dreams of the nation were riding on the United States Senate when it moved to this chamber in 1859. I was deeply moved by a passage in Kentucky Senator John Crittenden's inspiring speech on that January day. In closing, I should like to read from it to my colleagues:

. . . wherever we sit we shall be the Senate of the United States of America—a great, a powerful, a conservative body in the government of this country, and a body that will maintain, as I trust and believe, under all circumstances and in all times to come, the honor, the right, and the glory of this country. Because we leave this Chamber, we shall not leave behind us any sentiment of patriotism, any devotion to the country which the illustrious exemplars that have gone before us have set to us. These, like our household gods, will be carried with us; and we, the representatives of the States of this mighty Union, will be found always equal, I trust, to the exigencies of any time that may come upon our country. No matter under what sky we may sit; no matter what dome may cover us; the great patriotic spirit of the Senate of the United States will be there and I have an abiding confidence that it will never fail in the performance of its duty, sit where it may, even though it were in a desert.[26]

Crittenden's words are as profound and meaningful today as they were when spoken more than a century and a quarter ago.

CHAPTER 19

The Senate Press Galleries

November 24, 1980*

Mr. President, it is reported that Napoleon once said, "Three hostile newspapers are more to be feared than a thousand bayonets." [1] Another giant of history attesting to the power and importance of newspapers was Thomas Jefferson, who, in his letter to Colonel Edward Carrington on January 16, 1787, wrote: "The basis of our government being the opinion of the people, the very first object should be to keep that right; and were it left to me to decide whether we should have a government without newspapers, or newspapers without a government, I should not hesitate a moment to prefer the latter." [2]

Over the past several months, I have been speaking about the variety of elected and appointed officials of the Senate and their diverse responsibilities. I have discussed the majority and minority leaders, the party whips, the secretary of the Senate and sergeant at arms, the chaplain, the reporters of debates, and the pages. Today, I shall speak about another group that maintains its offices here in the Capitol and has the run of the building with all of its privileges, from parking spaces to special elevators and dining facilities. But, while this group is with us, they are not of us. They are not salaried employees of the Senate. I am speaking of the press corps that occupies the Senate press gallery, where sit the molders and shapers of that "opinion of the people" which, in Jefferson's estimation, was the bedrock of our representative democracy.

One hundred years ago, Frank G. Carpenter, who covered Washington for the *Cleveland Ledger* under the name of "Carp," described the press corps as one of "two Congresses" in the Capitol:

One sits on the floor of the House and the Senate; the other has seats in the galleries. One makes its speeches to the members of the two lawmaking bodies, the other talks to the nation. One sits but a few months a year; the other is in session all the time, weekdays and Sunday, year in and year out. The latter criticizes the former and praises or condones its actions. It has much to say of the future of great men.

Carp's description remains true, except that Congress, like the press, now works almost continually rather than for "a few months a year." [3]

From here, inside the Senate chamber, we look up at the press behind their wooden desks along the northern gallery, even as they peer down at us from over the parapets. Beyond those desks, and through the etched glass doors, is the Capitol's own news room. Banks of telephone booths, clattering ticker-

* Updated April 1989

Reporters in the press gallery took notes and watched the proceedings during a Senate session in 1939.
U.S. Senate Historical Office

tape machines and typewriters, and squads of reporters in shirt sleeves turning out tomorrow's news—all these create an atmosphere reminiscent of a scene from "The Front Page." There is something incongruous about the Minton tiles, marble walls, and decorated ceilings in this news room, but, from the signs of clutter, I gather that the reporters have made themselves comfortable anyway.

There are actually four press galleries in the Senate: a gallery for newspaper reporters, a periodical gallery for magazine reporters, a press photographers' gallery, and a radio and television gallery. I will be talking about the origins and functions of these galleries and about some of the more prominent men and women who have served there. It is usually their job to report on my activities as a sena-

tor. Today, I will turn the tables and report on them.

Members of the press galleries are aware that the Senate did not always open its doors to them, did not always provide them space in and near the chamber to facilitate their work. The first meetings of the Senate were conducted behind closed doors. Until December 1795, there were no galleries for the public and the press, and, although an annual journal of Senate proceedings was published, the daily news of the Senate's activities filtered out only indirectly.

Even after public galleries were constructed and the doors were opened, reporters had no special place to sit apart from other interested spectators. Nor were all of the sessions open to them. All executive business—nominations and treaties—was carried on in closed session, a practice which lasted until 1929. A journalist named William Duane, for instance, was hauled before the Senate and interrogated by the presiding officer, Vice President Jefferson, in 1800 for publishing the text of a bill which had not been debated in public. The Senate permitted him to depart and subsequently issued a warrant for his arrest, but, after the Federalists lost their majority in the Senate, his interrogation was never resumed.[4]

William Duane was by no means the only journalist ever taken to task for his publication of congressional documents and activities. In 1812, the House of Representatives called in the editor of the *Alexandria* (Virginia) *Herald*, Nathaniel Rounsavell. He was cited for publishing a secret message that President James Madison had sent to the House regarding an embargo of American merchant ships on the eve of America's second war with Great Britain. Rounsavell refused to divulge the names of his sources, on the grounds that he had simply overheard their conversation, and the House ultimately dropped the matter.[5]

In March 1848, the Senate ordered its sergeant at arms to arrest a *New York Herald* reporter, John Nugent, when he published a secret text of the treaty of Guadelupe-Hidalgo, which ended the Mexican War. Nugent refused to reveal his sources and was confined for several weeks in the Committee on Territories room, here in the Capitol Building. The prisoner ate his breakfasts and lunches in the committee room but accompanied the sergeant at arms home each evening for supper. Nugent steadfastly refused to talk, and the Senate finally released him on April 28, for health reasons.

There were two other reporter-prisoners in the Capitol. In 1871, Zebulon White and Hiram Ramsdell, reporters for the *New-York Tribune*, were arrested and locked in the Pacific Railroads Committee room. They had published the secret Treaty of Washington, which settled several Civil War-era claims between the United States and Great Britain. White and Ramsdell also refused to divulge their sources and were finally released shortly before the Senate session was due to adjourn. Their imprisonment does not appear to have been a harsh one. Accounts indicate that their wives and friends, including several senators, visited them every day; that they received books and fresh flowers; that they ate meals sent in from the Senate restaurant; and that they were entrusted with the key to their "prison" door.[6]

As long as the practice of routinely holding executive sessions of the Senate behind closed doors continued, so, too, did the problem of leaks to newspapers. It was a rare executive session that was not followed by copious articles and relatively accurate tallies of votes in the next day's newspapers. Some wags suggested that the Senate held so many sessions in secret in order to guarantee better newspaper coverage. The press, they said, was less interested in reporting the open sessions than the closed ones.

Finally, in 1929, the Senate revised its rules to hold executive sessions in public, except in extraordinary instances. The reason for this belated change was a controversy that arose over an Associated Press story which gave the vote tally on the nomination of former Senator Irvine Lenroot to the United States Court of Customs and Patent Appeals. As it happened, the published tally was slightly incorrect, and several senators called for an investigation of the Associated Press' chief Senate reporter, Paul Mallon. On the Senate floor, Mallon was defended by Senator Robert M. La Follette, Jr., of Wisconsin, who opposed the secrecy rule and called the attempts to punish Mallon a suppression of freedom of the press. Finally, La Follette pointed out the obvious: that the sources for all these stories on secret sessions

PUCK.

THEY HATE THE LIGHT, BUT THEY CAN'T ESCAPE IT.

Cartoonist Joseph Keppler depicted the press as casting the light of publicity on a secret session of the Senate.
Keppler/Puck, c. 1895

of the Senate had to be the senators themselves. On June 18, 1929, the Senate finally voted to make further secret sessions the exception rather than the rule.[7]

In retrospect, we can say that it was regrettable that the Senate conducted so much of the public business behind closed doors. The practice only bred suspicion in the public's mind and fostered ill will between the press and the Senate. Today, after passage of several so-called sunshine reforms, we have grown accustomed to carrying on our activities under the full light of public scrutiny. During the entire period since the end of World War II, for instance, the Senate has met in secret session twenty-seven times,

primarily to discuss highly sensitive military issues, using classified documents.[8] Even in those few instances, sanitized versions of the discussions were printed soon after in the *Congressional Record.*

Even though the Senate's legislative sessions were open to the public by the time the government moved from Philadelphia to Washington in 1800, the body still did not provide a separate location for use by the press in general. At that time, reporting on the activities of Congress was carried out exclusively by the *National Intelligencer,* which won a position on the Senate floor. Reports printed in the *Intelligencer* were then clipped out and reprinted in other papers throughout the nation. While the *Intelligencer* retained its privileged position on the floor for many years, it soon had competition from other papers. As early as January 1808, the Philadelphia Federalist paper *United States Gazette* was printing accounts under such by-lines as: "Reported for the *United States Gazette*" and "From our Correspondents at Washington." [9]

The Capitol press corps as a continuing body dates from 1827. According to historian Frederick B. Marbut in his book *News From The Capital*, "Since the session which began in December of that year, every Congress has had its proceedings reported in some paper, somewhere in the country, by its own correspondent." Among the reporters who watched over the Senate's debates in that year was James Gordon Bennett, who would soon found the *New York Herald*, one of the most influential newspapers of the nineteenth century, which pioneered many of the features that are standard in newspapers today.[10]

It was Bennett who later challenged the Senate's practice of awarding special press facilities on the floor to reporters from Washington papers while relegating other correspondents from out-of-town papers to the public galleries. In 1841, Bennett's *Herald* attempted to place its own stenographers at desks on the Senate floor. In those days, a senator's desk was his office, and the chamber was often crowded and noisy. Adding more reporters to the floor would have made conditions even worse. When the *Herald*'s request was rejected, Bennett published a scathing editorial, writing: "We have to record this day one of the most outrageous, high-handed, unconstitutional acts ever perpetrated by any legislative assembly in a free land—an act of despotism, tyranny and usurpation against the liberty of the press." In large part because of Bennett's crusade, the Senate later that year adopted a change

Newspaperman Horace Greeley, who regularly reported on the Senate, himself served briefly in the House of Representatives.   *Library of Congress*

in its rules to "cause suitable accommodations" to be prepared in the eastern gallery for such reporters as might be admitted by the rules of the Senate. The gallery immediately above the presiding officer's chair would be set aside for two reporters from each Washington paper and one from each out-of-town paper that sent a correspondent. Crosby Noyes, one of the founders of the *Washington Star*, came to Washington as a correspondent for the *Lewiston* (Maine) *Journal* in 1847 and later recalled his first impressions. "The Senate chamber was the center of interest," wrote Noyes, "and the reporters who congregated there were comfortably accommodated in a single row of seats, or rather stools, in a narrow gallery." That was our first Senate press gallery.[11]

In those days, it would not have been unusual to find the nation's leading editors in the gallery during the sessions of Congress. The "editorial correspondence" they sent back to their papers was a powerful force in shaping public opinion and national legislation. There, one would find James Watson Webb of the *New York Courier and Enquirer*, Thomas Ritchie of the *Richmond Enquirer*, Henry B. Anthony of the *Providence Journal*, and Thurlow Weed of the Albany *Evening Journal*. Horace Greeley, perhaps the most famous newspaperman of his generation, came to the Senate press gallery often to send back his own dispatches. Even during Greeley's three-month term in Congress, from 1848 to 1849, he continued to file reports for the *New-York Tribune*. Another early correspondent in the Senate press gallery was Whitelaw Reid, who eventually became editor of the *Tribune* and a prominent statesman in his own right.

Also in the 1840's came the introduction of the telegraph, which revolutionized the reporting of the news. The first long-distance demonstration of the telegraph, as we all know, took place on the first floor of the Capitol on May 24, 1844, when Samuel Finley Breese Morse sent the first message, "What hath God wrought!" from Washington to Baltimore. Returning from Baltimore to Washington came news of the Democratic convention, then being held in Baltimore. Morse posted his dispatches on a bulletin board in the Capitol Rotunda, creating what we might call the first "wire service." Shortly afterwards, the New York Associated Press was established, placing its telegraph reporters in every city in the country. In Washington, its chief reporter was Louis A. Gobright, who studiously followed the business of the Senate and the House. The expense of sending telegraph messages, and the variety of papers which would carry Associated Press reports, made Gobright one of the first practitioners of "objective journalism" in Washington. Whereas earlier reporters had colored their stories—as they do sometimes even today—with partisan editorializing, Gobright believed it was his business merely to communicate the facts. "I do not act as a politician belonging to any school," he explained, "but try to be truthful and impartial. My dispatches are merely dry matters of fact and detail."[12]

During the Civil War, newspapers from all over the northern states sent correspondents to report on the conduct of the war, both militarily and administratively. Reporters swarmed over Washington, and, when the war was over, many of them stayed in the capital. A "Newspaper Row" developed along Fourteenth Street at Pennsylvania Avenue, between the White House and the Capitol, flanked by the Willard and Ebbitt House hotels (the site of the current National Press Club). After a day at the Capitol, reporters would retire there to their various news bureaus to file their reports and make the rounds of the hotel bars, picking up additional information. "From nine o'clock in the evening until after midnight," reported one correspondent in the 1870's, "unless there is a night session at the Capitol, Newspaper Row is a busy place." On any given evening when the Congress was in session, it would not be unusual to find senators and congressmen visiting Newspaper Row to give personal interviews to favored papers from their home states.

The real news in those days came from Congress, not the president. Presidents had no press secretaries and did not even maintain a news room in the White House until the beginning of the twentieth century. Presidents made formal speeches and statements, but otherwise often spoke to the press through senior senators from their

Reporters seeking news surrounded senators outside the chamber during the impeachment trial of President Andrew Johnson.
Frank Leslie's Illustrated Newspaper, May 30, 1868

party. Lincoln, it is true, did give informal, nonattributed interviews during the war, and his immediate successor, Andrew Johnson, gave the first attributed presidential interview to a newspaper. For the most part, however, correspondents found the White House and executive agencies far less productive of news than was the Congress. As a result, the chief correspondents of each paper spent the greatest part of their time in the Senate and House press galleries and at congressional committees. "At other times," wrote Ben: Perley Poore, the dean of the Washington press corps in those years, "they are generally to be seen in the anterooms to the reporters' galleries, where they hold informal sessions of their own, often indulging

in comments on what is going on in the halls nearby in a manner not overly complimentary to those honorable Senators and Representatives who are there engaged in legislation." [13]

In 1902, Crosby Noyes looked back over his fifty years of association with the congressional press galleries and called them a "training school for the production of able editors, statesmen, financiers, railroad magnates, generals, governors, poets, novelists, magazinists, and men of mark in all lines." [14] Reading through the roster of reporters who have served in the Senate press gallery, one becomes aware of the accuracy of Noyes' remarks. I, for one, was surprised to find among the nineteenth-century reporters the

In the 1890's, an artist sketched a group of reporters in the press gallery.

name of Samuel Clemens, who, of course, wrote under the pseudonym of Mark Twain. In November 1867, Twain had just returned from a voyage to the Holy Land, about which he would soon publish his first book, the celebrated *Innocents Abroad.* Hoping to have some time to finish the book, earn a little money, and polish his skills as a lecturer, Twain signed on as a secretary to Senator William M. Stewart of Nevada. At the same time, he was also a "letter writer" to the *Alta Californian* of San Francisco and the *Chicago Republican.* For an individual to work both on a Senate staff and as a reporter was not unusual in those days, when salaries for both positions were considerably lower than they are today.[15]

Of course, Twain's reporting was more in the vein of humorous observation than hard news. Many of his comments, based on observing the Senate in action from the galleries, still carry a witty message. As an example, let me read from his letter to the *Alta Californian* on February 11, 1868, in which he imparted this "fatherly advice" to a new senator:

He ought not to spend millions in the purchase of volcanoes and earthquakes [this was a reference to the purchase of Alaska] and then "retrench" by cutting off the Senate's stationery supplies.

He ought not to keep mean whiskey at his rooms and tell his constituents it is forty years old.

He ought not to draw a salary for his pet Newfoundland dog, under the name and style of "Clerk of the Senate Committee on So-Forth and So-Forth."

He ought not to get the handsome girls places in the Treasury Department, and tell all the homely ones the places are all full.

He ought not to palm off old speeches from the *Congressional Globe* for 1832 as original, for behold, old speeches are even a more shameless fraud than new whiskey.

He ought not to shirk important votes and then plead those threadbare "sick relatives" in expiation and explanation. Something fresh must be tried. . . .

He ought to write a signature that another man can read, without direct inspiration from heaven.

And finally, let him never make a speech until he has something to say. This last is about the hardest advice to follow that could be offered to a senator, perhaps.[16]

When Twain left Washington in March 1868, he published a delightful essay on his experiences with the Senate, "My Late Senate Secretaryship," in which he claimed to have been fired for writing outrageous and indiscreet letters to Senator Stewart's Nevada constituents. The truth was more prosaic. He had simply returned to California to protect his copyright on *Innocents Abroad*, the book which would shortly make him the most famous of all American humorists.

Five years later, Twain published his first novel, *The Gilded Age,* based heavily on the men and events he had observed from the Senate press gallery. This novel introduced the public to the pious but conniving Senator Abner Dilworthy, the expansive but ineffective schemer Colonel Beriah Sellers, and the beautiful lobbyist Laura Hawkins, who all became popular stage characters in theatrical performances in the late nineteenth century. (For more about these colorful Twain characters, see Chapter 21.) [17]

Mr. President, if Mark Twain had the most wicked wit of all congressional correspondents, Ben: Perley Poore possessed the most jovial spirit and the greatest treasure-trove of anecdotes about Washington's political history. Poore's two volumes of *Reminiscences* treat the Senate and House far more kindly than did Twain's *Gilded Age.* [18] In many ways, Ben: Perley Poore personified the "Bohemian" spirit of the Washington press corps in those post–Civil War years. Those were the days when correspondents would dress in top hat and tails to appear in the press gallery for the opening day of Congress and then manage to look quite disreputable for the rest of the session. Back then, correspondents, as well as senators, contributed to the cigar smoke that hung heavy in this chamber, and spittoons were more than ornamental relics.

Reporters in that Bohemian era often developed close ties to politicians, for mutual benefit. Poore, for instance, reported for the *Boston Journal,* a rock-ribbed Republican paper that was known as the "family Bible" all

Ben: Perley Poore, shown here in Masonic regalia, served simultaneously as a newspaper reporter and as clerk of the Senate Committee on Printing Public Records. *Library of Congress*

across New England. But he was also clerk of the Senate Committee on Printing Public Records, a committee chaired by Rhode Island's Republican Senator Henry B. Anthony. The *Boston Journal* paid Poore only for those few months that the Congress was in session, while the clerkship of the Senate committee supplemented his income for the rest of the year. As I have noted, this was not at all an uncommon arrangement in those days. But what a clerk the Senate had in Ben: Perley Poore! In 1865, he took over the printing of the *Congressional Directory* and established the format of that most handy reference publication which, in revised and expanded version, continues on today. He was also responsible for the monumental task of listing the nation's public documents in his *Descriptive Catalog of Government Publications of the United States, 1774–1881 (1885),* and *The Federal and State Constitutions, Colonial Charters and Other Organic Laws of the United States,* two volumes still very much in use.[19]

It was, by the way, Ben: Perley Poore who devised an entomological classification of congressional correspondents. He arranged them into "busy bees," "useless butterflies," "stinging wasps," "buzzing mosquitoes," and "hum-bugs." I shall not venture to assess the contemporary appropriateness of such a classification.[20]

Mr. President, this Bohemian era of the Washington press corps that I have been describing was also a period of large-scale and rapid postwar industrialization, of financial wheeling and dealing, and of considerable economic and political corruption. Lobbyists and "claims agents"—who pressed the claims of Civil War veterans, widows and orphans, and businessmen who had suffered war losses—often posed as newspaper reporters to gain access to senators and to cover their own lobbying activities. Some legitimate reporters also engaged in lobbying, as historian Frederick Marbut has noted, using their press gallery privileges and contacts "to branch out into such profitable sidelines as lobbying, pressing claims and selling tips to lobbyists and speculators."[21]

Each of the two houses of Congress attempted to deal with this problem. As early as 1852, the House of Representatives had adopted a rule to deny press credentials to anyone acting as a claims agent. Three years later, the House expelled a reporter who had been paid for winning a claim in favor of the Colt revolver patent. In 1857, the House also expelled a *New York Times* reporter for lobbying in favor of a Wisconsin land bill. In 1875, the House investigated four reporters who

had received large cash payments for their work on behalf of legislation subsidizing the Pacific Mail Steamship Line. As a result of these abuses, the House adopted a resolution to revoke the gallery credentials of any reporter who received a fee in connection with any legislation pending before Congress.

In those days, the presiding officer of each house determined who should be admitted to the press gallery. In 1873, the Senate shifted this responsibility to the Select Committee on Rules, and, in 1877, the House experimented with a novel idea for self-policing of the press galleries. The Speaker of the House met with a group of reporters to devise a system whereby congressional newsmen would elect a Standing Committee of Correspondents to determine that only *bona fide* reporters were admitted. This arrangement worked well enough, and, in 1884, the Senate Rules Committee also recognized the right of the standing committee to police the Senate press gallery. Since 1888, the rules adopted by the standing committee have been published in the *Congressional Directory.*[22]

The current rules require, among other things, that a person admitted to the press galleries must establish "to the satisfaction of the Standing Committee":

(b) That he or she is not engaged in paid publicity or promotion work or in prosecuting any claim before Congress or before any department of the government, and will not become so engaged while a member of the galleries.

(c) That he or she is not engaged in any lobbying activity and will not become so engaged while a member of the galleries.[23]

The standing committee performed—and still performs—most admirably. It negotiates with the Architect of the Capitol for space and maintenance of its quarters in the Capitol and Senate office buildings, selects the press gallery superintendents, and arranges for press facilities at committee hearings.

To illustrate a magazine article, an artist depicted "The Anteroom of the Reporters' Gallery During a Stupid Speech." *Harper's New Monthly Magazine, January 1874*

Similar functions are performed by the Standing Committee of Press Photographers and by the executive committees of the radio and television and the periodical press galleries. The most important function of these committees has been to determine the qualifications of reporters applying for admission to the press galleries and to protect Congress from lobbyists acting in the guise of reporters. Since this regulatory function has created a certain exclusiveness in the galleries, the Senate has had to act in the role of an appeals court, from time to time, to liberalize the rules.

An early rule of the standing committee, for instance, limited access to only those reporters who filed their dispatches by telegraph. This eliminated from the press galleries all women correspondents, of whom

there were as many as eleven in the 1870's. Since the women were all letter writers who submitted their columns too infrequently to justify the expense of telegraphed dispatches, they were thus shut out of the press galleries. Senators and representatives, however, always made room for the women correspondents in the family galleries, rather than relegate them to the crowded public galleries.

I should note that the first woman to gain access to the press gallery was Jane Grey Swisshelm, who, in 1850, marched into Vice President Millard Fillmore's office and demanded that, as a correspondent for the *New York Tribune*, she be seated in the press gallery. Fillmore, she reported, tried to dissuade her, saying that the place would be unpleasant for a lady, but he finally relented and as-

An autograph album of sketches collected by press gallery superintendent James D. Preston includes this inside view of the press gallery by artist Art Young.   *James D. Preston Papers, Archives of American Art, Smithsonian Institution*

signed her a seat along with the other reporters. Her first appearance in the press gallery touched off quite a commotion, but she wrote that she "felt that the novelty would soon wear off, and that women would work there and win bread without annoyance."

Mrs. Swisshelm filed only four columns during her stay in the Senate press gallery, but they were dramatic ones concerning the events of the Compromise of 1850. When Senator Henry Foote of Mississippi drew a pistol on Senator Thomas Hart Benton of Missouri on the Senate floor, Jane Swisshelm reported to her readers: "I sat in the reporters' gallery, directly opposite the gentlemen, and saw it all." Unfortunately, Mrs. Swisshelm's last letter from the galleries was an unsubstantiated attack on the personal life of Senator Daniel Webster, repeating gossip common to the press galleries, but which other reporters thought it wiser not to put into print. The incident embarrassed editor Horace Greeley of the *Tribune* and caused

Mrs. Swisshelm to leave Washington, although she carried on her career as a journalist in Pennsylvania and Minnesota.

Slowly, over the years, as women began to be employed as regular reporters filing telegraphic dispatches, they reappeared in the press galleries. Gender discrimination remained, however, although it was primarily imposed by their newspapers. Mary Hornaday, a Washington correspondent for the *Christian Science Monitor* in the 1930's and 1940's, recalled that women reporters did not receive the choicer assignments until World War II, when many of the male reporters were sent overseas to cover the war. Today, as Jane Swisshelm had predicted, women reporters are no longer a novelty, but take their place as regular members of the Senate press corps.[24]

For many years, black journalists were also excluded from the press galleries on the grounds that they reported for weekly rather than daily newspapers. In 1943, the standing committee rejected the application of a member of the Associated Negro Press on those grounds and acted similarly on the application of Louis R. Lautier in 1947. In the latter case, however, the Senate Committee on Rules and Administration met the next day and voted to overrule the Standing Committee of Correspondents, issuing a press card to Mr. Lautier (who, by the way, later became the first black reporter to be admitted to membership in the National Press Club). Although its members protested this "arbitrary" action, the standing committee, on May 8, 1947, revised its rules, opening the press galleries to reporters for any news service which regularly provided news of national affairs to weekly papers.[25]

Representatives of the new broadcast media were a third group who, for a time, found themselves shut out of the press galleries. Daily newspaper reporters reacted suspiciously to the new medium and complained that their quarters in the Capitol were already too crowded to accommodate radio news gatherers. Only those radio reporters who were already accredited through newspaper work were able to view the proceedings from the press galleries and make use of its facilities.

Still, radio was a natural medium for United States senators; it was perfectly attuned to the sonorous voices, elaborate vocabularies, and beautiful diction of senators from the 1920's and 1930's. In 1923, only three years after the beginning of commercial radio, the opening of Congress and the State of the Union message by President Calvin Coolidge were broadcast over the radio from the House chamber. Radio facilities were also tied into a microphone system in the House of Representatives, but the system was abandoned a year later because congressmen complained that the microphones produced a "brassy, ringing sound, and they are a great obstacle to hearing." The

first radio broadcast from the Senate chamber occurred on March 3, 1929, an occasion when retiring Vice President Charles Dawes and incoming Vice President Charles Curtis both spoke. When the first coast-to-coast network hookup was established in 1930, Senator William E. Borah of Idaho made the first nationwide address. (Incidentally, the first loudspeaker system in this chamber was installed in May 1933 for the impeachment trial of Judge Harold Louderback.)

Not until 1939, however, were radio reporters successful in establishing their own press gallery. A group led by radio commentator Fulton Lewis, Jr., bypassed the standing committee and petitioned the Senate Rules Committee. The committee held hearings and eventually proposed a revision of Senate Rule XXXIV, which in its current form as Rule XXXIII permits *bona fide* reporters . . . for daily news dissemination through radio, television, wires, and cables, and similar media of transmission." That same year, a portion of the gallery was set aside for radio reporters, and offices were created for them on the gallery floor. Broadcast booths were also set up for live and taped interviews with senators.[26]

Not until 1953 was "television" added to the radio and television gallery, but television reporters were in evidence around Capitol Hill for years before that. As early as 1947, President Truman's State of the Union message was televised. The National Broadcasting Company also had used the radio gallery that year to broadcast the first panel discussion direct from the Capitol. Senator Tom Connally of Texas, ranking minority member of the Foreign Relations Committee, was one of the first senators to be interviewed on camera at the Capitol. He arrived home that night in time to see his face on the television screen and afterwards became a strong proponent of televised broadcasting. Other senators returned from the campaign

During a press conference in November 1948, reporters listened to Vice President-elect Alben Barkley.
U.S. Senate Historical Office

trail in 1950 enthusiastic about the new medium, marveling that they could reach more voters in one broadcast than in months of personal appearances in their states.[27]

Televised committee hearings go back to 1947, when General George C. Marshall testified on the Marshall Plan to reconstruct postwar Europe. In 1950, the Senate's Kefauver crime investigation hearings were broadcast from New York City. When the cameras trained on the nervous hands of witness Frank Costello, they made an eloquent statement that deeply affected audiences everywhere. In 1954, the American Broadcasting Company decided to provide live coverage of the Army-McCarthy hearings,

and was the only network to do so. Commentators and historians have since judged that those televised hearings had more to do with swinging the tide of public opinion against the antics of Senator Joseph R. McCarthy than any other factor. Television coverage in 1957 of the Jimmy Hoffa hearings by the Senate Select Committee on Improper Activities in the Labor and Management Field (known as the "Rackets Committee") helped to advance the presidential candidacies of Senators John F. Kennedy and Barry Goldwater. It also brought to public attention the committee's chief counsel, Robert F. Kennedy. In more recent years, we recall the dramatic impact of the Ervin committee's televised hearings in the Watergate investigation and of the House Judiciary Committee's deliberations on the impeachment of President Nixon.[28]

For years, the House of Representatives banned television from its committee rooms, while Senate hearings and investigations were televised. Now, both houses of Congress permit TV cameras in their committee hearings. In 1979, the House decided to permit televising of its floor proceedings.

In 1973, I called for televising, on a trial basis, the floor proceedings of the Senate, saying that "the time has come for a new look at the possibility of using the electronic media to bring the Senate and the people closer together." I was also involved with the planning for televising two anticipated events on the floor. The first was the possible impeachment trial of President Richard Nixon. The second was the final Senate vote in 1975 on the contested election for senator from New Hampshire between Louis C. Wyman and John A. Durkin. The Senate Rules Committee considered both of these occurrences of such historical significance that it recommended lifting the ban on televising. Of course, neither event took place—President Nixon resigned rather than face impeachment, and a new election was held in New Hampshire. One event in the Senate chamber that was televised occurred on December 19, 1974, when Nelson A. Rockefeller was sworn in as vice president of the United States. As acting majority leader in the absence of Senator Mike Mansfield at that time, I helped to make this televised event possible.

Only in 1978 did the Senate permit radio broadcasts of floor debate during consideration of the Panama Canal treaties. At that time, I was majority leader, and, believing that the broadcasting of those proceedings would constitute a service to the people of the country, I pressed for Senate authoriza-

James Preston served as the first official superintendent of the Senate press gallery.   *Library of Congress*

tion. The radio broadcast coverage brought to the citizens better, more accurate information regarding the reasons senators voted for and against the treaties. The positive response to those broadcasts also contributed significantly to the Senate's decision in 1986 to permit regular television and radio broadcasting of floor proceedings.

Mr. President, in my discussion of the historical relationship between the Senate and the press, I must include the first official superintendent of the Senate press gallery, James D. Preston. For over fifty years, until his retirement in 1955, Jim Preston was a dedicated servant of the Senate. Senator Arthur Vandenberg of Michigan once told him, "You and the Senate Press Gallery are as indivisible as the Capitol and its dome." Jim Preston, the son of a Washington correspondent, and himself briefly a Washington reporter for the *Boston Journal,* became superintendent of the Senate press gallery in 1897. Prior to that time, the superintendent's job had been an unofficial one, limited mostly to keeping the inkwells filled and supplying the reporters with writing paper. Not satisfied with those mundane responsibilities, Preston began gathering copies of bills and committee reports for reporters, and followed the proceedings of the Senate himself in order to provide the correspondents with background information and other items that would help them in filing their dispatches. He also began coaxing senators to make texts of their prepared speeches available in advance. When one considers the tons of advanced texts and other press releases that senators' offices now post in the press galleries, one wonders if Preston knew what a Pandora's box he was opening!

Jim Preston's wealth of knowledge about committee meetings and the status of bills, together with his ability to dredge up factual information at a moment's notice, built him a reputation among the correspondents as "the Socrates of the press gallery," the "sage of the Senate," and "Old Man Senate." He also proved most helpful to new senators trying to learn the ropes. Georgia's distinguished Senator Walter George recalled that on his first day in the Senate, in 1922, he was expected to eulogize his deceased predecessor and send to the desk several resolutions, but he realized he did not know the first thing about getting started. "While I'm brooding," Senator George told the story, "suddenly there looms up this tall, thin fellow who walked like a pair of scissors. 'Need any help, buddy?' he asks. I spilled all my beans to him and he gave me the right answers. I depended on him for years until I could stand alone." [29]

Mr. President, as of April 26, 1989, there were over 6,400 people accredited to the various congressional press galleries—reporters and photographers not only from every state in this country but also from nations around the globe—and the number was, at that time, increasing at a rate of approximately 50 per month. Only about 650 of these, however, were actually covering Capitol Hill on a regular basis. These included correspondents from the major national news magazines, newspapers, and television and radio broadcast networks, many of whom are familiar faces on our television screens every evening and in various weekly television news analyses. Perhaps two-thirds of the regular congressional press corps are not national reporters. Instead, they cover news of importance to local papers and stations in particular states or regions. These reporters must satisfy editors who, as one correspondent complained, are only interested in "floods, military bases, and foreign imports." I, for one, do not wish to minimize their importance, for all senators know well the reporters from their "home town" papers, who interpret how national events will influence local affairs. They are among our most direct communications links to our constituents, and their value cannot be overemphasized.

The truth is that the Senate needs the press corps to keep the public informed about our legislative business. No amount of speeches, newsletters, or personal correspondence could ever equal the impact of their daily reporting, although we are not always pleased with the results. Students of journalism have confirmed long-held suspicions on Capitol Hill that the press as a whole devotes far more space and attention to the executive branch than to the legislative branch. Senators are disappointed if their speeches and legislative victories sometimes receive insufficient coverage, if complicated legislative proposals are miscon-

In the late 1860's, newspaper reporter and novelist Mark Twain, shown here, *center*, with two fellow correspondents, also worked as secretary to a senator.

Library of Congress

strued, or if they are occasionally misquoted. Senators may complain, but they cannot censure the press for these differences of opinion. This is all part of what is called the "adversary" relationship between us, which makes for independence of the press. Perhaps a better word for the relations between Congress and the press is "symbiotic," indicating a close association between two dissimilar organisms which is usually, but not always, of mutual benefit.

Let me close by quoting once more from Mark Twain, who, in a letter written in January 1868, discussed an offer he had received to serve as a congressional correspondent. "Mr. Bennett of the New York *Herald* tells me that if I will correspond twice a week from Washington, I may abuse and ridicule any body and *every* body I please." [30] Senators may, of course, suspect that there are correspondents in the galleries who carry similar licenses today. But, while we do not always see things alike, we usually work together, the senators on the floor and the correspondents in the galleries, because those who make the news and those who report it are both trying to reach the same audience.

Mark Twain's fictitious altercation with his boss ran as follows:

My Late Senatorial Secretaryship

I am not a private secretary to a senator any more now. I held the berth two months in security and in great cheerfulness of spirit, but my bread began to return from over the waters then—that is to say, my works came back and revealed themselves. I judged it best to resign. The way of it was this. My employer sent for me one morning tolerably early, and, as soon as I had finished inserting some conundrums clandestinely into his last great speech upon finance, I entered the presence. There was something portentous in his appearance. His cravat was untied, his hair was in a state of disorder, and his countenance bore about it the signs of a suppressed storm. He held a package of letters in his tense grasp, and I knew that the dreaded Pacific mail was in. He said:

"I thought you were worthy of confidence."

I said, "Yes, sir."

He said, "I gave you a letter from certain of my constituents in the State of Nevada, asking the establishment of a post-office at Baldwin's Ranch, and told you to answer it, as ingeniously as you could, with arguments which should persuade them that there was no real necessity for an office at that place."

I felt easier. "Oh, if that is all, sir, I *did* do that."

"Yes, you *did*. I will read your answer for your own humiliation:

" 'Washington, Nov. 24
" 'Messrs. Smith, Jones, and others.
" 'GENTLEMEN: What the mischief do you suppose you want with a post-office at Baldwin's Ranch? It would not do you any good. If any letters came there, you couldn't read them, you know; and, besides, such letters as ought to pass through, with money in them, for other localities, would not be likely to *get* through, you must perceive at once; and that would make trouble for us all. No, don't bother about a post-office in your camp. I have your best interests at heart, and feel that it would only be an ornamental folly. What you want is a nice jail, you know—a nice, substantial jail and a free school. These will be a lasting benefit to you. These will make you really contented and happy. I will move in the matter at once.
" 'Very truly, etc.,
" 'MARK TWAIN.
" 'For James W. N——, U.S. Senator.'

"That is the way you answered that letter. Those people say they will hang me, if I ever enter that district again; and I am perfectly satisfied they *will*, too."

"Well, sir, I did not know I was doing any harm. I only wanted to convince them."

"Ah. Well, you *did* convince them, I make no manner of doubt. Now, here is another specimen. I gave you a petition from certain gentlemen of Nevada, praying that I would get a bill through Congress incorporating the Methodist Episcopal Church of the State of Nevada. I told you to say, in reply, that the creation of such a law came more properly within the province of the state legislature; and to endeavor to show them that, in the present feebleness of the religious element in that new commonwealth, the expediency of incorporating the church was questionable. What did you write?

" 'Washington, Nov. 24
" 'Rev. John Halifax and others.
" 'GENTLEMEN: You will have to go to the state legislature about the speculation of yours—Congress don't

know anything about religion. But don't you hurry to go there, either; because this thing you propose to do out in that new country isn't expedient—in fact, it is ridiculous. Your religious people there are too feeble, in intellect, in morality, in piety—in everything, pretty much. You had better drop this—you can't make it work. You can't issue stock on an incorporation like that—or if you could, it would only keep you in trouble all the time. The other denominations would abuse it, and "bear" it, and "sell it short," and break it down. They would do with it just as they would with one of your silver-mines out there—they would try to make all the world believe it was "wildcat." You ought not to do anything that is calculated to bring a sacred thing into disrepute. You ought to be ashamed of yourselves—that is what *I* think about it. You close your petition with the words: "And we will pray." I think you had better—you need to do it.

" 'Very truly, etc.,

" 'Mark Twain,
" 'For James W. N——, U.S. Senator.'

"*That* luminous epistle finishes me with the religious element among my constituents. But that my political murder might be made sure, some evil instinct prompted me to hand you this memorial from the grave company of elders composing the board of aldermen of the city of San Francisco, to try your hand upon—a memorial praying that the city's right to the water-lots upon the city front might be established by law of Congress. I told you this was a dangerous matter to move in. I told you to write a noncommittal letter to the aldermen—an ambiguous letter—a letter that should avoid, as far as possible, all real consideration and discussion of the water-lot question. If there is any feeling left in you—any shame—surely this letter you wrote, in obedience to that order, ought to evoke it, when its words fall upon your ears:

" '*Washington, Nov. 27.*
" '*The Honorable Board of Aldermen, etc.*

" 'Gentlemen: George Washington, the revered Father of his Country, is dead. His long and brilliant career is closed, alas! forever. He was greatly respected in this section of the country, and his untimely decease cast a gloom over the whole community. He died on the 14th day of December, 1799. He passed peacefully away from the scene of his honors and his great achievements, the most lamented hero and the best beloved that ever earth hath yielded unto Death. At such a time as this, *you* speak of water-lots!—what a lot was his!

" 'What is fame! Fame is an accident. Sir Isaac Newton discovered an apple falling to the ground—a trivial discovery, truly, and one which a million men had made before him—but his parents were influential, and so they tortured that small circumstance into something wonderful, and, lo! the simple world took up the shout and, in almost the twinkling of an eye, that man was famous. Treasure these thoughts.

" 'Poesy, sweet poesy, who shall estimate what the world owes to thee!

" ' "Mary had a little lamb,
    its fleece was white as snow—
  And everywhere that Mary went,
    the lamb was sure to go."
" ' "Jack and Gill went up the hill
  To draw a pail of water;
  Jack fell down and broke his crown,
  And Gill came tumbling after."

" 'For simplicity, elegance of diction, and freedom from immoral tendencies, I regard those two poems in the light of gems. They are suited to all grades of intelligence, to every sphere of life—to the field, to the nursery, to the guild. Especially should no Board of Aldermen be without them.

" 'Venerable fossils! write again. Nothing improves one so much as friendly correspondence. Write again—and if there is anything in this memorial of yours that refers to anything in particular, do not be backward about explaining it. We shall always be happy to hear you chirp.

" 'Very truly, etc.,

" 'Mark Twain,
" 'For James W. N——, U.S. Senator.'

"That is an atrocious, a ruinous epistle! Distraction!"

"Well, sir, I am really sorry if there is anything wrong about it—but—but it appears to me to dodge the water-lot question."

"Dodge the mischief! Oh!—but never mind. As long as destruction must come now, let it be complete. Let it be complete—let this last of your performances, which I am about to read, make a finality of it. I am a ruined man. I *had* my misgivings when I gave you the letter from Humboldt, asking that the post route from Indian Gulch to Shakespeare Gap and intermediate points be changed partly to the old Mormon trail. But I told you it was a delicate question, and warned you to deal with it deftly—to answer it dubiously, and leave them a little in the dark. And your fatal imbecility impelled you to make *this* disastrous reply. I should think you would stop your ears, if you are not dead to all shame:

" 'Messrs. Perkins, Wagner, et al.

" 'GENTLEMEN: It is a delicate question about this Indian trail, but, handled with proper deftness and dubiousness, I doubt not we shall succeed in some measure or otherwise, because the place where the route leaves the Lassen Meadows, over beyond where those two Shawnee chiefs, Dilapidated-Vengeance and Biter-of-the-Clouds, were scalped last winter, this being the favorite direction to some, but others preferring something else in consequence of things, the Mormon trail leaving Mosby's at three in the morning, and passing through Jawbone Flat to Blucher, and then down by Jug-Handle, the road passing to the right of it, and naturally leaving it on the right, too, and Dawson's on the left of the trail where it passes to the left of said Dawson's and onward thence to Tomahawk, thus making the route cheaper, easier of access to all who can get at it, and compassing all the desirable objects so considered by others, and, therefore, conferring the most good upon the greatest number, and, consequently, I am encouraged to hope we shall. However, I shall be ready, and happy, to afford you still further information upon the subject, from time to time, as you may desire it and the Post-office Department be enabled to furnish it to me.

" 'Very truly, etc.,

" 'MARK TWAIN,
" 'For James W. N. ———, U.S. Senator.'

"There—now *what* do you think of that?"

"Well, I don't know, sir. It—well, it appears to me—to be dubious enough."

"Du—leave the house! I am a ruined man. Those Humboldt savages never will forgive me for tangling their brains up with this inhuman letter. I have lost the respect of the Methodist Church, the board of aldermen—"

"Well, I haven't anything to say about that, because I may have missed it a little in their cases, but I *was* too many for the Baldwin's Ranch people, General!"

"Leave the house! Leave it forever and forever, too."

I regarded that as a sort of covert intimation that my service could be dispensed with, and so I resigned. I never will be a private secretary to a senator again. You can't please that kind of people. They don't know anything. They can't appreciate a party's efforts.[31]

And so, Mr. President, this is the way it was, and is, and will continue to be—the Mark Twains, the Ben: Perley Poores, the Jane Grey Swisshelms, the Horace Greeleys of yesteryear; and the Walter Cronkites, the Walter Lippmanns, the Katharine Grahams of our own day and time—they all, yes, even the muckrakers, too, constitute the mighty Fourth Estate, that guardian of our liberties and shaper of the "opinion of the people," which, "in the Reporters' Gallery yonder," is, said Edmund Burke, "more important than they all."

CHAPTER 20

The Botanic Garden and Capitol Landscape

January 29, 1981 *

Mr. President, in my series of statements on the United States Senate, I have given special attention to a description of this body's meeting places here in the Capitol. I have spoken of the statuary, the paintings, and the architecture that so distinguish the inside of this building. Today, I shall discuss the Capitol's exterior beauty, focusing on the Botanic Garden and the landscaping of the surrounding 214.7 acres.

Looking back over the past one hundred years, there have been major changes to both the Botanic Garden and the Capitol grounds. Undoubtedly, the coming century will bring additional alterations. Today, I shall speak about the efforts, over many years, to bring to this place the natural beauty that surrounds us.

Countless hours of planting, weeding, watering, spraying, pruning, separating, and planning—as well as worrying about bugs and slugs, beetles and worms, droughts and rains, hail and frost—go into making Capitol Hill the glorious splash of greenery and color that we know and love. Most of the people who do all of this weeding and worrying, who try to keep our trees alive and our grass green, work in the Botanic Garden or for the landscape architect, under the supervision of the architect of the Capitol.

There is no lovelier oasis from the rigors of legislative life than the Botanic Garden, only a block away. The idea for a botanic garden in the nation's capital can be traced back to the eighteenth century. In 1796, the commissioners of the District of Columbia corresponded with Representative James Madison and President George Washington in Philadelphia regarding the possibility of constructing a botanic garden as part of the national university that was envisioned for the new capital city.[1]

The idea of a botanic garden lay fallow until January 1814, when Dr. William Thornton, who had designed the Capitol and was, at that time, superintendent of the Patent Office, suggested to President Madison that a botanic garden be built without waiting for the creation of a university. Fearing that some native plants might soon become extinct, Thornton warned:

By clearing lands, whole families of plants are likely to be lost to the world, but a greenhouse would preserve what the Almighty has given. . . . If a university be ever established . . . the botanic garden would be a necessary appendage.[2]

* Updated March 1989

An aerial view of the Capitol grounds in 1980 shows the Botanic Garden, *right foreground*, the U. S. Grant memorial, and the reflecting pool, *left foreground*, with the Taft Carillon rising above the trees on the left.

Architect of the Capitol

Six more years would pass, however, before anything was done to make the botanic garden a reality. In 1820, Congress granted five acres of land at the eastern end of the mall to the Columbian Institute for the Promotion of Arts and Sciences, a scientific organization dedicated to collecting, cultivating and distributing "the various vegetable production of this and other countries whether medicinal, esculent, or for the promotion of arts and manufactures." [3] While the institute did collect and distribute plants, it was dependent on private donations and never had the funds to develop its garden adequately. After 1837, the Columbian Institute itself ceased to exist.

On August 18, 1838, an event occurred that would affect the botanic garden's future. That day, the six ships of the United States' Exploring Expedition to the South Seas, under the command of Lieutenant Charles Wilkes, set sail from Hampton Roads, Virginia. According to Wilkes, the principal objective of his 1838 expedition was "the promotion of the great interest of commerce and navigation, yet all occasions will be taken, not incompatible with the great purpose of the undertaking, to extend the bounds of science and to promote the acquisition of knowledge." Among those aboard for the latter purpose was William D. Brackenridge, a horticulturist. [4]

Nearly four years later, in June 1842, the Wilkes expedition returned to the United States and put into New York harbor. Wilkes had traveled some 85,000 miles, exploring the Pacific Ocean from the coast of North America south to Australia and Antarctica. Throughout the voyage, Brackenridge had been busy collecting specimens, and the holds of the returning ships contained ten thousand species of plant materials and more than 250 species of live plants. This treasure-trove of flora became the basis for the nation's Botanic Garden. [5]

The original conservatory of the Botanic Garden stood near the Capitol in 1859. *Architect of the Capitol*

Soon after the expedition's return in 1842, Congress appropriated funds for a greenhouse to shelter the collection, near what was then the Patent Office in downtown Washington. William Brackenridge himself took over the care of these precious plants. Displayed for the first time in the United States were exotic sights like the beautiful bird-of-paradise flower and species of the mimosa tree, which we see throughout suburban Washington today.

In 1849, the Patent Office needed the space occupied by the greenhouse, and Congress paid for construction of a new greenhouse at the eastern end of the mall on the site of the old Columbian Institute garden. Once the exotic plant collection was moved to its new location, it became an attraction for both city dwellers and tourists. Some years later, *Harper's Weekly* proclaimed, "There are few places in Washington city more interesting to visitors than the Botanic Garden at the foot of Capitol Hill." [6]

Congress officially recognized the collection in 1856, naming it the United States

Botanic Garden and placing it under the jurisdiction of the Joint Committee on the Library. Since that time, the garden has been funded through annual congressional appropriations.[7]

In 1854, William R. Smith, who later replaced Brackenridge as superintendent of the gardens, prepared a catalog of the plants in the conservatory and noted that "the majority of the plants in this list are the results of the United States Exploring Expedition." One of Smith's duties at that time was to gather seeds from the garden's collection for distribution to interested horticulturists.[8]

William R. Smith was an interesting character. As official keeper of the coconuts and cyclamens, he occupied a little brick house buried in the jungle of rare and exotic plants. Visitors undoubtedly enjoyed treading the garden's shaded walks, and little children would peep in at the flowers through the iron fence that enclosed it, but, for almost sixty years, William R. Smith actually lived there.

In the early 1850's, while Brackenridge was still chief horticulturist, the young Smith, fresh from Scotland, was hired as the director's assistant. When Brackenridge resigned in 1863, Smith became superintendent of the garden. During his long tenure there, the cuttings he had planted with young hands grew into lofty trees.[9]

Seeds from the plants brought back by Wilkes' expedition were not the only things Smith gathered and distributed. He returned from one of his trips to England with a clipping of what is called "Boston ivy," which he proceeded to cultivate and introduce across the nation. The *Washington Star* of October 20, 1907, reported:

Among the treasures in vegetation which grow in the National Botanic Garden in addition to the memorial trees is the *Ampelopsis veitchii*, the parent of millions of the same vine and the ancestral vine of all of them in the United States. The vine is an English immigrant. It was brought to this country many years ago by William R. Smith, Superintendent of the Botanic Garden. Hence Mr. Smith is the foster father of a vine that climbs and clasps uncounted walls from sea to sea—the foster father of the most popular city vine in America.[10]

One of the best-known landmarks of the Botanic Garden is not a plant, but the famous thirty-foot-tall Bartholdi fountain, which now stands in the outdoor garden off Independence Avenue and First Street, Southwest. It has been part of the garden, although not always in the same spot, since 1878. Designed for the 1876 Philadelphia Centennial Exposition by Frédéric Auguste Bartholdi, the French sculptor of the Statue of Liberty, the fountain was purchased for the Botanic Garden by the United States government at the conclusion of the exposition.

The enormous fountain, with its huge basins, strange sea creatures spitting water, and its three graceful, eleven-foot-high caryatids, represents water and light. Indeed, the fountain was a major nighttime attraction in late nineteenth-century Washington, since its twelve Victorian gas lamps provided one of the earliest public displays of outdoor lighting in the city.[11]

Ironically, the future of the Botanic Garden became threatened by a project designed to beautify the mall area. Unveiled in 1901, the "McMillan Plan"—named for Senator James McMillan of Michigan—proposed creating an unbroken swath of green stretching from the Washington Monument to the Capitol. Achieving this goal would require removal not only of unsightly railroad buildings and underbrush at the foot of Capitol Hill but also of the Botanic Garden. Under the plan, the site was needed for a large memorial to President Grant, which the designers insisted must be in that exact location to achieve the desired symmetry.[12]

In 1910 the Bartholdi fountain was located in front of the original Botanic Garden conservatory. *Library of Congress*

Friends of the Botanic Garden objected strenuously, because the plan also called for destroying an entire grove of beautiful large memorial trees. The *Washington Star* launched a series of articles denouncing the Grant memorial and pleading that the trees be spared the ax. Among the endangered trees was an oak grown from an acorn taken from the tree over Confucius' grave, as well as memorial trees honoring Presidents Hayes and Garfield, and trees planted by, or honoring, several members of Congress.[13]

The protesters succeeded in blocking the project for two decades, but eventually, in the 1920's, the Botanic Garden had to be relocated, and the Grant memorial was built. The commemorative trees and many others were destroyed. There was some discussion about moving the Botanic Garden to the suburbs, away from the bustling city, but this idea, fortunately for us today, made little headway. Instead, it was finally decided to recreate the Botanic Garden only slightly to the south of its old location.

The current conservatory building, at Maryland Avenue and First Street, SW, was begun in 1931 and completed in 1933. In addition, a little fan-shaped building was constructed to serve as a home for the director of the garden. In 1934, when the garden was placed under the jurisdiction of the architect of the Capitol, this attractive little house became the garden's offices. The Bartholdi fountain, too, found a new home, as the centerpiece of a garden across Independence Avenue from the conservatory.[14]

While the most visible feature of the new Botanic Garden is the soaring glass conserva-

The humid interior of the Botanic Garden's present conservatory enables tropical plants to thrive and grow to dramatic heights. *Architect of the Capitol*

tory dome of the palm room, its most unique feature is less apparent. The conservatory represents the first time that aluminum was used in the construction of a building this size. Even more amazing, the thirty-one tons of aluminum parts have been virtually maintenance-free for over fifty years.[15]

Stepping into the aluminum-ribbed conservatory is like entering another world. On a snowy February day, just a few steps can transport one to the tropical lushness of the South Seas where bananas grow in profusion, or to the hot, dry Mexican desert where cacti grow in bizarre shapes. Roaming through the conservatory's nearly 29,000 square feet of growing space, through the palm house, the fern house, the citrus, cactus and bromeliad houses, or by the little stream full of goldfish, a visitor sees many kinds of strange and exotic plants. At a glance, one

can learn both their common and Latin names and their country of origin. Some of the plants on display in the conservatory are as old as the original Botanic Garden. There is a juju date tree that arrived in a five-gallon tub in the hold of one of Wilkes' ships in 1842. The progeny of many of those original plants are still flourishing.

One of the rarest plants at the Botanic Garden is an enormous vessel fern that measures twenty feet across. And there are palms so big that they push the window panes right out of the palm room's one hundred-foot-high roof. Heat and humidity collect right under the ceiling and, once the palms grow tall enough to reach this pocket of warm, moist air, they just take off. There are banana trees in this room, too. Each tree yields only one bunch of bananas in its lifetime and then dies, but a new tree shoots up on the same spot. Right next to the bananas are palms over 150 years old. There are also the amazing, if more junior, century plants. These palms are said to bloom only once after a century of growth; then they die.

The Botanic Garden's beautiful orchid collection is one of the largest in the world, with more than fifteen thousand specimens. Major attractions of the orchid display are the tiny yellow orchids, delicate white ones, and the large purple Mother's Day type. Some of the orchids in the garden's collection are exceedingly rare. Because of the Botanic Garden's excellent and well-deserved reputation for good care of its plants, some private orchid breeders give one of the only two existing plants of a new breed to the garden for protection.

While some plants are very rare and very old, others are simply fun to look at. There are painted fingernail plants from Brazil whose tips appear to have just received a fresh coat of fuchsia lacquer. One of the plants that children like best is the chenille plant from Malaysia, which sends out fuzzy pink tongues that resemble the chenille in bedspreads and bathrobes. Some plants look rather creepy, as though they would like to wrap their tendrils around you when your back is turned. And some, like the pincushion cactus from Mexico, leave no question that you had better not touch.

There is the mother-in-law plant, which has a slightly poisonous taste and will make your tongue sore. And there is the prayer plant, which, each night when darkness comes on, folds its leaves like a child at its bedside entering into prayer; when the light returns, the leaves again open.

All of these living plants, just like children, need the constant and careful supervision provided by the conservatory's staff of seven gardeners and three nighttime engineers. A broken window, a sudden drop in temperature, lightning, fire, or the failure of a heating unit, could destroy the collective growth of several centuries. In 1957, the Botanic Garden, normally open every day except Christmas and New Year's Day, had to close for a brief period because of damage done by a windstorm. Dozens of panes of glass shattered, but only a few plants were lost—even the most delicate orchid was saved.

Although more than two million people a year, including 800,000 children in school groups, pass through the gardens, there is little vandalism. A few visitors, however, cannot seem to resist leaving their mark. In the cactus room, several venerable giants bear the indignity of having names and hearts gouged into their sides. Foreign dignitaries and horticulturists are drawn to the gardens with great regularity. What these visitors most delight in seeing is a familiar plant so far from home, like the banyan tree of India, where it is considered sacred.

While most visitors to the Botanic Garden generally behave themselves, some do not. Birds and squirrels seem to know when the windows atop the conservatory are going to be opened to regulate temperature and humidity. In 1941, a red squirrel wandered in, stayed for years, and was finally named "Charlie." There are mockingbirds that spend the winter inside the conservatory— and who can blame them? Once, a few years ago, someone turned a pet iguana loose in the garden, reasoning, no doubt, that it would be more at home there among the lush tropical foliage than in a basement. The iguana did seem to enjoy the change but terrified the tourists. Only by turning off all the water was the staff able to coax the creature out of hiding and capture it.

During the summer, the outside as well as the inside of the conservatory is ablaze with color. Tubs of impatiens and baskets of begonias invite visitors to picnic or rest on the benches. Across the street, the Bartholdi fountain is surrounded by one of the prettiest gardens this side of West Virginia. There are daisies, snapdragons, white and yellow sundrops, silvery dusty millers—incidentally, that is the name of a fiddle tune, also, "The Dusty Miller"—and gorgeous climbing clematis. The walkways are bordered with Senator Everett Dirksen's beloved marigolds. In summers past, there has been a lovely twenty-two-foot butterfly-shaped arrangement in the garden, made from flowering plants. For the bicentennial celebration in 1976, there was a magnificent map of the United States made of plants.

Dispensing information, part of the Botanic Garden's mandate, means answering the dozens of calls and letters that come into the garden office each week. Staff members keep a list of poisonous plants by their desks to answer the calls of distraught parents who fear, sometimes correctly, that their children have eaten harmful plants. Often, however, plants are the victims of children, instead of the reverse. One woman worried that her young son had killed her prize cactus by dousing it with dishwashing detergent. A staff member reassured her that the brand her child selected was biodegradable.

Each day's mail brings requests for help, samples of sickly leaves and sometimes squashed bugs. After consultation, these specimens are quickly destroyed before whatever did them in can start to feed on the garden's delicacies. The late J. Edgar Hoover, school children, and members of the Senate and House have all brought their plant problems to the Botanic Garden. Hoover's problem was ailing gardenias. Children have asked how to grow a mango tree from the large, ugly mango seed. (It is very difficult.) A public official once brought in two wilted geraniums planted in chamber pots.

Members of the House and Senate get not only advice but also actual plants on loan from the Botanic Garden to brighten their offices. If one of their wards becomes ill while on loan, the garden staff will retrieve it and nurse it back to health. But sometimes it is too late. One representative's secretary edged his stationery in black and wrote, "We regret to inform you of the demise of the two plants which were in four inch pots."

All of the plants in members' offices, as well as all of the poinsettias and chrysanthemums and the hundreds of marigolds and begonias that adorn the garden, are grown at the garden's Poplar Point nursery, twenty-two acres of gardens and greenhouses in the District of Columbia's Anacostia section.

The Poplar Point nursery also provides the thousands of plants that decorate the grounds of the Capitol and the Library of Congress, and I shall now shift the focus of my remarks from the Botanic Garden to the Capitol grounds. The lawns and gardens surrounding the Capitol are the domain of the architect of the Capitol and of landscape architect Paul Pincus and his staff of eighty. Not a day goes by when the gardeners cannot be seen tugging at weeds, pruning

trees, or tenderly setting out tiny new plants. Thanks to them, from early spring to late fall, those who work and visit here enjoy a veritable wonderland of color.

It is hard to believe that, lovely as they are today, the Capitol grounds were once sadly neglected. It was not until 1874, when portions of the Capitol were already three-quarters of a century old, that Congress turned its attention to the surrounding grounds. When it finally decided to act, however, Congress hired the most famous landscape architect in America, Frederick Law Olmsted, who had designed New York City's Central Park.

Olmsted found the acres he was to work his magic on in sad shape. No single plan for their improvement had been consistently followed. The Capitol grounds had been enclosed and encircled by a road in the early 1800's, but these improvements were obliterated by the burning of the Capitol in 1814. When the House and Senate wings were added at mid-century, the huge quantity of earth removed for the foundations was heaped into geometric outlines and sodded, but the grass had died and rain had eroded the mounds.[16]

Some attention had been given to the east front, but the west front was a barren, bumpy stretch of earth. Because Congress had always thought the city of Washington would grow to the east, it considered the east front most important. By 1874, however, it was apparent that this was not to be. Washington lay to the west, and the Capitol looked as if it had turned its back on the executive branch and the people of the federal city. It was time, Olmsted told Congress, to clean up the "back yard." [17]

Although the terribly uneven grade of the west front presented a challenge, Olmsted's worst enemy was the soil itself. Like much of Washington's soil, it had a heavy clay base. Shortly after the government moved to the

In 1858, the new House and Senate wings of the Capitol were nearing completion, while construction continued on the dome. This view, which also includes the original Botanic Garden, illustrates the neglected state of the western grounds.   *Architect of the Capitol*

new capital in 1800, an observer described the soil as *"exceedingly stiff* clay, becoming dust in dry and mortar in rainy weather." Olmsted ordered the ground on both the east and west fronts plowed up, regraded, drained, and covered over with two feet of top soil. To make sure that the thousands of trees and bushes he had ordered for the new grounds would grow, he had added to the topsoil doses of oyster-shell lime, stable manure, and "swamp muck." [18]

Olmsted's plans for the Capitol were largely completed by the mid-1880's, and all of Washington marveled at the change. No longer did the gleaming white Capitol seem to rise from a flat and ugly plain of dull brown, nor did it appear in imminent danger of sliding off its hill. Instead, its base was softened by graceful groves of trees. A long, sweeping lawn of green joined it to the rest

of the city to the west. The lovely configuration of the grounds we see today, and the terrace completed in 1892, are Olmsted's magnificent legacy.

It is always sad to see summer fade and the flowers die. The red cannas and the yellow chrysanthemums on the east and west fronts are some of the last to go. But we can rest assured that spring will always bring a new burst of color to Capitol Hill. Until the mid-1960's, however, members of Congress had to wait almost until June to see much color up here. We may thank our late colleagues Hubert Humphrey of Minnesota and Everett Dirksen of Illinois for having some of spring's earliest harbingers planted on the grounds.

No one had a way with words quite like Senator Humphrey. On April 25, 1962, he rose in the Senate and lamented:

The broad terraces designed by Frederick Law Olmsted for the west front of the Capitol offer a panoramic view of the Mall and the Washington Monument.

The calendar tells us that spring has come. If we step outside right now, we can feel that it is spring. The flowers which are blooming in the private yards and gardens throughout the Washington area tell us it is spring. The gardens surrounding the center of the executive branch of our Government—the White House—tell us it is spring. Even the leaves and the trees surrounding the Capitol tell us rather plaintively that it is spring.

But there are no flowers in the eastern area of the Capitol Grounds to tell us that it is spring.

What he wanted, Senator Humphrey said, was to

nudge my colleagues out of their deep, somber concern for earthshaking budgets and policy deliberations for a few moments to consider a small—but important— need in the front yard of the Nation's Government.[19]

As it turned out, Senator Humphrey had chosen to speak out on flowers when his colleague, Senator Dirksen, an expert horticulturist and no mean orator himself, was present. Senator Dirksen applauded Senator Humphrey's plea for more plants but cautioned him of the danger of frost. While noting that he had planted his own cannas at home that weekend, Senator Dirksen urged Senator Humphrey to be patient. Said Senator Dirksen:

Certainly in due time there will be cannas and dahlias and princesfeathers and, in due time, all the other beautiful flowers, that somehow engender a kind of introspection, assuage all the turbulence of the soul, and bring peace to the hearts of all those who labor here and of all the thousands who come here to visit. So, Mr. President, all in its own good time will be brought to pass.[20]

But Senator Humphrey would not be put off. What about all those flowers already blooming in Maryland, "far enough away from the Capitol so that the air out there is not quite as warm as it is here," he challenged. Senator Dirksen suggested that perhaps Senator Humphrey had gotten his flowers mixed up with early shrubs like forsythia, to which Senator Humphrey indignantly replied that he certainly did know the difference. *Flowers* were blooming in Maryland and at the White House!

There the matter rested, but only until the following day when Senator Humphrey, delighted to find his friend Senator Dirksen also in the chamber, announced that he had done a little research overnight. He had before him, he proudly announced, Pamphlet No. 309 from the National Arboretum and went on to list the variety of plants that could have been blooming on the Capitol grounds that very minute if only they had been planted the previous fall! Several other senators jumped in, noting that their states' flowers bloomed early in the spring as well. While Senator Dirksen continued to insist that his colleague still did not know the difference between a flower and a shrub, all finally agreed that perhaps some effort could be made to beautify the Capitol in the springtime. I must add here that one of the shrubs that does its part to add color to Capitol Hill in the spring is the beautiful rhododendron, the state flower of West Virginia.[21]

That fall, the gardeners put in the tulip and daffodil bulbs that blossomed the next spring. By 1973, the staff of landscape architect Paul Pincus was planting more than thirty thousand bulbs each October. And this past October, between sixty and seventy thousand tulips, hyacinths, daffodils, cro-

A lover of flowers, Senator Everett Dirksen championed the marigold. *U.S. Senate Historical Office*

cuses, and narcissuses were planted. In the middle of February, when the cold winds whip across the lawn, we should take heart at the thought of all those wonders of nature growing beneath the frozen soil, preparing for their spring debut.

Sometimes, the gardeners must wonder if they do too good a job of enticing the public to come and look at nature's handiwork. Whole azalea bushes are known to have been dug up and carted off during the night. One summer, there was an especially high disappearance rate among some beautiful ornamental pepper plants planted in the gardens.

As majestic as the flowers at our feet, are the trees that tower over our heads as we cross the Capitol grounds. Among the trees of over one hundred species that grace Capitol Hill are some California redwoods, Chi-

Azaleas bloom each spring near the east front of the Capitol.

U.S. Senate Historical Office

From spring through fall, the Capitol grounds are bright with flowers, as shown in these views of, *left*, a trolley stop on the Capitol's east plaza and a fountain on the north side. *Above*, a grotto nestled amid a stand of trees on the northwest Senate lawn offers visitors a tranquil, shady oasis. *U.S. Senate Historical Office*

nese saucer magnolias, umbrella trees, cucumber trees, cherry trees, redbuds, and pines. These grounds are a squirrel's paradise because of all the nut trees: hickory, pecan, walnut, and oak.

I spoke earlier about the old memorial trees at the base of Capitol Hill which were destroyed to make way for the Grant monument. Since the early 1900's, more than one hundred more memorial and historic trees have been planted on the Capitol grounds.

Until 1978, the oldest trees on Capitol Hill were a trio of stately elms. The trio are now a duo. Some of us remember the sad day in 1978 when we heard the buzz of the saw signaling the demise of another tree—one of these elms, on the Capitol's northeast lawn. Seventeen feet in circumference, the tree was so badly diseased that it had to be taken down. When it was cut down, its rings showed that the elm was more than 110 years old. Generations of tourists had posed for pictures beneath its branches. Its life spanned the administrations of at least twenty-two presidents.

This elm was not one of the official memorial trees, but Senator Edward Kennedy delivered a fine eulogy to it the day after it was felled. Although it bore no official name, the senator said his brother, John, when a young senator himself, liked to call it the "Humility Tree," because senators always had to duck their heads when they passed under its low branches on their way to the Capitol.[22]

The two old elms that remain are on the House side of the grounds. Both are over one hundred years old. While the one on the east front is unnamed, the other, just to the south of the House wing, is the Cameron elm. It honors Senator Simon Cameron of Pennsylvania, who saved its life. One day in the mid-1870's, Senator Cameron was crossing the lawn when he saw workmen about to chop down a perfectly healthy tree. The tree,

he learned, stood in the middle of the new walkway that landscape architect Frederick Law Olmsted had planned through the grounds, and it had to go. Cameron stood in front of the tree and ordered the workmen to leave it alone. Today, you can see how the concrete sidewalk curves right around the tree's base. Now eighty feet tall, the old elm is ailing. Its insides are filled with tons of concrete and steel cables to hold its major branches off the ground.

Another man who loved his tree was Speaker Sam Rayburn. In October of 1949, a Texas white oak was planted in his honor. Many a day, as Speaker Rayburn left the Capitol, he would walk over to his tree with a tape measure to see how it was doing.

There are trees on the grounds honoring many states and a variety of former members and organizations. There are several redwood trees. One was planted on the west front of the Senate side in 1966 by a delegation of Cherokee Indians. In 1976, the citizens of Maryland presented the Capitol with a seedling of their state's great Wye Oak, the oldest white oak in America. Also in 1976, the citizens of Paw Paw, West Virginia, planted a pawpaw tree on the grounds.[23]

In looking over the list of memorial and historic trees, I was struck by an entry listing five crab apple trees, planted in 1952, that are dedicated to the Sullivan brothers. No one who is old enough to remember World War II could forget their sad story.

The Sullivan brothers—George, Francis, Joseph, Madison, and Albert—were young men from Waterloo, Iowa, who all enlisted in the navy together after Pearl Harbor. Coming from a close-knit family, they requested that they all be assigned to the same ship. They were assigned to the U.S.S. *Juneau* in the Pacific. On November 13, 1942, the *Juneau* was struck by a Japanese torpedo and went down near the Solomon Islands. All five brothers went down with the ship. I shall never see those five crab apples on the Senate side of the east front without thinking of those brave boys.

The Sullivan crab apples, Senator Cameron's elm, Sam Rayburn's white oak, Senator Dirksen's marigolds, Senator Humphrey's daffodils—they are all a part of the history that surrounds the United States Senate here on Capitol Hill. It is not just a history cast in stone and bronze; it is also a green past that continues to grow today and will grow verdantly on into the future, with its

Daffodils
That come before the swallow dares, and take
The winds of March with beauty.[24]

CHAPTER 21

The Senate in Literature and Film

May 15, 1987

Mr. President, today in my continuing series of addresses on the history of the United States Senate, I would like to devote some attention to a special group of senators. Although widely known in their time, I dare say these senators are completely unfamiliar to most current members. They were a colorful, vibrant, compelling group who captured national attention by thrilling deeds—and misdeeds. Some were heroes, some were scoundrels, some were buffoons, and some were larger-than-life examples of how the Senate really operates. I am talking about such senators as Silas Ratcliffe, Abner Dilworthy, Cale Caldwell, Jefferson Smith, Melvin Ashton, Seab Cooley, and Solomon Spiffledink.

Senator Solomon *who*? I can see puzzled expressions on senators' faces, and there may be some perplexed clerks thumbing through their copies of the *Senate Manual*, looking under "S" for "Spiffledink." There is a Senator Spencer and a Senator Spong but no Spiffledink between them. Instead of the *Senate Manual*, they will have to consult a novel published in 1927 by a reporter in the press

gallery named Louis Ludlow. The novel is *Senator Solomon Spiffledink*, and, yes, the title character is totally fictitious, as are Senators Ratcliffe, Dilworthy, Caldwell, Smith, Ashton, and Cooley.

Over the years, the Senate has attracted the talents of many novelists, from Mark Twain to Margaret Truman, as well as Hollywood film makers, from Frank Capra to Otto Preminger, who have created memorable fictional senators and unforgettable cinematic images of the Senate. In some cases, the films and novels mirrored reality; in other cases, they distorted it for humor, suspense, satire, and pure entertainment. I suspect that more than a few senators formed their first impressions of this institution, long before their elections, by viewing *Mr. Smith Goes to Washington* or reading *Advise and Consent*. Numerous visitors in our galleries were probably influenced by those same movies and books and, consequently, have felt disappointed by the less than dramatic proceedings they might have witnessed on the Senate floor. It is hard for real life senators to compete with the likes of Jimmy

Two illustrations from *The Gilded Age* show "Senator Dilworthy," *left*, addressing the Sunday School and, *right*, giving Laura his blessing.
M. Twain and C.D. Warner, The Gilded Age, 1902 ed.

Stewart, William Powell, and Charles Laughton. But now, with their movies showing on other channels against the televised proceedings of the Senate, it is time we took a look at the great fictitious senators of our history.

The line between reality and fiction can be quite thin, and political novelists have regularly based their characters and stories on actual individuals and events. The *roman à clef,* a novel which makes little pretense or apology about depicting thinly disguised real people, is a mainstay of Washington literature. Indeed, part of the fun of reading this type of novel comes from trying to guess which well-known figures served as the

book's models. We can see this device in Mark Twain's and Charles Dudley Warner's classic novel of Capitol mayhem, *The Gilded Age,* first published in December 1873.

In *The Gilded Age,* Twain drew a wonderfully malicious portrait of Senator Abner Dilworthy, as pious a fraud as ever served in the Senate. Twain introduced the senator as he was giving an uplifting speech, replete with allusions to "the genius of American Liberty, walking with the Sunday School in one hand and Temperance in the other up the glorified steps of the National Capitol." One of his young protégés thought that the more he watched the senator in action, "the more he honored him, and the more conspicuously the moral grandeur of his character appeared to stand out." But much of the story's plot involves Dilworthy's efforts to win congressional approval of an unsavory private bill from which he and his friends would benefit handsomely. In these efforts, the senator was assisted by a beautiful and crafty female lobbyist, Laura Hawkins. At one point, Miss Hawkins expressed her concern that critical newspaper editorials would defeat their bill, but Dilworthy gave her a lesson in Gilded Age political science:

Oh, not at all, not at all, my child. It is just what we want. . . . Give us newspaper persecution enough, and we are safe. Vigorous persecution will alone carry a bill sometimes, dear; and when you start with a strong vote in the first place, persecution comes in with double effect. It scares off some of the weak supporters, true, but it soon turns strong ones into stubborn ones. And then, presently, it changes the tide of public opinion. The great public is weak-minded; the great public is sentimental. . . . In a word, the great putty-hearted public loves to "gush," and there is no such darling opportunity to gush as a case of persecution affords.

The bill moved inexorably through the House of Representatives, but suddenly the unexpected occurred—just as his state legislature was on the verge of reelecting Dilworthy, Mr. Noble, a member of the legislature, produced seven thousand dollars which he claimed the senator gave as a bribe for his vote. Shocked, the legislature elected another candidate, and the Senate rejected Dilworthy's private bill. "Newspapers, and everybody else," called the senator "a pious hypocrite, a sleek, oily fraud, a reptile who manipulated temperance movements, prayer meetings, Sunday Schools, public charities, missionary enterprises, all for his private benefit." Just when all seemed lost for the senator, however, he brazenly offered a resolution appointing a special Senate committee to investigate the allegations against him.

When the resolution carried and the committee was appointed, the newspapers immediately attacked the ploy and reviled the Senate with blistering force:

Under the guise of appointing a committee to investigate . . . Dilworthy, the Senate yesterday appointed a committee to *investigate his accuser, Mr. Noble*. . . . That Mr. Dilworthy had the effrontery to offer such a resolution will surprise no one, and that the Senate could entertain it without blushing and pass it without shame will surprise no one. We are now reminded of a note which we have received from the notorious burglar Murphy, in which he finds fault with a statement of ours to the effect that he had served one term in the penitentiary and also one in the U.S. Senate. He says, "The latter statement is untrue and does me great injustice." After an unconscious sarcasm like that, further comment is unnecessary.

Instead of castigating their fellow member for his gross violation of senatorial ethics, Dilworthy's colleagues on the committee turned their fire on his accuser, Mr. Noble, for having received a bribe! Dilworthy finished out his term and returned home to a "grand ovation" from his friends who declared "that he was still good enough for them." [1]

Now, Mr. President, we might say: "My goodness, what a fertile imagination Mark Twain had! Surely no United States senator could have been so hypocritical, so cynical, so boldly corrupt, and no Senate committee could have behaved so outrageously. This must be an example of literary license—a broad, sweeping satire." But, alas, the sad truth is that Senator Abner Dilworthy was based on a very real United States senator, Samuel Pomeroy of Kansas. And, for the most part, the events Mark Twain described in *The Gilded Age* actually took place.

During the winter of 1867–1868, Mark Twain sat in the press gallery in this chamber, writing articles for newspapers, acting as personal secretary to Nevada's Senator Wil-

The fictional "Senator Dilworthy" was based on the real Senator Samuel Pomeroy.

U.S. Senate Historical Office

liam Stewart, and collecting material he would later incorporate into his first novel. In 1870, Twain returned to Washington and there, by chance, had dinner with Senator Pomeroy.

Samuel Pomeroy was one of the breed known in those days as a Radical Republican, meaning that he supported rigorous reconstruction of the South. He also made a name for himself in the temperance and Sunday school movements, but this pious reputation was ingloriously stripped away when, in 1873, just as Twain was writing his book, Pomeroy was accused of offering an eight-thousand-dollar bribe to ensure his reelection to the Senate. His party convention unanimously refused to renominate him, but a select Senate committee declined to condemn Pomeroy's attempted bribery and attacked his accusers instead. As Justin Kaplan, Twain's biographer, wrote, "Senator Abner Dilworthy of *The Gilded Age* is Pomeroy undisguised, unmistakable to contemporary

readers." Kaplan added that "Pomeroy-Dilworthy became a comic-corrupt archetype which Mark Twain jeered at all his life and which survives today." [2]

Seven years after *The Gilded Age* appeared, Henry Adams anonymously published a shining gem of a Washington novel, entitled *Democracy*. The great-grandson of President John Adams and grandson of President John Quincy Adams, Henry Adams felt alienated from an America that was madly pursuing wealth and ignoring the old patrician class that he represented. The evolution of the United States from General Washington to General Grant, said Adams in a famous quip, proved Darwin wrong. Brooding in his home on Lafayette Square over this course of events, Adams wrote *Democracy* to express his dismay over American national politics. His chief senatorial protagonist, Senator Silas Ratcliffe, resembled Twain's Abner Dilworthy in several respects: both were venal politicians masquerading as pious statesmen and both were immensely popular and powerful political leaders. Both were brought low by the end of the novel and both were drawn from real life senators. Senator Silas P. Ratcliffe, "the Prairie Giant of Peoria," clearly depicted Senator James G. Blaine, "the Plumed Knight of Maine."

Democracy tells the story of Mrs. Lightfoot Lee, a socialite widow who decided to spend the winter in the city of Washington. Mrs. Lee was eager to see how the tremendous forces of government worked, but what she really wanted was power. She differed much from her sister Sybil in dress, ornaments, tastes, and interests. To Sybil, politics was of little interest, and although she was once induced to go to the Capitol and to sit ten minutes in the Senate gallery, according to Adams: "to her mind the Senate was a place where people went to recite speeches, and she naively assumed that the speeches were useful and had a purpose, but as they did not

[476]

interest her she never went again. This is a very common conception of Congress; many congressmen share it."

Mrs. Lee, however, was more patient and bolder. She visited the Capitol from time to time and read the debates in the *Congressional Record*. Interested in the machinery of government, she sought to understand its operation and the quality of the men who controlled it.

Presently, Mrs. Lee met power in the form of Silas Ratcliffe. "What a pity he is so dreadfully senatorial," she remarked, "otherwise I rather admire him." Senator Ratcliffe, however, was immediately infatuated with the lady, it being "a historical fact that elderly senators have had a curious fascination for young and handsome women," and proceeded to instruct her in the ways democratic government actually works. Things are not always what they seem, he explained. Once, as governor of his state during the Civil War, he rigged an election, but his purpose was to prevent the "peace party" from carrying his state and denying Lincoln's election. "I am not proud of the transaction," he told her, "but I would do it again, and worse than that, if I thought it would save this country from disunion."

In the novel's most memorable vignette, Mrs. Lee journeyed to Mount Vernon with Senator Ratcliffe, where they discussed the first president's monumental character. Mrs. Lee asked, "Was he then the only honest public man we ever had?" Ratcliffe responded:

Public men cannot be dressing themselves today in Washington's old clothes. If Washington were President now, he would have to learn our ways or lose the next election. Only fools and theorists imagine that our society can be handled with gloves or long poles. One must make one's self a part of it. If virtue won't answer our purpose, we must use vice, or our opponents will put us out of office, and this was as true in Washington's day as it is now, and always will be.

By the end of the book, Senator Ratcliffe proposed marriage. "In politics we cannot keep our hands clean," he prefaced his proposal by explaining. "I have done many things in my political career that are not defensible."

Adams' disappointment in the American political scene and in the politicians of his day was reflected in the musings of Mrs. Lee as she searched both soul and conscience for the answer to Ratcliffe's proposal of marriage:

The audacity of the man would have seemed sublime if she had felt sure that he knew the difference between good and evil, between a lie and the truth; but the more she saw of him, the surer she was that his courage was mere moral paralysis, and that he talked about virtue and vice as a man who is colorblind talks about red and green; . . . Was it politics that had caused this atrophy of the moral senses by disuse?

But Ratcliffe suggested that she could help him reform politics and enjoy a taste of the power she craved. As she wavered over this intriguing offer, Mrs. Lee discovered another of the senator's past political intrigues, a case in which he demanded money to move certain legislation out of a committee he chaired—an incident similar in some respects, although different in details, from the real Senator James G. Blaine's financial transactions with the railroads. When confronted with this story, Ratcliffe, as usual, had a rationalization. In this case, he claimed that he was just raising campaign money to keep the government from passing "into the bloodstained hands of rebels," but Mrs. Lee rejected the excuse. When the senator desperately offered to leave politics and become minister to England, thus giving his new wife high social position in London, she interpreted this suggestion as a "gross attempt to bribe her with office." Spurned, Senator Ratcliffe rushed out of the house and, on the front steps, received a final humiliation from

Senator James G. Blaine served as the model for the character of "Senator Silas P. Ratcliffe."

Keppler/Puck, February 22, 1888

an elderly diplomat who struck him with his cane. One suspects that Henry Adams, descendant of an old and cast-aside political family, who detested James G. Blaine and the new class of politicians he represented, took particular pleasure in writing this scene. But the novel ends without triumph, with Mrs. Lee concluding that "nine out of ten of our countrymen would say I had made a mistake." [3]

Mr. President, to my list of thinly disguised fictional senators from the nineteenth century, I should like to add one more: Senator Norton, who appeared in the obscure Washington novel, *A Man and His Soul*, written in 1894 by Theron Crawford. Like Mark Twain, Crawford served for a time as a newspaper correspondent in the Senate press gallery, but there the comparison stops. Crawford lacked Twain's talent, and his books have been forgotten. Yet, this particular book is valuable because its author, as a newspaper correspondent, had things he wanted to say that he could not put into his dispatches. There was always the threat of libel, of physical retribution, and of losing one's sources. In a novel, the correspondent could write more freely.

Theron Crawford reported for Democratic newspapers but had grown close to the Republican James G. Blaine, making him a character in the novel. But the Blaine depicted in *A Man and His Soul* differs markedly from the detestable Silas Ratcliffe of *Democracy*. Here he appears as Ralph Granger, cabinet member and personal friend of the book's journalist-hero (Blaine served as secretary of state in the Garfield, Arthur, and Harrison administrations). Secretary Granger "had too much intelligence to be involved in . . . vulgar intrigue for place," the journalist wrote, but Granger's wife was "so ambitious of social position as to be absolutely reckless in reaching for the object of her desires. . . . Her husband's modest fortune must have

been insufficient to satisfy her requirements, and I had noticed, within the last year, associated with her, from time to time, the oily and diplomatic stars of political intrigue, the aristocratic purveyors of position." Their nearness to Mrs. Granger had led the reporter "to think that she was in danger of selling her fair name and the honorable position of her husband in her reckless desire to have money." In reality, Blaine and his wife Harriet lived and entertained considerably beyond the earnings of a public servant, and it was the need for outside sources of income that had led Blaine into his many private and politically disastrous financial dealings.

The villain of Crawford's book was neither Granger nor his wife, but the fictional Senator Norton who discovered financial irregularities in Secretary Granger's department and used this knowledge during his power struggle with the president of the United States. Senator Norton was quite a character. Here is how Crawford introduced him, in the lobby of a posh Washington hotel:

There came into the group about the open fire a statesman, long famed, in the House, for his cynical ability, his wit, his readiness in debate and his colossal vanity, which made him more cruel and ungrateful than a peacock. . . . His spare, slight figure was clothed in evening dress, over which he wore a long fur-lined overcoat, which descended nearly to his heels. His dark, olive-tinted, hard-lined face was shadowed by a long mustache and short beard. A dark evening hat was cocked rakishly over one ear. A dark perfecto cigar was held tightly in one corner of his grinning mouth.

Isn't that a perfect description of one of those villains who was always tying the heroine to the railroad tracks in stage melodramas? But, in fact, the passage also described New York Senator Roscoe Conkling, Blaine's chief political enemy.

Should anyone challenge my interpretation of Conkling as Norton, let me cite this

According to author Theron Crawford, Senator Roscoe Conkling, depicted here as Mephistopheles, "swaggered through the debate of Congress."

Keppler/Puck, October 3, 1877

passage from *A Man and His Soul*, in which Crawford described the reporter's view from the press gallery: "Senator Norton came into his seat, fresh from one of the bath-rooms below the Senate, curled and perfumed by the official barber, radiant with health, physical superiority and intellectual pride. He fairly swaggered down the aisle of the Senate chamber, and took his seat with an aggressive air of insolence." What a vivid picture! Compare that description of Norton with one of Roscoe Conkling, taken from a biography of James G. Blaine that Crawford had published a year earlier. Before Conkling's great speeches, Crawford wrote, the senator always appeared "fresh from a plunge in the marble bath-tubs in the basement of the Capitol building; curled, scented and insolent, he swaggered through the debate of Congress." The descriptions, of course, are strikingly similar. This was the senator whom one woman admirer called "the Apollo of the Senate" and whom enemies dubbed "the curled darling of Utica."

Beyond his bathing habits, the fictitious Senator Norton further resembles the real Senator Conkling in his monumental battle with a president of his own party over patronage. Crawford described a meeting with Norton in the senator's lavish hotel suite, filled with potted plants from the government's Botanic Garden. Norton, he said, "divided the world into two classes: those who adhered to him, and those who opposed him. For the former, he was always willing to work; for the latter, he was untiring in his ferocious energy to destroy. It was not enough for him to defeat an enemy. It was necessary for his complete satisfaction to absolutely annihilate him." Pacing up and down in the room, speaking in a low tone that gradually increased in volume, Norton outlined his relations with the president, who had once been one of his political lieutenants. One might easily imagine that

Crawford was alluding to Chester A. Arthur, the accidental president. Arthur had, as one of Conkling's top political henchmen, previously presided over the New York Customs House, which formed Conkling's principal power base with its enormous patronage booty of more than a thousand jobs. A quirk of fate had elevated Arthur to the White House, where he was trying to chart an honorable, independent course in espousing civil service reform. The fictional senator accused the president of forgetting "all past alliances, all previous friendships, all prior obligations of duty and loyalty."

Senator Norton expressed outrage at this unexpected presidential independence. He insisted that, if the president failed to make certain appointments, he would expose the financial irregularities in Secretary Granger's department and drive Granger from the cabinet. Although the president depended greatly on Granger's advice, he was a weak but proud man who had "no loyalty of character, and would sacrifice Granger tomorrow, in a moment, if he could do it without scandal, rather than make the slightest concession to Norton." Through a devious channel, word reached Secretary Granger, who took the blame to cover for his wife's crimes but rebuked her sharply. The mortified woman staggered to her room, collapsed, struck her head on the mantle, and fell dead in the fireplace—this was a Victorian novel, after all!

The journalist-author delivered his own rebuke to Conkling and other senators of the era in the lament of one of his characters, who complained: "I have never known a time in the history of the Senate when there was so much silly, boyish quarreling about nothing, and such an absolute forgetting of all of our real duties." Crawford's observations about the senators' failure to adhere faithfully to the rules of their own august body in the days antedating our own century were quite correct, as we can see from his reference to the executive sessions in which nominations and treaties were considered.

> The executive sessions of the Senate are secret only in name . . . , their transactions might as well be conducted in open day. The senators are, practically, on their honor, not to tell what occurs during these sessions; but no method has ever been discovered for making more than fourscore men keep secrets, and so full details of everything leaks out, in some irregular way, within the shortest possible time after each session is closed.[4]

Thus, these three Gilded Age political novels indicted the Senate for conduct unbecoming a national legislature. In their way, these books helped to reshape public opinion and prepare for direct election of senators and other reforms of the Progressive Era.

Mr. President, I have used these three novels as a small sample of the popular Washington *roman à clef*. I would like to turn now to a different genre of political novel: the senatorial murder mystery. Nearly everyone loves a good mystery as an occasional diversion. Intricate plots, littered with clues and frequent red herrings, engage our attention, no matter what the literary merits of the book at hand. Not all mystery stories take place in English country houses or on isolated islands. The Capitol Building has housed many a foul and treacherous crime, according to certain mystery writers, and senators have been likely suspects as murderers—and victims. An old stage adage says that, if you introduce a gun in a plot, it has to be fired during the performance. That seems to be equally true for senators: they are too significant to be just another member of the cast. If you put a senator into a whodunit, he probably did it. What awful motive would lead a United States senator to commit such a crime? Surprisingly, senatorial murders are more often provoked by family quarrels than political struggles. One suspects that novelists just cannot believe that any political or ideological issue matters enough to serve as a motive for murder. They ought to spend some time in our cloakrooms!

Let me offer three sinister examples of this fictional Senate, beginning in chronological order with perhaps the greatest American detective novelist, Dashiell Hammett. Hammett is most famous for his creation of Sam Spade in *The Maltese Falcon* and Nick and Nora Charles in *The Thin Man*, but let us focus instead on Senator Ralph Bancroft Henry, who appeared in *The Glass Key*, published in 1931. Senator Henry, "one of the few aristocrats left in American politics," was running for reelection and desperately needed the support of party boss Paul Madvig. The boss also happened to be dating the senator's daughter—much to the disgust of the senator's son, Taylor. When Taylor was found dead, his skull crushed by a blunt instrument, Boss Madvig became the prime suspect. Ned Beaumont, a special investigator for the district attorney's office, set out to clear his friend.

Who killed Taylor Henry? Although it is considered poor form to give away the ending of a murder mystery, I hope I will be forgiven for revealing that Beaumont fingered Senator Henry as the perpetrator. The motive remained ambiguous. Although the senator finally confessed to killing his son accidentally, after the young man had chased the boss out into the street, Beaumont suspected that the senator acted in a fit of anger because his son interfered with his chances for reelection.[5]

Unfortunately for Dashiell Hammett, *The Glass Key* was not his last encounter with the United States Senate. Hammett's politics were far to the left of center and, during the 1930's, he had flirted with communism. During the dark days of the Red Scare of the 1940's and 1950's, the author was called up before the House Un-American Activities Committee and the Senate Permanent Sub-

Author Dashiell Hammett made a senator a main character in his novel *The Glass Key*.
National Portrait Gallery

committee on Investigations to answer for his political beliefs and to name his associates. Senator Joseph McCarthy of Wisconsin shamelessly grilled Hammett, who held no government post and was hardly in a position to subvert his country. McCarthy's henchmen Roy Cohn and David Schine toured United States Information Agency libraries overseas, urging them to remove such nonpolitical books as *The Maltese Falcon* from their shelves. Hammett went to prison rather than name names. This was one case where truth was stranger than fiction.

Unlike Hammett's homicidal Senator Henry, Senator Leander Rhodes was an innocent victim, blown to bits by an exploding log in the fireplace of his Massachusetts Avenue mansion. This shocking crime occurred in Edgar Box's 1953 novel *Death Before Bedtime.* I chose this mystery because Edgar Box was the alias for Gore Vidal, grandson of United States Senator Thomas P. Gore of Oklahoma. Vidal has also written about many real-life senators in his four historical novels *Lincoln, Burr, 1876,* and *Washington, D.C.* (Hubert Humphrey even made an appearance in Vidal's bizarre novel *Duluth*).

In *Death Before Bedtime,* Vidal created the reactionary Leander Rhodes, chairman of the Senate Spoils and Patronage Committee, described at one point as having a "face red from speechmaking, his gray hair tangled above his bloodshot eyes." The senator was preparing to announce his candidacy for president in a speech before the National Margarine Council but, before he could make the announcement, he stopped to light the fateful fire at his Massachusetts Avenue home. Since Vidal described Rhodes as "a near-idiot with a perfect Senate record of obstruction," his demise is hard to mourn. The only surprise is that the senator was done in by a member of his family, rather than by some irate citizen determined to save the Republic.[6]

From a mystery by Senator Thomas Gore's grandson, let me turn to one by President Harry Truman's daughter. In 1981, Margaret Truman published *Murder on Capitol Hill,* one of a series of mysteries in which she has strewn bodies throughout Washington, from the White House to the Supreme Court and from the Smithsonian to Georgetown. In this tale, we find the Senate majority leader, Cale Caldwell, stabbed to death with an ice pick at a Senate reception! Not just your ordinary, run-of-the-mill majority leader, Senator Caldwell was also chairman of the "Appro-

priations Committee on the Interior and Related Agencies." I submit that anyone who tried to serve as majority leader and, simultaneously, to chair a major standing committee would find himself violently threatened by members of his own party! I would have advised the police to begin their investigation by interviewing members of the Appropriations Committee, in order of seniority. But, in the end, it turned out that the senator's family was behind the murder, rather than his colleagues. The moral of these senatorial mysteries, one gathers, is that we should avoid getting so wrapped up in our work that we neglect our homelife—it could be dangerous to our health.[7]

Mr. President, I might also mention *Washington Post* reporter Lawrence Meyer's murder mystery *A Capitol Crime,* in which a former United States senator persuaded a fanatical admirer to bump off an investigative reporter and stuff his body down a manhole in the Capitol basement. Now this is an interesting scenario—one which many members of the Senate may have contemplated over the years. Granted that a few congressmen, generally in the nineteenth century, of course, responded to criticism in the press by using their fists and canes on the heads of offending journalists, members of Congress, for the most part, have acted with admirable restraint. Not one of them has ever killed or conspired to kill a representative of the fourth estate! On the other hand, in 1890, a reporter by the name of Charles E. Kincaid did shoot a former member of the U.S. House of Representatives from Kentucky named William Preston Taulbee inside this Capitol Building. Taulbee died from the effects of the wounds eleven days later. Their feud was personal with considerable provocation on the former congressman's part, but I understand that some members of the House press gallery have formed a Kincaid society to commemorate his crime. I point out this inci-

This scene from *Mr. Smith Goes to Washington* takes place in a replica of the Senate chamber as it appeared in the 1930's.   *Courtesy of Columbia Pictures*

dent only to alert future mystery writers not to be so quick to pin blame on the senators.[8]

Turning from these grisly stories to more pleasant images, I would like to mention the way motion pictures have made the United States Senate their stage and senators their players. The three films I have chosen for home entertainment viewing on videocassette are those that were shown recently in "The Senate Goes to the Movies" series, sponsored by the Senate Commission on Art. I shall briefly describe each of the three: *Mr. Smith Goes to Washington*, *The Senator Was Indiscreet*, and *Advise and Consent*.

Has there ever been a better movie about the Senate than Frank Capra's 1939 classic *Mr. Smith Goes to Washington*? To briefly summarize the plot, the naive, idealistic Jefferson Smith, played by James Stewart, was appointed to fill out the term of a senator who died unexpectedly. Smith placed himself under the care and supervision of his silky

senior senator, Joseph Paine, portrayed by Claude Rains. The party bosses expected to control Smith but, when they arrived in Washington, he eluded them to go off sightseeing at all the patriotic memorials, and they discovered that they had their hands full with their junior senator. Unbeknownst to Senator Smith, his senior colleague was pushing legislation to build a dam which would financially benefit the state political boss of their party (the dam was to be located on the very site where Smith intended to build a Boy Rangers' camp). When Smith uncovered the truth, Senator Paine maneuvered to discredit him and have him expelled from the Senate. In a last desperate effort, Smith launched a filibuster to stall Senate action until he could demonstrate that the public (and the Boy Rangers) supported him.

The movie includes many shots actually taken in the Russell Senate Office Building and in the vicinity of the Capitol, and much

[484]

of the action takes place in a magnificent reproduction of the Senate chamber. In fact, if we wish to see how this chamber, in which we meet today, looked before its massive renovation in 1950, *Mr. Smith* gives us that opportunity. Technically, the movie is authentic, accurate, and generally true to the procedures of that day, thanks to the advice that James Preston, superintendent of the Senate press gallery, provided to the movie crew. In the climactic scenes of the movie, Senator Smith's secretary—indeed his only staff person—played by Jean Arthur, sat just to the right of the press gallery, signaling down to the senator which rules would enable him to hold the floor, much to the bemusement of the vice president, who was presiding. Finally, the strain became too great, and Senator Smith collapsed, here on the floor, in front of the Republican leader's desk. So shaken was Senator Paine by this performance, that, in the cloakroom, he attempted to shoot himself. At the movie's end, he admitted his guilt, clearing Jefferson Smith, who still lay crumpled on the floor. There is not a dry eye left in the house, but it is safe to say that no such scene ever has taken place, or ever will, in this chamber.

Similarly, there has never been a senator quite as foolish as Melvin Ashton, the lead role in George Kaufman's 1947 movie *The Senator Was Indiscreet.* Played by William Powell, Melvin Ashton may have looked senatorial, but, clearly, no coherent thought had ever passed through his head. Nevertheless, Senator Ashton was determined to run for president. The movie opens in a New York hotel where the senator was to make a speech and, incidentally, be made an honorary Indian chief. During the ceremony, the senator's irate party chairman arrived and demanded to know how he could take such a step without party approval. Kissing babies was one thing, but becoming an Indian chief was strictly for presidential candidates.

Moreover, Ashton had been denying in public that he would be a presidential candidate, and the party boss pointed out that only real candidates were permitted to deny their candidacies.

Senator Ashton refused to be dissuaded. He announced that he had been keeping a diary, recording everything that he had seen and exposing party machinations. The shaken party leader, realizing that publication of such a diary could topple his machine, agreed to let Ashton run. To everyone's surprise, the senator moved quickly to the top of the public opinion polls. Among his campaign slogans: he opposed both inflation and deflation and, instead, stood for "flation." As a publicity stunt, he rode in the locomotive of his campaign train, which he managed to wreck, but then received credit for helping to rescue the survivors! At the last minute, when it appeared that this improbable senator might become an even more improbable president, a newspaper reporter spirited away his diary and published its shocking revelations. The senator and his cohorts fled to Pago Pago and anywhere else without an extradition treaty.

It must come as a surprise to audiences—especially since the movie's advertisements show the senator in his pajamas—that Ashton's indiscretion was merely that he kept a diary. In fact, I'm sad to say, diary keeping has been a rare art in the Senate. One thinks of William Maclay of Pennsylvania, John Quincy Adams of Massachusetts, Henry Fountain Ashurst of Arizona, and George Aiken of Vermont, who maintained and published diaries. But most members are simply too busy to keep such a record. Senatorial diaries, of course, are tremendous resources for future historians and political scientists, and I sincerely hope that this delightfully funny movie will not dissuade any senator from committing such an "indiscretion."

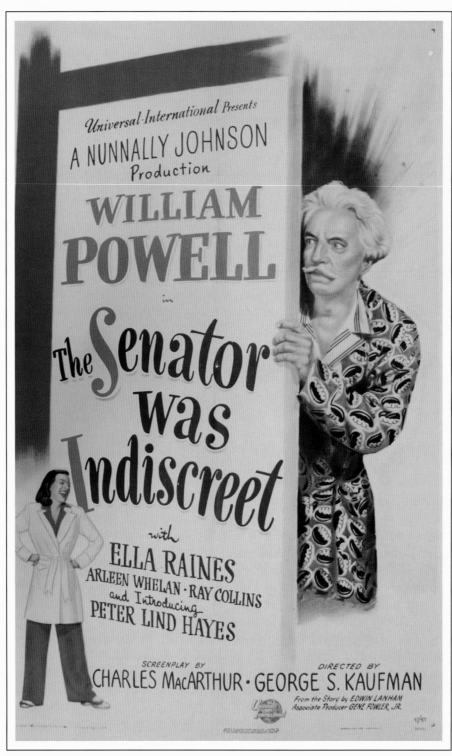

The fictional "Senator Ashton" in *The Senator Was Indiscreet* kept a diary implicating his party bosses in political chicanery. *Copyright 1947, Universal Pictures Co., Inc.*

The final film that I would like to highlight is the late Otto Preminger's 1962 masterpiece *Advise and Consent*, the movie version of Allen Drury's Pulitzer prize-winning novel of the same name. As with the nineteenth-century *roman à clef*, part of the joy of Drury's novel, and Preminger's movie, is guessing who is really who. Like Mark Twain and Theron Crawford, Allen Drury served as a reporter in the Senate press gallery, where he collected many of his ideas, characters, and situations. A few years after he published *Advise and Consent*, Drury also published a diary (shades of Melvin Ashton!) which he kept while covering the Senate during World War II. This diary provides a road map for his novel, with numerous directional signs. One may fancy that the aging fictional president strongly resembles Franklin D. Roosevelt at the end of his presidency. The vice president, Harley Hudson, could be seen as Harry Truman. The dashing majority leader, something of a lady's man, seems to be Alben Barkley of Kentucky, and the upright minority leader, Orrin Knox, appears to be Ohio's Robert Taft. Old Seab Cooley, the southern senator who is played so magnificently by Charles Laughton in the movie, is a dead ringer for Kenneth McKellar of Tennessee, and Cooley's battle with presidential nominee Robert Leffingwell resembles McKellar's campaign against David Lilienthal, with perhaps the nomination of Henry Wallace to be secretary of commerce thrown in for good measure. The overzealous Senator Fred Van Ackerman is a caricature of Joseph McCarthy, and the tragic Brigham Anderson, who kills himself in his Senate office, reminds us of Senator Lester Hunt of Wyoming, who took his life in the Russell Building in 1954.[9]

For those of us who love the United States Senate, *Advise and Consent* is a special treat. There are scenes of the Senate's old wicker subway cars, of the trolleys that used to run down Constitution Avenue, of the Senate Caucus Room, and even of the tour guides in the Capitol. And again, much of the action takes place in the Senate chamber, lovingly recreated by Hollywood. Although this new set reflected the renovations made to the Senate chamber in 1950, *Advise and Consent* was able to utilize the same Senate chamber desks and chairs that were constructed for *Mr. Smith Goes to Washington*.

Both the book and the movie *Advise and Consent* center on the president's nomination of Robert Leffingwell to be secretary of state. Leffingwell was a bright but prickly figure, deeply resented by Senator Seab Cooley for an old slight. The Senate majority leader was also not happy with the nomination, since he had not been consulted, but he loyally agreed to lead the fight for confirmation. Senator Brigham Anderson of Utah chaired the Foreign Relations Committee's subcommittee handling the nomination. During the course of the hearings, Seab Cooley produced a witness who swore that Leffingwell once belonged to a Communist cell. Although the charge was true, Leffingwell—who had long since changed his political philosophy—covered up his past and discredited his accuser. Meanwhile, Senator Van Ackerman, an extreme peace promoter who had embraced Leffingwell's nomination, uncovered a terrible secret in Anderson's past, which he used to blackmail the subcommittee chairman. Rather than submit to blackmail, yet unable to face the public humiliation, Senator Anderson committed suicide. The vote in the Senate on the nomination was tied, and Vice President Hudson was preparing to cast the deciding vote when he received a message that the president had died. Hudson withheld his vote, thus allowing the Leffingwell nomination to be rejected, on the grounds that he would want to appoint his own secretary of state. He then left the Senate chamber to go to the White House.

[487]

Otto Preminger is shown directing the action on the set of the Senate chamber during the filming of *Advise and Consent*.

As with *Mr. Smith Goes to Washington, Advise and Consent* is technically quite accurate. The studio went to great pains to recreate the appropriate settings and made every effort to capture the flavor of the Senate. The actions of the senators and presiding officer are a bit exaggerated, however, and, in several instances, not in keeping with the rules of the real Senate, as when Senator Van Ackerman couples a discharge motion, which must lie over for a day, with a motion to vote on the discharged nomination "here and now." Such a motion would be declared out of order by the presiding officer of the Senate. Also somewhat unreal was the vice president's question, stated three times: "Do I hear a request for the yeas and nays?" This is a question which is never asked by the chair in the Senate. Then, too, the majority leader's motion that the Senate stand adjourned "until further notice" would be difficult to envision under the circumstances, since it would hardly conform to the constitutional requirement that neither house shall, without the consent of the other, adjourn "for more than three days." But what the heck! Perhaps these peccadilloes can be forgiven on the basis that too rigid a conformity to the real-life Senate would be intensely boring and, thus, hurtful to box-office receipts in the motion picture industry!

The only remaining criticism, then, that one might have of both films is that they show the chamber almost always filled with

Actor Charles Laughton, *in white suit*, was filmed on location outside the Russell Senate Office Building for the movie *Advise and Consent*.

senators, all sitting at their desks. Anyone who has spent any time in the galleries knows that this is somewhat unreal in that only a few senators are present on the floor at almost any given time. The rest are off at committee hearings and any number of other official duties. Great numbers of senators are on the floor, generally, only during votes. Even then, instead of sitting orderly at their desks, they tend to mill about in groups, conversing with their colleagues, waiting to cast their votes and learn the outcome of the tally. Apparently, such a scene was too confusing for the movie companies to recreate. I expect, however, that after the public has been conditioned to our behavior by viewing our own proceedings on television, the next major movie about the Senate will be able to portray this aspect of the chamber in a way that is more true to life.

Mr. President, my brief literary and cinematic tour of the Senate has included merely a few examples. There are so many other works that could be cited, among them the great Appalachian writer Harry Caudill's *The Senator from Slaughter County*, Allen Drury's *Senator Mark Coffin*, and the Alan Alda film *The Seduction of Joe Tynan*. Most likely, other senators have their own favorite Senate novels and movies. I would like to conclude my remarks, however, by returning to Senator Spiffledink. More full of bunk than Melvin Ashton, more naive than Jefferson Smith, more hypocritical than Abner Dilworthy,

This illustration of "Senator Solomon Spiffledink" shows the senator "as he is today, at the full meridian of his powers." *L. Ludlow, Senator Solomon Spiffledink*

I freely admit that this child of my brain, *Senator Solomon Spiffledink,* shows Congress at its worst. That is exactly what it is intended to do. But it also shows that, even at its worst, Congress is only afflicted with some of the human frailties and is not so very bad after all. . . . In presenting *Senator Solomon Spiffledink* to a critical public, I ask my readers not to regard Solomon as any particular individual, for the truth is that he is a composite, nor to make this book a basis for too harsh a judgment of Congress until they have read its forthcoming companion piece, *Senator John Law.* When John makes his appearance in literary garb I shall hope to see the scales exactly balanced.[10]

more vainglorious than Senator Norton, Solomon Spiffledink was a wicked caricature by—whom else?—a reporter in the press gallery, Louis Ludlow. I will not attempt to summarize this amusing little book but would like to quote from the author's introduction. Ludlow writes:

That is a nice sentiment, Mr. President, but, in fact, no such novel as *Senator John Law* was ever published. It seems to be easier to lampoon the Senate than to praise it. News reporting and political novels generally lean towards the spectacular and the negative, leaving history and political science to remind us of the positive. Those who have been fortunate enough to serve in the United States Senate have to expect such treatment, and we hope we have thick enough skins to laugh along with other readers and movie-goers at the egregious foibles of fictional senators. Sometimes, however, the tables can be turned. One reason why Ludlow never wrote *Senator John Law,* other than our suspicion that a name like that would signify a perfectly dreadful novel, was that, in 1928, Ludlow himself was elected to the United States House of Representatives, where he served for twenty years. More recently, movie actors have also begun running for national office and winning. So, perhaps, the moral of this story for the artistic community is: be careful about how you portray Congress in your novels and films, for you never know when you may decide to run for office yourself. You may wind up as the subject of your own barbs.

CHAPTER 22

Lobbyists

September 28, 1987*

Mr. President, in 1869, a newspaper correspondent published this vivid description of a monster in the Capitol building: "Winding in and out through the long, devious basement passage, crawling through the corridors, trailing its slimy length from gallery to committee room, at last it lies stretched at full length on the floor of Congress—this dazzling reptile, this huge, scaly serpent of the lobby." What was this awful creature? It was intended as the embodiment of lobbyists, who were proliferating in the years after the Civil War and who, many believed, were corrupting the Congress. Even today, the media tend to portray legislative lobbyists as some form of monster. And yet, we realize that lobbyists play an important and essential role in the legislative process. Today, in my continuing series of addresses on the history of the Senate, I shall attempt to penetrate some of the myths and mysteries surrounding lobbyists over the past two hundred years.[1]

Citizens of the United States, whether as individuals or in organizations, have both direct and indirect interest in legislation considered by Congress. They make their interests known by electing sympathetic senators and representatives and by petitioning for or against specific legislation. This is a right

guaranteed them by the First Amendment to the Constitution. Roy Swanstrom, in his study of the Senate's early years, noted that the first petitions and memorials came from a variety of groups: shipwrights concerned about the effects of the tariff; merchants desiring an end to the tax on molasses; federal clerks requesting an increase in pay; military officers who sought reimbursement for personal funds expended during the Revolution; as well as from chambers of commerce, taxpayers' committees, veterans, and even state legislatures. In those days, the Senate might appoint a committee to consider a petition or refer it to a committee already dealing with similar legislation. Petitions that ran contrary to the wishes of the majority were tabled or pigeonholed in some way and forgotten.[2]

With so many interests competing for congressional attention, petitioners sought ways of attracting notice. In April 1798, on the motion of Senator Samuel Livermore of New Hampshire, a large committee of Philadelphia citizens was admitted to the Senate floor to present a petition in support of the administration's policies toward France. Senator Humphrey Marshall of Kentucky objected to this procedure and won passage of a resolution to prohibit individuals or delegations from presenting such petitions in such

* Updated June 1989

[491]

a way in the future. Entertainment was another means adopted from the start by those interested in influencing legislation. During the First Congress, Pennsylvania Senator William Maclay wrote in his diary that New York merchants employed "treats, dinners, attentions" to delay passage of a tariff bill. Of the influences and pressures brought upon the members regarding legislation, Maclay wrote:

In the Senate Chamber this Morning Butler said he heard a Man say he would give [John] Vining a 1,000 Guineas for his Vote. but added I question whether he would do so in fact— so do I too, for he might get it for a 10th part of the Sum. I do not know that pecuniary influence has actually been Used, but. I am certain, That every other kind of management. has been practised, and Every tool at Work that could be thought of. Officers of Government, Clergy Citizens [Order of] Cincinnati, and every Person under the influence of the Treasury.[3]

Lobbyists have been at work from the earliest days of the Congress. William Hull was hired by the Virginia veterans of the Continental army to lobby for additional compensation for their war services. In 1792, Hull wrote to other veterans' groups, recommending that they have their "agent or agents" cooperate with him during the next session to pass a compensation bill. In 1795, a Philadelphia newspaper described the way lobbyists waited outside Congress Hall to "give a hint to a Member, teaze or advise as may best suit."[4]

As early as the closing years of the eighteenth century, there were widespread suspicions that large, well-financed interests were receiving special attention from the government. During the first half century of our Republic, the most distrusted and despised special interest was the Bank of the United States, a private bank chartered by the federal government. Critics of the bank pointed out that a number of sitting senators served as its directors, a clear case of conflict of interest. James Madison wrote to Thomas Jefferson in 1791, "Of all the shameful circumstances of this business, it is among the greatest to see the members of the Legislature [Congress] who were most active in pushing this Job, openly grasping its emoluments."[5] On December 21, 1833, Senator Daniel Webster of Massachusetts wrote from Washington to the bank's president, Nicholas Biddle: "Since I arrived here, I have had an application to be concerned, professionally, against the Bank, which I have declined, of course, although I believe my retainer has not been renewed, or *refreshed*, as usual. If it be wished that my relation to the bank should be continued, it may be well to send me the usual retainer."[6] That is stating it plainly, isn't it?

The perception of impropriety that the bank fostered was a contributing factor to President Andrew Jackson's decision to remove government funds and to veto attempts to extend its charter.[7]

In the early days, tariff legislation had the greatest impact on society as a whole and stimulated the greatest amount of lobbying. It is interesting to note, in light of the press' traditional suspicion of lobbyists, that some of Washington's first newspaper correspondents were, in certain respects, tariff lobbyists. Merchants and shippers in New England, and planters in the South, sent correspondents to the capital to serve as representatives throughout the congressional session, to keep them informed on the progress of tariff legislation, and to assist their representatives in fighting for their interests. This arrangement is not surprising when we consider that a critical aspect of lobbying has been to supply information, both to members of Congress and to those interested in stopping or promoting a bill.[8]

Complementing the freewheeling attitude which many government officials in those days took towards the relationship between public office and private enterprise was the reality of living and working in the Washington of the early nineteenth century. The embryonic capital bore no resemblance to the cosmopolitan centers of Philadelphia and New York, let alone the great European capitals. The city was dusty and malaria-ridden in the summer, damp and cold in the winter. Social and cultural amenities were few. Many senators left their families at home and took rooms in the boardinghouses that surrounded the Capitol Building. It was an atmosphere in which the so-called "social lobby" could thrive, and thrive it did. Clubs, brothels, and "gambling dens" became natural habitats of the lobbyists, since these institutions were occasionally visited by members of Congress, who, far from home, came seeking good food, drink, and agreeable company.

The excesses of ante-bellum lobbying reached their height in the early 1850's when Samuel Colt sought passage of a bill to extend his patent for seven years. A congressional investigation later disclosed that, in addition to staging lavish entertainments for wavering senators, "more than one" of Colt's agents "have at different times presented pistols to certain members," including "a handsome Colt pistol, as a present," to a representative's "little son, only eleven or twelve years of age." [9]

The select committee's report noted that:

The money has been used, as the evidence shows, in paying the costs and charges incurred in getting up costly and extravagant entertainments, to which ladies and members of Congress and others were invited, with a view of furthering the success of this measure. The ladies, having been first duly impressed with the importance of Colt's pistol extension by presents of Parisian gloves, are invited to these entertainments; and the evidence shows that, while there, members of Congress are appealed to by them to favor this particular measure. [10]

Colt's principal lobbyist was characterized by the committee as having adopted the rule that

To reach the heart or get the vote,
The surest way is down the throat. [11]

—an altogether appropriate epigram for the lobbying of the period.

The House report also referred to a practice in those days whereby certain persons affiliated with the press were allowed to obtain seats on the House floor. The report revealed that these persons, in contravention of promises to the contrary and in violation of House rules, would lobby the representatives concerning such matters as claims or bills. According to the following excerpt from the report:

The evidence shows another important fact, that the letter-writers for the daily press who have been admitted to desks on the floor of the House are very generally regarded as the most efficient agents who can be employed by those who have measures to advance. Although these letter-writers, before they can obtain a seat within the House, are required to give a personal pledge of honor that they are not "employed as agents to prosecute any claim pending before Congress," yet we find that, in utter disregard of this pledge and its spirit, they have been employed in many of the railroad, patent, and other schemes which have engaged the attention of Congress during the present session. [12]

Mr. President, this practice has been discontinued, as we all know.

By the 1850's, railroad construction, largely underwritten by federal land grants and other subsidies, further increased the presence of lobbyists in Congress. Their numbers multiplied geometrically with the outbreak of the Civil War and with the industrial development that followed. Lobbying, as both an institution and a danger, impressed itself most strongly upon the public conscience in the decade after the war. As Professor David J. Rothman has written, "In the 1870's, when

Railroad lobbyist William E. Chandler later became a U.S. senator. *U.S. Senate Historical Office*

party did not yet superintend the course of Senate affairs, lobbying for the first time became a vital element in government." Lobbyists like William E. Chandler accepted large retainers from a great number of railroads seeking government assistance. The corporations themselves often resented the many lobbyists, whom they called "strikers," seeking their money. Railroad magnate Collis P. Huntington, for whom the city of Huntington, West Virginia, was named, complained: "The damned strikers [lobbyists] are so numerous that if we should endeavor to put the matter [of purchasing government property in San Francisco's harbor] before Congress this session I have no doubt it would cost us more than it would be worth. . . . The Strikers, or Third House members, are very quick and hungry in Washington this winter." [13]

Businesses hired lobbyists to gain a sympathetic hearing for their legislative aims.

Because a single lobbyist often did not possess wide enough contacts, they were forced to hire several different agents. Collis Huntington estimated that his rival railroad operator, Tom Scott, had hired two hundred lobbyists for the congressional session of 1876–1877. The cost of so many agents was enormous, and the results were far from certain. Tom Scott, for instance, did not win congressional support for his railroad. Businessmen felt caught in a bind; not always certain that a lobbyist possessed the influence he claimed, an entrepreneur, nevertheless, feared that not hiring him might cause lucrative government support to slip away. The correspondence of leading businessmen is filled with complaints about lobbying costs, including hotel accommodations, entertainment, cigars, and champagne. According to Professor Rothman, railroad passes were freely distributed in the effort to win supporters. Again, Huntington complained: "When in Washington, I had to give out many passes, mostly at the request of Senators and Members of Congress, and since Congress adjourned I think we have averaged six letters per day from Senators and Members of Congress asking for passes over the road. . . . This giving free passes is all wrong." Sometimes it also meant direct payments to members of Congress. Collis Huntington argued, "We must take care of our friends." [14]

Periodically, lobbying scandals broke into the press and caught public attention. The Crédit Mobilier scandal of 1872 revealed that a member of the House, Representative Oakes Ames, had distributed railroad stocks to senators and representatives in return for their support for railroad legislation. In 1883, when the chief lobbyist of the Southern Pacific Railroad died, his widow sued the company for a larger property settlement. To support her case, she introduced his correspondence as evidence. Newspapers seized upon the material and reprinted it widely, further muddying the reputations of lobbyists as a whole.

By far the most famous lobbyist of the era was Sam Ward, popularly known as the "King of the Lobby." Ward was originally hired by Treasury Secretary Hugh McCulloch, who was trying to restore order and stability to the nation's finances after the Civil War. The treasury secretary wanted to retire the $450 million in greenback currency issued during the war, but Congress feared the political consequences of such a deflationary action. In order to educate legislators on the need to improve the nation's credit, Sam Ward gave dinners. As his biographer explained, Ward "proceeded upon the comfortable axiom that the shortest distance between a pending bill and a Congressman's 'aye' lies through his stomach." Washington was not at that time a city of first-class restaurants. Many congressmen still lived and ate in boardinghouses, tellingly named "messes," and even official dinners were often dismal affairs. Ward, however, provided the finest foods and wines, and the most sparkling conversation and entertainment, at a rumored cost to the Treasury Department of twelve thousand dollars!

Ward worked for other clients as well—individuals, corporations, and foreign governments—helping them move bills through Congress and promoting their claims before government bureaus. To demonstrate his influence, he frequently used the stationery of congressional committees. And he always kept stores of wine, liquor, and cigars to make friends and influence people. Ward could often be found at Welcher's restaurant, coaching its cook, and serving as unofficial maître d'hôtel for congressional customers. Ward would escort legislators to a table, recommend the best items on the menu, and seat them near those who had business to conduct.

Sam Ward managed to steer clear of suspicion in the multitude of lobbying scandals of the era, but, in 1875, he was called to testify before a congressional investigation of subsidies for the Pacific Mail Steamship Company. Newspapers charged that Ward had distributed over a hundred thousand dollars to bribe correspondents, House doorkeepers, and other federal officials. Ward defended his actions and gave us his insights into Gilded Age lobbying. Here are excerpts from his candid and humorous testimony:

This business of lobbying, so called, is as precarious as fishing in the Hebrides. You get all ready, your boats go out—suddenly there comes a storm, and away you are driven. . . . Everybody who knows anything about Washington, knows that ten times, aye, fifty times, more measures are lost than are carried; but once in a while a pleasant little windfall of this kind recompenses us, who are always toiling here, for the disappointments. I am not ashamed—I do not say I am proud, but I am not ashamed—of the occupation. It is a very useful one. In England it is a separate branch of the legal profession; there they have parliamentary lawyers who do no other business. There the committees sit all day to hear these lawyers, and they sit in Parliament at night, whereas here committees are only allowed to sit for an hour and a half; so that it is very hard to get through four thousand bills in a session. The disappointments are much more numerous than the successes. I have had many a very pleasant "contingent" knocked away when everything appeared prosperous and certain, and I would not insure any bill, if I were paid fifty per cent, to secure its passage. . . .

I was retained, I suppose, because "the king's name is a tower of strength," and I am known as the "King of the Lobby." . . .

We who are of the "regular army" know when we are whipped. But gentlemen of little experience come down here, and peg on . . . until the end of the session, and never understand when they had better go home. . . . To introduce a bill properly, to have it referred to the proper committee, to see that some member in that committee understands its merits, to attend to it, to watch it, to have a counsel to go and advocate it before the committee, to see that members of the committee do not oversleep on the mornings of important meetings, to watch for the coming in of the bill to Congress day after day, week after week, to

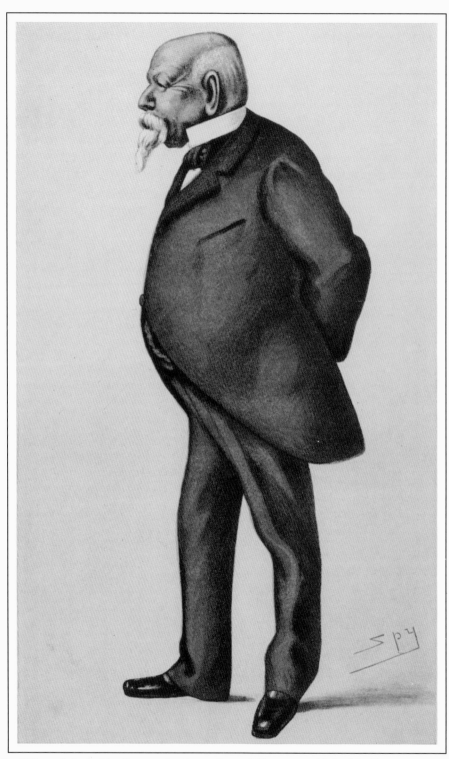

Sam Ward, the "King of the Lobby," entertained members of Congress with lavish dinners.

Vanity Fair, January 10, 1880

have your men on hand a dozen times, and to have them as often disappointed; to have one of those storms which spring up in the Adriatic of Congress, until your men are worried, and worn, and tired, and until they say to themselves that they will not go up to the Capitol today—and then to have the bird suddenly flushed, and all your preparations brought to naught— these, these are some of the experiences of the lobby.[15]

Some of the lobbying techniques of the Gilded Age were not unlike those of today, with speeches supplied, analyses prepared, opposition arguments suggested, personal contacts with key members, appearances before committees, and grassroots campaigns generated by lobbyists. Time and circumstance have conspired to render other scenes from the Gilded Age unfamiliar to the current observer. Gone are the elegant parlors of society matrons where senators and representatives were lavishly entertained by winsome female lobbyists. Ben: Perley Poore wrote, for example:

. . . the most adroit lobbyists belong to the gentler sex. . . . They are retained with instructions to exert their influence with designated Congressmen.

To enable them to do their work well, they have pleasant parlors, with works of art and bric-a-brac. . . . Every evening they receive, and in the winter their blazing wood fires are often surrounded by a distinguished circle. Some treat favored guests to a game of euchre, and as midnight approaches there is always an adjournment to the dining-room, where a choice supper is served[:] A cold game pie, broiled oysters, charmingly mixed salad, and one or two light dishes, . . . with iced champagne or Burgundy at blood heat. Who can blame a Congressman for leaving the bad cooking of his hotel or boarding-house, with the absence of all home comforts, to walk into the parlor web which the cunning spider-lobbyist weaves for him?[16]

In 1869, *The Nation* defined a lobbyist as "a man whom everybody suspects. . . . and whose employment by those who have bills before a legislature is only resorted to as a disagreeable necessity."[17] That sentiment was repeated throughout the literature of the Gilded Age. As we have seen in Chapter 21, Mark Twain and Charles Dudley Warner's novel *The Gilded Age*, which gave its name to the era, told the story of Colonel Beriah Sellers' tawdry efforts to lobby for a bill that would make him rich.[18]

Subsequent novels and scholarly studies of the nineteenth-century Congress have tended to portray the most venal aspects of lobbying. By contrast, Margaret Susan Thompson's *The "Spider Web": Congress and Lobbying in the Age of Grant* argued that lobbyists became the scapegoats for other congressional ills, and that, even during the Gilded Age, lobbyists performed beneficial services. She wrote that Congress was unprepared for the vast economic changes occurring in the nation and needed all the help it could get. As the predominant branch of government, Congress had overextended itself. Henry Adams asserted that "Congress is inefficient, and shows itself more and more incompetent, as at present constituted, to wield the enormous powers that are forced upon it." Turnover of membership was high; levels of parliamentary expertise were correspondingly low. Neither house had formal floor leadership. There was practically no staff, either for committees or for individual members.[19]

At the same time, pressures on the federal government were steadily increasing. The more crowded the congressional agenda became—with issues of finance, industry, internal improvements, and international relations—the more interests demanded to be heard. This is the nub of what political scientists call "pluralistic democracy." Although we often hear a hue and cry about "special interests," everyone, in a sense, belongs to a multitude of these interests: we are defined by our gender, race, age, ethnicity, religion, economic status, educational background, and ideological bent. Some groups are better

HALF-TONE PLATE ENGRAVED BY R. C. COLLINS.

AN APPEAL IN THE LOBBY.

In the Gilded Age, women were increasingly included among the capital's most effective lobbyists.

The Century Illustrated Monthly Magazine, May 1902

CHAIRMAN OF COMMITTEE, $10,000.

MALE LOBBYIST $3,000.

HIGH MORAL SENATOR $3,000.

FEMALE LOBBYIST $3,000.

Illustrations from Mark Twain and Charles Dudley Warner's novel *The Gilded Age* indicate the costs claimed by one lobbyist in seeking the passage of a client's bill.
M. Twain and C.D. Warner, The Gilded Age, 1902 ed.

funded or better organized than others: corporate interests, organized labor, New Right political action committees. Some groups, especially the very young, the very old, the very poor, are the least organized and the least able to make their needs heard. Nevertheless, they all have a "special interest" in congressional actions. Members of Congress, of course, attempt to represent all of the various interests within their constituencies, but they must establish some priorities. Lobbyists attempt to shape those priorities by reminding them of the needs of specific groups.

Thus, Margaret Thompson defined lobbying as "the process by which the interests of discrete clienteles are represented within the policy-making system." She defined lobbyists as "representatives who act concurrently with, and supplement the capabilities of, those who are selected at the polls. Lobbyists fill roles that in many ways are comparable to those of legislators: helping to transmit and obtain satisfaction for demands upon the government, thereby advancing the substantive interests of those whom they have taken it upon themselves to serve." [20]

What, then, is the problem? Money lies at its root. A group's chances of being heard were improved by hiring a lobbyist, which cost money. The more money available, the higher the number and caliber of lobbyists

who could be hired. As a lobbyist in the 1870's, William E. Chandler of New Hampshire, who later became a cabinet member and a senator, drew the unheard-of retainer of ten thousand dollars from Jay Gould, and Gould was not his only client. As Thompson pointed out, "Establishing access, particularly if one's demand was individual and basically indistinguishable from hordes of others, was time-consuming, debilitating, and practically impossible unless someone was continuously on the scene to oversee it." She noted that, during the Forty-third Congress from 1873 to 1875, 2,666 private pension bills were introduced, and only 441, or 16.6 percent, were enacted. How did the members of the Invalid Pension Committee determine which pensions to accept and which to reject? Personal contact improved one's chances. Those who could afford it hired lobbyists; the less affluent prowled the halls of Congress for themselves. [21]

This type of self-lobbyist was described by the Washington *Evening Star* in 1891. Noting that visitors to the Capitol searched for the beautiful female claims agent they had read about in novels, the *Star* suggested that the real case was

a poorly clad, nervous, wistful, and frightened woman. She has some claim before Congress, perhaps, or is interested in some other measure. She goes to see the

In 1882, a cartoonist contrasted the life of a senator plagued by numerous lobbyists with earlier days when members simply made patriotic speeches.

members or senators because she thinks it will help her interests and not because she wishes to. It is as disagreeable to her to visit them as it is to them to receive her visit. She shrinks at a rough word and she is grateful for kind usage. This is one kind of female lobbyist, and if she succeeds in getting anything it is because men take pity on her.

Far more significant were the professional lobbyists, hired by others to handle their claims or to promote their legislative causes. The *Star* broke them into three categories. One was the occasional lobbyist, who came to Washington to promote a certain measure and then went home. Largely inexperienced, these occasional lobbyists were the least ef-fective. Then, there were the "clever fellows with smooth tongues," who peddled their familiarity with Congress to any individual or group that could afford to hire them. "If they are not employed by one side, they will work on the other side in order to be bought off." That is, wealthy interest groups would pay them not to work against their legislative aims. Finally, there was a third group which the *Star* termed "the worst of all." These were the agents of large corporations and monopolies. "They have unlimited means and they usually employ lesser lobbyists under them. They are often fine men in other respects and men of talent. They do unquestionably exert an influence on legislation and they resort not only to bad means to accomplish their ends, but to diplomatic means as well. These are the most dangerous lobbyists of all."[22]

During the second half of the nineteenth century, the practice of lobbying shifted from the former to the latter type of agent described by the *Star*. As the issues themselves became more complex, they required more constant and sophisticated attention. In many ways, the lobbying techniques that developed during this period are still with us. Lobbyists analyzed bills, prepared arguments in defense of their clients, drafted speeches, contacted committee members, and orchestrated grassroots campaigns in favor of their bills.[23]

Now, we accept these lobbying tools as legitimate. Back then, they were suspect, in part, because they were new and, in part, because interests and lobbyists were indiscreet with their use of money to sway votes. As lobbying became perceived as dangerous and a corrupting influence, Congress responded with a variety of reforms. The first effort to regulate lobbyists took place in 1876 when the House required all lobbyists to register with the clerk of the House. In 1879, members of the press galleries in the Senate and House chambers followed suit. They proposed rules of admission to the galleries that would bar all lobbyists posing as journalists, and they created a Standing Committee of Correspondents to police the galleries. Those rules, and that committee, are still in operation today.[24]

Despite the criticism of lobbyists, nineteenth century senators came to appreciate the help they could offer. Especially in defending the high protective tariff, which directly affected numerous industries, senators turned to the representatives of those industries. Senator Francis Warren of Wyoming knew that as soon as he stood up to defend the high tariff on wool, his opponents would

fire back with statistics against him. "I want *facts* to build up my arguments," Warren told a lobbying group. One representative of the sugar industry, under investigation for its lobbying practices, protested, "How can a Senator know about a great question unless he keeps himself informed by those who have devoted their lifetime to it and have a lifelong interest in it?"[25]

The growing importance of lobbying drew many former members of Congress into the profession. They held several important advantages: they understood the legislative process; they knew key members of Congress; and they had access to the floors of the chambers. In fact, by 1897, there were so many former members mingling on the floor of the Senate in behalf of clients that Maine Senator Eugene Hale proposed barring from the floor any nonsenator who had an interest in any pending legislation. The rule was not adopted.[26]

The turn of the century saw the rapid consolidation of American industry and the formation of "trusts," which offered a new challenge to congressional government. Between 1897 and 1904, the number of trusts in the United States grew from 12 to 318 (representing a consolidation of more than five thousand manufacturing plants). These giant trusts, including Standard Oil, American Tobacco, and U.S. Steel, could all afford extensive lobbying in Washington. They seemed to carry the most weight with the United States Senate—the house of Congress not then directly elected by the people. A number of senators were closely identified with major trusts. Editorial cartoonists began picturing the Senate chamber filled with overblown figures representing corporate interests; newspapers referred to the Senate as a "Millionaire's Club"; and David Graham Phillips published his muckraking series, *The Treason of the Senate*, naming senators allegedly beholden to corporate interests.[27]

Lobbyists lingered in the corridors of the Capitol, waiting to appeal to passing senators.

The Century Illustrated Monthly Magazine, May 1902

Progressive presidents like Theodore Roosevelt and Woodrow Wilson took advantage of these popular images of lobbyists and business corruption as leverage for their reform legislation. In seeking public support for lower tariff rates, President Wilson trained his fire on the lobby with this sharply worded attack: "Washington has seldom seen so numerous, so industrious, or so insidious a body. The newspapers are being filled with paid advertisements calculated to mislead the judgment of public men not only, but also the public opinion of the country itself. There is every evidence that money without limit is being spent to sustain this lobby, and to create an appearance of a pressure of public opinion antagonistic to some of the chief items of the tariff bill. . . .

It is thoroughly worth the while of the people of this country to take knowledge of this matter. Only public opinion can check and destroy it." Here is an excerpt from one of Wilson's press conferences in 1913:

WILSON: . . . I should think you [reporters] were missing a lot of stories about the extraordinary lobbying in this town at this time.

QUESTION: There is a good deal written about it, Mr. President.

WILSON: Somehow you haven't got hold of it so that the country could notice it. This town is swarming with lobbyists, so you can't throw bricks in any direction without hitting one, . . . That is the most concerted and as concentrated an effort, I dare say, as has ever been made to influence governmental legislation by the pressure of private interests. . . .

QUESTION: Do you refer especially to sugar?

WILSON: Sugar, wool—those in particular. Those have the biggest lobbies. . . .

In 1917, members of the Woman's Christian Temperance Union held a rally on the Capitol steps.

QUESTION: I think the country knows pretty well that lobbyists are here.

WILSON: I know, but. . . . [t]here is a good deal more than the usual scenery in view. . . .

QUESTION: You mean, Mr. President, there is a corrupt lobby here?

WILSON: I don't know that they could approach Congress in that way, but [there is] just a systematic misrepresentation of the facts.[28]

Wilson's prodding of the press produced the headlines he desired—and helped the Democrats achieve a sharply lowered tariff. The *New York World* ran an exposé on the questionable lobbying tactics of an agent for the National Association of Manufacturers, which led the House of Representatives to launch an investigation. The investigating committee proposed legislation requiring all lobbyists to register with the clerk of the House. Although the House supported the bill, the Senate was not yet ready to go along. Slowly but surely, lobbying reforms were enacted. Democrats and progressive Republicans prevailed on the Senate Judiciary Committee to investigate lobbying activities in 1913, and each senator publicly revealed any personal finances that might benefit from a change in the tariff. In 1919, Congress prohibited any lobbying effort with appropriated funds. This move was designed to prevent agency officials from conducting public relations campaigns, such as stimulating letters and telegrams, in order to influence the passage of legislation.[29]

By the 1920's, Washington lobbying had begun to develop many of the features we associate with it today. Lobbying broadened its scope beyond financial and commercial interests, and the free-lance lobbyist was supplanted by collective action in the form of membership associations, which had been growing and developing since the beginning of the century. In addition, lobbying techniques began to change. For example, the telephone, telegraph, and radio intensified the development of grassroots lobbying.

In 1928, the Senate enacted a bill requiring lobbyists to register with the secretary of the Senate and clerk of the House, but this time the House balked. The movement for some form of regulation gained further impetus during a lobbying scandal the next year. Newspapers revealed that Connecticut Senator Hiram Bingham had placed on the Senate payroll, as a clerk, Charles L. Eyanson, a lobbyist for the Connecticut Manufacturers Association. Moreover, Eyanson accompanied Senator Bingham into closed sessions of the Senate Finance Committee, which was then drafting the Smoot-Hawley Tariff. After an investigation by the Judiciary Committee, the Senate censured Bingham by a vote of 54 to 22, condemning his action as "contrary to good morals and senatorial ethics" and tending "to bring the Senate into dishonor and disrepute." The censure, however, did not spur any legislative response to lobbying.[30]

In 1930, a subcommittee of the Senate Judiciary Committee continued investigating lobbying practices. Among the senators involved was Hugo Black of Alabama, who was not a member of the Judiciary Committee. Because Black was concerned about lobbying efforts regarding the private development of Muscle Shoals (which later became the public power program known as the Tennessee Valley Authority), Chairman George Norris of Nebraska invited him to sit with the committee during the investigation. The hearings were often stormy. At one point, a witness called Senator Black a "contemptible cur" and the senator responded, "I'll see you outside about that." The investigation derailed corporate efforts to exploit Muscle Shoals but achieved no consensus on how to deal with lobbying. The experience, however, formed strong opinions in the mind of Hugo Black, who five years later reexamined Congress' "hidden persuaders."[31]

By 1935, Senator Black had acquired a reputation as a persistent and talented Congressional investigator. For years, he had been advocating that lobbyists publicly register their names, objectives, salaries, and monthly expenses. Then, in the spring of 1935, lobbyists for public utility companies led a particularly furious assault on the Wheeler-Rayburn bill that was designed to break up public utility holding companies. The mountain of letters and telegrams that covered Capitol Hill bore all the evidence of an orchestrated campaign, inspiring Black to launch an investigation.

The hearings made headlines when Senator Black called in Western Union officials, who testified that the 816 telegrams one representative received were all dictated and paid for by a lobbyist for the Associated Gas and Electric Company. Evidence of large payments for propaganda activities was also uncovered. In a radio address, Black told listeners that Americans had a constitutional right to petition, but that no "sordid or powerful group" had a right to present its views "behind a mask concealing the identity of that group." He denounced the "high-powered, deceptive, telegram-fixing, letter-framing, Washington-visiting" utility company lobby, and argued that funds for such activities came from citizens' utility bills. "Just contemplate," said Senator Black, "what a good time people are having on your money in Washington!"[32]

As a result of his efforts, the Public Utilities Holding Company Act was amended to provide for registration of all company agents. Black also introduced legislation for registration of all lobbyists, which passed the Senate and House in different versions. Although efforts to reconcile the two bills failed, Congress was willing to regulate lobbying on an industry-by-industry basis, adding registration provisions to the Merchant Marine Act of 1936 and the Foreign Agents Registration Act of 1938. At the same time, many states enacted lobbying disclosure laws.[33]

Immediately after World War II, the Joint Committee on the Organization of Congress studied ways to make Congress more efficient. During the course of its hearings, the joint committee heard loud complaints about lobbying pressures on Congress, and several groups, including the American Political Science Association, recommended some form of lobbyist disclosure. "Congress is handicapped in the performance of its proper function," the political scientists argued, ". . . by the importunities of special-interest groups which tend to divert legislative emphasis from broad questions of public interest." The joint committee also became concerned that concentrated lobbying efforts by a vocal minority could distort national legislation. The joint committee's staff director, George Galloway, who believed that "the strongest pressures from outside are essentially minority pressures representing particular local interest or specific occupational groups," urged that Congress "turn the spotlight of publicity on lobbying activities."

At the joint committee's recommendation, Congress adopted the Federal Regulation of Lobbying Act, which became Title III of the Legislative Reorganization Act of 1946. This act defined a lobbyist as any person "who by himself, or through any agent or employee or other persons in any manner whatsoever, directly or indirectly, solicits, collects, or receives money or any other thing of value to

be used principally . . . to influence, directly or indirectly, the passage or defeat of any legislation by the Congress of the United States." Anyone meeting this description was required to register name, address, salary, and expenses with the secretary of the Senate and the clerk of the House, and to file quarterly reports on funds received or spent, "to whom and for what purpose" those funds were paid, "the names of newspapers and magazines in which the lobbyist 'caused to be published' articles or editorials," and the proposed legislation the lobbyist was employed to support or oppose. Lobbyists were also required to keep detailed accounts of all contributions of five hundred dollars or more made to members of Congress. Criminal penalties were assigned for any violation of this act.[34]

In 1954, the Supreme Court upheld these lobbying registration requirements in the case of *U.S.* v. *Harriss*. The Court defined the legislation narrowly, however, finding that it did not apply to groups or individuals who spent their own money to lobby Congress directly. It also exempted groups whose principal purpose was something other than lobbying. In the *Harriss* case, the Court reasoned that:

Present-day legislative complexities are such that individual members of Congress cannot be expected to explore the myriad pressures to which they are regularly subjected. Yet full realization of the American ideal of government by elected representatives depends to no small extent on their ability to properly evaluate such pressures. Otherwise the voice of the people may all too easily be drowned out by the voice of special interest groups seeking favored treatment while masquerading as proponents of the public weal. This is the evil which the Lobbying Act was designed to help prevent.[35]

Only two lobbyists have ever been convicted under the Federal Regulation of Lobbying Act. In 1956, Republican Senator Francis Case of South Dakota charged that he had been given a $2,500 campaign contribution to influence his vote. A Senate investigation followed, leading to fines of $2,500 and one-year suspended sentences for two Superior Oil Company lobbyists and a $10,000 fine for their employer.

Calls to strengthen the lobbying law were heard in the wake of the Watergate scandal and the activities of Korean lobbyist Tong-sun Park. In 1976, the Senate drafted and passed more specific definitions of lobbyists and lobbying practices, but intensive lobbying pressures—principally arguing that the new requirements would violate the free speech rights of lobbyists—kept the measure from passing the House. During the 1980's, the Senate Governmental Affairs Committee continued to hold hearings on lobbying registration and to consider new approaches to this old issue. In the Ninety-ninth Congress, the committee produced an excellent report, containing a discussion of the history of lobbying. I recommend the report, *Congress and Pressure Groups: Lobbying in a Modern Democracy*, to all those interested in the subject.

Today's lobbying is more diverse than ever before, with an organized lobby formed, seemingly, around virtually every aspect of American social and economic life. No longer do the lobbying groups come solely from Washington's great law firms and associations. Public relations companies, consulting groups, and specialized accounting, medical, and insurance firms have joined their ranks. All these, and others, engage in a multitude of activities, from raising money for election campaigns to conducting technical studies, with the ultimate goal of influencing the course of legislation and government policy.

Modern technology has made it possible for far-flung group members to stay in almost constant contact with their lobbying representatives in Washington. The explosion in the electronic media and the televis-

ing of House and Senate debates have resulted in better-informed interest groups, who, in turn, more readily communicate their message to their members, legislators, and other targets. Congressional offices are frequently flooded with telegrams, telephone calls, letters and postcards (sometimes preprinted), as a "grassroots" campaign moves into full swing, mobilized by one or another interest group on a given issue. Among the most effective interest groups today in bringing such organized pressure to bear upon legislators are the labor unions, the banking interests, the gun lobby, the pro-Israel lobby, anti-abortion and freedom-of-choice groups, civil rights organizations, environmentalists, and consumer interests.

The past fifteen years have witnessed a political phenomenon: the development and proliferation of political action committees (PACs). These PACs are formed by special interest groups for the purpose of funneling contributions to the political campaigns of members of Congress and other office-seekers, and they constitute a subtle but sophisticated form of lobbying. Spiraling campaign costs in this electronic age have made members of Congress increasingly dependent upon PAC contributions. Incumbents and challengers alike, unless they are inordinately wealthy, besiege scores of PACs in every election for money to finance their ravenous advertising and other political expenditures. The demand for funds to wage a successful political campaign has now become so excessive that the average cost of winning a Senate seat in the 1988 election was roughly four million dollars. This means that a senator is forced to raise an average of more than twelve thousand dollars every week over a six-year term in order to remain in public service. And this is just the average! In the more populous states, the cost is far greater—exceeding ten million dollars per candidate in some instances—and the costs

A lobbyist waits near the Senate chamber.   *George Tames/New York Times*

are rising with each election year. The threat to our representative form of democracy is clear and needs no elaboration here.

The need for congressional campaign financing reform is, likewise, obvious. But just because it is obvious does not mean that it is easy to attain, as was demonstrated by our inability to enact reform legislation during the One-hundredth Congress. As the then-majority leader, I filed a cloture motion eight times (the most ever) to shut off a filibuster and failed eight times to get the necessary three-fifths majority. The "money chase" has gotten out of hand, and the practice of providing campaign contributions in return for "access" to the policy-making process does nothing to remove the negative image that clouds the legitimate side of interest representation.

Another problem is that special interest groups often wield an influence that is greatly out of proportion to their representation in the general population. This type of lobbying, in other words, is not exactly an equal opportunity activity. One-person, one-vote does not apply when the great body of citizens is under-represented in the halls of Congress compared to the well-financed, highly organized special interest groups, notwithstanding the often plausible objectives of such groups.

It should be clear from my remarks that Congress has always had, and always will have, lobbyists and lobbying. We could not adequately consider our work load without them. We listen to representatives from the broadest number of groups: large and small; single-issue and multi-purposed; citizens groups; corporate and labor representatives; the public spirited and the privately inspired. They all have a service to fulfill. At the same time, the history of this institution demonstrates the need for eternal vigilance to ensure that lobbyists do not abuse their role, that lobbying is carried on publicly with full publicity, and that the interests of all citizens are heard without giving special ear to the best organized and most lavishly funded. As for the lobbyists themselves, they would probably agree with Sam Ward, the nineteenth-century King of the Lobby, that the disappointments are greater than the successes. They spend many hours and considerable shoe leather trying to convince 535 members of Congress of the wisdom or folly of certain legislation. They face vigorous competition. They still bear the brunt of press criticism and take the blame for the sins of a small minority of their numbers. But they have a job to do, and most of them do it very well indeed. It is hard to imagine Congress without them.

CHAPTER 23

Women Senators

February 26, 1985 *

Mr. President, today, in my continuing series of addresses on the Senate's history, I shall discuss the history of women senators. Clearly, women have come a long way since the days when they could only view Senate deliberations from the galleries, where the rustling of their crinolines sometimes grew so loud that it drew stern remonstrances from the presiding officer. But, while women have moved from passive observers to active participants in the Senate, it is also clear from their small numbers among us that theirs has been, and continues to be, a long and rocky road to reaching the Senate.

The arrival of the first women in Congress coincided with the height of the suffrage movement and the ratification, in 1920, of the Nineteenth Amendment granting women the right to vote. The long struggle to win the vote brought many women to Washington for the first time—not yet as members of Congress but as vocal, militant protesters. Their actions, such as chaining themselves to the White House fence, were designed to attract attention—and they did. They certainly got the attention of the senators and representatives assembled in joint session to hear President Woodrow Wilson's annual address on December 5, 1916. Five suffragists, members of the National Woman's Party, had smuggled a huge yellow satin banner into the front row of the House chamber's visitors' gallery. As President Wilson was speaking, the suffragists dramatically unfurled the banner over the side of the railing. The banner read: "Mr. President, What Will You Do For Woman Suffrage?" The president was only momentarily distracted, and a House employee leaped up and tore down the offending banner.[1]

The Nineteenth Amendment, stating: "The right of citizens of the United States to vote shall not be denied or abridged by the United States or by any State on account of sex," was ratified and certified as a part of the Constitution in 1920, but the first female member of Congress actually arrived more than three years before its passage. Several states, led by Wyoming, had already recognized women's right to vote, and one of these states—Montana—made history in 1916 when its voters elected suffragist and reformer Jeannette Rankin to the House of Representatives.

* Revised September 1989

Supporters of woman suffrage paraded on Pennsylvania Avenue in 1913.   *Library of Congress*

WE DEMAND AN
AMENDMENT TO THE
CONSTITUTION OF THE
UNITED STATES
ENFRANCHISING THE
WOMEN OF THIS COUNTRY

During her first term in the House, Miss Rankin dramatically cast her vote against American entry into World War I. After her initial term, Representative Rankin ran unsuccessfully for the Senate. Nearly a quarter of a century later, on the eve of World War II, she returned to the House as a member. Still an ardent pacifist, she opposed America's entry into the conflict. This time, Representative Rankin was the only member of either house of Congress to vote against entering the war. In 1943, at the end of this second term, Miss Rankin retired from Congress and devoted the rest of her life to working for world peace.[2]

A total of 127 women from forty states have served in Congress, beginning with the election of Jeannette Rankin in 1917. Of this number, 16 have been senators, including our colleagues Senator Nancy Kassebaum of Kansas and Senator Barbara Mikulski of Maryland. Senators Margaret Chase Smith of Maine and Barbara Mikulski hold the distinction of being the only women to serve in both chambers. Nearly every Congress since the Sixty-fifth, when Miss Rankin arrived, has seen an increase in the number of women members. Nevertheless, 127 represents a mere 1 percent of the almost 12,000 people who have served in Congress in two hundred years.[3]

Women, like their male colleagues, have found their way into Congress by a variety of means and for varying lengths of time. Two of the sixteen women senators, for example, were never sworn in because Congress was not in session between their dates of election and the expiration of their brief terms.

One woman sat in the Senate for only one day—a record for brevity. Several women were appointed or elected to fill unexpired terms and served in Congress for less than a year. Only six women have been elected to full Senate terms. In an excellent article with

Jeannette Rankin of Montana made history in 1916 by becoming the first woman elected to Congress.
Library of Congress

the somewhat macabre title "Over His Dead Body: A Positive Perspective on Widows in the U.S. Congress," historian Diane Kincaid noted that most women have made their way to Congress via the so-called "widow's mandate," or "widow's succession," the practice by which the widow of a deceased member is awarded his seat to keep it "safe" until the next general election. The widow's mandate has brought 70 percent of the women senators and 50 percent of the women representatives to Congress.[4] As women have become more active in politics at all levels, the congressional tradition of the widow's mandate has weakened. And, as we know today, both Senators Kassebaum and Mikulski were elected on their own.

The women who have served in Congress are remarkably diverse in their party affiliations, philosophy, and backgrounds, just as are their male counterparts. As Hope Chamberlin wrote in her book on women in Congress entitled *A Minority of Members*:

Most members of this numerically select group were reared in modest economic circumstances; almost all attended college; only a few never married. The majority have been white, Anglo-Saxon, and Protestant. Beyond hard work and the gift of intuition, however, they have had little else in common. The laws of chance, if nothing else, argue against parallels. . . . their precongressional careers, if any, span a broad spectrum: teaching, stenography, journalism, social work, broadcasting, the theater, law—even cowpunching.[5]

The history of women in the Senate has clearly been a bipartisan one—the tally, thus far, stands at nine Democrats, seven Republicans.[6]

The very first woman senator, Rebecca Latimer Felton, actually holds three Senate records: She was the first woman senator; she had the shortest Senate service—one day; and—at eighty-seven years of age—she was the oldest person ever to be sworn into the Senate for the first time. Obviously, this was no ordinary person. Her biography, by John Talmadge, is aptly subtitled *Nine Stormy Decades*, and, indeed, they were.[7]

Rebecca Latimer Felton took her oath of office on November 21, 1922. Less than two months earlier, on October 3, 1922, the date of her senatorial commission, few would have expected Mrs. Felton to achieve this special honor. The sudden death of controversial Senator Thomas E. Watson gave Georgia Governor Thomas Hardwick an unexpected opportunity. Hardwick's opposition to the Nineteenth Amendment while serving in the House of Representatives had not endeared him to women voters. It apparently occurred to him that, if he were to name a woman—the first woman—to the Senate, he might regain the favor of the newly enfranchised women. There was little danger of alienating male constituents, since a man was almost certain to be chosen in the

The first woman senator, Rebecca Latimer Felton of Georgia, held office for one day in 1922.
Georgia Department of Archives and History

election that was scheduled to be held before the Sixty-seventh Congress reconvened.

When Governor Hardwick announced his selection of Mrs. Felton, he also announced that he would be a candidate for the unexpired term in the coming primary. Although he described Mrs. Felton as a "noble Georgia woman, now in the sunset of a splendid useful life," he added, "It is unfortunate that an elected successor will prevent her from being sworn in."[8]

Governor Hardwick obviously underestimated Mrs. Felton's vitality in her sunset years. She had been in Georgia politics too long not to know a gentlemanly power play when she saw one. In her telegram of acceptance, she thanked the governor for the honor "on behalf of the thousands of Georgia women who will reward you at the ballot box." [9]

On October 7, the governor officially presented the certificate of appointment to Mrs. Felton at a ceremony witnessed by a crowd of her friends and neighbors. Although he had opposed woman suffrage, the governor explained, he now accepted it as the law and, as a sign of good faith, was appointing Mrs. Felton to the brief interim term. [10]

Rebecca Felton took advantage of the forum to reiterate her views on the political role of women, declaring: "The biggest part of this appointment lies in the recognition of women in the government of our country. It means, as far as I can see, there are now no limitations upon the ambitions of women. They can be elected or appointed to any office in the land. The word 'sex' has been obliterated entirely from the Constitution." [11]

Newspapers in the North and South praised Mrs. Felton but questioned the governor's motives. The *Pittsburgh Gazette-Times* dismissed the appointment as "merely a pretty sentiment . . . an empty gesture." The governor, it asserted, "did not appoint a woman because he has respect for women in politics, but actually to smooth his own path to the Senate." According to the *St. Louis Star*, "Other governors who may be studying the health charts of United States senators should take full note of Governor Hardwick's strategy." [12]

Behind the scenes, with Mrs. Felton's blessing, suffragists across the country launched a campaign to see that Mrs. Felton was officially seated in the Senate chamber. The appointment of the first woman senator, they believed, must be acknowledged on a national stage. But how to unblock the road to Washington? There seemed only two alternatives: either the president would have to be persuaded to call a special session of Congress or the Senate must consent to her being sworn in before her elected successor took his seat.

The suffragists tried the presidential path first. President Warren Harding was flooded with messages urging him to give Mrs. Felton her day in the Senate. But the president refused, claiming that it would be too expensive to summon Congress back just to seat a single senator.

When Georgia Democrats chose Walter George, not Governor Hardwick, as their candidate in the primaries (tantamount to election in Georgia, at the time), the suffragists shifted their approach. They urged George to put off presenting his credentials until Mrs. Felton could be seated. George pointed out several obstacles, most seriously the Seventeenth Amendment that stated, in essence, that the term of an appointed senator ended the day a successor was elected, but, if Mrs. Felton was willing to risk rejection, George said he was willing to step aside to allow her to precede him.

Although hospitalized with a throat ailment in late October, Mrs. Felton continued her efforts, again asking President Harding to call a special session of Congress. As it happened, circumstances required such a session to deal with a ship subsidy bill, and Harding called one for November 20. Mrs. Felton began to prepare for the journey.

Her decision to set off for an uncertain fate in Washington surprised no one in Georgia. Few expected her to change after more than fifty years of charting her own course. For a half century, she had campaigned across the state, opposing graft and bribery and pressing for her many causes: woman suffrage, temperance, prison reform, compulsory school attendance, vocational education, and care for expectant mothers. Like many of her contemporaries, Mrs. Felton also shared the anti-Negro prejudice of her section of the country to the point of obsession and was well known as a champion of white supremacy and segregation. If anyone could convince the Senate to seat her, it was strongminded "Mother" Felton.[13]

Rebecca Latimer was born in DeKalb County, Georgia, in 1835, in the latter half of Andrew Jackson's second administration. Her father was a Whig leader in the area and instilled in his children a lively interest in current events. In her autobiography entitled *My Memoirs of Georgia Politics,* she recalled visiting the local stagecoach stop with her father to learn the latest news. After the stagecoach departed, "it was the most natural thing in the world for my father (also the postmaster) to read aloud [from the *Southern Recorder*] to the eager people, who learned all they knew of national politics in that way. I became familiar also with 'Tippecanoe and Tyler too!' "[14]

Rebecca's father believed in the education of women and saw to it that his daughter received the best available in Georgia. When she was sixteen, she was enrolled in Madison Female College, a strict Methodist institution which her mother had attended. Graduating with honors in 1852, she was on the committee that selected as the commencement speaker William Harrell Felton, an eloquent Methodist minister and physician. Fifteen months later, Rebecca Latimer and Dr. Felton, an advocate of rights for women, were married.

The Feltons lost their sons, their farm, and their fortune during the Civil War and spent the years afterwards trying to regain their former prosperity. In 1874, Dr. Felton, bucking the "Bourbon" Democrats, ran for a House seat from Georgia's Seventh District as an Independent. Mrs. Felton entered the fray with relish:

> From the beginning to the end, I was in the thick of my husband's campaign. . . . I wrote hundreds of letters all over fourteen counties. I wrote night and day, and for two months before the close kept a man and a horse at the door to catch every mail train three miles away. . . . At one time my health broke down, but I was propped up in bed with pillows and wrote ahead. I made appointments for speaking, recruited speakers, answered newspaper attacks, contracted for the printing and distribution of circulars and sample ballots.[15]

The campaign's success proved a great tonic to Mrs. Felton's health. For the next six years, she served as her husband's secretary and clerk in Washington. Constituents who benefited from her capable services began to call her the "Second Representative from the Seventh."

Her husband's campaigns for reelection, in the autumns of 1876 and 1878, were bitter ones, and her presence at his side became a campaign issue. Political rallies of that era were rough, coarse affairs, considered unfit for the ears of Georgia ladies. Consequently, her presence was denounced by the Democratic press in editorials that called her attendance a "disgusting spectacle." Enemy editors thundered: "There is a nobler, higher sphere for women. Fill it!"[16]

When Dr. Felton was defeated in 1880, he and his wife began a newspaper, the *Cartersville Free Press,* to push reform measures they held dear. When, in 1884, Dr. Felton was elected to the first of three terms in the state assembly, his wife was again at his side, pushing her own agenda and garnering the support of women's groups for measures her husband introduced. When William Felton died, in 1909, it was only natural that Rebecca Felton should travel the reformer's route alone.

As she traveled to Washington in November 1922, eighty-seven-year-old Mrs. Felton wondered about the reception that awaited her in the capital. How would her fellow senators in the third session of the Sixty-seventh Congress react to a woman colleague? According to the *New York Times,* some senators, fearing a precedent for ac-

Rebecca Felton was photographed at her desk during her one day as a senator.   *Library of Congress*

cepting women in the Senate, threatened to object to her taking the oath. That view was not unanimous, however. A Republican quoted in the *Atlanta Journal* contended: "It will be a brave man that objects. I'm not a candidate for the job." [17]

To cheers from women crowding the gallery, Rebecca Felton arrived early for her great moment. Taking a vacant seat, she waited for Vice President Calvin Coolidge to call the Senate to order at noon on November 20. To her disappointment, the Senate adjourned after only twelve minutes, out of respect for the deceased Tom Watson. "I'll be back tomorrow," Mrs. Felton assured waiting reporters. [18]

She was back the next day, and, once more, women from a number of female-rights organizations filled the galleries. Mrs. Felton blew them a kiss as she marched in to occupy Watson's vacant seat.

After three other new senators were sworn in, Mrs. Felton listened as senior Georgia Senator William Harris stated Felton's case and expressed the hope that there would be no objections. Hardly had Harris finished speaking when a voice called out, "Mr. President!" It was Thomas J. Walsh of Montana, who rose to urge that Mrs. Felton not be seated. It was not the lady herself, he made clear, whom he opposed, but the irregularity of her seating. Walsh was prepared to speak at length, but a message came from the House that the president was ready to address the joint session on changes in the merchant marine. Mrs. Felton went along with the rest of the senators and sat through the president's speech; she then returned with them to the Senate chamber.

Once again, Thomas Walsh rose and delivered a long discourse. Although he cited the Constitution and a host of other authorities, he acknowledged that he was not lodging a formal objection, only informing his colleagues of the gravity of the situation. Finally, he finished. There was silence. When no one else moved to speak, the president pro tempore asked the clerk to read Mrs. Felton's credentials. Mrs. Felton sighed and smiled as she took Senator Harris' arm and proceeded to the dais to be sworn in.

When she responded, "I do," in a clear voice, the galleries erupted in applause, in which even some of the senators joined. There was no opportunity for Mrs. Felton to speak that day but, having waited for weeks, she was willing to be patient for one more day.

At the Wednesday session, Senator Felton proudly answered the roll call, then arose and was recognized as the "junior senator from Georgia." After thanking her colleagues, especially Senator George, who would be sworn in as soon as she finished speaking, she addressed herself to the future. Looking gravely at the male senators who surrounded her, she said, "When the women of the country come in and sit with you, though there may be but a very few in the next few years, I pledge you that you will get ability, you will get integrity of purpose, you will get exalted patriotism, and you will get unstinted usefulness." [19]

With that, her brief Senate career ended but not her career as an activist. Until her death in 1930, at the age of ninety-five, Rebecca Felton remained active, voting in every state, local, and national election and urging other women to do likewise.

Rebecca Felton was right in predicting that more women would follow her into the Senate and that they would be women of quality. She was also correct in stating that their numbers would be few. An entire decade elapsed before the next woman arrived. This was Hattie Caraway of Arkansas, the first woman ever elected to this body. In the journal she kept while a senator, edited by Diane Kincaid and entitled *"Silent Hattie" Speaks*, Mrs. Caraway noted that she had been given the same desk Rebecca Felton had used for just a day. "I guess," she observed dryly, "they wanted as few of them contaminated as possible." [20]

Hattie Caraway established many Senate firsts. In addition to being the first woman elected to the Senate, she was also the first woman to vote in the Senate, to preside over the Senate (on October 19, 1943), to chair a Senate committee (Enrolled Bills), and to preside over Senate hearings.

Hattie Wyatt was born in Tennessee in 1878. When she graduated from Dickson Normal College in 1896, she became engaged to Thaddeus Horatius Caraway. After their marriage in 1902, Thaddeus pursued a career in politics and law in Arkansas, while Hattie's life centered around their children and their home. In 1912, Thaddeus Caraway was elected as a Democrat to the first of his three terms in the U.S. House of Representatives. Then, in 1920, he was elected to the Senate, where he particularly supported the interests of poor farmers. A committed Democrat and a forceful debater, Caraway served in the Senate until his unexpected death on November 6, 1931.

The timing of his death presented Arkansas politicians with a dilemma. Since more than a year remained until the next general election, Arkansas law required the governor to make an immediate appointment and then

Louisiana Senator Huey Long campaigned for Arkansas Senator Hattie Caraway in 1932 and was credited with her victory. *Collection of the Louisiana State Museum*

Washington still grieving, and on December 9, 1931, was sworn into the Senate. On January 12, 1932, she became the first woman elected to the Senate by winning the contest for the remaining year of her husband's term.

While Senator Caraway was busy in Washington, six well-known Arkansas Democrats prepared to run in the general election for the seat they expected would soon be empty. But they had miscalculated. Two days before the filing deadline for the primary, Hattie Caraway recorded in her diary, "because I really want to try out my own theory of a woman running for office I let my check and pledges be filed." Although the Arkansas newspapers played the story prominently—"Bombshell Explodes in Arkansas Politics," "Jonesboro Senator Springs Surprise by Announcing for Office"—the six men who had also filed did not consider her a serious threat.[21]

After all, there was no indication that Senator Caraway had made any campaign preparations at all. But her opponents' nonchalance turned to concern when, in July, they learned that Mrs. Caraway was going to be assisted in her campaign by popular Senator Huey Long of Louisiana, the father of our former colleague, Russell Long. An avowed enemy of Arkansas' senior Senator Joseph T. Robinson, Long proclaimed the "brave little woman senator" who sat beside him in the chamber—and who had frequently voted for his "share the wealth" proposals—the true heir to the egalitarian philosophy of her late husband.[22]

A magazine article that fall described the scene when Senator Long arrived in Arkansas on August 1:

Seven motor trucks and Senator Long's private automobile composed the campaign caravan. Two of the trucks were the specially designed and built sound trucks developed by him for his Louisiana forays. Each is equipped with four amplifying horns. . . . On the

to hold a special election for the final year of the term.

Several candidates were considered, but all were more interested in the full six-year term up for grabs in the general election little more than a year away. All agreed with the governor that naming Thad Caraway's widow as the interim appointee, as well as the Democratic candidate in the special election for the remaining year, would be the safest route to follow. It was assumed that Mrs. Caraway would have no interest in running for the full term, and the contending male Democrats could battle over the seat in the 1932 election. Hattie Caraway seemingly accepted these arrangements, returned to

Speaking Announcements

Senator Hattie D. Caraway
and
Huey P. Long
U. S. Senator (former Governor) of Louisiana

MONDAY, AUGUST 1st, 1932

MAGNOLIA	9:00 A. M.	Court House
EL DORADO	11:00 A. M.	Court House
CAMDEN	2:30 P. M.	Court House
FORDYCE	4:30 P. M.	Political Park
PINE BLUFF	8:00 P. M.	Mo. Pacific Park

TUESDAY, AUGUST 2nd, 1932

STRUTTGART	9:00 A. M.	East of Court House
BRINKLEY	11:00 A. M.	City Park
FORREST CITY	1:30 P. M.	Court House
WYNNE	3:00 P. M.	Railroad Park
HARRISONBURG	5:00 P. M.	Court House
JONESBORO	8:00 P. M.	Court House

WEDNESDAY, AUGUST 3rd, 1932

WALNUT RIDGE	9:00 A. M.	Band Stand
NEWPORT	11:30 A. M.	Remmel Park
BATESVILLE	2:30 P. M.	Fair Grounds
SEARCY	4:30 P. M.	Court House
LITTLE ROCK	9:00 P. M.	Band Shell

THURSDAY, AUGUST 4th, 1932

RUSSELLVILLE	11:00 A. M.	Court House
BOONEVILLE	3:00 P. M.	Court House
FT. SMITH	8:00 P. M.	Andrews' Field

FRIDAY, AUGUST 5th, 1932

MENA	11:00 A. M.	City Park
MT. IDA	3:00 P. M.	Court House
HOT SPRINGS	9:00 P. M.	Whittington Park

SATURDAY, AUGUST 6th, 1932

MALVERN	9:00 A. M.	Court House
ARKADELPHIA	11:00 A. M.	Next to Library
PRESCOTT	2:00 P. M.	Court House
HOPE	4:00 P.M.	Municipal Auditorium
TEXARKANA	8:00 P. M.	Court House Lawn

Hattie Caraway and Huey Long kept a grueling schedule during their 1932 campaign travels.
Hattie Caraway Papers, Special Collections, University of Arkansas

roof of each truck is a slatted platform with two of the four amplifying horns on each side, and with nested take-down iron railings and a portable stairway. . . .

Of the remaining five trucks, one is the small advance car, whose crew of two men finds sites for meetings, distributes handbills, drums up local chairmen. . . . The other four cars are heavy vans for transporting tons of literature, automobile windshield stickers, posters and similar printed matter. The heavy cars work in two units, a sound truck and two literature vans to each.[23]

Thus equipped, Long and Caraway stumped the state together. Senator Long was a charismatic speaker and electrified the crowds. "We're here to pull a lot of pot-bellied politicians off a little woman's neck," he told the audience. Mrs. Caraway spoke less often but in the same vein, appealing to the poverty-stricken farmers she represented. Their combined message was unmistakable: Senator Caraway had her constituents' interests at heart, and they should return her to Washington.[24]

In their week-long, two-thousand mile campaign tour, the two senators visited thirty-one counties and delivered nearly forty speeches. Their efforts proved highly successful, for Hattie Caraway received 44.7 percent of the vote in the primary, a plurality, and went on to an election victory in November.[25]

Hattie Caraway returned to the Senate, where she quietly and diligently represented her depression-stricken constituents and became a firm supporter of New Deal legislation. In 1938, she decided to run for reelection. Even without the help of Huey Long, who had been assassinated three years earlier, she defeated Representative John McClellan—whose slogan was "Arkansas Needs Another Man in the Senate"—by eight thousand votes and won her second six-year term.[26]

For another six years, Senator Caraway continued to serve her constituents and to support President Roosevelt's programs. In 1943, she cosponsored the proposed Equal Rights Amendment to the Constitution, the first woman member of Congress to endorse it. Then, in 1944, the sixty-six-year-old Hattie Caraway was denied a third Senate term when former University of Arkansas President J. William Fulbright defeated her in the Democratic primary.

In February 1936, another "first" for women occurred in the Senate when Rose McConnell Long of Louisiana was sworn in, bringing the number of women in the chamber to two for the first time. Unfortunately, the circumstances that brought Mrs. Long were tragic—the brutal assassination of her

Women who served in the U.S. Senate during the 1930's and 1940's included Rose McConnell Long of Louisiana, *center*; Dixie Bibb Graves of Alabama, *right*; and Vera Bushfield, *upper left*, and Gladys Pyle, *lower left*, both of South Dakota.
U.S. Senate Historical Office and South Dakota State Historical Society [Bushfield]

husband in the Louisiana state capitol building. The Long family holds an unmatched Senate distinction: Senator Huey Long, Senator Rose Long, and our former colleague Senator Russell Long form the only father-mother-son combination in the history of this institution. Currently, we have the sons of several former senators in the Senate: Senators Simpson, Dodd, and Gore are all the sons of former senators, but the parent in the Senate, in each instance, was the father. Only Senator Russell Long can claim both parents as United States senators.

Mrs. Long was not the first choice of the Louisiana Democratic machine to inherit her husband's Senate seat. When the front-runner, Governor O. K. Allen, died before he could be sworn in, his successor, Governor

James Noe, promptly appointed Mrs. Long, in order to avoid a divisive intraparty struggle. Governor Noe claimed, "This is the proudest moment of my life." Hattie Caraway of Arkansas—perhaps remembering the assistance she received from Huey Long— was delighted, declaring, "It will be nice to have a woman's company in the Senate." [27]

Succeeding her colorful and famous husband in the Senate presented Mrs. Long with a challenge. Her approach was far more low key than his, focusing on her committee responsibilities. Of the five Senate committees to which she was appointed, she concentrated principally on Public Lands and Surveys, taking great pride in leading the efforts to enlarge Chalmette National Historical Park on the site of the Battle of New Orleans.

Mrs. Long understood politics well enough to accept her role as simply the legatee of her husband's political estate. When the Seventy-fourth Congress ended in January 1937, she quietly left Washington, for Shreveport and home.[28]

In mid-1937, another woman joined Senator Caraway in the Senate. Dixie Bibb Graves of Alabama arrived amid a storm of controversy. Her husband, Governor Bibb Graves, appointed her to fill the Senate vacancy created by Hugo Black's appointment to the Supreme Court. Defending his decision, the governor contended that "she has as good a heart and head as anybody." But the governor's mansion was inundated with mounting criticism over the apparent flagrant abuse of personal patronage.[29]

In fact, Mrs. Graves was not without political experience, gained in campaigning for such causes as temperance and woman suffrage. According to the *New York Times*, she had a strong political influence on her husband and was "at home with deep-sea fishing tackle, a shotgun, a garden spade, or a silver ladle at the banquet table."[30]

Despite the skepticism and anger she left back home, Mrs. Graves, escorted by Alabama's senior Senator John Hollis Bankhead II, was sworn in on August 20, 1937, and took her seat in the Seventy-fifth Congress with Hattie Caraway looking on. As a freshman Democratic senator, Mrs. Graves was assigned a seat at the rear of the chamber, in a section known as the "Cherokee Strip." Because there were seventy-six Democratic senators in 1937, some had to be seated on the Republican side, where they were said to be "off their reservation," in an area reminiscent of Oklahoma's original Cherokee Strip that belonged neither to the Indians nor to the government. "I'm supposed to be seen, perhaps," Mrs. Graves told a radio audience on one occasion, "but certainly not heard."[31]

Mrs. Graves did speak, however, and spoke loudly enough on issues close to the hearts of voters in Alabama that a write-in campaign was launched to change her status from interim senator to full-fledged candidate. Mrs. Graves declined the honor, however, and, with an almost perfect attendance record to her credit, ended her Senate career after less than five months in office by resigning on January 10, 1938.

In 1938, the first Republican woman senator, Gladys Pyle of South Dakota, came to Washington. In November 1938, she was elected to the Senate to fill the remaining two months in the vacancy caused by the death of Senator Peter Norbeck. She was, in fact, the first woman elected to the Senate in her own right without prior service under appointment. Although Congress was not in session during the two months Gladys Pyle served as a senator, she was determined to take the appointment seriously. She would not be sworn in or receive any committee assignments, but she chose to travel to Washington anyway, "because I wouldn't feel like a senator unless I did." When she arrived at the capital, she established herself in the Senate Office Building. Then, in the two months during which she was a senator, she began calling on all the top government officials who might be able to aid depression-ravaged South Dakota.[32]

It was ten more years before another woman came to the Senate, and, like Gladys Pyle, she was from South Dakota. "Honored, that's how I feel," said Vera Bushfield in 1948 when South Dakota's governor appointed her to serve out the three months remaining in the term of her late husband, Senator Harlan Bushfield, a former governor of that state. "The appointment is being made," the governor told the people of South Dakota, "with the understanding that shortly before the 80th Congress reconvenes she will resign and thus enable me to give seniority rights to the new senator-elect." The governor left no question: this was to be a short Senate career.[33]

Like Gladys Pyle, Mrs. Bushfield had to decide whether or not to go to Washington, since Congress was in recess at the time of her appointment. Because she would not be sworn in even if she went, Mrs. Bushfield chose to stay home in Pierre. "I can serve the constituency best," she explained, "by making myself as accessible as possible." Keeping her promise to the governor, Mrs. Bushfield resigned on December 27, 1948, giving senator-elect Karl Mundt a few days' seniority over the other freshmen in the Eighty-first Congress.[34]

The next woman to enter the Senate is one many of us have been privileged to know personally. I vividly recall that she was the only woman in the Senate when I came here in 1959 and that she always wore a beautiful red rose. When I arrived, she had already been in the Senate for a decade. I refer to Margaret Chase Smith of Maine, who holds at least two Senate records. She is the first woman in history to be elected to both the House and the Senate, and she holds the record for the longest Senate service by a woman—four terms or twenty-four years. In 1960, she attained the highest vote percentage of all Republican senatorial candidates nationally. She was also the first woman elected to a leadership post in the Senate, being unanimously elected chairman of the Republican Conference in 1967 and, again, in 1969 and 1971.

"If I am to be remembered in history," said Margaret Chase Smith, "it will not be because of legislative accomplishments but for an act I took as a legislator in the United States Senate when on June 1, 1950 I spoke in the Senate in condemnation of McCarthyism at a time when the then Junior Senator from Wisconsin had the Senate paralyzed with fear that he would purge any Senator who

Maine's Margaret Chase Smith, the first woman elected to both the House and the Senate, served twenty-four years as a senator. She is shown here with Lyndon B. Johnson.   *U.S. Senate Historical Office*

disagreed with him." Mrs. Smith is probably right. What came to be known as her "Declaration of Conscience" speech is probably the act for which she is most remembered, but it is only one important incident in a very long and distinguished career.[35]

Declaration of Conscience is also, fittingly, the title of Margaret Chase Smith's autobiography, highlighting the importance the element of conscience played in her political career. Speaking out strongly against McCarthy's tactics, she declared:

I do not like the way the Senate has been made a rendezvous for vilification, for selfish political gain at the sacrifice of individual reputations and national unity. . . . I do not want to see the Party ride to political victory on the Four Horsemen of Calumny—fear, ignorance, bigotry and smear.[36]

Senator Smith's willingness to take on Senator McCarthy, who was finally censured by the Senate four years later, left no doubt about her independent spirit. She was no novice at politics, having arrived in the Senate with almost a decade of experience in the House of Representatives behind her. In 1940, she had been elected to the House to fill the vacancy caused by the death of her husband, Clyde H. Smith. She was reelected four times.

Military preparedness was one of Senator Smith's primary interests during her service in both the House and the Senate. While in the House, she had earned the nickname "Mother of the WAVES" for her introduction of legislation to establish the women's branch of the navy. She also worked indefatigably for increases in appropriations for medical research.[37]

In 1964, Senator Smith sought the Republican nomination for president. "I have few illusions and no money, but I'm staying for the finish," she said. She became the first woman in history to have her name placed in nomination for president at a major political party convention. Once, before Senator Smith's bid for the presidency, an interviewer asked her, "Suppose you woke up one morning and found yourself in the White House, what would you do?" "Well," responded Mrs. Smith, "I'd go straight to Mrs. Truman and apologize, and then I'd go home."[38]

Proud of her perfect attendance record and of answering to 2,941 consecutive roll-call votes, Margaret Chase Smith consistently refused to campaign when the Senate was in session, and she kept her campaign expenditures at a minimum. This practice proved successful until 1972. Running on her record turned out to be a dangerous strategy in that year when many senior incumbents lost to their younger opponents. Since Mrs. Smith was seventy-four at the time, many voters may have interpreted her failure to campaign as a sign that she was too old for the job. At

any rate, her opponent outspent, outtraveled, and outpolled her.

"I hate to leave when there is no indication another qualified woman is coming in," Senator Smith lamented. "We've built a place here for quality service. If I leave and there's a long lapse, the next woman will have to rebuild entirely." Four women had come and gone in the Senate during Senator Smith's long tenure, and, to her relief, she did not have to wait too long for other qualified women to follow.[39]

Back in April 1954, Senator Smith had written in her syndicated column "Washington and You": "Gov. Robert B. Crosby did the women of America as well as the women of Nebraska a great honor in appointing Mrs. Eva Bowring to the vacancy created by the death of Sen. Dwight Griswold." In addition to a long career of Republican party work, Mrs. Bowring, who owned a ten-thousand-acre cattle ranch, frequently worked alongside her ranch hands.[40]

At a press conference to accept the proffered Senate seat, Mrs. Bowring announced that she was going home to the Bar 99 "to kiss the cattle goodbye" and then she would be off to Washington to begin her six-month career as a senator. When sworn in, she became the thirteenth female member of the Eighty-third Congress. She did not consider the number unlucky at all. "Prepare yourself," she declared, "there will be more and more women."[41]

For six months, Eva Bowring devoted herself to her Senate duties, especially supporting President Eisenhower's farm policies; then she set off to oversee the cattle roundup at her ranch.[42]

When Mrs. Bowring retired, one woman succeeded another as a United States senator for the first time in history. Hazel Abel had been elected to fill the two-month vacancy in Nebraska's Senate seat created by a technicality in the state's election law. Consider-

From 1954 to 1989, nine women entered the Senate: *top row, left to right*, Maryon Allen of Alabama, Hazel H. Abel and Eva K. Bowring, both of Nebraska; *center row*, Paula Hawkins of Florida, Nancy Kassebaum of Kansas, and Muriel Humphrey of Minnesota; *bottom row*, Maurine Neuberger of Oregon, Elaine Edwards of Louisiana, and Barbara Mikulski of Maryland.   *U.S. Senate Historical Office and Library of Congress*

ing the shortness of the term, it was surprising that anyone campaigned hard for it, but Mrs. Abel and sixteen others did. "Why bother?" she was asked. "To me it was more than a short term in the Senate. I wanted Nebraska voters to express their approval of a woman in government. I was sort of a guinea pig." [43]

On November 8, 1954, Hazel Abel took her oath of office as senator. To honor the occasion, Eva Bowring had made the trip to Washington in order to escort her successor to the dais for the swearing in. Senator Abel's brief service began dramatically, for, on November 10, the Senate started censure proceedings against Senator Joseph McCarthy. After reviewing the evidence, Hazel Abel voted with the majority to censure Senator McCarthy.

In 1960, another woman joined Senator Smith in this chamber. When Senator Richard Neuberger died, the Oregon voters elected his widow, Maurine, to succeed him. The decision to run had been a difficult one. Her husband had died just two days before the filing deadline for the upcoming election, and Governor Mark Hatfield had appointed a former state supreme court justice, Hall S. Lusk, to serve in the interim. But petitions signed by several thousand Oregonians urging her to put her name on the ballot, plus a supportive telephone call from Senator Smith, convinced Mrs. Neuberger to toss her hat into the ring.

A former two-term member of the Oregon house of representatives, Mrs. Neuberger was recognized as a seasoned politician and campaigner, as well as an advocate of the liberal Democratic politics espoused by her late husband. As a senator, she took on the tobacco lobby and pressed Congress into authorizing the Federal Trade Commission to regulate cigarette advertising. Maurine Neuberger served until 1966, when she chose not to seek reelection.

For three short months in 1972, there was another woman in the Senate: Democrat Elaine Edwards of Louisiana. Like Dixie Bibb Graves of Alabama, she was appointed by her husband, Louisiana Governor Edwin Edwards. She was to complete the term of the late Senator Allen J. Ellender, who had been elected in 1936 to succeed Louisiana's first woman senator, Rose McConnell Long.

In her three months in office, Senator Edwards focused on issues of concern to her state, such as financing for new highway construction in Louisiana, a provision in the Omnibus Rivers and Harbors bill easing the financial burden on local governments, and a bill appropriating funds for the Allen J. Ellender Fellowships for needy high school students and teachers.

After Senator Edwards resigned in November 1972 and Senator Margaret Chase Smith left the Senate the following January, five years passed before another woman sat in the Senate. Many of us who were in the Senate at the time remember with great sadness that two senators arrived because of the deaths of their husbands. In January 1978, Muriel Humphrey was appointed by the governor of Minnesota to fill the vacancy caused by the death of Senator and former Vice President Hubert Humphrey. A few months later, in June, the death of Senator James Allen of Alabama brought his widow, Maryon, to the Senate.

Both Senators Muriel Humphrey and Maryon Allen left this body in November 1978, but that month also brought us another woman senator under happier circumstances. In the November elections that year, our colleague Senator Nancy Kassebaum became the fourteenth woman senator. She became only the fourth woman ever to win election to a full six-year term, and the first woman to win election to the Senate who was not preceded in Congress by a spouse. In 1980, Paula Hawkins of Florida won a Senate seat and joined Senator Kassebaum, for six years, as the fifteenth woman senator. In November 1986, our colleague Senator Barbara Mikulski was elected to the Senate from Maryland and became the sixteenth woman senator and only the second woman ever to have been elected to both houses of Congress. There have never been more than two women in the Senate at any one time. But surely it will be just a matter of time before this record, too, will be broken and another Senate "first" added to the record books.

CHAPTER 24

Black Senators

March 28, 1985*

Mr. President, in the first two centuries of our government under the Constitution, sixty-five black Americans have been elected to the United States Congress. Among this number, sixty-two served in the House, including five women; only three have served in the Senate. In 1870, Hiram Revels of Mississippi became the first black senator and the first black to serve in the United States Congress. He was followed, in 1875, by a second black senator, Blanche Kelso Bruce, also of Mississippi.[1] In 1966, Massachusetts elected Edward Brooke to the Senate, the first black to serve in this body in eighty-six years and the first ever elected to the Senate by popular vote.

Once emancipated and granted citizenship, American blacks moved into public office enthusiastically. They played prominent roles in the Reconstruction governments of several southern states and then advanced onto the national scene. In the three decades after Hiram Revels broke the color line in 1870, a steady stream of black legislators followed him to Washington. During the period from 1870 to 1897, twenty-two blacks were elected to Congress—twenty to the House and two to the Senate. All were

from southern states that were parts of the military districts created by various Reconstruction acts. All were Republicans.[2]

These twenty-two members of the late 1800's have been portrayed in many ways: as the ignorant tools of corrupt white politicians, as corrupt politicians themselves, and as the noblest leaders of their race. In truth, they were as diverse as their white congressional colleagues. If some were corrupted and some were corrupt, they were no more so than some of their white contemporaries.

These early black legislators represented a wide variety of trades and professions, which ranged from bricklayers to teachers. Education had clearly been a crucial stepping stone, for, even though most had been born in slavery, many had managed to acquire some college training, and five held college degrees. Before their service in Congress, most of them had gained political experience as state legislators and local government officials. Afterward, many went on to hold prestigious positions as educators and administrators.[3]

All required—and displayed—courage, tenacity, and perseverance to overcome the obstacles set in their paths. The legal status

---

* Revised October 1989

THE FIRST COLORED SENATOR AND REPRESENTATIVES.
In the 41ˢᵗ and 42ⁿᵈ Congress of the United States.

Hiram R. Revels, the first black senator, *seated far left*, appears in an 1872 Currier and Ives print with black members of the House of Representatives.

National Portrait Gallery

of their elections was continually challenged, their supporters were intimidated and, in some cases, even murdered.[4]

Toward the end of the nineteenth century, the enforcement of discriminatory laws, combined with local prejudices, effectively blocked blacks from voting. By 1902, black Americans no longer had a voice in Washington, and nearly three decades passed before blacks were again elected to Congress. Since 1929, there has been a slow, steady increase, both in the number of black legisla-

tors and in the states or districts they represent. Over the past six decades, forty black members have been Democrats and only three have been Republicans. In the present 101st Congress, there are twenty-four black representatives.[5]

Let us now examine the careers of the three black men who have served in the Senate. We begin with Hiram Rhodes Revels of Mississippi who, on February 23, 1870, arrived in this Senate chamber. Mississippi had just been readmitted to the Union, and its

A former minister, Hiram R. Revels of Mississippi began his Senate career in 1870.   *Library of Congress*

legislature had elected him to serve the remaining year of an unexpired Senate term. Before he could be sworn in, however, he would have to endure a heated debate among his future colleagues over whether he should be seated. As Revels awaited the outcome, he knew that some of the oratory to follow would surely be bitter and uttered by men who opposed him for his race alone.[6]

Hiram Revels was born in Fayetteville, North Carolina, on September 27, 1827.[7] Born of free parents, with Indian blood as part of his heritage, Revels and his brothers and sisters were part of a substantial community of free blacks in North Carolina before the Civil War. Despite the meager educational opportunities for blacks in the state, his parents worked hard to educate their children. Revels learned all he could at a small school run by a black woman and then taught the younger children in his

family at home while supporting himself as a barber.

Revels, who began preaching the gospel while still a teenager, became a minister of the African Methodist Episcopal Church in Baltimore after studying at a Quaker seminary in Indiana. He taught and preached in a number of midwestern and border states—both slave and free. Late in life, Revels recalled the difficulties of these years:

At times, I met with a great deal of opposition. I was imprisoned in Missouri in 1854 for preaching the gospel to Negroes, though I never was subjected to violence. According to the slave code no free Negroes had even any right to remain in that state . . . but in large towns and cities, this was seldom enforced.[8]

Revels eventually settled in Baltimore, where he served as minister of a church. During the Civil War, he organized two black regiments and went to Mississippi to assist with education for the freedmen. After the war, he returned to the pulpit, serving churches in Kansas, in New Orleans, and, finally, in Natchez, Mississippi. There, in a state occupied by federal troops, where more than half the population was black, he found a political climate that was encouraging blacks to move into politics through the Republican party.

Revels began his political career in 1868 as an alderman in Natchez. Then, in 1869, he won a seat in the reconstructed Mississippi state senate, which convened in January 1870. In preparation for the state's return to the Union, the legislature needed to elect three United States senators: two to terms that would expire in 1871 and 1875, and one to a full term starting in 1871. The full term went to former Confederate General James Alcorn, and the next longest went to the carpetbagger governor, Adelbert Ames. After three days of debate and seven ballots, Revels won the short, fourteen-month term.[9]

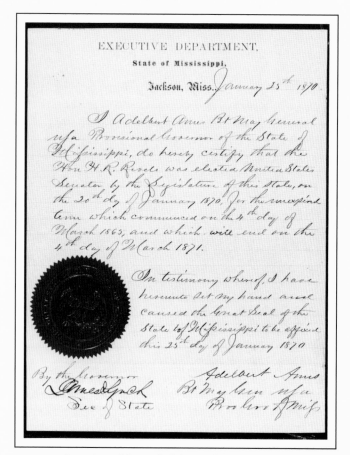

A series of heated debates followed Hiram Revels' presentation of his credentials to the Senate on February 23, 1870. *National Archives*

Revels and Ames traveled to Washington together, arriving in late January. Revels, by now a national celebrity, was besieged by reporters who found him "a dark mulatto of large stature, easy and self-possessed in manner, and [who] talks well." Revels told the press that he intended "to look after the interests of his race in Congress." [10]

Hoping to get right to work, Revels rented rooms in the Capitol Hill home of George T. Downing, the former caterer and restaurateur from New York who managed the restaurant of the House of Representatives and was reported to be the wealthiest black man in the nation. [11]

On February 23, 1870, with both Revels and Ames present, Senator Henry Wilson of Massachusetts rose and declared, "I present the credentials of Hon. H.R. Revels, Senator-elect from Mississippi, and I ask that they be read, and that he be sworn in." [12]

The fight was on. Since the Republicans solidly controlled the Senate, there was no doubt that the credentials would eventually be approved. Still, the opposition was prepared to spend considerable energy in its losing cause. Senator Willard Saulsbury of Delaware, a Democrat, immediately challenged Revels' credentials, contending that a provisional military governor did not have the authority to certify a United States senator. Saulsbury's opposition was hardly unexpected, for he had already introduced a memorial "praying such legislation as will secure the Government of the United States to the white race." [13]

Democrats Saulsbury, Garrett Davis of Kentucky, and John Stockton of New Jersey tried to avert what they considered the calamity of Revels' seating by claiming that the Mississippi legislature could not legally elect a senator until after the state's readmission to the Union. The attack came as no surprise to the Republicans or to Revels. Davis was known as a white supremacist and had been among the most outspoken foes of the 1866 Civil Rights Act. [14]

Revels' supporters, who included influential Senators Roscoe Conkling of New York and Lyman Trumbull of Illinois, effectively countered each charge. Finally, after hours of haggling, the opposition senators turned to the more promising tactic of questioning whether Revels had been a United States citizen for the requisite nine years. This raised a genuine issue, since, prior to passage of the 1866 Civil Rights Act, even free blacks were not legally considered to be citizens.

Debate dragged on for two days, with Davis leading the opposition. Determined to bar Revels from the Senate, Davis raged: "I do not know why the law of the universe permitted that race to be brought here; and above all, I do not know why the Yankees were made their instruments to bring them here, unless it was to curse and to create another devil for the white man! . . . I say that Revels is not a citizen under your legislation." [15]

Senator James Nye, a Nevada Republican, charged that Davis' opposition was simply "the same old story of prejudice against the colored man." Senator Henry Wilson and Ohio Senator John Sherman observed that Revels had been a voter, and thus a citizen, in Ohio at least twenty years before.[16]

Finally, and conclusively, Charles Sumner of Massachusetts entered the debate. "Mr. President," Sumner intoned, "the time has passed for argument. Nothing more need be said. For a long time it has been clear that colored persons must be Senators, and I have often so declared." [17]

The senators agreed with Sumner, and the issue was brought to a vote. The *New York Times* reported that "there was not an inch of standing or sitting room in the galleries, so densely were they packed; and to say that the interest was intense gives but a faint idea of the feeling which prevailed throughout the proceedings." [18] The atmosphere in the chamber was electric as Vice President Schuyler Colfax called for the votes. Visitors strained to hear each senator's reply as his name was called. The final tally showed a straight party vote of 48 to 8 in Revels' favor. The nation's first black senator would be seated.[19]

Realizing that his historic moment had arrived at last, Revels strode to the dais to be sworn in. Senator Wilson accompanied him down the aisle, since there was no senior Mississippi senator to provide the usual escort.

Newspaper reaction to Revels' seating was mixed, and even the most favorable journals displayed the paternalism with which newly

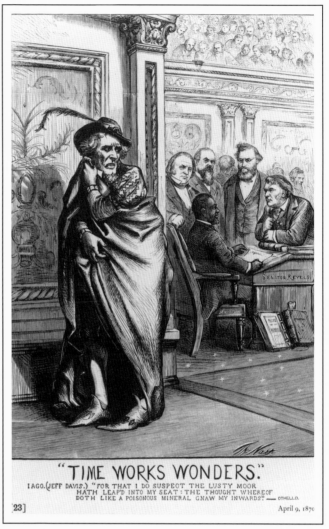

"TIME WORKS WONDERS."

IAGO.(JEFF DAVIS.) "FOR THAT I DO SUSPECT THE LUSTY MOOR HATH LEAP'D INTO MY SEAT: THE THOUGHT WHEREOF DOTH LIKE A POISONOUS MINERAL GNAW MY INWARDS". — OTHELLO.

[23]   April 9, 1870

Thomas Nast portrayed former Mississippi Senator Jefferson Davis as Shakespeare's Iago, to Hiram Revels as Othello.   *Harper's Weekly, April 9, 1870*

enfranchised blacks had to contend. The *Philadelphia Inquirer*, however, pronounced the matter closed, observing: "The colored United States Senator from Mississippi has been awarded his seat, and we have not had an earthquake, our free institutions have not been shaken to their foundations, nor have the streets of our large cities been converted to blood. . . . All the speeches made concerning Revels' race were in the interests of a political shibboleth that is as dead as slavery itself." [20]

Revels soon found that it was one thing to be admitted to the Senate but quite another to be effective here. He made his first attempt to influence legislation only a month after taking his oath, when he rose to speak against a bill that could lead to the barring of black officeholders in Georgia. Believing that he must act as a representative of black citizens throughout the country, Revels eloquently urged defeat of the legislation. To his sorrow, however, the Senate passed the bill readmitting Georgia to the Union with the offensive amendment permitting state control of all seating in the state legislature. This provision effectively excluded Georgia's blacks from holding office in the state and national legislatures.[21]

Revels' first taste of failure would unfortunately be repeated often in his short Senate career. Although he labored hard at his assignments on the Education and Labor Committee and the Committee on the District of Columbia, his legislative efforts bore no fruit. He lent support to measures proposed by his more formidable colleagues, such as Sumner, for desegregation of schools and the lifting of political restrictions against blacks, but, time after time, these initiatives went nowhere.

When Revels' brief Senate term ended, on March 3, 1871, he returned to Mississippi to head Alcorn College. During 1873, he briefly served as interim secretary of state of Mississippi, then returned to the presidency of Alcorn from 1876 until 1882, when he retired and devoted himself to church work. Hiram Rhodes Revels died on January 16, 1901, at the age of seventy-eight. In spite of the prejudice he faced, Revels had made history as the first black man to serve in the Congress of the United States.

When Blanche Kelso Bruce of Mississippi took the oath of office on March 4, 1875, he became the second black senator in history, and the only former slave to serve in this body. He went on to become the first black to serve a full six-year term, the first to preside over the Senate, and the first to chair a Senate committee.[22]

On March 1, 1841, Bruce was born in slavery on a Virginia plantation. The youngest of eleven children, he was chosen to be the special playmate of his master's son, and, when the white child was tutored, Blanche sat in on the lessons and proved the more able student. During Bruce's childhood, his owner moved from state to state, taking his family and slaves with him. They lived twice in Missouri and once in Mississippi, with Bruce and his brothers working in tobacco fields and factories at each stopping place. When the Civil War began, Bruce and two of his brothers headed for Hannibal, Missouri, to try to join the Union army, while his owner went south to join the Confederacy. Since the Union army did not yet accept black recruits, Bruce spent the war teaching school, starting out in Kansas, which was a free state. Once Missouri emancipated its slaves, Bruce returned to Hannibal and opened a school for black children. Thus, as Bruce later wrote, he had simply emancipated himself. He received his only formal education in a few months spent at Oberlin College in Ohio; then, short of money, he left to work as a porter on a riverboat.[23]

Having decided to try politics as a career—and recognizing the opportunities offered to blacks by Republican control in defeated Confederate states like Mississippi—Bruce kept moving south. In 1868, he arrived in Floreyville, Mississippi, with only seventy-five cents but also with boundless energy and ambition. He progressed rapidly over the next six years, both politically and financially, serving in a series of appointive and elective local offices, from county elections supervisor to sheriff. At the same time, Bruce began purchasing land, first obtaining several lots in town and later, in 1874, buying a

Born in slavery, Blanche Kelso Bruce of Mississippi became the second black senator in 1875. *Library of Congress*

640-acre cotton plantation. This purchase became the foundation of a fortune in real estate that grew as his career progressed.[24]

In February of 1874, the state legislature elected Bruce to the United States Senate seat that had long been his goal. As had happened with Revels earlier, Bruce's election drew national newspaper attention. The *Vicksburg Times* complimented and cautioned him, "One newly-elected senator, although colored and formerly a steamboat porter, is a man of liberal and comprehensive views . . . , he fully realizes the necessity for adoption by his race and by the white Republicans of an honest and liberal policy."[25] The *New York Times* approved of his election, stating, "Mr. Bruce [is] possessed of intelligence, an irreproachable private character, and is perhaps quite as well qualified to perform the duties of the position as almost any fairer skinned aspirant." The *Louisianian*, a black-owned newspaper, also applauded the choice, declaring, "Senator Bruce is of fine address, easy and graceful in his carriage, thoughtful and matured in his intellect, and a man of sterling and acknowledged integrity."[26]

Blanche Bruce's Senate term began in March 1875, more than a year after his election. Although his credentials were not challenged, as Revels' had been, he did experience some coolness in the Senate chamber. As he later recalled:

When I came up to the Senate I knew no one except Senator [J.L.] Alcorn [of Mississippi] who was my colleague. When the names of the new Senators were called out for them to go up and take the oath, all the others except myself were escorted by their colleagues. Mr. Alcorn made no motion to escort me, but was buried behind a newspaper, and I concluded that I would go it alone. I had got about half-way up the aisle when a tall gentleman stepped up and said: "Excuse me, Mr. Bruce, I did not until this moment see that you were without an escort, permit me. My name is Conkling," and he linked his arm in mine and we marched up to the desk together.[27]

The other focus of public attention in the Senate that day was former President Andrew Johnson, who had barely escaped removal from office in an impeachment trial seven years before in the same chamber. Johnson had just returned to the Senate as a freshman member from Tennessee.

One of the causes that Bruce espoused early in his Senate career was that of fellow black Republican P.B.S. Pinchback, who had been elected to the Senate by the Louisiana legislature. In March 1873, when Pinchback's term was due to begin, opponents claimed that the legislature that chose him had been elected fraudulently. A rival claimant for the seat also appeared and presented his credentials. The Senate referred the credentials of both to the Committee on Privileges and Elections, and parliamentary maneuvering prevented the matter from coming to the floor for three years.[28]

During the 1875 special session that followed his swearing in, Senator Bruce made quiet efforts on Pinchback's behalf, but, when the matter remained unresolved at the beginning of the regular session the next year, he tried a more public approach. Delivering his first speech on the Senate floor, Bruce responded to opponents, who charged that there had been voting fraud in the election of both the legislature and the governor and that Pinchback's election by the questionable legislature could not be valid. "Shall we admit by our action on this case that for three years the State of Louisiana has not had a lawful Legislature; that its laws have been made by an unauthorized mob; that the President . . . and Congress . . . have sustained and perpetuated this abnormal, illegal, wrongful condition of things?" Bruce asked. He contended that, even if there had been problems in the election of the legislature, "Mr. Pinchback is a representative of a majority of the legal voters of Louisiana, and is entitled to a seat in the Senate."[29] Despite

Bruce's efforts, when the matter came to a vote in March 1876, the Senate refused to seat Pinchback.

In the Senate, Bruce served on the Pensions and Manufactures committees, as well as the Committee on Education and Labor. He also chaired a select committee on the Mississippi River. Much of his time was spent carefully drafting bills calling for desegregation of the army and pensions for black veterans of the Civil War. Like Revels before him, however, Bruce had little luck getting any of his bills passed.

Bruce also addressed the controversy over Mississippi's 1875 election, which had been marred by violence and the murder of several blacks. Bruce gave an impassioned speech, graphically depicting the terrorism used to intimidate blacks from voting. He pleaded for a federal investigation, which was authorized, although its damning findings were ignored.

On February 14, 1879, Senator Bruce became the first black to preside over the Senate, a milestone that was duly reported in the press. The *New-York Tribune* announced: "This is the first time a colored man ever sat in the seat of the Vice-President of the United States. Senator Bruce is universally respected by his fellow senators and is qualified both in manners and character to preside over the deliberations of the most august body of men in the land." [30]

The three congresses in which Senator Bruce served saw a steady erosion in Republican strength and black membership. There were seven black representatives in the Forty-fourth Congress, only three in the Forty-fifth, and none in the Forty-sixth. Bruce never had a black colleague in the Senate. In the elections of 1878, the Democrats swept both houses of Congress, placing the Republicans in the minority and depriving Bruce of his Mississippi River committee chairmanship. It was while he was in the mi-

nority, however, that Bruce performed his most valuable service to black Americans. He headed an investigation into the failure of the Freedmen's Savings and Trust Company, which had been chartered by Congress. Bruce's committee exposed the venality and mismanagement that had caused the collapse and recommended a plan that enabled the bank's seventy thousand black depositors to recover more than half of their money. [31]

In January 1880, a newly elected Democratic legislature in Mississippi chose a Democrat as Bruce's successor. Although he would still represent the state in the Senate for another year, Bruce recognized that, since federal troops were no longer present to protect black voters, Mississippi would cease to provide a political base for blacks and Republicans. Accordingly, he decided to settle in Washington.

When Bruce's single Senate term ended on March 3, 1881, there was some talk that he might be offered a cabinet office in the administration of incoming President James Garfield. The cabinet post did not materialize, but, during Garfield's brief administration and those that followed, Bruce held a series of federal patronage jobs, including register of the treasury and recorder of deeds in the District of Columbia. He served as a trustee of Howard University, which awarded him an honorary LL.D. degree in 1893. Bruce was register of the treasury when he died, in 1898, at the age of fifty-seven.

Eighty-six years after Senator Bruce left this chamber, the nation's third black senator, Edward W. Brooke of Massachusetts, was sworn in. He was the first black senator since Reconstruction, the first from a northern state, and the first popularly elected to the Senate. [32]

Senator Brooke was born in the city of Washington, D.C., on October 26, 1919. The family had already made considerable progress, from his great-grandfather Brooke,

The third black senator, Edward W. Brooke III of Massachusetts, was elected in 1966.

U.S. Senate Historical Office

who had been a slave in Virginia, to his father, who served for half a century as a lawyer with the Veterans Administration. Brooke attended Washington's Dunbar High School, which was then a segregated school. Anticipating a career in medicine, he earned a bachelor of science degree, in 1941, from Howard University. Then, in World War II, Brooke served in Italy as a second lieutenant. After a quick course in Italian, he performed dangerous, valuable service as a liaison officer with the Italian partisan guerrillas under the code name of Captain Carlo.

When the war was over, Brooke decided to study law instead of medicine and graduated from Boston University Law School. He was

building a private law practice when friends from army days urged him to run for the state legislature. Brooke claimed he had not cast his first vote until the age of thirty, but he entered both the Republican and Democratic primaries, won the GOP nomination, and remained with that party throughout his political career.

Having lost his first two bids for the state legislature, Brooke withdrew from politics until 1960, when he ran for Massachusetts secretary of state. Although he narrowly lost the election, his new visibility won him the chairmanship of the Boston Finance Commission, a municipal watchdog group, where he proved to be a vigorous crusader for government reform. As a result, he was elected state attorney general in 1962 and reelected in 1964. Often criticized for not using his office to push forward the civil rights movement, Brooke responded: "I am a lawyer and . . . the attorney general of Massachusetts. I can't serve just the Negro cause. I've got to serve all the people of Massachusetts." [33]

When Leverett Saltonstall's retirement opened up a U.S. Senate seat from Massachusetts, Brooke entered the race and, in November 1966, defeated a strong Democratic opponent to win a striking victory. As his winning margin mounted on election night, Brooke happily announced that "the people of Massachusetts judge you on your worth alone," and he promised to merit their faith.[34]

Brooke took his Senate oath in January 1967. Our colleagues Mark Hatfield and Ernest Hollings were members of that class. Senator Edward Kennedy escorted the junior senator from Massachusetts to the dais to be sworn in. Reminded by the press of the acrimony and hoopla that had surrounded the arrivals of Senators Revels and Bruce, Brooke noted with satisfaction: "There was no special fanfare for me. . . . I felt like a member of the club." That Brooke's election

Senator Brooke, a Republican, is pictured here with Senate Republican Leader Everett Dirksen.

U.S. Senate Historical Office

was viewed as a meaningful and positive achievement by blacks across the country was demonstrated by the congratulatory letters that poured into the Massachusetts freshman's office at the rate of 350 a day.[35]

Brooke set about making himself known to the nation. During his two terms in the Senate, he held seats on such visible committees as Appropriations and Banking, plus a host of subcommittees and special and select committees. In 1968, President Lyndon Johnson appointed Brooke and ten others to investigate that summer's urban violence and to try to find answers to the problems that lay behind it. The report of the Commission on Civil Disorders warned that the nation was becoming seriously divided along racial lines and urged increased government aid for education, housing, and employment to help the inner cities. Although the president did not act on its proposals, Brooke and others here in the Senate were able to incorporate some of the commission's recommendations into subsequent civil rights legislation.

Brooke received his first extended national coverage and established his reputation as a national civil rights advocate during Senate consideration of President Nixon's nominees to seats on the Supreme Court. After warning the president, in vain, in 1969, that his choice of Judge Clement Haynsworth was an insupportable one for many Republican senators, Brooke fired the initial Senate volley in the ultimately successful fight to keep Haynsworth off the high bench. Early in the following January, Brooke again found himself unable to support the president's next nominee, Judge G. Harrold Carswell, and again successfully led the fight within his party to defeat the nomination. Brooke's actions in these instances set a pattern that he was to follow for the next several years: in general, he opposed President Nixon on domestic policy and supported him on foreign policy. In 1973, however, Brooke became one of the first Republican senators to urge President Nixon to resign.

At the heart of Brooke's legislative agenda was his belief in a pressing need for reconciliation in America: reconciliation between blacks and whites, between generations, between ideologies, between the civil and military functions of the government. He pursued this reconciliation through a variety of avenues, including tax reform, aid to education, and fair housing. Alerted, while attorney general of Massachusetts, to the problems facing consumers, Brooke strongly supported truth-in-lending legislation and other consumer protection measures. Above all, throughout his time in the Senate, Senator Brooke continued his low-pressure efforts to persuade the federal government to use its power to wipe out racial injustice in America. In 1978, Edward Brooke was defeated in his bid for a third Senate term. He now practices law in Washington, D.C.

Mr. President, there is a heartening progress evident in the careers of these three men, Senators Revels, Bruce, and Brooke. Hiram Rhodes Revels was seated by the Senate, in 1870, only after days of bitter, divisive debate, which was an embarrassment to Revels, to the Senate, and to the nation. When Blanche Kelso Bruce took his seat in 1875, he suffered no overt racial slurs but also had little chance for longevity here. Edward Brooke, sworn in eighty-six years after Bruce's departure, became the first black senator since Reconstruction, the first from the North, the first from an overwhelmingly white state, and, perhaps most important, the first to be elected by the citizens rather than by a state legislature. Brooke took office with little fanfare in 1967, won reelection, and, for twelve years, served the Senate and the people of Massachusetts with distinction.

ROBERT C. BYRD'S SENATE
A Thirty-Years' View

After two hundred years, [the Senate] is still the anchor of the Republic, the morning and evening star in the American constitutional constellation. . . . It has weathered the storms of adversity, withstood the barbs of cynics and the attacks of critics, and provided stability and strength to the nation during periods of civil strife and uncertainty, panics and depressions. In war and peace, it has been the sure refuge and protector of the rights of a political minority. And, today, the Senate still stands—the great forum of constitutional American Liberty!

ROBERT C. BYRD, 1989

I considered it necessary to inform Soviet leaders that the Senate would not act to rubber-stamp any treaty; that it shared a responsibility with the president in the making of treaties; that it would fulfill its constitutional role without fear or favor; and that inflammatory editorials and statements coming from Moscow would hinder rather than speed treaty approval by the Senate.

ROBERT C. BYRD, 1989

Many new senators come here thinking that they will quickly make their mark on the institution. Soon, however, they learn that it is the institution that makes its mark on them. The Senate goes on, like Tennyson's brook, forever, and it is far greater than the sum of its one hundred parts.

ROBERT C. BYRD, 1989

CHAPTER 25

Robert C. Byrd's Senate

The Education of a Senator
1917–1958

In 1989, at the completion of my twenty-two years as a Senate party leader, Senate Historian Richard Baker asked me to participate in a series of oral history interviews to offer my observations on leadership in the modern Senate. Chapters 25, 26, and 28 present a distillation of those interviews.

According to genealogical records, a William Sale came to America from England in the year 1657 and settled in Rappahannock County, Virginia. On November 20, 1917—260 years later—his ninth generation descendant, Cornelius Calvin Sale, Jr., was born in North Wilkesboro, North Carolina, the son of Cornelius and Ada (Kirby) Sale. On Armistice Day, November 11, 1918, Ada Sale died of influenza, her widower husband being left with four sons and a daughter. In accordance with the dying mother's request, the father gave the baby son to the father's sister and her husband, Mr. and Mrs. Titus Dalton Byrd, who adopted the baby as their own and gave it the name Robert Carlyle Byrd.

Having no recollection of my mother, because she died when I was less than a year old, I grew up believing that the Byrds were my true parents. They brought me to West Virginia when I was about three years old, and we lived in various rural and coal-mining areas until I graduated from high school, got a job, and married my high-school sweetheart, Erma Ora James, a coal miner's daughter. On May 29, 1987, Erma and I celebrated our fiftieth wedding anniversary.

My foster parents were hard working, honest, and religious. They were poor, but they gave me their love and their good name, and they taught me how to live. Although I strayed from their teachings from time to time, still, through the years, I have found that the basic values and principles by which they lived were right. I am convinced that the man who wrote the old song "Faith of Our Fathers" knew what he was talking about, and so do I.

Starting to school in a two-room schoolhouse in Mercer County, West Virginia, and growing up in the years of the Great Depression, I determined early to try to excel—both in the classroom and in the workplace. Graduating from high school in 1934 when times were hard, I could not go on to college but had to go to work. Although finding a job was not easy, I finally landed one at a gas station four miles away, which paid a salary of fifty dollars a month. I walked the distance when I could not hitch a ride on a bread truck.

Later, I worked as the "produce boy" in the coal company store, and then I became a meat cutter. When I married, I was making seventy dollars a month—and I earned every penny of it! Jobs were hard to get, and I was glad to have one. I cannot remember ever missing a day's work because of sickness.

During World War II, I worked as a shipyard welder in Baltimore, Maryland, and in Tampa, Florida. When the war ended, I took Erma and our two daughters back to southern West Virginia and worked again as a meat cutter. Then, I began a new career: politics.

My interest in politics awakened during World War II. In 1946, I filed for a seat in the West Virginia house of delegates, the lower house of the state legislature. One of thirteen candidates in that race for the three delegate seats from Raleigh County, I was politically unknown. My foster father was not a politician, not a banker or businessman, not someone with money or influence who could give me a big start in politics. He was a poor coal miner. I had to make it on my own, and, inasmuch as I was working as a meat cutter at the time, I did not have much going for me.

A Republican lawyer named Oppie Hedrick, from Beckley, West Virginia, took an interest in my candidacy. He advised me: "Make your fiddle case your brief case. Everywhere you go, carry that fiddle case. Your identity will become known. You make yourself a little speech, and they won't forget you because of that violin."

I took his advice. I would go to meetings—just any kind of meeting—Odd Fellows, Fraternal Order of Moose, the Elks, women's garden club meetings, Kiwanis, Rotary,

Lions. I would play a few tunes, quote some poetry, and then briefly state why I thought I should be elected to the legislature. I campaigned for better schools and rural roads and for liberalization of workmen's compensation laws.

The outcome of the election was a surprise: I led the entire field of thirteen, incumbents included. The headline in the August 12, 1946, Beckley newspaper read, "Butcher Fiddled While Others Smiled and Led Democratic Ticket." I was not surprised to have won a seat in the legislature, because I had worked very hard to win, but to lead the ticket was most gratifying. I had campaigned assiduously and had called on all the Democratic county executive committee members and other politicos. I would go to their homes, sometimes as late as nine or ten o'clock at night, and take my violin with me. I would tell them I was running for office, and, before leaving, I would ask, "Would you like me to play a tune on my violin?" They would say, "Yes." And it caught on quickly. I also used a little campaign jingle to aid voters in remembering my name:

> BYRD by name,
> BYRD by Nature;
> Let's send BYRD
> To the legislature.

I did not have an automobile of my own. (I was thirty-two years old and in the West Virginia senate before I owned a car and learned to drive.) But I had a coal miner friend named Dallas Radford who had an automobile. In the late afternoons, after working all day in the mine, he would drive me around the county to see political leaders, county officials, and precinct workers. He never charged me anything; I just paid for the gasoline. I have never forgotten that coal miner friend, who had known me since I was a boy, believed in me, and just wanted to see me get ahead in politics.

Scenes from the early life of Robert C. Byrd include, *clockwise from upper left*: young Robert Byrd with his foster father, Titus D. Byrd (c. 1923); Vacation Bible School students at the community church in Stotesbury, West Virginia, in 1927 (Robert Byrd is in front row, wearing bow tie); young Robert Byrd with his violin (c. 1929); and a group of coal miners at Stotesbury (c. 1932), including Titus Byrd, *circled at left*, and Mrs. Byrd's father, Fred James, *circled in center*. *Office of Senator Robert C. Byrd*

In those days, the state legislature met only two months in every two years, and the annual salary was five hundred dollars. When I went to Charleston for the session, my wife remained at Crab Orchard, Raleigh County, where I was employed. The pastor of my church, Colonel Shirley Donnelly, had a sister who lived across the street from the state capitol at Charleston. He suggested that I rent a room at her house, in order to be close to the capitol and away from the hotels where most of the legislators gathered. He believed, rightly, that it would be a better influence on me.

I also selected a good legislative attaché from Raleigh County—a fine old gentleman named Granville Bennett. He had served as foreman on juries, knew his way around the courthouse, and had been active in the Democratic party for a long time. Bennett, who boarded nearby in Charleston, would come up to my room in the evenings, and we would go over the calendar bills together and decide how I should vote on them. He was a good influence on me. I did very well at that session of the legislature.

Right after the election and before the session had begun, George Titler, president of the United Mine Workers in District 29 (Beckley), asked to see me at his office. He told me that he wanted me to vote for Walter Vergil Ross, a member of the house of delegates, for Speaker. Titler was a rough, tough old-time labor leader. But I replied, "No, I can't vote for Mr. Ross. I have already promised my vote to his opponent, Mr. John Amos." This incurred Titler's wrath, and he assured me that, when the time came for my reelection in two years, he would urge the coal miners to vote against me.

During my first term in the legislature, in 1947, I introduced a bill to liberalize workmen's compensation payments. Having grown up in a coal miner's home, I knew the needs of the miners, and I knew the time had come to increase workmen's compensation benefits. I introduced the legislation, and it passed the house. The only speech I made during the session was on that bill, for I had been advised not to talk too much or too often. I was told that, whenever I had something to say, I should say it and say it well— be prepared, and let it go at that.

I received the plaudits of more than half the members of the house of delegates that night. At that time, there were two former United States senators serving in the West Virginia house of delegates. One was Rush D. Holt. The other was Joseph Rosier, appointed in 1941 to fill the unexpired term of Senator Matthew M. Neely, who had been elected governor. I felt that I was walking in some pretty high cotton, with two former United States senators sitting in that legislature. When I concluded my speech, Rosier asked unanimous consent that it be made part of the house *Journal*. Unlike the U.S. Senate, where speeches automatically appear in the *Congressional Record*, a speech in the West Virginia legislature was not recorded in the *Journal* unless unanimous consent was granted.

My wife Erma and I opened a small grocery store of our own at Sophia (Raleigh County) in June 1948. When the time came for me to run for reelection that year, George Titler, the UMWA president, kept his promise. He really went after me. I campaigned with my fiddle, and I met him head on. I explained to the voters: "Mr. Titler tried to tell me how to vote, and I did not intend to be told how to vote. I had already made a commitment, and I did not intend to break my promise. Moreover, I felt I was voting for the better man for the job of House Speaker."

The 1948 election was one to remember. President Truman was running for election, and there were various county races for sheriff and other local offices, but my campaign for reelection attracted more attention than all of the other contests in Raleigh County because of the Byrd-Titler feud.

I was reelected by a huge vote. At that time, the United Mine Workers was a potent political organization, with around 120,000 coal miners in West Virginia. But the miners demonstrated that they, too, would not be told how to vote by their leader. They voted their sentiments and supported me strongly.

In 1950, I ran for the West Virginia senate. The ninth senatorial district included Wyoming County, which adjoined my home county of Raleigh. Titler vigorously opposed my candidacy in Wyoming County, where I was not as well known, and campaigned hard against me. But I worked that county from one end to the other, won the race for state senate, and won it big. I defeated Clay S. Crouse, a Beckley lawyer, in the primary by a vote of 9,819 to 4,818, and went on to defeat Republican A.D. Cooke in the fall elections, 23,843 to 12,355.

While a member of the lower house of the legislature, I had enrolled in 1950 at Morris Harvey College (now Charleston University), near the state capitol, hoping eventually to earn a baccalaureate degree. I had graduated from high school sixteen years earlier, in 1934, during the Great Depression, at a time when it was not possible for me to go on to college. As a member of the state senate in 1951, I pressed ahead with my studies, driving to and from the college, more than sixty miles away, while Erma ran the store at Sophia. During the summer, I attended Concord College at Athens, fifty miles away.

In 1952, while serving in the state senate, I ran for a seat in the U.S. House of Representatives. That opportunity came when the Sixth District's congressman, Dr. Erland H. Hedrick, decided to run for governor rather than seek reelection to Congress. I seized the occasion. I knew that if I did not run at that point, I might not have a good opportunity again—or certainly for a long time—to run for an open seat in Congress.

From the beginning, I knew it would be a tough primary campaign, with five other men running, including a competitor from my own county who was sure to split that county's vote. I realized I would have to work extra hard in the congressional district's other three counties. At the time, I was attending Marshall College (now Marshall University) in Huntington, West Virginia, but I withdrew and plunged headlong into the campaign.

I knew that my chances for obtaining the Democratic nomination could be jeopardized if I alienated any of the several factions within the party that were contending for the governorship. The state's attorney general, William C. Marland, attracted powerful support from the party's "statehouse faction," and Congressman Erland Hedrick drew his own potent following from the mine workers' union. I was not interested in getting caught in that crossfire, for I needed votes from all sides.

At one point, I learned of a meeting of Dr. Hedrick's supporters at Van, a mining community in Boone County. I had not been invited, but I decided to attend anyway. Arriving after the meeting had begun and making my way up to the front row, I introduced myself to Woodrow Hendricks, a lawyer who was acting as master of ceremonies. I told him I was a candidate for Congress and was taking no sides in the governor's race. Hendricks was a little cool toward me, but, finally, when all the other candidates had spoken, he introduced me as a candidate for Congress. "He is a butcher," said Hendricks, "he is a fiddler, and here he is."

His calling me a butcher and a fiddler was not exactly intended to be complimentary, I felt. His manner and tone led me to believe that I need not expect much help from him. I suppose he thought that I would simply stand, wave at the crowd, and sit down. But I did not sit down so easily. I began by saying, "This man has introduced me as a butcher. Shakespeare worked in his father's meat shop [which I later learned was not accurate], so what's wrong with being a butcher? Mr. Hendricks has also introduced me as a fiddler. Thomas Jefferson, one of the greatest presidents and a founder of the Democratic Party, was also a fiddler. So, what's wrong with being a fiddler?" Then I said, "The gentleman who introduced me is a lawyer. If it's the last thing I ever do, I intend to get a law degree, if for no other reason than to show a man like this that a coal miner's son can do what he did." The crowd loved it. They ate it like ice cream!

When Hendricks finally got the floor again, he announced that the next meeting of Hedrick supporters would be at Nellis—a few miles away—the following Saturday night and stated that William Blizzard, president of the United Mine Workers in District 17 (Charleston), would be the speaker. "Y'all come," he urged.

The next Saturday night, I rounded up a banjo picker and a guitar player and headed for Nellis. When we arrived at the schoolhouse rally, Bill Blizzard was already making a stem-winding speech. Blizzard, like George Titler, was a rough-and-tumble labor leader of the old school. A mine-worker chieftain in those days had to be a tough customer, and Bill was no exception.

When I walked into the crowded room and took a chair, Blizzard pointed his finger at me and said, "Now, I want to say to you coal miners, when any of these candidates ask you for your vote, ask them where they stand in the governor's race; if they're not for Dr. Hedrick, don't you vote for them—no matter what the office, all the way from Congress to constable." After Blizzard had finished a long fire-and-brimstone speech, Woodrow Hendricks, who again was the

master of ceremonies, announced that, following the benediction, some refreshments—ice cream, cake, and sodas—would be served out in the hall. "Go and help yourself," he said. Just then, a grizzled coal miner in the back of the room shouted, "We want to hear Byrd!" Hendricks responded, "You can hear Byrd some other time. We're going to have the benediction now."

There was no stopping that. The local preacher pronounced the benediction. As the audience filed out, I sent my two friends to the car for the banjo, fiddle, and guitar. While the people were having refreshments, we tuned up our instruments and played "Old Joe Clark," "Cripple Creek," "Turkey in the Straw," and other favorites. The people began coming back into the room, bringing their cake and ice cream with them. I asked them to move in, take chairs, and not block the doorway. The room was soon filled again, with every person who had been there earlier returning for the music.

I then put my fiddle down and said, "Now this is *my* meeting. I drove seventy-five miles to come here tonight, I am a candidate for Congress, and I think I'm entitled to be heard. Mr. Blizzard has told you to ask every candidate which man he's going to support in the governor's race."

At that moment, Bill Blizzard walked back in, pointed his finger at me, and shouted, "Where do you stand in the governor's race? Are you for Hedrick?" I said, "Just have a seat, Mr. Blizzard. I'll tell you where I stand." I went on to say that I had paid my own filing fee; Dr. Hedrick had not paid it; Bill Blizzard had not paid it. I had paid it. I was on my own. I declared, "There are six of us running for the nomination for Congress. I'd be foolish to take sides publicly for any one of the candidates in the governor's race, because, if I did, I would lose support in my own race. Any good politician knows better than to do that. I don't expect Dr. Hedrick to choose sides in my race; he's running his own race, and I'm running mine!"

Then I addressed the crowd: "I grew up in a coal miner's home; married a coal miner's daughter; ate from a coal miner's table; slept in a coal miner's bed. Are you going to vote against a man like that?"

"No!" the mining crowd roared.

"When the controversial Fire Boss bill came up in the state senate," I continued, "I had an ulcer of the stomach and was in bed at a hospital. It was a bill that you coal miners were very interested in. I didn't have to go up to the senate and vote. I had a perfect excuse, if I had wanted one. I could have shown by a doctor's slip that I was in the hospital. But I didn't take the easy way out. I got a cab, went up to the capitol and voted with you, the coal miners of West Virginia, on that bill. Are you going to turn down a man like that who stands up for you?"

"NO!" came the chorus back.

I told the crowd, "I had a little grocery store at Sophia. The strike came and coal miners couldn't buy food because they couldn't get credit. I didn't have much on the shelves, but I let 'em have what I had. I fed their children. Some of that money I was able to collect; some I won't ever collect. Are you going to turn down a man who stood by the children of coal miners when the miners couldn't get credit anywhere else?"

"NO!" The chorus kept getting louder.

Bill Blizzard, by then, saw that he was licked. So, I concluded, "When I finish talking, I'm sure Mr. Blizzard will have something more to say to you, and when he finishes, I, too, will have something more to say. Stick around."

Well, Bill Blizzard got back up on the stage and struck a conciliatory note: "Bob Byrd, we can't turn against you; your labor record is too good. But we do wish that you would support Dr. Hedrick for governor." When he had finished, I quoted a poem and dedicated

it to Bill Blizzard, and we all went away friends that night. I had won the crowd— lock, stock, and barrel!

If it had not been for my violin, I would not have been given an opportunity to address that meeting. It was the violin that made it possible for me to speak to the crowd that night in 1952 about my candidacy for a seat in Congress. Almost forty years later, it is still the most famous fiddle in West Virginia.

In the course of the 1952 primary campaign, the Ku Klux Klan story broke. I had joined the Klan in the early 1940's when I was in my early twenties. Because I was opposed to communism and so was the Klan, I became a member—a mistake I could never erase and would always regret. Ironically, my interest in running for political office had its genesis in a suggestion to me by a retired Methodist minister who was a Grand Dragon in the Klan from Arlington, Virginia. The minister, who initiated me into the organization, suggested that I should "some day" run for Congress but that I should begin at the "bottom of the ladder: the House of Delegates." That suggestion was the spark that put me to thinking about public office. I got others to join and had signed up 150 new members before I went off to work as a welder in the Baltimore, Maryland, shipyards. Two of these former klansmen went public with the story shortly before the 1952 primary election. I admitted that I had been a member in the early 1940's and also admitted that I had made a mistake. I weathered the storm and won the nomination.

In the race for general election, however, a letter was brought out that I had written to the imperial wizard in Atlanta, whom I did not know personally. In that letter, I had recommended that the Klan be revived in West Virginia. I was very naive. I had written that letter at the request of a man who lived in Beckley, West Virginia, the county seat of

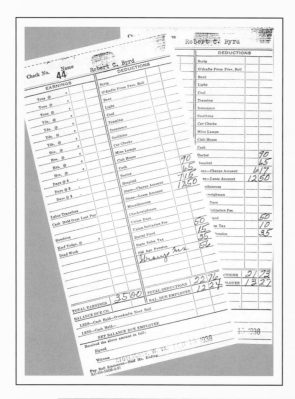

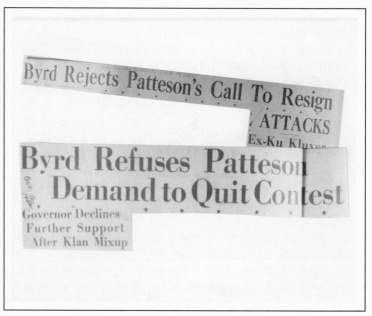

Pay stubs from Robert C. Byrd's days as a coal company store "produce boy" in 1938 show the deductions from his seventy-dollar monthly salary; he served from 1947 to 1952 in the West Virginia legislature at the state capitol in Charleston, West Virginia, *bottom*; newspaper headlines during the 1952 campaign for the House of Representatives reflect Byrd's rift with Governor Okey Patteson. *Office of Senator Robert C. Byrd and Library of Congress*

my county, and who wanted to be a kleagle in the Klan. I foolishly wrote the letter in 1946 and forgot about it. That letter surfaced in the fall campaign after I had indicated in the primary contest that I had been a member back in the early 1940's and had since lost interest. I had forgotten about that 1946 letter. The letter created quite a stir. It was one of several letters that I had written at the time in the belief that the Klan could be an effective force in the struggle against communism and in the promotion of traditional American values.

During the fall campaign, my Republican opponent attacked me about the Klan. As the November election drew near, Democratic Governor Okey Patteson called me to the state capitol on a Saturday night. When I reached his office, he said, "Bob, I've been away on vacation, and I've had to return earlier than I intended because of three problems: I have the miners' strike in Widen, at which there have been some shootings; I have the West Virginia turnpike problem; and I've got your Klan problem. I don't mind telling you, Bob, that your problem is giving me more headache than the other two problems put together." He went on, "I am asking you to get off the ticket. You pull out of this race, serve out your term in the state senate, and then you can run for Congress when this whole thing blows over." "Governor," I said, "if I pull out of the race now, I'm as close to Congress as I'll ever get. The people who are supporting me expect me to run, and I won't get out of the race." He replied, "Well, I can't force you out. There is no law under which I can force you to get off the ticket. But I'll have to withdraw the party's support from you."

I responded, "Well, I understand that. Just don't fight me if you can avoid it. If you have to withdraw your support, fine. You're the titular head of the party in the state, and you're under a lot of pressure. I understand

that. But just don't make it any harder than that on me." "Well, Bob," he said, "I won't do anything to hurt you. As a matter of fact, if I were a voter in your congressional district, I'd vote for you." He was a very nice man, a popular governor.

The next morning, the newspaper headlines read, "Byrd Refuses Patteson Demand to Quit Contest." Phone calls started coming in from people, urging, "Stay in there. Don't get off the ticket." Public interest had been aroused. With the Democratic party apparatus shunning me, I ran my own race. I defeated the Republican candidate, Latelle M. La Follette, by 21,000 votes, receiving 55.6 percent of the ballots cast. I then resigned from the state senate, having served half of the four-year term. I was on my way to Washington!

My race for a seat in Congress had been a difficult and trying one, and its outcome was a testament, as I saw it, to the willingness of the voters to listen to all sides, to weigh the facts, and to forgive. I was happy and grateful for the outcome. My convictions concerning hard work had also been reinforced.

When I became a member of the House of Representatives in January 1953, I had a five-member staff. In those days, there was none of the advanced electronic equipment that we now have. Along with my staff, I operated the mimeograph machine, the robotyper, the typewriters, and other office equipment. We worked long hours.

As one of the new members of the House and a member of the minority party, I was not in a position to receive significant assistance from that body's leadership. During the six years that I served in the House, I did not build much seniority, and I never came to know a wide range of members.

My interests were mainly the parochial ones that impacted on my own congressional district. I worked my district hard and returned to it often. Some of my detractors predicted that I would be only a one-term congressman, and I tried hard to lay that notion to rest, giving my constituents good service, with prompt attention to their problems. As a result, I became strongly entrenched in my congressional district. Coal mining was the backbone of the economy, and, consequently, I was very interested in legislation that affected coal, the miners and their families.

In my first House term in 1953, I was appointed to the House Administration Committee—a housekeeping committee. In 1955, at the start of my second term, I was assigned to the Foreign Affairs Committee and given membership on the Subcommittee on the Far East and the Pacific. The first time I ever traveled overseas was in 1955 as a member of that subcommittee. Its chairman was Clement J. Zablocki of Wisconsin. On the subcommittee trip, in addition to Zablocki and myself, were Marguerite Stitt Church of Illinois, Ross Adair of Indiana, John Jarman of Oklahoma, Richard Wigglesworth of Massachusetts, and Dr. Walter Judd of Minnesota. We traveled around the world in an old Constellation, a four-motored propeller plane that was slow in comparison with today's aircraft. Visiting more than twenty countries in Europe, the Middle East, Southeast Asia, and the Far East, we were gone sixty-six days—from October 11 to December 15, 1955. The trip was quite an education for me in international affairs.

When I was first elected to the House, Harley M. Kilgore and Matthew M. Neely were West Virginia's two U.S. senators. Because Senator Kilgore was from Beckley, the county seat of my home county, I was better acquainted with him than with Senator Neely, who was from the northern part of the state.

Senator Kilgore advised me to enter law school. At that time, I did not possess a college degree, but I had acquired seventy hours of college work before coming to Washington, and I wanted to get a law degree. Although I did not expect to practice law, I wanted the kind of reading and class experience that would go with such a degree. In January 1953, I enrolled in night classes at George Washington University law school. There, I built up more than twenty credit hours before transferring to American University's Washington College of Law, after learning that George Washington University would not give me a law degree because I lacked the prerequisite baccalaureate degree. Having been advised to see Dean John Myers at American University, I asked for an appointment.

Dean Myers told me that American University also required a prerequisite degree. But he said, "I'll tell you what I'll do. You have seventy hours of straight-A college work. If you can complete the required courses in law with no lower than a 'B' average, I will recommend you for an LL.B. degree." That was a challenge, and it gave me a chance to obtain a law degree.

Over a period of ten years, attending law school at night, I managed to finish the required courses with a high "B" average or a low "A." When I graduated *cum laude* in 1963, at the age of forty-five, I had the honor of receiving the certificate of that LL.B. degree from President John F. Kennedy, the commencement speaker.

Having to face reelection every two years when I was in the House significantly delayed my legal studies. During each election year, I concentrated heavily on my congressional district, keeping my political fences mended and serving my constituents. Once elected to a six-year term in the Senate, however, I was able to speed up the pace and finish my law school work—the only time in history that anyone has both begun and completed law school while serving in Congress.

When I ran for the U.S. Senate in 1958, the incumbent senator, Republican W. Chapman Revercomb, was up for reelection. He was suave, urbane, and courtly and had twice served in the Senate. Incumbents were hard to defeat then, as they are today. From the House, I saw the Senate as a broader field of opportunity, and I wanted to serve all of West Virginia, not just one congressional district. I knew I could do more for my state as a senator than as a member of the House.

I had begun to explore the possibilities of running for the Senate, aware that Senator Revercomb would be running for a new term in 1958. In the fall of 1957, after Congress had adjourned, I traveled around the state to measure my strength as a potential candidate for the Senate. One evening, when I was in West Virginia's northern panhandle, I received a telephone call from Washington. The caller was Robert Howe, the United Mine Workers' liaison to the House of Representatives. He asked when I would be back in Washington, and I told him I planned to remain in West Virginia for several weeks. He said he wanted to see me because he had a message to deliver from "the Boss," meaning John L. Lewis, president of the United Mine Workers of America. I told him I would come to Romney, in the eastern part of West Virginia, one evening the following week to speak at a civic club meeting. Howe agreed to drive to Romney, about 115 miles from Washington, to meet with me.

When I met with Robert Howe in Romney, he got right down to business. Howe said that Lewis wanted me to know that he planned to support former Governor William C. Marland for the U.S. Senate in the campaign of 1958 and that Lewis did not want me to run for the Senate but wanted me, instead, to run for reelection to the House. According to Howe, Lewis recognized that I had a good labor record but

believed that the miners' union owed it to Marland to support him in the race for Revercomb's Senate seat.

I replied, "Well, the UMWA paid its debt last year [1956] to Mr. Marland in the election for U.S. Senate. That's the reason Mr. Revercomb is a senator now." In the race to fill the two years remaining in the term of Senator Kilgore, who had died in February 1956, the miners' union had supported Marland against Revercomb that year, but Marland had lost. "You supported him, and he lost," I contended. "Now, we have Mr. Revercomb in the Senate. I should have my chance at it." Well, he was sorry, Howe said, but that was the message from the UMWA president. Lewis would come into West Virginia and campaign for Marland and against me if need be. I told him, "I will be back in touch with you."

That night, after my speech to the civic organization, I made my way southward to Beckley. Along the way, a few miles from Romney, I entered Petersburg, the county seat of Grant County. There, I stopped my car and went to a telephone booth. The snow was up around my ankles, and it was cold in the booth. I called my wife, who was at home in the Washington area, and said, "Well, Erma, I've made my decision." "What decision?" she asked. I said, "To run for the United States Senate." "How did you come to make it?" "Mr. John L. Lewis helped me to make it," I said. "He sent me a message today telling me not to run for the Senate. He is going to come into the state and campaign for Marland for the Senate, so I am going to run."

I then drove on to Raleigh County, arriving in Beckley at about three o'clock in the morning. Later that morning, I was up early, calling some of the political leaders in southern West Virginia.

I first called Judge R.D. Bailey in Pineville, Wyoming County, to say I was running for

Robert C. Byrd is shown with members of his family, *clockwise from upper left*: with his older daughter, Mona, in 1939; with his wife Erma and daughters Mona, *left*, and Marjorie, *right*, in 1958; and playing the fiddle for his grandchildren in the 1970's.

Office of Senator Robert C. Byrd

the Senate. Having represented Raleigh and Wyoming counties in the state senate, I knew Judge Bailey well. He had once been a candidate for governor and was highly respected throughout the state.

I then called Sidney Christie in McDowell County, which, at that time, had the third largest population of any of the state's fifty-five counties. It was a coal-mining population. Because the Christie brothers were the political kingpins in that county, I called Sidney, who was the most politically active of the brothers (and whom, in later years, I would successfully promote for a federal district judgeship), to tell him I was announcing for the United States Senate. Christie's reaction, like Judge Bailey's, was positive. After that, I called other political leaders, and the consensus was, "Go to it. We're with you."

Later that day, I publicly announced that I was running for the United States Senate against Chapman Revercomb and that former Governor Marland would be a candidate against me in the primary. I also announced that John L. Lewis, chief of the United Mine Workers, would support Marland and would come into the state and campaign for him.

As it later developed, Senator Neely died in January 1958, opening up the other Senate seat in the 1958 election. John D. Hoblitzell, Jr., was appointed by Republican Governor Cecil Underwood to fill that vacant seat for several months until the general election that fall. With the opening of Neely's Senate seat, Marland chose not to file against me but, instead, filed to fill the unexpired term of Senator Neely. Jennings Randolph—who had served seven terms as a West Virginia member of the U.S. House of Representatives and who had lost for reelection in 1946, after which he had become an executive with Capital Airlines—also entered the race for Neely's seat. The primary election for Neely's seat thus became a hot contest that

also included a former president of the West Virginia Senate, Arnold M. Vickers. I had two primary opponents: Fleming N. Alderson of Charleston and Jack R. Delligatti of Fairmont.

In the meantime, before the second Senate seat became vacant, the coal miners had become aroused by the news that John L. Lewis would oppose me for the Senate. But when the opportunity opened for a second Senate seat and William Marland decided to enter that race, the tension between Lewis and myself was relieved. I was then contacted again by Bob Howe and by Jim Mark, the UMWA liaison to the Senate, whom I also knew. Both suggested that I pay a visit to Lewis, because no confrontation was now going to take place and Lewis would be supportive of my candidacy. It would be good for me, they thought, if I smoked the peace pipe with the formidable mine workers' chieftain. So, I went to see Lewis.

When I arrived at the UMWA headquarters, Howe and Mark took me to the office of John L. Lewis, who opened the discussion. "Young man," he began, "when you announced you were going to run for the United States Senate, you also announced that former Governor William C. Marland would be a candidate against you; and you took the liberty of announcing that I would support Mr. Marland and would come into West Virginia and campaign for him." Measuring his words, Lewis said, "I want you to know, young man, that I am in the habit of making my own press announcements, and I resented your presuming to make such a public statement involving me." His eyes twinkled; they were icy blue beneath his bushy eyebrows, and they seemed to bore right through me.

I listened respectfully. Then, when he had finished talking, I told my side of the story. I had always admired John L. Lewis, I said. He was a great labor leader. My foster father was a coal miner, and I had married a coal miner's daughter. I could remember when there was no union in the coal fields and how the men had to work from daylight until dark to eke out a meager living. I had seen the union come into being, I said, and knew that Lewis and the union had done much to improve the pay and working conditions of miners.

I further responded to Lewis, "I'm a politician; and when I was considering running for the Senate, you sent Mr. Howe to West Virginia to inform me that you would not support me if I ran for the Senate. You told me to run for the House again, for which you would support me, but that you were going to support Marland in the Senate race, even to the extent of coming to West Virginia and campaigning for him." Continuing, I said, "I resented the message that you sent to me by Mr. Howe, and that made up my mind to run for the Senate. I knew that your opposition to my candidacy would elevate the visibility of my race, and I was running to win, so I decided to play my trump card: announce that Marland was going to run against me, that you would support him, and that you would campaign for him in West Virginia against me. I would have been foolish to sit there and say nothing concerning your opposition to my candidacy." I then concluded, "It gave the kind of visibility to my race that brought support from people who, otherwise, probably wouldn't have even known I was running. So, I played my trump card— early."

Lewis wound up by saying that he was going to back me for the Senate and that I would make a fine senator. That ended the meeting on a happy note. I had a feeling of satisfaction about this meeting, having faced up to John L. Lewis and stood my ground firmly, just as I had done with George Titler a decade earlier. I had also developed a greater respect for Lewis.

On the way back up the hill to my office on the House side, Jim Mark said to me, "Mr. Lewis admires somebody who has the courage to stand up to him. You demonstrated that, and you did it in a nice way. I have a feeling that when I get back to the office, I'm going to hear some good things about you."

Later that afternoon, Jim Mark called me on the phone and said, "Well, it's just as I had thought. You really made a hit with Mr. Lewis. He likes you. That was a great thing you did, coming down and meeting with him. Glad you all got everything smoothed out."

John L. Lewis kept his word. He supported me, and he also supported Marland. But Jennings Randolph won the nomination in the other Senate race, beating Marland and the others handily. Randolph and I, together, became the Democratic nominees for the two U.S. Senate seats, and we both went on to win in the general election in November. John L. Lewis remained a strong supporter of mine in my future campaigns for reelection to the Senate, as did George Titler.

Since 1946, I had been able to win election campaigns with only meager financial resources. In the early years, I had broken into politics by campaigning hard for the house of delegates and by using my violin as an attention-getter. It had been the same when I went on to become a state senator and, later, a member of the U.S. House of Representatives. My trusty fiddle had opened doors for me many times and in many places, and it did so again in the U.S. Senate race.

Jennings Randolph and I ran in 1958 on a combined "war chest" of not more than $50,000. Since we were not opposing each other, we decided to run as a team. The Democratic Senatorial Campaign Committee allotted a few thousand dollars to my campaign and to Randolph's. In those days, campaigning in West Virginia consisted mainly of traveling around the state, speaking at courthouse rallies and family reunions, in union halls and on street corners, as well as appearing before civic organizations. We also used highway billboards; our campaign motto was, "Byrd and Randolph will build West Virginia in the U.S. Senate."

We ran a few radio and newspaper ads but used very little television. Randolph won the election for the two-year term, defeating John Hoblitzell by a margin of 117,657 votes. With a margin of 118,573 votes, I defeated Chapman Revercomb for the full six-year term and became the 1,579th person to serve in the U.S. Senate since its beginning in 1789.

I was elated with this victory, deeply grateful to the voters of West Virginia, and determined—more than ever—to work hard to justify their faith and confidence in me.

CHAPTER 26

Robert C. Byrd's Senate

Rise to Leadership
1959–1977

In January 1959, I moved into what was then known as the Old Senate Office Building—later named the Richard B. Russell Building. My staff in the House was familiar with congressional casework and moved to the Senate with me. I had a very competent administrative assistant, Virginia Yates, and, with the addition of executive secretary Ethel Low, we lost no time in adding to the staff and setting up shop in a larger space.

It was like a new door, opening to wider horizons. When I came to the Senate, there were, of course, many well-known members here. Senator Joseph Clark of Pennsylvania would soon refer to most of them as "the Senate establishment." Such senators as Richard Russell of Georgia, Margaret Chase Smith of Maine, Everett Dirksen of Illinois, J.W. Fulbright of Arkansas, Harry Flood Byrd, Sr., of Virginia, Lister Hill of Alabama, Paul Douglas of Illinois, Strom Thurmond of South Carolina, James Eastland of Mississippi, Estes Kefauver of Tennessee, Sam Ervin of North Carolina, Russell Long of Louisiana, Bob Kerr of Oklahoma, Stuart Syming-

ton of Missouri, Joseph O'Mahoney of Wyoming, and Lyndon Johnson of Texas were familiar figures throughout the country, most of them having been around for a long time.

As a three-term member of the House, I had not become acquainted with members of the Senate. I had met Lyndon Johnson on one occasion while I was still in the House, but only following my election to the Senate. I recall that he was standing in the middle aisle of the Senate chamber when someone introduced me to him and we shook hands. His coat pockets were bulging with papers, and I thought his trousers were a bit too long. I was later to learn a lot more about Johnson—his personality, his legislative tactics and ability, and his leadership style.

My West Virginia colleague, Jennings Randolph, and I visited with Lyndon Johnson in the majority leader's office to make our case for committee assignments. Randolph requested membership on the Committee on Labor and Public Welfare and the Committee on Public Works. I requested an Appropriations seat. That was the only com-

Robert C. Byrd entered the U.S. Senate in 1959.   *Office of Senator Robert C. Byrd*

mittee I really wanted, because I believed it would enable me to do more for West Virginia. Stating that it would be somewhat unusual to place a freshman senator on the Appropriations Committee, Johnson advised me to talk with its chairman, Arizona Senator Carl Hayden, and also with Richard Russell, the senior senator from Georgia, which I did. Senator Randolph ended up getting the two committee assignments he sought, and I got Appropriations.

I became a strong supporter of Lyndon B. Johnson because he had arranged for me to obtain the committee assignment I wanted. It is fair to say that Johnson's influence, as majority leader, was what counted most in Democratic assignments to committees in those days, although he acted in consultation with other so-called establishment senators. I know that he talked such matters over with Senators Russell and Hayden. Once they reached a meeting of the minds, that pretty much decided any in-house matter. At that time, the Senate Democratic Steering Committee, which formally made the committee assignments, was smaller than its modern successor and was dominated by Johnson, Russell, and other southern senators.

Most members' access to the majority leader was somewhat limited. Junior senators did not simply walk in unannounced and have an extended conversation with Lyndon Johnson. As a new member of the Senate, I was very well aware of the importance of seniority here, and I did not attempt to push myself on anyone. I was willing to await my turn.

The senator for whom I developed the greatest respect was Richard Russell. I felt that he was, so to speak, the "father" of the Senate. I served with him from January 1959 until he died on January 21, 1971, and he was the one senator whom I never addressed by his first name or nickname during all those years.

As a newcomer to the Senate, Robert Byrd had particular respect for Senator Richard Russell, *left*.
Office of Senator Robert C. Byrd

Senator Russell was a patrician type, respected for his knowledge of the rules and precedents and for his enduring good judgment. Never going out of his way to develop a friendship or acquaintance, he, nevertheless, was easy to talk with. I would sometimes ask him about the rules or customs of the Senate and would seek his judgment on some of the key issues. Urbane and scholarly, he was not an orator. He was courtly and polite, never overly partisan. Senator Russell was a Christian gentleman.

My second major committee assignment in 1959 was the Banking Committee. I did not particularly want to be on Banking, but I took it as a second committee for the time being.

My third assignment was to the Senate Committee on Rules and Administration, which I requested on the advice of Senator Russell; otherwise, I probably would not have shown much interest in it. After serving on that committee for two years, I became chairman of its subcommittee on the Senate restaurants—not exactly an impressive position. In 1969, I moved to the chairmanship of the subcommittee on rules. Soon thereafter, I recommended that all subcommittees of the Senate Rules Committee be abolished, because I considered them to be unnecessary. My recommendation was followed, and the subcommittee functions were shifted to the full committee.

The Senate Rules Committee lacks the prerogatives and powers of the House Rules Committee, the Senate being a different institution in so many ways. Nonetheless, I considered it an important committee because of its jurisdiction over the Senate rules and regulations, the Senate offices and buildings, and the Senate side of the Capitol. Being on that committee has allowed me to keep an eye on the rules. Its current chairman, Senator Wendell Ford of Kentucky, is one of the most genial and dedicated chairmen under whom I have served, and he does his work thoroughly, competently, and well. His is certainly not the easiest job in the Senate.

In our very first year as senators, Jennings Randolph and I each cast a critical vote, and President Dwight D. Eisenhower suffered the humiliation of a cabinet-level defeat, when the Senate rejected Admiral Lewis Strauss to be his secretary of commerce. Admiral Strauss had previously served as chairman of the Atomic Energy Commission. Never a tactful man, he had alienated many senators, especially Senator Clinton Ander-

son of New Mexico, who launched a campaign to defeat Strauss' nomination.

It is interesting to know what impact irrelevant and extraneous factors may sometimes have on a senator's vote. I was leaning toward supporting Lewis Strauss but had not fully made up my mind when, one morning, I read a newspaper column by the late Drew Pearson stating that John L. Lewis, head of the United Mine Workers of America, was supporting the Strauss nomination and had the votes of both West Virginia senators in his pocket.

As soon as I read this, I made up my mind to vote against Lewis Strauss, although I was sure he had had nothing to do with the content of the column. The columnist had been misinformed. I picked up the telephone, called Senator Randolph, my senior colleague, and told him what I had just read in the newspaper. He had read it, too, and we agreed, then and there, that we would both vote against Strauss.

The United Mine Workers was a potent organization, politically, in West Virginia at that time, and Lewis was a powerful labor leader. Thus, it was no small matter for the two West Virginia senators to take an opposing position. But when I read that Lewis had my vote in his pocket, I decided I could not vote for Strauss, because nobody should be led to believe that I would be the captive of any person or group in the casting of my vote.

A tiny straw, sometimes, on the waves of the political sea of history can bring about a sea change. Strauss was defeated 46 to 49. He would have been confirmed had my West Virginia colleague and I voted for him.

During my early years in the Senate, I devoted most of my attention to committee work and to the needs of my constituents. In 1961, my Senate education gained a great boost when I became chairman of the District of Columbia appropriations subcommittee. I did not have to lobby for that assignment; it just fell into my lap! Rhode Island Senator John Pastore had chaired the subcommittee when I first served on it, but, in 1961, he became chairman of another subcommittee and I succeeded him. The position was not an enviable one or one that I would have wanted, but I have always believed strongly in living up to the scriptural admonition, "Whatsoever thy hand findeth to do, do it with thy might." So, I did it with all my "might." I worked at the job as though it were the best subcommittee in the Senate. Washington did not have home rule at that time, and its government was headed by a trio of appointed commissioners rather than an elected mayor.

I knew every statistic in the District of Columbia appropriation bill, down to the bottom dollar. I had a good memory, and I was able to present the whole budget, from "ankle to forelock," without any notes at all. I had time in those days to master the District of Columbia budget, and master it I did.

I remember the advice I received from Senator John Stennis of Mississippi when I took over that subcommittee. He said, approvingly, "You'll make a big job out of that, young man. That's a small job; but you'll make a big job out of it." And he had occasion to make the same comment to me a few years later when I became the secretary of the Democratic Conference: "That's a job that a lot of people don't think is very significant. But you'll make it an important job, Robert. You'll make it an important job. I've seen'ya do it before." Senator Stennis was someone who would take time out of a busy day to give me a note of encouragement. He was one of my all-time favorite senators—a paradigm of fairness, rectitude, and integrity. He looked upon Senator Russell with the same respect and reverence as I did and was always very deferential to Senator Russell. That told me a lot about both men.

I discovered when I was on the subcommittee that there were many people in the District of Columbia who were drawing welfare checks but who did not qualify. The way I saw it, I did not make the welfare regulations, but I did have the responsibility of chairing the subcommittee and exercising prudence in the appropriation of the taxpayers' money to the District of Columbia. I felt that unqualified welfare recipients were taking money that did not belong to them, dollars that ought to go for other purposes in the District, and that the ineligibles should be removed from the rolls. This was not a popular thing to do. I received a great deal of criticism from some quarters for my efforts to clean up the welfare rolls, the *Washington Post* being a frequent and bitter critic.

At one point, I put into effect a 13-percent increase, across the board, in payments to those on welfare who were truly qualified under the regulations governing eligibility. I also expanded the number of social workers in the welfare department and raised their grade levels, so they could earn higher pay for their work. I increased the funding for schools and recreation facilities, beefed up the police department, and increased the appropriations for health services in the federal city. A majority of Republicans and Democrats in the Senate supported my efforts to reshape the District of Columbia's spending priorities.

I served as chairman of the D.C. appropriations subcommittee for seven years—longer than any other chairman of the subcommittee in this century. Finally, an opportunity came for me to chair another subcommittee, and I took it—gladly. After I moved out of the chairmanship, the welfare caseload, which had been decreasing throughout my tenure, began to rise again.

At the time I became chairman of the District of Columbia appropriations subcommittee in 1961, I also replaced Lyndon Johnson on the Senate Armed Services Committee when he became vice president. I am sure he had put in a good word for me with Senator Russell, who then chaired the committee.

I took an active part in deliberations on the 1963 nuclear test ban treaty with the Soviets. Ultimately, I voted against it, based on what I had learned from the committee's hearings. I was particularly influenced by Dr. Edward Teller's testimony in opposition to the treaty.

Senator Russell was a strong and able chairman of the Armed Services Committee. The members trusted his judgment; the military services respected him; everyone saw him as somebody who was there to do what was best for the country.

Today, the Senate Armed Services Committee is chaired by another able Georgian, Senator Sam Nunn. Elected to the U.S. Senate in 1972 to complete the unexpired term after Senator Russell's death, Senator Nunn has admirably filled his predecessor's shoes.

Having received a law degree in 1963, I decided to seek assignment to the Senate Judiciary Committee. In 1969, I went on that committee, at which time I gave up my seat on the Armed Services Committee.

Incidentally, with regard to my replacing Lyndon Johnson on the Armed Services Committee in 1961, I am reminded of an interesting experience that gave me a close-up insight into his legendary arm-twisting techniques, one which expanded my education as a United States senator. During the Kennedy administration, I had asked President Kennedy to appoint Sidney Christie of McDowell County, West Virginia, to a federal district judgeship. After President Kennedy's assassination, President Johnson called me on the telephone one day, and the following conversation ensued:

"Bob, I'm calling you about your federal judgeship. I want you to send down another name."

"Well, Mr. President, why?"

"Because he's too old."

"He's only sixty-one."

"We don't like to name them when they are beyond age sixty."

"He wasn't beyond age sixty when I sent his name down there."

"Send us another name. He's not qualified."

"Mr. President, he is highly qualified. And I want him."

"How bad do you want him?"

"Well, I want him. I am 100 percent for him."

"Send us another name."

I said, "Mr. President, you may recall that, when you were seeking the party nomination for president, I ran for delegate to the convention as a publicly declared Johnson supporter. I didn't look for any rock to hide under. I was for Lyndon Johnson and said so from the steeple top."

I continued my reference to the 1960 Los Angeles convention, where most of the West Virginia delegates were for John F. Kennedy. At the convention, I had been asked by a news reporter whether, when the roll call got down to West Virginia and if West Virginia's votes would put Kennedy over the top, would I then change my support from Johnson and vote for Kennedy. My answer, I reminded the president, was:

No! I came here to vote for Lyndon B. Johnson. I ran as a Johnson delegate, and I will not climb on any bandwagon for anyone else. It might run over me, but I won't get on it. I came here to vote for Lyndon B. Johnson, and there are only three circumstances which could cause me not to vote for him: one, if Johnson were to take himself out of the running; two, if *he* were to have a heart attack; and three, if *I* were to have a heart attack.

I then said, "Mr. President, I wasn't 85 percent for you. I wasn't 90 percent. I was

100 percent for you. That is the way I feel about Sidney Christie. I am not 80 percent. I am not 90 percent. I am 100 percent."

"Well," the president said, "where do you stand on the [1964] civil rights bill?"

"There are some parts of it I can support," I said, "and some parts of it I can't; therefore, I will be against the bill, because we don't have the votes to get amendments adopted."

President Johnson then suggested, "Why couldn't I send you off on a mission somewhere in the world, and you could be absent when the cloture vote occurs?"

I responded, "Mr. President, one of the reasons I supported you at the convention was because you appointed me to the Senate Appropriations Committee when you were majority leader, and I can go anywhere in the world today as a member of that committee. I will be there when the roll is called," I said, "and I'm not going to vote for cloture."

"Why?" he asked.

"Mr. President, if a man breaks into your house and you don't have anything but a stick of stovewood, you'll use that on him. All we have is the filibuster. We don't have the votes to amend this bill. That's all we've got—that stick of stovewood."

I told him, "I'll vote with Senator Russell when the time comes, even if they have to bring me in on a stretcher."

He said, "You love me as much as you love Dick Russell don't you?"

I said, "Yes, Mr. President, I do; but I can't carry water on both shoulders. I will be there, if I'm living; and I will vote against cloture."

We had been talking, I suppose, for about twenty minutes, when the president concluded by saying, "Well, Bob, I still love you. Christie's name will be sent up there one day next week." Lyndon Johnson was true to his word, and I was true to mine. He sent Christie's nomination to the Senate, and I voted against cloture on the civil rights bill.

A very different aspect of my education as a senator involved intensive study of Senate rules and procedures. When I came to the Senate, I learned about floor procedure gradually and by observing other senators. Of course, parliamentary procedure was not entirely foreign to me, for I had served twelve previous years in three legislative bodies. But the U.S. Senate is different from all other legislative bodies in the world.

I did not take much interest in parliamentary rules and practices, however, until 1967, when I was elected secretary of the Senate Democratic Conference. I had not thought of running for a Senate leadership position until one day in 1966, when I noticed in the newspapers that Senator George Smathers of Florida, who was Democratic Conference secretary, had decided not to run for that post again. I thought I might have a good chance to win because the southerners seemed to like me, and the fact that I had been a staunch opponent of invoking cloture on civil rights legislation pretty much threw the whole southern bloc into my camp.

First, I went to see Senator Russell and then Senator Hayden, Senator Stennis, and Majority Leader Mike Mansfield. Two other senators announced their candidacies for the job: Joe Clark of Pennsylvania and Fred Harris of Oklahoma. With the southern bloc in my camp and the race being a three-way split, I was not at any disadvantage. I also got support from some border-state senators who generally worked well with Richard Russell. The southerners spoke a good word here and there that helped me with senators outside that region, thus enabling me to pick up some westerners. The race was decided not on personalities but, largely perhaps, on ideology. I was viewed as being a conservative; Clark and Harris were seen as liberals. In fact, ideology probably played a greater role in that race than in any subsequent race I was ever in. Senator Harris eventually with-

As secretary of the Democratic Conference, Robert Byrd joined other members of the Senate leadership in meeting with President Lyndon Johnson. Here, Byrd, *left*, Majority Leader Mike Mansfield, *center*, and Democratic Whip Russell Long, *back to camera*, confer with Johnson in October 1967. *Office of Senator Robert C. Byrd*

drew from the race, and I defeated Senator Clark 35 to 28—a majority of 7 votes. One senator was absent from the conference and did not submit a proxy.

About a week after I had won that race, I met George Smathers on the Senate floor. He said, "Well, what are you doing back in your office? You won this job. You're supposed to stay here on the floor." I guess he was kidding me, but his comment had an effect. I said to myself, "I belong here on the floor. If I'm going to do this job right, I ought to be here." So, from that day forward until the day I relinquished the post of majority leader—twenty-two years later—I was there on the Senate floor practically all the time, early and late, day in and day out.

I entered the conference secretary's job without a clear sense of its responsibilities or its limitations. I said to Mike Mansfield, "If there is anything I can do, I want you to know I'm here to help. I'll watch the floor while you're busy at other things. You tell me what you want done. I'll see to it." I did not think that Mansfield particularly liked

floor work, and he seemed glad to have somebody there helping to mind the store. I began to study the book of precedents and the book of rules, and soon I came to know some things about floor work. As a result, I became proficient in the use of the rules.

The job involved more than floor work, I was soon to learn. As a member of the Senate leadership, I joined Majority Leader Mike Mansfield and Majority Whip Russell Long at a White House breakfast with the president on the morning of February 6, 1968. The House Democratic leadership also attended. It was right after the January 1968 Tet offensive in Vietnam, and we had lost a lot of men. After listening to an extended discussion of the subject, I finally spoke up and raised a question as to the quality of the intelligence information we had been given. I said, "It seems to me that we fell short on our intelligence information. We should have known. We should have foreseen what happened."

This comment made Johnson very angry. He really let me have it, and with both barrels. When he finished, I responded, "Mr. President, I didn't come here to be lectured. I thought you wanted my frank opinion." He then came on harder than ever. When he finished, I said again, "Mr. President, I didn't come here to be lectured. I'm no 'yes man.' I have spoken my candid feelings. I thought that's what you expected us to do."

I felt badly about this exchange, and, when I returned to my office, I dictated the following note of apology:

Dear Mr. President:
  I apologize for my closing remark about not being a 'yes man.' It was uncalled for. It was not in good taste, and I regret it. No remark I made was meant to question your own veracity or your own personal judgment. I only meant to convey the sincere feeling and the strong conviction that the information on Vietnam which you have been getting in certain respects and on which you must make your decisions, may not have been sound or may not have been properly evaluated by people upon whom you have to depend.
                    ROBERT C. BYRD, U.S. SENATOR

After dictating the telegram, I decided I would just call the president. What I had prepared in the telegram, I said to him on the phone in a conversational tone. The president listened, and then he replied, "Well, Bob, I owe you an apology. You can understand how much this is bearing on my mind and on my heart. I was uptight and tense. I overreacted."

We had both said we were sorry for the hot words. He was a strong individual, a big man on the inside as well as on the outside. Lyndon Johnson had a soft heart, and he was my friend.

To show how a senator may change his mind overnight, I cite my vote on President Johnson's 1967 nomination of Thurgood Marshall to the United States Supreme Court. Marshall was the first black to be named to the highest court in the land.

I had carefully considered the nomination and concluded, after much thought and sev-

eral discussions with my staff, that I would vote for Marshall's confirmation. Having once been a member of the Ku Klux Klan, for which I had received much criticism, and also having filibustered against the 1964 Civil Rights Act, I felt that I should vote to confirm Marshall. It would be politically smart to do so; and it would go a long way, I thought, toward erasing the bad marks against me by virtue of my Klan background. Therefore, I asked a member of my staff to prepare a Senate floor speech in support of Marshall.

Although I had not opposed Marshall's nomination to the U.S. Court of Appeals for the Second Circuit, I did not like his voting record on the court, considering it far too liberal. Moreover, I believed that his many years of close association with the National Association for the Advancement of Colored People (NAACP), as director-counsel of that organization's legal defense and education fund, would unduly influence his decisions on the Supreme Court. Nonetheless, I decided to vote for him. It was strictly a political decision.

When I went to bed on the night before the vote, however, I thought about the nomination before going to sleep. It suddenly occurred to me that, if Marshall were white, I would vote against his confirmation because of his voting record on the bench. I said to myself, "If he were white, my decision would be an easy one; I would vote against him. Then, why should I vote for him just because he is black?" I decided, therefore, to vote against him. The next morning, I went to the office, rewrote my speech, and voted against the confirmation of Thurgood Marshall.

In 1971, two years after I was assigned to the Senate Judiciary Committee and four years after my vote on Thurgood Marshall, President Richard Nixon indicated that he was considering me for appointment to fill a vacancy on the Supreme Court. He wanted to appoint conservative judges, and the Senate had just rejected two of his nominees: Clement Haynsworth and G. Harrold Carswell. Some of my Senate Republican colleagues suggested that the president appoint me because I was perceived as one who would be a conservative on the Court and could be confirmed by the Senate.

On Friday, October 8, President Nixon invited me to accompany him on his plane to a speaking engagement in Elkins, West Virginia. On the way, he asked me a few questions, such as where I had attended law school. I told him I had attended American University College of Law but had never practiced. He said, "I want you to know I am considering you very strongly for appointment to the Supreme Court. You've got a lot of people boosting you, a lot of senators." He mentioned Senators Robert Griffin of Michigan, Clifford Hansen of Wyoming, and Strom Thurmond—all Republicans—and Democrat Russell Long. He also included Treasury Secretary John Connally as one of my supporters.

The next day's *Washington Daily News* carried the headline, "Robert Byrd, Nixon's Next Court Choice"; and on October 11, the headline in the *Washington Evening Star* read, "Sen. Byrd Viewed as Heading Nixon List for High Court." The *New York Times* of October 11, under the headline "Evidence Grows that Byrd Will Get High Court Seat," ran a subheading stating, "Senator Said to Be Nixon's First Choice, and Easy Confirmation Is Predicted."

I had told the president I was interested. But a couple of days went by, and the more I thought about it, the more I came to doubt that I would really like the job. One night at dinner, I said to my wife Erma, "The more I think about this, the more I'm afraid of it. I think I would just wither away. As a judge, I'd be off in some room, reading all day long,

cloistered and living like a recluse; and I think the atmosphere would just be too stuffy for me. I like the legislative branch, and I just don't believe I'd like to be cooped up all the time. Of course, the salary is better; and a member of the Supreme Court will sometimes affect the course of the country more than will one of a hundred senators. But," I said, "I don't think I'd like it, although it's a lifetime job with no campaigning." My wife asked, "Then why don't you let the president know?"

The next day, I went to see Senator John Pastore. "John," I said, "I'm not sure Mr. Nixon will appoint me, of course; but he is considering me, and I really don't want to be on the Supreme Court, the more I think about it. I've never practiced law, and I might not turn out to be a good Supreme Court justice. I'd work at the job, but I just don't think I would like it."

"Well," he said, "you ought to let the president know. If he were to appoint you, he'd be embarrassed if you turned it down. Why don't you get in touch with him? Don't go down to the White House, because the press will see you going in and they will be all over you."

I then phoned John Connally and said, "I don't know whether or not the president plans to nominate me. Maybe he does; maybe he doesn't. But I don't want him to appoint me. I've thought about it, and I wouldn't be happy."

Connally responded, "Well, I want you to know that I don't agree with what you say; but, if that's the way you want it, I'll let him know." That was the end of it, and I never heard any more about it. Subsequently, in December 1971, the president nominated Lewis Powell and William Rehnquist to the two existing vacancies, and they were both confirmed.

I served as secretary of the Democratic Conference for four years, from 1967 to

1971. In 1969, Senator Edward Kennedy of Massachusetts defeated Senator Russell Long for the job of Democratic whip. During the next two years, I gave much consideration to making a run for the whip's post. My four years of floor work as conference secretary gave me the experience I needed for the job, and my daily contacts with Democratic colleagues during those four years had put me in a good position to make the challenge.

I had been assured of Senator Richard Russell's proxy, which was delivered to the Democratic Conference on the morning of January 21, 1971, when the Senate leadership was to be chosen for the Ninety-second Congress. For several days, there was concern that Senator Russell, who was gravely ill, might not live. Anticipating that he would not be able to attend the conference, I had worked with Senator Russell's colleague from Georgia, Senator Herman Talmadge, to obtain the proxy.

I was not absolutely certain of having a majority of the votes for the whip's post, but I left my house in nearby Arlington early that morning and heard the news on the radio that Senator Russell had made it through the night. I drove to my office and made a few calls by way of last-minute efforts.

When I left my home that morning, I told my wife Erma that I was not sure I would run. Even when I left my office in the Senate office building to go to the 10:00 a.m. conference in the Capitol, I was still not sure. But by the time I reached the elevator at the end of the long corridor from my office, I had made up my mind to run. The deciding factor leading to my decision was this thought: "Here is a man at Walter Reed Hospital on his death bed. He has the confidence and faith in me to openly announce to the world, by written proxy, that he is for Robert C. Byrd and, in his failing handwrit-

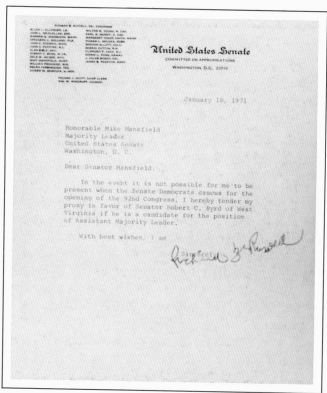

The support of ailing Senator Richard Russell influenced Robert Byrd's decision to run for the post of Democratic whip in 1971. *Office of Senator Robert C. Byrd*

ing, has signed a proxy vote for me. To merit that kind of faith, therefore, I ought to have the courage to run. Win, lose or draw, I owe it to Senator Russell to run."

I went into the party conference and had short conversations with several senators, nailing down the vote of one last senator before the meeting began. I had a prearranged understanding with Senator Randolph, my senior West Virginia colleague, that, if I decided to run, I would give him an indication—by way of a nod—and he would rise and put my name in nomination. Otherwise, he would not do so. I gave him the nod, and he nominated me for the whip's post.

The vote was 31 to 24—again, coincidentally, I had won by a margin of 7 votes, the same as in my election four years earlier to the office of conference secretary. In later years, Senator Kennedy became one of my best, most loyal supporters. He has long been my friend, and he is today one of the Democratic senators I most admire for his courage, ability, and dedication. Much of the significant social legislation enacted in the One-hundredth Congress came from the Senate Committee on Labor and Human Resources, of which he is chairman, and bears his imprint. His tenacity and consistency in championing the interests of the working people, the poor, the disadvantaged, and his support for legislation beneficial to the education and health of all Americans are acknowledged universally. Senator Edward M. Kennedy would have been one of the outstanding senators in any era of the Senate's two-hundred-year history.

I had been on the Senate Judiciary Committee for four years when, in the latter part of February 1973, President Nixon indicated his intention to nominate the acting director of the Federal Bureau of Investigation, L. Patrick Gray, to be the permanent successor to the late J. Edgar Hoover, who had headed the FBI since its inception. I immediately expressed opposition to the nomination, believing that Gray's appointment was unwise and would be bad for the FBI. More than just intuition, my objections to Gray were based on previous newspaper and magazine articles charging that under Gray the FBI had: (1) directed twenty-one FBI offices in fourteen states to gather information against Democrats that might help President Nixon to win reelection; (2) dragged its heels in investigating the bugging of Democratic headquarters at the Watergate building in Washington; and (3) made little or no attempt to investigate sabotage and espionage activities against the Democrats.

Moreover, I remembered that federal Judge John J. Sirica, after sitting through the Watergate trial in which two defendants were convicted and five pleaded guilty to conspiracy charges, had publicly criticized the Justice Department's investigation of the matter. Since the FBI is the Justice Department's investigating arm, I sensed that Gray's performance as acting director of the FBI was due for a public examination. I charged Gray with "political partisanship" in his conduct as acting director; cited political speeches he had made while in that job; and stated that the FBI, with its "vast intelligence network" and "thousands of computerized dossiers," should not be under the control of "a politicized director." I further accused Gray of having waged only a limited investigation of the Watergate affair.

On Thursday, March 22, under my intensive grilling, Gray admitted that John W. Dean III, President Nixon's top legal counsel, had probably lied to the FBI during its investigation of the Watergate case.

"He [Dean] lied to the agent, didn't he?" I asked.

"Looking back, I would have to conclude that your judgment is probably correct," replied Gray.

This was a startling revelation. At the White House's request, Gray had subserviently shipped the FBI's Watergate files to presidential counsel John Dean, even after he knew that Dean might have had too close a relationship with some of the accused men in the Watergate case, and even after Dean, by Gray's own testimony, appeared to have misled the FBI agent.

Gray's chances had been damaged beyond repair. On April 5, 1973, President Nixon announced that he was withdrawing the nomination of L. Patrick Gray to be director of the FBI, at Gray's request. The nomination, which was at first regarded almost universally as a "shoo-in," had fallen. My hunch—that Judge Sirica had touched a raw nerve with his criticism of the Justice Department's handling of the Watergate investigation—had proved correct. Another skein in the tangled Watergate web had unraveled.

In 1976, I briefly stepped into the national political arena when, on January 9, I announced my candidacy for the Democratic presidential nomination and thus became the eleventh announced candidate. I also declared my intention to file for reelection that year to a fourth term in the Senate. Stating that I would run in West Virginia's presidential preference primary in May, I said I would not rule out the possibility of entering other state primaries, although I did not consider it "a necessity" to do so. As I viewed the national political situation at the time, I believed there was a strong likelihood that the Democrats would end up picking a candidate at a brokered convention and, in that event, I stood a chance perhaps of becoming the choice for the first or second spot on the national ticket. In the words of the *New York Times* of January 10, "His [Byrd's] aim appeared to be to try to hold West Virginia's 33 delegates, plus any others he might pick up, for brokerage purposes at the nominating convention in New York City in July."

Because my whip duties in the Senate kept me busy during daily sessions, I limited my presidential campaign interests mostly to West Virginia, making appearances in other states only on weekends or holidays. Although I received sufficient contributions from the required number of states around the country to qualify for federal campaign funds, I declined to accept the federal funds. I knew that to make an all-out effort for the nomination would require giving it my full-time attention seven days a week. To do this, I would have to slack my whip responsibilities, thus jeopardizing a virtually sure shot for Senate majority leader the following January, while having only a long-shot chance of winning the national prize. With Arizona Congressman Morris K. Udall, California Governor Edmund G. Brown, Jr., and Idaho's U.S. Senator Frank Church all in the race, and with Georgia Governor Jimmy Carter

Senator Byrd became a candidate for the Democratic presidential nomination in 1976.
Jim Dent/The Charleston Gazette, January 9, 1976

and Alabama Governor George Wallace also picking up delegates across the nation, particularly in the South where I might otherwise have developed a base, I saw myself only as a potential darkhorse in a deadlocked convention.

Running on the campaign theme, "Restore America's Greatness," I defeated George Wallace in West Virginia, 89 percent to 11 percent, and won the support of thirty-one of the state's thirty-three delegates. I later released all my delegates when it became clear that Carter—who chose not to enter the West Virginia primary, the only state primary he skipped—had the nomination sewed up. Meanwhile, I was unopposed for reelection to the U.S. Senate.

During the 1976 presidential race, Robert Byrd defeated George Wallace in the West Virginia primary.

Jim Dent/The Charleston Gazette, November 3, 1975

Prior to the convening of the Ninety-fifth Congress in January 1977, the race for Senate majority leader had been gathering steam for several months. Majority Leader Mike Mansfield had informed me, before making a public announcement, that he did not plan to seek reelection in 1976, which gave me a head start in locking up commitments for the post. Other contenders for the job were Hubert Humphrey of Minnesota, Edmund Muskie of Maine, and Ernest "Fritz" Hollings of South Carolina. Both Muskie and Hollings subsequently withdrew from the race, thus limiting the field to Humphrey and me. Humphrey, a former vice president, was popular and extremely able. Even though he had recently undergone a very serious operation for bladder cancer, he insisted on making it a race to the finish. He conducted a vigorous and spirited campaign, but, well in advance, I had stacked up more than enough commitments to win.

The race was an attention-getter almost down to the wire, and there was considerable guessing about the eventual outcome. Much of the speculation was wide of the mark,

In January 1977, Senate Democrats elected Robert C. Byrd as majority leader.

Jim Dent/The Charleston Gazette, December 1, 1976

with newspapers quoting an unidentified "top aide" as saying, "One of the most important aspects—maybe the most important—is that it is a secret ballot. In a very private way, senators with public commitments to Byrd have let it be known that they are going to vote for Humphrey." What the so-called top aide failed to reckon was that senators who make their commitments publicly are virtually sure to live up to such commitments, even on a secret ballot. Moreover, my own personal knowledge of senators was such that I could distinguish a *real* commit-

ment from words that might *appear* to be a commitment. I never counted "soft" commitments or "undecideds" as being *my* votes; I always figured they would vote for my opponent on a secret ballot. If I erred, I intended to err on the conservative side, preferring to end up with a few extra votes rather than fall a few short.

On the evening prior to the day of the Democratic Conference vote, Senator Humphrey called to say he would withdraw from the race if I were willing to relinquish the chairmanship of the Democratic Conference to him. Others had made the same suggestion to me on his behalf. It was difficult for me to say no to Hubert, but I did. I knew I had the votes to win, and by an impressive margin, even if Humphrey stayed in the race. I also knew that the conference chairmanship would be vitally important to me once I became majority leader.

The next morning, prior to the conference vote on the leadership, Senator Humphrey called me to say he was withdrawing. He told reporters, "I felt I did not have sufficient votes, and it was in the interest of the Democratic majority to come out of this caucus united." Hubert Humphrey moved that my election as majority leader be by acclamation. From the Republican side came the news that Tennessee's Howard Baker had been chosen over Michigan Senator Robert Griffin to lead the minority.

Of Senator Humphrey, I spoke with admiration, saying that the Minnesotan did not need any titles to be a national leader, "He is a national leader, he has been a national leader, and he will always be a national leader." I then appointed a three-member ad hoc committee, headed by Connecticut Senator Abraham Ribicoff, to report to the Democratic Conference with recommendations for institutionalizing the role of former presidents or vice presidents who become senators. The conference, on the following day, accepted the committee's recommendations that such a person—Senator Humphrey in this instance—be given a salary equal to that of the majority leader, as well as a chauffeured car, additional staff, an office in the Capitol, and the title: deputy president pro tempore of the Senate. Hubert was pleased, "It gives me a chance to serve on the leadership team that meets with the President and his Cabinet—and sit in on the development of policy and its implementation." Then he added, "That's why I wanted to be majority leader."

The vote for majority leader occurred on January 4, 1977. Senator Hubert Humphrey died a year later, on January 13, 1978.

CHAPTER 27

Robert C. Byrd's Senate

The Democratic Leader and Foreign Policy
1977–1989*

Mr. President, although the framers of our Constitution did not foresee the post of majority leader, the office has evolved during this century into one of preeminence within the United States Senate. Indeed, it has become one of the most significant positions within the entire United States government. Few institutional "powers" come with the job, other than the power of first recognition: the presiding officer recognizes the majority leader before other senators. In addition, the majority leader has the authority to schedule action on legislation and other matters. Consequently, the position of majority leader is largely what each occupant is able to make of it through diligence, knowledge of the rules, and good working relations with other senators. The majority leader must also establish a relationship with the president of the United States, regardless of his party. And, given the Senate's unique role in American foreign policy, Senate majority leaders have increasingly sought to develop contacts with key world leaders.

It is this foreign policy component of the role that I shall address here, based on my own years as Senate Democratic leader. In so doing, I emphasize that it is critically important for a Senate leader to develop a broad perspective on world affairs and to become acquainted with international officials in order to deal more knowledgeably with the host of diplomatic and military issues that reach the Senate.

Between 1977 and 1989, it was my privilege to meet and talk with Great Britain's Margaret Thatcher, German Chancellor Helmut Kohl, Egyptian President Anwar Sadat, Soviet leaders Leonid Brezhnev and Mikhail Gorbachev, Israel's Prime Ministers Menachem Begin and Yitzhak Shamir, French President François Mitterrand, Chinese Premier Hua Guofeng, and many other world leaders. My discussions with such leaders were an essential part of my efforts as Senate Democratic leader to develop an independent viewpoint on foreign and defense matters through both the Carter and Reagan administrations.

As Senate majority leader, I believed it essential to assert and uphold the Senate's proper constitutional role in foreign affairs. While I worked closely with President Jimmy Carter, I often maintained an inde-

* Prepared December 1989

pendent position and did not automatically support the policies of his administration, even though it was Democratic. Similarly, I supported President Ronald Reagan's administration on some issues and strongly opposed it on others.

During 1977, which was both my first year as majority leader and the first year of the Carter administration, my actions on two issues helped to establish the pattern of independence that I sought. The first occurred on June 16, 1977, when the administration's plan for a phased withdrawal of United States troops from South Korea faced a Republican-sponsored amendment to the State Department authorization bill. This amendment, which seemed likely to pass, would have barred the administration from acting and would have been seen as a sharp rebuke to the new president on one of the first foreign policy issues considered by Congress during his administration. To avoid such a serious setback, I negotiated a compromise between the White House position and those who wanted to flatly prohibit any U.S. withdrawal. My suggested language said that "United States policy toward Korea should continue to be arrived at by joint decision of the President and Congress" and that "any implementation of the foregoing policy should be done in regular consultation with the Congress." Acceptance of the amendment spared the administration an embarrassing defeat, and it also established the theme for all my other dealings with Democratic and Republican administrations. I have consistently advocated the constitutionally sound notion that foreign policy is the joint responsibility of Congress and the president, and that arbitrary, controversial, or secretive unilateral presidential actions do not produce a sound, sustainable foreign policy.

Later in 1977, I played an entirely different role in regard to the proposed sale of the Airborne Warning and Control System

(AWACS) to Iran. On July 22, 1977, I hand-delivered to President Carter a letter asking him to withdraw notification of the proposed sale of the AWACS. My actions were, in part, governed by the Senate schedule. Congress was moving toward a statutory recess, due to begin on August 5. The Senate was then tied up with a Republican filibuster against a bill for public financing of congressional elections. Under the Arms Export Control Act, Congress had only thirty days to act on the sale. In my letter to President Carter, I said, "In view of the limited time remaining, and the schedule facing the Senate, it will be impossible for the Senate to give the proposal the careful and serious consideration it deserves." But I also expressed serious reservations about the sale. I was troubled over the potential security risk involved, warning that we would be taking "an unnecessary risk of compromising the highly sophisticated technology which is critical to our own national defense." In addition, I argued that the sale ran contrary to our interest in a stable military balance and limited arms proliferation in the Middle East.

Administration officials worked hard to persuade me to back down, but I insisted that Congress deserved time to consider the sale thoughtfully. When the president would not agree to my request for a delay, I enlisted the support of the Republican minority leader, Howard Baker of Tennessee. We personally appeared before the Foreign Relations Committee to urge a disapproval resolution. We asserted that this was an institutional issue and that such a disapproval resolution was the only way to ensure that the Senate had sufficient time to weigh the sale on its merits. Senator Baker, who in fact favored the sale, agreed with me on the institutional principles involved.

Although the White House recognized the probability of a Senate defeat, it believed that the sale would be approved by the

House. (Both houses had to vote disapproval resolutions in order to kill the plan.) But the House Foreign Affairs Committee surprised the administration by voting to disapprove the transaction. At that point, the administration notified me that it had decided to temporarily withdraw the sale. President Carter also agreed to make some modifications in the AWACS package to reduce potential security risks and to meet the Senate's other concerns. Having received these assurances, Congress allowed the proposed sale to go through as modified when it returned in September from its summer recess.

In a Senate speech on October 7, 1977, I again expressed my reservations about "the immense quantity of sophisticated military equipment" we were selling to Iran. Pointing to some $18 billion in arms sales to Iran over the previous five years, I called for a moratorium on such transactions and suggested that Congress consider requiring explicit legislative approval, rather than resolutions of disapproval, for sales valued at more than $200 million to any one nation. Considering that the shah of Iran lost power only two years later, and that his vast stockpiles of U.S.-provided military equipment were taken over by a regime overtly hostile to our country, I believe that my concerns were amply justified. Although the AWACS sale was the last major sale to Iran that was approved before the shah was deposed, the planes had fortunately not been delivered before the Iranian revolution. Yet, the fact that those sophisticated aircraft came so close to falling into the hands of an unfriendly government surely demonstrated the dangers that I had been pointing out.

The major foreign policy issue facing the Senate in 1977 and 1978 was the debate over the Panama Canal treaties, which represented my trial by fire as the new majority leader. Signed by President Carter and Panamanian leader General Omar Torrijos on September 7, 1977, the two treaties—the Panama Canal Treaty and the Neutrality Treaty—were designed to replace the original 1903 Panama Canal Treaty, which had been slightly modified in 1936 and 1955. Discussions of a new agreement had been underway in Democratic and Republican administrations for thirteen years, during which time I had expressed opposition to any new treaty. There had been considerable tension between the U.S. and Panama over the canal, and, after careful study of the treaties and the history and negotiations leading up to their signing, I decided to support them if certain conditions and changes were incorporated in the resolution of ratification. The Carter administration hoped that the Senate would approve the new treaties before its fall adjournment, but, as majority leader, I thought it unrealistic and unwise to talk of Senate action on the treaties that year. Hearings would consume much time, and the Senate already had a full schedule of other pressing issues. I believed that all senators needed ample time to study the treaties carefully. When I explained these points to President Carter, he agreed to leave the matter of timing strictly to me.

At that time, sentiment throughout the country ran overwhelmingly against the Panama Canal treaties. I knew that a strong groundwork would have to be laid if the Senate was to give its approval to the ratification. Along with other senators, I voiced my own concern about ambiguities in the treaties. On October 11, 1977, Minority Leader Baker, six other senators, and I met with President Carter, Secretary of State Cyrus Vance, and National Security Adviser Zbigniew Brzezinski. We were especially concerned about two points: the United States' right to protect the neutrality of the canal; and the right of U.S. ships to "go to the head of the line" in the event of an emergency. We warned the president that, without some clarification, the treaties' chances of approval were remote. As a result of that session, President Carter met with General Torrijos and agreed to a Statement of Understanding which clarified the interpretations concerning these two points.

After the Senate adjourned, I organized a delegation of seven Democratic senators to visit Panama from November 9 through 12, 1977. The others in the delegation were Senators Paul Sarbanes of Maryland, Donald Riegle of Michigan, Howard Metzenbaum of Ohio, Walter Huddleston of Kentucky, Spark Matsunaga of Hawaii, and Jim Sasser of Tennessee. I noted that the Senate's constitutional responsibility to provide advice and consent in the making of treaties imposed upon senators the obligation to become as knowledgeable as possible about the treaties and related issues. Our delegation went to Panama, as I said then, "to listen and learn; to discuss the issues directly with Panama's highest government officials; to hear all interested parties, including Americans and Panamanians, opposed to and in support of the treaties; and to see for ourselves the Canal and related facilities." At a dinner party given by American Ambassador William J. Jorden, I explained to the Panamanian guests that "any senator voting for these treaties will pay a high political price. He will gain absolutely nothing personally by doing so. Therefore, you have to be tolerant and patient in bringing people around to understanding these problems and to taking this difficult decision."

The Panama trip set a standard which would characterize my future travels abroad: substantive discussions with high-level leaders, following intense advance preparation. The members of the press who went along were unanimous in saying that it was not a fun trip or a junket; it was a working trip. We set our own schedule, rather than have the State Department arrange it for us. We

went to see what we wanted to see and to hear what we wanted to hear from all sectors of the Panamanian population—both Americans and Panamanians—who were for or against the treaties, or undecided.

The centerpiece of the trip was a series of discussions with General Torrijos and a day spent with the Panamanian leader visiting different parts of the country. The talks with General Torrijos were frank and wide ranging. The senators expressed concerns about various aspects of the treaties, and Torrijos engaged in an animated exchange with the delegation as we stopped at several locales and talked aboard the aircraft between stops. Responding to a flurry of questions from the delegation, General Torrijos said that he felt "like a baseball catcher catching pitches from seven different pitchers."

From the beginning, I was personally impressed with Torrijos and his sincerity. He had an easygoing manner and was amiable, yet tough and self-confident. Our whole delegation took a liking to General Torrijos, and I sensed that he reciprocated the feeling.

At the last stop prior to returning to Panama City, we visited Farallon, the general's seaside residence. Walking through the massive crowd that had us packed in like sardines, we noticed that General Torrijos walked freely among the people, with his pistol on his hip. Yet, he showed no anxiety or concern. To us, it was an indication of his strength and popularity with Panamanians. That was a factor of no little significance in our deliberations over the treaties. At dinner that night, General Torrijos reaffirmed the Statement of Understanding, although he emphasized that the U.S. right of intervention should not imply the right to intervene in Panama's internal affairs. But, he said, there was no doubt about the United States' right to defend the canal.

The delegation also took a helicopter flight over the canal and engaged in lengthy dis-

General Omar Torrijos, shown here on his arrival at a provincial town, accompanied U.S. senators on a tour of his country in 1977.

W.J. Jorden, Panama Odyssey/photo by Rogelio Achurra

cussions with Lieutenant General Dennis McAuliffe, commander in chief of the U.S. Southern Command. When the delegation asked him about General Torrijos' comment that he (Torrijos) was sitting on a powder keg, General McAuliffe replied that it was, indeed, a highly emotional situation. If the treaty were not approved, there would probably be outrage and increased anti-United States demonstrations among the Panamanians. Once such demonstrations started, radical elements would attempt to take advantage of the situation. They would say, "If we can't have the canal, you can't either."

On the final night of that memorable Panamanian trip, our delegation was given a reception and dinner at the *Presidencia* by Panama's President Demetrio Lakas. In his book *Panama Odyssey*, Ambassador Jorden described how he had told the president that my favorite hobby was playing the fiddle. Wrote Jorden:

During the meal, Lakas and Byrd got along famously and, after the toasts had been exchanged, the president pressed his visitor to honor the others with a tune. Byrd finally relented and a violin was commandeered from the orchestra. The West Virginia statesman played "Turkey in the Straw" and the prolonged applause led to several encores. People were tapping their feet and drumming on the table. The Panamanian *presidencia* had never seen anything quite like it. When Byrd finally returned the violin to its owner, Lakas took off his necktie and handed it to the majority leader as a gesture of thanks, and of friendship. Byrd reciprocated.*

The intense interest of the senators in the Panama situation was evidenced all along the way by their incisive questions. The members of the delegation were highly dedicated and conscientious in their approach to the solemn duty of approving or disapproving the ratification of the treaties. In considerable measure, the outcome of the long debate was assured because these senators went to Panama. They were trusted, knowledgeable members, who spoke with authority when they engaged in the Senate debate on the treaties.

On January 26, 1978, I appeared as the final witness before the Senate Foreign Relations Committee, at the conclusion of its lengthy series of hearings on the treaty. I had previously announced that it would be necessary to guarantee at least two important points in order to gain public support for, and Senate approval of, the treaties: (1) the right of the United States to guarantee neutral access to the canal at all times beyond the year 2000; and (2) head-of-the-line passage for U.S. military and auxiliary vessels. I reiterated that position before the committee and ended my statement with these comments:

The Panama Canal, as David McCullough has written, is an expression of that old and noble desire to bridge the divide, to bring people together. Certainly, the canal has done this in many respects. Now, however, the time has come to bridge the divide between

---

* William J. Jorden, *Panama Odyssey* (Austin, TX, 1984), p. 486.

Panama and the United States, and for the two nations to work together in seeing that the canal continues to serve the people of the United States and Panama and the world.

As time for the Senate debate drew near, I conceived a plan, in conjunction with other key senators, that I hoped would be instrumental in securing the treaties' approval. An important element of this strategy was to obtain agreement from the Foreign Relations Committee that it would not take any formal action on proposed changes in the treaties. Normally, the committee would have reported the treaties with whatever amendments or reservations its members thought appropriate. In their book *Invitation to Struggle*, Cecil Crabb, Jr., and Pat Holt noted that the focus on the treaty had been through the office of the majority leader rather than through the committee, adding, "Byrd was more assertive of his prerogatives as majority leader than had been any of his recent predecessors, with the exception of Senator Lyndon B. Johnson." Only a few amendments could be approved without endangering the treaty ratification, and I believed that the greatest support for the treaty could be gained by giving all senators the opportunity to cosponsor a few beneficial floor amendments that would draw widespread approval from the Senate.

The two amendments that Senator Baker and I favored, and which were left open for broad cosponsorship on the Senate floor, were known as the "leadership amendments." Discussions between Senator Baker and myself led to the recommendations that the principles of the Statement of Understanding be the basis for amending Articles IV and VI of the Neutrality Treaty. Those amendments attracted a total of seventy-eight cosponsors. Senator Baker and I also agreed that, contrary to the general assumption, the Senate should consider the Neutral-

ity Treaty first, ahead of the Panama Canal Treaty. I believed that reversing the order would be vital, given the significance of the "leadership amendments" and the fact that these amendments applied to the Neutrality Treaty.

On February 8, the Senate began its formal consideration of the treaties, which continued through April 18, to the virtual exclusion of all other business. This was the longest Senate treaty debate since the Treaty of Versailles in 1919. I had, at one point, entertained the hope that the floor debates could be broadcast to the country by live telecasts, and Minority Leader Howard Baker shared this desire as a way of enlightening the public and enlisting support for the treaties. Technical problems appeared to be too great at the time, however, and on January 28, I announced that live radio broadcasts of the debates would be carried daily by National Public Radio through 210 stations. This audio transmission of gavel-to-gavel Senate floor debate would be unprecedented, but both Baker and I thought it necessary in order to combat the vast amount of misinformation that was being spread throughout the country by opponents of the treaties.

Opponents centered their efforts on winning approval of "killer amendments." I made it clear, however, that only the leadership amendments and certain clarifying reservations and understandings would be acceptable. Opponents attempted to circumvent this strategy by offering amendments that were phrased in such a way that senators would find them difficult to turn down. At first glance, many of these amendments seemed innocuous and "pro-American." Had they succeeded, however, they would have effectively killed the treaty.

In all, 145 amendments, 26 reservations, 18 understandings, and 3 declarations—for a total of 192 changes—were proposed; 88 of these were voted upon. In the final analysis,

In 1977 and 1978, the Senate insisted on thoroughly debating the Panama Canal treaties before approving their ratification.   *Charles Erkman/Charleston Daily Mail, October 17, 1977*

nothing passed that was not acceptable to the joint leadership. I adopted the strategy in most cases of moving to have the amendments tabled, rather than forcing senators to cast up-or-down votes on the proposals. This kept treaty proponents from having to vote against what appeared on the surface to be very desirable amendments.

On March 16, 1978, the Senate agreed to vote on the Neutrality Treaty, and, after approving the leadership amendments, gave its consent to ratification by a vote of 68 to 32. My vote was the sixty-seventh in favor of the treaty. But just hours before the treaty vote, the Senate took an action that threatened to jeopardize the carefully structured strategy for approval of the two treaties. Senator Dennis DeConcini of Arizona of-

fered a reservation, which was "okayed" by the White House, to provide that the U.S. or Panama could independently take steps "including the use of military force in Panama" to reopen the canal or restore the canal to operation. I was informed that President Carter, thinking that the outcome might depend upon Senator DeConcini's vote, had reluctantly agreed not to oppose his reservation. As word circulated that the White House had approved the reservation, senators assumed that the administration had considered the ramifications. The reservation was therefore approved by a 75 to 23 vote, and a few hours later the first treaty was approved.

The Panamanians found the DeConcini reservation totally unacceptable, considering it to be inconsistent with the spirit of the treaties. Angry statements from Panama seemed to threaten the whole package. Panama might well reject the treaties if the DeConcini reservation stood; but if it were modified enough to cause the defection of Senator DeConcini and others, the treaties might well be defeated. In collaboration with Assistant Secretary of State Warren Christopher and former Assistant Secretary of State William D. Rodgers, Senators Frank Church of Idaho, Paul Sarbanes, and I sought to find a compromise that would satisfy both Washington and Panama.

A marathon series of meetings ensued to prepare an alternative proposal. Finally, at a Sunday morning meeting in the Capitol, we drafted a new "leadership reservation." The Panamanian ambassador, Gabriel Lewis, was also present at that meeting, and, by the next morning, word came that his government approved the new language. The reservation provided that the United States would take unilateral action "only for the purpose of assuring that the canal shall remain open, neutral, secure, and accessible, and shall not have as its purpose or to be interpreted as a right of intervention in the internal affairs of the Republic of Panama or interference with its political independence or sovereign integrity." With Senator DeConcini as a cosponsor, the leadership reservation was then approved 73 to 27.

At 6 p.m. on the evening of April 18, 1978, the roll was called on the Panama Canal Treaty. It was approved by precisely the same vote as the Neutrality Treaty had been a month earlier—68 to 32. I was proud to have played a role as majority leader in bringing about this courageous vote to approve the treaty. As I had said during the debate:

Nothing can be politically right if it is morally wrong. In my judgment, it is not only economically right, not only commercially right, not only right from the standpoint of the security interests of our country, not only politically right, but it is morally right that we vote to ratify these treaties, and thus live up to the principles that we have so long espoused among nations.

The overall strategy, combined with the bipartisan leadership effort, the audio broadcasts to the nation, and hard work, had overcome the strong nationwide hostility toward the treaties, and they proceeded to their ratification.

Within only a few weeks after the approval of the Panama Canal treaties, the Senate was locked in another foreign policy dispute over the proposed sale of arms to three Middle Eastern nations. This time, the sale involved $4.8 billion worth of jet aircraft to Egypt, Israel, and Saudi Arabia. But the principal fight was over the Saudi component of the package, which some saw as a threat to Israeli security. With signs of opposition mounting in the Senate, the Carter administration pledged that the Saudi F-15's would be based outside striking distance of Israel and would not be equipped with bomb racks or air-to-air missiles that would give them offensive power. Nevertheless, the Foreign Relations Committee sent a resolution of disapproval to the Senate floor. After the administration agreed not to outfit the planes with offensive equipment, I concluded that the sale was "consistent with our national interests and with our efforts to help bring about peace in the Middle East." After ten hours of debate, and after a rare closed-door session of the Senate to discuss classified matters related to the sale, the Senate rejected the disapproval resolution, 44 to 54, and allowed the sale to go through.

In 1978, as majority leader and special emissary of President Carter, I visited several NATO nations in Western Europe. During that trip, I met with the heads of government in Spain, Belgium, West Germany, and the United Kingdom to exchange views on international issues, particularly concerning NATO modernization. I found these discussions most valuable when the Senate later debated such matters as western security and arms control.

Stopping first in Spain, I met with Prime Minister Adolfo Suarez to discuss Spain's future relationship with NATO. I expressed strong support for the steps that Spain had taken to establish a visible and vigorous democracy after the death of General Francisco Franco in 1975. The Spanish leaders made clear that, although their primary interests at the moment were domestic, related to strengthening their new government, they placed great importance on continued close relations with the United States. We discussed the 1976 Treaty of Friendship and Cooperation between our two nations, and I informed the Spanish officials that the United States would welcome the entry of Spain into NATO but would never presume to tell the Spanish people what to do.

Three principal themes dominated the discussions during the remainder of that European trip. First was the European attitude toward long-term defense programs of NATO. Second was the need for early and decisive action on U.S. energy policy—a matter of particular concern to West German Chancellor Helmut Schmidt and British Prime Minister James Callaghan. Third was the embargo that the United States had imposed in 1974 and 1975 on shipping arms to Turkey, which European leaders wanted lifted as soon as possible.

A major element of my trip was a visit to NATO headquarters near Brussels and to the Supreme Headquarters of the Allied Powers in Europe (SHAPE) near Mons, Belgium. I met with NATO Secretary General Joseph Luns and then helicoptered to SHAPE for sessions with General Alexander Haig. Both men stressed the importance of lifting the arms embargo on Turkey. At that time,

NATO officials made clear their concern about the continuing buildup of the Soviet-Warsaw Pact forces. Trends in the military balance of conventional forces seemed to be moving strongly to NATO's disadvantage and, if left unchecked, could undermine Western deterrence and stability.

While in Brussels, I met with leaders of the Belgian government, including Prime Minister Leo Tindemans and Defense Minister Paul Vanden Boeynants. With them, I emphasized the importance of Belgium's meeting its commitments to NATO's common defense efforts, particularly a three-percent real growth in defense spending. Although both men expressed strong and continuing support for NATO, they pointed to economic and political problems that acted as major constraints on increased defense spending.

In London, I had a lively discussion with Prime Minister James Callaghan at 10 Downing Street. I recall that we compared the legislative roles of the U.S. Congress and the British Parliament. We also discussed prospects for an arms control agreement. Callaghan told me that he thought the proposed SALT II Treaty would benefit both the West and the Soviets and also be good for Europe. By contrast, I found West German Chancellor Helmut Schmidt concerned about the "gray areas" not covered in SALT II, notably Soviet intermediate-range missiles.

On security affairs, the German leaders expressed their appreciation for my statements concerning the U.S. commitment to NATO. Like other European leaders, however, Schmidt believed that the U.S. embargo on arms to Turkey posed an increasing problem for NATO. I also discussed the enhanced radiation (or neutron) warhead—which could kill people without destroying buildings—with the West German leaders, who saw it as a matter of great sensitivity. They were willing to see the weapon deployed, but believed it must be handled with great care.

Defense Minister Hans Apel told me that it would be very difficult to win public support in West Germany for moving ahead with this weapon, since public attitudes had shifted against it. A debate on the neutron warhead "could be a disastrous event," he warned. Chancellor Schmidt expressed his concern about Soviet activities around the world, although both he and Foreign Minister Hans-Dietrich Genscher strongly supported U.S. efforts towards a SALT II agreement with the Soviets.

Having been strongly impressed by the European emphasis on the need to end the embargo on arms for Turkey, I immediately began work to get it lifted when I returned to Washington. The Carter administration was also committed to trying to have the embargo lifted, believing that its continuation was damaging to American interests. The Foreign Relations Committee, however, had already voted against a proposal to terminate the embargo, and prospects for a reversal of that action were thought to be very slim. Senator George McGovern indicated that he planned to try again to lift the embargo when the security assistance bill was taken up on the Senate floor in late July. Learning of McGovern's intention, I arranged a meeting with the South Dakota senator and told McGovern of my interest in working for repeal of the embargo, stating that I would offer an amendment for that purpose. McGovern deferred to me as majority leader. I then enlisted the support of Democrat Lloyd Bentsen of Texas and Republican John Chafee of Rhode Island, and the disparate coalition of Byrd, McGovern, Bentsen, and Chafee backed the amendment.

In arguing for termination, I noted that I had earlier supported the embargo: "There was an important point to be made in response to the Turkish use of U.S. weapons in Cyprus [during the Turkish military action in Cyprus in 1974]. That point has been made—clearly and unmistakably. Now, we must look forward. The embargo has become counterproductive. . . . For Turkey the embargo has assumed enormous—and highly negative—symbolic significance. . . . The embargo seriously undermines our collective security arrangements."

Although the primary intent of the amendment was to end the embargo, it also provided that the president should report to Congress on progress toward resolving the Cyprus issue, and it provided equal amounts of military sales credits for Turkey and Greece.

My cosponsors and I made personal appeals to our colleagues, and I organized a series of meetings in which members of the Joint Chiefs of Staff and top administration officials briefed senators and answered questions. I concentrated my efforts on newer members who had not been in Congress at the time of the earlier battles over Turkey. Meetings and briefings for staff members were also organized. I repeatedly emphasized that my efforts were not anti-Greece or pro-Turkey, but in the interests of both countries and of the U.S., NATO, and U.S. friends in the Middle East.

"Our goal is to have two strong and friendly nations in the Eastern Mediterranean, to maintain the strength of NATO, and to make possible a just and lasting Cyprus settlement," I said in introducing the amendment on July 25, 1978.

The amendment was fiercely debated, but, thanks to my intensive efforts and those of my colleagues, as well as to the strong backing of President Carter, it was approved in the Senate by a surprisingly large 57 to 42 margin on July 25, 1978. The House, on August 1, adopted a somewhat similar amendment offered by House Majority Leader Jim Wright, on a 208 to 205 vote. Both houses subsequently agreed to the conference report, and President Carter signed the legislation into law on September 26, 1978.

The SALT II Treaty was not signed until June 1979, and I paid close attention to the negotiations prior to its signing. Administration officials briefed me periodically. In regular Friday afternoon sessions, I met with such experts on arms control and strategic issues as Secretary of Defense Harold Brown, who supported the treaty, and Paul Nitze, who opposed it. To further prepare myself for what I expected would be a key role in moving the SALT II Treaty through the Senate, I planned a trip to the Soviet Union. Before leaving, I was briefed by the director of the Central Intelligence Agency, the chairman of the Joint Chiefs of Staff, the secretary of defense, and others.

My plan to go to Moscow was precipitated by inflammatory warnings, issued by the Communist party newspaper *Pravda*, that the Senate should not amend the treaty. The Soviets took the line that no Senate amendments would be acceptable and that, if any were adopted, the Soviets would not return to the negotiating table. I considered it necessary to inform Soviet leaders that the Senate would not act to rubber-stamp any treaty; that it shared a responsibility with the president in the making of treaties; that it would fulfill its constitutional role without fear or favor; and that inflammatory editorials and statements coming from Moscow would hinder rather than speed treaty approval by the Senate.

In Leningrad, I explained that I had come to the Soviet Union neither to praise nor to condemn the treaty but to create a better understanding of the treaty in the Senate and to explain to the Soviets the Senate's constitutional role in treatymaking. These were themes that I emphasized throughout my visit. One moving experience during that trip came when I laid a wreath at the monument to the defenders of Leningrad, which stands in a cemetery containing the mass graves of citizens who died during the nine-hundred-day Nazi siege of the city. It was clear that that wartime experience remained a vivid and dominant memory for the people of Leningrad.

After meeting with members of the Supreme Soviet in Moscow, I visited the summer residence of Soviet President Leonid Brezhnev in the Black Sea region, arriving on the Fourth of July. I was accompanied only by my staff adviser on foreign affairs, Hoyt Purvis, and a State Department translator, William Krimer. The Soviets had arranged to have a special plane fly us from Moscow to Simferopol—I recall that everything save the paneling in the forward compartment was appropriately covered in bright red. Brezhnev had sent his car to meet me at the airport and drive me to Yalta. As we whizzed through Simferopol, it became obvious that all traffic had been stopped in both directions. Cars, trucks, buses, even the electric trolley buses, had been pulled over to the side of the road. Absolutely nothing was moving except for the three cars in our motorcade.

The ninety-minute drive took us up into the Crimean mountains, offering some stunning views of the Black Sea coastline. I rode with Victor Sukhodrev, who told me he had served as translator for summit meetings since Premier Nikita Khrushchev's meeting with President John F. Kennedy in Vienna. We also talked about former President Richard Nixon, whom he respected. The Russians felt that, despite Nixon's anticommunist background, he had been able to improve relations between the United States and the Soviet Union. The Watergate scandal held little meaning for the Soviets, who were far more interested in foreign affairs than in American domestic politics. Along the route, Sukhodrev also pointed out to me the location of the Yalta conference where Roose-

"Why is it, Yuri, that after years of struggle by two mighty nations to achieve a SALT agreement, the entire matter is now in the hands of some person called Bobby Byrd?" read the caption to this cartoon about Senator Byrd's trip to the Soviet Union.

James Stevenson/The Washington Star, July 15, 1979

velt, Stalin, and Churchill had met. All of this reminded me of the long and arduous history of diplomatic negotiations between our two nations since the Second World War.

After lunch, we drove to Brezhnev's compound in a heavily wooded pine forest. President Brezhnev was waiting in a lawn chair when we arrived, and he invited me to join him in another chair on the plush green lawn. That beautiful mountain setting was reminiscent of West Virginia, and I took the occasion to present Brezhnev with my record album, "Mountain Fiddler," receiving in return a book of his speeches. We then moved to a handsome conference center, where we sat across from each other at a long

conference table. President Brezhnev was flanked by an aide and an interpreter; Purvis and Krimer were with me on my side of the table. The Soviet leader and I took turns speaking, but on several occasions he interrupted my remarks, and our discussion was lively and frank.

I was determined to explain the U.S. Senate's role in the treaty process, pointing out that the Senate, which had rejected the Versailles Treaty, zealously guarded its prerogatives. "The Senate will not be intimidated," I told Brezhnev. "It will not act out of fear; it will not act in haste." Brezhnev accepted my advice that Soviet leaders should cease making inflammatory statements that could be counterproductive. "We will be patient," he agreed. At the conclusion of my remarks, I raised one further issue, asking that the Soviet leader give compassionate consideration to those dissidents seeking to leave the Soviet Union. Brezhnev accepted a list of these names from me but made no commitments. Later, I was pleased to learn that two of the people on the list received visas to leave the Soviet Union and that I was the first American notified of the decision.

At the end of our discussion, Brezhnev offered an Independence Day toast to the friendship between Americans and Soviets. I returned the gesture with a toast to his health, to continued friendship between our countries, and to peace in the world. As we walked back outside, Brezhnev insisted on conducting us on a brief tour of the grounds. Clearly this was unplanned, and the compound's staff could be seen scampering around in preparation. Moving in a slow shuffle and with some assistance from me, Brezhnev led us up to a log cabin several hundred yards from the conference center. This rustic structure, plainly but handsomely furnished, had been built for Stalin, to his specifications, although Brezhnev did not think that Stalin had ever used it. As we walked back to our cars, Brezhnev carried on an animated conversation, pointing out various features of the compound. I mentioned that my wife Erma and my staff had remained behind in Moscow, and I asked if I might have some of the chocolate bars we had seen on the table to take back to the ladies in my party. Brezhnev quickly dispatched a staff member to bring several candy bars. "Ladies like chocolate," Brezhnev chuckled, ". . . when it is presented by a man."

Back in Moscow the next day for a meeting with Foreign Minister Andrei Gromyko, I found that pictures from the Yalta meeting appeared on the front pages of Soviet newspapers.

In Moscow, I met with top Soviet officials at the Presidium of the Supreme Soviet in the Kremlin and with Foreign Minister Andrei Gromyko. Our discussions were wide-ranging, but the central topics were arms control and defense spending. The Soviets believed that any reduction in strategic arms beyond those in SALT II needed to be viewed in the context of such "other factors" as China. Nikolay Inozemtzev, director of the Institute of World Economics and International Relations, assured me that the essence of Soviet policy was to go forward "in a resolute manner" toward significant reductions in strategic arms, based on the principle of equity. Our discussion of defense budgets underscored the difficulties in making comparisons between our fundamentally different economic systems. Soviet officials claimed that their defense budget was only one-fifth that of the United States, a ridiculous assertion. Differing accounting methods, radical differences in pay scales for military personnel, and the very nature of the socialist system obscured any common ground for an accurate comparison.

My two-and-a-half-hour meeting with Foreign Minister Gromyko covered a number of international topics and aspects of U.S.-Soviet relations, but most of the discussion centered on the role of the U.S. Senate in the treaty-ratification process. Just two weeks earlier, Gromyko had warned the Senate not to suggest any changes in the treaty, saying that Senate failure to approve SALT II would mean the end of Soviet-American arms negotiations. I stressed the Senate's constitutional role, and told the foreign minister that it would be in the best interest of all concerned if Soviet leaders refrained from any further inflammatory statements. Gromyko, who had by then been foreign minister for more than twenty years, acknowledged the truth of what I had said regarding the need for coolness, moderation, and reason on both sides. He promised that, if again tempted to respond to "hot-headed" statements in the United States, he would use one hand to restrain the other from reaching for pencil and paper or instruct his staff to break the tape in his tape recorder if he dictated a sharp response. Gromyko kept his word, as did Brezhnev, and as long as prospects for the treaty remained alive, Soviet leaders refrained from making critical public comments.

At a press conference in Moscow, I described the discussion as very helpful to me, stating that it had been "a way of contributing to a better understanding by the Soviets of those matters of concern to my colleagues as we develop this internal debate." One press report observed, "The red-carpet treatment given Byrd shows that the Kremlin does understand that the treaty is probably doomed without his active support."

Returning from Moscow, I stopped in Paris to obtain the views of French officials about the SALT II Treaty and other issues of importance in East-West relations. At the Elysée Palace, my aide Hoyt Purvis and I met with President Valéry Giscard d'Estaing. The president told me that France judged the SALT II Treaty on its merits, rather than on the basis of France's relationship to the United States. French experts had therefore deemed it a balanced treaty. In response to my questions about the consequences if the treaty were rejected, the French president replied that rejection would create political uncertainty in Western Europe about the United States. Some would cast the United States as extreme, and the Soviets would undoubtedly attempt to move closer to Europe and to dissociate Europe from the United States. The American ability to lead as a stable power would be questioned, and there would be fears in Europe of a new arms race and a renewed cold war. While Giscard d'Estaing made clear his support for ratification

of SALT II, however, he called for realistic efforts to alter the existing imbalance of intermediate range missiles in Europe.

My visit to Moscow and my talks with Soviet leaders had served their intended purpose, as I later reported to President Carter and others in his administration. What none of us had any way of knowing, however, was that rapidly changing international situations would prevent the Senate from debating the SALT II Treaty. In August, the State Department announced that it had discovered some two to three thousand Soviet troops in Cuba, and Senator Frank Church, chairman of the Foreign Relations Committee, postponed the SALT hearings to deal with reports of the Soviet brigade in Cuba. I must say that I was immediately skeptical of this brouhaha. It seemed to me premature to take any action before ascertaining the facts. In what the *Washington Post* called an "unprecedented initiative by a Senate leader," I arranged a meeting with Soviet Ambassador Anatoly Dobrynin in my office on Sunday, September 23, 1979. As it developed, the Soviet brigade had been in Cuba since the 1960's and had long been "forgotten" before it was rediscovered. It was all what I called a "pseudo-crisis" that distracted attention from the real merits of the treaty. I then worked with the administration and with other senators to assure that the United States would move ahead with modernization of our strategic and conventional forces, measures which helped the SALT II Treaty to regain some of its lost momentum. Later, the Foreign Relations Committee recommended approval of the treaty by the narrow vote of 9 to 6.

Then, events in Iran and Afghanistan intervened. In November 1979, U.S. embassy personnel in Teheran were taken hostage by Iranian militants. In December, the Soviets sent troops to Afghanistan to quell the Moslem rebellion there. Under the circum-

Democratic President Jimmy Carter and Democratic Majority Leader Robert C. Byrd are depicted here support-ing the SALT II treaty with the Soviet Union, while Minority Leader Howard Baker is portrayed as fearing that supporting the treaty could endanger his planned presidential campaign. *Jim Dent/Charleston Gazette, October 27, 1979*

stances, President Carter and I agreed that Senate consideration of the SALT II Treaty should be suspended. "It would not be con-ducive to the SALT process to bring up the treaty at this point," I said, telling the presi-dent, "the votes are not there." President Carter then publicly asked the Senate to postpone consideration of the SALT II Treaty. The Soviet invasion of Afghanistan had sealed the treaty's doom.

Looking back upon the international scene of 1979 and 1980, the tumultuous events in Iran come vividly to mind. As majority

leader, I had visited Iran in November 1978, when conditions in that country were be-coming increasingly chaotic. Earlier that month, civil disorder and demonstrations had led the shah, Muhammad Reza Pahlavi, to install a military government. A curfew was in effect during my visit, and security conditions were extremely tight. Driving from Teheran airport to the embassy, there was virtually no traffic on the streets, and military troops were much in evidence. A car was turned on its side and burning near the embassy entrance. My wife Erma and I were given rooms in the embassy compound, where, within less than a year, Americans would be taken hostage.

Minutes after our arrival, I met with Ambassador William Sullivan and began a long briefing session that reviewed recent developments in Iran. At that time, the U.S. supported the shah and believed he would prevail, but the ambassador warned that the situation was unpredictable. We had a serious exchange about how far the United States should go in encouraging the shah, and whether he was capable of saving the situation. National Security Adviser Zbigniew Brzezinski had urged me to tell the shah that the president and Congress stood behind him and were "unequivocal in our support." He also suggested that I encourage the shah to take his case directly to the Iranian people by radio and television. However, on the morning of November 27, when my wife and I visited with the Fatemi family, the Iranian family of my son-in-law, we heard a far less optimistic prognosis. I concluded that the shah had lost so much public support that pushing him to make more public appearances would be unwise. There was a danger of further polarizing Iranian society, so that the only alternative would then be the religious opposition led by the Ayatollah Ruhollah Khomeini.

My first official meeting was with General Gholam Reza Azhari, the military chief of staff, who, three weeks earlier, had been appointed by the shah as prime minister under the military government that had just been established. Azhari was preoccupied with what might occur during the Shi'ite Moslem holy days of Moharram, which would begin in less than a week and were viewed as a possible climactic confrontation between the military government and the religious forces. He said the people now seemed to believe that all of their problems had come from the shah, a claim Prime Minister Azhari believed

to be incorrect but, nonetheless, a fact to be reckoned with. "The people must be assured that the past is the past," Azhari declared.

Following the meeting with the Iranian prime minister, my staff and my wife and I helicoptered to Nivavran Palace, where the shah greeted us in a lavishly furnished suite. I began the private conversation by relaying President Carter's assurance that the United States supported his leadership, adding my own support for the shah's efforts to move toward representative democracy and to restore domestic stability and order. I also told the shah that the United States would not interfere with Iran's internal affairs, nor would we tolerate interference from the Soviet Union. The shah expressed thanks for these comments and then offered his own assessment of the crisis. He admitted that the speed with which events had developed had taken him by surprise, particularly the growing influence of the religious leaders. Iran had seemed "like a rock" only a year earlier when President Carter referred to it as an island of stability.

The shah rather dispassionately discussed the various options open to him, but he had not clearly determined what course of action to take. He believed that he had made a mistake by concentrating his efforts on progress without paying careful enough attention to public opinion. Efforts to develop a political party system had floundered, and political talent had remained idle. "We need a machinery for democracy," he told me. "I don't know if we can do it, but I will try." He described the opposition as "riding on a wave of dissatisfaction" but considered many of them "out of touch with reality" and completely lacking in experience to govern. The shah never referred to Ayatollah Khomeini by name, only as "this fellow in Paris," who was constantly sending Iranians directives for disobedience. Acknowledging that the ayatollah had a strong following, the shah held out the hope that Khomeini was losing ground. The shah said he himself had been caught in a vicious cycle: "Shall we establish law and order first and then democracy? Who can guarantee that if we brought a coalition to power, they would not yield too much, either to the extreme left or extreme right? If we continue clamping down, this may or may not end the disorder."

In answer to my question as to whether his government was adequately prepared to deal with events that might occur during Moharram, the shah responded, "The answer cannot be no."

I then met with the shah alone. I had decided not to push hard on the idea of urging the shah to use the mass media to appeal to the Iranian people. My reasons were: (1) it could make the shah appear weak; (2) the appointment of General Azhari as prime minister had been viewed by many as a bad decision; (3) the shah and his government lacked credibility; and (4) the situation had deteriorated so rapidly that the need was for action, not television appearances.

Following the meeting, the shah and Empress Farah hosted a luncheon attended by Ambassador and Mrs. Sullivan, Hoyt Purvis, my wife Erma and myself. The conversation was pleasant but generally serious and subdued. Empress Farah spoke of her son, who was in pilot training in the United States. The shah, not surprisingly, seemed preoccupied. He did say he was weighing options and searching for solutions.

My meetings with the shah and officials in the Iranian government and with our own Ambassador Sullivan convinced me that, while the situation was not entirely hopeless, events were rapidly approaching a climax of critical and fateful proportions, and I was pessimistic of its outcome. I urged the shah to be firm, fair, and determined, judicious but strong. He thanked me and asked me to tell President Carter and all agencies of the

In 1978, Robert C. Byrd visited Egyptian President Anwar Sadat. *Office of Senator Robert C. Byrd*

U.S. government—by which I understood him to mean the Central Intelligence Agency—to support him "in what they do as well as in what they say."

Ambassador Sullivan later wrote that, while the White House had trouble accepting the reality of the problems in Iran, "one of those who must not be trapped into unreality was Senate Majority Leader Robert Byrd. I believe he left Teheran understanding the true nature of the situation we faced." Indeed, less than two months after my departure, the shah himself left on "an extended vacation," and shortly thereafter Ayatollah Khomeini returned to Iran from his fifteen-year exile.

When I left Iran, I flew to Egypt for private meetings with President Anwar Sadat. As Senate majority leader and, in this undertaking, as President Carter's emissary and with his approval, I hoped to encourage support among other countries in the Middle East for Sadat's courageous peace initiative. President Sadat, a gracious man, became quite emotional and even angry in his comments about Israeli intransigence in the peace process. I stressed to him the admiration in which the American people held him and told him that this good will was reflected in Congress. I re-

Israeli Prime Minister Menachem Begin greeted Robert C. Byrd in Tel Aviv in 1978.
USIA, U.S. Embassy, Tel Aviv/Matty Stern

peatedly urged him to accept the draft treaty with Israel and not to let the process unravel.

Flying from Cairo to Tel Aviv, I met with Prime Minister Menachem Begin, who was equally vigorous in arguing the Israeli side of the treaty negotiations. I stressed to Begin the importance of avoiding public statements that might create misunderstandings or lead to a hardening of positions. "The United States cannot accept a 'take it or leave it' attitude on the part of either party," I warned. However, I assured Begin and Defense Minister Ezer Weizmann that there was no question about the United States' commitment to Israel's security.

While in Jerusalem, I met with various West Bank leaders and heard their pleas for self-determination. I next flew on to Jordan, where I met with King Hussein, who also spoke of the plight of the Palestinians. I urged the king to become part of the Middle

East peace talks that had begun with the Camp David accords. I importuned him to become involved, "put your fingerprints on the peace process," and help to shape its course. Leaving Jordan, I flew to Syria—at the special request of President Carter—for a scheduled meeting with President Hafiz al-Assad, only to find, upon my arrival in Damascus, that the meeting had been canceled. I was both puzzled and angered but I left word that I would return following my visit to Saudi Arabia and would expect the promise of a meeting to then be fulfilled. Persistence had its reward and, upon my return from a visit with the Saudi Arabian leaders, I stopped in Syria and, this time, the desired meeting with President Assad took place. Again, I urged participation and support in the peace effort. Despite Syria's sharp differences of views over the Camp David accords, I found the Syrians clearly interested in maintaining a dialogue with the United States.

In Saudi Arabia, I had had a three-hour meeting with Crown Prince Fahd, who was already the effective head of the Saudi government. We talked of peace, oil, and overall United States-Saudi relations. I urged the Saudis to support President Sadat's courageous peace initiative, and, although the Saudis were reluctant to support publicly the Camp David agreements, Prince Fahd wanted America's efforts to succeed.

Except for my apprehensions and concern about Iran, I returned from the Middle East modestly encouraged about the prospects for peace. Stopping in London, I met with Secretary of State Cyrus Vance, who was then on his way to the Middle East, to give him a preliminary report of my findings, and in Washington I presented to President Carter a confidential report on the trip. In my public report to the Senate, I said that the most encouraging aspect of my discussions was the degree to which Middle Eastern leaders in general were convinced that all of their nations and the United States shared the objective of achieving peace and stability in that region.

As we look back from another decade's perspective, that moment in the late 1970's was the closest that the Middle East has come to achieving peace and stability in our times. President Carter's effort to bring Israel and Egypt together was undoubtedly the high point of his presidency, for which he deserves lasting credit. It is a tragedy that the momentum begun at Camp David was disrupted by the Iranian revolution, the assassination of President Sadat, and the continuing, mindless, bloody civil war in Lebanon that has claimed so many lives and still holds so many innocent hostages. My journey through the Middle East proved valuable to me as Senate majority leader, giving me personal insights into those countries and their leaders that continued to assist me throughout the next decade. It also left me with a deep sense of regret over what might have been.

Concern with international affairs also took me to the People's Republic of China. In 1978, President Carter informed me that negotiations were underway to establish formal diplomatic ties with China. I knew that the supporters of Taiwan in Congress might seize upon this action as an opportunity to embarrass the administration, undercut its policies, and damage the prospects for improved relations with the People's Republic. I had already paid one visit to China in 1975 and had met with Deng Xiaoping in 1979 when he visited Washington, where we discussed the future of relations between the United States and China. Also in 1979, I received an invitation from the National People's Congress to visit the People's Republic, a trip that I made in July 1980.

Five years had passed since my previous visit, and I noticed many changes in China. It seemed evident that the country was moving away from the rigid, statist Soviet model toward a more decentralized approach, incorporating incentives and greater market flexibility. I not only visited with government leaders in Beijing but also made visits to communes, hospitals, and military facilities in several Chinese provinces. In Beijing, I met with Premier Hua Guofeng and Vice-Premier Zhao Ziyang. We spoke especially about the Chinese opposition to the Soviet intervention in Afghanistan. I pointed out that a resolution I had introduced in the Senate demanding withdrawal of all Soviet troops from Afghanistan had passed unanimously. We talked also of the common interests between our nations. "We do not view this relationship as a momentary thing," Hua told me, "but from the perspective of our long-range strategic interests." I sought to allay Chinese anxieties over any change in American foreign policy toward China if Ronald Reagan were to be elected president. Stating that the vast majority of Americans wanted a continued normalization of relations between our two countries, I told the Chinese leaders, "There is no turning the clock back."

During this visit, I was especially impressed with Vice Premier Zhao Ziyang, who seemed to be emerging as the key figure in the younger generation of Chinese leaders. Indeed, two months later he replaced Hua Guofeng as premier. Zhao made it clear that his view of China's modernization depended upon economic improvements. He said that China would adopt more Western methods of organizing production and that industrial enterprises would be given more autonomy. China was introducing an economy regulated more by the market than by state planning.

On my way back to the United States, I stopped in Tokyo to discuss these matters with Mike Mansfield, the American ambassador and my predecessor as Senate majority leader. In Washington, I told the Senate that "the United States has a real stake in helping China to strengthen its economy. . . . A strong, secure, peaceful, and modernizing China is vital to stability in the Asian-Pacific area." I was convinced then, and still believe, that the United States should "continue the course of steady, gradual growth in our relations with China." I regret that, in promoting the economic modernization of their country, the Chinese leadership did not realize the parallel need for greater political democracy, as demanded by the younger generation of Chinese. The massacre of student protesters in Tiananmen Square in 1989 and the fall of Zhao Ziyang as general secretary were great setbacks, both for China and for U.S.-Chinese relations. It is terrible when any political regime becomes so ossified that it can tolerate no change and would fire upon its own people. We can only hope that China, having taken this giant step backwards, will regain its footing and move forward toward the modernization and democratization that its people fundamentally desire.

My role as Senate Democratic leader changed considerably in 1981, when a Republican president occupied the White House and the Democrats became the minority party in the Senate. From a position of guiding the president's program through the Senate and marshalling the majority's forces, I found myself and my minority party in opposition to many of the new president's foreign policy initiatives. In 1981, for instance, I opposed President Reagan's proposed sale of AWACS planes to Saudi Arabia, arguing that it would destabilize the situation in the Middle East. I also opposed the president's decision to inject American peacekeeping forces into the Lebanese civil war, a decision that proved fatal to 241 U.S. Marines in one day in October 1983, and I was relieved

when President Reagan withdrew the remainder of those troops in 1984.

As Democratic leader, I supported the president whenever in good conscience I could but strongly opposed any signs of unilateral and secretive foreign policy action on the part of the executive. As minority leader, I felt it extremely important to monitor world events and maintain contact with world leaders. In 1985, when the United States and the Soviet Union resumed negotiations on a limitation of intermediate-range nuclear forces, I was eager to meet the new Soviet leader, Mikhail Gorbachev. In August of that year, I led a bipartisan delegation of eight senators on a visit to the Soviet Union. The other participants were Senators Strom Thurmond of South Carolina, Claiborne Pell of Rhode Island, Paul Sarbanes of Maryland, John Warner of Virginia, Sam Nunn of Georgia, George Mitchell of Maine, and Dennis DeConcini of Arizona. En route to Moscow, we stopped in London to meet with the British minister of state for foreign and commonwealth affairs, in order to learn the British impressions of the new Soviet leader and of developments in Soviet policy. From London, the delegation flew to Hungary, a Soviet ally that was already showing signs of movement toward a creative domestic economic policy, the forerunner of much of the dramatic change we have witnessed in Eastern Europe during the closing weeks of 1989. We met with government leaders in Budapest and had a good exchange of views. Finally, in Moscow, we met with Mikhail Gorbachev. The appearance that same day of the September 2, 1985, issue of *Time* magazine, containing a lengthy interview with Gorbachev, convinced the delegation that we were dealing with a Soviet leader skilled in modern public relations.

Gorbachev started the meeting by asking me how I liked Moscow. I replied that I liked the city and that I had also liked Kiev, with

In September 1985, a bipartisan delegation of senators visited Mikhail Gorbachev at the Kremlin. Shown are, *from left*: Senators Strom Thurmond, Sam Nunn, and Robert C. Byrd with Gorbachev, *far right*, and two Soviet officials. *Office of Senator Robert C. Byrd*

its greenery, clean streets, and warm hospitality. Gorbachev replied that there were many beautiful cities in the Soviet Union, that it was a vast land of diverse regions and cultures much like the United States, and that there were places in the Soviet Union he had never seen. Vastness, he said, left an impact on the national character and thinking of a people, so that the large-scale thinking of the United States and the Soviet Union were shaped by the large scale of our nations. "We more than any other nation are able to understand your nation and to build a bridge from the other side," he assured us.

He conceded that relations between the United States and the Soviet Union had not improved during the previous five years and

that he was determined to move relations "off dead center." This would take effort from both sides. Although there were many radical differences between our two nations, he insisted, we should not allow our differences to bring us into confrontation. "I cannot imagine a future of our two countries without cooperation," he told us. He spoke of his hopes for his forthcoming summit meeting with President Reagan and expressed concern about "those groups in the U.S. and Congress and those surrounding the President who tried to prevent the meeting."

During our dialogue, I raised our concern about the presence of Soviet troops in Afghanistan. Gorbachev interrupted to com-

[593]

plain that "Congress appropriates money to continue the fighting. The money sacks are all open and you spend no time to untie the money sacks." To this, I replied, "If there are any money sacks, it is easy to resolve. There will be no money sacks if the Soviets leave Afghanistan." When I completed my statement, Gorbachev replied that he had heard nothing new. Then, for about an hour and fifteen minutes, he responded with remarks that were defensive and argumentative but that continued to emphasize the need for political dialogue between our nations to end the arms race, to create a serious system of verification, and to prevent the militarization of space. He returned frequently to President Reagan's "Star Wars" plan, the Strategic Defense Initiative. "An arms race in space," said Gorbachev, "this is what bothers us and concerns us most of all." Of the continuing arms negotiations, he said, "We are all people well-steeled in the art of sitting at long meetings, but our time is drawing short." We needed greater cooperation between our nations in economic, scientific, and cultural fields. "The U.S. have their own way of life," he said. "The Soviets have their own way of life. . . . As the proverb goes, you should not go into another's monastery with your own charter." We needed to respect each other's own domestic matters.

When Gorbachev had finished, I responded that I was sorry he had "heard nothing new" in the statement that I had read on behalf of the delegation, because I believed it did express something new. I further stated:

You heard a fair and sound statement representing the feelings of the American people, and you heard for the first time the viewpoint of the U.S. Senate. After all, under our Constitution, while the President negotiates and we do not, no treaty can go into effect unless two-thirds of the members of the Senate—not the House, not Mr. McFarlane (the President's national security adviser), not the White House, but the Senate—vote to approve the resolution of ratification of a treaty. The Senate is no rubber stamp for any President.

To add bipartisan support for my comments, the vice chairman of the delegation, Senator Strom Thurmond, noted that he fully endorsed my statement. He said that, while the United States and the Soviet Union had differences in the past, there was "no reason why we cannot iron out these differences and work together for world peace," particularly if the Soviet Union "would get out of Afghanistan, Angola, Ethiopia, and Central America."

Our delegation came away with no sure signs that the Soviet position had shifted on any substantive foreign policy issue. Yet, as we reported to the Senate, "There is a new sense of self-confidence [in the Soviet leadership] which makes Mr. Gorbachev a formidable negotiating partner, whose skills at organizing his arguments and presenting them were demonstrated convincingly."

This meeting was very important for me as well as for other members of the delegation in forming our assessments of the new Soviet leader. Indeed, a little over two years later, President Reagan and General Secretary Gorbachev signed the Intermediate-Range Nuclear Forces Treaty to eliminate all INF missiles. This was the first major arms reduction agreement in over a decade. Moreover, it came before the Senate during the One-hundredth Congress, when the Democrats had been returned to the majority and I was once again majority leader. The INF Treaty was the culmination of a long, bipartisan process dating back to the Carter administration, when NATO's dual-track policy of weapons deployment and negotiation was initiated. Missiles were placed in European countries—despite the opposition of some citizens—at the same time that NATO leaders expressed their willingness to discuss with the USSR ways of reducing the number of weapons on both sides. NATO's tenacity in pursuing this policy, at some political cost to various European leaders, provided the leverage needed to bring the Soviets to negotiate at Geneva.

On the day that the One-hundredth Congress opened in January 1987, I offered a resolution, on behalf of myself and Minority Leader Bob Dole of Kansas, reauthorizing the Arms Control Observer Group. This unique group supplemented the activities of the Foreign Relations Committee by providing a more regular and systematic involvement of the full Senate in any arms control negotiations between the United States and the USSR. This bipartisan group followed the arms control process and provided the Senate with valuable insights into the negotiations, in line with the Senate's duty to advise and consent on treaty ratification. I also met with Senators Pell, Nunn, and David L. Boren of Oklahoma—the chairmen of the Foreign Relations Committee, the Armed Services Committee, and the Intelligence Committee, respectively—to ask them to work together and coordinate their efforts on the treaty. On February 17, 1987, the Senate approved a resolution expressing its full support for the president's commitment to achieve mutual, equitable, balanced, verifiable, and stabilizing nuclear arms reduction agreements with the Soviet Union.

Because of the critical importance of the INF Treaty to the NATO alliance, I led a bipartisan delegation of senators to Europe in February 1988. The delegation—consisting of Senators Nunn, Pell, Boren, Warner, and myself—visited with government leaders in London, Paris, Bonn, Rome, and Ankara. We found these leaders, including Margaret Thatcher, François Mitterrand, and Helmut Kohl, united in their view, although for different reasons, that the Senate should approve the INF Treaty. In the meantime, the three Senate committees—Foreign Relations,

Armed Services, and Intelligence—had begun to examine the treaty, calling expert witnesses in public and executive sessions. The Armed Services Committee and the Intelligence Committee identified issues requiring further clarification. Although I was under public pressure from the White House and Senate Republicans—and some of my Democratic colleagues—to call up the treaty for floor action, I stated, in early May, that floor debate would not begin until it was clear that the United States and the Soviet Union had resolved the issues and concerns raised by the two committees.

The problems identified by the two committees included ambiguities over the definition of "weapon" and whether futuristic weapons, not mentioned in the treaty, were covered by it. Also at issue was the ability to verify an implied ban on futuristic weapons, and there were differences of opinion on the procedures governing the conduct of on-site inspections. An additional concern was whether the administration was adequately committing itself to the updating of eavesdropping satellites and other technical means of intelligence. Only after Secretary of State George Shultz and Soviet Foreign Minister Eduard Shevardnadze met in Geneva and resolved all of the issues, and only after the concerns of the Armed Services and Intelligence Committees had been satisfied, did I call up the treaty and allow the floor debate to begin.

The Senate adopted a controversial condition on treaty interpretation that I offered on behalf of myself, Senator Dole, and the chairmen and ranking minority members of the three committees. This bipartisan amendment provided that, in interpreting the INF Treaty's terms, President Reagan or any future president would be bound not only by the treaty's text but also by the "common understanding" arrived at jointly by the Senate and the executive branch

British Prime Minister Margaret Thatcher greeted a delegation of U.S. senators at No. 10 Downing Street. *From left*: Senators David Boren, Sam Nunn, and Claiborne Pell; Mrs. Thatcher; U.S. Ambassador Charles H. Price; and Senators John Warner and Robert C. Byrd. *London Pictures Service*

through testimony by administration officials in hearings on the treaty. The amendment also provided that any reinterpretation of the treaty by the Reagan administration or any future administration would have to be approved by the Senate. This provision ensured that the Senate's constitutional role would not be undermined by a subsequent unilateral executive branch reinterpretation of the treaty, as had happened earlier when the Reagan administration declared that the 1972 Anti-Ballistic-Missile (ABM) Treaty would not prohibit testing of portions of

the proposed Strategic Defense Initiative program.

Taking the view that the Senate's role in the making of treaties would be meaningless if presidents could reinterpret treaties after the Senate approved them, I said, "The preservation of the institutional role of this Senate in making treaties is more important than this treaty because there will be other treaties." The amendment was adopted by a vote of 72 to 27.

Speaking to reporters after the vote on the amendment, I stated, "This Senate's action

At the invitation of President Reagan, Majority Leader Robert Byrd and Minority Leader Bob Dole attended the formal ratification of the INF Treaty in Moscow in June 1988.   *Office of Senator Robert C. Byrd*

on this treaty should be a clear signal to the Administration, to any future Administration and to the Soviet Union that this Senate will not roll over and play dead on any treaty for any President or be a rubber stamp for any President."

After two weeks of intense debate, on May 27, 1988, the Senate voted 93 to 5 to approve the resolution of ratification. In recognition of the key role played by the joint Senate leadership in successfully concluding debate on the INF Treaty, President Reagan invited Senator Dole and me to attend the

summit in Moscow, where the INF Treaty was formally ratified on June 1, 1988. The White House chief of staff, former Senator Howard Baker, also attended the ceremony. I was proud to be there and proud that the Senate's scrutiny had strengthened and improved this important treaty.

There were some aspects of the Reagan foreign policy that I found deeply troubling. For instance, during most of the 1980's, the administration devoted much time and energy to a narrowly focused, one-track military-oriented policy as a way of confronting the Sandinista regime in Nicaragua. This overemphasis on a single element of our hemispheric foreign policy resulted in a lack of adequate attention to the many serious social and economic problems faced by neighboring Mexico and the nascent democratic governments in South America.

After almost seven years of regional warfare, the presidents of Costa Rica, El Salvador, Guatemala, Honduras, and Nicaragua met in Esquipulas, Guatemala on August 7, 1987. There, under the leadership of President Oscar Arias Sanchez of Costa Rica, they signed an accord designed to end the fighting in Nicaragua and El Salvador and to seek a diplomatic and political settlement of the regional conflict. This so-called Esquipulas Agreement was followed up on March 23, 1988, when representatives of the Nicaraguan government and the Contras met at Sapoa, Nicaragua. There, in accord with the provisions of the Arias peace plan, they signed an agreement to negotiate both a cease-fire and the terms beginning a process of national reconciliation.

On August 10, 1988, the Senate approved an amendment which I offered to the fiscal year 1989 Defense appropriation bill on behalf of myself and Senators Christopher Dodd of Connecticut, David Boren of Oklahoma, John Stennis of Mississippi, Bennett Johnston of Louisiana, and Lawton Chiles of Florida. Offered as an attempt to form a bipartisan consensus to protect United States security interests while promoting peace and stability in the region, the amendment had resulted from protracted three-way negotiations among Senate Democrats, Senate Republicans, and the White House. Despite the successful resolution of every issue under negotiation, however, the White House withdrew its support for the amendment at the last minute—indeed, while the amendment was pending on the Senate floor. Still, the votes of Senate Democrats were enough

to adopt the provision by a vote of 49 to 47 over the opposition of the White House and all of our Republican colleagues.

The amendment provided $27 million in humanitarian assistance to the Contras through March 31, 1989, as well as a $5 million package of assistance to civilian victims of the war, to be administered by the Catholic church in Nicaragua. It also provided that the president could request and receive expedited action for the release of $16.5 million of previously authorized military aid for the Contras, if he certified to Congress that such an expedited vote was necessary to protect the Contras from an attack or a Sandinista action that threatened the peace and security of the region. Additionally, the amendment included economic incentives to encourage the Sandinistas to reach a general peace settlement with the Contras. The amendment put the Sandinistas on notice that Congress supported diplomatic solutions to the conflict in Central America, but it also sent them a message that we were prepared to return to military pressure if they failed to keep their word to democratize their government. It gave clear notice to the Sandinistas that they had reached a crucial point and that it was time to comply with the provisions of the Arias peace accord and to move to a genuinely pluralistic democratic process in Nicaragua.

A bipartisan accord was reached on March 24, 1989, in which the new administration under President George Bush joined the bipartisan congressional leadership in endorsing what had been the essential ingredients of the Byrd amendment, in effect making it affirmative administration policy for the first time. In a side letter to the accord, Secretary of State James Baker agreed to obligate funds beyond November 30, 1989, in the same formulation as set out in the amendment, if such an expenditure had been "affirmed via letters from the bipartisan leadership of

Congress and the relevant House and Senate authorization and appropriations committees." Accordingly, such a letter of approval was signed on November 27, 1989. In essence, the letter affirmed that the process of democratization in Nicaragua was proceeding as hoped, and the aid program set out in the Byrd amendment was being administered according to the spirit of the amendment.

The Byrd amendment represented the essential, critical rejection of the Reagan administration's single-minded devotion to military victory through the use of the expatriate army, known as the Contras, that was settled on the Honduran-Nicaraguan border. The amendment's successful implementation validated the support within the United States political system for the democratic and diplomatic road to peace that the presidents of the five Central American governments took when they signed the Esquipulas Agreement on August 7, 1987.

Another aspect of the Reagan administration's foreign policy that troubled me involved events in the Persian Gulf, which, by 1987, had become a sea of horrors. The decision of the Reagan administration to increase the United States' naval presence in the Persian Gulf at the height of the war between Iran and Iraq raised the question of whether the War Powers Resolution should be invoked. The administration steadfastly refused to acknowledge that it had placed American forces into a situation where involvement in hostilities was imminent and, therefore, refused to be bound by the limitations of that statute. The Senate spent considerable time debating this point.

On May 21, 1987, the Senate adopted an amendment that I offered with Senator Dole to the supplemental appropriation bill regarding the Persian Gulf. This amendment required the secretary of defense to make a comprehensive report and assessment of the

security situation in the gulf before providing military assistance to reflagged Kuwaiti shipping. We also dispatched special Senate investigating missions to the region, consisting of Senators Jim Sasser, John Glenn, and John Warner.

While some questioned the Senate's extensive oversight in regard to U.S. naval operations in the gulf, the configuration of this country's naval forces there was dramatically upgraded as a result of Senate prodding, and larger, more capable ships were deployed, making less likely a repetition of the Iraqi jet fighter's mistaken attack on the U.S.S. *Stark* that had occurred in May 1987. Furthermore, the Senate's involvement helped stimulate U.S. allies in Europe and around the Persian Gulf to increase their participation in the region.

On several occasions, the Senate attempted to express its will on the Persian Gulf but was unable to obtain the sixty votes needed to limit debate. Many senators were reluctant to pass legislation invoking the War Powers Resolution, in part because it would require the automatic withdrawal of forces from the Persian Gulf within sixty days, unless their continued deployment was authorized. This impasse lasted until October 1987, when the Senate narrowly passed a joint resolution, which I introduced with Senator John Warner, to require the president to provide a comprehensive report about the objectives of the specific military missions upon which he was embarking. Unfortunately, the resolution, which, in many ways, duplicated the requirements of the War Powers Resolution, was not acted upon in the House.

During the 1980's, the conflict in Afghanistan was an important factor in U.S.-Soviet relations. The Soviet invasion scuttled the chances of Senate approval of SALT II in 1979 and affected the relationship over the next decade. Throughout the period, the

Senate played a central role in relations between the two countries. After the invasion, the first such Soviet forcible military incursion into a sovereign independent nation since World War II, a strong bipartisan and bicameral consensus sustained a high level of military and economic assistance to the mujahedeen, the Afghan resistance fighters. The fiercely independent mujahedeen fought against great odds: a Soviet proxy regime, well-oiled with Soviet military hardware, and a five-hundred-thousand-man occupying army.

Over the decade of the 1980's, the consistent factor in the U.S. legislative-executive partnership to aid the mujahedeen was the U.S. Congress, which not only insisted on high levels of assistance, but even dominated American decision-making on specific weapons systems to be provided. A striking example of this congressional effort was the provision of "Stinger" hand-held surface-to-air missiles to the Afghan resistance, over the reluctance of the administration, an action which is credited with turning the tide of the war against the Soviets. Hundreds of Soviet aircraft and helicopters were brought down with this lethal and compact weapon, denying the Soviets the complete air dominance that they had earlier enjoyed. The Soviets were forced to withdraw their army from a war that had become increasingly unpopular among their population and that had led to an unending stream of casualties and a painful stalemate, bringing them substantial international costs, particularly in the Muslim world.

The Senate repeatedly expressed its unflinching endorsement for the cause of the Afghan resistance by adopting resolutions of continued support. In 1988, I authored a crucial resolution to prevent the administration from carrying out its intention to cut off American lethal aid as part of negotiations in Geneva on accords designed to end the conflict. Unfortunately, it became clear that the Soviets intended to continue giving heavy military support and guidance to their proxy regime in Kabul, even after the withdrawal of most of their ground forces. A cutoff of U.S. military aid would thus have left the resistance in an untenable position. The Senate resolution condemned any such U.S. cutoff and reiterated strong Senate support for continued U.S. military aid to the mujahedeen as long as the Soviets maintained their overwhelming assistance to Kabul. The resolution passed by a unanimous vote on February 29, 1988, and the accompanying debate was highly critical of the administration, particularly the State Department. The resolution received wide publicity, and, under the Senate's pressure, the administration hastily reformulated its policy in order to require "symmetry"—continuing U.S. military aid to the resistance so long as the Soviets provided similiar aid to their client regime in Kabul.

The Soviets denounced the Senate action, but the result demonstrated the impact of long and detailed Senate watchfulness over the course of the Afghan conflict. Because the Soviets were unwilling to abandon the Kabul regime and the Senate was adamantly opposed to removing key American support, the conflict became one of irresolute painful attrition. The Soviets apparently expected U.S. attention to fade over the long run and thus provide them the political victory in Afghanistan that they had been unable to secure with their own invading army. The final outcome remains to be seen.

This overview of a majority leader's dealings with American foreign policy has not covered all of the events and issues of the times or all the leaders with whom I dealt. I went to Ankara, for instance, to meet with Prime Minister Bulent Ecevit in 1978 about lifting the U.S. embargo on arms shipments to Turkey, and to Tokyo to discuss interna-

Members of the Iran-Contra committee heard testimony from hundreds of witnesses. *Office of Senator Robert C. Byrd*

tional affairs with Japanese Prime Minister Noboru Takeshita. There were also a host of other issues regarding Africa, South America, Asia, and Europe.

I cannot close this discussion, however, without referring to the notorious Iran-Contra affair and its implications for executive-legislative relations in foreign affairs. Like other senators, I was appalled at the news, in November 1986, that Reagan administration officials and private citizens had been involved in selling U.S. weapons to Iran in exchange for Iranian intercession with groups in Lebanon holding American citizens hostage. Although President Reagan repeatedly and publicly denied any knowledge of such transactions, the facts were clearly otherwise, as evidenced by the surfacing of a presidential "finding," which bore the signa-

ture "Ronald Reagan" and was dated January 17, 1986. The document stated:

> I hereby find that the following operation in a foreign country . . . is important to the national security of the United States, and due to its extreme sensitivity and security risks, I determine it is essential to limit prior notice, and direct the Director of Central Intelligence to refrain from reporting this finding to the Congress . . . until I otherwise direct.

What were the description and purpose of the "operation" as outlined by President Reagan? According to the presidential finding, the purposes were to:

> Assist selected friendly . . . third countries and third parties which have established relationships with Iranian elements . . . for the purpose of . . . (3) furthering the release of the American hostages held in

Beirut. . . . by providing these elements [within and outside the government of Iran] with arms, equipment and related materiel.

The president had publicly stated that he would countenance no deals with hostage takers and would not exchange arms for hostages. He had also publicly urged other industrialized nations to join in an embargo against providing arms to Iran.

It was also discovered that the proceeds from these arms sales apparently were being diverted to support anti-Sandinista forces in Nicaragua in flagrant violation of the Boland amendments, which Congress had adopted in 1982 to prohibit such assistance.

It was ironic that, as we prepared to celebrate the bicentennial of our Constitution, this bizarre stunt should come to light. It had been shrouded in secrecy and duplicity that had no place in an open, democratic society governed by laws, not men. The secret arms-for-hostages scandal damaged the presidency and the credibility of the United States with friends and allies. Moreover, it undermined the trust between the executive and legislative branches of the government.

When the One-hundredth Congress convened, one of the Senate's first acts was to vote 88 to 4 to adopt a resolution I had crafted and introduced, with Senator Dole as a cosponsor, creating a Select Committee on Secret Military Assistance to Iran and the Nicaraguan Opposition. I appointed Senator Daniel Inouye of Hawaii to serve as chairman, and I also appointed Senators George Mitchell of Maine, Sam Nunn of Georgia, Paul Sarbanes of Maryland, Howell Heflin of Alabama, and David Boren of Oklahoma to the committee. Minority Leader Dole appointed Senator Warren Rudman of New Hampshire to serve as vice chairman, together with Senators James McClure of Idaho, Orrin Hatch of Utah, William Cohen of Maine, and Paul Trible of Virginia. The Senate committee, working in conjunction with a similar select committee of the House, heard hundreds of witnesses and examined thousands of pages of documents. The story that unfolded was a sorry tale of White House arrogance and disdain for Congress, the American people, and the rule of law.

The Iran-Contra affair represented everything that I had fought against as majority leader and as minority leader. American foreign policy is not the exclusive domain of the presidency. The Constitution implicitly, but nonetheless clearly, provides that the executive and the legislative branches share power over foreign policy. The Senate, with its advice and consent authority and its participation with the House in the appropriations process, has a constitutional duty to remain fully informed about American foreign policy and to help steer it in a wise direction.

The full extent of President Reagan's own personal involvement in the arms deal for hostages and the Iran-Contra fiasco may never be fully revealed, but the American people had been badly misled and disserved by the president and his subordinates, who—although they may have believed their objectives to be noble—ignored the Constitution; lied to Congress; and conducted a secretive, arbitrary, and unchecked foreign policy. Had the proper congressional committees been informed of these actions at the time, they could have spared the president the acute embarrassment to which he was exposed when the scheme unraveled, because Congress would not have gone along with such a perverse undertaking. Years later, the courts are still trying the Iran-Contra defendants, some of whom have been found guilty and sentenced. One hopes that future presidents will remember the lesson of Iran-Contra: that in the making of foreign policy, they would be wise to look upon Congress as a partner rather than as an enemy.

Disagreement between the branches over specific issues of foreign policy is not a source of weakness but of potential strength. From the Panama Canal Treaty to the INF Treaty, Senate objections have helped to avoid mistakes and clarify ambiguities. Foreign leaders do not always understand our system of division of powers or appreciate the Senate's role in the ratification of treaties, but personal meetings of the type I have described between foreign leaders and the Senate leadership can be instructive for all parties and satisfy those leaders' concerns. As for United States senators, we must continue to take very seriously the separation of powers, recalling the wise words of James Madison in *The Federalist*, "In framing a government which is to be administered by men over men, the great difficulty lies in this: You must first enable the government to control the governed; and in the next place, oblige it to control itself."

CHAPTER 28

Robert C. Byrd's Senate

Reflections of a Party Leader

Thanks to the voters of West Virginia, I have had the opportunity to serve in the Senate longer than any of the twenty-nine other United States senators from my state. In this chapter, I wish to share my reflections on the Senate as it enters its third century. I must leave to others the task of assessing my leadership and contributions. My purpose here is simply to set forth my views about the Senate and my experiences as a Senate leader—as well as some personal observations—in the context of the themes established within these two volumes.

IN THE MAJORITY

When I was elected as the new majority leader in January 1977, I had already been handling the actual floor work for the majority party in the Senate for a decade. This equipped me with more floor experience than any other senator in history prior to assuming the top job. Such a background in working with the Senate's complex rules and precedents served me well during the periods of my majority leadership in the Ninety-fifth, Ninety-sixth, and One-hundredth congresses. Since a full description of the Senate's legislative contributions during

those years is available as part of this body's official record, I shall only mention some of the highlights here.*

The Senate of the Ninety-fifth Congress (1977–1978) faced many domestic and international challenges and achieved solutions to many of the most complex issues of modern times. That Congress enacted the first and only comprehensive energy program in history, created the Department of Energy, enacted an increase in the minimum wage, approved financial assistance to New York City in the form of a long-term federal loan guarantee, and passed two multi-billion-dollar tax cuts and a refinancing of the Social Security system to make it solvent into the next century. It approved the ratification of the Panama Canal treaties and provided the first comprehensive overhaul of the Civil Service system in almost a century. It also implemented a major reorganization of Senate committee jurisdictions and required financial disclosure by senators and Senate employees, as well as by all executive branch officials and top-level federal employees.

I was reelected without opposition as majority leader for the Ninety-sixth Congress (1979–1980). That Congress enacted impor-

---

* U.S., Congress, Senate, *Summary of Legislative Achievements,* 95th Cong., 2d sess., S. Doc. 95-132; 96th Cong., 2d sess., S. Doc. 96-78; 100th Cong., 2d sess., S. Doc. 100-47.

tant laws to further U.S. energy independence from foreign sources, strengthen our national defense, improve the rules of international trade, and reduce burdensome federal regulation. It also created the Department of Education and passed a crude oil windfall profit tax, intelligence oversight legislation requiring the executive branch to consult with Congress on critical intelligence activities, and superfund legislation dealing with the cleanup of toxic wastes. Unfortunately, under the Reagan administrations, much of the national energy program that was established during the Ninety-fifth and Ninety-sixth congresses was dismantled and rendered ineffective.

The One-hundredth Congress (1987–1988) compiled a record of accomplishments that, by most accounts, had not been surpassed—and perhaps not equalled—in the previous two decades. At the close of that Congress, in October 1988, the *New York Times* reported that "Congress regained its voice in the 1987–1988 session, enacting groundbreaking legislation in areas as diverse as trade policy and welfare reform, civil rights and arms control." The *Times'* report continued, "Much of the major legislation adopted in the two sessions closely tracks an agenda mapped out by Democratic leaders in January." *

Among the major accomplishments of that historic Congress were:

Omnibus Trade and Competitiveness Act
Intermediate Range Nuclear Forces (INF) Treaty
Catastrophic Health Insurance Act
Welfare Reform Act (first reform in fifty years)
Plant Closing Notification
Civil Rights Restoration Act (over the president's veto)
Fair Housing Act Amendments
Elementary and Secondary Education Act
Emergency Drought Relief
Clean Water Act (over the president's veto)
Endangered Species Act

Budget Summit Agreement
Omnibus Anti-Drug bill
U.S.-Canada Free Trade Agreement
Surface Transportation Act (over the president's veto)
Creation of Veterans' Affairs Department
Homeless Assistance
AIDS Research/Service
Housing Authorization
Tax Technical Corrections Act
Legislation to implement the Genocide Convention
Passed all thirteen appropriations bills in 1988 before the beginning of the new fiscal year, for the first time in twelve years

In April 1988, I announced that I would not be a candidate for Democratic party leader in the 101st Congress. I had long debated with myself whether I should seek a seventh term as leader, having announced in late 1987 that I would reach a decision in early 1988. Meanwhile, twenty-two of my Democratic colleagues had voluntarily asked me to run again, and I knew where the remaining votes were to be found in order to put together a majority for one more leadership win. But, after weighing the matter carefully over a period of several months, I reached my decision not to run. I did so for the following reasons: (1) my wife Erma had asked me not to run again for the position of Democratic leader; and (2) a telephone canvass of various newspaper editors and political leaders in West Virginia revealed that over 80 percent of them preferred that I take the chairmanship of the Appropriations Committee, which would become available to me since the then chairman, Senator John C. Stennis of Mississippi, had announced that he would retire at the end of the One-hundredth Congress. My constituents believed that I could do more for West Virginia as Appropriations chairman than as party leader. I had always felt that when the time finally came for me to relinquish the leadership post, I wanted to walk away from it by

* *New York Times*, October 24, 1988.

my own choice and on my own terms. That time had come. I had led my party through the valley of despair when we were six years in the minority, and we were again the majority party and scaling the peaks of successful achievements in the One-hundredth Congress. I had reached the mountaintop, with Congress well on its way to compiling an impressive record; I would be seventy-one years old in November—exceeding even the Psalmist's promised three-score years and ten; it was time to go, and I went. And I have never been sorry.

At the beginning of the 101st Congress, in January 1989, my colleagues elected me to the office of Senate president pro tempore—a constitutional officer—and I also became, by seniority and by Senate approval, the chairman of the Senate Committee on Appropriations.

Thus, on January 3, 1989, at the beginning of my thirty-first year in the Senate, I had served twenty-two years in the elected leadership of my party and had been honored with more Senate leadership offices than had any other senator in the two-hundred-year history of the Senate. For all of these high honors, I say to my colleagues and peers: Thank you! I shall always be grateful, and, in the chosen words of Paul the Apostle: "I thank my God upon every remembrance of you." (Phil. 1:3)

LEADERSHIP STYLE

I do not have any regrets as far as my leadership years are concerned. I always did my best, and I think I was an effective leader. When the going became tough, I worked all the harder. I seldom suffered a defeat as majority leader. One of the few times that I was not successful in achieving an objective, however, was when I tried to bring campaign financing reform legislation to a vote during the One-hundredth Congress. I worked hard at it; I believed in it; and I was disappointed that I was unable to get such reform legislation enacted.

My party colleagues elected me to be the leader, and I meant to be the leader. I did not hesitate to do things my way, although I realized that others sometimes did not like my approach. If I felt that the Senate ought to stay in session to get the job done, we stayed and got the job done. If Hamlet had been the Senate majority leader, he might well have soliloquized: "To be loved, or to be respected? That is the question." If there had to be such a choice, I chose to be respected. The Senate could not march to the tune of a hundred different drummers; senators would have to adjust their individual schedules to accommodate the Senate's needs. The work of the Senate came first; the "quality of life" for senators was secondary. I did my duty, and the record of Senate accomplishments during my two separate tenures as majority leader is a record that denotes a working Senate.

I believe that the Senate was an effective force in both foreign and domestic policy during those years. This tide ebbs and flows, of course; but I believe that, throughout my majority leadership, the Senate, when necessity indicated it, exercised an independent voice from that of the administration in formulating and implementing foreign policy, as well as in enacting domestic legislation and confirming nominations.

"Just stand aside and watch yourself go by," said a poet, but it is always difficult to see oneself as others see one. In leadership style, I think I was somewhere between Lyndon Johnson and Mike Mansfield, but more in the Johnson mold. I was energetic in pushing legislation and did not hesitate to use the Senate rules to force legislation forward and bring it up on the floor. On occasions when I could not get the consent of the minority to take up a bill, I used the rules to do so. To me, the Senate rules were to be used, when necessary, to advance and expedite the Senate's business. I had spent years in trying to master them because I believed that, to be an effective leader, one ought to know the rules and precedents and understand how to use them.

When I first became majority leader in 1977, I established an informal advisory panel of committee chairmen. I viewed them as the leaders of the little legislatures—the committees—who knew what legislation was moving in their committees.

I met often with my Democratic colleagues in small groups, sounding them out on the politics of different approaches to domestic and international problems, thus ascertaining the center of political gravity and facilitating the shaping of consensuses. Consensus politics does not unfailingly result in the sagest policy or the best legislative product, because consensus can mean taking the line of least resistance. Still, considering the fact that Senate leaders possess no patronage or other effective tools of discipline, they generally must rely on the incubative process of developing a line of general agreement and then coalescing the votes to win. It is an exercise that requires skill, hard work, and especially perseverance when the going is rough. I particularly respected the political judgment of such senators as Lloyd Bentsen, Wendell Ford, Daniel Inouye, Henry Jackson, Edward Kennedy, Russell Long, George Mitchell, Pat Moynihan, Sam Nunn, Paul Sarbanes, and James Sasser.

As a result of frequent meetings with senators of diverse viewpoints in my party, I was able to develop a collective sense of where we should go and how we should get there. I always tried to have an agenda in mind and to push hard during the sessions to accomplish the goals on my list. To develop such agenda, I depended a great deal on my committee chairmen, who helped me to determine the Senate legislative program, when we should schedule certain legislation, and what our overall legislative objectives ought to be in a given year and in a given Congress.

PRESS RELATIONS

I seldom sought out the media, recognizing that there were others who had better television skills than I. I came up in a political era when television was not the factor in politics that it is today. In those early years, politicians generally were judged by what they could do for their people, how hard they worked at the job, and how they voted on the issues, whereas so many of the careers of today's politicians seem to be based on their ability to deliver ten-second sound bites for the television cameras and on how much money they can raise for their election campaigns. And they are good at doing both.

I had trouble with television because TV demands oversimplification of the issues. I would spend hours mastering the details of a subject, and I found it frustrating to have to answer complex questions in one or two short sentences. But I held my own and did the interviews and appeared on the talk shows when I felt it was my responsibility to do so, and I did a good many of both over the years. Still, I felt that there were other leadership duties that I could perform much better than that of making TV appearances. Television was not my forte. I think one can be on television too much and can talk too much. In fact, senators usually do talk too much, thus staking out public positions for themselves, often without first carefully considering an issue in depth or waiting to learn what the interests of party unity may require on that issue. It is then too late to extricate themselves from their press statements, with the result that party leaders search in vain for votes. All of which is to say that frequently there are too many generals and not enough corporals, sergeants, and foot soldiers to win the big battles.

During the Carter administration, when the Democrats controlled both houses and I was Senate majority leader, I held regular Saturday morning press conferences in my Capitol office that were popular and drew considerable attention.

The press often tried to get me to predict the outcome of votes, but I knew the risks in attempting to foretell the outcome of a controversial matter. During the Reagan administration, for example, I saw the House Democratic leadership predict a victory on more than one occasion, confident of the votes that they were counting, only to see their votes slip away. I knew that the White House had certain unique advantages when it came to twisting arms and nailing down votes.

I was never comfortable in trying to present important issues to reporters who became quickly bored with details. My interest was in putting the ball across the goal line and the score on the board. That often took a lot of work in the back rooms talking with other senators, and I gave it priority over running up to the press gallery and trying to make a headline. I recognized the importance of informing the people through the media, but I believed that putting the Senate on TV had gone a long way toward satisfying that requirement. I felt that my primary duty as leader was to attend to the people's business by making the Senate run. As each piece of legislation was passed, another was waiting in line.

As the Democratic leader, I had certain responsibilities to the press: not to mislead it and to answer the questions where I could—and wanted to. According to my own blueprint, effective leadership was 5 percent press relations and 95 percent hard work behind the scenes in hammering out time agreements, preparing policy initiatives, molding consensuses among my colleagues, and doing the floor work. It can be argued

that I was mistaken in assigning that kind of rough balance. But in addition to not being particularly gregarious by nature, I felt constrained because I had to represent diverse elements in my party, and I often sought to temper my own personal views, at least publicly.

In the Minority

When the Ninety-seventh Congress convened on Monday, January 5, 1981, the Republicans had seized control of the Senate with a 53 to 47 majority. I ran unopposed and was elected leader of the Democratic minority. I had seen warning signs in 1980 that some of my Democratic colleagues were in trouble, judging by the polls and other indicators, and I had predicted as far back as the previous April that the Senate might switch to Republican control. Yet, I was surprised at the size of the margin by which the shift took place. When asked by a news reporter what advice I would have for the new Republican majority, both in the Senate and at the White House, and what they would have to learn, I responded, "That's for them to worry about; that's for someone else to teach. I'm not in the habit of giving unsolicited advice." I went on to say that, as minority leader, "I'll give it my best shot." And I did. I worked hard and gave it my best, sure that the Democrats would one day regain control of the Senate and believing that I would again become majority leader—all of which did, in due time, come to pass. During the years 1981 through 1986, I worked harmoniously with Republican Majority Leaders Howard Baker of Tennessee and Robert Dole of Kansas, cooperating with them whenever I could cooperate, and opposing them when I felt I had to do so. I saw the need for Senate Democrats to regroup, develop unity, propose alternatives to Republican programs, develop initiatives of our own, and, in general, prepare for the time—which would surely come—when the voters would swing back to the Democrats.

Meanwhile, I was reelected without opposition as minority leader at the beginning of the Ninety-eighth Congress, in January 1983.

In December 1984, I was confronted with my first leadership challenge in eight years, when Senator Lawton Chiles of Florida announced he would run for leader of the Senate Democrats. Chiles offered himself as a "new face," someone who would be more telegenic. News stories stated that Chiles "and his supporters were counting on senators committed to Byrd to switch on the secret ballot." I had been preparing for a challenge for some time and was not surprised when it came, because Senate Democrats had chafed under their minority status and some of them probably thought that a super-TV personality could restore their control and bring back their committee and subcommittee chairmanships. I did not, however, expect the challenge to come from Chiles. Apparently, his candidacy was the result of a sudden decision on his part, for he was reported as saying that when his "inner voice . . . tells me to move, I got to move."

I was confident that I had more than enough commitments to win, as it was never my style to wait until faced with an opponent before making preparations for a challenge. I always started long before the next leadership election rolled around. Faced with the Chiles challenge, I responded to press inquiries, saying, "When the votes are counted, that will be the end of it."

Chiles was a worthy contender, able and amiable, and he waged a clean fight. I took the position that he had as much right to seek the leadership post as I had, and I harbored no ill will for his doing so. Asked by a reporter about a statement by Chiles' press secretary that Senate Democrats were restless because they were in the minority and it was time to "bring in a new horse," I re-

sponded to this personal criticism by saying, "It's not going to be a cliffhanger. Aides don't vote in the Senate."

When the conference vote came on December 12, 1984, I was reelected leader of the Senate Democrats, by a vote of 36 to 11, with proxies counted. The "old face" had won again.

As the 1986 elections approached, Senate Democrats sensed that the political winds were blowing their way and that at high tide in November their ship would come in—as indeed it did. As Democrats contemplated being the majority party again, Senator J. Bennett Johnston of Louisiana announced on June 12 that he would challenge me for the leadership of the party in the One-hundredth Congress, which would convene the following January. Whereas the Chiles challenge to my leadership in the preceding Congress had, according to some observers, begun too late, this time the challenge came early—six months in advance. And whereas Senator Chiles had opined that the Democratic leadership in the Senate was in need of a "new face," Senator Johnston said that the Democrats "need a brand new image . . . I think we need a little passion out there on the floor." My response was, "This is not a Johnny Carson show." It was accomplishments, not image, I said, that counted. The Johnston challenge was a vigorous one, but, as Senator Johnston had said from the beginning, it was "friendly competition." On November 11, 1986, Senator Johnston dropped his bid for the office of majority leader in the coming One-hundredth Congress. In doing so, he said, "If you don't have the votes, you might as well not make your friends walk the plank." He had fought a good fight and was gracious in withdrawing from the contest. On November 20, I was elected Democratic leader for the sixth time by my party. It was my sixty-ninth birthday, and I was grateful to my colleagues for the gift: Senate majority leader for the One-hundredth Congress, marking two hundred years of the Senate's history.

Through the first six years of Ronald Reagan's administrations, when we were in the minority in the Senate, I developed a unity among Democrats that would serve well when we could again become the majority. This solidarity was not always easy to accomplish because of the wide diversity within the Democratic party in the Senate and because of the immense popularity of Ronald Reagan. I tried to mold a spirit of unity among my Democratic colleagues so that when we stood together, although in the minority, we could sometimes make a difference. When it came to speaking out on the issues, I was usually content to let other senators have the front seat and the front row.

In addition to attempting to build unity among Democrats, I considered it the responsibility of the minority party to develop alternate proposals to some of the legislation that was being pressed by the White House and the Senate Republican leadership.

As minority leader, I had much less to say publicly than when I was majority leader, and I received and accepted fewer invitations to be on television during that period. It was a matter of simple arithmetic: as the minority party, we did not have the votes. Having a popular president of the other party in the White House is not the most enviable position for a minority leader to be in. Unaccustomed to being out of power, the Democratic party in the Senate was demoralized and frustrated. Ronald Reagan's popularity seemed unshakable; and Senate Democrats appeared to have lost their way.

Conversely, the Democrats in the House, during those years, were in the majority, and Speaker Thomas P. "Tip" O'Neill, Jr., was in a position to say what legislation would or would not be scheduled and what the House majority would be able to deliver. Thus, the House Democrats overshadowed Senate Democrats; the House was where the action was. Being in the minority on the Senate side, I did not think that I should show up on television attempting to predict what would or would not happen in the Senate. It made a great deal of difference that I had no control of the schedule, did not have the votes, and had a dispirited bunch of Democrats looking to me for leadership in what was, in the usual sense, a no-win situation. In fact, we had to learn a new definition of "winning." Winning now often meant moderating the extremes. Winning now meant sticking together and trying to do the right thing, even when we knew we would lose.

As I said many times to my colleagues in our Tuesday conferences, "Let's go on the floor and offer this amendment because it's right. We won't win. But it's not so much how it will look today as how it will appear a year from now, when our position will have been proved right. That is what will count in the end."

To have a Republican president was bad enough for Senate Democrats, but to have Ronald Reagan in the White House was far, far worse. Reagan seemed to have a passion for kicking Congress around. He blamed Congress for everything. Confrontation was the order of the day. It appeared to me that he knew but little about the federal government when he came to Washington and that he knew little more when he left. I liked him personally and thought he was a charming man, but I believe that his fiscal and budgetary policies and his "hands-off" method of governing nearly ruined this country.

The 1981 25-percent tax cuts—5 percent the first year and 10 percent in each of the following two years—which benefited mostly the rich and high-income taxpayers, reduced the nation's revenues by the hundreds of billions in the ensuing years, while additional billions of dollars went for science-fiction-type, exotic weapons. Meanwhile, education and research programs were cut back, the nation's infrastructure was allowed to deteriorate, and the country went on living for today at the expense of tomorrow.

In a visit to the White House oval office prior to the 1981 tax cut, I told President Reagan that, in my opinion, we could not have a massive tax cut, proceed with a massive military buildup, and balance the budget in the foreseeable future. I recommended that the third year of the proposed triple-year tax cuts be dropped, at least for the time being or until two years further down the road when we would be in a better position to assess the deficit trend and evaluate the impact of the first- and second-year tax cuts on the economy. The president did not have a ready response to my suggestion, which I continued to press. Finally, he turned to Edwin Meese III, counselor to the president, who maintained that it was necessary to include the third-year tax cut in the 1981 enactment so as to provide predictability and assurance to the investment community that the cut was indeed coming. This approach would enable investors to plan for a longer period, thus providing a spur to the economy and, ultimately, an overall increase rather than a decrease in revenues to the treasury. I left the oval office with my head bloody but unbowed.

During the Reagan presidency, the federal deficits were in the trillions annually—for the first time ever—and so were trade deficits. The national debt soared, going from just under a trillion dollars to almost three trillion, and the United States went from being the greatest creditor nation in the world to become the world's largest debtor. All of this in just eight years!

Although I never rated Ronald Reagan as a first-class movie actor, he was certainly first class when it came to projecting his message on television. To a considerable extent, he had the American people fooled—not that he particularly intended to fool them; I think he really believed what he was saying. He accepted the scripts that were handed to him by his budget director, David Stockman, and others and apparently did not bother to ask questions. The public liked his "feel good" messages, and the media seemed reluctant to develop the facts and challenge his misstatements. In this case, I believe the media really fell down on the job. No other president in recent times had been let off the hook as much by the press as this one. The softball treatment of Reagan by the press was a serious disservice to the public. It was difficult for us Democrats in the Senate to compete with him, because we could not get our message across, especially being in the minority as we were. Since we did not control the committees, we lacked the institutional forums in which to project our views effectively, fashion policy, and craft implementing legislation.

Because I believed that we could not just criticize the president without having some solutions of our own, I tried wherever possible to fashion Democratic alternatives. On a number of important issues, I established Democratic task forces. These were intended to give Democrats a sense of having some influence over the course of events after having lost their committee and subcommittee chairmanships and to enable Democrats to hammer out the details of our alternatives. We had some successes.

During our six years in the minority, fairness was our battle cry as we attempted to moderate what we considered to be extreme Reagan policies. We offered alternative tax and budget plans. We attempted to make nutritious school lunches available to the two million children cut off by the Reagan administration. In order to reduce budget deficits and pay for needed infrastructure programs, we tried to suspend the third year of Reagan's three-year tax cut in 1981, and we also offered a Democratic jobs package to finance our crumbling roads and sewers, fund public works projects to employ unemployed workers, and retrain dislocated workers during a period of high unemployment and deep recession. We were defeated in these efforts, but we developed a record on which we could appeal to the voters at the ballot box, because we were advocating things that were clearly in the best interests of the country.

We sought to stress the vital need for real economic growth and competitiveness, and we tried to address the farm crisis which was devastating the family farm. Only by threatening to hold up the nomination of Edwin Meese for attorney general could the Democratic leadership secure an agreement even to consider a proposal for emergency assistance for American farmers. Congress approved this legislation, but the president vetoed it.

In foreign affairs, we opposed the administration's disastrous policy in Lebanon and sought to clarify the nation's objectives in Central America. But the administration rejected these initiatives, and the United States was left with tragedy in Lebanon and uncertainty in Central America.

We had a positive impact on foreign policy by encouraging the administration to support democracy in the Philippines, by pushing for renewed efforts at arms control, and by supporting the Afghans in their war against Soviet invaders.

We were successful in forcing the establishment of an independent inspector-general to look for waste in the Department of Defense, but perhaps our greatest success in those years was in turning the administration around in its attempt to slash the minimum social security benefit for three million retirees. In party-line vote after party-line vote, Democrats demonstrated a deep commitment to maintaining the minimum benefit, and President Reagan finally capitulated.

A minority leader in the Senate who does not have a president of his own party in the White House can do little to chart the Senate's course and is limited to engaging the opposition in rear-guard actions as a way of influencing the final legislative product. In looking back, I have often wondered why anyone would want to be a minority leader in such circumstances, except I did believe that the Democrats would eventually regain majority status; and I tried to prepare the party to assume that responsibility when it ultimately happened.

I thought that the Senate Republicans in 1981 handled their new role as the Senate's majority party very well. Of course, they had their own president to help them corral votes, which makes a world of difference. I thought they demonstrated a somewhat different approach from that of the Democrats in the way the committees and the Senate operated, but that was to be expected, considering that the two parties differ in their philosophy as to the responsibilities of government. Moreover, the Democrats had been in control of Congress for so long that, from the institutional standpoint, running the Senate was probably easier for us, simply because we had had more experience and practice in doing it. But Howard Baker and, later, Bob Dole proved to be effective majority leaders in pushing the Reagan administration's agenda. Many of the president's successes during the years 1981 through 1986 can be largely attributed to the legislative acumen of those two leaders in the Republican-controlled Senate, as well as to some exceptionally bright and effective senators such as Pete Domenici of New Mexico, James McClure of Idaho, and Ted Stevens of Alaska.

Many people think it is a good idea to have the White House controlled by one party and Congress controlled by the other, so that the two branches can keep an eye on each other. In my view, however, the resulting confrontation is not good for the country. The government works best when one and the same party is in control of both the executive and legislative branches, thus assuring responsibility and accountability. There is too much rank partisanship when the government is divided, and it leads all too often to a paralysis in formulating and implementing effective policy. Difficult problems often go unsolved because the players find it easier to assign blame than to find solutions. It is almost a sure prescription for government gridlock.

Leaders of the legislative branch must cooperate with the executive for the good of the nation. The president is the leader of the country. But even when he was of my own party, I always considered myself to be a Senate man—the Senate leader—and I felt an independence from the executive branch. I could never picture myself as being any president's "man" in the Senate, and I said so publicly. President Carter respected my viewpoint in this regard, and I tried to be helpful to him where I could. I occasionally differed with the president—not often—but I knew the Senate and I knew where the votes were. The president knew he could depend on me to be forthright with him, and he knew that I could keep a secret. I had, and still have, a great respect for President Carter. I think that history will recognize Jimmy Carter as having been a good president. He worked hard and accomplished some things that were good for the country. History will be kinder to him than were his contemporaries, including myself.

Television Coverage

One of the Senate actions during the years of the Republican majority in which I played a leading role, and of which I am particularly proud, was the institution of live television coverage of the United States Senate.

The Senate Press Galleries chapter in this volume discusses the Senate's evolution from a body that met behind closed doors to one whose proceedings may now be watched live on television by viewers across the country. In the process, it describes my efforts during the 1970's to move toward the broadcasting of Senate proceedings. Here, I shall add some details about the activities in the 1980's that finally achieved this goal.

As our nation forged through the tumultuous, controversial decades of the 1960's and 1970's, it became increasingly clear to many of us that the legislative branch of our government was in danger of being left in the historical dust. We began to understand that the ability to communicate with and influence the public is directly related to the exercise of power in a democratic society. An essential prerequisite to molding public opinion is the necessity of informing the citizens. By the early 1980's, we could see that the public in general did not understand the Senate's crucial role in our governmental processes. The president had immediate access to the media whenever he desired and could explain his actions to the American people as he wished; starting in 1979, the House broadcast its proceedings on television from gavel to gavel; but, without televised proceedings, the Senate was relatively invisible.

In the Ninety-fifth Congress, I submitted a resolution which would have authorized the installation of closed-circuit television from the Senate chamber to senators' offices, but it died in the Rules Committee.

Senator Howard Baker was a strong proponent of televising the Senate, and, in the first week of the Ninety-seventh Congress, he submitted a resolution to permit television cameras in the Senate. It was reported by the Rules Committee in August 1981, and the Senate took up the matter in February 1982. The resolution was before the Senate intermittently for the next two and one-half months. But the combination of senators who had always opposed television in the Senate, and others, like myself, who were trying to adjust to our newly acquired minority status and were not certain about how the process would function, kept the resolution far short of the sixty votes needed to close debate. The effort was abandoned for the remainder of that Congress.

Senator Charles Mathias of Maryland and Majority Leader Baker persisted in their efforts during the Ninety-eighth Congress. With several cosponsors, they submitted a resolution in February 1983, which the Rules Committee, chaired by Senator Mathias, reported in June 1983. When Senator Baker sought to bring up the issue in September 1984, the Senate invoked cloture by a vote of 73 to 26 and agreed to the motion to consider the proposal by a vote of 67 to 32. Two days later, however, the Senate failed to invoke cloture on the resolution itself, by a vote of 37 to 44, far short of the 60 votes needed. The bill was returned to the calendar.

On the first day of the Ninety-ninth Congress, January 3, 1985, I introduced a resolution to provide for television and radio coverage of the Senate and for certain facilitative changes in the Senate rules. Senator Mathias still chaired the Rules Committee, and the committee ordered the measure reported in October of that year. In February 1986, Senator Dole, who by then had become majority leader, called up the resolution, which was debated by the Senate during most of the month of February. A good portion of the debate centered not on television but on various other rules change proposals included in the resolution.

On February 27, the Senate agreed to a substitute amendment that I offered jointly with Senators Dole, Mathias, William Arm-

strong of Colorado, Albert Gore of Tennessee, and Pete Wilson of California. This amendment incorporated the rules changes that could be agreed upon, as well as the ground rules for a trial period to test televising the Senate. The Senate adopted the amended resolution by a vote of 67 to 21.

Under the resolution, the Senate tested internal broadcasts to Senate offices during the month of May 1986, followed by a period of trial broadcasts to the nation during June and July. When the Senate finally voted on July 29, 1986, to make television and radio coverage of the Senate's proceedings permanent, a very long struggle had been won.

In 1986, I stated on the Senate floor that the coming of television to the United States Senate was not an occurrence to be feared—it was an opportunity to be seized. It was a chance to improve the standing of the Senate in the eyes of the public, the media, and the students of this country who were watching video-taped curriculums on Congress in which they saw only the House of Representatives.

The people have a right to know, to see and hear, and to understand how Congress works. I believe that we have done remarkably well in fulfilling these goals, and I look forward to improving on what we have already accomplished. After more than three years of experience with televised proceedings, we know that television has not changed the way we do business in this chamber. But it has given a vast audience of the American people the opportunity to follow the legislative proceedings that will, in so many ways, affect their lives.

FUND RAISING

A corrupting influence has evolved in recent years that creates an environment for scandal and threatens to destroy the integrity of the legislative branch—not only the Senate but also the House. It is the current campaign-financing system, which will surely erode the confidence of the American people with the passage of time. When the public trust is undermined, then the structure is weakened. When the structure is sufficiently weakened, the edifice will fall.

Senators these days do not spend as much time in the chamber as was customary and possible in the past, partly because they are too busy with fund raising. Raising exorbitant amounts of money for campaigns has become the inexorable thief of time in the Senate, and it will ultimately become the thief of honor as well. The necessity of traveling from Capitol Hill around the city and around the country to raise funds for the next campaign keeps senators from doing their work on the floor and in committees and also takes them away from their families. They do not spend as much time in being senators as they did when I first came to the Senate.

The work load has also increased and will become heavier as the years pass. The population of the country is growing; new problems and new issues arise constantly and unexpectedly; and senators have too many committee assignments. Like most other senators, I serve on two major committees and one minor committee. Several senators are on more. I could easily spend all of my time with the work of one committee, which is the way it ought to be. But we senators are greedy when it comes to committee assignments. If the folks back home see a member's name on stationery that lists several prestigious committee, subcommittee, and other assignments, it tends to convey an aura of power, which, in reality, is exaggerated. Politically, it may be attractive, but when it comes to attending committee meetings, no senator can be in two or more places at once.

Will Rogers once said, "Politics has got so expensive that it takes a lot of money even to

get beat with." Today, it is difficult for most members to be full-time senators. Those senators who are not rich but who hope to continue public service in the Senate are reduced to being part-time legislators and full-time fund raisers. The voters are not yet fully aware of how much time senators spend away from their duties here because of the necessities of campaign fund raising.

Both as majority leader and as minority leader, I had to deal with the daily consequences of this incessant and growing "money chase." Senators were constantly reminding me of their need to be somewhere else on a particular day in order to raise money for their own campaigns or for those of their colleagues. Often, a group of six or eight senators was scheduled to go to New York or to California or elsewhere on a given day to raise money. Such trips took them away from their Senate duties and slowed the business of the Senate. When several senators are out of town for fund-raising events, the majority leader—although painfully aware of their need to raise money for campaign purposes—finds it difficult to schedule the Senate's work, since those senators will not be present to manage legislation on the floor, offer amendments, or vote.

Most senators probably do not understand the degree to which campaign fund-raising activities interfere with the operation of the Senate as fully as do the leaders, who have to deal with the problems of the whole Senate and are responsible for scheduling legislation for action, keeping the process moving, and getting the Senate's work done. The current method of financing campaigns not only interferes with the Senate's business and takes senators away from their families, as I have said, but it also is demeaning and will eventually result in shame and disgrace for some unlucky senator who will be brought down by it. It is a discredit to the American political system, and it seriously undermines public confidence in the institution, which, increasingly, is coming under the control of special interest groups, such as the Israeli lobby, the gun lobby, and the senior citizens' lobby, to name but three of the most powerful. Such Washington-based lobbying organizations often do not accurately represent the views of the membership they claim to be working for. They sometimes promulgate misinformation and frequently use scare tactics to whip up their members to pressure Congress. The solution, I believe, is for congressional elections to be publicly financed and for fund-raising political action committees (PACs) to be relegated to the dustbin of history, thus assuring that members of Congress would vote for the people's interests rather than for the special interests that supply the money for the members' campaigns. Money talks, and while it may not actually "buy" the votes of officeholders, it certainly gets their attention and limits their vision.

A system of public financing for congressional campaigns through voluntary contributions by taxpayers similar to that used for presidential campaigns, combined with a limitation on campaign spending, would constitute a bargain for the American people. In return, they would gain a higher quality of representation and be saddled with fewer laws and fewer costly programs enacted at the behest of special interests and pressure groups.

The Item Veto

As I look ahead to the Senate's third century, I see before us a proposal fraught with great danger to the legislative branch. This proposal would hand to the president the power to rescind or veto individual items within an appropriation act, rather than accepting or rejecting the entire measure.

If Congress were to adopt this ill-conceived proposal, the people's branch of government would suffer a self-inflicted wound that would penetrate to the heart of the constitutional system of checks and balances and separation of powers. It would destroy Congress' exclusive power of the purse, articulated in Article I, section 9, of the Constitution, which states, "No money shall be drawn from the Treasury, but in Consequence of appropriations made by Law." Under our national charter of government, only the legislative branch can make the law; thus, only the legislative branch can appropriate moneys.

Such a shift in power would radically unbalance the delicate system of separation of powers and checks and balances that constitutes the very foundation of our constitutional form of government.

The fifty-five delegates who attended the federal convention had themselves been British subjects prior to the American Revolution. Most were well versed in the development of the unwritten English constitution, and were thoroughly conversant with the story of sacrifice by Englishmen long before their own battle to establish representative government. The framers knew that the power over the purse had been safely vested in the English Parliament only after five hundred years of struggle, and that the price had sometimes been paid in blood that had flowed from the point of a sword. They knew that Magna Carta, signed in 1215 by a reluctant king, included a clause prohibiting the levying of taxes without the consent of the prelates and greater barons.

By the close of the fourteenth century in England, it had become customary to place conditions on money grants, so that to obtain funds from Parliament, the king had to agree to the attached conditions. Parliament often insisted that the money granted would be spent only for specific purposes. Here, over four centuries before the Constitutional Convention met in Philadelphia, was the beginning of our modern system of appropriations.

Throughout the seventeenth century, the English Parliament fought with a succession of kings to maintain the power over the purse. Finally, in 1689, Parliament declared William III and Mary to be joint sovereigns, but only after it prepared a Declaration of Rights, which they agreed to accept. This charter limited the monarch's powers in certain ways, among which was a restriction on levying money "without grant of parliament, for longer time or in other manner than the same is or shall be granted." Later that year, the Declaration was incorporated into a statute entitled the Bill of Rights. The supremacy of Parliament had, at last, been assured.

The power over the purse was the basic guarantee undergirding the rights and liberties of Englishmen. As the members of the Philadelphia convention prepared a written constitution for the fledgling American republic, they were guided by the long and painful history of both the motherland's unwritten constitution and the colonial experience under British rule.

With the light of seven hundred years as a lamp unto our feet, let us not now cavalierly cast aside the lessons of the past by lending voice or vote to a massive shift of power from the legislative branch to the executive. This would be the pernicious result of a line-item veto or enhanced rescissions powers for any president. Lord Byron said it best, "A thousand years scarce serve to form a state; an hour may lay it in the dust."

To concede to the executive the authority to excise items from appropriation bills, either by item vetoes or—even worse—by "enhanced" rescissions, would be an act fraught with far-reaching and dangerous consequences. The system of checks and balances established by the Constitution would be seriously altered and impaired. The executive would be strengthened while the legislative branch would be correspondingly weakened.

The influence of the president in our governmental system has already exceeded the fondest hopes of men like Hamilton, who desired a powerful executive. Two factors have especially contributed to the growth of executive power. Both were unforeseen by the Constitution's framers. The first is the emergence and growth of political parties and party patronage, with the president as titular head of his own party. The second is the expansion of the means of communication through the advent of television and radio. With ready access to these media, the president is able, from his "bully pulpit," to go over the heads of Congress and appeal directly to the people. Power to veto or rescind items, provisions, and sections of appropriation bills would enable a president to control Congress, as individual members of the Senate and House would be forced to bargain with the president in order to obtain appropriations for their states and districts. Two of the constitutionally conferred powers which help to make the Senate the unique body that it is—the treaty power and the confirmation power—could be greatly compromised by such enlarged bargaining leverage in the hands of the president, thus vitiating the checks and balances ensured by these powers.

A senator who exercised his own conscience and reflected the views of his own constituents on a given treaty or nomination could risk the loss of appropriations for roads, education, public housing, flood prevention, or airport facilities in his state. To argue that the president would not use such a "blackjack" on members of Congress is to ignore political reality.

The president would be assured of dominance over a subservient Congress. Presidents Ulysses Grant, Ronald Reagan, and others have advocated a line-item veto, but

President William Howard Taft expressed an opposing view: "The veto power does not include the right to veto a part of a bill . . . I think the power to veto items in an appropriation bill might give too much power to the president over congressmen."

Those who advocate a federal line-item veto cite the fact that forty-three of the states have it. Such an analogy is not compelling—or even relevant. The principle of separation of powers is more sharply drawn at the national level than at the state level. State constitutions and state governments deal with local problems or, at the most, problems common to the immediate region. Here, we are dealing with the federal Constitution, which binds together fifty states and the District of Columbia in a common bond. This Republic is based on a system of separation of powers that are distributed among three equal branches acting under checks and balances that operate, each against and with the other. The government of the nation must decide and implement policy, not for just a single state but, rather, for fifty states and territories. Congress, unlike a state legislature, must provide for the common defense and general welfare of the United States; wrestle with international policies affecting trade, commerce, immigration, alliances, treaties, and finance; raise and support armies and maintain a navy; establish post offices and highways; and formulate fiscal and monetary policy that will keep the economy strong and interest rates stable.

Moreover, most state legislatures—unlike Congress—meet for only brief periods during a year, or every two years, and lack the budget, oversight, and policy-making tools that fall within the realm of the national legislature. Under such circumstances, the responsibility at the state level rests more with the executive to do the budget paring— a burden, incidentally, that is made easier by the flow of federal funds into the state through the congressional pipeline that runs from Washington.

A study of the discussions involving the veto power that took place at the Constitutional Convention will produce no mention whatever of an item veto, nor was there any reference to such in any of the Federalist papers written by Madison, Hamilton, and Jay that explained the Constitution and advocated its ratification by the states. The convention debates on the veto concerned principally the issues of whether it should be an absolute or qualified negative; whether the votes necessary to override should be two-thirds or three-fourths of both houses; and whether the negative should be vested in the executive alone, or jointly in the executive and the judiciary.

As Hamilton later explained in *The Federalist*, No. 73, "The primary inducement to conferring the power in question upon the executive, is to enable him to defend himself; the secondary one is to encrease the chances in favor of the community, against the passing of bad laws, through haste, inadvertence, or design."

The framers, in their wisdom, decided against giving to the executive an absolute veto. Yet, a line-item veto would essentially amount to an absolute veto. Only in rare instances has Congress overridden the president's veto, even when he has chosen to veto a bill of general interest to the country at large. To expect two-thirds of both houses to override a veto of appropriation items of interest only to a few states or congressional districts is quite unrealistic.

On many occasions, provisions are included in legislation which, if they stood alone, would be vetoed, but, because they are part of a bill containing other provisions that the president wants, he declines to exercise the veto power. Such a bill, if stripped of the provisions objectionable to the president, would no longer be what Congress intended or envisioned when it voted to give its approval. The altered bill, which the president would then sign, would become a law different from the legislation which Congress had passed. Thus, to place in one man's hands the power to revise and amend a bill or resolution by striking language therefrom or by rescinding appropriations set forth therein, would be to make the president not only the chief executive but also the chief legislator.

Clothing the president with such legislative power would be counter to the letter and the spirit of Article I, section 1, of the Constitution, which vests *all* legislative powers in Congress. The framers clearly intended that the president's choice be limited either to a veto of the whole bill or to letting it become law.

I shall now turn briefly to the politics of the so-called item veto. I say "so-called" because there is much disagreement as to what is meant by the word *item* when it is used in this context. The proposal for an item veto is not something new; it has been around for a long time—long before Ronald Reagan, perhaps its most passionate devotee among the presidents, came to town. The item veto came into being during the Civil War, first in the provisional constitution of the Confederate States of America. It was then adopted by Georgia in 1865 and by Texas in 1866. Following the Civil War, almost every new state admitted to the Union adopted the item veto, and most of the older ones did likewise. As the states adopted the item veto, the agitation for engrafting such a veto onto the federal Constitution increased, and the proposal has been a matter of debate from its early advocacy by President Grant down to the present time.

Many who support the item veto are well-intentioned people who see it as an elixir for the disease of bloated federal deficits. Others, who have not taken the time for se-rious thought and study of the matter, simply think it is a good idea. Advocates in the legislative branch—who ought to know better—advance it as a panacea for deficit paring when, in reality, they are playing the demagogue by attempting to shift to the president a responsibility that is theirs, but which they lack both the will and the courage to carry out.

The proposal for an item veto at the national level has its appeal, and it is understandable that it would rank high in the polls. But average Americans, concerned with raising their families, advancing in their jobs, and putting the daily bread on the table, may have neither the time nor the inclination to examine and sift through the crosscurrents of history and arcane political theory in order to become fully familiar with the pros and cons of this debate. It thus becomes our responsibility, as members of the Senate and House, not to selfishly play upon an innocent ignorance, but to put aside political gimmickry. We must do what we can to inform the nation of the impracticality and the gross imprudence of giving either line-item veto or enhanced rescission power to the executive.

Madison's words in *The Federalist*, No. 63, are worth repeating here:

. . . [T]here are particular moments in public affairs, when the people stimulated by some irregular passion, . . . or misled by the artful misrepresentations of interested men, may call for measures which they themselves will afterwards be the most ready to lament and condemn. In these critical moments, how salutary will be the interference of some temperate and respectable body of citizens, in order to . . . suspend the blow meditated by the people against themselves, until reason, justice and truth, can regain their authority over the public mind? What bitter anguish would not the people of Athens have often escaped, if their government had contained so provident a safeguard against the tyranny of their own passions? Popular liberty might then have escaped the indelible reproach of decreeing to the same citizens, the hemlock on one day, and statues on the next.

Madison was illustrating the utility of a Senate in the establishment of the national character. From his penetrating observations, we may derive a true sense of our duty as senators to the states and to the people.

Let us then do our duty, forgetting not that the power over the purse, as Madison wrote in *The Federalist*, No. 58, "may in fact be . . . the most compleat and effectual weapon with which any constitution can arm the immediate representatives of the people, for obtaining a redress of every grievance, and for carrying into effect every just and salutary measure."

ADVICE TO A NEW SENATOR

If a newly elected senator were to ask for my views on how best to serve the Senate and the nation and for my advice on how to get ahead in this institution, I would recommend: stay in touch with your constituents, don't speak too often, keep your hands clean, wear no man's collar but your own, and work hard.

I believe that what is sometimes considered to be the result of genius is more the result of persistence, perseverance, and hard work. To be a good senator, one has to work at it. My advice would be to heed the Scriptural instruction, "Whatsoever thy hand findeth to do, do it with thy might." Whatever assignment one is given, work hard at the job. Master the subject. The Biblical proverb speaks of the reward: "Seest thou a man diligent in his business? He shall stand before kings."

Senators are quick to applaud the work that another senator does when he demonstrates a thorough grasp of the subject matter. A senator will be listened to if his colleagues perceive him as one who does his homework. That is the way to gain the recognition and respect of one's peers. Senators are quick to distinguish between a workhorse and a show horse.

I would also suggest to new senators that when they come to Washington they not be too easily swayed by the local media—the Washington press. Many of the pundits in Washington know little and care less about the opinions and views of people outside the Washington area. A senator will soon be out of tune with the rest of the country if he listens too much to the people who sit in Washington's ivory towers. The political winds outside Washington often blow in very different directions from the prevailing opinions purveyed by the political and journalistic wise guys in this media-hyped city—sometimes referred to as the ego capital of the world. Every editorial is the opinion of its anonymous author—and Washington's editorial writers and columnists are not the constituents back home who vote. Listen instead to the people back in the hills and hollows and up the creeks. There is more real wisdom gathered around a pot-bellied stove in an old country store on a cold day in January than may be found in all of the cocktail circuit here in this city throughout the whole year. And besides, the country gathering is far less boring and the surroundings are a lot safer.

Someone has said that politics is a dirty business. It is not a dirty business. Politics is a noble calling. But dirty politicians have given it a bad name. The ancient usurper of the throne and today's corrupt politician have at least one thing in common: unclean hands. The one's hands were imbrued with blood; the other's are stained with the currency of gain that is ill gotten. The usurper resorted to the sword to wrest the diadem and don the royal purple and then exterminated or exiled the kinsmen of the former occupant of the throne; the politician's course

Senators of the One-hundredth Congress gathered
for their official photograph on the steps of the U.S.
Capitol, July 26, 1988.
John O. Hamilton/U.S. Senate Historical Office

is more subtle—he uses words to defame his adversary and disarm the voters, and all the people suffer.

The man—or woman—who is elected to office, at any level of government, has been vested with a high honor and will never get rich solely on the salary of that office declared by law. If he uses his office for ill-gotten gains, he violates the people's trust, disgraces himself, casts shame upon his family and future generations of his bloodline, and dishonors all politicians at all levels of government.

Another politician who places an indelible stain upon his profession is one who sees all other politicians as demagogues and knows himself to be a demagogue but pretends to be something else. In a sense, he is as bad as the corrupt holder of office. He takes advantage of the gullibility of his constituents, plays upon their emotions and excites their passions, and deliberately—or at least knowingly—misleads them. He is clever, cunning, and cruel. He, as much as the venally corrupt politician, gives politics a bad name, because through him the people see all politicians as false.

Perhaps those who should bear the most guilt for "dirty politics" in the American political system are the people themselves. As some perceptive sage has said, "An elected official is one who gets 51 percent of the vote cast by 40 percent of the 60 percent of voters who registered." How true! Yet, I have to say to the newly elected senator, to myself, and to all other holders of public office, the burden and the duty are first upon *us*: keep your hands—and your conscience—clean; politics is *not* a dirty business!

SOME PERSONAL VIEWS—HOME-SPUN

We, the people of these United States, live in a country whose greatness seems to have been foreordained by her fortunate geography and rich natural resources, her agreeable and temperate climate, and by the hardy and industrious race of men and women who hewed her forests, cultivated her fields, bridged her rivers, built her cities, and created the American Dream that has excited the envy and won the admiration of mankind around the globe. How blessed we are to have inherited this pearl of great price! And how thankful we should be to the provident hand of that omnipotent Being who has favored our undertakings from the pre-dawn infancy of the colonial experience to the present-day meridian of the American Republic!

Let us not forget, however, that a nation's ascendancy to the heights of power carries with it no assurance that fortune's smile will never turn away. The pages of history are replete with the instructive accounts of other great civilizations that, in their prime, strode like colossuses upon the sands of time. Yet, they declined and fell—many without a trace. A hundred generations have since dropped, like the leaves of autumn, into the silence of the grave, leaving only a few decaying monuments, or fragments thereof, to testify to their bygone greatness.

For example, the mighty Roman empire was for centuries the wonder of the world. Her far-flung provinces stretched from Britain in the west to the waters of the Euphrates in the east; from the Rhine and the Danube in the north to the pyramids of Egypt and the deserts of Africa and Arabia in the south. Her temples and triumphal arches, her roads and aqueducts were among the noblest monuments to her engineering and creative genius. Commerce from all points of the compass flowed through her ports and over her highways into her thriving cities. Her forts and garrisons and her intrepid legions, bearing the glittering standard of the golden eagle at their head, protected her vast dominions against the marauding barbarians of the north and defeated the invading armies of Persian monarchs from beyond the Euphrates.

But, as Edward Gibbon tells us, the Roman empire's decline began when the Praetorian guards succumbed to the luxuries of the baths and theaters and easy living, and disobedience and relaxed discipline weakened the Roman legions. The decline was assured when public virtue and patriotism gave way to immorality and sedition, and when Roman citizens demanded free bread and public shows. The Roman Senate lost its dignity and its honor; corruption and venality were enthroned in high places; laziness and indolence were rewarded; emperors were assassinated and their wives and children exiled or put to death; and citizens were massacred in the civil wars fought to benefit tyrants ambitious to secure the throne and wear the purple.

A lesson to be drawn from the brilliant works of Gibbon is that the enemies of Rome were within her bosom, and they paved the way for the empire's collapse and fall—first, to the relentless barbarian invaders in the west and, a thousand years later, to the Turks in the east.

Many of the early symptoms that heralded the Roman empire's decline may be seen in our own nation today: the ubiquitous violence and immorality so pervasive throughout our society; the prevalence of corruption, dishonesty, and greed in government and in business circles; too much money in politics; the apathy of the governed toward the selection of those who govern; laziness, the love of easy living, the loss of pride in our work product, the exit of discipline from the schoolroom, the "government-owes-me-a-living" syndrome; and the decline of religion and family values. All of these, as I have watched them come about over a lifetime now of more than seventy years, are the early but sure signs of a decay in our society and institutions and in our national life. In my view, they bode ill for the future of our country. Like Edwin Markham, an American poet and lecturer, in his poem "The Fear for Thee, My Country":

> I fear the vermin that shall undermine
> Senate and citadel and school and shrine—
> The Worm of Greed, the fatted Worm of
>   Ease,
> And all the crawling progeny of these—
> The vermin that shall honeycomb the towers
> And walls of State in unsuspecting hours.

Markham's words are prophetic, and I believe it is our duty—as senators, as citizens who care and to whose hands the stewardship for the future has been entrusted—to do all we can to reverse, or at least arrest, the national decline in moral and religious values and in educational and professional standards, and go back to the basic virtues that made America "the land of the heart's desire."

The Biblical proverb admonishes us, "Remove not the ancient landmark, which thy fathers have set." Sometimes I fear that we have about lost sight of the old verities and values that made this a great country. My old "Mom" would probably say we have gotten above "our raisin'." Some of us have become so "sophisticated" that we look with scorn upon others who still hold onto the old beliefs: that rights and responsibilities go hand in hand; that honor and reward are to be found in honest toil; and that mediocrity is not good enough in anything, anywhere, or anytime. Ours is becoming a nation of hardened cynics. We ought to return to our beginnings, go back to the hills, look up at the treetops and the open sky, and gain a renewed sense of God's presence in our personal lives and in the life of the nation.

My foster parents on their knees influenced my life from my early beginnings. We may stray from what we were taught, but if we have had fundamental values ingrained in us from the outset, we will return to those early lessons. As senators, we especially need to remember the old values—such as faith in God, obedience to law, respect for the flag, honesty and thrift—and, as leaders, we should commend those values to the young people of America.

We senators should never forget that the roads that led us to Washington also lead back home. It is the people out there in the hills and hollows and what *they* think that counts. The farmer with his hand on the plow and the miner with his pick and shovel; the women who stay after the church meetings to wash the dishes; the teacher in the schoolroom; the fisherman in his boat on the stormy deep; the driver of a dog team in the frozen wastes of the far North; the lonely policeman who keeps the midnight watch—these are just plain folks, the people who count. They live near the bone and marrow of life, and they struggle daily to make a living.

> Their's is a song of little men,
> Whose strength is iron and leather,
> Who have no time for gold and fame
> While holding a world together.

I know that the hour is late and that "the world is too much with us," as Wordsworth said, but there is yet time and we should not "lay waste our powers." One senator, one teacher, one man or woman may set in motion today the forces that will change tomorrow's world. As leaders of the nation, we have a responsibility to urge our people to excel—in the workplace and in the classroom. Education is the best insurance for old age. One should never stop trying to learn. All of man's learning has barely scratched the surface of even the best brain. Aristotle said that "the fate of empires depends on the education of youth." Any nation that honors its ballplayers more than its scholars does not have its head screwed on straight, to use a familiar idiom. No ball game ever changed the course of history.

Regarding both the rewards of education and the cultivation of wholesome values in our national life, major network television, which can be, and is, a tremendous force for *good* in our society, often is just the opposite. On most nights, with the flick of a remote-control device, the living rooms of American families can be treated to a melange of foul-mouthed brats uttering language for which any stranger entering those same living rooms and uttering that same language would probably be thrown out bodily, and the use of which in any polite company would earn its user a reputation as a boor and a lout. The crudeness, profanity, vice and violence, and the semipornographic visualization of so much that is being broadcast over the airwaves for public consumption, are eroding our traditional mores and values and benumbing the nation's conscience. By the current tolerance of this diminution of taste and values on television we are teaching our children that the basest level of human behavior is the accepted norm. I consider it a duty to speak out in protest of such degradative programs.

This amazing electronic medium *could* be one of the greatest of all forces for the advancement of excellence in learning; yet, its pitch to the audience seems geared to a common denominator pegged to the lowest point on the mediocrity scale. While television does serve the nation in many ways, so much of its programming is quality-minus, filled with inane clutter, and has a corrosive effect on the nation's character. Little wonder that discipline has exited from the classroom, our students have fallen behind those of other industrialized countries, and America's moral fabric is not just becoming frayed around the edges but is falling apart at the seams.

All of the junk television and junk movies can never be worth the price of one good book. Violence, drugs, and booze are not the way to happiness and long life, and four-letter words are neither "in" nor right nor smart. Let's keep our values straight. Just because they may seem old fashioned doesn't mean that they are not good.

In these confusing days, "The time is out of joint." Each of us is duty "born to set it right," and our compass and our anchor today, as in the days of old, should be the Book our fathers read.

Far from the madding crowd's ignoble strife,
Their sober wishes never learned to stray;
Along the cool sequester'd vale of life
They kept the noiseless tenor of their way.*

* Thomas Gray, "Elegy Written in a Country Churchyard."

The Senate

The Senate of ancient Rome was the supreme council of the state and consisted, originally, of 100 nobles, chosen by Romulus, the legendary founder of Rome circa 1000 to 750 B.C. Later the number was 200, then 300 by the time the Roman Republic was established in 509 B.C. Lucius Cornelius Sulla increased the number to 600, Julius Caesar to 900. Augustus decreased it to 600. At first, the Roman Senate was wholly patrician, but at an early date plebeians were appointed. Its powers were originally only advisory, but later were extended to include administrative and legislative functions.

Senates in the provinces were common under the Roman Empire. Edward Gibbon related that Julian, a Roman emperor from 360 to 363 A.D., sent the whole Senate of Antioch, consisting of two hundred of the most noble and wealthy citizens, under guard from the palace to prison, though they were permitted, before the close of evening, to return to their homes.

There were other ancient senates. Plutarch tells us that the senate of Sparta was the first and most important institution created by Lycurgus the Lawgiver. The Spartan Senate had twenty-eight members and, according to Plato, it had equal authority with the kings and was the means of keeping them in check.

The American Senate, in my opinion, was the premiere spark of brilliance that emerged from the collective intellect of the Constitution's framers. It was not intended to function like the House of Representatives. It was meant to be a deliberative body, but it can act quickly when necessity requires it to do so. Haste makes bad legislation.

One of the Senate's greatest institutional strengths resides in its rules. For example, there is no limit on Senate debate except through cloture or by unanimous consent. The fact that the Senate can amend House-passed legislation is also important, for not every upper legislative body has the power to amend the actions of the lower body. The Senate can also originate legislation—except in the instance of revenue-raising measures, which, under the Constitution, must originate in the House, but which can be amended in the Senate. Appropriation bills, customarily, also originate in the House.

The Senate not only has the power to legislate. It also has the power to investigate, to approve the ratification of treaties, to confirm nominations, and to try impeached persons. Thus, it has judicial, legislative, executive, and investigative powers.

This combination of powers makes the Senate unique. It is also a continuing body, unlike the House, in the sense that two-thirds of its membership always carries over from one Congress to the next. Thus, there is a steadfast and constant membership mass that gives the Senate an enduring stability. These, too, are among its strengths.

As for the Senate's weaknesses, one is bound to observe that "the fault, dear Brutus, is not in our stars, but in ourselves, that we are underlings." If something seems wrong with the Senate from time to time, we, the members, might try looking into the mirror; there, in all probability, we will see where the problem lies. Those who weaken the Senate are members who, in one way or another, bring discredit on the institution; those who never quite understand it; and those who lack the institutional memory that fosters an appreciation of its history, its customs, its traditions, its rules and precedents, and a pride in having been chosen to serve in it.

Originally consisting of only twenty-two members, the Senate had grown to a membership of ninety-eight by the time I was sworn in as a new senator in January 1959. After two hundred years, it is still the anchor of the Republic, the morning and evening star in the American constitutional constellation. It has had its giants and its little men, its Websters and its Bilbos, its Calhouns and its McCarthys. It has been the stage of high drama, of comedy and of tragedy, and its players have been the great and the near-great, those who think they are great, and those who will never be great. It has weathered the storms of adversity, withstood the barbs of cynics and the attacks of critics, and provided stability and strength to the nation during periods of civil strife and uncertainty, panics and depressions. In war and in peace, it has been the sure refuge and protector of the rights of the states and of a political minority. And, today, the Senate still stands—the great forum of constitutional American liberty!

Notes

POWERS

Divider Page Quotations

[1] *Notes of Debates in the Federal Convention of 1787 Reported by James Madison* (Athens, OH, 1984), p. 193.

[2] Jacob E. Cooke, ed., *The Federalist* (Middletown, CT, 1961), p. 394.

[3] U.S., Congress, Senate, *Annals of Congress*, 8th Cong., 2d sess., p. 71.

[4] U.S., Congress, Senate, *Congressional Globe*, 31st Cong., 1st sess., p. 476.

CHAPTER 1

Treaties

[1] George H. Haynes, *The Senate of the United States: Its History and Practice* (Boston, 1938), 2:572, 574.

[2] Denna Frank Fleming, *The Treaty Veto of the American Senate* (New York, 1930), pp. 3–15.

[3] Jacob E. Cooke, ed., *The Federalist* (Middletown, CT, 1961), pp. 503–9.

[4] U.S., Congress, Senate, *The United States Senate, 1787–1801: A Dissertation on the First Fourteen Years of the Upper Legislative Body*, by Roy Swanstrom, S. Doc. 100-31, 100th Cong., 1st sess., 1988, pp. 24–25.

[5] Ibid., p. 113.

[6] Henry Cabot Lodge, "The Treaty-Making Power of the Senate," in Henry Cabot Lodge, *A Fighting Frigate and Other Essays and Addresses* (New York, 1902), pp. 231–32.

[7] Linda Grant De Pauw, ed., *Senate Executive Journal and Related Documents, Documentary History of the First Federal Congress of the United States of America*, vol. 2 (Baltimore, 1974), pp. 17, 24; John C. Fitzpatrick, ed., *The Writings of George Washington* (Washington, DC, 1939), 30:369–75.

[8] Fitzpatrick, 30:375–79.

[9] De Pauw, p. 30.

[10] Kenneth R. Bowling and Helen E. Veit, eds., *The Diary of William Maclay and Other Notes on Senate Debates, Documentary History of the First Federal Congress of the United States of America*, vol. 9 (Baltimore, 1988), pp. 128–30; see also U.S., Congress, Senate, *The Senate, 1789–1989*, by Robert C. Byrd, vol. 1, S. Doc. 100-20, 100th Cong., 1st sess., 1988, p. 14.

[11] Bowling and Veit, pp. 130–31.

[12] Ibid.

[13] Swanstrom, pp. 121–22.

[14] Ibid., pp. 122–23.

[15] Ibid., pp. 135–43.

[16] Arthur M. Schlesinger, Jr., *The Imperial Presidency* (Boston, 1973), pp. 79–80.

[17] U.S., Congress, Senate, *Executive Journal*, 29th Cong., 1st sess., pp. 84–85.

[18] James D. Richardson, ed., *Compilation of the Messages and Papers of the Presidents, 1789–1897*, H. Mis. Doc. 210, 53d Cong., 2d sess., 1907, 6:81–82.

[19] Ibid., 7:166.

[20] George Frisbie Hoar, *The Autobiography of Seventy Years* (New York, 1903), 2: 47–50.

[21] *Francis O. Wilcox, Chief of Staff, Senate Foreign Relations Committee, 1947–1955*, Oral History Interviews, February 1–June 13, 1984 (U.S. Senate Historical Office, Washington, DC), pp. 27–29.

[22] U.S., Congress, Senate, Committee on Foreign Relations, *Executive Sessions of the Senate Foreign Relations Committee Together with the Senate Armed Services Committee (Historical Series)*, vol. 9, 85th Cong., 1st sess., 1957 (Washington, DC, 1979), pp. 701, 722–27.

[23] *Francis O. Wilcox*, p. 205.

[24] Haynes, 2:660.

[25] Congressional Research Service, Library of Congress; Counts of treaties and treaty actions may vary because of differing methods and judgments, such as whether to count a protocol to a treaty as a separate treaty.

[26] For a discussion of the issue of executive agreements, see U.S., Congress, Senate, Committee on Foreign Relations, *Treaties and Other International Agreements: The Role of the United States Senate*, S. Print 98-205, 98th Cong., 2d sess., 1984.

[27] See Duane A. Tananbaum, *The Bricker Amendment Controversy: A Test of Eisenhower's Political Leadership* (Ithaca, NY, 1988), chapter 10.

[28] *Treaties and Other International Agreements*, pp. 39–40.

[29] Ibid.

[30] "Senate Blocks Treaty Limiting Recoveries in Air Disasters," *Congressional Quarterly Weekly Report* 41 (March 12, 1983), p. 516.

CHAPTER 2

Nominations

[1] Buckley et al. v. Valeo, Secretary of the United States Senate, *U.S. Reports* 424 (30 January 1976), pp. 121, 124.

[2] Jane Butzner, *Constitutional Chaff: Rejected Suggestions of the Constitutional Convention of 1787* (Port Washington, NY, 1972; reprint of 1941 ed.), pp. 107–11; Jacob E. Cooke, ed., *The Federalist* (Middletown, CT, 1961), p. 449.

[3] U.S., Congress, House, *Formation of the Union of the American States*, H. Doc. 398, 69th Cong., 1st sess., 1927, pp. 153, 430.

[4] Cooke, p. 512.

[5] Ibid., p. 513.

[6] Goldwin Albert Smith, *A History of England* (New York, 1966), pp. 184–86.

[7] Linda Grant DePauw, ed., *Senate Executive Journal and Related Documents, Documentary History of the First Federal Congress of the United States of America*, vol. 2 (Baltimore, 1974), pp. 8–9.

[8] George H. Haynes, *The Senate of the United States: Its History and Practice* (Boston, 1938), 2:724–25.

[9] Ibid., 2:726; U.S., Congress, Senate, *The United States Senate, 1787–1801: A Dissertation on the First Fourteen Years of the Upper Legislative Body*, by Roy Swanstrom, S. Doc. 100-31, 100th Cong., 1st sess., 1988, p. 98.

[10] Swanstrom, pp. 98–99; DePauw, pp. 17, 29–30.

[11] See F.B. Marbut, *News from the Capital: The Story of Washington Reporting* (Carbondale, IL, 1971).

[12] Haynes, 2:725; Swanstrom, pp. 99–100.

[13] DePauw, pp. 24–25; Joseph P. Harris, *The Advice and Consent of the Senate: A Study of the Confirmation of Appointments by the United States Senate* (Berkeley, CA, 1953), pp. 40–41.

[14] Swanstrom, p. 109.

[15] Thomas Jefferson to Gideon Granger, March 29, 1801, *The Writings of Thomas Jefferson*, ed. Paul L. Ford (New York, 1892–1899), 8:44, quoted in Noble E. Cunningham, Jr., *The Process of Government Under Jefferson* (Princeton, NJ, 1978), p. 165.

[16] Harris, pp. 48–50.

[17] Gaillard Hunt, ed., *The Writings of James Madison* (New York, 1908), 8:331–32.

[18] Harris, pp. 54–57; see also Donald B. Cole, *Martin Van Buren and the American Political System* (Princeton, NJ, 1984), pp. 216–32.

[19] Harris, pp. 62–64.

[20] Ibid., pp. 66–67.

[21] Ibid., pp. 69–70.

[22] Margaret Susan Thompson, *The "Spider Web": Congress and Lobbying in the Age of Grant* (Ithaca, NY, 1985), p. 158.

[23] Allan G. Bogue, *The Congressman's Civil War* (New York, 1989), p. 34.

[24] President Franklin D. Roosevelt's attempt to dismiss a member of the Federal Trade Commission was rejected by the Supreme Court in the 1936 case *Humphrey's Executor (Rathbun)* v. *U.S.*; See William E. Leuchtenburg, "The Case of the Contentious Commissioner: *Humphrey's Executor v. U.S.*," in Harold M. Hyman and Leonard W. Levy, eds., *Freedom and Reform: Essays in Honor of Henry Steele Commager* (New York, 1967), pp. 276–367.

[25] William S. McFeely, *Grant: A Biography* (New York, 1981), pp. 290–95.

[26] Harris, pp. 74–75.

[27] Ibid., pp. 84–87; Robert Rienow and Leona Train Rienow, *Of Snuff, Sin and the Senate* (Chicago, 1965), pp. 75–92.

[28] Harris, pp. 88–90.

[29] Ibid., pp. 99–103.

[30] Ibid., pp. 104–14.

[31] *Congressional Quarterly's Guide to Congress*, 3d ed. (Washington, DC, 1982), p. 206.

[32] U.S., Congress, Senate, Committee on Rules and Administration, *Senate Manual*, S. Doc. 101-1, 101st Cong., 1st sess., 1989, pp. 885–86.

[33] See my more extended discussion of Dawes' rush to the Capitol in U.S., Congress, Senate, *The Senate, 1789–1989*, by Robert C. Byrd, vol. 1, S. Doc. 100-20, 100th Cong., 1st sess., 1988, pp. 442–44.

[34] Richard Allan Baker, "A Slap at the 'Hidden-Hand Presidency': The Senate and the Lewis Strauss Affair," *Congress and the Presidency* 14 (Spring 1987): 1–16.

[35] Pat M. Holt, *Chief of Staff, Foreign Relations Committee*, Oral History Interviews, September 9 to December 12, 1980 (U.S. Senate Historical Office, Washington, DC), p. 223.

[36] Linda Greenhouse, "Steering Nominees Over Capitol Hill," *New York Times*, August 18, 1986.

[37] Peter B. Kovler, "Consent without Advice," *Commonweal* 5 (July 7, 1978): 430–33; "Senate Confirmation Process: Half Rubber, Half Stamp," *Washington Post*, September 10, 1977.

[38] Cooke, p. 513.

CHAPTER 3
Rules

[1] U.S., Congress, House, *House Rules and Manual, 100th Congress, Jefferson's Manual of Parliamentary Practice* (Washington, D.C., 1987), pp. 113–14.

[2] Ibid., pp. 115–16.

[3] Kenneth R. Bowling and Helen E. Veit, eds., *The Diary of William Maclay and Other Notes on Senate Debates, Documentary History of the First Federal Congress of the United States of America*, vol. 9 (Baltimore, 1988), pp. 403–4.

[4] Ibid., p. 405.

[5] U.S., Congress, Senate, Committee on Rules and Administration, *History of the Committee on Rules and Administration, United States Senate*, S. Doc. 96-27, 96th Cong., 1st sess., 1980, pp. 5–6.

[6] U.S., Congress, Senate, *The United States Senate, 1787–1801: A Dissertation on the First Fourteen Years of the Upper Legislative Body*, by Roy Swanstrom, S. Doc. 100-31, 100th Cong., 1st sess., 1988, p. 189.

[7] *History of the Committee on Rules*, pp. 5–6.

[8] U.S., Congress, Senate, *Congressional Record*, 44th Cong., 1st sess., pp. 220, 309–10, 517–20, 1020–24. The twenty-two joint rules of 1871 are found in the *Senate Manual* (Washington, DC, 1871), pp. 173–78. For a discussion of the abrogation of the joint rules, see Asher C. Hinds, *Hinds' Precedents of the House of Representatives of the United States*, vol. 4 (Washington, DC, 1907), pp. 311–13.

[9] Robert F. Thornton, "Evolution of the 'Rules of Procedure and Practice in the Senate when Sitting on Impeachment Trials,'" American Law Division, Congressional Research Service, The Library of Congress, Washington, DC, September 3, 1974, pp. 1–23.

[10] U.S., Congress, Senate, *Procedure and Guidelines for Impeachment Trials in the United States Senate*, by Floyd M. Riddick, S. Doc. 93-102, 93d Cong., 2d sess., 1974; U.S., Congress, Senate, *Amending the Rules of Procedure and Practice in the Senate When Sitting on Impeachment Trials*, S.

Rept. 99-401, 99th Cong., 2d sess., 1986; *Congressional Record*, pp. S11902–3 (Daily Edition, August 15, 1986).

[11] U.S., Congress, Senate, *A Compilation of Points of Order and Decisions Thereon*, comp. William J. McDonald, (Washington, DC, 1881).

[12] U.S., Congress, Senate, *Precedents Related to the Privileges of the Senate*, ed. George P. Furber, (Washington, DC, 1893).

[13] U.S., Congress, Senate, *Digest of Decisions and Precedents of the Senate and House of Representatives of the United States*, ed. Henry H. Smith, Mis. Doc. 278, 53d Cong., 2d sess., 1894.

[14] U.S., Congress, Senate, *Precedents: Decisions on Points of Order with Phraseology in the United States Senate*, comp. Henry H. Gilfry, Doc. 129, 61st Cong., 1st sess., 1909.

[15] Ibid., p. 480.

[16] U.S., Congress, Senate, *Senate Procedure: Precedents and Practices*, comp. Floyd M. Riddick, S. Doc. 97-2, 97th Cong., 1st sess., 1981, p. xi.

[17] Bowling and Veit, p. 401.

[18] *Congressional Record*, 54th Cong., 2d sess., p. 2932.

CHAPTER 4
Impeachment
The Historical Development of Impeachment, 1376–1789

[1] U.S., Congress, Senate, *Congressional Record*, 101st Cong., 1st sess., p. S14636 (Daily Edition, November 3, 1989).

[2] Raoul Berger, *Impeachment: The Constitutional Problems* (Cambridge, MA, 1973; Bantam edition, 1974), p. 4.

[3] U.S., Congress, House, *Formation of the Union of the American States*, H. Doc. 398, 69th Cong., 1st sess., 1927, p. 691.

[4] Berger, p. 57.

[5] Ibid., p. 1.

[6] Quoted in Goldwin Albert Smith, *A History of England* (New York, 1966), pp. 141–42.

[7] Ibid., p. 298.

[8] Berger, p. 32.

[9] Smith, p. 320.

[10] Berger, pp. 33–34.

[11] Ibid., pp. 34–37.

[12] Smith, pp. 321–22.

[13] Berger, p. 34.

[14] Ibid., pp. 104–5.

[15] Peter Charles Hoffer and N.E.H. Hull, *Impeachment in America, 1635–1805* (New Haven, CT, 1984), p. xiii.

[16] Ibid., p. xii.

[17] Quoted in ibid., p. 12.

[18] Ibid., pp. 9–11, 13.

[19] Ibid., pp. 15, 17.

[20] Ibid., pp. 17–21.

[21] Ibid., p. 25.

[22] Ibid., p. 41.

[23] Ibid., pp. 64, 68.

[24] Ibid., pp. 84–85.

[25] Ibid., pp. 78–80, 83.

[26] Ibid., p. 85.

[27] Ibid., pp. 85–86.

[28] Ibid., p. 68.

[29] Berger, p. 338.

[30] Quoted in ibid., p. 79.

[31] Hoffer and Hull, pp. 68–70, 76.

[32] Ibid., pp. 96–97.

[33] *Formation of the Union of the American States*, pp. 118–19.

[34] Ibid., pp. 141–44.

[35] Ibid., pp. 202–3.

[36] Ibid., pp. 205–6.

[37] Ibid., pp. 215–25.

[38] Ibid., pp. 226–34, 236.

[39] Ibid., p. 417–21.

[40] Ibid., pp. 465, 471, 478–79.

[41] Ibid., pp. 573–74, 596, 621, 624–25.

[42] Ibid., pp. 655, 659–61.

[43] Ibid., pp. 179, 395.

[44] Hoffer and Hull, p. 99.

[45] Ibid.

[46] *Formation of the Union of the American States*, p. 663.

[47] Ibid., pp. 144, 202, 236, 458, 469, 225, 418, 421, 479, 621, 574, 661.

[48] Ibid., pp. 691–93.

[49] Hoffer and Hull, pp. 101–2.

[50] *Formation of the Union of the American States*, pp. 691–92.

[51] Ibid., pp. 694, 702, 721.

[52] Ibid., p. 741.

[53] Jonathan Elliot, ed., *The Debates in the Several State Conventions, on the Adoption of the Federal Constitution* (Washington, DC, 1836), 4:113–14.

[54] Ibid., 4:126–27, 48.

[55] Ibid., 4:281, 276.

[56] Ibid., 3:498, 500, 516.

[57] Ibid., 4:17.

[58] Jacob E. Cooke, ed., *The Federalist* (Middletown, CT, 1961), pp. 439–41.

[59] Quoted in Hoffer and Hull, pp. 119–20.

[60] Ibid., pp. 123, 144.

[61] Ibid., p. 145.

Impeachment Trials in the Senate, 1789–1989

[1] Peter Charles Hoffer and N.E.H. Hull, *Impeachment in America, 1635–1805* (New Haven, CT, 1984), pp. 151–63.

[2] Quoted in ibid., p. 208.

[3] Ibid., pp. 206–17; U.S., Congress, Senate, *Annals of Congress*, 8th Cong., 1st sess., pp. 319–64; George H. Haynes, *The Senate of the United States: Its History and Practice* (Boston, 1938), 2:849–50.

[4] Hoffer and Hull, pp. 217–20.

[5] Ibid., p. 231.

[6] Ibid., pp. 218–55.

[7] U.S., Congress, House, Committee on the Judiciary, *Constitutional Grounds for Presidential Impeachment*, 93d Cong., 2d sess., House Committee Print, 1974, pp. 45–46.

[8] Ibid., pp. 46–47; Philip Kurland, "Watergate, Impeachment, and the Constitution," *Mississippi Law Journal* 45 (May 1974): 553.

Michael Les Benedict, *The Impeachment and Trial of Andrew Johnson* (New York, 1973), pp. 1–25.

[10] Ibid., pp. 89–125.

[11] Ibid., pp. 126–80; see also *Trial of Andrew Johnson, President of the United States, On Impeachment, By the House of Representatives For High Crimes and Misdemeanors* (New York, 1970; reprint of 1868 ed.), vol. 2.

[12] Kurland, p. 556; *Congressional Quarterly's Guide to Congress*, 3d ed., (Washington, DC, 1982), p. 246.

[13] Kurland, p. 556; Haynes, 2:861.

[14] Haynes, 2:875–77; U.S., Congress, Senate, *Congressional Record*, 99th Cong., 2d sess., pp. S16350–53 (Daily Edition, October 15, 1986).

[15] Haynes, 2:861–62, 875–77; *Congressional Record*, 99th Cong., 2d sess., p. S16352 (Daily Edition, October 15, 1986).

[16] *New York Times*, May 17–25, 1933; Kurland, pp. 556–57.

[17] *Congressional Record*, 99th Cong., 2d sess., p. S16352 (Daily Edition, October 15, 1986).

[18] Haynes, 2:861; *New York Times*, April 18, 1936; Kurland, p. 557.

[19] *Floyd M. Riddick, Senate Parliamentarian*, Oral History Interviews, June 26, 1978 to February 15, 1979 (U.S. Senate Historical Office, Washington, DC), pp. 284–343; U.S., Congress, Senate, S. Res. 479, 99th Cong., 2d sess., August 16, 1986; U.S., Congress, Senate, *Procedure and Guidelines for Impeachment Trials in the United States Senate*, by Floyd M. Riddick, S. Doc. 93-102, 93d Cong., 2d sess., 1974.

[20] *Congressional Record*, 99th Cong., 2d sess., pp. S15760–61 (Daily Edition, October 9, 1986).

[21] Ibid., pp. S15760–62.

[22] *Congressional Record*, 100th Cong., 2d sess., p. H6193 (Daily Edition, August 2, 1988); *Congressional Record*, 101st Cong., 1st sess., pp. S2802–3 (Daily Edition, March 16, 1989).

[23] *Congressional Record*, 101st Cong., 1st sess., pp. S13783–87 (Daily Edition, October 20, 1989).

[24] U.S., Congress, Senate, *Proceedings of the United States Senate in the Impeachment Trial of Alcee L. Hastings*, S. Doc. 101-18, 101st Cong., 1st sess., p. 683; *Congressional Record*, 101st Cong., 1st sess., pp. S13783–88 (Daily Edition, October 20, 1989).

[25] Ibid., p. 13787.

[26] Ibid., May 10, 1989, pp. H1802–11; "Senate Convicts Judge Nixon, Removes Him From Bench," *Congressional Quarterly Weekly Report* 47 (November 4, 1989): 2955.

[27] *Congressional Record*, 101st Cong., 1st sess., pp. S14635–36 (Daily Edition, November 3, 1989).

[28] Ibid., p. S14634.

[29] *Proceedings . . . . Alcee L. Hastings*, pp. 905–18, 1245–49.

[30] Raoul Berger, *Impeachment: The Constitutional Problems* (Cambridge, MA, 1973; Bantam edition, 1974), pp. 64, 71.

[31] Ibid., pp. 64, 71–72, 74.

[32] Ibid., pp. 73–74.

[33] U.S., Congress, House, *In the Matter of the Impeachment Inquiry Concerning U.S. District Judge Alcee L. Hastings, Hearings Before the Subcommittee on Criminal Justice of the Committee on the Judiciary, House of Representatives*, 100th Cong., 1st sess., 1987, Appendix 1, Serial No. 11, p. 351.

[34] *Congressional Record*, 99th Cong., 2d sess., p. S15506 (Daily Edition, October 7, 1986).

[35] Joseph Story, *Commentaries on the Constitution of the United States* (Boston, 1891), 1:586–87.

[36] Berger, p. 339.

[37] Ibid., p. 85.

[38] *Congressional Record*, 101st Cong., 1st sess., March 15, 1989, pp. S2552, 2555, 2554.

[39] Ibid., p. S2558.

[40] Ibid., March 16, 1989, p. S2802.

[41] Ibid., March 15, 1989, p. S2560.

[42] Berger, pp. 3–4.

[43] U.S., Congress, House, *Miscellaneous Materials, Hearings Before the Subcommittee on Criminal Justice of the Committee on the Judiciary, House of Representatives*, pursuant to H. Res. 128, 100th Cong., 2d sess., 1989, Appendix V, Serial No. 11, pp. 903–4.

[44] U.S., Congress, Senate, *Report of the Senate Impeachment Trial Committee on the Articles Against Judge Walter L. Nixon, Jr., Hearings Before the Senate Impeachment Trial Committee, United States Senate*, 101st Cong., 1st sess., 1989, Part 4B, pp. 583–85.

[45] John Bartlett, *Familiar Quotations*, 15th ed. (Boston, 1980), p. 343.

[635]

CHAPTER 5

Extended Debate

Filibusters, 1789–1917

[1] *Congressional Quarterly's Guide to Congress*, 3d ed. (Washington, DC, 1982), p. 92; Robert Luce, *Legislative Procedure* (Boston, 1922), p. 283.

[2] John Langhorne and William Langhorne, *Plutarch's Lives* (New York, 1855), p. 499.

[3] Georg Jellinek, "Parliamentary Obstruction," *Political Science Quarterly* 19 (December 1904):580.

[4] Lindsay Rogers, *The American Senate* (New York, 1926), p. 123.

[5] Jellinek, p. 581.

[6] Seth Ames, ed., *Works of Fisher Ames* (Boston, 1854), 1:71.

[7] Kenneth R. Bowling and Helen E. Veit, eds., *The Diary of William Maclay and other Notes on Senate Debates, Documentary History of the First Federal Congress of the United States of America*, vol. 9 (Baltimore, 1988), p. 157.

[8] Ibid., pp. 162–63.

[9] U.S., Congress, Senate, *Annals of Congress*, 11th Cong., 3d sess., p. 1092.

[10] Franklin L. Burdette, *Filibustering in the Senate* (Princeton, NJ, 1940), p. 17.

[11] *Niles' Weekly Register* 30 [or 6, third series] (Baltimore, 1826):452–53, 455–56.

[12] Burdette, p. 21.

[13] U.S., Congress, Senate, *Congressional Globe*, 26th Cong., 2d sess., pp. 242–43, 247–48.

[14] Burdette, pp. 22–24.

[15] Ibid., p. 25.

[16] Ibid., pp. 25–27.

[17] Ibid., p. 28.

[18] Ibid.

[19] Ibid.; See also U.S., Congress, Senate, *The Senate, 1789–1989*, by Robert C. Byrd, vol. 1, S. Doc. 100-20, 100th Cong., 1st sess., 1988, pp. 187–88, 197–98.

[20] *Congressional Globe*, 37th Cong., 3d sess., p. 518.

[21] Ibid., p. 549.

[22] Ibid., p. 550.

[23] Ibid., pp. 552–53.

[24] Ibid., pp. 558–59.

[25] Ibid., p. 584.

[26] Ibid., pp. 1436–37.

[27] Ibid., p. 1477.

[28] Ibid., pp. 1490, 1494.

[29] Burdette, p. 34.

[30] U.S., Congress, Senate, *Congressional Record*, 46th Cong., 1st sess., pp. 2123–55.

[31] Ibid., p. 2172.

[32] Ibid., pp. 2172–75.

[33] Burdette, p. 39.

[34] See Byrd, pp. 323–26.

[35] *Congressional Record*, 51st Cong., 2d sess., p. 819.

[36] Ibid., p. 1443.

[37] Ibid., pp. 1440–42.

[38] Ibid., pp. 1565, 1567–68.

[39] Ibid., p. 1740.

[40] Burdette, p. 59.

[41] Ibid., p. 68.

[42] *Congressional Record*, 54th Cong., 2d sess., pp. 2736–37.

[43] Ibid., pp. 2754–2930.

[44] Burdette, pp. 69–72.

[45] Ibid., p. 72.

[46] *Congressional Record*, 57th Cong., 2d sess., pp. 3058–59.

[47] Ibid.

[48] Burdette, pp. 78–79.

[49] Ibid., p. 84.

[50] *Congressional Record*, 60th Cong., 1st sess., pp. 7161–7201, 7220–26.

[51] Ibid., pp. 7195–96.

[52] Ibid., pp. 7158–59.

[53] Robert M. La Follette, *La Follette's Autobiography* (Madison, WI, 1913), p. 474.

[54] Congressional Record, 60th Cong., 1st sess., p. 7259.

[55] Burdette, pp. 90–91.

[56] *New York Times*, January 30, 1915.

[57] *Congressional Record*, 63d Cong., 3d sess., p. 2600.

[58] *New York Times*, January 30, 1915.

[59] *Congressional Record*, 63d Cong., 3d sess., pp. 3229–3412.

[60] Ibid., p. 3321.

[61] Ibid., p. 3314.

[62] Ibid., p. 3321.

[63] Ibid., p. 3339–40.

The Cloture Rule

[1] U.S., Congress, Senate, Committee on Rules and Administration, *Senate Cloture Rule*, by Congressional Research Service, S. Prt. 99-95, 99th Cong., 1st sess., 1985, p. 11; Thomas Jefferson, *A Manual of Parliamentary Practice, Jefferson's Parliamentary Writings, The Papers of Thomas Jefferson*, Second series (Princeton, NJ, 1988), p. 395.

[2] *Senate Cloture Rule*, p. 11; W.C. Ford, ed., *Journals of the Continental Congress, 1774–1789*, vol. 11, 1778 (Washington, DC, 1908), p. 534.

[3] Gaillard Hunt, ed, *Journals of the Continental Congress, 1774–1789*, vol. 20, 1781 (Washington, DC, 1912), p. 479.

[4] *Jefferson's Parliamentary Writings*, p. 395.

[5] U.S., Congress, Senate, *The United States Senate, 1787–1801: A Dissertation on the First Fourteen Years of the Upper Legislative Body*, by Roy Swanstrom, S. Doc. 100-31, 100th Cong., 1st sess., 1988, pp. 210–11.

[6] Ibid., p. 211.

[7] Ibid.

[8] Ibid.

[9] Seth Ames, ed., *Works of Fisher Ames* (Boston, 1854), 1:80.

[10] George H. Haynes, *The Senate of the United States: Its History and Practice* (Boston, 1938), 1:393–94; U.S., Congress, Senate, *The Previous Question: Its Standing as a Precedent for Cloture in the United States Senate*, by Joseph Cooper, S. Doc. 87-104, 87th Cong., 2d sess., 1962, pp. 2–13.

[11] *Senate Cloture Rule*, p. 12.

[12] U.S., Congress, Senate, *Congressional Globe*, 41st Cong., 3d sess., p. 28.

[13] *Senate Cloture Rule*, pp. 14–15.

[14] Ibid., p. 15.

[15] U.S., Congress, Senate, *Congressional Record*, 51st Cong., 2d sess., p. 852.

[16] *Senate Cloture Rule*, pp. 15–16.

[17] Henry Cabot Lodge, "The Struggle in the Senate," *The North American Review* 157 (1893):527–28.

[18] *Congressional Record*, 63d Cong., 3d sess., p. 3787.

[19] David P. Thelen, *Robert La Follette and the Insurgent Spirit* (Boston and Toronto, 1976), pp. 64–65.

[20] *New York Times*, January 30, 1915.

[21] Democratic National Committee and Democratic Congressional Committee, *Democratic Campaign Textbook, 1916* (New York and Chicago, 1916), p. 20; Democratic National Committee and Democratic Congressional Committee, *Democratic Campaign Textbook, 1920* (New York and Chicago, 1920), pp. 19–20.

[22] *New York Times*, February 23, 1917.

[23] *Congressional Record*, 64th Cong., 2d sess., p. 4273.

[24] Ibid., pp. 4512–25.

[25] Franklin L. Burdette, *Filibustering in the Senate* (Princeton, NJ, 1940), p. 117.

[26] *Congressional Record*, 64th Cong., 2d sess., p. 4569.

[27] Ibid., pp. 4744, 4781.

[28] Ibid., p. 4878.

[29] Ibid., pp. 4894–95.

[30] Ibid., pp. 4898–99.

[31] Ibid., pp. 4988–89.

[32] Ibid., pp. 4999, 5002.

[33] Ibid., p. 5002.

[34] Ibid., p. 5005.

[35] Ibid., p. 5008.

[36] Burdette, p. 120.

[37] *Congressional Record*, 64th Cong., 2d sess., pp. 5018–20.

[38] James D. Richardson, comp., *A Compilation of the Messages and Papers of the Presidents* (New York, 1917?), 16:8217–18.

[39] Thomas W. Ryley, *A Little Group of Willful Men* (Port Washington, NY, 1975), pp. 147–48.

[40] Burdette, pp. 127–28.

[41] *Congressional Record*, 65th Cong., special sess., pp. 20–21.

[42] Ibid., p. 41.

[43] Ibid., p. 40.

[44] *Congressional Record*, 67th Cong., 3d sess., p. 388.

[45] *Congressional Record*, 69th Cong., special sess., pp. 3–4.

[46] Ibid., p. 9.

[47] *New York Times*, April 19, 1925.

[48] *Washington Star*, May 15, 1925.

[49] *Senate Cloture Rule*, pp. 18–19.

[50] *Senate Cloture Rule*, p. 20; *Congressional Record*, 80th Cong., 2d sess., p. 9603.

[51] *Senate Cloture Rule*, p. 23.

[52] Ibid., pp. 23–24.

[53] Ibid., p. 24; *Congressional Record*, 85th Cong, 1st sess., p. 179.

[54] *Senate Cloture Rule*, p. 25.

[55] *Congressional Record*, 88th Cong., 2d sess., p. 95.

[56] Ibid., pp. 250, 253.

[57] Ibid., pp. 1072, 1076.

[58] *Senate Cloture Rule*, p. 27.

[59] Ibid.

[60] *Congressional Record*, 91st Cong., 1st sess., p. 593.

[61] *Senate Cloture Rule*, p. 30; *Congressional Record*, 94th Cong., 1st sess., p. 3835.

[62] *Senate Cloture Rule*, p. 31.

[63] *Congressional Record*, 94th Cong., 1st sess., pp. 4371, 4817.

[64] *Senate Cloture Rule*, p. 31.

[65] *Congressional Record*, 94th Cong., 1st sess., pp. 5252, 5262, 5612, 5652.

[66] *Congressional Record*, 96th Cong., 1st sess., p. 3036.

[67] *Congressional Record*, 99th Cong., 2d sess., p. S3156 (Daily Edition, February 27, 1986).

[68] Ibid., pp. 3131, 3157.

Filibusters, 1917–1964

[1] U.S., Congress, Senate, *Congressional Record*, 66th Cong., 1st sess., p. 8413.

[2] Ibid., pp. 8548–49.

[3] Ibid., pp. 8555–56.

[4] Ibid., pp. 8786–87.

[5] Ibid., pp. 8802–3.

[6] *Congressional Record*, 67th Cong., 3d sess., p. 288.

[7] Ibid., pp. 325–32.

[8] Ibid., p. 393.

[9] Ibid., p. 396.

[10] Ibid., p. 441.

[11] Ibid., p. 450.

[12] *Congressional Record*, 67th Cong., 4th sess., p. 277.

[13] Ibid., pp. 283–96.

[14] Ibid., pp. 3314–15.

[15] *New York Times*, February 21, 1923.

[16] *Congressional Record*, 67th Cong., 4th sess., p. 4852.

[17] Ibid., p. 4735.

[18] *Congressional Record*, 69th Cong., 1st sess., p. 2106.

[19] Ibid., pp. 2106–15.

[20] Ibid., p. 2298.

[21] Ibid., p. 2575.

[22] Ibid., pp. 2678–79, 2825.

[23] Franklin L. Burdette, *Filibustering In The Senate* (Princeton, NJ, 1940), pp. 154–55.

[24] Ibid., p. 160.

[25] *Congressional Record*, 70th Cong., 2d sess., p. 4865.

[26] Ibid., p. 4873.

[27] Burdette, p. 172.

[28] *Congressional Record*, 72d Cong., 2d sess., p. 1452 (quotation from Isa. 5:8).

[29] Ibid., p. 1459.

[30] Ibid., p. 1462 (quotation from James 5:1–3).

[31] Ibid. (quotation from James 5:4).

[32] Ibid., pp. 1462–63.

[33] Ibid., pp. 1579–80.

[34] Ibid., p. 1581.

[35] *Congressional Record*, 74th Cong., 1st sess., pp. 7913–14.

[36] Ibid., p. 7941.

[37] Ibid., p. 9096.

[38] Ibid., p. 9098.

[39] Ibid., p. 9100.

[40] Ibid., pp. 9122–23.

[41] Ibid., p. 9123.

[42] Ibid., pp. 9128–31.

[43] Ibid., pp. 9091–9175.

[44] Ibid., p. 9188.

[45] *New York Times*, June 14, 1935.

[46] *Congressional Record*, 74th Cong., 1st sess., p. 14719.

[47] Ibid., pp. 14726–27.

[48] Ibid., p. 14736.

[49] Ibid., p. 14744.

[50] Ibid., p. 14748.

[51] Ibid., p. 14738.

[52] U.S., Congress, Senate, *Biographical Directory of the United States Congress, 1774–1989*, Bicentennial Edition, S. Doc. 100–34, 100th Cong., 2d sess., 1989, p. 1388.

[53] *Congressional Record*, 74th Cong., 2d sess., p. 10543.

[54] Ibid., pp. 10544–46.

[55] *Congressional Record*, 83d Cong., 1st sess., p. 3749.

[56] Ibid., pp. 3766, 3775, 3764.

[57] Ibid., p. 3791.

[58] Ibid., p. 3848.

[59] *New York Times*, April 26, 1953.

[60] "History, Techniques of Senate Filibusters," *Congressional Quarterly Almanac*, vol. 13 (Washington, DC, 1957), p. 570. See also *Washington Post*, June 15, 1978.

[61] *Congressional Record*, 85th Cong., 1st sess., p. 16456.

[62] Ibid., pp. 16456–57, 16478.

[63] *Washington Post*, September 30, 1981.

[64] *Congressional Record*, 97th Cong., 1st sess., pp. 22178, 22263.

[65] Ibid., p. 22178.

Filibusters, 1964–1989

[1] U.S., Congress, Senate, *Congressional Record*, 88th Cong., 2d sess., pp. 13133–219.

[2] Ibid., p. 13327.

[3] Ibid., pp. 13308–9.

[4] Ibid., pp. 13319–20.

[5] Ibid., p. 14511.

[6] *Congressional Record*, 95th Cong., 1st sess., pp. 30809–10

[7] Ibid., pp. 31927–28.

[8] Ibid., pp. 31929–30.

[9] Ibid., pp. 31930–31.

[10] Ibid., pp. 31916, 31919–20.

[11] Ibid., p. 31927.

[12] Ibid., pp. 31923–24.

[13] Ibid., pp. 31926–27.

[14] *Congressional Record*, 100th Cong., 1st sess., pp. S8007–8 (Daily Edition, June 11, 1987).

[15] Ibid., pp. S7865–66 (Daily Edition, June 9, 1987).

[16] Ibid., pp. S8126, S8236, S8307, S8363 (Daily Edition, June 16–19, 1987).

[17] Ibid., p. S11148 (Daily Edition, August 3, 1987).

[18] Ibid., p. S11935 (Daily Edition, September 10, 1987).

[19] Ibid., pp. S12063–64 (Daily Edition, September 15, 1987).

[20] *Congressional Record*, 100th Cong., 2d sess., pp. S1113–14 (Daily Edition, February 23, 1988).

[21] Ibid., p. S1122.

[22] U.S., Congress, Senate, *Journal*, 100th Cong., 2d sess., p. 103.

[23] *Congressional Record*, 100th Cong., 2d sess., pp. S1121, S1144, S1149, S1152–53, S1156 (Daily Edition, February 23, 1988).

[24] Ibid., p. S1356.

[25] Ibid., p. S1517.

[26] Ibid., p. S1534 (Daily Edition, February 26, 1988).

[27] Ibid., p. S1559.

[28] Ibid., p. S1344 (Daily Edition, February 23, 1988).

[29] Ibid., p. S1535 (Daily Edition, February 26, 1988).

[30] Congressional Quarterly, Inc., *Vital Statistics on Congress, 1989–1990 Edition*, by Norman J. Ornstein, Thomas E. Mann, Michael J. Malbin (Washington, DC, 1990), p. 163; "Trivialized Filibuster is Still a Potent Tool," *Congressional Quarterly Weekly Report* 45 (September 5, 1987): 2115–20.

[31] Richard R. Beeman, "Unlimited Debate in the Senate: The First Phase," *Political Science Quarterly* 83 (September 1968), 3:419.

LEADERSHIP

Divider Page Quotations

[1] Edwin P. Whipple, ed., *The Great Speeches and Orations of Daniel Webster* (Boston, 1880), p. 229.

[2] Quoted in *Time*, March 20, 1964, p. 22.

[3] "Leadership: An Interview with Senate Leader Lyndon Johnson," *U.S. News and World Report*, June 27, 1960, p. 89.

[4] See Chapter 7, "Party Floor Leaders," p. 194.

CHAPTER 6

The President Pro Tempore

[1] Linda Grant De Pauw, ed., *Senate Legislative Journal, Documentary History of the First Federal Congress of the United States of America*, vol. 1 (Baltimore, 1972), pp. 7–8, 21.

[2] Margaret C.S. Christman, *The First Federal Congress, 1789–1791* (Washington, DC, 1989), pp. 66, 283–84; Dumas Malone, ed., *Dictionary of American Biography* (New York, 1946; reprint of 1935 ed.), 9: 587–88.

[3] U.S., Congress, Senate, *The United States Senate, 1787–1801: A Dissertation on the First Fourteen Years of the Upper Legislative Body*, by Roy Swanstrom, S. Doc. 100-31, 1988, pp. 253–57; Alvin M. Josephy, Jr., *On the Hill: A History of the American Congress* (New York, 1979), p. 79.

[4] Swanstrom, pp. 257–58.

[5] Ibid., p. 259; *Dictionary of American Biography*, 18: 354–55.

[6] George H. Haynes, *The Senate of the United States: Its History and Practice*, (Boston, 1938), 1:256–57.

[7] Hans L. Trefousse, "Ben Wade and the Failure of the Impeachment of Johnson," *Historical and Philosophical Society of Ohio Bulletin* 18 (October 1960): 241–52.

[8] Haynes, p. 257.

[9] Ibid., pp. 257–58; "The Great Senate Deadlock," *Senate History* 9 (July 1984): 1, 9.

[10] U. S., Congress, Senate, *Congressional Record*, 47th Cong., special sess., p. 505; see also Willard King, *Lincoln's Manager: David Davis* (Cambridge, MA, 1960).

[11] *Congressional Record*, 49th Cong., 1st sess., pp. 103–4, 180–82.

[12] Harry S. Truman, *Memoirs by Harry S Truman*, vol. 1: *Year of Decisions* (Garden City, NY, 1955), pp. 22–23, 487.

[13] D.B. Hardeman and Donald C. Bacon, *Rayburn: A Biography* (Austin, TX, 1987), p. 313.

[14] Ibid., p. 326.

[15] *Congressional Record*, 50th Cong., 2d sess., pp. 2144–50.

[16] Burton J. Williams, *Senator John J. Ingalls: Kansas' Iridescent Republican* (Lawrence, KS, 1972), pp. 6, 9.

[17] David S. Barry, *Forty Years in Washington* (Boston, 1924), p. 95.

[18] Ibid., pp. 49, 98.

[19] Walter B. Stevens, "A Day and Night with 'Old Davy': David R. Atchison." *Missouri Historical Review* 31 (January 1937): 129–39.

[20] William E. Gienapp, *The Origins of the Republican Party, 1852–1856* (New York, 1987), p. 107.

[21] David J. Rothman, *Politics and Power: The United States Senate, 1869–1901* (Cambridge, MA, 1966), p.17.

[22] David Graham Phillips, *The Treason of the Senate*, eds. George E. Mowry and Judson A. Grenier (Chicago, 1964; reprint of 1906 ed.), pp. 200–201.

[23] Haynes, 1: 251–52; *Congressional Record*, 62d Cong., 1st sess., pp. 1182–89.

[24] Richard Lowitt, *George W. Norris: The Persistence of a Progressive, 1913–1933* (Urbana, IL, 1971), pp. 223–26, 385.

[25] Haynes, 1: 253–54.

[26] *Warren Featherstone Reid, Assistant to Warren G. Magnuson*, Oral History Interviews, July 1, 1981 to July 23, 1981 (U.S. Senate Historical Office, Washington, DC), p. 170.

[27] Ibid., p. 174; see also Thomas H. Neale, "The President Pro Tempore of the U.S. Senate: The Historical Development of the Office and a Synopsis of its Duties and Responsibilities," CRS Report No. 81-114 GOV, Congressional Research Service, Library of Congress, Washington, DC, 1981.

CHAPTER 7

Party Floor Leaders

[1] George Goodwin, Jr., *The Little Legislatures: Committees of Congress* (Amherst, MA, 1970), p. 222.

[2] U.S., Congress, Senate, *Majority and Minority Leaders of the Senate*, by Floyd M. Riddick, S. Doc. 100-29, 100th Cong., 2d sess., 1988, p. 1.

[3] Ibid.

[4] Goodwin, p. 223.

[5] Riddick, p. 2.

[6] Ibid., pp. 1–2.

[7] Kenneth R. Bowling and Helen E. Veit, eds., *The Diary of William Maclay and Other Notes on Senate Debates, Documentary History of the First Federal Congress of the United States of America*, vol. 9 (Baltimore, 1988), p. 400.

[8] Quoted in Riddick, p. 2.

[9] U.S., Congress, Senate, *Congressional Globe*, 27th Cong., 1st sess., p. 48.

[10] U.S., Congress, Senate, *William Boyd Allison: Memorial Addresses*, 60th Cong., 2d sess., 1909, p. 31; U.S., Congress, Senate, *Biographical Directory of the United States Congress, 1774–1989*, S. Doc. 100-34, 100th Cong., 2d sess., 1989, p. 530.

[11] U.S., Congress, Senate, *The Senate, 1789–1989*, by Robert C. Byrd, vol. 1, S. Doc. 100-20, 100th Cong., 1st sess., 1988, p. 374.

[12] Woodrow Wilson, *Congressional Government: A Study in American Politics* (Cleveland, OH, 1965; reprint of 1885 ed.), p. 147.

[13] Riddick, p. 3.

[14] Quoted in ibid.

[15] Ibid., p. 5.

[16] Ibid., pp. 3–4.

[17] Ibid., p. 5.

[18] Ibid.

[19] Ibid.

[20] Ibid., p. 13.

[21] Senate Rule XXVI, par. 5(a).

[22] U.S., Congress, Senate, *Congressional Record*, 75th Cong., 1st sess., p. 8840.

[23] "Leadership: An Interview with Senate Leader Lyndon Johnson," *U.S. News and World Report*, June 27, 1960, p. 89.

[24] Ibid., p. 88.

[25] Allen Drury, *Advise and Consent* (Garden City, NY, 1959), p. 40.

[26] Riddick, pp. 8–9.

[27] *Time*, March 20, 1964, p. 23.

CHAPTER 8

Party Whips

[1] Robert Luce, *Legislative Procedure* (Boston, 1922), p. 501.

[2] U.S., Congress, Senate, *Majority and Minority Whips of the Senate*, by Walter J. Oleszek, S. Doc. 98-45, 98th Cong., 2d sess., 1985, p. 3.

[3] Luce, p. 502.

[4] Oleszek, pp. 1–2.

[5] Francis Pym, Chief Whip, Conservative Party, British House of Commons, to Senator Robert C. Byrd, March 23, 1971,Robert C. Byrd papers.

[6] U.S., Congress, Senate, *Congressional Record*, 43d Cong., 1st sess., p. 2488.

[7] *Congressional Record*, 74th Cong., 2d sess., p. 7046.

[8] Claude G. Bowers, *The Life of John Worth Kern* (Indianapolis, IN, 1918), p. 351.

[9] Oleszek, p. 5.

[10] Bowers, p. 352.

[11] Oleszek, p. 15.

[12] Ibid., pp. 17–18.

[13] *Congressional Record*, 74th Cong., 2d sess., p. 7046.

[14] Marvin E. Stromer, *The Making of a Political Leader* (Lincoln, NE, 1969), p. 46.

[15] Robert C. Byrd, CBS, "Face the Nation," January 31, 1971; *Congressional Record*, 92d Cong., 1st sess., p. 1374.

[16] Oleszek, p. 11.

[17] Ibid., p. 10.

[18] *Congressional Record*, 92d Cong., 1st sess., p. 3447.

[19] *New York Times*, January 12, 1966, p. 15.

[20] Oleszek, pp. 8–9.

[21] Cecil Holland, "Senator Russell Long—Acumen, Affability, Ambition," *Washington Sunday Star*, October 2, 1966.

CHAPTER 9

The Committee System

Committees, 1789–1845

[1] Woodrow Wilson, *Congressional Government: A Study in American Politics* (Cleveland, OH, 1965; reprint of 1885 ed.), pp. 69, 82.

[2] Lauros G. McConachie, *Congressional Committees: A Study of the Origins and Development of Our National and Local Legislative Methods* (New York, 1898), pp. 7–9; and J. Franklin Jameson, "The Origin of the Standing Committee System in American Legislative Bodies," *Annual Report of the American Historical Association*, 1893, Senate Miscellaneous Documents 104, 52d Cong., 2d sess.

[3] Noble E. Cunningham, "Congress as an Institution, 1800–1850," paper delivered at the Project 87 Conference in Washington, DC, February 1981.

[4] Neil MacNeil, *Forge of Democracy: The House of Representatives* (New York, 1963), p. 150.

[5] U.S., Congress, Senate, *Standing Rules of the Senate*, S. Doc. 97-10, 97th Cong., 1st sess., 1981, Rule VII, part 6.

[6] U.S., Congress, Senate, *The United States Senate, 1787–1801: A Dissertation on the First Fourteen Years of the Upper Legislative Body*, by Roy Swanstrom, S. Doc. 100-31, 100th Cong., 1st sess., 1988, p. 223.

[7] Ibid., pp. 224–25; U.S., Congress, Senate, *Annals of Congress*, 3d Cong., 1st sess., p. 147.

[8] McConachie, p. 267; Kenneth R. Bowling and Helen E. Veit, eds., *The Diary of William Maclay and Other Notes on Senate Debates, Documentary History of the First Federal Congress of the United States of America*, vol. 9 (Baltimore, 1988), pp. 75, 91, 116.

[9] Swanstrom, pp. 226–27; Joseph Ralston Hayden, *The United States Senate and Treaties, 1789–1817* (New York, 1920), pp. 171–72.

[10] Swanstrom, pp. 227–28; McConachie, p. 267.

[11] Charles Francis Adams, ed., *The Memoirs of John Quincy Adams* (Freeport, NY, 1969; reprint of 1874–1877 ed.), 1:482.

[12] Thomas Jefferson, *A Manual of Parliamentary Practice*, *Jefferson's Parliamentary Writings* (Princeton, NJ, 1988), p. 382.

[13] Swanstrom, p. 231; Adams, pp. 329–30, 496.

[14] Mary Giunta, "The Public Life of William Branch Giles, Republican, 1790–1815" (Ph.D. dissertation, Catholic University, 1980), pp. 209–11.

[15] *Annals of Congress*, 7th Congress, 1st sess., pp. 23–24.

[16] Alex B. Lacy, Jr., "Jefferson and Congress: Congressional Method and Politics, 1801–1809" (Ph.D. dissertation, University of Virginia, 1964), p. 45.

[17] Ibid., p. 48.

[18] *Annals of Congress*, 7th Cong., 1st sess., p. 155.

[19] Lacy, pp. 105–6.

[20] Swanstrom, p. 232.

[21] *Annals of Congress*, 10th Cong., 1st sess., p. 19.

[22] Ibid., p. 21.

[23] Ibid., p. 39.

[24] Adams, pp. 478–81.

[25] George Goodwin, Jr., *The Little Legislatures: Committees of Congress* (Amherst, MA, 1970), p. 12.

[26] Ibid., p. 7.

[27] U.S., Congress, Senate, Committee on Finance, *History of the Committee on Finance*, S. Doc. 97-5, 97th Cong., 1st sess., 1981, pp. 16–17.

[28] *Annals of Congress*, 14th Cong., 2d sess., pp. 19–20, 32–33.

[29] U.S., Congress, Senate, Committee on Commerce, *History, Membership and Jurisdiction of the Senate Committee on Commerce From 1816–1966*, S. Doc. 100, 89th Cong., 2d sess., 1966, p. 2.

[30] Walter Kravitz, "Evolution of the Senate's Standing Committee System," *The Annals of the American Academy of Political and Social Science* 411 (January 1974): 30.

[31] McConachie, p. 275.

[32] Ibid., pp. 276–86.

Committees, 1845–1900

[1] Glenn Brown, *History of the United States Capitol* (New York 1970; reprint of 1900–1902 ed.).

[2] Ibid., Plate 237.

[3] U.S., Congress, Senate, Office of the Senate Curator, "The Senate Appropriations Committee Capitol Suite," October 1981, unpublished manuscript in the files of the U.S. Senate Historical Office, Washington, DC, pp. 2–4.

[4] Ibid., pp. 4–7.

[5] Ibid., p. 7.

[6] Lauros G. McConachie, *Congressional Committees: A Study of the Origins and Development of Our National and Local Legislative Methods* (New York, 1898), pp. 294, 296.

[7] Ibid.

[8] Jerrold Zwirn, *Congressional Publications: A Research Guide to Legislation, Budgets, and Treaties* (Littleton, CO, 1983), pp. 169–75.

[9] U.S., Congress, Senate, *History of Senate Committees, 1789–1863*, 38th Cong., special sess., 1863, p. 15.

[10] McConachie, pp. 284–86.

[11] U.S., Congress, Senate, *Congressional Globe*, 35th Cong., 1st sess., pp. 39–42.

[12] *Congressional Globe*, 38th Congress, special sess., p. 1554.

[13] *Congressional Globe*, 38th Congress, 1st sess., pp. 15–16.

[14] Robert W. Johannsen, *Stephen A. Douglas* (New York, 1973), pp. 685–88.

[15] David Donald, *Charles Sumner and the Rights of Man* (New York, 1970), pp. 444–97.

[16] David J. Rothman, *Politics and Power: The United States Senate, 1869–1901* (Cambridge, MA, 1966), pp. 20–21; Thomas G. Belden and Marva R. Belden, *So Fell the Angels* (Boston, 1965), p. 250.

[17] Clarence Berdahl, "American Government and Politics: Some Notes on Party Membership in Congress," *American Political Science Review* (April 1949), pp. 313–14.

[18] Michael Les Benedict, *Compromise of Principle: Congressional Republicans and Reconstruction, 1863–1865* (New York, 1974), pp. 36–37.

[19] U.S., Congress, Senate, *Congressional Record*, 48th Cong., 1st sess., pp. 266–69.

[20] U.S., Congress, Senate, Committee on Appropriations, *Committee on Appropriations, 100th Anniversary, 1867–1967*, S. Doc. 21, 90th Cong., 1st sess., 1967, pp. 7–8.

[21] *Congressional Record*, 48th Cong., 1st sess., p. 308.

[22] Ibid., p. 309.

[23] Ibid., p. 312.

[24] Ibid., p. 334.

[25] U.S., Congress, Senate, Committee on Finance, *History of the Committee on Finance*, S. Doc. 97-5, 97th Cong., 1st sess., 1981, pp. 32–44.

[26] Rothman, pp. 58–74.

[27] Woodrow Wilson, *Congressional Government: A Study in American Politics* (New York, 1956; reprint of 1885 ed.), pp. 155–57.

Committees, 1900–1946

[1] John Braeman, *Albert J. Beveridge: American Nationalist* (Chicago, 1971), p. 43.

[2] Claude G. Bowers, *Beveridge and the Progressive Era* (New York, 1932), pp. 115–16.

[3] Robert M. La Follette, *La Follette's Autobiography* (Madison, WI, 1913), pp. 375–76.

[4] U.S., Congress, *Congressional Directory*, 57th Cong., 1st sess., 1901, pp. 168–70.

[5] Ibid., pp. 176–83.

[6] Ibid., pp. 146–63.

[7] Walter Kravitz, "Evolution of the Senate's Committee System," *The Annals of the American Academy of Political and Social Sciences* 411 (January 1974): 33.

[8] U.S., Congress, Senate, *Congressional Record*, 60th Cong., 2d sess., pp. 3067–69.

[9] *Congressional Record*, 66th Cong., 2d sess., pp. 7715–16.

[10] Kravitz, pp. 35–36.

[11] *Congressional Record*, 67th Cong., 1st sess., p. 204; *New York Times*, April 19, 1921.

[12] *Congressional Record*, 68th Cong., 1st sess., pp. 159, 747.

[13] Ralph K. Huitt and Robert L. Peabody, *Congress: Two Decades of Analysis* (Westport, CT, 1969), pp. 121–23.

[14] George H. Haynes, *The Senate of the United States: Its History and Practice* (Boston, 1938), 1:291; Patrick J. Maney, *"Young Bob" La Follette: A Biography of Robert M. La Follette, Jr., 1895–1953* (Columbia, MO, 1978), pp. 42–43.

[15] Eleanor E. Dennison, *The Senate Foreign Relations Committee* (Stanford, CA, 1942), p. 111; George F.

Sparks, ed., *A Many-Colored Toga: The Diary of Henry Fountain Ashurst* (Tucson, AZ, 1962), p. 153.

[16] Information drawn from U.S., Congress, *Congressional Directory*, 72d Cong., 2d sess., 1933, and 73d Cong., 2d sess., 1934.

[17] See Nancy Weiss, *Farewell to the Party of Lincoln: Black Politics in the Age of FDR* (Princeton, NJ, 1983).

[18] Martha H. Swain, *Pat Harrison: The New Deal Years* (Jackson, MS, 1978), pp. 33–122.

[19] Ernest R. May, "Writing Contemporary International History," *Diplomatic History* 8 (Spring 1984): 104.

[20] Telford Taylor, *Grand Inquest: The Story of Congressional Investigations* (New York, 1955), p. 67.

[21] See Michael Wreszin, "The Dies Committee, 1938," in *Congress Investigates: A Documented History, 1792–1974*, eds. Arthur M. Schlesinger, Jr., and Roger Bruns, 5 vols. (New York, 1975), 4:2923–56.

[22] Kravitz, p. 35.

[23] U.S., Congress, Joint Committee on the Organization of Congress, *Organization of Congress*, 79th Cong., 1st sess., 1945, pp. 164–67.

[24] *Francis O. Wilcox, Chief of Staff, Senate Foreign Relations Committee, 1947–1955*, Oral History Interviews, February 1 to June 13, 1984 (U.S. Senate Historical Office, Washington, DC).

Committees, 1946–1989

[1] U.S., Congress, Senate, *Guide to the Records of the United States Senate at the National Archives, 1789–1989*, S. Doc. 100-42, 100th Cong., 2d sess., 1989; Congressional Information Service, *U.S. Congressional Hearings Index* and *CIS Index to Unpublished Senate Committee Hearings*.

[2] See U.S., Congress, Senate, *The Senate 1789–1989*, by Robert C. Byrd, vol. 1, S. Doc. 100-20, 100th Cong., 1st sess., 1988, pp. 537–50.

[3] Public Law 79-601.

[4] *The Legislative Reorganization Act of 1946, Statutes at Large* 60, sec. 136, 832 (1946).

[5] Lindsay Rogers, "The Staffing of Congress," *Political Science Quarterly* 61 (March 1941): 1–22.

[6] *Legislative Reorganization Act*, pp. 834–35.

[7] Congressional Quarterly, Inc., *Vital Statistics on Congress, 1989–1990 Edition*, by Norman J. Ornstein, Thomas E. Mann, Michael J. Malbin (Washington, DC, 1990), pp. 136, 138.

[8] Walter Oleszek, "Overview of the Senate Committee System," in U.S., Congress, Senate, Commission on the Operation of the Senate, *Committees and Senate Procedures* (Washington, DC, 1977), pp. 5–10.

[9] *Francis O. Wilcox, Chief of Staff, Senate Foreign Relations Committee, 1947–1955*, Oral History Interviews, February 1 to June 13, 1984 (U.S. Senate Historical Office, Washington, DC), pp. 25–26.

[10] Ibid., p. 36.

[11] Ibid., pp. 40–41.

[12] U.S., Congress, Senate, *Committee on Foreign Relations, United States Senate, 170th Anniversary, 1816–1986*, S. Doc. 99-21, 99th Cong., 2d sess., 1986, pp. 35–38; *Pat M. Holt, Chief of Staff, Foreign Relations Committee*, Oral History Interviews, September 9 to December 12, 1980 (U.S. Senate Historical Office, Washington, DC), pp. 45–50.

[13] U.S., Congress, Senate, Committee on Expenditures in the Executive Departments, *Legislative Reorganization Act of 1946, Hearings, June 1951*, 80th Cong., 2d sess., pp. 33–36.

[14] Ibid., p. 63.

[15] Ibid., p. 84.

[16] U.S., Congress, Senate, Committee on Expenditures in the Executive Departments, *Organization and Operation of Congress, Hearings before the Committee on Expenditures in the Executive Departments*, 82d Cong., 1st sess., 1951, pp. 66–67; see also George Galloway, "Next Steps in Congressional Reform," *University of Illinois Bulletin* 50 (December 1952); and Galloway, *Congressional Reorganization Revisited* (College Park, MD, 1956).

[17] *Organization and Operation of Congress*, pp. 611–12.

[18] Ibid., p. 635.

[19] Ibid., pp. 72, 629.

[20] The following joint committees were created in the three decades following 1945: Atomic Energy (1946); the Economic Report (1946); Defense Production (1950); Foreign Economic Cooperation; Indian Administration; Immigration and Nationality Policy (1952) [this last committee never met and was abolished in 1970]; Housing (1947); Construction of a Building for a Museum of History and Technology for the Smithsonian Institution (1955); Labor-Management Relations (1948); Navajo-Hopi Indian Administration (1950); Organization of Congress (1965); Congressional Operations (1970); Arrangements for the Commemoration of the Bicentennial of the United States of America (1975).

[21] *Organization and Operation of Congress*, p. 630.

[22] William S. White, *Citadel: The Story of the U.S. Senate* (New York, 1957), pp. 180–81, 185.

[23] Joseph S. Clark, *The Senate Establishment* (New York, 1963), p. 17.

[24] Roger H. Davidson, "Two Roads to Change: House and Senate Committee Reorganization," *Congressional Studies* 7 (Winter 1980): 15; see also Roger H. Davidson, "Representation and Congressional Committees," in *Changing Congress: The Committee System, The Annals of the American Academy of Political and Social Science* 411 (January 1974): 48–62; U.S., Congress, Joint Committee on the Organization of the Congress, *Organization of Congress*, part 1, 89th Cong., 1st sess., 1965, pp. 744–51.

[25] Congressional Quarterly, Inc., *Congress and the Nation*, vol. 3 (Washington, DC, 1973), pp. 382–96.

[26] U.S., Congress, Senate, *Toward a Modern Senate: Final Report of the Commission on the Operation of the Senate*, S. Doc. 94-278, 94th Cong., 2d sess., 1976, pp. 1–6; U.S., Congress, Senate, Commission on the Operation of the Senate, *Committees and Senate Procedures*, 94th Cong., 2d sess. (Committee Print), 1976.

[27] Judith H. Parris, "The Senate Reorganizes Its Committees, 1977," *Political Science Quarterly* 95 (Summer 1979): 319–37; for a summary of the pre-1977 situation by a key Senate participant, see Bill Brock, "Committees in the Senate," in *Changing Congress: The Committee System*, pp. 15–26.

[28] Parris, pp. 321–23.

[29] U.S., Congress, Senate, *First Report with Recommendations of the Temporary Select Committee to Study the Senate Committee System*, S. Rept. 94-1395, 94th Cong., 2d sess., 1976.

[30] U.S., Congress, Senate, Committee on Rules and Administration, *Committee System Reorganization Amendments of 1977, Hearings*, 95th Cong., 1st sess., 1977.

[31] Davidson, "Two Roads of Change," pp. 11–16, 22–32.

[32] For a recent scholarly treatment of the broad context of congressional committee reform since 1970, see Leroy N. Rieselbach, *Congressional Reform* (Washington, DC, 1986), chapters 3 and 4.

[33] Parris, p. 330.

[34] Ibid., p. 320.

[35] Ibid., p. 330.

[36] Ibid.

[37] Ibid., pp. 330–31.

[38] Ibid., p. 331.

ORGANIZATION

Divider Page Quotations

[1] U.S., Congress, Senate, *Annals of Congress*, 13th Cong., 3d sess, p. 23.

[2] Christian F. Eckloff, *Memoirs of a Senate Page*, ed. Percival G. Melbourne (New York, 1909), pp. 12–13.

[3] *F. Nordy Hoffmann, Senate Sergeant at Arms, 1975–1981*, Oral History Interviews, June 28 to August 30, 1988 (U.S. Senate Historical Office, Washington, DC), p. 224.

CHAPTER 10

Secretary of the Senate

[1] For an enumeration of the secretary's current responsibilities, as established by statute and Senate rules, see the "Secretary of the Senate" entry in U.S., Congress, Senate, Committee on Rules and Administration, *Senate Manual*, S. Doc. 101-1, 101st Cong., 1st sess., 1989, pp. 959–60.

[2] Kenneth R. Bowling, "Good-by Charlie: The Lee-Adams Interest and the Political Demise of Charles Thomson, Secretary of Congress, 1774–1789," *Pennsylvania Magazine of History and Biography* 100 (July 1976): 314–35.

[3] Kenneth R. Bowling and Helen E. Veit, eds., *The Diary of William Maclay and Other Notes on Senate Debates, Documentary History of the First Federal Congress of the United States of America*, vol. 9 (Baltimore, 1988), p. 5.

[4] Ibid., p. 27.

[5] Ibid., p. 29.

[6] Ibid., p. 134.

[7] Ibid., p. 141.

[8] Ibid., pp. 141–42.

[9] Ibid., p. 66.

[10] Ibid., p. 187.

[11] Ibid., p. 213.

[12] Ibid., p. 370.

[13] U.S., Congress, *Debates and Proceedings in the Congress of the United States*, 13th Cong., 3d sess., 1814, p. 23.

[14] Quoted in Ruth Ketring Nuermberger, "Asbury Dickins (1780–1861): A Career in Government Service," *The North Carolina Historical Review* 24 (July 1947): 309–10.

[15] For a detailed accounting of Dickins' duties as secretary, see ibid., pp. 302–13.

[16] Ibid., p. 302.

[17] John A. Garraty and Mark C. Carnes, eds., *Dictionary of American Biography*, Supplement 8 (New York, 1988), pp. 35–37; Lewis Wood, "Sage of Capitol Hill," *New York Times*, August 26, 1945; Ernest Barcella, "They Call Him Mr. Baffle," *Colliers*, January 29, 1949, pp. 27, 61–62.

[18] Lucy Salamanca, "Halsey is Guide for Senate," *Washington Star*, January 2, 1937; "Seniors in U.S. Service," *Washington Star*, December 11, 1943; *Washington Star*, January 29, 1945.

[19] William S. White, "Old Guard of the Old Guard," *New York Times*, June 8, 1947; Carl A. Loeffler, "Recollections of a Lifetime with the Senate," 1949, unpublished manuscript in the files of the U.S. Senate Historical Office, Washington, DC.

[20] Quoted in Nuermberger, p. 308.

CHAPTER 11

Sergeant at Arms

[1] Kenneth R. Bowling and Helen E. Veit, eds., *The Diary of William Maclay and Other Notes on Senate Debates, Documentary History of the First Federal Congress of the United States of America*, vol. 9 (Baltimore, 1988), pp. 226–27.

[2] Linda Grant De Pauw, ed, *Senate Legislative Journal, Documentary History of the First Federal Congress of the United States of America*, vol. 1 (Baltimore, 1972), p. 700.

[3] Jonathan Elliot, *The Debates in the Several State Conventions on the Adoption of the Federal Constitution* (New York, 1836), 4:130.

[4] Quoted in U.S., Congress, Senate, *The United States Senate, 1787–1801: A Dissertation on the First Fourteen Years of the Upper Legislative Body*, by Roy Swanstrom, S. Doc. 100-31, 100th Cong., 1st sess., 1988, p. 190; U.S., Congress, Senate, Committee on Rules and Administration, *Senate Manual*, S. Doc. 101-1, 101st Cong., 1st sess., 1989, p. 5.

[5] Swanstrom, p. 201.

[6] George H. Haynes, *The Senate of the United States: Its History and Practice* (Boston, 1938), 1:354.

[7] William H. Masterson, *William Blount* (Baton Rouge, LA, 1954), pp. 320–23; U.S., Congress, Senate, Committee on Rules and Administration, *Senate Election, Expulsion and Censure Cases from 1793 to 1972*, S. Doc. 92-7, 92d Cong., 1st sess., 1972, p. 3; Swanstrom, p. 52.

[8] U.S., Congress, Senate, *Annals of Congress*, 5th Cong., 1st sess., pp. 496–97.

[9] Swanstrom, p. 52.

[10] *Annals of Congress*, 5th Cong., 2d sess., p. 589; U.S., Congress, Senate, *Journal*, 19th Cong., 1st sess., p. 402; 22d Cong., 1st sess., p. 354.

[11] *National Intelligencer*, September 5, 1811.

[12] U.S., Congress, Senate, *Congressional Globe*, 38th Cong., 1st sess., pp. 2088–90; Haynes, 1:352.

[13] *Congressional Globe*, 42d Cong., 2d sess., pp. 2627–29.

[14] U.S., Congress, Senate, *Congressional Record*, 44th Cong., 2d sess., pp. 690–93.

[15] *Congressional Record*, 47th Cong., 2d sess., p. 3180.

[16] *Congressional Record*, 51st Cong., 2d sess., pp. 1440–42.

[17] Ibid., p. 1443.

[18] *Congressional Record*, 63d Cong., 3d sess., pp. 3354–55; 63d Cong., special sess., pp. 19–48.

[19] *New York Times*, February 24, 1927; *Washington Evening Star*, February 24, 1927; *Congressional Record*, 69th Cong., 2d sess., p. 4454–56.

[20] *Congressional Record*, 77th Cong., 2d sess., p. 8839.

[21] Richard Riedel, *Halls of the Mighty* (Washington, DC, 1969), pp. 89–90; *New York Times*, November 15, 1942; *Washington Evening Star*, November 15, 1942. The unserved arrest warrants and related materials may be found in Records of the Senate, Office of the Sergeant at Arms, 1942, Record Group 46, National Archives, Washington, DC.

[22] *Congressional Record*, 81st Cong., 2d sess., p. 8409.

[23] *Congressional Record*, 94th Cong., 2d sess., p. 34585.

[24] F. Nordy Hoffmann, *Senate Sergeant at Arms, 1975–1981*, Oral History Interviews, June 28 to August 30, 1988 (U.S. Senate Historical Office, Washington, DC), p. 224.

[25] *Congressional Record*, 100th Cong., 2d sess., February 23, 1988, pp. 1152–55.

[26] *Washington Post*, February 25, 1988.

[27] Ibid., April 29, 1951.

[28] F.B. Marbut, *News from the Capital: The Story of Washington Reporting* (Carbondale, IL, 1971), pp. 89–90, 145.

[29] *Hoffmann*, pp. 212–15.

[30] David S. Barry, *Forty Years in Washington* (Boston, 1924); and Donald A. Ritchie, " 'The Loyalty of the Senate:' The Washington Correspondents in the Progressive Era," *The Historian* 51 (August 1989): 574–91.

[31] David S. Barry, "Over the Hill to Demagoguery," *The New Outlook* 161 (February 1933): 40–42; *Congressional Record*, 72d Cong., 2d sess., pp. 3269–82, 3511–30; see also U.S., Congress, Senate, Committee on the Judiciary, *David S. Barry, Sergeant-at-Arms, United States Senate*, S. Rept., 72d Cong., 2d sess., 1933.

[32] *Congressional Record*, 95th Cong., 2d sess., pp. 34628–29; U.S., Congress, Senate, *Tributes to F. Nordy Hoffmann, Sergeant at Arms and Doorkeeper of the Senate*, S. Doc. 96-77, 96th Cong., 2d sess., 1981.

[33] *Hoffmann*, p. 234; *New York Times*, November 9, 1981.

[34] *Congressional Record*, 99th Cong., 1st sess., p. S7203 (Daily Edition, April 2, 1985).

CHAPTER 12

Senate Chaplain

[1] Psalm 127:1.

[2] *Notes of Debates in the Federal Convention of 1787 Reported by James Madison* (Athens, OH, 1966), pp. 209–10.

[3] Charles Francis Adams, ed., *Letters of John Adams Addressed to His Wife* (Boston, 1841), 1:23; W.C. Ford, ed., *Journals of the Continental Congress, 1774–1789*, vol. 1 (Washington, DC, 1904), p. 26.

[4] Adams, 1:24.

[5] Linda Grant De Pauw, ed., *Senate Legislative Journal, Documentary History of the First Federal Congress of the United States of America*, vol. 1 (Baltimore, 1972), p. 12.

[6] Kenneth R. Bowling and Helen E. Veit, eds., *The Diary of William Maclay and Other Notes on Senate Debates, Documentary History of the First Federal Congress of the United States of America*, vol. 9 (Baltimore, 1988), p. 13.

[7] See Martin J. Medhurst, "From Duché to Provoost: The Birth of Inaugural Prayer," *Journal of Church and State* 24 (Autumn, 1982): 573–88.

[8] U.S., Congress, Senate, *Annals of Congress*, 6th Cong., 2d sess., p. 728.

[9] Margaret Bayard Smith, *The First Forty Years of Washington Society in the Family Letters of Margaret Bayard Smith*, ed. Gaillard Hunt (New York, 1965; reprint of 1906 ed.), pp. 13–14.

[10] Ibid., pp. 16–17.

[11] U.S., Congress, House, *Chaplains in Congress and in the Army and Navy*, H. Rept. 124, 33d Cong., 1st sess., 1854, pp. 6–7.

[12] U.S., Congress, Senate, *Congressional Globe*, 35th Cong., 1st sess., p. 13.

[13] Ibid., p. 14.

[14] *Congressional Globe*, 36th Cong., 1st sess., pp. 97–98.

[15] U.S., Congress, Senate, *Congressional Record*, 86th Cong., 1st sess., p. 1.

[16] *Congressional Record*, 88th Cong., 1st sess., p. 22693; Edwin Markham, "Lincoln, the Man of the People," in Edwin Markham, *The Book of American Poetry* (Miami, FL, 1977).

[17] *Congressional Record*, 76th Cong., 1st sess., p. 1150; *Congressional Record*, 86th Cong., 2d sess., p. 3709.

[18] *Congressional Record*, 80th Cong., 1st sess., p. 7116.

[19] *Congressional Record*, 91st Cong., 2d sess., p. 29611.

[20] *Congressional Record*, 44th Cong., 1st sess., p. 3093.

[21] *Congressional Record*, 94th Cong., 2d sess., pp. S7463–66 (Daily Edition, May 19, 1976); *New York Times*, July 2, 1987.

CHAPTER 13

Reporters of Debates and the Congressional Record

[1] U.S., Congress, Senate, *The United States Senate, 1787–1801: A Dissertation on the First Fourteen Years of the Upper Legislative Body*, by Roy Swanstrom, S. Doc. 100-31, 100th Cong., 1st sess., 1988, pp. 67–69, 238–52.

[2] F.B. Marbut, *News from the Capital: The Story of Washington Reporting* (Carbondale, IL, 1971), pp. 14–27, 37–38.

[3] Allen C. Clark, "Joseph Gales, Junior, Editor and Mayor," *The Records of the Columbia Historical Society* 23 (1920): 113; Elizabeth Gregory McPherson, "The History of Reporting the Debates and Proceedings of Congress" (Ph.D. dissertation, University of North Carolina at Chapel Hill, 1940), p. 32.

[4] McPherson, pp. 118–75; Marbut, pp. 39–53.

[5] U.S., Congress, Senate, *Tributes to James W. Murphy, Senior Official Reporter of Debates in the Senate of the United States, July 26, 1956*, S. Doc. 147, 84th Cong., 2d sess., 1956, pp. 3–4.

[6] U.S., Congress, Senate, *Congressional Record*, 88th Cong., 1st sess., p. 13746.

[7] "Address of Hon. Huey P. Long," National Shorthand Convention, Washington, DC, August 21, 1935, in the files of the U.S. Senate Historical Office, Washington, DC.

[8] Robert D. Stevens, "But is the Record Complete? A Case of Censorship of the *Congressional Record*," *Government Publications Review* 9 (January–February 1982): 75–80.

[9] *Congressional Record*, 63d Cong., 1st sess, pp. 5382, 5911.

[10] *Francis J. Attig, Reporter of Debates*, Oral History Interview, April 5, 1978 (U.S. Senate Historical Office, Washington, DC), p. 34.

[11] Ibid., pp. 42, 46.

[12] *Floyd M. Riddick, Senate Parliamentarian*, Oral History Interviews, June 26, 1978 to February 15, 1979 (U.S. Senate Historical Office, Washington, DC), pp. 30–61.

[13] James Nathan Miller, "Congress' License to Lie," *Reader's Digest* (February 1983), pp. 73–77; Barbara Rehm, "Editing the Congressional Record," *Freedom of Information Center Report No. 508*, School of Journalism, University of Missouri, Columbia, MO, March 1985, p. 5.

[14] Irving H. Bartlett, *Daniel Webster* (New York, 1978), p. 4; Claude Moore Fuess, *Daniel Webster* (Boston, 1930), 1:383.

[15] *Gregg v. Barrett*, 771 F.2d 539 (D.C. Cir 1985).

CHAPTER 14

Capitol Police

[1] U.S., Congress, House, Committee on House Administration, *A Statutory History of the United States Capitol Police Force*, 99th Cong., 1st sess., committee print, 1985, pp. 1–2.

[2] From "Letters of the Commissioners of Public Buildings," Records of the Office of Public Buildings and Grounds, Record Group 42, National Archives, vol. 7, p. 378, as quoted in "The Capitol Police: 1801–1950," manuscript copy in the files of the U.S. Senate

Historical Office, Washington, DC; U.S., Library of Congress, *Librarians of Congress, 1802–1974* (Washington, DC, 1977), p. 65; U.S., Congress, House, *Fire in the Library*, H. Rept. 22, 19th Cong., 1st sess., 1826, pp. 1–5.

[3] *A Statutory History*, pp. 3–4.

[4] Quoted in "As Old as The Star, Capitol Police Organized Fifty Years Ago," *Washington Star*, December 16, 1902.

[5] Ibid.

[6] Ibid.

[7] *Librarians of Congress*, pp. 86–89.

[8] *Washington Star*, December 16, 1902; *A Statutory History*, pp. 4–8.

[9] U.S., Office of the Commissioner of Public Buildings, "Rules and Regulations for the Government of the Capitol Police," April 11, 1862, copy in the files of the U.S. Senate Historical Office, Washington, DC.

[10] *A Statutory History*, pp. 10–11; *The Chicago Republican*, February 8, 1868.

[11] *A Statutory History*, p. 13; Samuel D. Wyeth, *Roose's Companion and Guide to Washington and Vicinity* (Washington, DC, 1882), pp. 64–65, cited in "The Capitol Police, 1801–1950," p. 13.

[12] *A Statutory History*, pp. 15–16.

[13] Ibid., pp. 16–17.

[14] *Washington Star*, November 7–8, 1898.

[15] *Washington Star*, July 3, 1915; *New York Times*, July 4–7, 1915.

[16] John Alexander, *Ghosts: Washington's Most Famous Ghost Stories* (Washington, DC, 1975), pp. 81–82.

[17] Ibid., p. 73.

[18] Ibid., p. 67.

[19] Ibid.

[20] *A Statutory History*, pp. 26–29; U.S., Congress, House, *Reducing the Number of Capitol Police*, H. Rept. 34, 62d Cong., 1st sess., 1911, pp. 6–8; *Washington Star*, October 6, 1902.

[21] *Washington Star*, December 16, 1902; *A Statutory History*, p. 29.

[22] *A Statutory History*, pp. 35–36.

[23] U.S., Congress, Senate, *Congressional Record*, 62d Cong., 2d sess., pp. 7606, 7610.

[24] Ibid., p. 7606.

[25] Ibid., pp. 7610–12; Minutes of the Senate Democratic Conference, Office of the Democratic Secretary.

[26] *Congressional Record*, 62d Cong., 2d sess., p. 7609.

[27] *Congressional Record*, 65th Cong., 2d sess., p. 5951.

[28] *Congressional Record*, 74th Cong., 1st sess., pp. 7396–97; U.S., Congress, House, *Legislative Establishment Appropriation Bill, 1936*, pp. 62–65, 180–83.

[29] *New York Times*, December 14, 1932; *Washington Evening Star*, December 14, 1932.

[30] *Washington Evening Star*, July 13–14, 1947; *New York Times*, July 13, 1947.

[31] Donald L. McMurry, *Coxey's Army: A Study of the Industrial Army Movement of 1894* (New York, 1968; reprint of 1929 ed.), pp. 121, 125–26; Carlos A. Schwantes, *Coxey's Army: An American Odyssey* (Lincoln, NB, 1985), chapter 11.

[32] I am indebted to William Manchester for his excellent account of the bonus march in *The Glory and the Dream: A Narrative History of America, 1932–1972* (Boston, 1974), pp. 3–19.

[33] *New York Times*, March 2–3, 1954; *Washington Star*, March 2–3, 1954.

[34] U.S., Congress, House, Committee on House Administration, *Capitol Police Reorganization Act of 1954*, hearing, June 22, 1954, pp. 13–38; U.S., Congress, House, *Capitol Police Reorganization Act of 1954*, H. Rept. 2267, 83d Cong., 2d sess., 1954.

[35] *A Statutory History*, pp. 90–91.

[36] Ibid., pp. 139–40.

[37] *Washington Post*, September 12, 1967; *New York Times*, September 12, 1967; *Congressional Record*, 90th Cong., 1st sess., p. 25116; *A Statutory History*, p. 106.

[38] *Washington Post*, March 2–3, 1971; *Washington Evening Star*, March 2–3, 8, 12, 1971.

[39] *Washington Post*, November 8–9, 1983; "Capitol Security Strengthened After Terrorist Bomb Explodes," *Congressional Quarterly Weekly Report* 41 (November 12, 1983), pp. 2355–58.

[40] Frederick M. Kaiser, "The U.S. Capitol Police and Supreme Court Police: Expanding Their Protective Mandates and Jurisdictions," *Police Studies* 11 (Summer 1988): 81–91.

CHAPTER 15
Congressional Salaries

[1] Sources consulted for this speech, in addition to the files of the Senate Historical Office and the Senate Library, include: Paul E. Dwyer and Frederick H. Pauls, "A Brief History of Congressional Pay Legislation," CRS Report 87–685 GOV, Congressional Research Service, Library of Congress, Washington, DC, 1987; Frederick H. Pauls and Paul E. Dwyer, "A Brief Report on Congressional Pay," CRS Report 86–1051 GOV, 1986; Mike Mills, "Raising Members' Pay." *Congressional Quarterly Weekly Report* 47 (February 4, 1989); "Proposed Amendment, Age 200, Showing Life," *Washington Post*, March 29, 1989; David C. Huckabee. "The Constitutional Amendment to Regulate Congressional Salary Increases," CRS Report 86–889 G, 1986.

[2] *Notes of Debates in the Federal Convention of 1787 Reported by James Madison* (Athens, OH, 1966), p. 30.

[3] Ibid., pp. 107–8.

[4] Linda Grant De Pauw, ed, *Senate Legislative Journal, Documentary History of the First Federal Congress of the United States of America*, vol. 1 (Baltimore, 1972), pp. 140–44; Kenneth R. Bowling and Helen E. Veit, eds, *The Diary of William Maclay and Other Notes on Senate Debates, Documentary History of the First Federal Congress of the United States of America*, vol. 9 (Baltimore, 1988), pp. 138–39.

[5] De Pauw, p. 144; Bowling and Veit, pp. 139–40.

[6] Linda Grant De Pauw, ed., *House of Representatives Journal, Documentary History of the First Federal Congress of the United States of America*, vol. 3 (Baltimore, 1977), pp. 200, 202–3; Charlene Bangs Bickford and Helen E. Veit, eds., *Legislative Histories, Documentary History of the First Federal Congress of the United States of America*, vol. 6 (Baltimore, 1986), pp. 1833–45.

[7] Bickford and Veit, pp. 1833–45.

[8] Ibid., 4:1.

[9] U.S., Congress, Senate, *Annals of Congress*, 4th Cong., 1st sess., March 1–4, 1796, pp. 48–50; *U.S. Statutes at Large*, 1:448–49.

[10] Based on information in U.S., Congress, Senate, *Biographical Directory of the United States Congress, 1774–1989*, Bicentennial Edition, S. Doc. 100-34, 100th Cong., 2d sess., 1989, pp. 83–94.

[11] U.S. Code, vol. 2, sec. 39 (1856).

[12] U.S., Congress, Senate, *Congressional Globe*, 42d Cong., 3d sess., pp. 2048–49.

13 Ibid., pp. 2046–47.

14 Ibid.

15 Ibid., pp. 2180, 2049.

16 Ibid., p. 2181.

17 Ibid., p. 2047.

CHAPTER 16

Archives and Records

1 Frank McAllister to Thomas M. Owen, Jr., February 12, 1937, Records of the Legislative Records Branch, Record Group 46, National Archives, Washington, DC.

2 Lewis Henry Machen to William C. Rives, September 12, 1836, William Cabel Rives Papers, Box 54, Library of Congress, Washington, DC; Buford Rowland, "Recordkeeping Practices of the House of Representatives," *National Archives Accessions* 53 (January 1957): 3–4.

3 "Preliminary Survey, United States Senate," [undated], Records of the Legislative Records Branch, Record Group 46, National Archives, Washington, DC.

4 Quoted in Ben Cole, "Document Sleuth," *Washington Evening Star* [c. 1950], copy in Senate Historical Office files.

5 Ibid.; "Transfer of Certain Records from the Senate Wing of the Capitol," April 1, 1937, Records of the Legislative Records Branch, Record Group 46, National Archives, Washington, DC; U.S., Congress, Senate, *Congressional Record*, 75th Cong., 1st sess., pp. 2670–71, 2735–36.

6 U.S., Congress, Senate, *Records Management Handbook for United States Senate Committees*, by Karen Dawley Paul, S. Pub. 100-5, 100th Cong., 2d sess., 1988.

7 Correspondence from Professor Judith Wellman to U.S. Senate Historical Office, Washington, DC, 1980.

8 U.S., National Archives and Records Service, "Annual Report of the Legislative Archives Division . . . for the Fiscal Year Ended September 30, 1987."

9 *Congressional Record*, 95th Cong., 1st sess., p. 5638.

10 U.S., Congress, Senate, S. Res. 474, 96th Cong., 2d sess.; U.S., Congress, Senate, *Relating to Public Access to Senate Records at the National Archives*, S. Rept. 96-1042, 96th Cong., 2d sess., 1980; Richard A. Baker, "The Records of Congress: Opportunities and Obstacles in the Senate," *The Public Historian* 2 (Summer 1980): 62–72.

11 U.S., Congress, Senate, *Final Report of the Study Group on the Commemoration of the United States Senate Bicentenary*, S. Doc. 98-13, 98th Cong., 1st sess., 1983, p. 4.

12 U.S., Congress, Senate, *Guide to the Records of the United States Senate at the National Archives*, S. Doc. 100-42, 100th Cong., 2d sess., 1989. The companion volume of House records is U.S., Congress, House, *Guide to the Records of the United States House of Representatives at the National Archives*, H. Doc. 100-245, 100th Cong., 2d sess., 1989.

13 U.S., Congress, Senate, Conference on the Research Use and Disposition of Senators' Papers, *Proceedings*, ed., Richard A. Baker (Washington, DC, 1979), pp. 7–8.

14 U.S., Congress, Senate, *Records Management Handbook for United States Senators and Their Repositories*, by Karen Dawley Paul, S. Pub. 99-4, 99th Cong., 1st sess., 1985.

15 U.S., Congress, Senate, *Guide to Research Collections of Former United States Senators, 1789–1972*, S. Doc. 97-41, 97th Cong., 2d sess., 1983.

16 Hannah Flagg Gould, "A Name in the Sand."

CHAPTER 17

Senate Pages

1 U.S., Congress, House, Select Committee on the Contingent Expenses of the House, *Contingent Expenses of the House of Representatives*, H. Rept. 30, 27th Cong., 2d sess., 1842, p. 6.

2 Ibid.

3 In addition to the specific sources cited, much of the information in this chapter is based on Bill Severn, *Democracy's Messengers: The Capitol Pages* (New York, 1975); Severn, pp. 13–14.

4 Ibid., pp. 14–15.

5 Christian F. Eckloff, *Memoirs of a Senate Page*, ed. Percival G. Melbourne (New York, 1909), p. 3; George H. Haynes, *The Senate of the United States: Its History and Practice* (Boston, 1938), 2:945.

6 Eckloff, pp. 42–43.

7 Ibid., p. 43.

8 Quoted in Severn, p. 15.

9 Eckloff, p. 7.

10 Edmund Alton, *Among the Law-Makers* (New York, 1892), p. 259.

[11] Baker A. Jamison, *Memories of Great Men and Events: 1840–1861* (New York, 1917), p. 6; Severn, p. 16.

[12] Jamison, p. 124.

[13] Eckloff, pp. 5–6.

[14] Jamison, pp. 124–25; Severn, pp. 16–17.

[15] Jamison, p. 125; Severn, p. 16.

[16] Jamison, pp. 122–24; Severn, p. 17.

[17] Severn, pp. 22–23.

[18] Ibid., pp. 22–24; for more on Arthur Pue Gorman, see John Lambert, *Arthur Pue Gorman* (Baton Rouge, LA, 1953).

[19] Ibid., pp. 24–25.

[20] Eckloff, p. 10; Severn, p. 26; Jamison, pp. 124–25.

[21] Eckloff, pp. 12–13.

[22] Alton, pp. 23–24.

[23] Ibid., p. 26.

[24] Ibid., pp. 31–32.

[25] Ibid., p. 176.

[26] Ibid., pp. 259–60.

[27] Ibid., pp. 176, 179.

[28] Ibid., pp. 175–76.

[29] Ibid., pp. 81–87; Jamison, pp. 125–26.

[30] Severn, p. 40.

[31] Richard Riedel, *Halls of the Mighty* (Washington, DC, 1969), p. 17.

[32] Severn, p. 29.

[33] Ibid., pp. 9–10.

[34] Alton, pp. 257–58, 260.

[35] Ibid., pp. 258–59.

[36] Ibid., p. 19.

[37] Riedel, p. 15.

[38] Bobby Baker, with Larry L. King, *Wheeling and Dealing* (New York, 1978), p. 31.

[39] Quoted in Severn, p. 41; Riedel, p. 188.

[40] Mildred L. Amer, "Pages of the United States Congress," CRS Report No. 84-73 GOV, Congressional Research Service, Library of Congress, Washington, DC, 1984, p. 17.

[41] Riedel, p. 19.

[42] Severn, p. 21.

[43] Amer, pp. 43–46.

[44] Severn, p. 56.

[45] Amer, p. 24.

[46] Severn, pp. 108, 112.

[47] Quoted in Amer, p. 38; Senator Burton's reference is to Charles Dickens' brutal "Dotheboys Hall" in *Nicholas Nickleby*.

[48] Amer, p. 39.

[49] Amer, p. 31.

[50] Quoted in Severn, p. 95.

[51] Ibid., pp. 95, 97.

[52] Ibid., p. 5.

[53] Carl A. Loeffler, "Recollections of a Lifetime with the Senate," unpublished manuscript, 1949, in the files of the U.S. Senate Historical Office, Washington, DC, p. 4.

SETTING

Divider Page Quotations

[1] Kenneth R. Bowling and Helen E. Veit, eds, *The Diary of William Maclay and Other Notes on Senate Debates*, Documentary History of the First Federal Congress of the United States of America, vol. 9 (Baltimore, 1988), p. 401.

[2] U.S., Congress, Senate, *The Old Senate Chamber: Proceedings in the Senate of the United States Upon Vacating their Old Chamber on January 4, 1859*, S. Doc. 67, 74th Cong., 1st sess., 1935, p. 3.

[3] Emily Edison Briggs, *The Olivia Letters* (New York, 1906), pp. 91–94.

CHAPTER 18

Meeting Places of the Senate

New York and Philadelphia, 1789–1800

[1] Paul A.W. Wallace, *The Muhlenbergs of Pennsylvania* (Philadelphia, 1950), p. 277; Louis Torres, "Federal Hall Revisited" *Journal of the Society of Architectural Historians* 29 (December 1970): 327–28.

[2] Quoted in Torres, p. 328.

[3] Ibid.

[4] Ibid., pp. 329–30.

[5] Ibid., p. 329.

[6] Ibid., p. 336.

[7] Kenneth R. Bowling and Helen E. Veit, eds., *The Diary of William Maclay and Other Notes on Senate Debates, Documentary History of the First Federal Congress of the United States of America*, vol. 9 (Baltimore, 1988), p. 169.

[8] Linda Grant DePauw, ed., *Senate Legislative Journal, Documentary History of the First Federal Congress of the United States of America*, vol. 1 (Baltimore, 1972), p. 490.

[9] Russel Blaine Nye, *The Cultural Life of the New Nation, 1776–1830* (New York, 1960), pp. 111–13, 125–28.

[10] U.S., Department of the Interior, National Park Service, *Congress Hall*, by Miriam Blimm (Washington, DC, 1976), pp. 2–3.

[11] Ibid., p. 3.

[12] "Furnishing Plan for the Second Floor of Congress Hall," unpublished manuscript prepared by the staff of Independence National Historical Park, Philadelphia, PA, October 1963, pp. C,I, 6–9.

[13] *American Daily Advertiser*, June 6, 1791, quoted in U.S., Department of the Interior, National Park Service, *The Most Splended Carpet*, by Susan H. Anderson (Philadelphia, 1978), p. 5.

[14] Anderson, p. 5.

[15] Blimm, p. 5.

[16] U.S., Congress, Senate, *Annals of Congress*, 6th Cong., 1st sess., p. 183.

Washington, 1800–1859

[1] Quoted in [William B. Webb and J. Woolridge] *Centennial History of the City of Washington, D.C.* (Dayton, OH, 1892), p. 93.

[2] Constance McLaughlin Green, *Washington: A History of the Capital, 1800–1950* (Princeton, NJ, 1962), p. 4.

[3] George Gibbs, ed., *Memoirs of the Administrations of Washington and John Adams Edited from the Papers of Oliver Wolcott, Secretary of the Treasury* (New York, 1971; reprint of 1846 ed.), 2:377.

[4] Green, pp. 18–19.

[5] Margaret Bayard Smith to James B. Bayard, October 5, 1800, Margaret Bayard Smith Papers, Library of Congress, Washington, DC.

[6] Quoted in Alvin M. Josephy, Jr., *On the Hill: A History of the American Congress* (New York, 1979), p. 115.

[7] U.S., Congress, Senate, *The United States Senate, 1787–1801: A Dissertation on the First Fourteen Years of the Upper Legislative Body*, by Roy Swanstrom, S. Doc. 100-31, 100th Cong., 1st sess., 1988, pp. 183–84.

[8] Green, pp. 23, 18.

[9] U.S., Congress, Senate, *Annals of Congress*, 6th Cong., 2d sess., p. 723.

[10] Glenn Brown, *History of the United States Capitol* (New York, 1970; reprint of 1900–1902 ed.), pp. 15–16.

[11] Report of James Hoban, May 20, 1799, in U.S., Congress, House, *Documentary History of the Construction and Development of the United States Capitol Building and Grounds*, H. Rept. 646, 58th Cong., 2d sess., 1904, p. 87.

[12] Report of James Hoban, November 18, 1799, in *Documentary History*, p. 88.

[13] G. Scott and W. Thornton to John Emory, July 9, 1800, in *Documentary History*, p. 91.

[14] Quoted in Swanstrom, p. 182.

[15] Brown, p. 25.

[16] *Annals of Congress*, 6th Cong., 2d sess., p. 731.

[17] Josephy, p. 116.

[18] Ibid., pp. 117–18.

[19] Ibid., p. 118.

[20] Ibid., pp. 119–20.

[21] Ibid., p. 120.

[22] Ibid.

[23] U.S., Congress, House, *The Capitol*, 8th ed., H. Doc. 96-374, 96th Cong., 2d sess., 1981, p. 8; Brown, p. 28.

[24] B. Henry Latrobe to the President of the United States, February 20, 1804, in *Documentary History*, p. 105.

[25] *The Capitol*, p. 8.

[26] B. Henry Latrobe to the chairman of the committee of the Senate . . . , February 18, 1809, in *Documentary History*, p. 154.

[27] Ibid.

[28] B. Henry Latrobe to the Vice President of the United States, June 12, 1809, in *Documentary History*, p. 156.

[29] Charles Jared Ingersoll, *Inchiquin, The Jesuit's Letters* (New York, 1810), p. 52, quoted in U.S., Congress, Senate, Commission on Art and Antiquities, *The Senate Chamber, 1810–1859* (Washington, DC, 1985), p. 3.

[30] *The Capitol*, p. 9.

[31] U.S., Congress, Senate, *Art and Artists of the Capitol of the United States of America*, by Charles E. Fairman, S. Doc. 95, 69th Cong., 1st sess., 1927, p. 23; Brown, p. 47.

[32] Brown, p. 48; Josephy, p. 149.

[33] James M. Goode, *Capital Losses: A Cultural History of Washington's Destroyed Buildings* (Washington, DC, 1979), p. 291.

[34] B. Henry Latrobe to the Commissioner of Public Buildings, November 28, 1816, in *Documentary History*, pp. 191–92.

[35] *The Senate Chamber, 1810–1859*, p. 5.

[36] Robert Mills, *Guide to the Capitol of the United States* (Washington, DC, 1834), p. 43.

[37] "The Senate Chamber Desks," typescript prepared by the offices of Senate curator and historian, 1979, in files of the U.S. Senate Historical Office, Washington, DC, pp. 1–2.

[38] U.S., Congress, Senate, S. Res. 469, 93d Cong., 2d sess.

[39] Isaac Bassett Papers in a private collection. Copies of the papers are housed in the office of the Senate curator. The Bassett collection is rich in Senate history and also contains material on the House of Representatives and Washington, D.C. It covers approximately the years 1830 to 1895.

[40] *Art and Artists of the Capitol*, pp. 93, 98.

[41] Margaret Bayard Smith, *The First Forty Years of Washington Society in the Family Letters of Margaret Bayard Smith*, ed. Gaillard Hunt (New York, 1965; reprint of 1906 ed.), p. 310.

[42] George H. Haynes, *The Senate of the United States: Its History and Practice* (Boston, 1938), 2:945.

[43] Quoted in Haynes, p. 943.

[44] Quoted in *The Capitol*, p. 12; quoted in *The Senate Chamber, 1810–1859*, p. 9.

[45] *The Senate Chamber, 1810–1859*, p. 9.

[46] Quoted in ibid., p. 14.

[47] Ibid., p. 16.

[48] *The Capitol*, pp. 13–14; *Congressional Quarterly's Guide to U.S. Elections*, 2d ed. (Washington, DC, 1985), p. 686.

[49] U.S., Congress, Senate, *Congressional Globe*, 35th Cong., 2d sess., p. 201.

[50] Ibid., p. 202.

[51] U.S., Congress, Senate, *The Old Senate Chamber: Proceedings in the Senate of the United States Upon Vacating their Old Chamber on January 4, 1859*, S. Doc. 67, 74th Cong., 1st sess., 1935, p. 2.

Washington, 1859–1989

[1] *New York Herald*, January 5, 1859.

[2] George H. Haynes, *The Senate of the United States: Its History and Practice* (Boston, 1938), 2:918.

[3] U.S., Congress, Senate, *Our Capitol: Factual Information Pertaining to Our Capitol and Places of Historic Interest in the National Capital*, 88th Cong., 1st sess., S. Doc. 22, 1963, p. 18.

[4] Ibid., p. 28; *New York Times*, September 23, 1950.

[5] U.S., Congress, Senate, *Congressional Record*, 83d Cong., 2d sess., pp. 14963–64.

[6] Quoted in *Our Capitol*, p. 21n.

[7] *New York Times*, December 6, 1916.

[8] U.S., Congress, Senate, *Vases Presented by the Republic of France: Proceedings in the Senate of the United States*, S. Doc. 246, 65th Cong., 2d sess., 1918, p. 3.

[9] *Our Capitol*, p. 9.

[10] Quoted in ibid., p. 10n.

[11] Ibid., p. 9.

[12] Myrtle Chaney Murdock, *Constantino Brumidi: Michaelangelo of the United States Capitol* (Washington, DC, 1950), p. 6.

[13] *Our Capitol*, p. 10; U.S., Congress, Senate, *Art and Artists of the Capitol of the United States of America*, by Charles E. Fairman, S. Doc. 95, 69th Cong., 1st sess., 1927, p. 491.

[14] "A Public Building," *Harper's New Monthly Magazine* 38 (January 1869): 209.

[15] *Our Capitol*, pp. 10–11.

[16] Richard H. Abbott, *Cobbler in Congress: The Life of Henry Wilson, 1812–1875* (Lexington, KY, 1972), p. 256.

[17] U.S., Congress, House, Architect of the Capitol, *Art in the United States Capitol*, H. Doc. 91-368, 91st Cong., 2d sess., 1976, p. 398.

[18] *Our Capitol*, p. 11.

[19] Glenn Brown, *History of the United States Capitol* (New York, 1970; reprint of 1900–1902 ed.), pp. 162–63.

[20] *Our Capitol*, p. 31.

[21] Ibid., p. 17.

[22] U.S., Congress, Senate, *Study of Desirable Improvements to Senate Chamber and Senate Office Building*, S. Rept. 1043, 77th Cong., 2d sess., 1942, p. 2; Bassett quoted in *Our Capitol*, p. 17n; U.S., Congress, Senate, Committee on Public Buildings and Grounds, *Acoustics, Redecoration, and Better Lighting System for the Senate Chamber, Hearings before a subcommittee of the Committee on Public Buildings and Grounds, U.S. Senate, on S. Res. 150*, 77th Cong., 1st sess., 1941, p. 4.

[23] *Acoustics, Redecoration, and Better Lighting System*, p. 6; U.S., Congress, Senate, *History of United States Senate Roof and Chamber Improvements and Related Historical Data*, S. Doc. 20, 82d Cong., 1st sess., 1951, pp. 10–11.

[24] *History of United States Senate Roof and Chamber Improvements*, p. 29; *Study of Desirable Improvements to Senate Chamber*, pp. 3–4.

[25] See *New York Times*, August 10, 1950.

[26] U.S., Congress, Senate, *The Old Senate Chamber: Proceedings in the Senate of the United States Upon Vacating their Old Chamber on January 4, 1859*, S. Doc. 67, 74th Cong., 1st sess., 1935, p. 3.

CHAPTER 19

Senate Press Galleries

[1] Burton Stevenson, *The Home Book of Quotations*, 10th ed. (New York, 1967), p. 1601.

[2] John Bartlett, *Familiar Quotations*, 15th ed. (Boston, 1980), p. 388.

[3] Frank Carpenter, *Carp's Washington* (New York, 1960), pp. 271–72.

[4] U.S., Congress, Senate, *The United States Senate, 1787–1801: A Dissertation on the First Fourteen Years of the Upper Legislative Body*, by Roy Swanstrom, S. Doc. 100-31, 100th Cong., 1st sess., 1988, pp. 304–8.

[5] F.B. Marbut, *News from the Capital: The Story of Washington Reporting* (Carbondale, IL, 1971), pp. 22–23.

[6] Ibid., pp. 85–93, 142–46; see also U.S., Congress, Senate, *Congressional Record*, 101st Cong., 1st sess., pp. S3291–92 (Daily Edition, April 4, 1989).

[7] Patrick J. Maney, *"Young Bob" La Follette: A Biography of Robert M. La Follette, Jr., 1895–1953* (Columbia, MO, 1978), pp. 63–65.

[8] The Senate holds three distinct types of secret sessions: executive, legislative, and impeachment. Executive sessions are conducted for the review of nominations and treaties and were routinely closed until 1929. Since that time, they have been closed infrequently. Legislative sessions may be closed at the request of two or more senators. When the Senate sits as a court of impeachment, it operates under a special set of impeachment rules that provide for closed sessions as necessary.

[9] Marbut, pp. 23–27.

[10] Ibid., pp. 30–31.

[11] Ibid., pp. 55–65; *Washington Evening Star*, December 16, 1902.

[12] Carleton Mabee, *The American Leonardo: A Life of Samuel F.B. Morse* (New York, 1943), pp. 251–60; U.S., Congress, House, Committee on the Judiciary, *Telegraph Censorship*, H. Rept. 64, 37th Cong., 2d sess., 1962, p. 3.

[13] [Benjamin Perley Poore] "Washington News," *Harper's Monthly* 10:8 (January 1874): 225–36.

[14] *Washington Evening Star*, December 16, 1902.

[15] Justin Kaplan, *Mr. Clemens and Mark Twain: A Biography* (New York, 1966), pp. 57–75.

[16] *Daily Alta Californian*, February 11, 1968; "Mark Twain in Washington" Scrapbook, Manuscript Division, Library of Congress, Washington, DC.

[17] Mark Twain and Charles Dudley Warner, *The Gilded Age: A Tale of Today* (Seattle, 1968; reprint of 1873 ed.).

[18] Ben: Perley Poore, *Perley's Reminiscences of Sixty Years in the National Metropolis* (New York, 1971; reprint of 1886 ed.).

[19] See Joseph Patrick McKerns, "Benjamin Perley Poore of the Boston Journal: His Life and Times as a Washington Correspondent, 1850–1887" (Ph.D. dissertation, University of Minnesota, 1979).

[20] [Poore], "Washington News," p. 226.

[21] Marbut, p. 154.

[22] Ibid., pp. 139–54.

[23] U.S., Congress, *Official Congressional Directory: 1987–1988*, S. Prt. 100-31, 100th Cong., 1987, p. 1205.

[24] See in general Maurine Hoffman Beasley, *The First Women Washington Correspondents* (Washington, DC, 1976).

[25] Marbut, pp. 162–63.

26 William Small, "Equal Access for Broadcast Journalism," in Robert O. Blanchard, ed., *Congress and the News Media* (New York, 1974), pp. 66–89; Marbut, pp. 213–18.

27 *Darrell St. Claire, Assistant Secretary of the Senate*, Oral History Interviews, December 1976 to April 1978 (U.S. Senate Historical Office, Washington, DC), pp. 225–29.

28 For a case-by-case analysis of television on Capitol Hill, see Ronald Garay, *Congressional Television: A Legislative History* (Westport, CT, 1984).

29 *New York Times*, March 1, 1953; *Washington Evening Star*, February 27, 1955.

30 Albert Bigelow Paine, ed., *Mark Twain's Letters* (New York, 1917), 1:145.

31 Charles Neider, ed., *The Complete Humorous Sketches and Tales of Mark Twain* (New York, 1985; reprint of 1961 ed.), pp. 94–98.

CHAPTER 20

The Botanic Garden and Capitol Landscape

1 Karen D. Solit, Draft of a brief history of the Botanic Garden, l980, in the files of the U.S. Senate Historical Office, Washington, DC, p. 1.

2 Quoted in ibid.

3 Quoted in ibid., p. 2.

4 Robert Park MacHatton, "Heritage of the Navy," *U.S. Naval Institute Proceedings* 68 (July 1942): 967.

5 Ibid.; Leonard D. White, *The Jacksonians* (New York, 1954), p. 497; U.S., Congress, Joint Committee on the Library, *History of the United States Botanic Garden, 1816–1990*, by Karen D. Solit (forthcoming, 1991), p. 24.

6 Solit (1991), p. 30; *Harper's Weekly*, June 26, 1869, p. 40.

7 Mary Hughes, "U.S. Botanic Garden Shines Brightly in Shadows of Bureaucratic Jungle," *Florists' Review*, September 28, 1978, p. 102; Solit (1991), p. 31.

8 Quoted in Solit (1991), p. 32n.

9 Ibid., pp. 31–32.

10 Quoted in Solit (1980), p. 5.

11 James M. Goode, *Outdoor Sculpture of Washington, DC* (Washington, DC, 1974), pp. 250–51.

12 Solit (1991), p. 39.

13 Hughes, p. 102.

14 Solit (1991), pp. 50–52; Goode, p. 250.

15 Hughes, p. 102.

16 U.S., Congress, *Annual Report of the Architect of the United States Capitol for the Fiscal Year Ending June 30, 1882* (Washington, DC, 1882), pp. 13–15.

17 Ibid., p. 14.

18 Ibid., pp. 13, 15.

19 U.S., Congress, Senate, *Congressional Record*, 87th Cong., 2d sess., p. 7162.

20 Ibid., p. 7163.

21 Ibid., pp. 7211–13.

22 *Congressional Record*, 95th Cong., 2d sess., pp. 19173–74.

23 U.S., Congress, House, *The Capitol*, 8th ed., H. Doc. 96-374, 96th Cong., 2d sess., 1981, pp. 36–37.

24 William Shakespeare, "The Winter's Tale."

CHAPTER 21

The Senate in Literature and Film

1 Mark Twain and Charles Dudley Warner, *The Gilded Age: A Tale of Today* (Seattle, 1968; reprint of 1873 ed.), pp. 170, 300, 408.

2 Ibid., xv.

3 Henry Adams, *Democracy* (New York, 1961, reprint of 1880 ed.), pp. 22, 25, 64, 80, 187, 191.

4 Theron Crawford, *A Man and His Soul* (New York, 1894), pp. 23, 63–72, 117, 137, 146; in comparison, see Theron Crawford, *James G. Blaine: A Study of His Life and Career* (New York, 1893), p. 139.

5 Dashiell Hammett, *The Glass Key* (New York, 1979; reprint of 1931 ed.), p. 9.

6 Edgar Box, *Death Before Bedtime* (New York, 1979; reprint of 1953 ed.).

7 Margaret Truman, *Murder on Capitol Hill* (New York, 1981).

8 Lawrence Meyer, *A Capitol Crime* (New York, 1977).

9 Allen Drury, *Advise and Consent* (Garden City, NY, 1959); and Drury, *A Senate Journal, 1943–1945* (New York, 1963).

10 Louis Ludlow, *Senator Solomon Spiffledink* (Washington, DC, 1927).

CHAPTER 22

Lobbyists

[1] Emily Edison Briggs, *The Olivia Letters* (New York, 1906), pp. 91–94.

[2] U.S., Congress, Senate, *The United States Senate, 1787–1801: A Dissertation on the First Fourteen Years of the Upper Legislative Body*, by Roy Swanstrom, S. Doc. 100-31, 100th Cong., 1st sess., 1988, pp. 213–14.

[3] Kenneth R. Bowling and Helen E. Veit, eds., *The Diary of William Maclay and Other Notes on Senate Debates, Documentary History of the First Federal Congress of the United States of America*, vol. 9 (Baltimore, 1988), p. 215.

[4] Quoted in Swanstrom, p. 214.

[5] Ibid., p. 215.

[6] Charles M. Wiltse, ed., *The Papers of Daniel Webster, 1830–1834* (Hanover, NH, 1977), 3:288.

[7] U.S., Congress, Senate, Committee on Governmental Affairs, *Congress and Pressure Groups: Lobbying in a Modern Democracy*, S. Print 99-161, 99th Cong., 2d sess., 1986, p. 2.

[8] F.B. Marbut, *News from the Capital: The Story of Washington Reporting* (Carbondale, IL, 1971), pp. 29–38.

[9] U.S., Congress, House, H. Rept. No. 353, 33d Cong., 1st sess., August 3, 1854, pp. 9, 15.

[10] Ibid., p. 4.

[11] Ibid.

[12] Ibid.

[13] David J. Rothman, *Politics and Power: The United States Senate, 1869–1901* (Cambridge, MA, 1966), pp. 191–94.

[14] Ibid., 195–203.

[15] Lately Thomas, *Sam Ward, "King of the Lobby"* (Boston, 1965), pp. 336–40, 367–73.

[16] Ben: Perley Poore, *Perley's Reminiscences of Sixty Years in the National Metropolis* (New York, 1971; reprint of 1886 ed.), 2:514–15.

[17] Quoted in Margaret Susan Thompson, *The "Spider Web": Congress and Lobbying in the Age of Grant* (Ithaca, NY, 1985), pp. 53–54.

[18] Mark Twain and Charles Dudley Warner, *The Gilded Age: A Tale of Today* (Seattle, 1968, reprint of 1873 ed.).

[19] Thompson, pp. 33–69.

[20] Ibid., pp. 139–40.

[21] Ibid., pp. 165–73.

[22] *Washington Evening Star*, January 31, 1891.

[23] *Congress and Pressure Groups*, p. 4.

[24] Marbut, pp. 153–58.

[25] Rothman, pp. 203–4.

[26] Ibid.

[27] Robert Rienow and Leona Train Rienow, *Of Snuff, Sin and the Senate* (Chicago, 1965), pp. 157–87.

[28] Arthur Link, ed., *The Papers of Woodrow Wilson* (Princeton, NJ, 1978), pp. 472–73.

[29] *Congress and Pressure Groups*, pp. 7–9; Alvin M. Josephy, Jr., *On the Hill: A History of the American Congress* (New York, 1979), p. 294.

[30] U.S., Congress, Senate, *Congressional Record*, 71st Cong., 1st sess., p. 5131.

[31] Virginia Van Der Veer Hamilton, *Hugo Black: The Alabama Years* (Baton Rouge, LA, 1972), p. 176.

[32] Ibid., p. 248.

[33] *Congress and Pressure Groups*, p. 10; See also Kenneth Crawford, *The Pressure Boys: The Inside Story of Lobbying in America* (New York, 1939).

[34] *Congress and Pressure Groups*, pp. 41–45.

[35] *U.S.* v. *Harriss*, 347 U.S. 625 (1964).

CHAPTER 23

Women Senators

[1] Inez Haynes Irwin, *The Story of the Woman's Party*, (New York, 1921), pp. 180–82.

[2] Hope Chamberlin, *A Minority of Members: Women in the United States Congress* (New York, 1974), pp. 5–18; "Jeannette Rankin," *Notable American Women* (Cambridge, MA, 1980), 4:566–68; Florence White, *First Woman in Congress: Jeannette Rankin* (New York, 1980); Hannah Josephson, *Jeannette Rankin: First Lady in Congress* (Indianapolis, IN, 1974).

[3] Statistic made available by the Congressional Caucus for Women's Issues; Mildred L. Amer, "Women in the United States Congress," CRS Report No. 89-332 GOV, Congressional Research Service, Library of Congress, Washington, DC, 1989.

[4] Diane Kincaid, "Over His Dead Body: A Positive Perspective on Widows in the United States Con-

gress," *Western Political Quarterly* 31 (March 1978): 96–104.

5 Chamberlin, pp. 3–4.

6 Amer, pp. 5–41. In all of the following brief biographies of these senators, I should note that I have been greatly aided by the work of many historians who have written about women in the Senate collectively and individually. Particularly helpful have been Hope Chamberlin's *A Minority of Members*, Susan J. Tolchin's *Clout: Womanpower and Politics* (New York, 1974), and U.S., Congress, Joint Committee on Arrangements for the Commemoration of the Bicentennial, *Women in Congress, 1917–1976*, 94th Cong., 2d sess., 1976. An updated edition of this latter work will be published in 1991 under the direction of the Commission on the Bicentenary of the U.S. House of Representatives.

7 John Talmadge, *Rebecca Latimer Felton: Nine Stormy Decades* (Athens, GA, 1960). The best sources on the life of Rebecca Felton, and the sources from which the following biography are drawn, include Talmadge; Chamberlin, pp. 119–36; Joel Williamson, *Crucible of Race* (Oxford, MS, 1984); and Rebecca Latimer Felton, *My Country Life in Georgia in the Days of My Youth* (Atlanta, GA, 1919).

8 *Atlanta Journal*, October 2 and 3, 1922; Chamberlin, pp. 19–20.

9 Chamberlin, p. 20.

10 Ibid.

11 Ibid.

12 Ibid., p. 21.

13 Ibid., pp. 21–22.

14 Felton, p. 18.

15 Chamberlin, p. 26.

16 Ibid., p. 28.

17 Ibid., pp. 31–32; *New York Times*, November 18, 1922; *Atlanta Journal*, November 18, 1922.

18 Chamberlin, p. 32.

19 Ibid., pp. 33–36; U.S., Congress, Senate, *Congressional Record*, 67th Cong., 3d sess., pp. 3–23.

20 The best accounts of the career of Hattie Caraway are found in Chamberlin, pp. 86–95 and in Hattie Caraway, *"Silent Hattie" Speaks: The Personal Journal of Senator Hattie Caraway*, ed. Diane Kincaid (Westport, CT, 1979); Caraway, p. 44.

21 Caraway, pp. 121, 8.

22 Ibid., p. 57n; Stuart Towns, "A Louisiana Medicine Show: The Kingfish Elects an Arkansas Senator," *The Arkansas Historical Quarterly* 25 (Summer 1966): 122.

23 Hermann B. Deutsch, "Hattie and Huey," *Saturday Evening Post*, October 15, 1932, p. 88; see also David Malone, *Hattie and Huey: An Arkansas Tour* (Fayetteville, AR, 1989).

24 Caraway, p. 9.

25 Ibid., p. 10; Towns, p. 126; Deutsch, pp. 6–7, 88–90, 92; *Arkansas Gazette*, August 1–9, 1932; T. Harry Williams, *Huey Long* (New York, 1960), pp. 583–618.

26 Caraway, p. 11.

27 Chamberlin, p. 118.

28 Ibid., p. 120.

29 Ibid., p. 121; *Women in Congress*, p. 66.

30 *Women in Congress*, p. 31.

31 Chamberlin, p. 123.

32 Ibid., pp. 126–27; *Women in Congress*, p. 66.

33 Chamberlin, p. 196.

34 Ibid., pp. 197, 199.

35 *Women in Congress*, p. 75; The best sources on the career of Margaret Chase Smith include her autobiography, *Declaration of Conscience*, edited by William Lewis, Jr. (New York, 1972) and Frank Graham, *Margaret Chase Smith: Woman of Courage* (New York, 1964).

36 *Women in Congress*, p. 75.

37 Ibid., p. 76.

38 Ibid.

39 Chamberlin, p. 351.

40 Ibid., p. 240; *Women in Congress*, p. 11.

41 Chamberlin, pp. 241–42.

42 *Women in Congress*, p. 11.

43 Ibid., p. 3.

CHAPTER 24

Black Senators

1 Mildred Amer, "Black Members of the United States Congress, 1789–1989," CRS Report No. 89-502 GOV, Congressional Research Service, Library of Congress, Washington, DC, 1989, pp. 1–2; "The Long Road Up The Hill: Blacks in the U.S. Congress, 1870–1981,"

checklist of exhibition of the National Archives, 1981, p. 1.

[2] "The Long Road Up The Hill," p. 1; Mabel M. Smythe, ed., *The Black American Reference Book* (Englewood Cliffs, NJ, 1976), p. 627.

[3] Maurine Christopher, *America's Black Congressmen* (New York, 1971), pp. ix–x; Smythe, pp. 628–29.

[4] Christopher, pp. ix–x; Smythe, pp. 628–29.

[5] "The Long Road Up The Hill"; statistics provided by the Congressional Black Caucus; Amer, pp. 1–2.

[6] Sources of information on Hiram Revels include: Christopher, pp. 1–14; Julius Thompson, *Hiram R. Revels: 1827–1901* (New York, 1982); Billy Libby, "Senator Hiram Revels of Mississippi Takes His Seat, January–February 1870," *The Journal of Mississippi History* (November 1975), pp. 381–94; Joseph H. Borome, "The Autobiography of Hiram Rhoads Revels," *The Midwest Journal* (Winter 1952–1953), pp. 79–92; Donald L. Singer, "For Whites Only: The Seating of Hiram Revels," *Negro History Bulletin* (March 1972), pp. 60–63.

[7] Scholars are not certain about the date of Revels' birth. Three different dates appear in the Revels citations: September 1, 1822, September 27, 1822, and September 27, 1827. Most scholars are inclined to accept September 27, 1827, the date Revels himself gave in his autobiography.

[8] Quoted in Christopher, p. 2.

[9] Ibid.

[10] Libby, p. 383.

[11] Ibid.

[12] The debates over the seating of Hiram Revels can be found in U.S., Congress, Senate, *Congressional Globe*, 41st Cong., 2d sess., pp. 1503–68.

[13] Libby, p. 386.

[14] Christopher, pp. 4–5.

[15] Ibid., p. 5.

[16] Ibid., pp. 5–6.

[17] Ibid., pp. 6–7.

[18] Quoted in Libby, p. 392.

[19] Christopher, p. 7.

[20] Quoted in Libby, p. 393.

[21] Christopher, pp. 8–9; *Congressional Globe*, 41st Cong., 2d sess., pp. 1986–88.

[22] Sources of information on Blanche K. Bruce include: Christopher, pp. 15–24; Samuel Shapiro, "A Black Senator From Mississippi: Blanche K. Bruce," *The Review of Politics* (January 1982), pp. 83–109; Kenneth Mann, "Blanche Kelso Bruce: United States Senator," *The Journal of Mississippi History* (May 1976), pp. 183–98; G. David Houston, "A Negro Senator," *The Journal of Negro History* 7 (1922): 243–56.

[23] Shapiro, p. 85.

[24] Christopher, p. 16.

[25] Quoted in ibid., p. 17.

[26] Quoted in Mann, p. 186.

[27] Quoted in Shapiro, p. 89.

[28] U.S., Congress, Senate, *Compilation of Senate Election Cases from 1789–1885*, by George S. Taft (Washington, DC, 1885), pp. 483–506.

[29] Quoted in Mann, p. 188.

[30] Quoted in Christopher, p. 21.

[31] Ibid., p. 22; Shapiro, p. 92.

[32] Sources of information on Edward Brooke include: Christopher, pp. 228–36; John Henry Cutler, *Ed Brooke* (New York, 1972); "An Individual Who Happens to be a Negro," *Time*, February 17, 1967, pp. 20–23.

[33] Quoted in Christopher, p. 231.

[34] Ibid.

[35] *Time*, February 17, 1967, p. 20.

Index